Introductory Econometrics
Second Edition

20.

Longman Economics Series
Series editors: Robert Millward, Michael T. Summer
and George Zis

Using mathematics in Economics, *R. L. Thomas*
Environmental and Resource Economics: An Introduction, *M. S. Common*
Macroeconomics Analysis: An Intermediate text, *D. Cobham*

Introductory Econometrics
Second Edition

R. L. Thomas

Longman
London and New York

Longman Group UK Limited
Longman House, Burnt Mill, Harlow,
Essex CM20 2JE, England
and Associated Companies throughout the world.

Published in the United States of America
by Longman Publishing, New York

First published 1985
Second Edition 1993
ISBN 0582 073782

British Library Cataloguing-in-Publication Data
A catalogue record for this book is available from the
British Library

Library of Congress Cataloging-in-Publication data
Thomas, R. L., 1942–
    Introductory econometrics: theory and applications/
R. L. Thomas. – – 2nd ed.
        p.   cm. – – (Longman economics series)
    Includes bibliographical references and index.
.   ISBN 0-582-07378-2
    1. Econometrics.   I. Title.   II. Series.
HB139.T52   1993
330′.01′5195– –dc20   92-28664
                                                 CIP

Set by 6HH in 10/11pt Times
Printed in Malaysia by VP

Contents

Note: * denotes a more difficult section in the text.

Preface to the second edition

Since publication of the first edition of this book the practice of econometrics, particularly in the United Kingdom, has seen striking changes. I have tried to make the second edition of this book reflect this. Central to this edition is an entirely new chapter on the specification and selection of models which includes material on D. F. Hendry's general to specific approach to modelling, error correction models, stationarity and cointegration. I have also included a separate chapter on maximum likelihood estimation. Students appear to have particular difficulty with this topic and it deserves special attention for this reason alone. In addition, however, many econometricians see maximum likelihood estimation as a more general approach to estimation than least squares and there are good reasons for approaching all estimation problems within such a framework.

I have also rearranged much of the other theoretical material in the first half of the book. Lagged variables now have a chapter on their own. In addition topics such as non-linear regression, dummy variables and parameter stability are now included in the chapter on extensions to the classical model and this chapter also contains extensive material on the testing of parameter restrictions. This has enabled me to include sections on likelihood ratio, Wald and Lagrange multiplier tests. Such tests are now frequently used but I find that few undergraduates have any intuitive understanding of them. I have tried to provide explanations that are accessible to the average third year undergraduate.

Some of the new topics introduced are complicated and at times this has necessitated a level of mathematics somewhat higher than that used throughout the first edition. While I have tried to limit the use of more difficult mathematics whenever possible, certain sections have been 'starred' as containing material that students with a limited maths background may find difficult. However such sections can be omitted without losing the thread of the development. As in the first edition, lack of space has limited the total amount of theoretical material that could be included and its range is again partly determined by the content of the later applied chapters.

The applied chapters have been updated to account for recent work of interest, with attention being paid to the use of error correction models and co-integration analysis. This has involved considerable rewriting, especially for the consumption and demand for money chapters. The empirical exercises at the end of each applied chapter have also been completely redesigned to reflect the changing approach of modern applied econometrics. The sheer quantity of recent applied work has exerted great pressure on available space and this has meant that, unfortunately, there was no room in this edition for a chapter on fixed capital investment.

As with the first edition, I am most grateful to those who have spent time reading and commenting on earlier drafts of various chapters. In particular I would like to thank M. T. Sumner, J. Stewart and an anonymous reader. Needless to say none of these can be held responsible for any errors that remain.

R. L. Thomas
July 1992

Acknowledgements

We are grateful to the following for permission to reproduce copyright material:

Cambridge University Press for Tables 9.1, 12.2, 12.3, 12.4; The Econometric Society for Table 7.2; the International Statistical Institute for Tables 13.2, 13.3 and Figure 13.1; John Wiley & Sons Ltd for Tables 7.1, 13.1; National Institute of Economic and Social Research for Table 13.4.

Whilst every effort has been made to trace the owners of copyright material, in a few cases this has proved impossible, and we take this opportunity to offer our apologies to any copyright holders whose rights we may have unwittingly infringed.

1 Introduction

Most economic theories have developed out of *a priori* reasoning based on relatively simple assumptions. However, different assumptions will lead to different theories. If we are to provide government with sensible policy prescriptions, we therefore require some way of distinguishing 'good' theories from 'bad' theories. The obvious way is to refer to 'the facts'. In the physical sciences a theory is judged by its ability to make successful predictions. Hypotheses are developed by a combination of *a priori* reasoning and empirical observations and are then used to generate predictions which can be tested against further data. If the predictions are judged 'correct', the hypothesis or theory still stands, while if the predictions are incorrect the hypothesis is either rejected or simply reformulated to take account of the new data. Such traditional 'scientific method' has served the physical sciences well over the past two centuries and one might hope that a similar approach was possible in economics. However, there are problems.

A major problem is that the economist can rarely, if ever, conduct a controlled laboratory experiment. Take two simple examples – one from physics and the other from economics. Suppose we were interested in the effect on the volume, V, of a gas of variations in its temperature, T, and the pressure under which it is kept, P. Specifically, we might wish to test the hypothesis that a given proportionate increase in the temperature of the gas, with pressure held constant, leads to a more than proportionate increase in its volume. That is, resorting to the terminology of economics, we ask the question – is the elasticity of volume with respect to temperature greater than unity? Suppose we assume that a relationship of the form

$$V = AT^\alpha P^\beta \qquad [1.1]$$

exists where A, α and β are constants. α measures the effect on volume of changes in temperature when pressure, P, is kept constant and β measures the effect on volume of changes in pressure when temperature, T, is held constant.[1]

Equation [1.1] is referred to as a *maintained hypothesis*. In hypothesis-testing situations, typically we make a number of assumptions not all of which are to be tested. Those assumptions we are prepared to accept and do not intend to test constitute the maintained hypothesis. We can never be certain that a maintained hypothesis is valid (e.g. a simpler linear formulation might be preferable to [1.1]), but some such assumptions are always necessary if hypothesis testing is to proceed at all. The form of equation [1.1] is, in fact, very suitable for the purpose at hand since α and β are, of course, elasticities. α is the elasticity of volume with respect to temperature under conditions of constant pressure. To measure α we would set up a laboratory experiment under which pressure is kept constant and we vary the temperature of the gas at will. We then observe the relationship between temperature and volume under these conditions and come to some conclusion about the size of α. Similarly, β is the elasticity of volume with respect to pressure under conditions of constant temperature. A further controlled experiment would be set up if we wished to come to some conclusion about the size of β.

Now consider a situation in economics where we are interested in the effect on a household's consumption expenditure, C, of variations in its disposable income, Y, and its stock of liquid assets, L. Specifically we might be concerned whether, for a given stock of liquid assets, the relationship between consumption and income was one of proportionality. Suppose we specified the maintained hypothesis

$$C = AL^{\alpha}Y^{\beta} \qquad\qquad [1.2]$$

where α now measures the elasticity of consumption with respect to liquid assets when income is constant, and β measures the elasticity with respect to income when the liquid asset stock is constant. Given the maintained hypothesis [1.2], testing whether the relationship between C and Y is one of proportionality simply involves testing the hypothesis

$$\beta = 1$$

Unfortunately, it is very unlikely that we will ever be able to set up controlled experiments in which, for example, we hold a household's liquid asset stock constant and observe the relationship between C and Y. In economics it is very rarely the case that we are able to collect data specifically generated for the purpose in hand. Rather, the economist has to make use of whatever data he can find. Such data can be classified into two kinds – *time series* data and *cross-sectional* data.

Time series data on an individual household would consist of observations on the income, consumption and liquid assets of the household for a series of successive periods, e.g. months or years. Although most published time series data on the consumption behaviour of households refers to aggregates (often economy-wide), of very many households. Unfortunately, there would be no way in which we could guarantee that the household's liquid asset stock remained constant while we observed the relationship between C and Y.

Cross-sectional data consist of observations on different households over the same period of time. For example, the Family Expenditure Surveys in the UK and general household surveys in other countries provide such data on many thousands of households. However, there would be no reason to expect household stocks of liquid assets to be constant over the cross-section. Moreover, as we are now dealing with different households, we would also be faced with the problem of variations in size, composition and background.

Clearly, whatever type of data is available for the investigation of [1.2] we are faced with the difficulty that both Y and L will be varying. This situation is, of course, the normal one in economics. Our data is almost invariably such that all variables we are interested in will be non-constant, the controlled experiment not being feasible.

A statistical technique exists that goes some way to overcoming the handicap of being unable to carry out controlled experiments. This technique, known as *multiple regression analysis*, enables us to 'estimate' quantities such as A, α and β in equation [1.2] simultaneously, without the need to hold variables constant artificially. Notice that if we take logarithms of equation [1.2] we obtain the linear equation

$$\log C = \log A + \alpha \log L + \beta \log Y \qquad [1.3]$$

The reader should be familiar with the *least squares technique* of estimating a simple linear relationship between two variables. This technique can, in fact, be extended to the estimation of linear relationships such as [1.3], although in the multiple regression case the estimated relationship cannot be depicted in a simple two-dimensional diagram. Multiple regression, then, is the economist's replacement for a controlled laboratory experiment. Often it may not be a very good replacement but it is normally the best we have and much *econometrics* involves its use in one form or another. Equations [1.2] and [1.3] suggest that an exact or *deterministic* relationship exists between the left-hand side or dependent variable and the two right-hand side or explanatory variables. However, economic relationships are never exact – human beings are unpredictable in their behaviour, and for this reason a random *disturbance* is usually added to such relationships. For example, a household may receive exactly the same income and possess exactly the same liquid asset stock in one week as it does in another. Yet its consumption may well differ for purely random reasons. We therefore rewrite equations such as [1.3] which we wish to estimate as

$$\log C = \log A + \alpha \log L + \beta \log Y + \varepsilon \qquad [1.4]$$

where ε is a random disturbance which may take either a positive or a negative value.[2] This disturbance can also be regarded as reflecting all other factors apart from Y and L which have some (hopefully slight) effect on household consumption. One cannot expect Y and L to encompass all influences on C.[3]

The fact that a random disturbance is included in economic relationships means that we cannot expect to measure quantities such as A, α and β in [1.4] exactly. This would be the case even if we were able to set up controlled experiments and hold Y and L constant because we would have no control over ε, the random factor. For example, if we held L constant in order to investigate β, then our findings from one experiment might well differ from those in another because of the different random responses of the household, reflected in different values for ε. Similarly, when applying the multiple regression technique, we might obtain one set of estimates for A, α, and β from one sample of observations on Y, L and C and a rather different set from another sample. In other words, the estimators are subject to sampling variability and have sampling distributions.[4] We cannot therefore estimate A, α and β exactly but are reduced to finding, for example, 95 per cent confidence intervals for their values. Similarly, we can never say with certainty that, for example, $\alpha \neq 0$ in equation [1.4], i.e. that liquid assets influence consumption. We can merely test statistically the hypothesis $\alpha = 0$ and reject it or not at, for example, the 5 per cent level of significance. It is when we reject $\alpha = 0$ that we say 'liquid assets are significant at the 5 per cent level'.

At this point it is worth considering the meaning of the term 'level of significance'. For example, to say that a hypothesis is rejected at 'the 5 per cent level of significance' is an admission that there is a probability of 5 per cent that it has been wrongly rejected. That is, that there is a probability of 5 per cent that the hypothesis was true all along and that the characteristics in the

3

data that led to its rejection occurred simply by chance. Hence, if we reject the hypothesis $\alpha = 0$ in [1.4] at the 5 per cent level of significance, we are saying that we believe liquid assets influence consumption but acknowledge a probability of 5 per cent that the statistical association that led us to this conclusion could have occurred by chance.

The fact that the significance level of a test is an admission of the existence of chance has one important implication. Suppose we were interested in other possible determinants of household consumption. Imagine that we tried adding, one at a time, twenty different variables to the right-hand side of [1.4]. Remember that, even if such a variable is of no importance in the determination of consumption, there is a 1 in 20, or 5 per cent, probability that it will appear 'significant at the 5 per cent level' purely by chance. Hence, if we try twenty such variables we must expect one of them to appear significant even if *none* of them are of real importance. The danger now is that we might forget the nineteen 'unsuccessful' variables and focus attention on the single 'significant' one, maintaining that we had uncovered evidence that it is an important determinant of consumption. What we would have done, however, is to have confused hopelessly the business of hypothesis *testing* with that of hypothesis *formulation*. The statistical relationship we have uncovered *may* reflect a genuine causal link but it is also possible that it represents a purely spurious relationship that happens to exist just in the data we have observed. We have *formulated* a hypothesis by 'observing' this data. What we cannot do is to *test* this by hypothesis using the *same* body of data and it is silly to claim that we have. A hypothesis formulated from one data set obviously needs to be tested on a *new* data set.

The above procedure is an extreme example of what is commonly referred to as 'data-mining'. Unfortunately, such data-mining, albeit in a less extreme form, appears to be a fairly common practice in much empirical economic research. One finds impressive-looking regression equations presented in many published papers. What should be realised is that the presented regressions are almost certainly the 'most successful' of a whole series of 'trial' regressions, the vast majority of which do not appear. The presenter may not have tried the twenty variables of the above example, but he will probably have tried two or three and also experimented with different definitions of the one that worked best.[5] Although it is probably an inevitable consequence of the paucity of economic data, there is therefore a tendency for hypothesis formulation and testing to get mixed up in economic research. Because of this it is probably wise to take many of the regression equations reported in the applied chapters of this book with just a slight pinch of salt and mentally downgrade the significance of variables and the overall performance of presented equations. The 'non-statistically minded' reader may have some difficulty in fully understanding what has just been said but, if this is the case, it would be a good idea if this introduction was returned to after a reading of the theoretical chapters.

The technique of multiple regression is described in Chapter 2. Because the existence of the random disturbance in relationships such as [1.4] means that this technique will yield only *estimates* of parameters like A, α and β, we are inevitably concerned with the quality of these estimates. *Estimates* are always obtained by the use of some estimating formula or *estimator* and we would obviously like this estimator to be a 'good' one in some sense. Part of Chapter 2 is therefore concerned with defining the properties that we would like our estimators to have. We then consider the conditions under which the least squares method most commonly used in multiple regression analysis will yield estimators possessing these properties. The necessary conditions make up what is frequently referred to as the *classical multiple regression model*. Unfortunately, they turn out to be rather restrictive conditions. Because of this, we introduce in Chapter 3 a method of estimation that is, nowadays, frequently used as an alternative to least squares. This is the method of maximum likelihood. The great advantage of this method is that it produces estimators that, provided samples are large, possess desirable properties under very general conditions. This is in contrast to the least squares method which is really only suitable when the assumptions of the classical model turn out to be valid. As we noted above, these classical assumptions are rather restrictive.

In fact, if least squares is to be an appropriate method of estimation, then first, as we shall see, it is necessary that disturbances such as ε in equation [1.4] should satisfy a whole series of assumptions many of which are unlikely to be met. Secondly, the manner in which we are normally forced to collect our data turns out to be important. Because we are unable to perform controlled experiments we are unable to fix for ourselves the sample values of explanatory variables such as Y and L in [1.4]. Instead, we have to accept any values thrown up by chance by the economic system we are observing. In the jargon, the explanatory variables are *stochastic* or *random* rather than *non-stochastic* or *non-random*. The consequences of this are often serious. Economic data series often display consistent trends, that is they move steadily upwards or downwards over time (the price level in the post-war UK is an obvious example). Such trend variables will be 'spuriously' correlated even if there is no causal link between them. Indeed, it turns out that many of the standard statistical procedures of the classical regression model become invalid when variables are trending in this way. Until recently, many applied econometricians paid little if any attention to such problems.

Another problem that arises when variables are stochastic, whether they are trending or not, is that the relationship we are interested in may well be but one in a simultaneous system of such relationships. This situation is common in economics and has important implications for the manner in which we estimate a relationship.

The consequences of breakdowns in the assumptions that make up the classical regression model and the alternative procedures that are available are considered in detail in Chapters 5 to 8. Indeed, the analysis of such breakdowns and the devising of alternative estimating procedures make up the main subject matter of theoretical econometrics. In Chapter 5 we examine the consequences of breakdowns in the classical assumptions concerning the disturbances and also take a preliminary look at the consequences of having stochastic explanatory variables. Chapter 6 is concerned with extending the analysis to cover situations where the effect of a change in one economic variable on another is not necessarily instantaneous. Effects may be 'lagged' in that it may be a number of periods before the full effect of a change in an explanatory variable is felt.

Chapter 7 is an important chapter in that it attempts to deal with the problem of how we should decide on the appropriate specification of the equations we estimate and how we should choose between alternative specifications. For example, which explanatory variables should be included in an equation? Should we be satisfied with a specification such as [1.2] for the 'consumption function', or should we consider adding further explanatory variables? In Chapter 7 we also indicate the methods that can be used nowadays in an attempt to tackle the spurious correlation problem described above. In Chapter 8 we concern ourselves with the problems, referred to above, arising out of the simultaneity of many economic relationships.

Chapters 9 to 12 each cover an important area of applied work in econometrics. Empirical exercises are included at the end of each of the applied chapters. These involve the use of actual data on the UK economy for estimating regression equations arising out of the material of the preceding chapter. Working with realistic data is a vital part of any course in econometrics since only by actually trying to estimate economic relationships will a student begin to acquire a 'feel' for the difficulties involved. Any of the various statistical packages, such as PCGIVE or MICROFIT, currently available in UK universities is suitable for tackling these exercises.

Finally, in Chapter 13, the structure and uses of the major UK macroeconometric models are discussed. We consider how such models are used in forecasting and as an aid to policy formulation. Successful forecasting and the provision of sensible policy prescriptions are two of the ultimate aims of econometrics.

When reading the applied chapters, the reader may be struck by the fact that there appears to be no coherent pattern in much of the econometric research work that has been undertaken in the various areas we cover. Unfortunately, much past empirical work in economics has suffered from the lack of a systematic and constructive research strategy. Work tended to proceed in virtual isolation, taking only token account of previous research in an area. Equations were often specified in a purely *ad hoc* manner, with sometimes little more than a precursory reference to economic theory. Fortunately, during the 1980s, several coherent research methodologies have been proposed. In the UK in particular, the methodology associated with Professor D. F. Hendry of the London School of Economics has come very much to the fore.

The Hendry research methodology is described in some detail in Chapter 7 but may be conveniently summarised as follows. First, any new 'model' should only supplant old 'models' if it can account not only for all previously accepted results but also explain some new phenomena that the old models cannot. Secondly, a new model must have a sound basis in economic theory. Thirdly, any new model must be able to account for *all* the properties of the data under consideration. In particular, it should be able to explain the results obtained by previous researchers using the same data set and also explain why their research methods led to such conclusions.

Another distinctive characteristic of the approach is to start with a very general formulation and then use the data evidence to simplify the estimating equation along lines consistent with economic theory. This contrasts with the more conventional approach adopted by many investigators where economic theory is used to specify an initial simple form for estimating equations which is then modified according to the characteristics of the data. It is possible to argue that the Hendry approach leaves so much scope for data-based simplification of general equations, by for example experimenting with various lag structures, that it verges on the data mining discussed earlier. However, such a possibility merely increases the necessity of testing any model, obtained by the Hendry approach, against new data that was not available when the model was constructed.

The Hendry research strategy is closely linked with the use of what are called error-correction models. Error-correction models are also dealt with in Chapter 7. Their great advantage is that, because they work predominantly in terms of the rates of change of variables rather than the levels of variables, they represent a possible answer to the spurious correlation problem. Working with the rates of change of variables will frequently remove trend elements (until recently the rate of change in the UK price level showed no definite trend either upwards or downwards). Spurious correlations can thus be avoided although there is a danger that unless equations are properly specified vital information relating to the levels of variables will not be made use of.

Having read the applied Chapters 9 to 12, the reader may well feel that the achievements of econometric researchers during the past forty years are hardly commensurate with the time and effort they have put in. Such feelings are by no means unjustified but it is to be hoped, given the new research methodologies now being adopted and given the greater willingness of present researchers to tackle the spurious correlation problem, that the next forty years will prove considerably more fruitful than the last. It will be noted that, in each of the applied chapters, the later work discussed involves use of the Hendry methodology and techniques.

At this stage the reader may find some difficulty in fully appreciating some of the issues just discussed. However, if this is the case then it should prove helpful to re-read this introduction once the book as a whole has been studied.

Notes

1. Those familiar with Charles' Law will recognise that the actual relationship between V, P and T is $PV/T = $ constant. Hence, since this implies $V = $ (constant) TP^{-1}, experimentation should yield $\alpha = 1$ and $\beta = -1$.
2. This implies that the original equation [1.2] should be rewritten as $C = AL^{\alpha}Y^{\beta}\theta$ where θ is the 'antilog' of ε, i.e. $\theta = e^{\varepsilon}$. θ must be assumed always greater than zero, otherwise consumption would be negative and $\varepsilon = \log \theta$ would not be defined.
3. ε may also reflect the fact that we cannot always measure variables with perfect accuracy. While a relationship such as [1.3] could hold for the true values of C, L and Y it may well not hold exactly for the data we obtain. Possible errors in the measurement of C, L and Y are thus another reason for adding a random disturbance to [1.3].
4. The situation is analogous to that when we attempt to estimate a population mean, μ, by the mean of a random sample, $\bar{x}$. The reader should be familiar with the fact that $\bar{x}$ is subject to sampling variability, i.e. that different random samples will yield different values for $\bar{x}$.
5. For example, the percentage annual rate of price inflation can be calculated in several ways. Similarly, there are alternative definitions for the 'broad money stock'.

2 Multiple regression analysis

In this chapter we shall be concerned with the so-called 'classical linear regression model'. A working knowledge of the two-variable regression model will be assumed and we shall deal mainly with what is known as multiple regression. However, we first revise some crucial aspects of simple two-variable regression analysis.

2.1 Revision of some important concepts in two-variable regression

In simple regression analysis a linear relationship is assumed between a *dependent* variable or *regressand*, Y, and an *explanatory* variable or *regressor*, X.

$$Y = \beta_1 + \beta_2 X + \varepsilon \qquad [2.1]$$

For example, Y might be the weekly consumption expenditure of a household of given size and composition and X the weekly disposable income of such a household. β_1 and β_2 are fixed constants and ε is a random *disturbance*. The disturbance reflects, first, all factors other than disposable income which influence the consumption expenditure of this type of household, e.g. its tastes, social and educational background, the size of its bank balance, and so on. ε may therefore be positive or negative. It might be positive for a household which because of past savings has a large positive bank balance and may be negative for a household which has incurred large debts. Secondly, the disturbance reflects the basic unpredictable or random nature of human behaviour. We do not expect two households with the same disposable income and identical in other respects to, necessarily, make exactly the same consumption expenditure. Neither can we expect a given household to make exactly the same consumption expenditure in two successive weeks even when the conditions under which it operates remain unchanged.

The disturbance ε may be regarded as a random variable with its own probability distribution and it is convenient to assume for the moment that its average or expected value is zero, i.e. $E(\varepsilon) = 0$. Taking expectations over equation [2.1], we then have for a household of given income X

$$E(Y) = \beta_1 + \beta_2 X \qquad [2.2]$$

Equation [2.2] is sometimes referred to as the *population regression line* and β_1 and β_2 are population parameters. $E(Y)$ may be regarded as the average or expected consumption expenditure of households with the given disposable income X. The parameter β_1, of course, represents the expected expenditure of a household with zero income while β_2 measures the change in expected expenditure per unit change in disposable income X. The population regression

2.1 Population and sample regression lines.

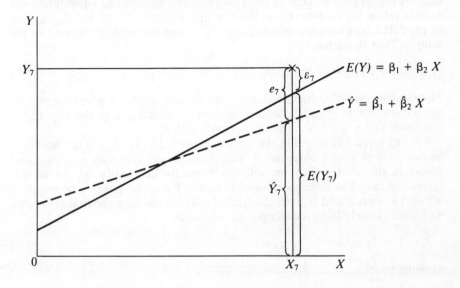

line is represented by the solid line in Fig. 2.1, β_1 and β_2 being the intercept and slope of this line.

Equation [2.2] refers to a population of households and in practice the investigator never discovers the exact position of this line, i.e. he never gets to know the precise values of the parameters β_1 and β_2. The population regression line has to be estimated from sample data.

Suppose a random sample of size n is available.[1] This consists of observations on Y and X for n households of the given type. The observations may refer to a 'cross-section' of households during a given week or alternatively they may be 'time series data' on a single household over n separate weeks. Provided [2.1] holds for the population of households from which the sample is drawn we may write

$$Y_i = \beta_1 + \beta_2 X_i + \varepsilon_i \qquad i = 1, 2, 3, \ldots, n \qquad [2.3]$$

where Y_i is the consumption expenditure of the ith household in the sample and X_i is its disposable income.[2] ε_i is the value of the disturbance for the ith household in the sample during the particular week in which it was observed. Notice that the sample provides no information on the sample values of ε. The ε_is are unknown and, since the exact values for β_1 and β_2 are never discovered, it can be seen from equation [2.3] that they will remain unknown even though the sample provides the values Y_i and X_i.

Equation [2.2], the population regression line, is estimated by a *sample regression line*. The estimation is performed by fitting (using some method which we need not yet specify), a line to a 'scatter diagram' of the sample values of consumption Y on income X. We shall write the sample regression line as

$$\hat{Y} = \hat{\beta}_1 + \hat{\beta}_2 X \qquad [2.4]$$

9

where $\hat{\beta}_1$ and $\hat{\beta}_2$ are estimates of the parameters β_1 and β_2 and $\hat{Y}$ is known as the fitted or *predicted value of Y*. $\hat{Y}$ is so called because, on substituting the sample values for income X, i.e. the X_is, into equation [2.4], we obtain a set of predicted consumption expenditures, $\hat{Y}_i$ – one for each household in the sample. That is, we have

$$\hat{Y}_i = \hat{\beta}_1 + \hat{\beta}_2 X_i \qquad i = 1, 2, 3, \ldots, n \qquad\qquad [2.5]$$

The sample regression line (with intercept $\hat{\beta}_1$ and slope $\hat{\beta}_2$) is represented by the broken line in Fig. 2.1. Since it is merely an estimate of the population regression line it will not normally coincide with it.

For any given household in the sample, predicted Y, i.e. $\hat{Y}$, will not normally be the same as actual observed Y. This is simply another way of saying that points in the scatter diagram will not normally lie exactly on the sample regression line. The difference between Y and $\hat{Y}$ may be positive or negative, is called a *residual* and is given the symbol e. There will be a residual associated with each household in the sample, i.e. we have

$$e_i = Y_i - \hat{Y}_i \qquad i = 1, 2, \ldots, n \qquad\qquad [2.6]$$

or using [2.5]

$$Y_i = \hat{\beta}_1 + \hat{\beta}_2 X_{9i} + e_i \qquad i = 1, 2, \ldots, n \qquad\qquad [2.7]$$

It is crucial to distinguish clearly between the residuals, i.e. the e_is, and the disturbances, i.e. the ε_is. The difference is illustrated in Fig. 2.1 for the seventh household in the sample. During the week it was observed, this household had consumption Y_7 and income X_7 and would be represented in a scatter diagram by the point (X_7, Y_7) designated by a cross in Fig. 2.1. The disturbance for this household, ε_7, is the difference between its actual consumption expenditure when observed, Y_7, and the average or expected expenditure of such households, which we may write as $E(Y_7)$, when they have an income of X_7. It is therefore, as illustrated in Fig. 2.1, the vertical distance between the designated point and the population regression line. As already mentioned ε_7 is, and remains, unknown. The residual for the seventh household, e_7, is the difference between actual consumption expenditure and the predicted value for such expenditure obtained by using the sample regression line. In Fig. 2.1 it is the vertical distance between the point and the sample regression line. Since the positions of both point and sample regression line are known, *the residual e_7 unlike the disturbance ε_7 can be calculated*. Since the sample regression line is an estimate of the population regression line, the residual e_7 can be regarded as an estimate of the unknown ε_7.

Summarising we have the following relationships for this seventh household. From the population regression line [2.2] we have the expected expenditure of a household with such an income

$$E(Y_7) = \beta_1 + \beta_2 X_7$$

Actual expenditure will not normally equal expected expenditure but

$$Y_7 = E(Y_7) + \varepsilon_7 = \beta_1 + \beta_2 X_7 + \varepsilon_7$$

From the sample regression line we have the predicted expenditure of a household with income X_7

$$\hat{Y}_7 = \hat{\beta}_1 + \hat{\beta}_2 X_7$$

Actual expenditure will not normally equal predicted expenditure but

$$Y_7 = \hat{Y}_7 + e_7 = \hat{\beta}_1 + \hat{\beta}_2 X_7 + e_7$$

Similar distances and residuals exist and similar relationships will of course hold for each of the n households in the sample.

We have deliberately said nothing up to this point about how the population regression line is estimated and the sample regression line obtained. It should be realised that whatever method is used (and there are many), a set of residuals will be generated – one for each household or observation. Different methods will yield different sets of residuals. It is assumed that the reader is aware that the most common method of estimation is the so-called *method of least squares*. That is, that sample regression line is chosen, i.e. those values for $\hat{\beta}_1$ and $\hat{\beta}_2$ are selected, which minimises the sum of the squared residuals, i.e. the quantity $\sum_{i=1}^{n} e_i^2$.

There is nothing inherently virtuous about the method of least squares. As we shall see later it will yield 'good' estimates of the parameters only when a relatively large number of rather restrictive assumptions are satisfied. However, it does have the advantage that it is still applicable when the dependent variable is influenced by more than one explanatory variable. Suppose, for example, that for households of the given type it was felt more appropriate to replace the population regression line [2.2] by

$$E(Y) = \beta_1 + \beta_2 X + \beta_3 L \qquad [2.8]$$

where L represents the stock of liquid assets of such households and β_3 is another parameter. Actual consumption of such households is now given by

$$Y = \beta_1 + \beta_2 X + \beta_3 L + \varepsilon \qquad [2.9]$$

where ε is a disturbance of the same nature as that in the previous discussion.[3]

Suppose the investigator is interested in the size of the parameters β_2 and β_3. β_2 measures the change in average or expected consumption expenditure, $E(Y)$, per unit change in disposable income when a household's stock of liquid assets remains constant. β_3 measures the change in $E(Y)$ per unit change in the stock of liquid assets when the household's disposable income remains constant.

In the physical sciences it would perhaps be possible for the investigator to set up a controlled experiment in which a variable such as L is held constant, the variable X is allowed to vary and the resultant values of Y are observed. Since L is held constant, equation [2.8] can be rewritten as

$$E(Y) = \beta_1' + \beta_2 X \qquad [2.10]$$

where $\beta_1' = \beta_1 + \beta_3 \bar{L}$ and $\bar{L}$ is the fixed value of L.

Equation [2.10] is formally equivalent to [2.2] so that we are back in the world of two-variable regression and estimates of the parameter β_2 may be obtained from the scatter diagram of Y on X. Similarly, if it were possible to set up a controlled experiment in which X were held constant, then the parameter β_3 could be estimated by observing the scatter of Y on L.

11

Most economic relationships involve more than two variables. It is very rarely the case that a population regression equation will contain just one explanatory variable. Unfortunately, however, in economics or econometrics controlled experiments are almost never feasible so that it is not possible in the above situation to hold variables such as X or L constant. In such a situation variations in, for example, the L variable, would make it extremely unlikely that 'good' estimates of the parameter β_2 could be obtained merely by observing the scatter of Y on X. Similarly, 'good' estimates of β_3 could not be obtained from the scatter diagram of Y on L. However, the method of least squares, so frequently used in two-variable regression, is also applicable to the estimation of parameters in equations such as [2.8]. It is to its use in so-called multiple regression that we now turn.

2.2 Least squares estimation with more than one explanatory variable

Assume that a linear relationship exists between a dependent variable or regressand Y and k explanatory variables or regressors, $X_1, X_2, X_3, \ldots, X_k$.

$$Y = \beta_1 X_1 + \beta_2 X_2 + \beta_3 X_3 \ldots \beta_k X_k + \varepsilon \qquad [2.11]$$

where ε is a disturbance of similar nature to that of the previous section and the β_js $(j = 1, 2, \ldots, k)$ are constants. It is often convenient to have a constant or intercept term in [2.11] and we can achieve this by specifying that the variable X_1 always takes the value unity, so that [2.11] becomes

$$Y = \beta_1 + \beta_2 X_2 + \beta_3 X_3, \ldots, + \beta_k X_k + \varepsilon \qquad [2.11A]$$

an equation with $k - 1$ 'genuine' explanatory variables.[4]

Assuming that $E(\varepsilon) = 0$, then by taking expectations over [2.11A] we have for a given set of values of the explanatory variables

$$E(Y) = \beta_1 + \beta_2 X_2 + \beta_3 X_3, \ldots, + \beta_k X_k \qquad [2.12]$$

Equation [2.12] is known as the *population regression equation* and the β_js as population regression parameters. For example, β_3 *measures the effect of a change in X_3 on $E(Y)$ when all the other explanatory variables remain constant.* Specifically it measures the change in $E(Y)$ per unit change in X_3 under these conditions. β_1 is sometimes called the *intercept* and $\beta_2, \beta_3, \ldots, \beta_k$ the regression *slope coefficients.*

The population regression equation is and remains unknown to the investigator. It has to be estimated from sample data. Suppose we have available a sample of n observations, each observation consisting of a value for the dependent variable Y and a set of corresponding values for the $k - 1$ regressors, X_2, $X_3, \ldots, X_k$. Provided [2.11A] holds for the population from which the sample is drawn we may write

$$Y_i = \beta_1 + \beta_2 X_{2i} + \beta_3 X_{3i}, \ldots, + \beta_k X_{ki} + \varepsilon_i \qquad i = 1, 2, 3, \ldots, n \qquad [2.13]$$

where Y_i is the value of Y pertaining to the ith sample observation and X_{ji} is the value of the jth explanatory variable pertaining to the ith observation. For example X_{38} is the value taken by the third X variable in the eighth sample observation. ε_i is the unknown disturbance associated with the ith observation.

Suppose (using some as yet unspecified method), the sample data is used to estimate the population regression equation [2.12] by a sample regression equation which we write as

$$\hat{Y} = \hat{\beta}_1 + \hat{\beta}_2 X_2 + \hat{\beta}_3 X_3, \dots, + \hat{\beta}_k X_k \qquad [2.14]$$

where $\hat{\beta}_1, \hat{\beta}_2, \hat{\beta}_3, \dots, \hat{\beta}_k$ are estimates of $\beta_1, \beta_2, \beta_3, \dots, \beta_k$ respectively. $\hat{Y}$ is again known as the predicted value of Y, since on substituting the sample values for the explanatory variables into [2.14] we obtain a set of predicted values for $\hat{Y}$ – one for each observation in the sample. We can write these predicted values as

$$\hat{Y}_i = \hat{\beta}_1 + \hat{\beta}_2 X_{2i} + \hat{\beta}_3 X_{3i}, \dots, + \hat{\beta}_k X_{ki} \qquad i = 1, 2, 3, \dots, n \qquad [2.15]$$

As in two-variable regression there is no reason why the actual sample Y values, the Y_is should be the same as the predicted values of Y, the $\hat{Y}_i$s. The difference is again referred to as a residual and given the symbol e. There will be a residual associated with each observation in the sample, i.e. we have

$$e_i = Y_i - \hat{Y}_i$$

or using [2.15]

$$Y_i = \hat{\beta}_1 + \hat{\beta}_2 X_{2i}, \dots, + \hat{\beta}_k X_{ki} + e_i \qquad i = 1, 2, 3, \dots, n \qquad [2.16]$$

Since the $\hat{\beta}_j$s, the actual sample values for Y and those for the X_js are known it is possible to calculate, using [2.16], each of the e_is. We stress again, however, that the corresponding disturbances, the ε_is, are and remain unknown. They cannot be obtained from [2.13] because the regression parameters, the β_js, are unknown.

The set of residuals we obtain will depend on the predicted values of Y and hence on the sample regression equation we use to estimate the population regression equation. Different sample regression equations will result in different sets of residuals. Ideally we would like the residuals to be in some sense 'as small as possible'.

If the method of least squares is adopted we select that sample regression equation, i.e. those values for $\hat{\beta}_1, \hat{\beta}_2, \hat{\beta}_3, \dots, \hat{\beta}_k$, which minimises the sum of the squared residuals, i.e. *as in two-variable regression we make the quantity* $\sum_{i=1}^{n} e_i^2$ *as small as possible.*

The least squares estimators for the multiple regression case may be derived as follows:

$$\text{Let } S = \sum_i e_i^2 = \sum_i (Y_i - \hat{\beta}_1 - \hat{\beta}_2 X_{2i} - \hat{\beta}_3 X_{3i}, \dots, - 1\hat{\beta}_k X_{ki})^2$$

13

Partially differentiating S with respect to each of the $\hat{\beta}_j$s in turn and equating these partial derivatives to zero we obtain

$$\frac{\partial S}{\partial \hat{\beta}_1} = -2 \sum_i (Y_i - \hat{\beta}_1 - \hat{\beta}_2 X_{2i} - \hat{\beta}_3 X_{3i}, \ldots, \hat{\beta}_k X_{ki}) = 0$$

$$\frac{\partial S}{\partial \hat{\beta}_2} = -2 \sum_i X_{2i}(Y_i - \hat{\beta}_1 - \hat{\beta}_2 X_{2i} - \hat{\beta}_3 X_{3i}, \ldots, \hat{\beta}_k X_{ki}) = 0 \qquad [2.17]$$

$$\vdots$$

$$\frac{\partial S}{\partial \hat{\beta}_k} = -2 \sum_i X_{ki}(Y_i - \hat{\beta}_1 - \hat{\beta}_2 X_{2i} - \hat{\beta}_3 X_{3i}, \ldots, \hat{\beta}_k X_{ki}) = 0$$

Notice, for future reference, that the set of equation [2.17] could be rewritten as

$$\sum_i e_i = 0, \quad \sum_i X_{2i} e_i = 0, \quad \sum_i X_{3i} e_i = 0, \ldots, \sum_i X_{ki} e_i = 0 \qquad [2.17A]$$

Rearranging [2.17] we obtain the so-called 'least squares normal equations'

$$\sum_i Y_i = \hat{\beta}_1 n + \hat{\beta}_2 \sum_i X_{2i} + \hat{\beta}_3 \sum_i X_{3i}, \ldots, + \hat{\beta}_k \sum_i X_{ki}$$

$$\sum_i X_{2i} Y_i = \hat{\beta}_1 \sum_i X_{2i} + \hat{\beta}_2 \sum_i X_{2i}^2 + \hat{\beta}_3 \sum_i X_{2i} X_{3i}, \ldots, + \hat{\beta}_k \sum_i X_{2i} X_{ki} \qquad [2.18]$$

$$\vdots$$

$$\sum_i X_{ki} Y_i = \hat{\beta}_1 \sum_i X_{ki} + \hat{\beta}_2 \sum_i X_{ki} X_{2i} + \hat{\beta}_3 \sum_i X_{ki} X_{3i}, \ldots, + \hat{\beta}_k \sum_i X_{ki}^2$$

Since the quantities $\sum Y_i, \sum X_{2i}, \sum X_{3i}, \sum X_{2i} Y_i, \sum X_{2i}^2$, etc. may all be obtained from the sample data and n is simply the sample size, [2.18] consists of a set of k linear equations in the k unknown $\hat{\beta}_j$s. These equations can be solved to yield a unique set of expressions for the $\hat{\beta}_j$s, provided two conditions are met:

1. the sample size exceeds the number of parameters being estimated, i.e. $n > k$;
2. as far as their sample values are concerned, none of the explanatory variables can be represented as an exact linear function of one or more of the other explanatory variables.

If either of these conditions is not met it is not difficult to show that the k equations in [2.18] are no longer all independent of one another and hence do not yield a unique solution for the $\hat{\beta}_j$s. By the second condition we mean that relationships such as, for example, $X_{2i} = 3 + 5X_{3i} - 8X_{5i}$ for all i, do not hold amongst the sample values of the explanatory variables. When such a relationship does hold we have a case of what is known as 'perfect multicollinearity'. We shall return to the topic of multicollinearity in the next chapter.

When the above conditions are met, the unique set of expressions for $\hat{\beta}_1, \hat{\beta}_2, \hat{\beta}_3, \ldots, \hat{\beta}_k$ obtained from [2.18] are known as the *ordinary least squares* (OLS) *estimators* of the parameters $\beta_1, \beta_2, \beta_3, \ldots, \beta_k$ respectively. They are termed 'ordinary' to distinguish them from the different sets of estimators which may be obtained by more complicated variants of the least squares method.

The solution of equations [2.18] is rarely, except in the two-variable case, attempted 'by hand'. Computer programs for calculating values for the OLS estimators are readily available and the reader is expected to use such programs in the empirical exercises later in the book.

To derive expressions for the OLS estimators we shall write the normal equations [2.18] in matrix form as

$$\mathbf{X'Y} = (\mathbf{X'X})\hat{\boldsymbol{\beta}} \qquad [2.19]$$

where
$$\mathbf{X} = \begin{bmatrix} 1 & X_{21} & X_{31} & ,\ldots, & X_{k1} \\ 1 & X_{22} & X_{32} & ,\ldots, & X_{k2} \\ 1 & X_{23} & X_{33} & ,\ldots, & X_{k3} \\ \vdots & \vdots & \vdots & & \vdots \\ 1 & X_{2n} & X_{3n} & & X_{kn} \end{bmatrix}, \quad \mathbf{Y} = \begin{bmatrix} Y_1 \\ Y_2 \\ Y_3 \\ \vdots \\ Y_n \end{bmatrix} \text{ and } \hat{\boldsymbol{\beta}} = \begin{bmatrix} \hat{\beta}_1 \\ \hat{\beta}_2 \\ \hat{\beta}_3 \\ \vdots \\ \hat{\beta}_k \end{bmatrix}$$

$\mathbf{X}$ therefore consists of an $n \times k$ matrix of all the sample values for the explanatory variables. Notice that the ith row of $\mathbf{X}$ consists of those values pertaining to the ith sample observation, while the jth column consists of the sample values for just the jth explanatory variable. Since X_1 is always unity the first column of X consists of a row of 1's. $\mathbf{Y}$ is an $n \times 1$ column vector containing the sample values for Y and $\hat{\boldsymbol{\beta}}$ is a $k \times 1$ vector containing the least squares estimators.

Premultiplying [2.19] by the inverse of the matrix $\mathbf{X'X}$, we obtain

$$\hat{\boldsymbol{\beta}} = (\mathbf{X'X})^{-1}\mathbf{X'Y} \qquad [2.20]$$

Thus the vector of least squares estimators is obtained by multiplying the inverse of the matrix product $\mathbf{X'X}$ into the matrix product $\mathbf{X'Y}$. It is instructive to consider the structure of these matrix products.

$$\mathbf{X'X} = \begin{bmatrix} n & \sum X_{2i} & \sum X_{3i}, \ldots, & \sum X_{ki} \\ \sum X_{2i} & \sum X_{2i}^2 & \sum X_{2i}X_{3i}, \ldots, & \sum X_{2i}X_{ki} \\ \sum X_{3i} & \sum X_{3i}X_{2i} & \sum X_{3i}^2, \ldots, & \sum X_{3i}X_{ki} \\ \vdots & \vdots & \vdots & \vdots \\ \sum X_{ki} & \sum X_{ki}X_{2i} & \sum X_{ki}X_{3i}, \ldots, & \sum X_{ki}^2 \end{bmatrix} \quad \mathbf{X'Y} = \begin{bmatrix} \sum Y_i \\ \sum X_{2i}Y_i \\ \sum X_{3i}Y_i \\ \vdots \\ \sum X_{ki}Y_i \end{bmatrix}$$

Thus $\mathbf{X'X}$ is a symmetric $k \times k$ matrix containing the sums of squares and cross-products of the sample values of the explanatory variables, while $X'Y$ is a $k \times 1$ vector containing the sums of cross-products of the dependent variable Y with each explanatory variable in turn.[5]

Equation [2.20] is probably the most famous formula in econometrics and it is worth considering the computational steps that have to be taken if it is to be used to obtain the values of the OLS estimators. The steps are

1. compute the matrix products $\mathbf{X'X}$ and $\mathbf{X'Y}$;
2. compute the inverse of the matrix product $\mathbf{X'X}$. Since $\mathbf{X'X}$ is of order $k \times k$, its inverse $(\mathbf{X'X})^{-1}$ will also be of order $k \times k$;
3. use equation [2.20] to compute the $k \times 1$ vector of OLS estimators $\hat{\beta}$.

It is step (2) of the above procedure that is most time-consuming from a computational point of view. For example, with four explanatory variables, $k = 5$, so that step (2) involves inverting a 5×5 matrix.[6] Inverting such matrices is a formidable task to undertake by hand and this is the reason why computer programs are necessary to compute the OLS estimators in the multiple regression case.

It is also clear from the nature of the above matrix products that expressions in terms of ordinary algebra for the OLS estimators, the $\hat{\beta}_j$s, will be extremely complicated and 'messy' except in the most simple of cases where there are only one or at most two explanatory variables. For this reason the more compact matrix expression [2.20] is usually preferred. However, as an example, we shall derive the least squares estimators in simple non-matrix terms for the case of one explanatory variable.

In two-variable regression the matrix products become

$$\mathbf{X'X} = \begin{bmatrix} n & \sum X_i \\ \sum X_i & \sum X_i^2 \end{bmatrix} \quad \text{and} \quad \mathbf{X'Y} = \begin{bmatrix} \sum Y_i \\ \sum X_i Y_i \end{bmatrix}$$

where we have replaced X_2 by the single explanatory variable X. Therefore, using [2.20]

$$\boldsymbol{\hat{\beta}} = \begin{bmatrix} \hat{\beta}_1 \\ \hat{\beta}_2 \end{bmatrix} = \begin{bmatrix} n & \sum X_i \\ \sum X_i & \sum X_i^2 \end{bmatrix}^{-1} \begin{bmatrix} \sum Y_i \\ \sum X_i Y_i \end{bmatrix}$$

$$= \frac{1}{n \sum X_i^2 - (\sum X_i)^2} \begin{bmatrix} \sum X_i^2 \sum Y_i - \sum X_i \sum X_i Y_i \\ -\sum X_i \sum Y_i + n \sum X_i Y_i \end{bmatrix}$$

Thus we see that $\hat{\beta}_2$, the OLS estimator of the slope of the population regression line [2.2], is given by the expression

$$\hat{\beta}_2 = \frac{n \sum X_i Y_i - \sum X_i \sum Y_i}{n \sum X_i^2 - (\sum X_i)^2} = \frac{n \sum x_i y_i}{n \sum x_i^2} = \frac{\sum x_i y_i}{\sum x_i^2}$$

where $x_i = X_i - \bar{X}$ and $y_i = Y_i - \bar{Y}$, $\bar{X}$ and $\bar{Y}$ being the sample means of the X_is and the Y_is.

The reader should be familiar with this expression for $\hat{\beta}_2$ but will probably be less familiar with the expression that can be obtained above for $\hat{\beta}_1$, the OLS estimator of the intercept of the population regression line. $\hat{\beta}_1$ is, in fact, usually and more conveniently calculated by using the first of the normal equations [2.18] which in the present case reduces to

$$\sum Y_i = \hat{\beta}_1 n + \hat{\beta}_2 \sum X_i$$

Dividing throughout by n and rearranging we have $\hat{\beta}_1 = \bar{Y} - \hat{\beta}_2 \bar{X}$ which may be used to obtain $\hat{\beta}_1$ once $\hat{\beta}_2$ has been calculated.

Multiple versus simple regression coefficients

Consider again the situation represented by equation [2.8] where household consumption, Y, is not only influenced by disposable income, X, but also by its stock of liquid assets, L. Suppose that the investigator estimates two regression equations, one containing the liquid assets variable and the other not

$$\hat{Y} = \hat{\beta}'_1 + \hat{\beta}'_2 X \qquad\qquad [2.21]$$

$$\hat{Y} = \hat{\beta}_1 + \hat{\beta}_2 X + \hat{\beta}_3 L \qquad\qquad [2.22]$$

One point should be clarified immediately. The OLS estimate $\hat{\beta}'_2$, obtained from [2.21] in the absence of the L variable, will *not* normally be the same as the $\hat{\beta}_2$ obtained from the estimation of an equation such as [2.22] which contains L.[7] In equation [2.21] no attempt is made to allow for the influence of liquid assets on consumption. In equation [2.22], however, the OLS estimate, $\hat{\beta}_2$, represents an attempt to assess the influence of a change in disposable income on consumption under the *ceteris paribus* condition that liquid assets are constant.[8] In the present case, it is likely that X and L will be positively correlated across households – high income households will tend to have large stocks of liquid assets. Thus, in equation [2.21], $\hat{\beta}'_2$ will reflect not only the influence of variations in disposable income but also that of the parallel variations in liquid assets. However, in [2.22], $\hat{\beta}_2$ reflects only the effect of variations in X under the *ceteris paribus* condition that L is constant. Hence, we are likely to find $\hat{\beta}'_2 > \hat{\beta}_2$. Such a result is quite usual. The addition of further variables to a regression equation will normally lead to changes in the values of the estimated coefficients attached to the variables already present.[9] For an excellent explanation of why the OLS estimation procedure can be regarded as an attempt to assess the *ceteris paribus* effects of changes in explanatory variables, see Stewart (1984:88–95).

Sampling variability of the ordinary least squares estimators

Once a set of OLS estimates has been computed from a given sample it must be realised that these estimates are specific to that particular sample. If it were possible to take a second and further samples and to compute OLS estimates for each such sample, there is no reason why any of these sets of estimates should coincide with those obtained from the first sample. Different samples will consist of different sets of observations and hence will yield different sets of estimates, i.e. the OLS estimators are subject to *sampling variability*.

Thus if repeated samples were taken (all of identical size n) we might obtain a wide distribution of values for $\hat{\beta}_1$, for $\hat{\beta}_2$, for $\hat{\beta}_3$, etc. As we shall see, each $\hat{\beta}_j$ is a random variable in its own right with its own sampling distribution. In economics of course normally only one, not many, samples can be taken. However, it is possible, given suitable assumptions, to derive theoretically the form of these sampling distributions and hence obtain expressions for certain parameters, e.g. their mean and variance, relating to them.

Knowledge of the sampling distributions of the $\hat{\beta}_j$s enables us to make inferences about the corresponding population parameters, i.e. the β_js. Thus if we know the sampling distribution of $\hat{\beta}_3$, for example, we could not only make a point estimate of β_3 but also: (a) test hypotheses concerning the value of β_3; (b) obtain confidence intervals for β_3. We shall return to these aspects of regression analysis later in the chapter.

At this point we should remember that there is nothing inherent in the method of least squares that ensures that estimators of population regression parameters so obtained are 'good' estimators. A number of assumptions concerning, in particular, the disturbance must be satisfied if this is to be so. However, before examining these assumptions it is necessary to consider in some detail what we might mean by the term 'good estimator'. The next section therefore consists of a digression on the desirable properties of estimators and their sampling distributions.

2.3 Small-sample and large-sample properties of estimators

Consider a random variable Y whose probability distribution has, as one of its parameters, β, which we wish to estimate. In other words, we have a population consisting of a 'very large number' of value for Y, and β is a characteristic of this population, e.g. β might be the population mean or alternatively the population variance.

The parameter β is to be estimated from a random sample consisting of n observations on the variable Y which we write as $Y_1, Y_2, Y_3, \ldots, Y_n$. An estimator of β, for which we use the symbol $\hat{\beta}$, has to be constructed by substituting the sample observations on Y into some expression involving all, or possibly only some, of these sample observations. Thus an estimator of β can be written as

$$\hat{\beta} = \hat{\beta}(Y_1, Y_2, Y_3, \ldots, Y_n) \qquad [2.23]$$

For example, if β is the population mean an estimator which might be employed is the sample mean in which case

$$\hat{\beta} = \frac{Y_1 + Y_2 + Y_3, \ldots, Y_n}{n} \qquad [2.24]$$

The reader should not need reminding that different random samples (of the given size n) will contain different values of the variable Y and hence, using [2.23], will yield different values for $\hat{\beta}$, i.e. different estimates of the parameter β. The estimator $\hat{\beta}$ is a random variable with its own probability distribution (normally called a sampling distribution). The distribution for $\hat{\beta}$ will have a mean, generally written $E(\hat{\beta})$ and a variance generally written

$$\sigma_{\hat{\beta}}^2 = E[\hat{\beta} - E(\hat{\beta})]^2$$

Properties of estimators such as $\hat{\beta}$ are generally classified into so-called *small sample* properties and so-called *large sample* or *asymptotic* properties. If the sampling distribution of an estimator possesses a certain property and possesses the attributes of this property no matter what the size of the samples from which estimates are derived, then that property is known as a small sample property. This is because the attributes of the property are possessed by the estimator *even for small samples*. It is implicitly understood that they are also possessed when the sample size is large. In contrast, if the sampling distribution of an estimator possesses the attributes of a property only when the sample size becomes very large or tends to infinity, then such a property is known as a large sample or asymptotic property. The attributes of such properties do not hold when the sample size is small.

18

Desirable small sample properties of an estimator

Unbiasedness

An estimator, $\hat{\beta}$, is said to be an *unbiased* estimator of β if and only if

$$E(\hat{\beta}) = \beta \qquad\qquad [2.25]$$

That is, $\hat{\beta}$ is unbiased if the mean of its sampling distribution is equal to β, the parameter being estimated.

A sampling distribution for an unbiased estimator is illustrated in Fig. 2.2. Since the illustrated distribution is symmetric (as is often the case) its mean is at the centre of the distribution and, because of the unbiasedness property, is equal to the parameter being estimated.

In everyday terms unbiasedness simply means that if repeated samples of a given size were taken, the 'average' value of the $\hat{\beta}$s obtained would equal β. Some of the values for $\hat{\beta}$ obtained would 'underestimate' β and others would 'overestimate' β but there would be no systematic tendency towards error in either direction.

If equation [2.25] does not hold for an estimator then the estimator is said to be *biased* and the quantity $E(\hat{\beta}) - \beta$ is known as the *bias*. If the bias is positive then $\hat{\beta}$ systematically overestimates β. If the bias is negative then $\hat{\beta}$ systematically underestimates β.

Finally, notice that in defining unbiasedness no reference was made to sample size. Thus when [2.25] holds for an estimator it holds regardless of sample size and in particular holds when the sample size is small. Thus unbiasedness is a small-sample property.

Efficiency

Unbiasedness alone is not a particularly reassuring property. If the variance of the sampling distribution of $\hat{\beta}$ were large then, even if $\hat{\beta}$ were unbiased, the values of $\hat{\beta}$ that would be obtained if repeated samples were taken would tend to be widely dispersed about β. Since in practice only one sample is generally

2.2 Sampling distribution for an unbiased estimator.

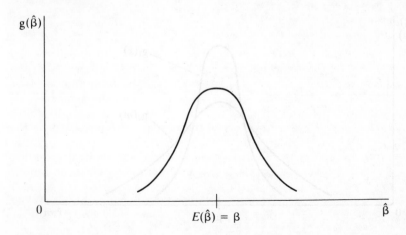

taken, it would therefore be quite possible for the specific value of $\hat{\beta}$ obtained from that one sample to be 'unluckily' very different from β, the parameter being estimated. Clearly then, we would like the variance of any unbiased estimator we use to be as small as possible. The smaller is this variance, i.e. the smaller the dispersion of the $\hat{\beta}$s about β, the lower is the probability of obtaining a specific value for $\hat{\beta}$ which is 'very different' from β.

An estimator, $\hat{\beta}$, is said to be an *efficient* estimator of β if and only if:

1. it is an unbiased estimator of β, i.e. $E(\hat{\beta}) = \beta$;
2. amongst all unbiased estimators it has the minimum variance, i.e. $\mathrm{var}(\hat{\beta}) \leqslant \mathrm{var}(\beta^*)$ where β^* is any other unbiased estimator.[10]

Notice that before an estimator can be efficient it must first be unbiased. For the reason outlined above an efficient estimator is also sometimes called a *best unbiased* estimator. Notice again that no reference to the sample size is involved in the definition of an efficient estimator. Hence efficiency is a small-sample property.

The word 'efficient' is sometimes used in a relative sense. Thus if two estimators are unbiased but one has a smaller variance than the other, then the first is said to be the more efficient. For example, both the sample mean, $\bar{X}$, and the sample median, m, are unbiased estimators of the mean, μ, of a univariate population, but the sample mean is the more efficient estimator since it has the smaller variance. This is illustrated in Fig. 2.3.

Whereas it is often quite simple to determine whether an estimator is unbiased or not it is a more complex matter to determine whether or not it is efficient. To establish efficiency we have to compare the variance of an estimator with the variances of all other unbiased estimators and there may be very many of these. For this reason it is sometimes convenient to restrict attention to a smaller subclass of unbiased estimators. For example, it is often relatively easy to find the unbiased estimator with the minimum variance if we restrict ourselves to considering only so-called *linear estimators*.

2.3 Sampling distributions for the mean and the median.

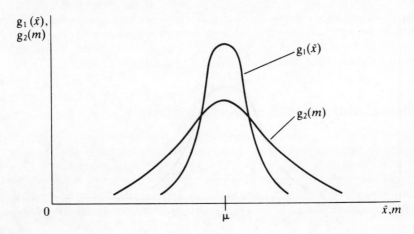

A linear estimator is an estimator which is a linear function of the sample observations. Therefore for $\hat{\beta}$ to be a linear estimator we must have

$$\hat{\beta} = \hat{\beta}(Y_1, Y_2, Y_3, \ldots, Y_n) = a_1 Y_1 + a_2 Y_2 + a_3 Y_3, \ldots, + a_n Y_n \qquad [2.26]$$

where the a's are constants. For example, the sample mean $\bar{Y}$ is a linear estimator of the population mean since

$$\bar{Y} = \left(\frac{1}{n}\right) \sum_i Y_i = \left(\frac{1}{n}\right) Y_1 + \left(\frac{1}{n}\right) Y_2 + \left(\frac{1}{n}\right) Y_3, \ldots, + \left(\frac{1}{n}\right) Y_n$$

where n is a constant, being the fixed sample size.

Restricting ourselves to linear estimators leads to the definition of a third small sample property.

Best linear unbiasedness

An estimator, $\hat{\beta}$, is said to be a *best linear unbiased estimator* (or BLUE) of β if and only if:

1. it is a linear estimator, i.e. $\hat{\beta} = \sum_i a_i Y_i$ where the a_is are constants;
2. it is unbiased, i.e. $E(\hat{\beta}) = \beta$;
3. amongst all linear unbiased estimators it has the minimum variance, i.e. $\text{var}(\hat{\beta}) \leqslant \text{var}(\tilde{\beta})$ where $\tilde{\beta}$ is any other linear unbiased estimator.

A BLUE estimator is not generally as 'good' an estimator as an efficient one. Except for the case where the efficient estimator is itself linear (in which case the BLUE and the efficient estimator are identical), there will be non-linear estimators with smaller variances than the BLUE. However, no unbiased estimator by definition can have a variance smaller than that of the efficient estimator. In many cases, however, the problems involved in finding the efficient estimator are such that we have to content ourselves with using (when it can be derived) the BLUE.

Finally, we should note that it must always be good sense when estimating a parameter to make use of all the information available to us. For example, it would be wise to estimate a population mean by the sample mean rather than the sample median since the median makes use only of the ranking of the sample observations and not their absolute size. For this reason the sample mean is, as we have seen, a more efficient estimator than the sample median. In fact, it can be shown that in general an estimator cannot be *the* efficient estimator unless it makes use of all available information.

Asymptotic distributions and probability limits

Before we move on to discuss some desirable large-sample properties of estimators the reader needs to be familiarised with the concepts of asymptotic distributions and probability limits. Consider the following example.

Suppose we are concerned with estimating the mean, μ, of a non-normal population of values for the random variable Y. We estimate μ by $\bar{Y}$, the mean of a random sample size n, so let us consider the sampling distribution for $\bar{Y}$.

For small values of n, since the population is non-normal, all we can say about the sampling distribution for $\bar{Y}$ is that it has a mean $E\bar{Y} = \mu$ and a variance $\sigma_{\bar{y}}^2 = \sigma^2/n$ where σ^2 is the population variance. However, as n becomes larger, we know by the central limit theorem that the sampling distribution for $\bar{Y}$ approaches a normal distribution with the above mean and variance

$$\text{i.e. as } n \to \infty \qquad \bar{Y} \to N(\mu, \sigma^2/n) \qquad\qquad [2.27]$$

The larger n becomes the more closely the distribution for $\bar{Y}$ can be approximated by the above normal distribution. This normal distribution is known as the *asymptotic distribution* of $\bar{Y}$. In general the asymptotic distribution of an estimator, $\hat{\beta}$, is that distribution which the sampling distribution for $\hat{\beta}$ approaches as the sample size tends to infinity.

However, this is not, in the present case, the final form taken by the sampling distribution. Clearly as $n \to \infty$ the variance of $\bar{Y}$, $\sigma_{\bar{Y}}^2 = \sigma^2/n$, tends to zero. Thus as $n \to \infty$ the sampling distribution of $\bar{Y}$ collapses onto a single point equal to μ, the population mean. (When $\bar{Y}$ is distributed with mean μ and zero variance, then $\bar{Y}$ can take only one value – that of μ.) When the sampling distribution of an estimator collapses onto a single point in this manner, that point is known as the *probability limit* of the estimator. Thus the probability limit of $\bar{Y}$ is μ. This is generally written

$$\text{plim } \bar{Y} = \mu \qquad\qquad [2.28]$$

Note that asymptotic distributions are not necessarily normal as in the above example (although in practice they often are). Also sampling distributions do not always collapse onto a single point as above (although they typically do). Furthermore, even if the sampling distribution does so collapse it may not, as in the above case, collapse onto the parameter being estimated.

The asymptotic distribution of an estimator will have a mean and a variance. The mean of the asymptotic distribution is called the *asymptotic mean* of the estimator and the variance of the asymptotic distribution is called the *asymptotic variance*. The asymptotic mean is generally easy to derive. We need merely consider what happens to the mean of the sampling distribution of the estimator as $n \to \infty$. In general, for any estimator $\hat{\beta}$ the asymptotic mean is given by $\underset{n \to \infty}{\text{Limit }} E(\hat{\beta})$. In the above example $E(\bar{Y}) = \mu$ and remains so as $n \to \infty$, so the asymptotic mean of $\bar{Y}$ is equal to μ.

The asymptotic variance is conceptually harder to derive. It is not equal to $\underset{n \to \infty}{\text{Limit var }} \hat{\beta}$. In the above case, for example. Limit var $\bar{Y}$ equals $\underset{n \to \infty}{\text{Limit }} \sigma^2/n = 0$, whereas the variance of the asymptotic distribution we know to be σ^2/n. The asymptotic variance is in fact defined as

$$\text{ass-var}(\hat{\beta}) = \frac{1}{n} \underset{n \to \infty}{\text{Limit }} [\text{var}(\sqrt{n}\hat{\beta})]$$

because, although var$(\hat{\beta})$ may tend to zero as $n \to \infty$, this is not generally the case for var$(\sqrt{n}\hat{\beta}) = n.\text{var}(\hat{\beta})$. For example, var$(\sqrt{n}\,\bar{Y}) = n.\text{var}(\bar{Y}) = \sigma^2$. Hence, using the above definition, ass-var$(\bar{Y}) = \sigma^2/n$ which we know to be the variance of the asymptotic distribution for $\bar{Y}$.

Desirable large-sample or asymptotic properties of estimators

Asymptotic unbiasedness

An estimator, $\hat{\beta}$, is said to be an *asymptotically unbiased* estimator of β if and only if

$$\hat{\beta} \to \beta \text{ as } n \to \infty \qquad \text{i.e. } \underset{n \to \infty}{\text{Limit}} E(\hat{\beta}) = \beta$$

Thus asymptotic unbiasedness implies that an estimator becomes unbiased as the sample size becomes very large. Its asymptotic mean is equal to the parameter being estimated. Note that unbiasedness, since that is a property which holds for *any* sample size, implies asymptotic unbiasedness. However, the converse need not be true. If an estimator is asymptotically unbiased (i.e. unbiased for large samples), it does not follow that it is unbiased for small samples. The most common example of an asymptotically unbiased but biased estimator is the sample variance

$$\hat{\sigma}^2 = \sum (Y_i - \bar{Y})^2 / n$$

when used to estimate the variance, σ^2, of a univariate population. It can be shown that

$$E(\hat{\sigma}) = \left(\frac{n-1}{n}\right)\sigma^2 \neq \sigma^2$$

Hence, $\hat{\sigma}^2$ is a biased estimator of σ^2. However, as

$$n \to \infty \qquad \left(\frac{n-1}{n}\right) \to 1 \qquad \text{and so } E(\hat{\sigma}^2) \to \sigma^2$$

Hence, $\hat{\sigma}^2$ is an asymptotically unbiased estimator of σ^2.

Consistency

As estimator, $\hat{\beta}$, is said to be a *consistent* estimator of β if and only if

$$\text{plim } \hat{\beta} = \beta$$

Thus an estimator, $\hat{\beta}$, is consistent, if, as $n \to \infty$, its sampling distribution collapses onto a single point (i.e. the probability limit of $\hat{\beta}$ exists) and that point coincides with the parameter being estimated. We have already come across one example of a consistent estimator at the beginning of this subsection. Since plim $\bar{Y}$ exists and is equal to μ, the sample mean is said to be a consistent estimator of the population mean. If plim $\hat{\beta} \neq \beta$ then $\hat{\beta}$ is said to be *inconsistent*.

A sufficient condition for an estimator to be consistent is that both its bias (when it is present) and its variance should tend to zero as the sample size n tends to infinity. Sampling distributions for such estimators are illustrated in Figs 2.4a and 2.4b. Figure 2.4a refers to an estimator which is biased for 'small' samples but for which both bias and variance tend to zero as the sample size increases. In Fig. 2.4b the estimator is unbiased for all sample sizes but the variance again tends to zero as n increases. The sampling distribution for $\bar{Y}$, mentioned above, provides an example of this latter sequence.

2.4a A biased but consistent estimator.

2.4b An unbiased and consistent estimator.

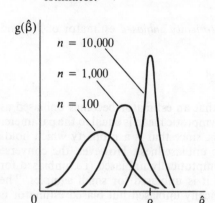

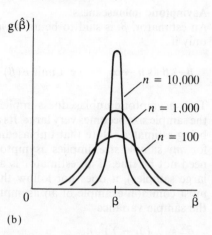

(a)

(b)

Consistent estimators possess some very useful properties which we shall make considerable use of in the rest of this book. These properties are listed below but are considered in more detail in the appendix to this chapter.

1. If $\hat{\beta}$ is a consistent estimator of β then $f(\hat{\beta})$ is a consistent estimator of the quantity $f(\beta)$. For example, if β can be consistently estimated by $\hat{\beta}$, then β^2, $\log \beta$, etc. can be consistently estimated by $\hat{\beta}^2$, $\log \hat{\beta}$, etc.
2. If $\hat{\beta}_1$ is a consistent estimator of β_1 and $\hat{\beta}_2$ is a consistent estimator of β_2, then $f_1(\hat{\beta}_1)f_2(\hat{\beta}_2)$ is a consistent estimator of $f_1(\beta_1)f_2(\beta_2)$ where f_1 and f_2 may be any functions of β_1 and β_2 respectively. That is, β_1/β_2, $\beta_1^2 \log \beta_2$, etc can be consistently estimated by $\hat{\beta}_1/\hat{\beta}_2$, $\hat{\beta}_1^2 \log \hat{\beta}_2$, etc.

These properties are sometimes described by the phrase 'consistency carries over'. However, it must be stressed that the properties of unbiasedness and asymptotic unbiasedness do not 'carry over' in this way. For example, just because $E(\hat{\beta}_1) = \beta_1$ and $E(\hat{\beta}_2) = \beta_2$ it is *not* generally true that $E(\hat{\beta}_1/\hat{\beta}_2) = \beta_1/\beta_2$.

Obtaining consistent or unbiased estimators is rarely simply a matter of estimating the equations 'suggested by theory'. This should become clear after the next few chapters but some inkling of the usefulness of the above properties can be obtained by considering the estimation of the following 'demand equation'

$$q = \alpha_0 + \alpha_1 p + \alpha_2 p^s + \alpha_3 x + \varepsilon \qquad [2.29]$$

where q and p are the demand for and price of some good, p^s is the price of a substitute good and x is some index of consumer income. As we shall discover in Chapter 8, the estimation of [2.29] is much complicated by the possible existence of a supply equation for the good in question. However, in section 9.3 we shall see that for certain goods whose supply can be considered as 'predetermined' in some manner, it is appropriate to invert [2.29] to obtain

$$p = -\left(\frac{\alpha_0}{\alpha_1}\right) + \left(\frac{1}{\alpha_1}\right)q - \left(\frac{\alpha_2}{\alpha_1}\right)p^s - \left(\frac{\alpha_3}{\alpha_1}\right)x - \left(\frac{\varepsilon}{\alpha_1}\right) \qquad [2.30]$$

and apply the OLS estimating procedure to [2.30] rather than [2.29]. Equation [2.30] can be rewritten as

$$p = A_0 + A_1 q + A_2 p^s + A_3 x + u$$

where the αs are related to the As as follows

$$\alpha_1 = \frac{1}{A_1} \qquad \alpha_0 = -\frac{A_0}{A_1} \qquad \alpha_2 = -\frac{A_2}{A_1} \qquad \alpha_3 = -\frac{A_3}{A_1} \qquad \text{[2.31]}$$

and

$$u = -\frac{\varepsilon}{\alpha_1}$$

Given a predetermined supply, we shall see that, while the application of OLS to [2.29] will yield biased and inconsistent estimators of the αs, its application to [2.30] will yield unbiased and consistent estimators of the As. Given such estimators of the As, an obvious idea is to obtain alternative estimators of the αs by substituting into the expressions [2.31]. For example, if $\hat{A}_1$ and $\hat{A}_2$ are the OLS estimators of A_1 and A_2, then we estimate α_2 by $\alpha_2^* = -\hat{A}_2/\hat{A}_1$. Since the property of consistency 'carries over' the resultant estimators of the αs will also be consistent. For example, since $\hat{A}_1$ and $\hat{A}_2$ are consistent estimators of A_1 and A_2, it follows that $\alpha_2^* = -\hat{A}_2/\hat{A}_1$ must be a consistent estimator of $\alpha_2 = -A_2/A_1$. Hence, we have a way of obtaining consistent estimators of the αs. Unfortunately, however, the estimators are not unbiased since this property does not 'carry over'. Just because $\hat{A}_1$ and $\hat{A}_2$ are unbiased estimators of A_1 and A_2 it does not follow that $-\hat{A}_2/\hat{A}_1$ is an unbiased estimator of $-A_2/A_1$. The estimators have desirable large-sample properties only.

Similar use will be made of the properties of consistent estimators in all the applied chapters of this book.

Asymptotic efficiency

An estimator $\hat{\beta}$ is said to be an *asymptotically efficient* estimator of β if and only if:

1. it is a consistent estimator of β, i.e. plim $\hat{\beta} = \beta$;
2. no other consistent estimator of β has a smaller asymptotic variance.[11]

This is the large-sample property that is probably the most difficult to grasp. An asymptotically efficient estimator is best viewed as that estimator, out of the class of all estimators that are consistent, whose sampling distribution collapses 'most quickly' as $n \to \infty$ onto the parameter being estimated. Clearly, if an estimator is consistent the more quickly it collapses as $n \to \infty$ the better. Since the smaller the variance of the asymptotic distribution, the nearer is the distribution to its final collapse for any given very large n, we prefer that consistent estimator that has the smallest asymptotic variance.

Finally, we must remember that when an estimator possesses the attributes of any of the large sample properties just discussed it becomes possessed of them only as the sample size tends to infinity. The same estimator will possess these attributes only approximately for large samples (large is not infinite!) and possibly not at all when the sample size is small.

2.4 The classical linear multiple regression model

In this section we list a series of assumptions which taken together comprise the so-called classical linear multiple regression model.

We assume, as in section 2.2, that a linear relationship exists between the dependent variable Y and the $k - 1$ explanatory variables (regressors), X_2, $X_3, \ldots, X_k$. Thus, given a sample of n observations we again have equation [2.13]:

$$Y_i = \beta_1 + \beta_2 X_{2i} + \beta_3 X_{3i}, \ldots, + \beta_k X_{ki} + \varepsilon_i \qquad i = 1, 2, 3, \ldots, n \qquad [2.13]$$

To complete the specification of the classical multiple regression model we add the following assumptions:

1. The explanatory variables or regressors are (a) non-stochastic, (b) have values fixed in repeated samples and (c) are such that

   as $n \to \infty$, $(1/n)\mathbf{X}'\mathbf{X} \to \mathbf{Q}$

   where $\mathbf{Q}$ is a non-singular matrix of finite constants.
2. $E(\varepsilon_i) = 0$ for all i.
3. $\mathrm{Var}(\varepsilon_i) = \sigma^2 = \text{const.}$ for all i.
4. $\mathrm{Cov}(\varepsilon_i, \varepsilon_j) = 0$ for all $i \neq j$.
5. Each ε_i is normally distributed.
6. The number of observations exceeds the number of parameters being estimated, i.e. $n > k$.
7. No exact linear relationship exists between the sample values of any two or more of the explanatory variables.

Provided these assumptions hold, the OLS estimators described in section 2.2 possess all the desirable large and small sample properties described in the previous section. However, if, as is often the case in econometrics, any of the listed assumptions become invalid, then the OLS estimators lose some or all of these desirable properties. We shall now discuss in turn the meaning of each of these assumptions, beginning with the first.

A stochastic or random variable is a variable the value of which is determined by some chance or random mechanism according to some given probability distribution. To say that an explanatory variable is non-stochastic implies that its values are not randomly determined but are in fact chosen or fixed beforehand by the investigator (usually to suit his own objectives). The first part of assumption 1, then, is simply a way of saying that the n sample values for each of the $k - 1$ explanatory variables, i.e. the X_{ji}s, have been chosen in this way. Notice, however, that no such control is assumed over the values of the dependent variable. From [2.13], the Y_is in the sample depend not only on the X_{ji}s but also on the n random disturbances, i.e. the ε_is. The investigator has no control over the ε_is and in effect, having chosen the values for the X variables, sits back and observes the values for Y which result from the combined influences of the Xs and the disturbance. The Y_is then, unlike the X_{ji}s are stochastic or random, deriving their randomness from the random nature of the ε_is.

The second part of assumption 1 merely establishes the framework within which the sampling distributions of the OLS estimators are to be set. The assumption is that, if repeated samples all size n were drawn, the values taken by the regressors (the X_{ji}s chosen by the investigator) would be the same for each and every sample, i.e. would be 'fixed in repeated samples'. For the reasons just outlined, however, the values for the dependent variable, the Y_is, *will* vary from sample to sample and, hence, so will the values obtained for the OLS estimators which depend on both the Y_is and the X_{ji}s. Sampling distributions for the OLS estimators will therefore still arise despite the fixed nature of the X_{ji}s. However, these sampling distributions are those that would be obtained when all samples taken contain identical values for the X-variables.

To interpret the last part of assumption 1 we refer to the structure of the matrix product $\mathbf{X'X}$, given below equation [2.20]. The elements in $\mathbf{X'X}$ consist of the sample size, n, and the sums of squares and cross-products of the X_{ji}s. It should be clear that as the sample size tends to infinity some of the elements of $\mathbf{X'X}$ will increase without limit. This is obviously the case for n and the sums of squares. However, the elements of $(1/n)\mathbf{X'X}$ need not increase without limit. The last part of assumption 1 requires that as n tends to infinity the elements of $(1/n)\mathbf{X'X}$ approach definite finite values. When combined with the rest of assumption 1 this addition is essentially trivial. Since the investigator chooses the values of the regressors, i.e. the X_{ji}s, then obviously he can ensure, or we can assume he would ensure, that as n increases the elements in $(1/n)\mathbf{X'X}$ do not increase without limit.

It is when the first part of assumption 1 breaks down and the X-variables are stochastic and outside the control of the investigator that the last part of the assumption is less likely to hold. This is particularly the case for time series data. Many economic variables exhibit strong upward trends over time. In such cases as n increases, and more time periods are included in the sample, some of the elements of $\mathbf{X'X}$ will increase sharply and at a rate greater than that of n. When this occurs the last part of assumption 1 will not hold. The relevance of this will become clear in later chapters.

While the assumption of non-stochastic explanatory variables might be not unreasonable in many situations in the physical sciences where controlled experiments are possible, it is quite clearly a non-starter in most economic-type situations. Controlled experiments are rarely possible in economics and the usual situation is that the dependent and explanatory variables are all stochastic. The explanatory variables take on values determined by some chance mechanism contained in the economic system the investigator is observing. The dependent variable is stochastic because it is determined jointly by the stochastic explanatory variables and the stochastic or random disturbance.

Given the implausibility of assumption 1, the reader may well ask what purpose there is in deriving properties for the OLS estimators which are dependent on such an assumption. However, provided we are prepared to make certain assumptions about the relationship between the explanatory variables and the disturbance, then, as we shall see in the next chapter, it is possible to relax the assumption of non-stochastic explanatory variables without affecting the properties of the OLS estimators. In the meantime, it is convenient for expository purposes to retain the assumption however unreasonable it may seem.

Assumptions 2–5 refer to the probability distributions of the disturbances, i.e. the ε_is. It is helpful here if we revert for the moment to the case of two-variable regression. In Fig. 2.5 the population regression line $E(Y) = \beta_1 + \beta_2 X$ is shown.

In the two-variable model, given assumption 1, the values for the single explanatory variable or regressor, X, i.e. $X_1, X_2, \ldots, X_n$, are predetermined

2.5 The population regression line.

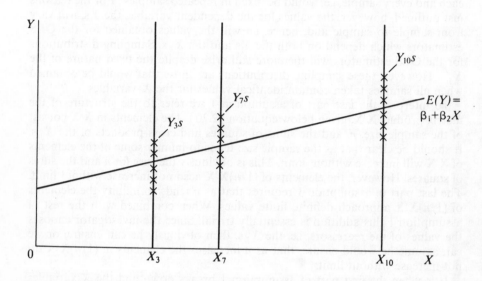

constants so that when repeated samples of size n are taken these values remain fixed. Consider, for example, the X value pertaining to the tenth observation in each of these samples, i.e. X_{10}. Whilst X_{10} does not vary from sample to sample, the disturbance associated with this tenth value, i.e. ε_{10}, of course, does vary. Assumption 2 simply specifies that the mean value of this disturbance, taken over very many samples all with the same X_{10}, is zero. Similarly, the mean values of the disturbances ε_3, ε_7, etc. associated with the fixed X_3, X_7 etc. are also assumed to be zero. We have, in fact, already made use of this assumption in more general form to move from equation [2.1] to the population regression line [2.2]. The assumption implies that the varying Y_3s, Y_7s and Y_{10}s, etc. obtained when repeated samples are taken are all 'equally spaced' above and below the population regression line as illustrated in Fig. 2.5 (remember that an ε_{10}, for example, is the distance between a Y_{10} and the population regression line). Notice that we are now treating Y_3, Y_7, Y_{10}, etc. as variables in their own right.

Assumption 3 specifies that the variance of the ε_{10}s obtained over many samples is the same as the variance of the ε_7s which in turn is the same as the variance of the ε_3s, etc., etc. This implies that the dispersion or 'spread' of the Y_{10}s about the population regression line is the same as that of the Y_7s and the Y_3s, etc.

When assumption 3 holds the disturbances are said to be *homoscedastic*. This assumption is probably most likely to break down when there is a large variation in the size of the n values of the explanatory variable. For example, returning to the consumption function example of section 2.1, suppose the $n X$ values referred to the disposable incomes of a cross-section of households, some with incomes close to subsistence level, others with much higher incomes. The consumption expenditures of the low-income households are unlikely to depart far from their mean value $E(Y)$, since such households do not possess the savings to finance high above-average expenditures whereas expenditures far below average would mean consuming below subsistence level. Thus the disturbances for such households are likely to be uniformly small and hence to have a small variance. High-income households, however, are not restricted by such constraints so that the disturbances for these households might have a much larger variance. Thus, in general the variance of the ε_is tends not to be constant but to vary directly with the size of the explanatory variable.

Assumption 4 specifies that the covariance and, hence, the correlation between any two of the disturbances taken over many samples is zero. Thus in repeated samples there is, for example, no tendency for samples with large positive ε_{10}s to also have large positive ε_7s. Similarly, there is no tendency for samples with large positive ε_{10}s to also have large negative ε_3s. Both positive and negative correlations are ruled out.

When assumption 4 holds the disturbances are said to be *non-autocorrelated*. This assumption is usually held to break down most frequently with time series data. Consider again the consumption function example but suppose each sample now consists of observations on a single household during n successive weeks. During certain weeks any household is likely to make consumption expenditures above the average for its current level of income because of, for example, illness, visitors or any other abnormal circumstance. It will therefore have positive disturbances during these weeks. However, the abnormal circumstance, if present during one week, will tend to be present in the following week and maybe even in the week after that. Thus if we consider a large number of samples, then those samples which happen to have large ε_3s, for example, will also tend to have large ε_4s and possibly large ε_5s. The assumption of non-autocorrelated disturbances therefore breaks down.

Assumption 5 specifies that, for example, the ε_{10}s that would be obtained if 'very many' samples were taken, are normally distributed about their zero mean. Similarly, for the ε_7s, the ε_3s, etc. This means that the Y_{10}s, the Y_7s, the Y_3s, etc. are all normally distributed about the population regression line. More precisely, each Y_i is normally distributed about its mean

$$E(Y_i) = \alpha + \beta X_i$$

The implication of this assumption is that there is only a small probability of obtaining values for a Y_i 'far away' from its mean but a much larger probability of obtaining values 'close' to the mean.

Finally assumptions 6 and 7 are included to ensure that it is possible to solve the normal equations [2.18] for a unique set of OLS estimators.

Properties of the OLS estimators

In this subsection it is implicitly assumed throughout that assumptions 6 and 7 holds so that an unique set of OLS estimators exists.

(a)   If assumption 1 holds then the OLS estimators are *linear estimators*, i.e. they are linear functions of the sample observations. Since the sample values for the explanatory variables are not 'observed' but are fixed constants, the sample observations consist simply of the values for the dependent variable Y, i.e. $Y_1, Y_2, Y_3, \ldots, Y_n$. If we consider [2.20] it is easy to see that the OLS estimators, the elements of the vector $\hat{\beta}$, are indeed linear estimators in the above sense. We can rewrite [2.20] as

$$\hat{\boldsymbol{\beta}} = \mathbf{CY}$$

where $\mathbf{C} = (\mathbf{X'X})^{-1}\mathbf{X'}$ is, given assumption 1, a $k \times n$ matrix of fixed constants. Thus we have that

$$\hat{\beta}_1 = C_{11}Y_1 + C_{12}Y_2 + C_{13}Y_3 + \ldots + C_{1n}Y_n$$
$$\hat{\beta}_2 = C_{21}Y_1 + C_{22}Y_2 + C_{23}Y_3 + \ldots + C_{2n}Y_n$$
$$\vdots$$
$$\hat{\beta}_k = C_{k1}Y_1 + C_{k2}Y_2 + C_{k3}Y_3 + \ldots + C_{kn}Y_n$$

where C_{ji} is the element in the jth row and ith column of the matrix $\mathbf{C}$ and, also, all such C_{ji}s are constants.

(b) If assumptions 1 and 2 hold the OLS estimators have the small sample property of *unbiasedness*, i.e. $E(\hat{\beta}_j) = \beta_j$ for all j, and the large sample property of consistency, i.e. plim $\hat{\beta}_j = \beta_j$ for all j. The property of unbiasedness is most easily derived in the multiple regression case by just noting that the set of equation [2.13] can be rewritten in matrix from as $\mathbf{Y} = \mathbf{X}\boldsymbol{\beta} + \boldsymbol{\varepsilon}$, where we have already defined the matrices $\mathbf{Y}$ and $\mathbf{X}$ and

$$\boldsymbol{\beta} = \begin{bmatrix} \beta_1 \\ \beta_2 \\ \vdots \\ \beta_k \end{bmatrix} \quad \text{and} \quad \boldsymbol{\varepsilon} = \begin{bmatrix} \varepsilon_1 \\ \varepsilon_2 \\ \vdots \\ \varepsilon_n \end{bmatrix}$$

are column vectors containing, respectively, the k population regression parameters and the n sample values for the disturbances. Substituting in [2.20] we have

$$\hat{\boldsymbol{\beta}} = (\mathbf{X'X})^{-1}\mathbf{X'Y} = (\mathbf{X'X})^{-1}\mathbf{X'}(\mathbf{X}\boldsymbol{\beta} + \boldsymbol{\varepsilon})$$
$$= (\mathbf{X'X})^{-1}\mathbf{X'X}\boldsymbol{\beta} + (\mathbf{X'X})^{-1}\mathbf{X'}\boldsymbol{\varepsilon} = \boldsymbol{\beta} + \mathbf{C}\boldsymbol{\varepsilon} \qquad [2.32]$$

The matrix equation [2.33] represents the set of equations

$$\hat{\beta}_1 = \beta_1 + C_{11}\varepsilon_1 + C_{12}\varepsilon_2 + C_{13}\varepsilon_3, \ldots, + C_{1n}\varepsilon_n$$
$$\hat{\beta}_2 = \beta_2 + C_{21}\varepsilon_1 + C_{22}\varepsilon_2 + C_{23}\varepsilon_3, \ldots, + C_{2n}\varepsilon_n$$
$$\qquad\qquad\qquad\qquad\qquad\qquad\qquad\qquad\qquad [2.32A]$$
$$\vdots$$
$$\hat{\beta}_k = \beta_k + C_{k1}\varepsilon_1 + C_{k2}\varepsilon_2 + C_{k3}\varepsilon_3, \ldots, + C_{kn}\varepsilon_n$$

where the C_{ji}s are as defined above. Taking expectations over each equation in [2.32A] and remembering that the C_{ji}s are all constants because of assumption 1 and that, by assumption 2, $E(\varepsilon_i) = 0$ for all i, we easily obtain $E(\hat{\beta}_j) = \beta_j$ for all j.

To prove that, given assumptions 1 and 2, the OLS estimators are also consistent is rather more complicated and interested readers are referred to Johnston (1972:274–5). We content ourselves here with noting that consistency implies that, as the sample size $n \to \infty$, the sampling distribution for each of the $\hat{\beta}_j$s will collapse onto the respective β_j being estimated.

(c) If assumptions 1–4 all hold it can be shown that the OLS estimators are BLUE, i.e. of all linear unbiased estimators they have the smallest variance.

The proof of this property is also rather complicated and a matrix proof for the multiple regression case is provided in Johnston (1984: 173–4). The variances of the OLS may be found by considering the following matrix

$$\sigma^2(\mathbf{X'X})^{-1} = \sigma^2 \begin{bmatrix} x^{11} & x^{12} & x^{13} & \cdots & x^{1k} \\ x^{21} & x^{22} & x^{23} & \cdots & x^{2k} \\ x^{31} & x^{32} & x^{33} & \cdots & x^{3k} \\ \vdots & \vdots & \vdots & & \vdots \\ x^{k1} & x^{k2} & x^{k3} & \cdots & x^{kk} \end{bmatrix} \qquad [2.33]$$

Note that in [2.33] x^{ij} is the element in the ith row and jth column of the *inverse* of the matrix product $\mathbf{X'X}$. Since $\mathbf{X'X}$ is symmetric (see below [2.20]) it follows that $(\mathbf{X'X})^{-1}$ is also symmetric so that $x^{ij} = x^{ji}$ for all $i \neq j$.

It can be shown that the variance of the OLS estimator $\hat{\beta}_j$ is equal to the jth diagonal element of the matrix [2.33]. That is

$$\text{var}(\hat{\beta}_j) = \sigma^2 x^{jj} \qquad j = 1, 2, 3, \ldots, k \qquad [2.34A]$$

where σ^2 is the constant variance of the ε_is. In fact for the expression [2.34A] to be valid only assumptions 1, 3 and 4 are necessary. The square root of $\text{var}(\hat{\beta}_j)$ is known as the *standard error* of $\hat{\beta}_j$.

The off-diagonal elements of the matrix [2.33] yield the covariances between the $\hat{\beta}_j$s that would be obtained if many samples were taken. That is

$$\text{covar}(\hat{\beta}_i, \hat{\beta}_j) = \sigma^2 x^{ij} \qquad \text{all } i \neq j \qquad [2.34B]$$

Because of [2.34A] and [2.34B] the matrix [2.33], that is $\sigma^2(\mathbf{X'X})^{-1}$, is known as the *variance-covariance matrix* for the OLS estimators.

As an example, consider again simple two-variable regression. In this case

$$(\mathbf{X'X})^{-1} = \frac{1}{n \sum_i X_i^2 - (\sum_i X_i)^2} \begin{bmatrix} \sum_i X_i^2 & -\sum_i X_i \\ -\sum_i X_i & n \end{bmatrix}$$

Thus applying [2.35] we have

$$\text{var}(\hat{\beta}_1) = \frac{\sigma^2 \sum X_i^2}{n \sum x_i^2} \qquad \text{and} \qquad \text{var}(\hat{\beta}_2) = \frac{\sigma^2}{\sum x_i^2}$$

expressions which the reader should be familiar with.

(d) If assumptions 1–5 all hold then it can be shown that (a) the OLS estimators are *efficient* and *asymptotically efficient*; (b) the OLS estimators are normally distributed. Thus, if we add the assumption of normally distributed disturbances to the first four assumptions then, first, the OLS estimators have the minimum variance not only of all linear unbiased estimators but of all unbiased estimators. Also since they are now asymptotically efficient, of all consistent estimators, the OLS estimators are the ones that collapse 'most quickly' onto the parameters being estimated as the sample size increases.

Secondly, given assumptions 1–5, the OLS estimators are normally distributed. Given assumption 1, we can treat all X-values as constants. Since, by assumption

5, each ε_i is normally distributed then, recalling equation [2.13]

$$Y_i = \beta_1 + \beta_2 X_{2i} + \beta_3 X_{3i}, \ldots, + \beta_k X_{ki} + \varepsilon_i \qquad i = 1, 2, 3, \ldots, n \qquad [2.13]$$

we see that each Y_i also has a normal distribution. This is because, under present assumptions, [2.13] implies that each Y_i is simply the sum of a constant plus a normally distributed ε_i. Since adding a constant to a random variable will merely change the position on the horizontal axis but not the shape or 'spread' of its probability distribution, it follows that, if repeated samples are taken, each sequence of Y_is obtained will be normally distributed. Since any linear function of normally and independently distributed variables is itself normally distributed, it follows that the sampling distributions for OLS estimators must also be normal. This in fact requires only assumptions 1 and 5. However, if assumptions 2–4 also hold then the OLS estimator of the regression parameter β_j, i.e. $\hat{\beta}_j$, is normally distributed with mean $E\hat{\beta}_j = \beta_j$ and variance $\sigma_{\hat{\beta}_j}^2 = \sigma^2 x^{jj}$. That is

$$\hat{\beta}_j \text{ is } N(\beta_j, \sigma_{\hat{\beta}_j}^2) \qquad \text{for} \qquad j = 1, 2, 3, \ldots, k \qquad [2.35]$$

As we have pointed out, whether or not the OLS estimators possess the properties just listed will depend on which, if any, of the assumptions of the classical regression model are valid. We shall examine in detail the consequences of breakdowns in these assumptions in Chapter 5.

Making inferences about the regression parameters

If σ^2, the constant variance of the disturbances, were known, then [2.35] could be used as the basis for either computing confidence intervals for any of the parameters or for testing hypotheses concerning their true value. In practice, of course, σ^2 is unknown and therefore has to be estimated. Since we may regard each e_i as an estimate of the corresponding ε_i, an obvious way of estimating the variance of the disturbances is to calculate the variance of the known sample residuals. That is, estimate σ^2 by the quantity

$$\hat{\sigma}^2 = \frac{\sum_i (e_i - \bar{e})^2}{n} = \frac{\sum_i e_i^2}{n}$$

where $\bar{e} = \sum_i e_i/n$, the mean of the sample residuals, is equal to zero from the first equation in [2.17A]. However, it can be shown[12] that $\hat{\sigma}^2$ is a biased estimator of σ^2 and that in fact $E\hat{\sigma}^2 = ((n-k)/n)\sigma^2$, i.e. $\hat{\sigma}^2$ tends to underestimate σ^2. An unbiased estimator of σ^2 is given by

$$s^2 = \left(\frac{n}{n-k}\right)\hat{\sigma}^2 = \frac{\sum_i e_i^2}{n-k}$$

since

$$Es^2 = \frac{n}{n-k} E\hat{\sigma}^2 = \sigma^2$$

Once an unbiased estimate of σ^2 has been obtained we may obtain unbiased estimates of the variances of the $\hat{\beta}_j$s by using $s_{\hat{\beta}_j}^2 = s^2 x^{jj}$ (cf. [2.34A]). The estimated standard error of $\hat{\beta}_j$ is then $s_{\hat{\beta}_j} = s\sqrt{x^{jj}}$ for all j.

From [2.35] we can see that $(\hat{\beta}_j - \beta_j)/\sigma_{\hat{\beta}_j}$ is a standard normal variable and it follows that, for all j,

$(\hat{\beta}_j - \beta_j)/s_{\hat{\beta}_j}$ has a student's t distribution with $n - k$, d.f.   [2.36]

We can now use [2.36] either:

1. to construct confidence intervals for any of the β_j. For example, a 95 per cent confidence interval for β_6 is given by

$$\hat{\beta}_6 \pm t_{0.025} s_{\hat{\beta}_6}$$

2. to test hypotheses concerning the true values of any of the β_j. For example, if we wished to test the null hypothesis $\beta_4 = 1$ against the alternative hypothesis $\beta_4 \neq 1$, the quantity $(\hat{\beta}_4 - 1)/s_{\hat{\beta}_j}$ may be used as a test statistic since when null is true it has a student's t-distribution.

Notice that the ability to make inferences about the regression parameters, the β_js, is dependent on the assumption that the disturbances, the ε_is, are normally distributed. Without this assumption [2.35] and hence [2.36] would not hold.

Presentation of regression results

In presenting OLS regression results it has become customary to write down the estimated sample regression equation with the estimated standard errors of the OLS estimators placed in parentheses beneath the corresponding OLS estimates. Thus, if we were estimating a simple consumption function with two regressors X_2 (income) and X_3 (liquid assets) we would present

$$Y = 246 + 0.643X_2 + 0.216X_3 \qquad R^2 = 0.992$$
$$\quad\ (54.6)\ \ (0.053)\quad\ (0.092)$$

where in the notation of the previous section

$\hat{\beta}_1 = 246,\ \hat{\beta}_2 = 0.643,\ \hat{\beta}_3 = 0.216$

$s_{\hat{\beta}_1} = 54.6,\ s_{\hat{\beta}_2} = 0.053,\ s_{\hat{\beta}_3} = 0.092$

and the meaning of R^2 is discussed in the next subsection.

Often in econometrics we are concerned with testing an hypothesis that a given regression parameter is zero. For example, in the above case we might wish to test the hypothesis that β_3, the liquid assets coefficient in the population regression equation, is zero. Such an hypothesis implies that liquid assets have no influence on consumption expenditure. From [2.36] we see that the test statistic for testing such a null hypothesis is of the simple form $\hat{\beta}_3/s_{\hat{\beta}_3}$, i.e. the ratio of the estimate $\hat{\beta}_3$ to its estimated standard error. Provided this ratio exceeds the relevant critical t-value we would reject the hypothesis that liquid assets have no influence on consumption. When this occurs it has become customary to say that the variable 'liquid assets' is 'statistically significant' in the determination of consumption expenditure.

The ratio of an estimate to its estimated standard error is often called a t-ratio and is sometimes presented in parentheses in place of the estimated standard error.

Suppose, as an example, the above regression result was based on a sample size $n = 20$. Then under the null hypothesis $\beta_3 = 0$, the test statistic or t-ratio has student's t-distribution with $n - k = 17$ degrees of freedom. Using a 0.05 level of significance and a one tail test the relevant critical t-value is $t_{0.05} = 1.74$. The t-ratio from the regression result is $0.216/0.092 = 2.35$. Hence, we would reject the null hypothesis and say that the liquid assets variable is 'significant at the 5 per cent level'.

Measures of 'goodness of fit'

The method of least squares ensures that the sample regression equation obtained is the equation that best 'fits' the sample observations in the sense that it minimises the sum of the squared residuals. However, the best 'fit' need not necessarily be a particularly good one and the residuals may still be relatively large. (In two-variable regression the sample regression line may not fit closely the points in the scatter diagram.) It is therefore usually desirable to have some measure of the 'goodness of fit' of a sample regression equation estimated by OLS. Such measures are naturally based on the sum of the squared OLS residuals, $\sum_i e_i^2$. One obvious measure is the so-called *standard error of the residuals* which is simply the square root of the residual variance, s^2, i.e.

$$s = \sqrt{(\sum e_i^2/(n - k))}$$

The problem with s is that once its value has been obtained we have no standard by which to judge whether its value is 'high' or 'low'. (The lower its value the better the 'fit' but does a value $s = 0.034$, for example, mean the 'fit' is 'good' or bad?) This problem can be overcome to a certain extent by the use of a measure based on the so-called decomposition of the sample variation in the Y variable. Just as in two-variable regression, the sample variation in Y or 'total sum of squares' is given by

$$\sum_i (Y_i - \bar{Y})^2 = \sum_i (\hat{Y}_i + e_i - \bar{Y})^2$$

$$= \sum_i (\hat{Y}_i - \bar{Y})^2 + \sum_i e_i^2 - 2\sum_i (\hat{Y}_i - \bar{Y})e_i$$

In multiple regression

$$\sum_i (\hat{Y}_i - \bar{Y})e_i = \sum_i (\hat{\beta}_1 + \hat{\beta}_2 X_{2i} + \hat{\beta}_3 X_{3i}, \dots, +\hat{\beta}_k X_{ki})e_i - \bar{Y}\sum_i e_i = 0$$

using the fact that the equations in [2.17] can be written as [2.17A].
We therefore obtain

$$\sum_i (Y_i - \bar{Y})^2 = \sum_i (\hat{Y}_i - \bar{Y})^2 + \sum_i e_i^2 \qquad [2.37]$$

Hence, as in two-variable regression, the total sum of squares (SST) can be decomposed into an 'explained sum of squares' (SSE) and the residual sum of squares (SSR). The explained sum of squares measures the variation in Y which can be attributed to the influence of the X variables.

A frequently used measure of 'goodness of fit' is the *coefficient of multiple determination* defined as

$$R^2 = \frac{\text{SSE}}{\text{SST}} = 1 - \frac{\text{SSR}}{\text{SST}} = 1 - \frac{\sum_i e_i^2}{\sum_i (Y_i - \bar{Y})^2} \qquad [2.38]$$

R^2 measures the proportion of the total variation in Y which can be explained by the sample regression equation, i.e. which can be attributed to the influence of the explanatory variables. Since R^2 is a proportion, it must be between zero and unity so that this gives us some standard by which we can judge whether a given value of R^2 is high or low, that is whether the 'fit' is good or bad. However, we are still faced with the problem of deciding how different from zero R^2 must be before we judge a 'fit' to be 'good'.

To provide a statistical answer to this question, notice from the definition of R^2 that it depends both on the Y_is and the e_is in the sample on which it is based. Therefore, if repeated samples were taken, R^2 would vary from sample to sample. R^2 is, in fact, a random variable with its own sampling distribution. Now suppose that the population regression equation [2.12] were such that all the β_js apart from β_1 were zero, i.e. the dependent variable was totally uninfluenced by the explanatory variables. This means that *for the population* the SSE must be zero and, hence, so must what we might call the 'population R^2'. However, since we observed a sample and not the population, even if the β_js are, in fact, all zero, we are unlikely to obtain OLS estimates which are exactly zero and, hence, unlikely to obtain a zero value either for the sample SSE or for the sample value of R^2.

Now what really concerns us is whether R^2 is sufficiently different from zero (i.e. whether the 'fit' is sufficiently 'good') for us to reject the null hypothesis that the 'population R^2' is zero, i.e. the hypothesis that the explanatory variables do not influence the dependent variable. To decide this we use the fact that under the above null hypothesis the sampling distribution for $\left(\dfrac{n-k}{k-1}\right)\left(\dfrac{R^2}{1-R^2}\right)$ has an F-distribution with $(k-1, n-k)$ degrees of freedom.

Clearly, if $R^2 = 0$ the above test statistic is zero and the larger the sample R^2 the larger the test statistic. If R^2 is sufficiently large for the test statistic to exceed the relevant critical F-value we reject the null hypothesis.

Summarising then, the coefficient of multiple determination, R^2, may be used to test the overall influence of the explanatory variables on the dependent variable – specifically, to test the joint hypothesis that

$$\beta_j = 0 \quad \text{for} \quad j = 2, 3, \ldots, k$$

At this point two notes of caution should be sounded. First, R^2 only measures the extent to which we can explain variations in Y when the method of estimation is OLS with an intercept. This is because the residuals only possess the properties [2.17A] when estimation is by standard OLS. For any other method of estimation, including OLS with intercept suppressed (see page 64), [2.17A] will not hold. When any of the properties [2.17A] are not valid, it is no longer possible to derive [2.37] and hence the expressions for R^2 given in [2.38] cannot be given their standard OLS interpretation. Alternative measures of goodness of fit must then be used.

Secondly, even for standard OLS, 'high' and 'significant' values for R^2 do not necessarily reflect any causal relationship between dependent variable and regressors. It is a simple matter to obtain high R^2 values when dependent variable and regressors all exhibit consistent trends, either upward or downward. Many economic variables show such trends but, as we shall stress in Chapter 7, correlations between trending variables are *at least partly spurious and may reflect no causal link*.

R^2 is also sometimes used as an aid in choosing between two alternative specifications of a regression equation. A simple example would be where the first specification involved two explanatory variables only and the second involved three such variables (one or two of which might be those involved in the first specification). It is obviously tempting invariably to choose that specification with the highest R^2.

However, when extra explanatory variables are added to a regression equation, R^2 cannot decrease and will almost certainly increase, regardless of the true importance of these variables in determining the values of the dependent variable. This should be clear from [2.38], since $\sum (Y_i - \bar{Y})^2$ remains unchanged when extra X variables are added and $\sum e_i^2$ cannot increase but will probably decrease. For this reason research workers often prefer to measure 'goodness of fit' by a quantity generally called the 'adjusted R^2', given the symbol $\bar{R}^2$ and defined as

$$\bar{R}^2 = R^2 - \left(\frac{n-1}{n-k}\right)(1 - R^2) \qquad [2.39]$$

The precise theoretical reasons for using the expression [2.39] need not concern us here and the reader need only note that the purpose of $\bar{R}^2$ is to assist 'goodness of fit' comparisons between regression equations which differ with respect to either the number of explanatory variables or the number of observations. Notice in particular that $\bar{R}^2 < R^2$, except in the case where $R^2 = 1$, that for given values of R^2 and n, $\bar{R}^2$ declines as k, the number of parameters being estimated increases, and that unlike R^2, $\bar{R}^2$ can take negative values (it generally does so when R^2 is very close to zero).

For the reasons just outlined it is possible that $\bar{R}^2$ may fall (unlike R^2) when extra variables are added to a regression equation. Thus, in comparing the 'goodness of fit' of different specifications of a regression equation, one is on firmer ground if one considers $\bar{R}^2$ rather than R^2.

Finally, two further warnings are necessary. First, comparisons of R^2 and $\bar{R}^2$ will not be appropriate when comparing equations with different dependent variables. For example, in the empirical appendices to the applied chapters of this book, we will be estimating equations both in the 'levels' of variables and in terms of their rates of change. R^2 in two such equations will be measuring different quantities – in the one case the proportion of variations in, for example, the level of consumption that can be explained and in the other the proportion of variations in the rate of change of consumption. The R^2s are not comparable and an alternative measure of goodness of fit is needed such as the standard error of the residuals mentioned at the beginning of this section.

Secondly, while comparisons of alternative specifications of a regression equation by means of R^2 and $\bar{R}^2$ are often a necessary part of applied work in econometrics, such procedures can be taken too far. There is a tendency for 'beginners' in such work to attach too much importance to the value of R^2. This is sometimes reflected by students adopting an 'everything but the kitchen sink' approach, trying variable after variable on the right-hand side of estimating equations, in a desperate attempt to obtain 'highly significant' values for R^2. We have already stressed that high R^2s are not necessarily an indicator of causality, but in addition readers should note that *such a procedure is nothing more than an example of the 'data-mining' warned against in Chapter* 1. High R^2s obtained by such techniques are virtually meaningless.

Further reading

For those who feel the need for a refresher course in basic statistics, Barrow (1988) provides a well-organised treatment of topics including probability, mathematical expectations, sampling distributions and two-variable regression. The two-variable regression model is also well covered in most introductory econometrics texts, e.g. Kmenta (1986), Johnston (1984) Kelejian and Oates (1989), and Stewart and Wallis (1981). A most readable discussion of the properties of estimators is to be found in Kmenta, Chapter 6. The classical multiple regression model is well covered in Kelejian and Oates and in Stewart and Wallis although those with an intense dislike of matrix algebra may prefer Kmenta. A 'fully-fledged' matrix treatment can be found in Johnston (1984). Finally, a more intuitive approach, providing many valuable insights, is provided by Stewart (1984).

Appendix: The properties of consistent estimators

We present here some intuitive and highly non-rigorous 'demonstrations' (they cannot be referred to as 'proofs') of the properties of consistent estimators mentioned in section 2.3.

1. *If $\hat{\beta}$ is a consistent estimator of β then* $f(\hat{\beta})$ *is a consistent estimator of* $f(\beta)$.
Consider the sampling distribution of $\hat{\beta}$. Since $\hat{\beta}$ is a consistent estimator of β, as $n \to \infty$ this sampling distribution 'collapses' onto the point β. In very non-technical terms[13] this means that for very large samples the estimator $\hat{\beta}$ actually equals β the parameter being estimated. Now, if $\hat{\beta} = \beta$ it follows that, again for very large samples, we must have $1/\hat{\beta} = 1/\beta$, $\log \hat{\beta} = \log \beta$, etc. and in general it will be true that $f(\hat{\beta}) = f(\beta)$.
Now consider the sampling distributions of the quantities $1/\hat{\beta}$, $\log \hat{\beta}$, etc. Since for very large samples $1/\hat{\beta} = 1/\beta$, the sampling distribution for $1/\hat{\beta}$ must 'collapse' onto $1/\beta$ as $n \to \infty$. Similarly, the sampling distribution for $\log \hat{\beta}$ must 'collapse' onto $\log \beta$ and in general, as $n \to \infty$, the sampling distribution for any $f(\hat{\beta})$ must 'collapse' onto $f(\beta)$. Thus if $\hat{\beta}$ is a consistent estimator of β, $1/\hat{\beta}$ is a consistent estimator of $1/\beta$, $\log \hat{\beta}$ is a consistent estimator of $\log \beta$ and in general $f(\hat{\beta})$ is a consistent estimator of $f(\beta)$.
Notice that such a property does not generally hold for unbiased estimators. For example, if $\hat{\beta}$ is an unbiased estimator of β it does not follow that $1/\hat{\beta}$ is an unbiased estimator of $1/\beta$. The following simple numerical example should make this clear.
Suppose $\beta = 4$ and the estimator $\hat{\beta}$ can take three possible values, 3, 4 and

5 with the following probabilities

$$P_r(\hat{\beta} = 3) = 0.25, \quad P_r(\hat{\beta} = 4) = 0.5, \quad P_r(\hat{\beta} = 5) = 0.25$$

β is clearly an unbiased estimator of β since $E(\hat{\beta}) = 4 = \beta$. Consider, however, the quantity $1/\beta = 0.25$ which we estimate by $1/\hat{\beta}$. The estimator $1/\hat{\beta}$ can take any of the values, $1/3$, $1/4$ and $1/5$, with

$$P_r(1/\hat{\beta} = 1/3) = 0.25, \ P_r(1/\hat{\beta} = 1/4) = 0.5, \ P_r(1/\hat{\beta} = 1/5) = 0.25$$

$1/\hat{\beta}$ can be seen to be a biased estimator of $1/\beta$ since

$$E(1/\hat{\beta}) = 1/3(0.25) + 1/4(0.5) + 1/5(0.25) = 0.258$$

2. *If $\hat{\beta}_1$ is a consistent estimator of β_1 and $\hat{\beta}_2$ is a consistent estimator of β_2 then $f_1(\hat{\beta}_1)f_2(\hat{\beta}_2)$ is a consistent estimator of $f_1(\beta_1)f_2(\beta_2)$.*
Consider the sampling distributions of $\hat{\beta}_1$ and $\hat{\beta}_2$. Since $\hat{\beta}_1$ and $\hat{\beta}_2$ are consistent estimators, as $n \to \infty$ the distribution for $\hat{\beta}_1$ 'collapses' onto β_1 and the distribution for $\hat{\beta}_2$ 'collapses' onto β_2. Non-technically we have that for very large samples $\hat{\beta}_1 = \beta_1$ and $\hat{\beta}_2 = \beta_2$. Therefore, for very large samples, $f_1(\hat{\beta}_1)f_2(\hat{\beta})$ must equal $f_1(\beta_1)f_2(\beta_2)$. For example

$$\hat{\beta}_1^2 \log \hat{\beta}_2 = \beta_1^2 \log \beta_2, \quad (\hat{\beta}_1)^{1/2}(\hat{\beta}_2)^{-1} = (\beta_1)^{1/2}(\beta_2)^{-1}, \text{ etc., etc.}$$

Consider next the sampling distributions for $\hat{\beta}_1^2 \log \hat{\beta}_2$, $(\hat{\beta}_1)^{1/2}(\hat{\beta}_2)^{-1}$, etc., etc. Since for very large samples, $\hat{\beta}_1^2 \log \hat{\beta}_2 = \beta_1^2 \log \beta_2$ the sampling distribution for $\hat{\beta}_1^2 \log \hat{\beta}_2$ must 'collapse' onto $\beta_1^2 \log \beta_2$ as $n \to \infty$. Similarly, the sampling distribution for $(\hat{\beta}_1)^{1/2}(\hat{\beta}_2)^{-1}$ must 'collapse' onto $(\beta_1)^{1/2}(\beta_2)^{-1}$ and, in general, as $n \to \infty$, the sampling distribution for $f_1(\hat{\beta}_1)f_2(\hat{\beta}_2)$ must 'collapse' onto $f_1(\beta_1)f_2(\beta_2)$. Thus $f_1(\hat{\beta}_1)f_2(\hat{\beta}_2)$ is a consistent estimator of $f_1(\beta_1)f_2(\beta_2)$.
Notice, again, that this second property does not hold in general for unbiased estimators. If $\hat{\beta}_1$ and $\hat{\beta}_2$ are unbiased estimators of β_1 and β_2 respectively it does not follow that $f_1(\hat{\beta}_1)f_2(\hat{\beta}_2)$ is an unbiased estimator of $f_1(\beta_1)f_2(\beta_2)$. First, as we have already noted, the fact that $E\hat{\beta}_1 = \beta_1$ and $E\hat{\beta}_2 = \beta_2$ does not generally mean that $Ef(\hat{\beta}_1) = f(\beta_1)$ and $Ef(\hat{\beta}_2) = f(\beta_2)$. Secondly, even if it did, it would not generally be true that

$$Ef_1(\hat{\beta}_1)f_2(\hat{\beta}_2) = f_1(\beta_1)f_2(\beta_2)$$

This equality would only hold for the special case where the variables $f_1(\hat{\beta}_1)$ and $f_2(\hat{\beta}_2)$ were independent.

Notes

1. For a discussion of such terms as 'random sample' and 'population' see: Kmenta (1986: 3–5).
2. We have used Y and X without subscripts as shorthand for the variables they represent. In two-variable regression analysis, when X and Y appear with subscripts, e.g. X_7 and Y_7, then they should be regarded as actual numbers taken by the variables concerned, e.g. Y_7 is the consumption of the seventh household in the sample. However, since, when repeated samples are taken, Y_7 will vary from sample to sample, it will sometimes be necessary to interpret Y_7 itself as a random variable. Similarly for all the X_i and Y_i. Whenever this second interpretation is adopted we shall draw attention to it.

3. Although it does not now, of course, include the influence of liquid assets.
4. The reader could regard equation [2.11a] as a generalisation of the simple consumption equation of section 2.1 but where we no longer restrict ourselves to households of a given size or composition. Thus X_2, X_3, X_4, and X_5 might refer to the income, liquid assets, size and composition, respectively, of households. The disturbance now reflects all *other* influences plus the random responses of households. Notice that in multiple regression when X_2, X_3, etc appear with a single subscript they are simply a shorthand for the variables, income, liquid assets, etc that they represent.
5. Remember that the first explanatory variable X_1 always takes the value unity. Hence, for example, the value in the top left-hand corner of $\mathbf{X'X}$ is given by $\sum_{i=1}^{n} 1 = n$.
6. By working in terms of the deviations of variables from their means, it is in fact possible to reduce the order of the matrix to be inverted from $k \times k$ to $(k-1) \times (k-1)$. Most computer programs adopt this approach.
7. Formulae such as those given by [2.20] into which we may substitute sample values to obtain estimates of population parameters are known as '*estimators*'. However, once the substitution has been performed and a specific value obtained that value is referred to as an '*estimate*' of the parameter.
8. It is actually an attempt to assess the results of a 'laboratory experiment' in which L is held constant and the effect of variations in X and Y examined.
9. The only exception in fact is when an additional variable is completely uncorrelated with the variables already present.
10. Although this definition is common in econometrics, some statisticians define efficiency differently. The mean square error of an estimator is defined as $E(\hat{\beta} - \beta)^2$ and can be shown to be equal to the sum of the variance of $\hat{\beta}$ and the square of its bias. Since both the variance and bias of an estimator are quantities we would like to be 'small', the efficient estimator is sometimes defined as that with the minimum mean square error. What we have defined as the efficient estimator is then referred to simply as the minimum variance or best unbiased estimator.
11. Strictly speaking $\hat{\beta}$ must be consistent in the sense that its bias and variance tend to zero as $n \to \infty$. Very occasionally one does meet other types of consistent estimator.
12. See, for example, Johnston (1984:180–1).
13. The difficulty here is that since $\hat{\beta}$ is a random variable we cannot, strictly speaking, talk about what happens to *the* value of $\hat{\beta}$ as $n \to \infty$ but only about what happens to the distribution of possible values for $\hat{\beta}$. Thus, while we can say that, as $n \to \infty$, the probability of $\hat{\beta}$ differing from β tends to zero, it is not correct to say that as $n \to \infty$ the value of $\hat{\beta}$ tends to β.

3 Maximum likelihood estimation

In this chapter, we attempt to give readers an initial grasp of a method of estimation that is frequently used nowadays in econometrics – *maximum likelihood estimation*. An intuitive appreciation of the method can be provided by a simple example. Suppose we have a normally distributed population of values for the random variable, Y, with mean μ and variance σ^2. For simplicity, suppose that we know that the variance $\sigma^2 = 20$, but wish to estimate the population mean, μ. A sample size $n = 5$, drawn from the population, is available and consists of the Y-values (12, 4, 10, 7, 6). Given such a small variance, it should be clear that a population with mean $\mu = 50$ is highly unlikely to have generated this sample. Similarly, a population with $\mu = 25$ is also rather unlikely to have done so. However, we might feel that $\mu = 10$ has a far greater 'likelihood' of being the actual value of the population mean. In colloquial terms, the *maximum likelihood estimator* (MLE) is that value of μ that is 'most likely' to have generated the sample values that have actually been obtained.

In practice, we are normally faced with the problem of estimating the population variance, σ^2, as well as μ. However, the principle of maximum likelihood estimation remains the same. The given sample values *could* have come from a population with any values of μ and σ^2, but clearly some values of μ and σ^2 are more likely to have generated the sample than others. The MLEs of μ and σ^2 consist of that pair of values for μ and σ^2 which are 'most likely' to have generated the given sample. As we shall see in the next section, 'most likely' is defined as meaning those values of population parameters which have the greatest probability of giving rise to the sample values actually obtained.

The advantage of the maximum likelihood (ML) method of estimation is that, under quite general conditions, MLEs are consistent and asymptotically efficient – that is, they have the desirable large sample properties described in the last chapter. While such estimators will not generally have any desirable small sample properties, we shall see later that in econometrics it is the exception rather than the rule for the OLS estimators of the last chapter to possess *any* desirable properties at all – large or small. Given such circumstances, MLEs frequently have an important role to play in multiple regression analysis.

3.1 Maximum likelihood estimation when variables are discrete

We can clarify the ideas just introduced by considering in more detail a sequence of examples. We begin with examples where the variable concerned is discrete, because these are probably more easily understood.

Suppose we have a population of values for a variable Y, which is 'binary' in nature. That is, the Y variable can take only the values zero or unity. We shall refer to the case $Y = 0$ as a 'failure' and the case $Y = 1$ as a 'success'.

For example, the population might consist of 'items' produced by a machine. A defective item might then be regarded as a failure for which $Y = 0$ and a 'good' item as a success for which $Y = 1$.

Let the proportion of successes in the population (i.e. the probability that $Y = 1$) be Π. Suppose that a random sample size n, represented by $(Y_1, Y_2, Y_3, \ldots, Y_n)$ is to be taken from the population. Consider, first, a situation where we do not know beforehand what the Y-values in this sample will be, merely that some will be zero and the rest unity. However, if Π were known, it would be possible to calculate the separate probabilities of drawing each of all possible sets of Y-values. For example, if the sample size were $n = 5$, then the probability of drawing the sample $Y_1 = 0$, $Y_2 = 1$, $Y_3 = 1$, $Y_4 = 0$, $Y_5 = 1$ would be

$$(1 - \Pi)(\Pi)(\Pi)(1 - \Pi)(\Pi)$$

Hence, if we knew that $\Pi = 0.3$, for example, then we would calculate the probability of drawing this particular sample as $(0.7)^2(0.3)^3 = 0.01323$.

Similarly, the probability of drawing the sample $Y_1 = 1$, $Y_2 = 1$, $Y_3 = 0$, $Y_4 = 1$, $Y_5 = 1$ would be

$$(\Pi)(\Pi)(1 - \Pi)(\Pi)(\Pi)$$

which if we knew $\Pi = 0.3$ would yield a value $(0.7)(0.3)^4 = 00567$. Obviously, the probability of any possible sample outcome can be calculated in this way if Π is known.

Now let us look at this situation in reverse. Suppose, as is more normally the case, the proportion of successes in the population, Π, is *unknown* but we wish to estimate it from a *single* sample for which the Y-values are *known*. We could then use the above procedure to calculate, for *alternative possible values* of Π, the probability of obtaining the known Y-values in the sample. The MLE of Π is that value for which this probability is the greatest. It is that value of Π that would generate the *given* sample most often if very many samples were taken. Colloquially, it is that value of Π that is 'most likely' to have generated the sample that was, in fact, drawn. For example, suppose again that $n = 5$, and that the sample actually drawn is $Y_1 = 1$, $Y_2 = 0$, $Y_3 = 1$, $Y_4 = 0$, $Y_5 = 1$. using the above procedure we can calculate, for alternative values of Π between 0 and 1, the probability of obtaining this particular sample outcome. Such probabilities, or sample likelihoods as they are called, are tabulated and illustrated in Fig. 3.1.

Both table and graph indicate that the sample likelihood is a maximum when $\Pi = 0.6$. Thus 0.6 is the MLE of Π – not altogether surprisingly, since the sample contained precisely 60 per cent successes. When $\Pi = 0.6$ we see that the sample likelihood, that is the probability of obtaining our given sample, is 0.0346. This value 0.0346 is known as the *maximised likelihood*.

In practice, MLEs are not calculated in the above arithmetical manner. An MLE is obtained by first deriving the *likelihood function*. This is a mathematical expression for the probability of obtaining a given sample. For example, in the above case, the probability or *likelihood*, L, obtained for drawing a particular sample will depend on the value given to the population parameter, Π, and on the Y-values in the sample. That is, for a sample size n

$$L = L(\Pi, Y_1, Y_2, Y_3, \ldots, Y_n) \qquad [3.1]$$

3.1 Sample likelihoods for varying values of π.

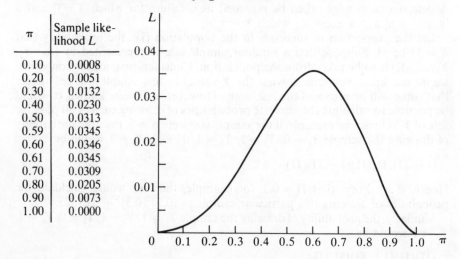

π	Sample likelihood L
0.10	0.0008
0.20	0.0051
0.30	0.0132
0.40	0.0230
0.50	0.0313
0.59	0.0345
0.60	0.0346
0.61	0.0345
0.70	0.0309
0.80	0.0205
0.90	0.0073
1.00	0.0000

In practice, the precise algebraic form of the likelihood function [3.1] is derived, expressing the exact manner in which L is dependent on Π and the Y-values. For the given Y-values in the sample, [3.1] is a function of Π alone and *the MLE of Π is simply that value of Π that maximises the likelihood function*. The maximisation of [3.1] is performed by differentiating L with respect to Π, setting the derivative to zero and solving the resultant equation for Π. During the maximisation, the given sample Y-values are treated as constants.

Frequently, the population from which our sample is drawn will be characterised by more than one parameter and we will require MLEs of all such parameters. The likelihood function will then take the form

$$L = L(\Pi_1, \Pi_2, \Pi_3, \ldots, \Pi_k, Y_1, Y_2, Y_3, \ldots, Y_n) \qquad [3.2]$$

where $\Pi_1, \Pi_2, \Pi_3, \ldots, \Pi_k$ are k population parameters. The MLEs of the Πs are now obtained by partially differentiating [3.2] with respect to each Π in turn, equating these partial derivatives to zero and then solving the resultant k equations for the Πs. The MLEs consist of that set of values for the Πs that, together, maximise the likelihood function [3.2].

Some non-numerical examples should make the above procedure clearer. First, consider the case where the variable Y has a Poisson probability distribution

$$f(Y) = \frac{\lambda^Y e^{-\lambda}}{Y!} \qquad [3.3]$$

Such a distribution might describe, for example, the frequency of calls per hour at a telephone exchange. Y would then be the number of calls per hour and $\lambda = E(Y)$. $e \approx 2.718$ is the exponential constant. Suppose we have data on the number of calls during n successive hours, Y, taking the values $(Y_1, Y_2, Y_3, \ldots, Y_n)$ during these hours. This data forms our sample size n, drawn from a population characterised by the single parameter, λ. We require the MLE of λ, the average call rate.

Assuming that the Ys in our sample are all independent of one another, the likelihood function is given by

$$L = f(Y_1)f(Y_2)f(Y_3)\ldots f(Y_n) \qquad [3.4]$$

where $f(Y_i)$ is simply the probability of obtaining the ith sample value, Y_i. Using [3.3] we obtain

$$L = \left[\frac{\lambda^{Y_1}e^{-\lambda}}{Y_1!}\right]\left[\frac{\lambda^{Y_2}e^{-\lambda}}{Y_2!}\right]\left[\frac{\lambda^{Y_3}e^{-\lambda}}{Y_3!}\right]\cdots\left[\frac{\lambda^{Y_n}e^{-\lambda}}{Y_n!}\right] \qquad [3.5]$$

The likelihood function [3.5] tells us, for any possible value of λ, the probability of obtaining the sample values $(Y_1, Y_2, Y_3, \ldots, Y_n)$ we have actually obtained. We require the value of λ that maximises this probability – that is we must find the value of λ that maximises the likelihood function [3.5].

Since the Ys in [3.5] are known constants, L is a function of λ only, so that a necessary condition for a maximised L is that $dL/d\lambda = 0$. However, the direct differentiation of L with respect to λ is cumbersome so, as is frequently the case with likelihood functions, it is convenient if we first take the natural logarithm of L. That is, remembering that $\log_e e = 1$,

$$l = \log L = [Y_1 \log \lambda - \lambda - \log Y_1!] + [Y_2 \log \lambda - \lambda - \log Y_2!]$$
$$+ [Y_3 \log \lambda - \lambda - \log Y_3!] + \cdots + [Y_n \log \lambda - \lambda - \log Y_n!]$$

Hence

$$l = \log L = (\log \lambda)\sum Y_i - n\lambda - \sum \log Y_i! \qquad [3.6]$$

Since $\log L$ is a monotonic increasing function of L (that is the larger is L the larger will be $\log L$), the value of λ that maximises $\log L$ will also maximise L. We can therefore find the MLE of λ by differentiating [3.6], the so-called *log-likelihood function*, with respect to λ and equating the result to zero. Remembering that the Y_is are given constants

$$\frac{dl}{d\lambda} = \frac{\sum Y_i}{\lambda} - n = 0 \qquad [3.7]$$

Solving [3.7] for λ yields the required MLE as

$$\tilde{\lambda} = \frac{\sum Y_i}{n} \qquad [3.8]$$

Since $d^2l/d\lambda^2 = -\sum Y_i/\lambda^2 < 0$, the second order condition for a maximum is met, so we can be sure that [3.8] does in fact maximise the likelihood function [3.5]. Thus the MLE of λ, the underlying population average call rate, is simply the average of the sample values – that is, the average number of calls per hour during the period for which we have data.

At this point the reader may feel that the MLE method merely produces answers that are intuitively obvious. However, the purpose of the simple examples we are at present considering is simply to illustrate the MLE method. In more complex situations ML estimators are by no means so obvious.

As a further example of ML estimation, suppose variable Y has a geometric probability distribution

$$f(Y) = (1 - \mu)\mu^Y \qquad 0 < \mu < 1 \qquad [3.9]$$

43

Such a distribution might describe the number of customers Y, in a simple queue with a single server. The mean length of the queue can be shown to be $EY = \mu/(1 - \mu)$. Suppose that n random checks on the length of queue yield the observations $(Y_1, Y_2, Y_3, \ldots, Y_n)$. These are the sample Y-values from which we have to obtain the MLE of the parameter μ.

The likelihood function in this case is

$$L = f(Y_1)f(Y_2)f(Y_3)\ldots f(Y_n)$$
$$= [(1 - \mu)\mu^{Y_1}][(1 - \mu)\mu^{Y_2}][(1 - \mu)\mu^{Y_3}]\ldots[(1 - \mu)\mu^{Y_n}] \qquad [3.10]$$

Taking logarithms, the log-likelihood function is

$$l = n\log(1 - \mu) + (\log \mu)\sum Y_i \qquad [3.11]$$

Differentiating with respect to μ and equating to zero,

$$\frac{dl}{d\mu} = -\frac{n}{1 - \mu} + \frac{\sum Y_i}{\mu} = 0 \qquad [3.12]$$

Solving [3.12] for μ gives the MLE as

$$\tilde{\mu} = \frac{\sum Y_i}{n + \sum Y_i} = \frac{\bar{Y}}{1 + \bar{Y}}$$

where $\bar{Y} = \sum Y_i/n$ is the mean of the sample observations. Since

$$\frac{d^2l}{d\mu^2} = -\frac{n}{(1 - \mu)^2} - \frac{\sum Y_i}{\mu^2} < 0 \qquad [3.13]$$

the second order condition for a maximum is again met, so $\tilde{\mu}$ is in fact the MLE of μ.

As an exercise, the reader should now return to the example concerning the binary population at the beginning of this section, obtain the log-likelihood function in this case and then demonstrate that the MLE of Π is indeed the sample proportion.

3.2 Maximum likelihood estimation when variables are continuous

Students frequently have difficulties with the maximum likelihood estimation method when variables are continuous, primarily because of the nature of probability distributions in such cases. Suppose a continuous random variable, Y, has a probability distribution $f(Y)$ sketched in Fig. 3.2.

Readers should be aware that it is not possible, as it is for discrete variables, to substitute a given value for Y, e.g. $Y = 10$, into $f(Y)$ and then interpret $f(10)$ as the probability that $Y = 10$. Rather, for continuous variables, one can use $f(Y)$ to determine the probability that Y lies between two given limits. For example, to find the probability that Y lies between 10 and 12, we have to find the definite integral of $f(Y)$ between these limits. That is

$$P_r(10 \leqslant Y \leqslant 12) = \int_{10}^{12} f(Y)\,dy \qquad [3.14]$$

3.2 Probability distribution for a continuous variable.

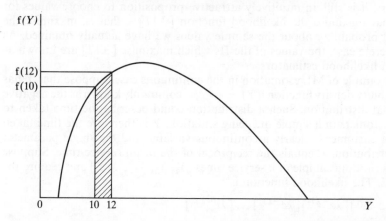

In evaluating (3.14) we are of course calculating the shaded area in Fig. 3.2 beneath the curve f(Y) and between $Y = 10$ and $Y = 12$. How then should we interpret quantities such as f(10) and f(12)? In fact, f(10) tells us the 'density' of probability at the point $Y = 10$. That is, if the variable Y is measured in centimetres, for example, then f(10) tells us the probability per centimetre at $Y = 10$. For example, if we require the probability that Y lies within the interval 9.995 to 10.005 cm, then this is approximately given by

$$P_r(9.995 \leqslant Y \leqslant 10.005) = f(10) \times (10.005 - 9.995) = 0.01f(10) \qquad [3.15]$$

That is, it is the density of probability over the interval multiplied by the length of that interval. The smaller the interval over which we wish to find the probability the better the approximation obtained.

Because, for continuous variables, a probability distribution like f(Y) tells us the density of probability at any value of Y, it is often referred to as a *probability density function*. In contrast, if a variable is a discrete variable, its probability distribution is normally called a *probability mass function*.

Suppose now that we have a population of values for a continuous variable, Y, with the distribution of Y described by the probability density function f(Y). Suppose further that we have a random sample, size n, consisting of the values $(Y_1, Y_2, Y_3, \ldots, Y_n)$ taken from this population and wish to estimate the k parameters $\Pi_1, \Pi_2, \Pi_3, \ldots, \Pi_k$ which characterise the population. As for discrete variables, we can construct a likelihood function for the sample observations by forming

$$L = f(Y_1)f(Y_2)f(Y_3) \ldots f(Y_n) \qquad [3.16]$$

Again, this likelihood function will take the form [3.2], reproduced here as [3.17],

$$L = L(\Pi_1, \Pi_2, \Pi_3, \ldots, \Pi_n, Y_1, Y_2, Y_3, \ldots, Y_n) \qquad [3.17]$$

Because the variable Y is now continuous, we cannot interpret [3.17] as yielding the probability of obtaining the sample values $(Y_1, Y_2, Y_3, \ldots, Y_n)$ for given values of the population parameters. Rather, [3.17] yields the density of

45

probability about these sample values. However, when estimating the population parameters, it is still an intuitively attractive proposition to choose values for the Πs that maximise the likelihood function [3.17] – that is, maximise the density of probability about the sample values we have actually obtained. As in the discrete case, the values of the Πs which maximise [3.17] are known as maximum likelihood estimators.

As an example of ML estimation in the continuous case, suppose that Y has the probability density function $f(Y) = \lambda e^{-\lambda Y}$ – commonly known as the negative exponential distribution. Such a distribution could describe the time taken to service customers in a simple queueing situation. Y is therefore the time taken to serve a customer – clearly a continuous variable and the single parameter in the distribution, λ, equals the reciprocal of the mean service time. Suppose we have a random sample of n service times ($Y_1, Y_2, Y_3, \ldots, Y_n$) and require the MLE of λ. The likelihood function is

$$L = [\lambda e^{-\lambda Y_1}][\lambda e^{-\lambda Y_2}][\lambda e^{-\lambda Y_3}] \ldots [\lambda e^{-\lambda Y_n}]$$

and the log-likelihood function

$$l = n \log \lambda - \lambda \sum Y_i \qquad [3.18]$$

Differentiating [3.18] with respect to λ and equating to zero,

$$\frac{dl}{d\lambda} = \frac{n}{\lambda} - \sum Y_i = 0 \qquad [3.19]$$

Solving [3.19] yields the MLE as $\tilde{\lambda} = n/\sum Y_i = 1/\bar{Y}$ where $\bar{Y}$ is the mean of the sample service times. Since $d^2l/d\lambda^2 = -n/\lambda^2 < 0$, the second-order condition for a maximum is met.

Notice that the procedure for finding MLEs in the continuous case is identical to that for discrete variables. As a final example in this section, let us return to the case considered at the beginning of the chapter, where we have a normally distributed population of values for the continuous variable Y and wish to estimate the population mean, μ, and population variance, σ^2. The probability density function for the normal distribution is

$$f(Y) = \frac{1}{(2\pi\sigma^2)^{1/2}} e^{-(Y-\mu)^2/2\sigma^2} \qquad [3.20]$$

Since the normal distribution is fully specified given its mean and variance, in this case we have two, but two only, parameters to estimate.

Since, remembering again that $\log_e e = 1$,

$$\log f(Y) = -\tfrac{1}{2} \log 2\pi - \tfrac{1}{2} \log \sigma^2 - \frac{1}{2\sigma^2} (Y - \mu)^2 \qquad [3.21]$$

the log-likelihood function for a random sample size n drawn from the normal population is

$$l = \sum \log f(Y_i) = -\frac{n}{2} \log 2\pi - \frac{n}{2} \log \sigma^2 - \frac{1}{2\sigma^2} \sum (Y_i - \mu)^2 \qquad [3.22]$$

For the given sample Y-values, l in [3.22] is a function of μ and σ^2 alone. Hence, to maximise l we partially differentiate with respect to μ and σ^2 and set the resultant derivatives to zero.

$$\frac{\partial l}{\partial \mu} = -\frac{1}{2\sigma^2} \sum 2(Y_i - \mu)(-1) = \frac{1}{\sigma^2} \sum (Y_i - \mu) = 0 \qquad [3.23A]$$

$$\frac{\partial l}{\partial (\sigma^2)} = -\frac{n}{2}\left(\frac{1}{\sigma^2}\right) + \frac{1}{2\sigma^4} \sum (Y_i - \mu)^2 = 0 \qquad [3.23B]$$

We can now solve [3.23A] and [3.23B] for μ and σ^2 to find the required MLEs. First, for a non-zero σ^2, [3.23A] implies

$$\sum (Y_i - \mu) = \sum Y_i - n\mu = 0$$

so that the MLE of μ is $\tilde{\mu} = \sum Y_i/n = \bar{Y}$, the mean of the sample observations.
Multiplying [3.23B] throughout by $2\sigma^4$ yields

$$-n\sigma^2 + \sum (Y_i - \mu)^2$$

so that given $\tilde{\mu} = \bar{Y}$ we obtain the MLE of σ^2 as $\tilde{\sigma}^2 = \sum (Y_1 - \bar{Y})^2/n$, the variance of the sample observations.

We can check whether these values for μ and σ^2 actually maximise the log-likelihood function by deriving the matrix of second order partial derivatives of l.

$$\begin{pmatrix} \dfrac{\partial^2 l}{\partial \mu^2} & \dfrac{\partial^2 l}{\partial \mu\, \partial(\sigma^2)} \\ \dfrac{\partial^2 l}{\partial(\sigma^2)\, \partial \mu} & \dfrac{\partial^2 l}{\partial(\sigma^2)^2} \end{pmatrix} = \begin{pmatrix} -\dfrac{n}{\sigma^2} & -\dfrac{1}{\sigma^4}\sum(Y_i - \mu) \\ -\dfrac{1}{\sigma^4}\sum(Y_i - \mu) & \dfrac{n}{2\sigma^4} - \dfrac{1}{\sigma^6}\sum(Y_i - \mu)^2 \end{pmatrix}$$

$$= \begin{pmatrix} -\dfrac{n}{\tilde{\sigma}^2} & 0 \\ 0 & -\dfrac{n}{2\tilde{\sigma}^4} \end{pmatrix} \qquad [3.24]$$

The second equality in [3.24] is obtained by substituting into each matrix element the solution to equations [3.23A] and [3.23B] that is $\mu = \tilde{\mu} = \bar{Y}$ and $\sigma^2 = \tilde{\sigma}^2 = \sum (Y_i - \bar{Y})^2/n$. From [3.24] it is clear that

$$\frac{\partial^2 l}{\partial \mu^2} < 0, \quad \frac{\partial^2 l}{\partial(\sigma^2)^2} < 0 \quad \text{and} \quad \frac{\partial^2 l}{\partial \mu^2}\frac{\partial^2 l}{\partial(\sigma^2)^2} > \left(\frac{\partial^2 l}{\partial \mu\, \partial \sigma^2}\right)^2$$

Thus, the second-order conditions for a maximum are met, so we have indeed maximised the likelihood function.

It is useful to stress two facts about ML estimation at this point. It should be obvious that the formulae for the various MLEs we have obtained depend entirely on the form of the distribution assumed for the parent population – that is, on whether the parent population is Poisson, Geometric, Exponential, etc. The first point then is that, unless we know the distribution of the parent population, maximum likelihood estimation is impossible. The second point is that although, as we shall see in the next section, MLEs very frequently have desirable large sample properties, they often do *not* possess the small sample properties we would ideally like estimators to have. For example, in

47

the last case considered, the MLE of the population variance σ^2 was found to be $\tilde{\sigma}^2 = \sum (Y_i - \bar{Y})^2/n$. However, $\tilde{\sigma}^2$ is a biased estimate of σ^2. Hence, here at once is an example of an MLE that does not possess the small sample property of unbiasedness.

3.3 Properties of maximum likelihood estimators

Although MLEs may not possess any of the desirable small sample properties of estimators, it can be shown that under very general conditions they can be relied on to possess the large sample properties of consistency and asymptotic efficiency. That is, first, as the sample size n tends to infinity, the sampling distribution for an MLE collapses on to the parameter being estimated. Secondly, of all such consistent estimators, the MLE's distribution collapses 'most quickly' as the sample size n increases. That is, the MLE has the smallest asymptotic variance of all consistent estimators of the parameter in question.

Recall, from section 2.3, that the asymptotic distribution of an estimator is the limiting distribution which the sampling distribution of that estimator approaches as the sample size increases. The asymptotic variance is simply the variance of this limiting distribution. It turns out that *the asymptotic distributions of MLEs are, again under very general conditions, normal distributions.* Moreover, the mean of the asymptotic distribution of an MLE always equals the parameter being estimated (since MLEs are asymptotically unbiased) and it is always possible to find an expression for the variance of an MLE's asymptotic distribution. Knowledge of this variance is important if we wish to test hypotheses concerning, or form confidence intervals for, the parameters we are estimating.

To illustrate how it is always possible to find the asymptotic variance of an MLE, consider again the k parameter case where the likelihood function for a sample size n is given by [3.2]. As usual, let $l = \log L$. Next consider the negative of the matrix of expected values of second-order partial derivatives

$$-\begin{pmatrix} E\left(\dfrac{\partial^2 l}{\partial \pi_1^2}\right) & E\left(\dfrac{\partial^2 l}{\partial \pi_1 \partial \pi_2}\right) & \cdots & E\left(\dfrac{\partial^2 l}{\partial \pi_1 \partial \pi_k}\right) \\[2ex] E\left(\dfrac{\partial^2 l}{\partial \pi_2 \partial \pi_1}\right) & E\left(\dfrac{\partial^2 l}{\partial \pi_2^2}\right) & \cdots & E\left(\dfrac{\partial^2 l}{\partial \pi_2 \partial \pi_k}\right) \\[2ex] \vdots & \vdots & & \vdots \\[2ex] E\left(\dfrac{\partial^2 l}{\partial \pi_k \partial \pi_1}\right) & E\left(\dfrac{\partial^2 l}{\partial \pi_k \partial \pi_2}\right) & \cdots & E\left(\dfrac{\partial^2 l}{\partial \pi_k^2}\right) \end{pmatrix} \qquad [3.25]$$

This normally symmetric matrix is known as the *information matrix*. It can be shown that the asymptotic variance of the MLE of the parameter Π_j is given by the jth diagonal element of the inverse of the information matrix, normally written I^{jj}. That is

asymptotic var $\Pi_j = I^{jj}$ $\qquad j = 1, 2, 3, \ldots, k$ $\qquad\qquad$ [3.26]

As an example, consider the case of a normally distributed population with mean μ and variance σ^2. Using [3.24] the inverse of the information matrix is

$$-\begin{pmatrix} E\left(\dfrac{\partial^2 l}{\partial \mu^2}\right) & E\left(\dfrac{\partial^2 l}{\partial \mu\, \partial(\sigma^2)}\right) \\ E\left(\dfrac{\partial^2 l}{\partial(\sigma^2)\, \partial \mu}\right) & E\left(\dfrac{\partial^2 l}{\partial(\sigma^2)^2}\right) \end{pmatrix}^{-1} = \begin{pmatrix} \dfrac{n}{\sigma^2} & 0 \\ 0 & \dfrac{n}{2\sigma^4} \end{pmatrix}^{-1} = \begin{pmatrix} \dfrac{\sigma^2}{n} & 0 \\ 0 & \dfrac{2\sigma^4}{n} \end{pmatrix} \qquad [3.27]$$

The asymptotic variances of the MLEs of μ and σ^2 are therefore σ^2/n and $2\sigma^4/n$ respectively. Thus, we can say that the MLE of μ, that is $\tilde{\mu} = \bar{Y}$, is asymptotically normally distributed with mean μ and variance σ^2/n. Similarly, the MLE of σ^2, that is $\tilde{\sigma}^2 = \sum (Y_i - \bar{Y})^2/n$, is asymptotically normally distributed with mean σ^2 and variance $2\sigma^4/n$.

It is in fact the case that, since we have a normally distributed population, the sample mean, $\bar{Y}$, is $N(\mu, \sigma^2/n)$ even for small samples. However $\tilde{\sigma}^2$ becomes $N(\sigma^2, 2\sigma^4/n)$ only as the sample size becomes large.

At this point, it should be noted that the diagonal elements of the inverse of the information matrix also provide *lower-bounds* for the *small sample* variances of any unbiased estimators of the relevant parameters. That is, if $\hat{\Pi}_j$ is any unbiased estimator of Π_j, then

$$\text{var } \hat{\Pi}_j \geqslant \Pi^{jj} \qquad j = 1, 2, 3, \dots, k \qquad [3.28]$$

In other words the variance of Π_j cannot be smaller than the relevant element in the information matrix.

The inequality [3.28] is known as the *Cramer–Rao inequality*. It makes possible the construction of a lower limit for the variance of any unbiased estimator, provided we know the form of the distribution of the parent population. This lower limit is referred to as the *Cramer–Rao lower bound*.

In section 2.3 we mentioned the difficulty, frequently experienced in determining *the* efficient estimator of a parameter, of determining from among all unbiased estimators, linear or non-linear, the one which has the smallest variance. The Cramer–Rao lower bound sometimes provides a way out of this difficulty. If we have an unbiased estimator, whose variance equals the lower bound I^{jj}, then this must be the efficient estimator, since we know no other unbiased estimator can have a smaller variance. For example, in the above example relating to a normally distributed population, readers should be aware that $\bar{Y}$ is an unbiased estimator of the population mean, μ, and moreover has a variance σ^2/n regardless of the sample size. The variance of $\bar{Y}$ therefore equals the Cramer–Rao lower bound. Hence $\bar{Y}$ is not merely asymptotically normally distributed with mean μ and variance σ^2/n, but possesses the small sample properties of unbiasedness and efficiency.

There are two reasons, however, why the Cramer–Rao lower bound cannot always be used to solve the problem of determining efficiency. First, if we do not know the distribution of the parent population then we cannot construct the information matrix and hence we will not know the lower bound. Secondly, even if we know the lower bound *it may not be attainable*. That is, there may be no unbiased estimator with a variance equal to the lower bound.[1] For example, in the case of a normally distributed population we know from [3.27] that the lower bound for unbiased estimators of the population variance,

σ^2, is $2\sigma^4/n$. That is, no unbiased estimator of σ^2 can have a variance smaller than $2\sigma^4/n$. Unfortunately, it turns out that there is no unbiased estimator with a variance equal to $2\sigma^4/n$ either. For example, the MLE $\tilde{\sigma}^2$ only attains the lower bound as the sample size becomes very large. When the Cramer–Rao lower bound is unattainable, finding the efficient estimator of a parameter can become an insuperable problem.

3.4   Maximum likelihood estimation and multiple regression

In section 2.2 we considered the OLS method of estimating the β_j parameters in the population regression equation [2.12]. In section 2.4 we then introduced the classical multiple regression model and considered the properties of the OLS estimators when the classical assumptions hold. In this section, we return to equation [2.12] and consider how and why we might estimate the β_j parameters not by OLS but by the method of maximum likelihood.

Recall that if assumption 1 of the classical model holds, so that the X variables are non-stochastic, then the sample observations consist of the values obtained for the dependent variable, Y, i.e. $Y_1, Y_2, Y_3, \ldots, Y_n$. Moreover, since each Y_i is determined by

$$Y_i = \beta_1 + \beta_2 X_{2i} + \beta_3 X_{3i} + \cdots + \beta_k X_{ki} + \varepsilon_i \qquad [3.29]$$

then, provided assumption 5 of the classical model holds, that is provided each ε_i is normally distributed, we recall that each Y_i has a normal distribution. This is because, under present assumptions, [3.29] implies that each Y_i is simply the sum of a constant plus a normally distributed ε_i.

Hence, given assumption 3 of the classical model (Var $\varepsilon_i = \sigma^2 =$ constant), when repeated samples are taken each sequence of Y_is obtained will be normally distributed with mean and variance

$$EY_i = \beta_1 + \beta_2 X_{2i} + \beta_3 X_{3i}, \ldots, + \beta_k X_{ki} \qquad [3.30]$$

$$\text{var } Y_i = \sigma^2 \qquad [3.31]$$

Knowing their distribution enables a likelihood function for the Y_is to be formulated. in this case, the sample likelihood will depend on the underlying parameters of the regression equation, i.e. the β_js *and* σ^2, and on the sample values obtained. That is

$$L = L(\beta_1, \beta_2, \beta_3, \ldots, \beta_k, \sigma^2, Y_1, Y_2, Y_3, \ldots, Y_n) \qquad [3.32]$$

From [3.30] and [3.31] we know that the probability density function for each Y_i has the normal form

$$f(Y_i) = \frac{1}{(2\pi\sigma^2)^{1/2}} e^{-(Y_i - EY_i)^2/2\sigma^2} \qquad [3.33]$$

EY_i being given by [3.30]. Hence

$$\log f(Y_i) = -\tfrac{1}{2}\log 2\pi - \tfrac{1}{2}\log \sigma^2 - \frac{1}{2\sigma^2}(Y_i - EY_i)^2 \qquad [3.34]$$

50

If we are to be able to write the likelihood function [3.32] in the customary form

$$L = f(Y_1)f(Y_2)f(Y_3) \ldots f(Y_n)$$ [3.35]

then it is necessary that all the Y_is be independent of each other. From [3.29] we know that each Y_i depends on the corresponding ε_i. Hence independence of the Y_is requires independence of the ε_is.

The classical assumption 4 that covar $(\varepsilon_i, \varepsilon_j) = 0$ for all $i \neq j$, combined with the assumption already made that each ε_i is normally distributed, ensures independence of the ε_is and hence the independence of the Y_is. Thus, provided these assumptions are valid, the log-likelihood function for the nY-values is

$$l = \sum \log f(Y_i) = -\frac{n}{2}\log 2\pi - \frac{n}{2}\log \sigma^2 - \frac{1}{2\sigma^2}\sum(Y_i - EY_i)^2$$ [3.36]

where, remember, EY_i is given by [3.30].

Rather than going through the normal procedure of differentiating l with respect to each parameter in turn, we simply note that, if we are to maximise l, then the minus sign in front of the last term in [3.36] implies that we must choose the values of the β_js so as to minimise the sum of squares $\sum(Y_i - EY_i)^2$. That is choose $\tilde{\beta}_j$s so that

$$\sum(Y_i - \tilde{\beta}_1 - \tilde{\beta}_2 X_{2i} - \tilde{\beta}_3 X_{3i}. \ldots - \tilde{\beta}_k X_{ki})^2$$ [3.37]

is a minimum. But, given the resultant $\tilde{\beta}_j$s, the term in brackets in [3.37] is simply the ith residual from the estimation. Hence, to maximise the likelihood function we have to choose our $\tilde{\beta}_j$s so as to *minimise the sum of squares of the resultant residuals*. But this is just what we do when we use the ordinary least squares estimation method. It is therefore apparent that *under present assumptions* the MLEs of the β_js must be identical to the OLS estimators of the β_js. That is

$$\tilde{\beta}_j = \hat{\beta}_j \qquad j = 1, 2, 3, \ldots, n$$ [3.38]

where the $\hat{\beta}_j$s are given by the matrix formula [2.20].

Unlike the OLS estimating method the ML method also provides an estimate of the disturbance variance σ^2. Differentiating [3.36] partially with respect to σ^2 and equating to zero yields

$$\frac{\partial l}{\partial \sigma^2} = -\frac{n}{2\sigma^2} + \frac{1}{2(\sigma^2)^2}\sum(Y_i - EY_i)^2 = 0$$ [3.39]

Substituting the MLEs (i.e. the $\tilde{\beta}_j$s) for the β_js in EY_i and solving [3.39] for σ^2, yields the MLE of σ^2 as

$$\tilde{\sigma}^2 = \frac{\sum e_i^2}{n}$$ [3.40]

where $e_i = Y_i - \tilde{\beta}_1 - \tilde{\beta}_2 X_{2i}. \ldots - \tilde{\beta}_k X_{ki}$ is the ith residual.

As we noted on page 32, $\tilde{\sigma}^2$ the MLE of σ^2 is a biased estimator, so this is another case where the ML method does not yield an unbiased estimator. However, $\tilde{\sigma}^2$ has the desirable large sample properties of consistency and asymptotic efficiency. As an MLE it is asymptotically normally distributed with mean σ^2 and, if the information matrix is derived in this case, the asymptotic variance of $\tilde{\sigma}^2$ is found to be $2\sigma^4/n$.

It may seem that since the MLEs and the OLS estimators are identical in this case, the method of maximum likelihood adds little that is useful to our treatment of multiple regression in the last chapter. However, the MLEs [3.38] were derived for the case where (a) the population regression equation takes the form [2.12] and (b) all the assumptions of the classical multiple regression model are valid. When this is the case, the two types of estimator do indeed coincide. But will they coincide if either the conditions (a) and (b) do not hold? We conclude this section by considering this question.

Consider, first, the population regression equation [2.12]. There is really no reason why economic relationships should take such a conveniently linear form as this and in practice we might wish to make EY some non-linear function of the explanatory X variables. Considering, for simplicity, the case of a single explanatory variable, suppose the population regression equation takes the form $EY = \beta_1 X_2^{\beta_2}$. Such an equation is said to be non-linear in the parameters β_1 and β_2.

Introducing a disturbance term obeying the usual classical assumptions, we then have for a sample size n

$$Y_i = \beta_1 X_{2i}^{\beta_2} + \varepsilon_i \qquad i = 1, 2, 3, \ldots, n \qquad [3.41]$$

It is possible to apply the least squares method to the estimation of [3.41]? We must choose $\hat{\beta}_1$ and $\hat{\beta}_2$ so as to minimise the sum of squared residuals, S, where now

$$S = \sum e_i^2 = \sum (Y_i - \hat{\beta}_1 X_{2i}^{\hat{\beta}_2})^2 \qquad [3.42]$$

To minimise S we differentiate partially with respect to $\hat{\beta}_1$ and $\hat{\beta}_2$ and equate the resultant derivatives to zero.[2]

$$\frac{\partial S}{\partial \hat{\beta}_1} = -2 \sum X_{2i}^{\hat{\beta}_2}(Y_i - \hat{\beta}_1 X_{2i}^{\hat{\beta}_2}) = 0 \qquad [3.43]$$

$$\frac{\partial S}{\partial \hat{\beta}_2} = -2\hat{\beta}_1 \sum X_{2i}^{\hat{\beta}_2} \log X_{2i}(Y_i - \hat{\beta}_1 X_{2i}^{\hat{\beta}_2}) = 0 \qquad [3.44]$$

Equations [3.43] and [3.44] comprise two equations in $\hat{\beta}_1$ and $\hat{\beta}_2$ which can in principle be solved to yield least squares estimators. Unfortunately, they are obviously highly non-linear and there exists no compact algebraic solution. However, computer algorithms exist for minimizing sums of squares such as [3.42] numerically. The resultant values of $\hat{\beta}_1$ and $\hat{\beta}_2$ are known as *non-linear least squares estimators*.

Now let us consider the estimation of [3.41] using a maximum likelihood approach. Provided the ε_i disturbances are normally distributed and obey the other classical assumptions, the sample Y_is will be normally and independently distributed with mean $EY_i = \beta_1 X_{2i}^{\beta_2}$ and variance σ^2. The log-likelihood function for the n sample Y-values therefore again takes the form [3.36] except that now $EY_i = \beta_1 X_{2i}^{\beta_2}$. Just as in the general linear case, maximising the likelihood function involves minimising $\sum (Y_i - EY_i)^2$. That is, in this case, we minimise

$$\sum (Y_i - \tilde{\beta}_1 X_{2i}^{\tilde{\beta}_2})^2 \qquad [3.45]$$

Hence, we must choose the MLEs, $\tilde{\beta}_1$ and $\tilde{\beta}_2$ so as to minimise the sum of squares of the resultant residuals.

Minimising [3.45] is obviously an identical problem to minimising [3.42]. Hence, as in the linear case, the maximum likelihood and least squares estimators turn out to be identical.

It should now in fact be clear that for *any* non-linear population regression line, provided the disturbances are normally distributed and obey the other classical assumptions, *the non-linear least squares and maximum likelihood estimators will be identical.* The log-likelihood function will always take the form [3.36], the only difference between individual examples being that the form of EY_i will depend on the precise type of non-linearity in the population regression equation. Maximising the log-likelihood function will therefore always involve minimising the sum of squares of the resultant residuals.

Although, then, there are no differences between the non-linear least squares and maximum-likelihood estimators under present assumptions, what of their properties? The properties of the OLS estimators, outlined in the middle part of section 2.4, depended very much on the implied assumption of a linear population regression equation. For non-linear regression equations we have *for each separate case* the problem of deriving (if possible) the properties of the relevant non-linear least squares estimators from scratch. In fact, it turns out that rarely, if ever, do non-linear least squares estimators have any of the desirable small sample properties described in section 2.3.

If, however, we view estimation within a maximum likelihood framework, then regardless of the precise non-linearity involved, we can in all cases fall back on the general properties of MLEs. We can be confident that our estimators will have the large sample properties of consistency, asymptotic normality and asymptotic efficiency. This is the major advantage of viewing estimation from a maximum likelihood angle.

MLEs and non-linear least squares estimators are identical provided all the classical assumptions concerning the disturbances are valid. But what if some or all of the classical assumptions fail to hold? We shall consider breakdowns in the classical assumptions in some detail in chapter 4. We shall find that, even with a linear population regression line, the ML and OLS estimators rarely coincide when the assumptions break down. Here we merely note that, it is the exception rather than the rule in econometrics for the OLS estimators to have any desirable properties at all – large or small sample. In such a situation the maximum likelihood method of estimation comes into its own, because it provides an established procedure for providing estimators which, under quite general conditions, possess the desired large sample properties of consistency and asymptotic efficiency.

3.5 The computation of maximum likelihood estimates

In regression analysis ML estimation generally involves the minimisation of sums of squares such as [3.37] and [3.45]. When these sums of squares involve non-linearities such as that in [3.45] it is not normally possible to obtain algebraic expressions for the MLEs. For example, the reader should try solving equations [3.43] and [3.44] for $\hat{\beta}_1$ and $\hat{\beta}_2$ in terms of the Y_is and X_{2i}s. Such sums of squares have to be minimised by numerical algorithms. Let us take as an example the sum of squares given by [3.42] or [3.45].

Notice first that, for a given value of $\hat{\beta}_2$, the population regression equation underlying [3.42] becomes linear in the parameters. That is, it takes the form $EY = \beta_1 Z$ where $Z = X_2^{\beta_2}$, while the sum of squares [3.42] becomes

$$S' = \sum (Y_i - \hat{\beta}_1 Z_i)^2 \qquad [3.46]$$

where the Z-values are constructed from the X_2-values using $Z_i = X_{2i}^{\hat{\beta}_2}$.

Minimising a sum of squares such as [3.46] for a given value of $\hat{\beta}_2$ is a simple matter. We simply construct the required Z-values from the X_2-values and minimise the sum of squares in the usual manner. We can therefore select a 'grid' of given values for $\hat{\beta}_2$ and perform the minimisation of [3.46] for each such value. For example, if β_2 was expected to lie between 0 and 1, then we could compute the value of $\hat{\beta}_1$ in [3.46] which minimised S' for each of the values $\hat{\beta}_2 = 0$, $\hat{\beta}_2 = 0.1$, $\hat{\beta}_2 = 0.2, \ldots, \hat{\beta}_2 = 1.0$. Having found the smallest minimum S', we could then conduct a second and finer 'grid search'. If, for example, $\hat{\beta}_2 = 0.4$ yielded the smallest minimum S' during our first search, we could carry out a second search using the values $\hat{\beta}_2 = 0.35$, $\hat{\beta}_2 = 0.36, \ldots, \hat{\beta}_2 = 0.45$. We would then select the smallest of the minimum S' values in the second search. If necessary an even finer search could then be performed. In this way we could find, numerically, the pair of values $\hat{\beta}_1$ and $\hat{\beta}_2$ that minimises the original sum of squares [3.42]. These values would be the non-linear least squares estimators and of course the MLEs of $\hat{\beta}_1$ and $\hat{\beta}_2$.

Minimising the sums of squares that arise in non-linear maximum likelihood estimation problems is not always as straightforward as in the above case. The numerical problems involved can be very complex. However, high-speed computer algorithms are available for dealing with such problems. These may either tackle the sum of squares directly or make use of derivatives such as [3.43] and [3.44]. They normally involve iterative procedures. That is, initial values for the estimates are found which are used, via some given rule, for computing new estimates which come closer to minimising the relevant sum of squares. The process is repeated until the estimates converge on their optimal values.

Until recently, any kind of non-linear maximum likelihood method of estimation was very time-consuming and costly. Such methods were therefore avoided if at all possible. Preference was given to alternative simpler estimators which, hopefully, could be demonstrated to be asymptotically equivalent to MLEs. However, the rapid development and increased availability of high-speed computers and algorithms, during the past five to ten years, now makes non-linear estimation a much more attractive proposition. This development, plus the fact that MLEs generally possess desirable large sample properties, has led some econometricians to favour approaching any estimation problem from a maximum likelihood viewpoint.

Further reading

Few books provide an elementary treatment of maximum likelihood estimation. However a more advanced introduction is provided by Silvey (1975) and a fuller treatment of the topic can be found in Kendall and Stuart (1973). A good introduction to ML estimation in multiple regression is provided by Stewart (1991).

Notes

1. Some statisticians would only refer to an estimator as efficient if its variance equalled the Cramer–Rao lower bound. If no such estimator had this property then the unbiased estimator with the smallest variance would be termed merely the minimum variance or best unbiased estimator.
2. Recall that if $z = y^x$ then $\log z = x \log y$, $(1/z)(dz/dx) = \log y$ and hence $dz/dx = y^x \log y$.

4 Some extensions of the classical linear model

4.1 Non-linear regression equations

It is frequently the case that economic relationships between variables are non-linear so that the standard equation [2.12] is often likely to be inappropriate. When it is suspected that the population regression equation is non-linear there are a number of simple non-linear functions by which we may attempt to approximate it. For example, in two-variable regression instead of $EY = \beta_1 + \beta_2 X_2$ we might specify

$$E(Y) = \beta_1 + \beta_2\left(\frac{1}{X_2}\right) \qquad\qquad [4.1]$$

or

$$E(Y) = \beta_1 + \beta_2 \log X_2 \qquad\qquad [4.2]$$

or

$$E(Y) = \beta_1 X_2^{\beta_2} \qquad\qquad [4.3]$$

These functions are illustrated for positive β_1 and β_2 in Fig. 4.1A, 4.1B and 4.1C respectively. It is left to the reader to determine the shape of these functions for negative values of their parameters.

Population regression equations such as [4.1] and [4.2] are linear in the parameters β_1 and β_2. That is, they can be 'transformed' into standard linear equations merely by defining new variables $1/X_2$ and $\log X_2$. Once transformed they can be estimated by OLS in the usual manner. That is, for example, once we have defined $Z_2 = 1/X_2$, [4.1] becomes[1]

$$E(Y) = \beta_1 + \beta_2 Z_2 \qquad\qquad [4.1A]$$

Equation [4.3], however, is non-linear in the parameters and its straightforward estimation by OLS requires the additional assumption that the disturbance is 'multiplicative' in form. That is, it enters the population relationship in the form

$$Y = (EY)(\varepsilon) = \beta_1 X_2^{\beta_2}\varepsilon \qquad\qquad [4.4]$$

rather than as

$$Y = E(Y) + \varepsilon = \beta_1 X_2^{\beta_2} + \varepsilon \qquad\qquad [4.4A]$$

Multiplicative disturbances may or may not be a reasonable assumption but, provided [4.4] is valid, we obtain by taking logarithms

$$\log Y = \log \beta_1 + \beta_2 \log X_2 + \log \varepsilon \qquad\qquad [4.5]$$

Equation [4.5] is linear in the logarithms of the variables. Hence, provided the *transformed* disturbance 'log ε' obeys the usual classical assumptions, we may safely apply OLS and regress the transformed variable 'log Y' on the transformed variable 'log X_2'. The only minor complication is that the intercept in this regression yields an estimate of log $β_1$ rather than $β_1$. Note, however, that [4.4A] cannot be transformed into a linear equation in this way so that the assumption of multiplicative disturbances is crucial for straightforward estimation by OLS. If the disturbance enters additively as in [4.4A] then the equation has to be estimated by the non-linear least squares procedure described in section 3.5. It is, in fact, normally the case that, when an equation is non-linear in the parameters, a non-linear procedure is necessary for estimation. Unless 'artificial' assumptions such as that of a multiplicative disturbance are made, it is usually not possible to transform the equation into standard linear form.

4.1 Non-linear relationships between EY and X.

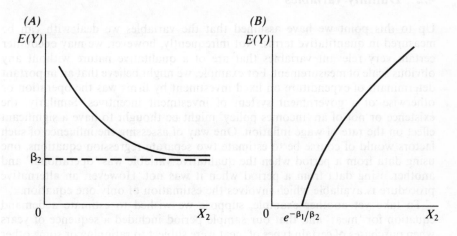

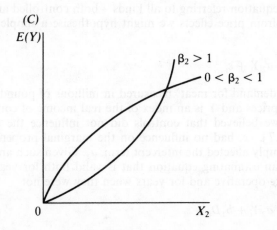

Equations such as [4.1]–[4.3] can easily be generalised for the multiple regression case. A favourite form is the generalisation of [4.4]

$$Y = \beta_1 X_2^{\beta_2} X_3^{\beta_3}, \ldots, X_k^{\beta_k} \varepsilon \qquad [4.6]$$

Like [4.4] this equation is linear in the logarithms. Also its parameters, the β_js $(j = 2, 3, \ldots, k)$, can be interpreted as the elasticities of the dependent Y variable with respect to each of the explanatory variables. This property makes [4.6] an obvious choice of estimating equation when such elasticities are of particular interest. For example, it is frequently used in the estimation of demand equations for a single good and for demand for money equations. Since the Cobb–Douglas production function is linear in the logarithms we shall also encounter equations such as [4.6] in Chapter 11. Notice again, however, that for straightforward OLS estimation of [4.6] we require the assumption of a multiplicative disturbance.

4.2 Dummy variables

Up to this point we have assumed that the variables we deal with can be measured in quantitative terms. Not infrequently, however, we may encounter certain very relevant variables that are of a qualitative nature without any obvious scale of measurement. For example, we might believe that an important determinant of expenditure on fixed investment by firms was the operation or otherwise of a government system of investment incentives. Similarly, the existence or not of an 'incomes policy' might be thought to have a significant effect on the rate of wage inflation. One way of assessing the influence of such factors would of course be to estimate two separate regression equations, one using data from a period when the qualitative variable was 'operational' and another using data from a period when it was not. However, an alternative procedure is available which involves the estimation of only one equation.

To take yet another example, suppose we wished to estimate a demand equation for 'meat' and that our sample period included a sequence of years when purchases of certain types of meat were subject to rationing or some other form of control. We do not have data on different kinds of meat but must estimate an equation referring to all kinds – both controlled and uncontrolled. Abstracting from price effects we might hypothesise a simple linear equation for year t

$$Q_t = a_1 + a_2 Y_t + \varepsilon_t \qquad [4.7]$$

where Q is 'demand for meat' measured in millions of pounds of expenditure at constant prices and Y is an index of the real income of consumers.

Suppose we believed that controls did not influence the parameter a_2 in equation [4.7], i.e. had no influence on the marginal propensity to consume meat, but simply affected the intercept term, a_1. Given such an assumption, we can specify an estimating equation that is valid both for years during which controls were operative and for years when they were not

$$Q_t = a_1 + a_2 Y_t + b_1 D_t + \varepsilon_t \qquad [4.8]$$

where $b_1 < 0$ and

$D_t = 1$ for 'controlled years' $D_t = 0$ for 'uncontrolled years'

Equation [4.8], combined with the definition of D, implies that during years when the purchase of meat was not controlled and $D_t = 0$, the demand equation was given by equation [4.7]. However, during other years when $D_t = 1$, we have

$$Q_t = (a_1 + b_1) + a_2 Y_t + \varepsilon_t \qquad [4.9]$$

To estimate an equation such as [4.8] simply involves constructing a 'dummy' variable D, taking the value unity whenever controls were operative and zero when they were not, and applying normal multiple regression techniques treating this variable just like any other. For example, suppose we estimated

$$\hat{Q}_t = 24 + 0.2Y_t - 5D_t \qquad [4.10]$$

This would simply imply

$$\hat{Q}_t = 24 + 0.2Y_t \qquad \text{for uncontrolled years} \qquad [4.11]$$

and

$$\hat{Q}_t = 19 + 0.2Y_t \qquad \text{for controlled years} \qquad [4.12]$$

Equations [4.11] and [4.12] are illustrated in Fig. 4.2. We see that, given our present model, the operation of controls on meat purchases results in a parallel downward shift in the demand function. This implies that introducing controls leads to a decrease in meat purchases of £5 m no matter what the level of income. To test whether this estimate of £5 m is significantly different from zero in the statistical sense we need simply examine the t-ratio on the coefficient D_t in equation [4.10].

4.2 A parallel downward shift in the demand function.

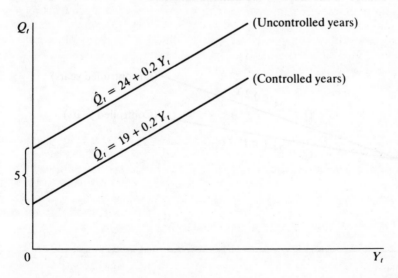

It may justifiably be argued that the imposition of controls on certain types of meat purchase might be just as likely to affect the marginal propensity to consume (MPC) meat, a_2, as it would the intercept in [4.7]. However, this situation may also be handled by specifying

$$Q_t = a_1 + a_2 Y_t + b_2 Y_t D_t + \varepsilon_t \qquad [4.13]$$

where b_2 is presumed to be negative and D_t is defined as before. This implies the equations

$$Q_t = a_1 + a_2 Y_t + \varepsilon_t \qquad \text{for uncontrolled years} \qquad [4.14]$$

and

$$Q_t = a_1 + (a_2 + b_2) Y_t + \varepsilon_t \qquad \text{for controlled years} \qquad [4.15]$$

Thus it is now the MPC that is smaller during years when controls operate. Equation [4.13] would be estimated simply by including the 'multiplicative' dummy variable $Y_t D_t$ in the estimating equation instead of the 'intercept' dummy D_t. $Y_t D_t$ would take the value zero when controls were not operative but take a value equal to Y_t in years when they were. Suppose, for example, we estimated

$$\hat{Q}_t = 24 + 0.2 Y_t - 0.05 Y_t D_t$$

This would imply the demand functions illustrated in Fig. 4.3. Now the slope rather than the intercept of the demand function varies according to whether controls are operative.

The dummy variable technique can easily be generalised to the case where we have more than one 'genuine' explanatory variable. For example, a more plausible specification for the demand equation for meat might be

$$Q_t = a_1 + a_2 Y_t + a_3 P_t + a_4 F_t + \varepsilon_t \qquad [4.16]$$

4.3 A change in the slope of the demand function.

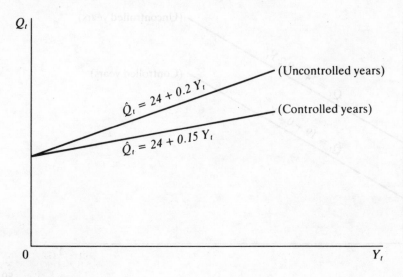

where P_t and F_t are indices of the price of meat and the prices of 'non-meat' foods. If we wished the intercept in [4.16] to change with the imposition of controls we could specify

$$Q_t = a_1 + a_2 Y_t + a_3 P_t + a_4 F_t + b_1 D_t + \varepsilon_t \qquad [4.17]$$

However, if we wished to consider the effect of controls on the parameters a_2, a_3 and a_4 we could specify

$$Q_t = a_1 + a_2 Y_t + b_2 Y_t D_t + a_3 P_t + b_3 P_t D_t + a_4 F_t + b_4 F_t D_t + \varepsilon_t \qquad [4.18]$$

and examine the significance of the estimates of b_2, b_3 and b_4.

Dummy variables represent a most useful extension to regression analysis since they enable us to allow for variables which cannot be measured in quantitative units. Their values need not be restricted to zero or unity. For example, in Chapter 10, we shall see that a number of recent papers on the UK consumption function seek to allow for a rescheduling of expenditures in anticipation of rises in indirect taxation. An intercept dummy is defined to take the value $+1$ in the quarter prior to the tax change, -1 in the quarter after the tax change but zero in all other quarters. Thus, the net effect of the dummy is zero but it influences the timing of expenditures. We shall encounter intercept-type dummies in all the applied chapters of this book. The use of multiplicative dummies to allow for changes in the slope coefficients of regression equations is more rare.

Seasonal dummies

It is sometimes necessary to introduce more than one dummy variable into a regression equation. The most frequent reason for doing so is to allow for seasonal variations. For example, if we thought that the intercept term in our demand for meat equation [4.7] varied from quarter to quarter (more meat might be purchased in the winter quarter) we could specify for quarter t.

$$Q_t = a_1 + a_2 Y_t + b_1 D_{1t} + b_2 D_{2t} + b_3 D_{3t} + \varepsilon_t \qquad [4.19]$$

where $D_{1t} = 1$ for winter quarter $D_{1t} = 0$ otherwise
        $D_{2t} = 1$ for spring quarter $D_{2t} = 0$ otherwise
        $D_{3t} = 1$ for summer quarter $D_{3t} = 0$ otherwise

This would imply the following demand equations

$$Q_t = a_1 + b_1 + a_2 Y_t + \varepsilon_t \qquad \text{(winter quarter)}$$
$$Q_t = a_1 + b_2 + a_2 Y_t + \varepsilon_t \qquad \text{(spring quarter)}$$
$$Q_t = a_1 + b_3 + a_2 Y_t + \varepsilon_t \qquad \text{(summer quarter)}$$
$$Q_t = a_1 + a_2 Y_t + \varepsilon_t \qquad \text{(autumn quarter)}$$

The significance of seasonal effects could then be determined by examining the t-ratios on the estimates of b_1, b_2 and b_3 in equation [4.19].

Notice that the seasonal effects are represented by three, not four dummy variables. *We do not need to include a fourth dummy to allow for the autumn quarter.*[3] In fact, if we attempted to introduce another dummy:

$D_{4t} = 1$ for autumn quarter $D_{4t} = 0$ otherwise

we would find our estimating procedures breaking down. This is because we would then have an exact linear relationship of the form

$$D_{1t} + D_{2t} + D_{3t} + D_{4t} = 1$$

between the dummy variables, holding during all quarters.

If it were thought that seasonal variations affected the marginal propensities to consume in [4.7] rather than the intercept, then this could be allowed for by introducing the winter, spring and summer dummies multiplicatively

$$Q_t = a_1 + b_1 Y_t D_{1t} + b_2 Y_t D_{2t} + b_3 Y_t D_{3t} + a_2 Y_t + \varepsilon_t \qquad [4.20]$$

Such an equation implies marginal propensities to consume of

$$a_2 + b_1, \quad a_2 + b_2, \quad a_2 + b_3 \quad \text{and} \quad a_2$$

during winter, spring, summer and autumn quarters respectively.

The use of seasonal dummies is easily extended to equations such as [4.16] which contain more than one 'genuine' explanatory variable.

4.3 Testing for parameter stability

There are often occasions in applied econometric work when we may wish to know whether an economic relationship has changed. For example, we might wish to test whether the parameters of a 'pre-war' consumption function differed from those of the post-war function. In recent years tests for parameter stability have been used very frequently in studies of the demand for money. The stability of demand for money functions has, of course, important implications for monetary policy.

The most well-known tests of parameter stability are probably those by Chow (1960b). To illustrate the idea behind these tests, suppose we suspect a sudden change or shift in the parameters of a demand for money function in the middle of our sample period. The first of the Chow tests proceeds as follows. Ordinary least squares regressions are run for the two sub-periods (i.e. for the periods before and after the suspected shift in the function) and also for the 'pooled' or full period. Suppose that the residual sums of squares for these regressions are $\sum e_1^2$, $\sum e_2^2$ and $\sum e_p^2$ respectively. Now consider the quantity

$$\frac{\sum e_p^2 - (\sum e_1^2 + \sum e_2^2)}{\sum e_1^2 + \sum e_2^2} \qquad [4.21]$$

[4.21] measures the proportionate increase in the sum of squared residuals that results from fitting a single regression to the full period rather than permitting the 'greater freedom' of fitting separate equations for each sub-period. Given the null hypothesis of parameter stability (i.e. no sudden shift in the function) we should expect this quantity to be 'small'. However, if a shift has occurred we must expect it to be 'larger'. The two cases are illustrated in Figs 4.4 and 4.5 where we abstract from any variables other than the demand for money and the rate of interest.

In both cases, points in the scatter referring to one sub-period are shown by crosses and to the other sub-period by dots. Figure 4.4 illustrates the scatter we might obtain when the function shifts. The two solid lines show the fitted

4.4 A change in parameter values.   4.5 No change in parameter values.

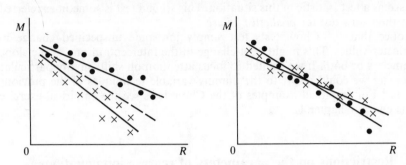

OLS equations for the two sub-periods. Clearly, if we were to restrict ourselves to fitting a *single* equation to all points (i.e. the dotted single line) there will be a large increase in the absolute size of residuals and, hence, in the sum of squared residuals for the whole period. Figure 4.5 illustrates a scatter we might obtain in the case of parameter stability. Now, replacing the two separate lines by a single line fitted to all points would lead to very little increase in the size of residuals.

The problem, of course, is to determine how large the quantity [4.21] should be before we can safely reject the hypothesis of parameter stability. Luckily, it is not difficult to show that, under the null hypothesis of parameter stability, the quantity

$$\left\{ \frac{\sum e_p^2 - (\sum e_1^2 + \sum e_2^2)}{\sum e_1^2 + \sum e_1^2} \right\} \left\{ \frac{n_1 + n_2 - 2k}{k} \right\} \qquad [4.22]$$

where n_1 and n_2 are the sizes of the two sub-samples and k is the number of parameters being estimated, has an F distribution with

$$(k, n_1 + n_2 - 2k)$$

degrees of freedom. Hence, it may be used as a test statistic and compared with the relevant critical F value.

The second of the two Chow tests covers the situation where the size of the second sample n_2 is less than k. It is then not possible to run an OLS regression for this second subsample. Consider, however, the quantity

$$\frac{\sum e_p^2 - \sum e_1^2}{\sum e_1^2} \qquad [4.23]$$

Equation [4.23] represents the proportionate increase in the sum of squared residuals that results from fitting an OLS regression to the pooled $n_1 + n_2$ observations rather than just to the first n_1 observations. The greater is this quantity, the more inclined we will be to reject the null hypothesis of parameter stability. In fact, given the hypothesis of parameter stability, the quantity

$$\left\{ \frac{\sum e_p^2 - \sum e_1^2}{\sum e_1^2} \right\} \left\{ \frac{n_1 - k}{n_2} \right\} \qquad [4.24]$$

has an F distribution with $(n_2, n_1 - k)$ degrees of freedom and may therefore be used as a test statistic in this situation. This second test is sometimes referred to as the Chow test for *predictive failure*.

Notice that the Chow tests test simply for some unspecified change in parameter values. This might be a change in the intercept, in one of the slope parameters or both. If we wanted to focus attention on shifts in any particular parameter we could resort to the dummy variable techniques of the previous section.[4] For empirical examples of the Chow tests see the empirical exercise at the end of Chapter 12.

4.4 Restrictions on the parameters of regresssion equations

In applied econometric work we may often believe that the parameters of a population regression equation should satisfy certain restrictions. One of the simplest examples of such a restriction is when we *suspect or require the intercept to be zero*. We shall encounter situations where we require this on a number of occasions in this book. For example, we shall see in Chapter 10 that all the main theories of the consumption function can lead to long-run equations that do not contain an intercept.

Consider the case of a single explanatory variable where, in the absence of an intercept, the population regression line becomes

$$EY = \beta_2 X_2 \qquad [4.25]$$

If we believe that the population regression line has no intercept, then obviously it makes sense to estimate it by a sample regression line, $\hat{Y} = \hat{\beta}_2 X_2$, without an intercept. Applying the OLS principle, this means minimising a sum of squared residuals given by

$$S = \sum e_i^2 = \sum (Y_i - \hat{Y}_i)^2 = \sum (Y_i - \hat{\beta}_2 X_{2i})^2 \qquad [4.26]$$

In effect we are choosing, out of all sample regression lines *that pass through the origin*, that which best fits the sample observations.

Differentiating [4.26] with respect to $\hat{\beta}_2$, the only coefficient we have to estimate, and equating to zero yields

$$\frac{dS}{d\hat{\beta}_2} = -2 \sum X_{2i}(Y_i - \hat{\beta}_2 X_{2i}) = 0 \qquad [4.27]$$

Solving [4.27] we obtain the OLS estimator of $\hat{\beta}_2$ as

$$\hat{\beta}_2 = \frac{\sum X_{2i} Y_i}{\sum X_{2i}^2} \qquad [4.28]$$

Notice that [4.28] has the same form as the normal OLS estimator of β_2 in two-variable regression, $\hat{\beta}_2 = \sum x_{2i} y_i / \sum x_{2i}^2$. The difference is that when the intercept is suppressed the deviations of Y and X_2 from their sample means are replaced by the actual values of Y and X_2. That is, $y_i = Y_i - \bar{Y}$ is replaced by Y_i and $x_{2i} = X_{2i} - \bar{X}$ is replaced by X_{2i}. A similar result, in fact, holds in multiple regression. With intercept suppressed, it can be shown that equation [2.20] (page 15) will still yield the OLS estimators of the slope coefficients provided we replace actual values of variables by deviations and redefine X as an $n \times (k - 1)$ matrix in which the column of ones in the original X matrix has been suppressed.

If, instead of simply accepting that the intercept be suppressed, we wished to test the validity of its suppression, the obvious procedure is to estimate the equation in the normal manner with intercept included. We can then test the hypothesis that β_1, the intercept in the population regression line, is zero by performing the normal t-test on our estimated intercept.

Restricted least squares

Normally, economic theory provides information, not about the precise value of individual regression parameters, but about relationships between them. It may suggest that the β_js in a population regression equation such as [2.12] (page 12) obey some *linear restriction*. For example, in section 9.1, we note that consumer theory suggests that all price and income elasticities in a demand equation should sum to zero. Hence, if we estimate a demand equation using the logarithmic form [4.6] then, since the β_js now represent elasticities, theory implies the *linear restriction* $\sum \beta_j = 0$. Similarly, in Section 11.1, we shall encounter the Cobb–Douglas production function. This can be written in the form

$$Q = BK^{\beta_2}L^{\beta_3}u \qquad [4.29]$$

where Q is output, K and L are capital and labour inputs and u is a multiplicative disturbance of the kind discussed in section 4.1. Taking logarithms yields

$$Y = \beta_1 + \beta_2 X_2 + \beta_3 X_3 + \varepsilon \qquad [4.30]$$

where $Y = \log Q$, $X_2 = \log K$, $X_3 = \log L$, $\beta_1 = \log B$ and $\varepsilon = \log u$. As is demonstrated in section 11.1, constant returns to scale in such a production function means that its parameters obey the *linear restriction*

$$\beta_2 + \beta_3 = 1 \qquad [4.31]$$

Consider a situation where we wish to estimate an equation such as [4.30] and where we believe that the restriction [4.31] is valid. That is, we believe a population relationship exists of the form

$$Y = \beta_1 + \beta_2 X_2 + (1 - \beta_2)X_3 + \varepsilon \qquad [4.32]$$

If we now attempt to estimate [4.32] by the normal OLS procedure, regressing Y on X_2 and X_3, we would obtain a sample regression equation

$$\hat{Y} = \hat{\beta}_1 + \hat{\beta}_2 X_2 + \hat{\beta}_3 X_3 \qquad [4.33]$$

We could now attempt to obtain estimates of the parameters β_1 and β_2 by comparing the coefficients in [4.32] and [4.33]. However, it should be immediately clear that we have a problem, since we would have *three* known coefficients, $\hat{\beta}_1$, $\hat{\beta}_2$ and $\hat{\beta}_3$ from which we would have to obtain estimates of *two* parameters, β_1 and β_2. Unless the estimates $\hat{\beta}_2$ and $\hat{\beta}_3$ obey the restriction $\hat{\beta}_2 + \hat{\beta}_3 = 1$, we will obtain two estimates of β_2, one equal to $\hat{\beta}_2$ and that other equal to $1 - \hat{\beta}_3$. Since, even if the *true* coefficients of X_2 and X_3 in [4.30] sum to unity, it is unlikely that their *estimates* $\hat{\beta}_2$ and $\hat{\beta}_3$ will do so, this will be the most common outcome. In fact, we have what is referred to in econometrics as an *overidentification problem*. If we are to obtain a unique estimate of β_2 some modification of the estimating procedure is necessary.

The OLS estimators $\hat{\beta}_1$, $\hat{\beta}_2$ and $\hat{\beta}_3$ in [4.33] are obtained by minimising the sum of squared residuals

$$\sum e_i^2 = \sum (Y_i - \hat{Y}_i)^2 = \sum (Y_i - \hat{\beta}_1 - \hat{\beta}_2 X_{2i} - \hat{\beta}_3 X_{3i})^2 \qquad [4.34]$$

If we are to obtain a unique estimate of β_2 then [4.34] has to be minimised *subject to the restriction that* $\hat{\beta}_2 + \hat{\beta}_3 = 1$. This can be achieved either using the Lagrangian multiplier method or, alternatively, substituting the constraint into [4.34] and then minimising in the usual way. The latter method is the more instructive since on substitution of $\hat{\beta}_2 + \hat{\beta}_3 = 1$ into [4.34], we then have to minimise

$$\sum e_i^2 = \sum \{ Y_i - \hat{\beta}_1 - \hat{\beta}_2 X_{2i} - (1 - \hat{\beta}_2) X_{3i} \}^2$$
$$= \sum \{ (Y_i - X_{3i}) - \hat{\beta}_1 - \hat{\beta}_2 (X_{2i} - X_{3i}) \}^2 \qquad [4.35]$$

However, choosing $\hat{\beta}_1$ and $\hat{\beta}_2$ so as to minimise [4.35] is exactly the same as choosing them so as to minimise the residual sum of squares when estimating a relationship of the kind

$$(Y - X_3) = \beta_1 + \beta_2 (X_2 - X_3) + \varepsilon \qquad [4.36]$$

Thus the simplest way of obtaining estimates that yield a unique value for $\hat{\beta}_2$ is to construct new variables $Y^* = Y - X_3$ and $X_2^* = X_2 - X_3$ and then use OLS to compute

$$\hat{Y}^* = \hat{\beta}_1 + \hat{\beta}_2 X_2^*$$

which is equivalent to

$$\hat{Y} = \hat{\beta}_1 + \hat{\beta}_2 X_2 + (1 - \hat{\beta}_2) X_3 \qquad [4.37]$$

The above method of estimation is known as *restricted least squares*. Notice that *the form of the equation eventually estimated*, [4.36], *is obtained simply by manipulating* [4.32]. Provided the classical assumptions hold when applied to [4.36], the restricted least squares estimators will possess all the usual desirable small and large sample properties.

The restricted least squares method may also be used to solve over-identification problems arising from the existence of more than one linear restriction on regression parameters. For example, suppose we believed the underlying population relationship was

$$Y = \beta_1 + \beta_2 X_2 + \beta_3 X_3 + \beta_4 X_4 + \beta_5 X_5 + \varepsilon \qquad [4.38]$$

where $\beta_2 = \beta_3$ and $\beta_4 + \beta_5 = 1$. This implies for the population

$$Y = \beta_1 + \beta_2 X_2 + \beta_2 X_3 + \beta_4 X_4 + (1 - \beta_4) X_5 + \varepsilon$$

so that if we compute the unrestricted sample regression equation

$$\hat{Y} = \hat{\beta}_1 + \hat{\beta}_2 X_2 + \hat{\beta}_3 X_3 + \hat{\beta}_4 X_4 + \hat{\beta}_5 X_5 \qquad [4.39]$$

we would again have an overidentification problem with just 3 independent parameters, β_1, β_2 and β_4 to obtain from the 5 estimated $\hat{\beta}$s in [4.39]. The solution to this problem is to estimate [4.39] subject to the two linear restrictions $\hat{\beta}_2 = \hat{\beta}_3$ and $\hat{\beta}_4 + \hat{\beta}_5 = 1$. The simplest way to do this is to note that [4.38] can be rearranged as

$$Y - X_5 = \beta_1 + \beta_2(X_2 + X_3) + \beta_4(X_4 - X_5) + \varepsilon \qquad [4.40]$$

Thus, we use our data to construct new variables

$$Y^* = Y - X_5, \quad X_2^* = X_2 + X_3 \quad \text{and} \quad X_4^* = X_4 - X_5,$$

and compute the sample regression equation

$$\hat{Y}^* = \hat{\beta}_1 + \hat{\beta}_2 X_2^* + \hat{\beta}_4 X_4^* \qquad [4.41]$$

which is equivalent to

$$\hat{Y} = \hat{\beta}_1 + \hat{\beta}_2 X_2 + \hat{\beta}_2 X_3 + \hat{\beta}_4 X_4 + (1 - \hat{\beta}_4)X_5 \qquad [4.42]$$

The restricted least squares estimates of β_1, β_2 and β_4 are then the $\hat{\beta}_1$, $\hat{\beta}_2$ and $\hat{\beta}_4$ in [4.41]. From the restrictions, the corresponding estimates of β_3 and β_5 are $\hat{\beta}_3 = \hat{\beta}_2$ and $\hat{\beta}_5 = 1 - \hat{\beta}_4$.

Testing linear restrictions

The *F*-test

It is rarely the case that we are prepared to accept without question an *a priori* restriction suggested by economic theory. Rather, the purpose of estimating 'restricted equations' such as [4.36] and [4.40] is normally to *test* the restrictions implied by them. Consider our first example, where the unrestricted sample regression equation was given by [4.33] and the restricted version, incorporating $\hat{\beta}_2 + \hat{\beta}_3 = 1$, by [4.37]. Since both these equations are estimated by OLS, it is possible in each case to split the total sum of squares in the dependent Y variable, SST, into an explained sum of squares and a residual sum of squares, as indicated by equation [2.38] (page 34). That is

$$\begin{aligned} \text{SST} &= \text{SSE}_U + \text{SSR}_U & \text{for the unrestricted equation} \\ \text{SST} &= \text{SSE}_R + \text{SSR}_R & \text{for the restricted equation} \end{aligned}$$

where in each case SSE represents that part of SST that can be explained by the explanatory X variables and SSR is the residual sum of squares, $\sum e_i^2$.

It should be intuitively clear that the residual sum of squares for an unrestricted equation such as [4.33] is likely to be smaller than for the corresponding restricted equation [4.37]. In [4.33] we consider all possible values for $\hat{\beta}_1$, $\hat{\beta}_2$ and $\hat{\beta}_3$ as we seek to minimise the residual sum of squares. However, in [4.37] we are permitted to consider only values for β_2 and β_3 which obey the restriction $\hat{\beta}_2 + \hat{\beta}_3 = 1$. To put it another way, we are likely to be able to explain more of the total variation in Y when we do not restrict our search than when we do restrict it. We can therefore expect

$$\text{SSR}_R > \text{SSR}_U \quad \text{and} \quad \text{SSE}_R < \text{SSE}_U \qquad [4.43]$$

However, the extent of the differences expressed in [4.43] will depend very much on whether or not the restriction imposed in [4.37] is valid, i.e. on whether the true underlying values of β_2 and β_3 obey the restriction $\beta_2 + \beta_3 = 1$. If the restriction is valid, then the unrestricted estimates of β_2 and β_3 are unlikely to differ much from the restricted estimates. Hence, we would be able to explain as much of SST with the restricted estimates as we could with the unrestricted ones. Therefore, there would be little difference between the residual sum of squares for the restricted equation, SSR_R, and that for the unrestricted equation, SSR_U. If, however, the restriction is not valid and $\beta_2 + \beta_3 \neq 1$, then we can expect the unrestricted estimates to sum to something different from unity and, hence, to differ from the restricted estimates which, of course, still satisfy $\hat{\beta}_2 + \hat{\beta}_3 = 1$. Thus, if the restriction is not valid we can expect a major difference between the restricted residual sum of squares SSR_R and its unrestricted equivalent SSR_U.

The above argument suggests that we should reject the null hypothesis $\beta_2 + \beta_3 = 1$ (i.e. that the restriction is valid) if the quantity $SSR_R - SSR_U$ is 'sufficiently large'. However, as it stands $SSR_R - SSR_U$ depends on the units of measurement we are working in. To obtain an expression independent of measurement units we can use instead $(SSR_R - SSR_U)/SSR_U$, but this, of course, still leaves the question of how large this ratio has to be before we reject the restriction. Fortunately, it is not difficult to show that, given the null hypothesis $\beta_2 + \beta_3 = 1$, the quantity

$$\frac{SSR_R - SSR_U}{SSR_U/(n-k)} \text{ has an } F \text{ distribution with } (1, n-k) \text{ degrees of freedom} \quad [4.44]$$

We can therefore use [4.44] as a test statistic and reject the null hypothesis if it exceeds the relevant critical F value.

Test statistics such as [4.44] are available for testing any linear restriction or restrictions. In the general case where we wish to test simultaneously the validity of h restrictions, then the test statistic

$$\frac{(SSR_R - SSR_U)/h}{SSR_U/(n-k)} \text{ has an } F \text{ distribution with } (h, n-k) \text{ degrees of freedom}$$

$$[4.45]$$

For example, if we wished to test the restrictions imposed on equation [4.38], i.e. that $\beta_2 = \beta_3$ and $\beta_4 + \beta_5 = 1$, then h would equal 2 and SSR_R would be the residual sum of squares associated with [4.41], while SSR_U would be that associated with the unrestricted equation [4.39]. The $n - k$ in the denominator of [4.45] refers to the degrees of freedom associated with the unrestricted equation [4.39], n being the sample size and k the number of *unrestricted* parameters.

When employing the above test the reader should always keep in mind the basic idea of the test. We reject a restriction or restrictions if the proportionate increase in the sum of squared residuals resulting from their imposition (i.e. $(SSR_R - SSR_U)/SSR_U$) is sufficiently large. Numerical examples of this test can be found in the appendices to Chapters 9 to 12.

A useful special case of the above test occurs where the restrictions specify simply that some or all of the parameters in the population regression equation are zero. For example, given a population relationship

$$Y = \beta_1 + \beta_2 X_2 + \beta_3 X_3 + \beta_4 X_4 + \beta_5 X_5 + \varepsilon \quad [4.46]$$

we might wish to test the joint hypothesis $\beta_3 = \beta_4 = \beta_5 = 0$. For example, the sample values of X_3, X_4 and X_5 might be highly correlated. As we shall see in section 5.3, when this is the case it may become difficult to disentangle the individual influences of X_3, X_4 and X_5 on Y. It is possible, for example, for all the estimates $\hat{\beta}_3$, $\hat{\beta}_4$ and $\hat{\beta}_5$ to appear insignificantly different from zero on the usual t-tests even when one or more of the corresponding βs is non-zero. If we reject the restriction $\beta_3 = \beta_4 = \beta_5 = 0$ we are saying that the combined influence of X_3, X_4 and X_5 is significant but that correlation between these variables is obscuring the true influence of at least one of them. In such a case we would estimate

$$\hat{Y} = \hat{\beta}_1 + \hat{\beta}_2 X_2 + \hat{\beta}_3 X_3 + \hat{\beta}_4 X_4 + \hat{\beta}_5 X_5 \quad \text{unrestricted equation} \quad [4.47]$$

$$\hat{Y} = \hat{\beta}_1 + \hat{\beta}_2 X_2 \quad \text{restricted equation} \quad [4.48]$$

The number of restrictions used in the test statistic [4.45] will in this case be $h = 3$, the number of variables whose combined influence we are testing for.

A final special case arises when we test the hypothesis that *all* the slope parameters in the population regression equation are zero. In equation [4.46] this would imply

$$\beta_2 = \beta_3 = \beta_4 = \beta_5 = 0$$

We would now be testing for the existence of any relationship at all between the explanatory X variables and Y. We might wish to do this if all the X variables were highly correlated with one another. In this case, since the restricted equation would contain *no* explanatory variables, the restricted *explained* sum of squares must be zero so that SSR_R must now equal the total sum of squares SST. The test statistic [4.45] therefore now becomes

$$\frac{(SST - SSR_U)/(k - 1)}{SSR_U/(n - k)} = \frac{SSE_U/(k - 1)}{SSR_U/(n - k)} \quad [4.49]$$

It is left for the reader to deduce that the test statistic [4.49] is, in fact, identical to that given in terms of R^2, the coefficient of multiple determination, at the conclusion of Chapter 2.

Large sample χ^2 tests
In the last subsection we relied entirely on intuitive arguments in deriving the test statistic [4.45]. However, in terms of statistical theory, the derivation is based on two facts. Firstly, it can be shown that

$$\frac{SSR_R - SSR_U}{\sigma^2} \text{ has a } \chi^2 \text{ distribution with } h \text{ degrees of freedom} \quad [4.45A]$$

and

$$\frac{SSR_U}{\sigma^2} \text{ has a } \chi^2 \text{ distribution with } n - k \text{ degrees of freedom} \quad [4.45B]$$

where σ^2 is the disturbance variance.

Secondly, it can be demonstrated that the above χ^2 variables are distributed independently of one another. Since the ratio of two independent χ^2 distributions, each divided by their respective degrees of freedom, forms an F distribution, [4.45] then follows.

If σ^2 were known, we could in fact test restrictions, such as the $\beta_2 = \beta_3$ and $\beta_4 + \beta_5 = 1$ imposed on [4.38], simply by calculating [4.45A] and rejecting the restrictions if the value of this statistic exceeded the relevant critical χ^2 value. Notice that we would again be rejecting the restrictions if the increase in the residual sum of squares, that arises from their imposition, is sufficiently large. Unfortunately, σ^2 is not known and that is why we based our test on the ratio of [4.45A] to [4.45B], since this causes the σ^2 to 'cancel out'. However, if σ^2 in [4.45A] is replaced by any consistent estimator of it, then the resultant statistic will still have a χ^2 distribution if the sample size is sufficiently large. Under the null hypothesis of valid restrictions, the MLE of σ^2 is $\tilde{\sigma}_R^2 = SSR_R/n$. Since this is a consistent estimator, it follows that, for large samples under the null hypothesis,

$$\frac{SSR_R - SSR_U}{\tilde{\sigma}_R^2} \text{ has a } \chi^2 \text{ distribution with } h \text{ degrees of freedom} \qquad [4.50]$$

A large sample test of the restrictions can therefore be based on [4.50].[5] The restrictions are rejected if [4.50] exceeds the relevant critical value taken from χ^2 tables.

The test in terms of nR^2

The large sample test statistic [4.50] can be expressed in an alternative and very simple form. Considering again the equations [4.39] and [4.41], let us represent the residuals from the restricted equation [4.41] by e_i^*. Hence $SSR_R = \sum e_i^{*2}$. Suppose now that [4.41] has been estimated and the e_i^*s obtained. Next, instead of estimating the unrestricted equation [4.39], suppose we regress e^* on X_2, X_3, X_4 and X_5 – that is on the explanatory variables in [4.39]. In other words we compute the regression

$$\hat{e}^* = \beta_1^* + \beta_2^* X_2 + \beta_3^* X_3 + \beta_4^* X_4 + \beta_5^* X_5 \qquad [4.51]$$

where the β^*s are the OLS coefficients. [4.51] is sometimes referred to as an *auxiliary regression*.

It is possible to show that *the residuals obtained from the auxiliary regression* [4.51] *are identical to the residuals obtained from the unrestricted* [4.39]. That is both [4.39] and [4.51] have the same residual sum of squares, SSR_U. However, the total sum of squares in [4.51] is $SST = SSR_R$. Thus in terms of the output from the auxiliary regression [4.51], we can express the test statistic [4.50] as

$$\frac{SSR_R - SSR_U}{\tilde{\sigma}_R^2} = \frac{SST - SSR}{SST/n} = nR^2 \qquad [4.50A]$$

It follows that one way of carrying out the large sample test for restrictions is

1. Estimate the restricted equation and retain the residuals.
2. Use these residuals as dependent variable in an auxiliary regression in which the explanatory variables are those in the unrestricted equation.
3. Take nR^2 for the auxiliary regression and compare it with the relevant critical χ^2 value.

Non-linear restrictions

Economic models are just as likely to suggest non-linear restrictions on the coefficients of estimating equations as they are to suggest linear restrictions. We shall encounter such non-linear restrictions in, for example, equation [9.29] (page 214) which refers to the demand for a durable good.

To illustrate the problems arising from non-linear restrictions, consider the estimation of a population relationship

$$Y = \beta_1 + \beta_2 X_2 + \beta_3 X_3 + \beta_2 \beta_3 X_4 + \varepsilon \qquad [4.52]$$

In [4.52] we have the non-linear restriction that the coefficient on X_4, β_4 *equals* $\beta_2\beta_3$. Clearly, if we estimate [4.52] by a sample regression equation of the form

$$\hat{Y} = \hat{\beta}_1 + \hat{\beta}_2 X_2 + \hat{\beta}_3 X_3 + \hat{\beta}_4 X_4$$

then we have an over-identification problem. Three parameters β_1, β_2 and β_3 have to be obtained from four estimated coefficients $\hat{\beta}_1$, $\hat{\beta}_2$, $\hat{\beta}_3$ and $\hat{\beta}_4$. There is no reason why the estimate of β_2 obtained from $\hat{\beta}_2$ should coincide with that obtained by taking the ratio $\hat{\beta}_4/\hat{\beta}_3$.

The difficulty, now, is that because of the non-linearity of the constraint, it is not possible to manipulate [4.52] in the way we were able to manipulate [4.32] and [4.38] to obtain [4.36] and [4.40] respectively. We can no longer incorporate the constraint into our underlying relationship so as to provide an estimating equation of convenient form that can be tackled by OLS. There is no alternative in this case than to attempt to minimise the residual sum of squares

$$\sum e_i^2 = \sum (Y_i - \hat{Y}_i)^2 = \sum (Y_i - \hat{\beta}_1 - \hat{\beta}_2 X_{2i} \hat{\beta}_3 X_{3i} - \hat{\beta}_4 X_{4i})^2 \quad [4.53]$$

subject to the restriction $\hat{\beta}_4 = \hat{\beta}_2\hat{\beta}_3$. The problem is that the 'normal equations' obtained from this minimisation are, not surprisingly, non-linear and do not lead to convenient expressions for the $\hat{\beta}$s that can be written down in algebraic form. They have to be solved by the purely numerical techniques described in section 3.5. In the present case this might involve selecting a value for, say, $\hat{\beta}_2$ and then finding the values for $\hat{\beta}_1$, $\hat{\beta}_3$ and $\hat{\beta}_4$ that minimise [4.53] given this value of $\hat{\beta}_2$. For example, if we set $\hat{\beta}_2 = 2$, then the constraint becomes $\hat{\beta}_4 = 2\hat{\beta}_3$ and [4.53] may be written as

$$\sum e_i^2 = \sum \{Y_i - \hat{\beta}_1 - 2X_{2i} - \hat{\beta}_3 X_{3i} - 2\hat{\beta}_3 X_{4i}\}^2$$
$$= \sum \{(Y_i - 2X_{2i}) - \hat{\beta}_1 - \hat{\beta}_3(X_{3i} + 2X_{4i})\}^2 \qquad [4.53A]$$

Since for the given $\hat{\beta}_2$ the restriction becomes linear, the minimisation of [4.53A] is straightforward, following the lines already described for linear restrictions. The minimisation, however, has to be performed for the whole range of possible values for $\hat{\beta}_2$ until the overall minimum value of $\sum e_i^2$ is found. The set of values $\hat{\beta}_1, \hat{\beta}_2, \hat{\beta}_3$ and $\hat{\beta}_4$ yielding this minimum are the *non-linear least squares estimators* for this case. The testing of non-linear restrictions will be discussed in the sections following.

4.5   The likelihood ratio test

The approach to the testing of parameter restrictions followed in the previous section follows on naturally from the OLS method of estimation. In the last

71

chapter, however, we considered an alternative method of estimation – that of maximum likelihood, and in this and the next two sections we consider three kinds of test which arise from this approach. We shall take as an example in each case the estimation of equation [4.38], which involved two restrictions $\beta_2 = \beta_3$ and $\beta_4 + \beta_5 = 1$. As we shall see, the first test – the likelihood ratio test – requires the estimation of both unrestricted and restricted versions of [4.38], that is equations [4.39] and [4.41]. The second test – the Wald test – requires only the estimation of the unrestricted equation [4.39], whereas the third test – the Lagrange multiplier test – requires only the estimation of the restricted equation [4.41].

Consider first the maximum likelihood estimation of the unrestricted version of equation [4.38]. The log-likelihood function takes the usual form [3.36] where in this case

$$EY_i = \beta_1 + \beta_2 X_{2i} + \beta_3 X_{3i} + \beta_4 X_{4i} + \beta_5 X_{5i} \qquad i = 1, 2, 3, \ldots, n \qquad [4.54]$$

On maximisation of the likelihood function, we obtain the MLEs of the β_js and of σ^2 the disturbance variance. Recall, from [3.38] and [3.40], that these MLEs of the β_js are identical to the unrestricted OLS estimators and that the MLE of σ^2 in this unrestricted estimation is $\tilde{\sigma}^2 = \sum e_i^2/n$. If we now substitute the MLEs we have obtained back into [3.36], we obtain a value for the *maximised log-likelihood*, l_u, for the unrestricted equation [4.39] of

$$l_U = -\frac{n}{2} \log 2\pi\tilde{\sigma}^2 - \frac{1}{2\tilde{\sigma}} \sum e_i^2 = -\frac{n}{2} \log 2\pi\tilde{\sigma}^2 - \frac{n}{2} \qquad [4.55]$$

Recall that MLEs are simply those values for the relevant parameters that maximise the probability (or probability density) of drawing the sample Y_is actually obtained. l_u is that maximum probability density.

Next consider the estimation of [4.38] subject to the restrictions $\beta_2 = \beta_3$ and $\beta_4 + \beta_5 = 1$. The log-likelihood function again takes the form [3.36] but now EY_i is replaced by

$$EY_i^* = \beta_1 + \beta_2 X_{2i}^* + \beta_4 X_{4i}^* \qquad i = 1, 2, 3, \ldots, n \qquad [4.56]$$

where $Y_i^* = Y_i - X_{5i}$, $X_{2i}^* = X_{2i} + X_{3i}$ and $X_{4i}^* = X_{4i} - X_{5i}$. Substituting the MLEs back into the log-likelihood function yields a maximised log-likelihood, l_R, for the restricted equation [4.41] of

$$l_R = -\frac{n}{2} \log 2\pi\tilde{\sigma}_R^2 - \frac{n}{2} \qquad [4.57]$$

where $\tilde{\sigma}_R^2$, the MLE of σ^2 in the restricted case, equals $\sum e_i^{*2}/n$ and the residuals, e_i^*, now being summed and squared are those obtained from the restricted equation [4.41].

Under the null hypothesis of valid restrictions, the maximised likelihoods, L_R and L_U, should be very similar[6]. That is the *likelihood ratio*, L_R/L_U, should be close to unity and its logarithm, $l_R - l_U$, close to zero. If at least one of the restrictions are invalid, however, then we expect $L_R/L_U < 1$ and hence $l_R - l_U < 0$. The idea behind the likelihood ratio test is that we reject the null hypothesis of valid restrictions if $l_R - l_U$ is 'sufficiently negative'. In the above case

$$l_R - l_U = -\frac{n}{2} \log(\tilde{\sigma}_R^2/\tilde{\sigma}^2) \qquad [4.58]$$

The problem of course is to decide what we mean by 'sufficiently negative'. For a given level of significance we require a critical value for the test statistic [4.58]. For the above example it is possible to link the test statistic [4.58] to the F-test statistic [4.45]. Recalling that, under present assumptions, OLS estimators and MLEs are identical, it follows that in the notation of the last section

$$\tilde{\sigma}_R^2 = \frac{SSR_R}{n} \qquad \text{and} \qquad \tilde{\sigma}^2 = \frac{SSR_U}{n}$$

Hence the test statistic [4.58] can be expressed as a function of the ratio SSR_R/SSR_U. However, it is easy to see that the test-statistic [4.45] (with $h = 2$ restrictions in the present case), can also be expressed as a function of this ratio and, in fact, a given value for [4.58] implies a unique given value for [4.45]. In this case it is therefore possible to obtain critical values for test statistic [4.58] by referring to the F-distribution.

Unfortunately, it is not always possible to obtain the small sample distribution of the relevant likelihood ratio test statistic. For example, it is particularly difficult to do so when the restrictions on parameters are non-linear. However for large samples it is possible to show that, under the null hypotheses that all restrictions are valid, the *likelihood ratio statistic*.

$$LR = -2(l_R - l_U) \text{ has a } \chi^2 \text{ distribution with } h \text{ degrees of freedom} \qquad [4.59]$$

where h is again the number of parameter restrictions being tested for. Restrictions are rejected if the test statistic LR is sufficiently positive, i.e. if it exceeds the relevant critical value taken from the χ^2 distribution. Clearly, such a procedure could be employed to test the non-linear restriction implied by equation [4.52]. The only minor difficulty here is that to compute [4.59] we require the maximised likelihood both for the unrestricted and the restricted estimated equations. As we saw in the last section, minimising [4.53] subject to the restriction $\hat{\beta}_4 = \hat{\beta}_2\hat{\beta}_3$ is not so straightforward. One way round the problem is to adopt a Wald test which *requires estimation of the unrestricted equation only*.

4.6 The Wald test

We shall introduce the Wald test by again considering the testing of the linear restrictions $\beta_2 = \beta_3$ and $\beta_4 + \beta_5 = 1$ in equation [4.38]. We then consider its use in the testing of non-linear restrictions.

First, we deal with the problem of testing single restrictions. Suppose, for example, we wish to test the restriction $\beta_2 = \beta_3$ when the only equation estimated is the unrestricted [4.39]. Clearly, if the restriction is valid, we expect $\tilde{\beta}_2 - \tilde{\beta}_3$ to be close to zero, where $\tilde{\beta}_2 = \hat{\beta}_2$ and $\tilde{\beta}_3 = \hat{\beta}_3$ are the ML/OLS estimators of β_2 and β_3. If $\tilde{\beta}_2 - \tilde{\beta}_3$ is sufficiently different from zero, we will reject the restriction as inconsistent with the data. The problem is to find a criterion for deciding what is 'sufficiently different from zero'.

We require the sampling distribution of $\tilde{\beta}_2 - \tilde{\beta}_3$. Provided the assumptions of the classical regression model hold, $\tilde{\beta}_2 - \tilde{\beta}_3$ will be normally distributed with a mean of $\beta_2 - \beta_3$ and a variance

$$\sigma_{23}^2 = \operatorname{Var} \tilde{\beta}_2 + \operatorname{Var} \tilde{\beta}_3 - 2 \operatorname{Covar}(\tilde{\beta}_2, \tilde{\beta}_3) \qquad [4.60]$$

Recall from equations [2.35A] and [2.35B] that we can obtain the variances of $\tilde{\beta}_2$ and $\tilde{\beta}_3$ and the covariance between them from the variance-covariance matrix [2.34]. (Remember that OLS and ML estimators are identical under present assumptions.) We can therefore write [4.60] as

$$\sigma_{23}^2 = \sigma^2(x^{22} + x^{33} - 2x^{23}) \qquad [4.61]$$

Clearly, since $\tilde{\beta}_2 - \tilde{\beta}_3$ is $N(\beta_2 - \beta_3, \sigma_{23}^2)$, it follows that, under the null hypothesis that the restriction $\beta_2 = \beta_3$ is valid, $(\tilde{\beta}_2 - \tilde{\beta}_3)/\sigma_{23}$ is $N(0, 1)$. This provides the basis for a so-called Wald test of the restriction because although σ^2 in [4.61], the variance of the disturbances, is unknown, we can replace it by its maximum likelihood estimator, $\tilde{\sigma}^2$, obtained from unrestricted estimation of [4.38], and obtain $\tilde{\sigma}_{23}^2 = \tilde{\sigma}^2(x^{22} + x^{33} - 2x^{23})$. Under the null hypothesis of a valid restriction, the Wald test statistic

$$W = \frac{\tilde{\beta}_2 - \tilde{\beta}_3}{\tilde{\sigma}_{23}} \qquad [4.62]$$

remains $N(0, 1)$ in large samples. We therefore reject the restriction if W in [4.62] lies outside the relevant critical values taken from standard normal tables.

Similarly, it is possible to construct a Wald test that the parameters of [4.38] satisfy the restriction $\beta_4 + \beta_5 = 1$. $\tilde{\beta}_4 + \tilde{\beta}_5$ is $N(\beta_4 + \beta_5, \sigma_{45}^2)$, where

$$\sigma_{45}^2 = \sigma^2(x^{44} + x^{55} + 2x^{45}) \qquad [4.63]$$

It follows that, under the null hypothesis that the restriction $\beta_4 + \beta_5 = 1$ is valid, $(\tilde{\beta}_4 + \tilde{\beta}_5 - 1)/\sigma_{45}$ is $N(0, 1)$. Replacing σ_{45}^2 by $\tilde{\sigma}_{45}^2 = \tilde{\sigma}^2(x^{44} + x^{55} + 2x^{45})$ yields the Wald test statistic

$$W = \frac{\tilde{\beta}_4 + \tilde{\beta}_5 - 1}{\tilde{\sigma}_{45}} \qquad [4.64]$$

Notice that, whereas in [4.62] W is based on the difference between $\tilde{\beta}_2$ and $\tilde{\beta}_3$, in [4.64] the test statistic, reflecting this restriction, is based on the difference between $\tilde{\beta}_4 + \tilde{\beta}_5$ and unity.

*Joint tests of more than one restriction

Wald tests can also be constructed to test, simultaneously, the validity of more than one restriction. Again all that is necessary is the estimation of the unrestricted equation. The idea is to construct an overall measure of the extent to which the unrestricted estimates of the β_js satisfy the various restrictions that are being tested. However, before deriving this combined test we need to introduce a useful general result.

Readers may be aware that if

$$z_i \text{ is } N(0, c_i^2) \qquad i = 1, 2, 3, \ldots, h \qquad\qquad [4.65]$$

then the quantity $\sum z_i^2/c_i^2$ has a χ^2 distribution with h degrees of freedom provided the z_i are independently distributed. Unfortunately, the normal distributions out of which Wald statistics such as [4.62] and [4.64] are constructed are not independently distributed, so we cannot obtain the χ^2 statistic simply by squaring and summing individual W-statistics. However, if [4.65] holds but

$$\text{Covar}(z_i, z_j) = c_{ij} \neq 0 \qquad i \neq j \qquad\qquad [4.66]$$

so that the z_i are not independent, then if we define the variance-covariance matrix $\mathbf{C}$ and the vector $\mathbf{z}$ as

$$\mathbf{C} = \begin{bmatrix} c_1^2 & c_{12} & c_{13} & \cdots & c_{1h} \\ c_{21} & c_2^2 & c_{23} & \cdots & c_{2h} \\ c_{31} & c_{32} & c_3^2 & \cdots & c_{3h} \\ \vdots & \vdots & \vdots & & \vdots \\ c_{h1} & c_{h2} & c_{h3} & \cdots & c_h^2 \end{bmatrix}, \quad \mathbf{z} = \begin{bmatrix} z_1 \\ z_2 \\ z_3 \\ \vdots \\ z_h \end{bmatrix}$$

then it can be shown that the quantity

$$\mathbf{z}'\mathbf{C}^{-1}\mathbf{z} \text{ has a } \chi^2 \text{ distribution with } h \text{ degrees of freedom} \qquad [4.67]$$

The result is a generalisation of that below [4.65] and in fact it is a trivial matter to show that, if $c_{ij} = 0$ for all $i \neq j$, then [4.67] reduces to the result below [4.65].

We can now use the result [4.67] to construct a Wald statistic for the joint testing of both the restrictions on equation [4.38] simultaneously. If we define

$$\boldsymbol{\beta} = \begin{bmatrix} \beta_1 \\ \beta_2 \\ \beta_3 \\ \beta_4 \\ \beta_5 \end{bmatrix}, \qquad \mathbf{R} = \begin{bmatrix} 0 & 1 & -1 & 0 & 0 \\ 0 & 0 & 0 & 1 & 1 \end{bmatrix}, \qquad \mathbf{r} = \begin{bmatrix} 0 \\ 1 \end{bmatrix} \qquad [4.68]$$

then the constraints $\beta_2 = \beta_3$ and $\beta_4 + \beta_5 = 1$ can be written together in matrix form as

$$\mathbf{R}\boldsymbol{\beta} = \mathbf{r} \qquad\qquad [4.69]$$

If $\tilde{\boldsymbol{\beta}}$ is the vector of OLS/ML estimators of the elements of $\boldsymbol{\beta}$, then we know from section 2.4 that the elements of $\tilde{\boldsymbol{\beta}}$ will be normally distributed, with means given by the respective elements of $\boldsymbol{\beta}$ and variance-covariance matrix $\sigma^2(\mathbf{X}'\mathbf{X})^{-1}$. That is, in matrix notation

$$\tilde{\boldsymbol{\beta}} \text{ is } N[\boldsymbol{\beta}, \sigma^2(\mathbf{X}'\mathbf{X})^{-1}] \qquad\qquad [4.70]$$

It follows that[7]

$$\mathbf{R}\tilde{\boldsymbol{\beta}} \text{ is } N[\mathbf{R}\boldsymbol{\beta}, \sigma^2\mathbf{R}(\mathbf{X}'\mathbf{X})^{-1}\mathbf{R}'] \qquad [4.71]$$

and, hence, that under the null hypothesis that the restrictions [4.69] are valid,

$$\mathbf{R}\tilde{\boldsymbol{\beta}} - \mathbf{r} \text{ is } N[o, \sigma^2\mathbf{R}(\mathbf{X}'\mathbf{X})^{-1}\mathbf{R}'] \qquad [4.72]$$

Treating the two elements of the vector $\mathbf{R}\tilde{\boldsymbol{\beta}} - \mathbf{r}$ as akin to the z_i in [4.65], we can now apply the result [4.67], which implies that, under the null hypothesis of valid restrictions,

$$W^* = \tilde{\sigma}^{-2}(\mathbf{R}\tilde{\boldsymbol{\beta}} - \mathbf{r})'[\mathbf{R}(\mathbf{X}'\mathbf{X})^{-1}\mathbf{R}']^{-1}(\mathbf{R}\hat{\boldsymbol{\beta}} - \mathbf{r})$$

has a χ^2 distribution with $h = 2$ degrees of freedom   [4.73]

The result [4.73] holds only for large samples since we have replaced the unknown σ^2 by its MLE, $\tilde{\sigma}^2$, obtained from the unrestricted estimation of [4.38].

[4.73] is the Wald statistic for the joint testing of the two restrictions $\beta_2 = \beta_3$ and $\beta_4 + \beta_5 = 1$. Notice that it is based on the vector $\mathbf{R}\tilde{\boldsymbol{\beta}} - \mathbf{r}$, the elements of which are $\tilde{\beta}_2 - \tilde{\beta}_3$ and $\tilde{\beta}_4 + \tilde{\beta}_5 - 1$ (cf. [4.62] and [4.64]). We are measuring the extent to which these quantities differ from zero, i.e. the extent to which the $\tilde{\beta}$ estimates fail to satisfy the restrictions. If they fail to do so by a sufficiently large extent, that is if the test-statistic [4.73] exceeds the relevant critical χ^2 value, then we reject the null hypothesis and regard the restrictions as inconsistent with the data.

It should be clear that by defining appropriate matrices, $\mathbf{R}$ and $\mathbf{r}$, as in [4.68], it is possible to test simultaneously any number of linear restrictions on the parameters of a regression equation using the Wald statistic [4.73]. However, in general the statistic will have h degrees of freedom where h is the number of restrictions being jointly tested.

*The Wald test for non-linear restrictions

As we noted earlier the big advantage of Wald tests is that they require estimation of the unrestricted equation only. This makes the approach well suited to the testing of non-linear restrictions. As an example, we take the testing of the restriction $\beta_4 = \beta_2\beta_3$ implied by equation [4.52]. Any restriction, linear or non-linear on the parameters of [4.52] can be written in the form[8]

$$f(\beta_1, \beta_2, \beta_3, \beta_4) = 0 \qquad [4.74]$$

For example, the restriction $\beta_4 = \beta_2\beta_3$ can obviously be written as $f = \beta_2\beta_3 - \beta_4 = 0$. Clearly, if a restriction is valid, then we expect $f(\tilde{\beta}_1, \tilde{\beta}_2, \tilde{\beta}_3, \tilde{\beta}_4) \approx 0$ where the $\tilde{\beta}$s are the OLS/ML estimators of the corresponding βs. For our restriction, for example, we would expect $\tilde{\beta}_2\tilde{\beta}_3 - \tilde{\beta}_4 \approx 0$. If $f(\tilde{\beta}_1, \tilde{\beta}_2, \tilde{\beta}_3, \tilde{\beta}_4)$ differs sufficiently from zero we reject the restriction.

To construct the required Wald statistic we employ, firstly, a Taylor series expansion of $f(\tilde{\beta}_1, \tilde{\beta}_2, \tilde{\beta}_3, \tilde{\beta}_4)$ about the true βs.

$$f(\tilde{\beta}_1, \tilde{\beta}_2, \tilde{\beta}_3, \tilde{\beta}_4) = f(\beta_1, \beta_2, \beta_3, \beta_4) + (\tilde{\beta}_1 - \beta_1)\frac{\partial f}{\partial \beta_1} + (\tilde{\beta}_2 - \beta_2)\frac{\partial f}{\partial \beta_2}$$

$$+ (\tilde{\beta}_3 - \beta_3)\frac{\partial f}{\partial \beta_3} + (\tilde{\beta}_4 - \beta_4)\frac{\partial f}{\partial \beta_4} \qquad [4.75]$$

Under the null hypothesis of a valid restriction, [4.74] holds so that [4.75] becomes

$$f(\tilde{\beta}_1, \tilde{\beta}_2, \tilde{\beta}_3, \tilde{\beta}_4) = \mathbf{F}'(\tilde{\boldsymbol{\beta}} - \boldsymbol{\beta}) \qquad [4.76]$$

where $\mathbf{F}'$ is a row vector containing the partial derivatives $\partial f/\partial \beta_i$, while $\tilde{\boldsymbol{\beta}}$ and $\boldsymbol{\beta}$ are column vectors with the usual interpretation. In our example $\mathbf{F}' = (\partial f/\partial \beta_1, \partial f/\partial \beta_2, \partial f/\partial \beta_3, \partial f/\partial \beta_4) = (0, \tilde{\beta}_3, \tilde{\beta}_2, -1)$.

Since we know that

$$\tilde{\boldsymbol{\beta}} - \boldsymbol{\beta} \text{ is } N[\mathbf{0}, \sigma^2(\mathbf{X}'\mathbf{X})^{-1}] \qquad [4.77]$$

it follows that under the null hypothesis of a valid restriction[9]

$$f(\tilde{\beta}_1, \tilde{\beta}_2, \tilde{\beta}_3, \tilde{\beta}_4) = \mathbf{F}'(\tilde{\boldsymbol{\beta}} - \boldsymbol{\beta}) \text{ is } N[\mathbf{0}, \sigma^2\mathbf{F}'(\mathbf{X}'\mathbf{X})^{-1}\mathbf{F}] \qquad [4.78]$$

A suitable Wald statistic for testing a single restriction of the form [4.74] is therefore

$$W = \frac{f(\tilde{\beta}_1, \tilde{\beta}_2, \tilde{\beta}_3, \tilde{\beta}_4)}{\tilde{\sigma}\sqrt{\mathbf{F}'(\mathbf{X}'\mathbf{X})^{-1}\mathbf{F}}} \qquad [4.79]$$

where σ is replaced by its MLE $\tilde{\sigma}$. For large samples [4.79] has a $N(0, 1)$ distribution. The restriction is rejected as inconsistent with the data if W lies outside critical values taken from standard normal tables. Notice that, as stated earlier, the test is based on considering whether $f(\tilde{\beta}_1, \tilde{\beta}_2, \tilde{\beta}_3, \tilde{\beta}_4)$ is sufficiently different from zero. Notice also that, since in our example $(\mathbf{X}'\mathbf{X})^{-1}$ is of order 4×4 and $\mathbf{F}$ is of order 1×4, the quantity under the square root sign in [4.79] is a scalar.

It is also possible to construct Wald tests for the simultaneous testing of more than one non-linear restriction. For example, for equation [4.52] with four parameters, the restrictions would be written in the form

$$f_i(\beta_1, \beta_2, \beta_3, \beta_4) = 0 \qquad i = 1, 2, 3, \ldots, h \qquad [4.80]$$

where there are h restrictions in all. A generalisation of [4.78] is then

$$\mathbf{f} = \mathbf{F}^{*'}(\tilde{\boldsymbol{\beta}} - \boldsymbol{\beta}) \text{ is } N[\mathbf{0}, \sigma^2\mathbf{F}^{*'}(\mathbf{X}'\mathbf{X})^{-1}\mathbf{F}^*] \qquad [4.81]$$

where $\mathbf{f}$ is an $h \times 1$ vector, the ith element of which is $f_i(\tilde{\beta}_1, \tilde{\beta}_2, \tilde{\beta}_3, \tilde{\beta}_4)$ and $\mathbf{F}^{*'}$ is now a matrix with h rows, one for each restriction. For equation [4.52], for example, the ith row of $\mathbf{F}^{*'}$ would be $(\partial f_i/\partial \beta_1, \partial f_i/\partial \beta_2, \partial f_i/\partial \beta_3, \partial f_i/\partial \beta_4)$.

Given [4.81] we can now use the result [4.67] to obtain the required Wald statistic,

$$W^* = \tilde{\sigma}^{-2}\mathbf{f}'[\mathbf{F}^{*'}(\mathbf{X}'\mathbf{X})^{-1}\mathbf{F}^*]^{-1}\mathbf{f} \qquad [4.82]$$

where $\tilde{\sigma}^2$ is again the MLE of σ^2. Under the null hypothesis of valid restrictions [4.82] has a χ^2 distribution with h degrees of freedom for large samples.

4.7 The Lagrange multiplier test

In contrast to the Wald test, the Lagrange multiplier test requires estimation only of the *restricted* equation. It is therefore particularly useful when imposition of the restrictions leads to a considerable simplification of the estimating equation. First, however, we will consider yet again the testing of the restrictions $\beta_2 = \beta_3$ and $\beta_4 + \beta_5 = 1$ on equation [4.38]. Consider, first, the log-likelihood function for this equation

$$l = \log L(\beta_1, \beta_2, \beta_3, \beta_4, \beta_5, \sigma^2, Y_1, Y_2, Y_3, \ldots, Y_n) \qquad [4.83]$$

For the unrestricted MLEs it must be the case that

$$\frac{\partial l}{\partial \beta_j} = 0 \qquad \text{for all } j \qquad [4.84]$$

If the restrictions are valid then we expect the restricted MLEs of the β_js to be very close to the unrestricted MLEs. Hence we expect the $\partial l / \partial \beta_j$s to be 'near' to zero when they are worked out for values of the β_js set equal to the restricted estimates. The idea of the Lagrange multiplier test is to reject the restrictions if a certain function of these $\partial l / \partial \beta_j$s differs sufficiently from zero. The function used is in fact

$$LM = \tilde{\sigma}^2 \mathbf{L}'(\mathbf{X}'\mathbf{X})^{-1}\mathbf{L} \qquad [4.85]$$

where $\mathbf{L}$ is a column vector containing as elements the $\partial l / \partial \beta_j$s, evaluated for values of the β_j *set equal to the restricted estimates*. For large samples, LM in [4.85] can be shown to have the same distribution as that for the likelihood ratio statistic, LR, in [4.59]. Under the null hypothesis of valid restrictions it therefore has a χ^2 distribution with h degrees of freedom, where h as usual equals the number of restrictions. The advantage of the LM statistic over the LR statistic however is that, while computation of the LR statistic requires estimation of both unrestricted and restricted equations, the LM statistic requires estimation only of the latter. We will discuss the actual computation of [4.85] in the next subsection.

At this stage it will be unclear why [4.85] should be referred to as a Lagrange multiplier statistic. However, if we required the restricted MLEs of the parameters in for example equation [4.38], the log-likelihood function [4.83] would have to be maximised subject to the restrictions $\beta_2 = \beta_3$ and $\beta_4 + \beta_5 = 1$. We must therefore form the Lagrangian

$$l^* = l + \lambda_1(\beta_2 - \beta_3) + \lambda_2(\beta_4 + \beta_5 - 1) \qquad [4.86]$$

where λ_1 and λ_2 are Lagrange multipliers. Solving the constrained maximisation problem involves setting the derivatives $\partial l^* / \partial \beta_j = 0$ for all j. That is

$$\frac{\partial l^*}{\partial \beta_j} = \frac{\partial l}{\partial \beta_j} + \lambda_1 \frac{\partial(\beta_2 - \beta_3)}{\partial \beta_j} + \lambda_2 \frac{\partial(\beta_4 + \beta_5 - 1)}{\partial \beta_j} = 0 \qquad \text{for all } j \qquad [4.87]$$

That is

$$\frac{\partial l}{\partial \beta_j} = -\lambda_1 \frac{\partial(\beta_2 - \beta_3)}{\partial \beta_j} - \lambda_2 \frac{\partial(\beta_4 + \beta_5 - 1)}{\partial \beta_j} \qquad \text{for all } j \qquad [4.88]$$

As we saw earlier, the idea behind the *LM* test is that we reject the restrictions if the $\partial l/\partial \beta_j$ are sufficiently far from zero when evaluated for the restricted estimates. But the values of the $\partial l/\partial \beta_j$ for the restricted case are given by equation [4.88]. Thus we see that the $\partial l/\partial \beta_j$s can only be far from zero if the Lagrange multipliers λ_1 and λ_2 are far from zero. Thus, effectively, we reject the restrictions if λ_1 and λ_2 differ sufficiently from zero. Readers familiar with the Lagrange multiplier procedure will be aware that the size of λ_1 and λ_2 reflects the effect on the maximum possible value of l of relaxing the constraints. If the constraints are valid, their relaxation will have little effect on the maximised likelihood so that λ_1 and λ_2 should be close to zero. Invalid constraints, however, will be reflected in values for λ_1 and λ_2, and hence for the $\partial l/\partial \beta_j$s, which are far from zero. For these reasons [4.85], which is a function of the $\partial l/\partial \beta_j$s, is referred to as the Lagrange multiplier statistic.

The computation of Lagrange multiplier statistics

Lagrange multiplier statistics for least squares regression can be reformulated in a most convenient way. They can in fact be directly related to the coefficient of multiple regression, R^2, obtained from what we shall refer to as the *auxiliary LM regression*. The form of the auxiliary *LM* regression depends on the restrictions being tested. Suppose, for example, we wish to test the restrictions $\beta_2 = \beta_3$ and $\beta_4 + \beta_5 = 1$ on equation [4.38]. The disturbances in the unrestricted version of [4.38] are given by

$$\varepsilon = Y - \beta_1 - \beta_2 X_2 - \beta_3 X_3 - \beta_4 X_4 - \beta_5 X_5 \qquad [4.89]$$

The explanatory variables in the auxiliary *LM* regression are simply given by

$$Z_j = -\frac{\partial \varepsilon}{\partial \beta_j} \qquad \text{for all } j \qquad [4.90]$$

For [4.89] finding the Z_j is trivial. The auxiliary *LM* regression explanatory variables are $(1, X_2, X_3, X_4, X_5)$. Normally, however, the derivatives in [4.90] have to be evaluated under the null hypothesis that the restrictions being tested are valid.

The dependent variable in the auxiliary *LM* regression consists simply of *the residuals obtained from OLS/ML estimation of the restricted equation*. The estimated restricted version of [4.38] is [4.41], so the required dependent variable is

$$e^* = Y - X_5 - \hat{\beta}_1 - \hat{\beta}_2(X_2 + X_3) - \hat{\beta}_4(X_4 - X_5) \qquad [4.91]$$

The auxiliary *LM* regression thus involves regressing the e^*s from [4.91] on the set of explanatory variables $(1, X_2, X_3, X_4, X_5)$. The value of unity for the first variable in this set implies that a constant should be included in the regression. If the quantity nR^2 is now computed for this auxiliary *LM* regression, then it can be shown that the value obtained is identical to the value of the *LM* statistic [4.85]. Under the null hypothesis of valid restrictions, nR^2 therefore has a χ^2 distribution with $h = 2$ degrees of freedom.

The reader will recall encountering a test statistic of the form nR^2 towards the end of section 4.4. Then, as now, we were considering the testing of linear restrictions of the kind $\beta_2 = \beta_3$ and $\beta_4 + \beta_5 = 1$. In fact, if you check back, you will find that the computations required to obtain the test statistic at the end of section 4.4 are identical to those necessary to compute nR^2 in this subsection. They involve using the residuals from the restricted equation as the dependent variable in an auxiliary regression.

When, as in the above case, the equations and restrictions involved are linear, the large sample χ^2 test of section 4.4 and the LM test are, in fact, identical. The advantage of the LM approach, however, is that it is still applicable when the equation involved is non-linear. The following example should make this clear.

Consider the non-linear equation

$$Y = \alpha + \beta\left(\frac{1}{X - \gamma}\right) + \varepsilon \qquad \beta > 0 \qquad\qquad [4.92]$$

If the parameter $\gamma = 0$, then Y tends to infinity as X tends to zero and there is no intercept on the Y-axis.[10] Suppose we wish to test the restriction $\gamma = 0$. A Lagrange multiplier test is particularly appropriate in this case because, although [4.92] is non-linear, the restricted equation is linear in the parameters and therefore very easy to estimate. That is, if we set $\gamma = 0$ in [4.92], we obtain

$$Y = \alpha + \beta X^* + \varepsilon \qquad\qquad [4.93]$$

where $X^* = 1/X$.

For all sample observations we have

$$\varepsilon = Y - \alpha - \beta\left(\frac{1}{X - \gamma}\right) \qquad\qquad [4.94]$$

The explanatory variables in the auxiliary LM regression are therefore obtained from

$$Z_1 = -\frac{\partial \varepsilon}{\partial \alpha} = 1 \qquad\qquad [4.95]$$

$$Z_2 = -\frac{\partial \varepsilon}{\partial \beta} = \frac{1}{X - \gamma} \qquad\qquad [4.96]$$

$$Z_3 = -\frac{\partial \varepsilon}{\partial \gamma} = \frac{\beta}{(X - \gamma)^2} \qquad\qquad [4.97]$$

Remembering that we must evaluate [4.95], [4.96] and [4.97] under the null hypothesis that the restriction $\gamma = 0$ is valid, we obtain for explanatory variables $(1, X^{-1}, \beta X^{-2})$.

The dependent variable as usual consists of the residuals from the OLS estimation of the restricted equation. That is, from [4.93]

$$e^* = Y - \hat{\alpha} - \hat{\beta}\left(\frac{1}{X}\right) \qquad\qquad [4.98]$$

The auxiliary LM regression in this case therefore involves the OLS regression of the e^*s from [4.98] on the variables X^{-1} and βX^{-2} with a constant included. However, since β is unknown, in practice the explanatory variables used would be X^{-1} and X^{-2}. This will not affect the value of R^2. The value of the LM statistic can, then, as usual, be found by computing nR^2 for the auxiliary LM regression.

A choice between LR, Wald and LM tests normally has to be made on grounds of computational convenience. On these grounds, the Wald and LM tests are generally preferred to the LR test, because the latter requires estimation of both restricted and unrestricted equations. Choice between the Wald and LM tests depends on whether restricted or unrestricted equation is the easier to estimate. However, even if it is feasible to employ all three tests, it must not be thought that they will always give the same result. The three-test statistics are asymptotically equivalent but can still give different results, particularly for small samples. In fact, for the classical regression model, it can be shown that the test statistics must obey the inequalities

$$W \geqslant LR \geqslant LM \tag{4.99}$$

[4.99] implies that only when an LM test leads to rejection of the null hypothesis of valid restrictions, or when a Wald test leads to a failure to reject null, will the three tests give the same result.

Further reading

Non-linear regression models and the use of dummy variables, both as dependent variables and as the only explanatory variables in a regression equation, are well covered in Kmenta (1986). An excellent treatment of the testing of non-linear restrictions on regression parameters is that of Stewart (1991). Estimation subject to non-linear restrictions is a topic not covered in many introductory texts but Kmenta provides an understandable introduction. LR, Wald and LM tests are covered in Kmenta, Stewart and also Maddala (1989).

Notes

1. All computer regression packages contain routines for forming transformed variables such as Z_2, once X_2 has been inputted.
2. It is, of course, possible to include both the multiplicative dummies and the intercept dummies in the estimating equation at the same time. However, this can be shown to be exactly equivalent to the estimation of two separate equations, one for controlled years and one for uncontrolled years.
3. An alternative to three dummies and an intercept is to include four dummies and no intercept.
4. In fact, if a full set of multiplicative and intercept dummies are included in the equation, then the F-test for their exclusion (see equation [4.45]) can be shown to be equivalent to the first Chow test.
5. Alternatively, σ^2 could be replaced by its unbiased estimator $s^2 = \text{SSR}_U/(n-k)$. Intuitively, it seems sensible to correct for degrees of freedom in this way when the sample size is small.

6. $\log L_R = l_R$ and $\log L_U = l_U$.
7. We are using, here, a generalisation of the result that if k is a constant, then for a single variable, x, var $kx = k^2$ var x. That is, if a vector of variables, $\mathbf{x}$, has variance-covariance matrix $\mathbf{C}$, then if $\mathbf{K}$ is a conformable matrix of fixed constants, the variance-covariance matrix of $\mathbf{Kx}$ is given by $\mathbf{KCK'}$.
8. Note that a function such as x^3y^2 can be written as $f(x, y, z)$ because $x^3y^2 = x^3y^2z^0$.
9. See note 7.
10. For example, [4.92] could represent a non-linear 'Phillips curve' relationship between the rate of wage inflation, Y, and the level of unemployment, X. $\gamma < 0$ would then imply some upper limit to the rate of wage inflation.

5 Breakdowns in classical assumptions

In section 2.4 we listed the series of assumptions which make up the classical linear regression model and described the properties possessed by the OLS estimators when these assumptions hold. In this chapter we shall be concerned with the consequences for OLS estimators of breakdowns in the classical assumptions and with what alternative estimating procedures, if any, should be followed when such breakdowns occur. We leave until Chapter 7 any consideration of the consequences of applying the normal OLS formulae under conditions where the classical assumptions 1–7 (page 26) all hold but where the population regression equation [2.12] has been incorrectly specified.

5.1 Stochastic explanatory variables

The first assumption of the classical model stated that each explanatory variable or regressor was non-stochastic in the sense that its sample values were fixed or chosen by the investigator. Given this assumption it was then possible to envisage a situation where, if many samples were taken, each sample would contain the same fixed X_{ji}s. This established the framework within which we viewed the sampling distributions of the OLS estimators. Finally, it was then a trivial extension of the assumption to assume that, as the sample size, n, tended to infinity, the matrix product, $(1/n)(\mathbf{X}'\mathbf{X})$, tended to a non-singular matrix of finite constants.

Non-randomness is obviously an implausible assumption for virtually all economic data. The investigator is almost always in the position of having to accept whatever data observations are available, rarely being able to fix the values of any of the variables in which he is interested. We must therefore consider the situation where the economic system under observation determines (in equation [2.13]) not only the values of the random disturbances (and hence the values of the dependent variable, Y), but also the values of the explanatory variables, i.e. the X_{ji}s. That is, we must consider a situation where the regressors are stochastic, thus abandoning the first two parts of assumption 1.

If we relax the first two parts of assumption 1, then we must reformulate the last part, regarding the matrix product $\mathbf{X}'\mathbf{X}$. Since $\mathbf{X}'\mathbf{X}$ now has stochastic elements, which have sampling distributions, we replace the last part of assumption 1 by

$$\text{plim} \frac{1}{n}(\mathbf{X}'\mathbf{X}) = \mathbf{Q} \text{ where } \mathbf{Q} \text{ is a non-singular matrix of finite constants} \quad [5.1]$$

That is, as the sample size, n, tends to infinity, the sampling distributions of the elements in $(1/n)(\mathbf{X}'\mathbf{X})$ collapse onto single points.

Although [5.1], like its equivalent in Chapter 2, will breakdown if any of the regressors exhibit upward trends over time, we retain this assumption for the moment. Its relevance should become clear shortly.

When the explanatory variables in a regression equation are stochastic, the consequences for the OLS estimators depend on the relationship between the explanatory variables and the disturbance – more precisely on the extent to which the X variables can be regarded as being independent of ε. It will be helpful if, for the moment, we refer back to simple two-variable regression where the underlying population regression line is given by $E(Y) = \beta_1 + \beta_2 X$. This is depicted in Fig. 5.1.

Suppose now that the single explanatory variable X and the disturbance ε are for some reason *positively correlated*. There will then be a tendency for 'high' sample values of X (high X_is) to coincide with 'high' sample values of the disturbance (high ε_is). Similarly there will be a tendency for 'low' X_is to coincide with 'low' ε_is. Since $E\varepsilon_i = 0$, a 'high' ε_i means a positive ε_i and a 'low' ε_i means a negative ε_i. Remembering that the ε_is represent the vertical distances of points in a scatter diagram from the population regression line, it should be clear that, under these conditions, any sample of values for Y and X is likely to result in a scatter diagram similar to that illustrated in Fig. 5.1. Points in the scatter will lie above the population regression line for 'high' values of X and below that line for 'low' values of X. The crucial point is that all the investigator ever observes is the scatter of points – he never gets to know the underlying population regression line. It follows that a sample regression line fitted to the scatter of points by the OLS method is likely to have a steeper slope than the unknown population regression line. Thus when X and ε are positively correlated the OLS estimators are likely to overestimate β_2, the slope, and underestimate β_1, the intercept, of the population regression line. Similar but opposite consequences follow from a negative correlation between X and ε. This case is illustrated in Fig. 5.2, where now it can be seen that the OLS estimators are likely to underestimate β_2 and overestimate β_1.

5.1 Positive correlation between disturbance and explanatory variable.

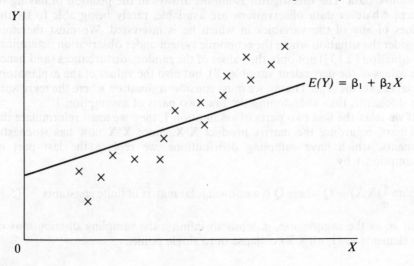

5.2 Negative correlation between disturbance and explanatory variable.

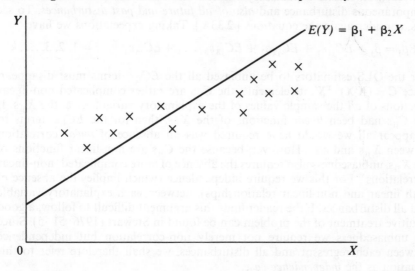

We may summarise the above arguments by saying that when the explanatory variable X and the disturbance ε are correlated, the OLS estimators of β_1 and β_2 are *biased*, the direction of the bias depending on the nature of the correlation. Furthermore, *this bias will persist even for large samples.* Under such conditions a larger sample will simply result in a larger number of points in the scatter, merely confirming the 'false impressions' given by the scatters in Figs 5.1 and 5.2. Hence, since no matter how large the sample size is made the bias in the OLS estimators persists, these estimators must not only lose the small sample property of unbiasedness but also the large sample property of consistency. It should be clear that under such conditions, if the sampling distributions for $\hat{\beta}_1$ and $\hat{\beta}_2$, the OLS estimators, collapse on to a single point as the sample size increases (i.e. if plim $\hat{\beta}_1$ and plim $\hat{\beta}_2$ exist) then these points cannot be equal to the true β_1 and β_2. Thus $\hat{\beta}_1$ and $\hat{\beta}_2$ must be inconsistent estimators of β_1 and β_2.

In multiple regression similar problems arise. It is not difficult to show that in this case the OLS estimators lose their desirable small and large sample properties whenever one or more of the explanatory variables or regressors is correlated with the disturbance. Since many econometric equations are estimated from time series data, with each observation referring to a different month, quarter or year, the sort of correlations we have been discussing above involve a relationship between the value of one of the regressors and the contemporaneous value of the disturbance. For this reason the above is often referred to as the *contemporaneously correlated case.*

If we ask ourselves under what conditions the above small and large sample biases will disappear, it is obvious that the absence of any contemporaneous correlations between the explanatory variables and the disturbance will help. However, the absence of such correlations is, in fact, sufficient only to restore to the OLS estimators the large sample property of consistency. In fact, if the OLS estimators are to retain the property of unbiasedness then it is necessary that each stochastic explanatory variable should be *independent* of the contemporaneous disturbance and *also of all future and past disturbances*. To see this, consider again the equations [2.33A]. Taking expectations we have

$$E\hat{\beta}_j = \beta_j + EC_{j1}\varepsilon_1 + EC_{j2}\varepsilon_2 + EC_{j3}\varepsilon_3, \ldots, + EC_{jn}\varepsilon_n \qquad j = 1, 2, 3, \ldots, k$$

For the OLS estimators to be unbiased all the $EC_{ji}\varepsilon_i$ terms must disappear. Since $\mathbf{C} = (\mathbf{X'X})^{-1}\mathbf{X'}$, its elements, the C_{ji}s are rather complicated non-linear functions of *all* the sample values of the explanatory variables, i.e. the X_{ji}s. If the C_{ji}s had been *linear* functions of the X_{ji}s, then for the $EC_{ji}\varepsilon_i$ terms to disappear all we would have required was an absence of *linear* correlation between X_{ji}s and ε_is.[1] However, because the C_{ji}s are non-linear functions of the X_{ji}s, unbiasedness also requires the absence of more complicated 'non-linear correlations'. For this we require independence (which implies the absence of both linear and non-linear relationships), between each explanatory variable and all disturbances. If the reader finds this argument difficult to follow, a good intuitive treatment of the problem can be found in Stewart (1976: 51–5). Since for unbiasedness we require not merely non-correlation but independence between each regressor and all disturbances, we shall therefore refer to this situation as the *independence case*.

An intermediate case, where the regressors are merely *contemporaneously uncorrelated* with the disturbance, arises when one of the regressors is a lagged value of the dependent variable. Consider for example the following equation

$$Y_t = \beta_1 + \beta_2 X_{2t} + \beta_3 X_{3t} + \beta_4 Y_{t-1} + \varepsilon_t \qquad t = 1, 2, 3, \ldots, n \qquad [5.2]$$

where we have replaced the usual i subscripts by t subscripts to indicate that the equation is to be estimated from time series data. The third regressor is simply the 'previous period's' value of the dependent variable Y. Equations such as [5.2] occur very frequently in econometrics. In particular, as we shall see in Chapter 6, they can arise in two very well-known economic models – the 'partial adjustment' model and the 'adaptive expectations' model. These models will appear regularly in the applied chapters of this book – particularly in those on consumption and the demand for money. However, we defer discussion of them until Chapter 6 and consider here only the econometric implications of lagged dependent variables.

If equation [5.2] is lagged by one period it becomes clear that Y_{t-1}, although it may be uncorrelated with ε_t, will, given the values of the regressors in period $t-1$, depend on ε_{t-1}. Hence, the third regressor in [5.2] is not independent of all *past* values of the disturbance. It follows, from the previous discussion, that the OLS estimators of the parameters of equations such as [5.2] will not be unbiased although, provided the condition [5.1] is valid, it can be shown that they will retain the large sample properties of consistency and asymptotic efficiency. It should be clear that similar conclusions must hold if, instead of, or in addition to, Y_{t-1}, variables such as Y_{t-2} or Y_{t-3} appear on the right-hand side of equation [5.2].

Summarising the above, the breakdown of the assumption of non-stochastic X-variables means that the OLS estimators retain both the properties of unbiasedness and consistency only when each and every explanatory variable or regressor is independent of all disturbance values, past, present and future. Indeed, we can see that non-stochastic explanatory variables represent a special case of the general independence case since, if the values of the X variables are fixed by the investigator, then they must necessarily be independent of all disturbance values.

At this point we give some initial consideration to the significance of the third part of assumption 1 in the classical model and its equivalent for stochastic regressors, the condition [5.1]. A fuller discussion appears in Chapter 7. As we have already noted, many economic time series exhibit trends. The condition [5.1] cannot hold for such 'non-stationary' time series and this has consequences for the large sample properties of the OLS estimators. For example, the conventional method of demonstrating that plim $\hat{\beta}_j = \beta_j$ for all j makes use of the condition [5.1]. If the condition does not hold, this does not necessarily mean that the OLS estimators are inconsistent but it does mean that we can no longer take their consistency for granted. As we noted above, many economic relationships contain, as regressors, lagged values of the dependent variable as in [5.2]. Under such circumstances, as we saw, the OLS estimators are biased and we are forced to fall back on such large sample properties as consistency. Hence, if the condition [5.1] fails to hold, and we cannot be certain that our estimators are even consistent, *then we can no longer say anything useful about the parameters we are trying to estimate.*

Another problem, likely to arise when the condition [5.1] breaks down because of trending regressors, is that of spurious correlation. When one of the regressors displays a distinct trend, it is often the case that movements in the dependent variable are also trend dominated. Even if trending variables are causally linked, much of the correlation between them is likely to be spurious and, when this is the case, it is clear that we cannot expect the OLS estimators to have their usual sampling distributions even for large samples.[2] The standard classical inferential procedures therefore *become inapplicable for any size of sample.*

The importance of the condition [5.1] should now be clear. Nevertheless, we shall assume implicitly that it is valid for the remainder of this chapter. Since [5.1] effectively rules out the possibility of non-stationary regressors, this also rules out the likelihood of spurious correlations.

Reformulation of assumptions concerning the disturbances

It is assumption 1 that is the most obvious 'non-starter' as far as most econometric investigation is concerned. It will therefore be helpful at this point to consider how the classical assumptions 2–5 concerning the disturbances may be reformulated for the case where we have stochastic rather than non-stochastic explanatory variables. Since the values of the explanatory variables can no longer be treated as fixed constants, we can now, strictly speaking, consider only *conditional* distributions of the ε_is, i.e. the distributions we would obtain for *given* sets of values for the X variables. It is possible that these distributions could differ, depending on the set of X values under consideration. This implies that, in *two-variable* regression, for example, we must reformulate assumptions 2–5 as:

2′ $E(\varepsilon_i \,|\, X_1, X_2, X_3, \ldots, X_n) = 0$ for all i

3′ $\text{Var}(\varepsilon_i \,|\, X_1, X_2, X_3, \ldots, X_n) = \sigma^2 = \text{const}$ for all i

4' $Cov(\varepsilon_i \varepsilon_j | X_1, X_2, X_3, \ldots, X_n) = 0$ for all $i \neq j$

5' For given $X_1, X_2, \ldots, X_n$ each ε_i is normally distributed

Consider the disturbances associated with, for example, the fourth and seventh sample observations, i.e. ε_4 and ε_7. Under the present alternative to assumption 1, we must envisage separate distributions for ε_4 and ε_7 for each and every possible set of X values. What assumptions 2', 3' and 4' now state, however, is that, for *each* of these given sets of X values, the expected values of ε_4 and ε_7 are both zero, the variances of ε_4 and ε_7 are both equal to the same constant, σ^2, and the covariance between ε_4 and ε_7 is zero. Finally, assumption 5' states that, for *each* given set of X values, ε_4 and ε_7 are both normally distributed. Assumptions 2'–5' have, of course, similar implications for all the ε_is.

Suppose we are able to assume that the explanatory variable is independent of the disturbance. Since for independent variables marginal (i.e. unconditional) and conditional distributions are identical, the conditional properties of the ε_is are then identical to the marginal or unconditional properties. Hence assumptions 2'–5' reduce to assumptions 2–5 so that no reformulation of these assumptions is necessary. If, however, we are unable to make the independence assumption then we must reformulate assumptions 2–5 as 2'–5'.

So far we have only considered the effect of stochastic X-variables on the unbiasedness and consistency properties of the OLS estimators. Clearly, however, if the small sample property of unbiasedness is lost – as it is in the contemporaneously correlated and uncorrelated cases, then the OLS estimators can no longer be efficient. They may still have a small sampling variance, but, from the definitions of section 2.3, unbiasedness is a necessary prerequisite if an estimator is to be efficient. Similarly, if the large sample property of consistency is also lost – as it is in the contemporaneously correlated case, then so, necessarily, must be the property of asymptotic efficiency.

For the 'independence case', where the properties of unbiasedness and consistency are retained, since the X variables are stochastic, the OLS estimators are no longer *linear* estimators in the sense that they can be expressed in the form $\sum a_i Y_i$ where the a_i are constants. The a_i are functions of the X_{ji}s – the sample values of the explanatory variables which can no longer be treated as predetermined constants. Hence the OLS estimators cannot, strictly speaking, be regarded as best *linear* unbiased estimators. However, they do retain the property of efficiency under these conditions – i.e. they have the minimum sampling variance of all unbiased estimators whether linear or non-linear. To see this, consider their sampling variances for a *given* set of specified values for the X-variables (i.e. their 'conditional' variances). That is, suppose we consider the population of all observations on Y and the explanatory X variables but concentrate for the moment just on that part of the population that contains the given specified set of X values. An infinite number of samples can be drawn from this 'subpopulation' all yielding different values for the OLS estimators. Since each such sample contains the same set of X values, these values can be treated *as if* they are constants. We know that the OLS estimators are efficient under such assumptions. However, they will be efficient whatever given set of X values we specify, i.e. whatever part of the full population we preselect. Since they are efficient for *any* preselected set of X values they must therefore be efficient in the fullest sense.

From the above discussion of the problems associated with stochastic explanatory variables it is clear that the greatest difficulties arise under the so-called contemporaneously correlated case. Unfortunately this is the case which probably arises most frequently in econometrics. We shall, in Chapter 8, examine in detail one factor which almost invariably gives rise to such contemporaneous correlations between explanatory variable and disturbance – the simultaneity of many economic relationships. Here, however, we turn to another aspect of econometric research which gives rise to the same problems – the question of *errors in the measurement of economic variables*.

Errors of measurement

Many economic data series represent only an approximation to the 'true' underlying values of the variable that the investigator really wishes to measure. Such errors of measurement could arise because totals are estimated only on a sample basis or maybe because data series measure concepts slightly different from those that appear in economic theory. Recall again the case of two-variable regression, where the underlying population regression line is given by $E(Y) = \beta_1 + \beta_2 X$. For a sample size n we have, for the 'true' values of the variables X and Y

$$Y_i = \beta_1 + \beta_2 X_i + \varepsilon_i \qquad i = 1, 2, 3, \ldots, n \qquad [5.3]$$

where the ε_is are disturbances obeying all the classical assumptions listed in the previous chapter. Suppose, however, that instead of observing the true X_i and Y_i we observe, for each i, X_i^* and Y_i^* where

$$Y_i^* = Y_i + v_i \qquad \text{and} \qquad X_i^* = X_i + \omega_i \qquad [5.4]$$

and v_i and ω_i represent errors in measuring the ith values of Y and X respectively. We shall assume that each v_i and ω_i has a zero mean and a constant variance, that errors made in observing X and Y at any one point of observation are independent of errors made at any other point, that the two errors are contemporaneously uncorrelated with one another and that they are contemporaneously uncorrelated with the disturbance in equation [5.3]. Such assumptions correspond to many situations that are likely to be found in the real world.

Suppose we attempt to estimate β_1 and β_2 using the observed Y_i^* and X_i^* instead of the true Y_i and X_i. Using [5.4] the regression equation [5.3] can be rewritten as

$$Y_i^* = \beta_1 + \beta_2 X_i^* + (\varepsilon_i + v_i - \beta_2 \omega_i) \qquad i = 1, 2, 3, \ldots, n \qquad [5.5]$$

This is a regression equation in the observable variables with a 'composite' disturbance given by the expression in parentheses. The problem is that this disturbance is dependent on the ω_is as are, (from [5.4]), the values of the explanatory variable, the X_i^*s. Thus, in equation [5.5], the explanatory variable and the disturbance are contemporaneously correlated so that application of the OLS method to this equation will lead to biased and inconsistent estimators of β_1 and β_2. The direction of the bias will depend on the nature of the correlation which, in turn, depends on the sign of β_2.[3]

Notice that it is the errors in the measurement of the explanatory X variable that cause the estimation problems. If the explanatory variable is observed without error, i.e. if $\omega_i = 0$ for all i, then [5.5] reduces to

$$Y_i^* = \beta_1 + \beta_2 X_i^* + (\varepsilon_i + v_i) \qquad i = 1, 2, 3, \ldots, n \qquad [5.6]$$

and we now have no contemporaneous correlation between explanatory variable and disturbance. Equation [5.6] in fact has the same statistical properties as the more familiar equation [5.3]. Equation [5.3] is sometimes referred to as an *errors-in-equation model* and equation [5.6] as a *generalised errors-in-equation model*, since [5.6] has a composite disturbance which behaves in an identical manner to the disturbance in equation [5.3].

Finally, consider the case where the disturbance in equation [5.3] is identically zero. This amounts to assuming that the relationship between Y and X is deterministic rather than stochastic. Since randomness is generally believed to be an intrinsic element in any economic relationship, this case is rarely likely to arise in econometrics. However, we shall have reason to refer to it when we discuss the empirical version of the so-called permanent income hypothesis in section 10.3 on the consumption function. The present case is generally known as the *errors in variables model* and here the only reason why points in a sample scatter diagram do not lie exactly on the underlying population regression line, $EY = \beta_1 + \beta_2 X$, is because of errors in measurement.

In the errors in variables model, since $\varepsilon_i = 0$, equation [5.5] reduces to

$$Y_i^* = \beta_1 + \beta_2 X_i^* + (v_i - \beta_2 \omega_i) \qquad i = 1, 2, 3, \ldots, n \qquad [5.5A]$$

and we again have a situation where disturbance and explanatory variable are contemporaneously correlated. The application of the OLS method to equation [5.5A] thus leads to biased and inconsistent estimators of β_1 and β_2.[4]

Although we have discussed errors of measurement in the context of two-variable regression, the various cases are exactly paralleled in multiple regression. Errors in the measurement of the dependent variable cause no problems. However, errors in the measurement of any of the explanatory variables mean that the OLS estimators lose both the properties of unbiasedness and that of consistency.

Instrumental variables

A method frequently adopted to overcome the problem of contemporaneous correlation, particularly when it arises as the result of measurement error, is that of *instrumental variable estimation*. To gain an intuitive grasp of this approach, consider the case of two-variable regression where the OLS normal equations [2.18] reduce to

$$\sum Y_i = \hat{\beta}_1 n + \hat{\beta}_2 \sum X_i$$
$$\sum X_i Y_i = \hat{\beta}_1 \sum X_i + \hat{\beta}_2 \sum X_i^2 \qquad [5.7]$$

We can regard the first equation in [5.7] as being obtained by summing [5.3] throughout and ignoring the term $\sum \varepsilon_i$. Similarly, the second equation can be obtained by multiplying [5.3] throughout by X_i and again summing, this time ignoring the term $\sum X_i \varepsilon_i$. Since $E\varepsilon_i = 0$, if the X variable in [5.3] is uncorrelated with the disturbance, then ignoring the $\sum \varepsilon_i$ and $\sum X_i \varepsilon_i$ terms is justifiable provided we are dealing with large samples. For this reason, the OLS estimators obtained by solving the normal equations [5.7] are consistent. However, when correlation exists between X and the disturbance we can no longer ignore the $\sum X_i \varepsilon_i$ term and the OLS estimators become inconsistent.

Suppose, however, we can find a so-called *instrument Z* which *while correlated with X is uncorrelated with the disturbance*. If in obtaining the second of the above normal equations we multiplied [5.3] throughout by Z_i rather than X_i, then (this time ignoring the term $\sum Z_i \varepsilon_i$) the normal equations would become

$$\sum Y_i = \beta_1^* n + \beta_2^* \sum X_i$$

$$\sum Z_i Y_i = \beta_1^* \sum Z_i + \beta_2^* \sum Z_i X_i \qquad [5.8]$$

Since Z is by assumption uncorrelated with the disturbance we are justified in ignoring the $\sum Z_i \varepsilon_i$ term for large samples. Hence the estimators of β_1 and β_2 obtained by solving [5.8] are consistent unlike the OLS estimators obtained by solving [5.7]. The solution to the equations [5.8] is in fact (letting $z_i = Z_i - \bar{Z}$):

$$\beta_2^* = \frac{\sum z_i y_i}{\sum z_i x_i} \quad \text{and} \quad \beta_1^* = \bar{Y} - \beta_2^* \bar{X} \qquad [5.9]$$

The expressions [5.9] are known as simple *instrumental variable* (IV) *estimators* of β_1 and β_2.

To avoid confusion, it should be noted at this point that in computing the IV estimators [5.9] we are not simply replacing X by Z and then regressing Y on Z. However, it can be shown that if we regress X on Z, save the predicted $\hat{X}$ values from this regression and then regress Y on $\hat{X}$, the resulting estimators will be identical to those given by [5.9]. In this process, while Z is still referred to as the instrument, $\hat{X}$ is known as the *instrumental variable*.

In selecting instrumental variables it is intuitively obvious that the correlation between 'instruments' and relevant explanatory variables should be as large as possible. While this is not necessary for consistency, *the larger are such correlations the smaller will be the asymptotic variances of the estimators obtained.* That is, the more rapidly will their sampling distributions collapse on to the parameters being estimated as the sample size increases.

In practice the problem of finding instruments which are sufficiently highly correlated with the explanatory variables and the necessity of checking whether these instruments are indeed uncorrelated with the disturbance somewhat reduces the theoretical attractiveness of the method. However, a favourite procedure is to use either the preceding or subsequent period value of an explanatory variable as its instrument. For example, if equations [5.5] and [5.5A] referred to time series data then, replacing i subscripts by t subscripts, either X_{t-1}^* or X_{t+1}^* would be used as the instrument for X_t^*. Since we assume that measurement errors at different observation points are independent of one another, we can regard such instruments as uncorrelated with the composite disturbances in [5.5] or [5.5A]. Hence, since both X_{t-1}^* and X_{t+1}^* are likely to be highly correlated with X_t^*, either would be a suitable instrument. Similarly, if [5.5] or [5.5A] refer to cross-sectional data then, writing X_{it}^* as the current period value of X^*, suitable instruments would be either the values X_{it-1}^* for all i, or the values X_{it+1}^* for all i. Notice, however, that this requires further data for the full cross-section (i.e. for all i) on either the preceding period values of X_i^* or the subsequent period values of X_i^*. Such data may not always be available.

It is not necessary to restrict the choice of instrument to a single variable. Suppose, for example, that when searching for an appropriate instrument for the X^* variable in [5.5] we discover m possible candidates, $Z_1, Z_2, Z_3, \ldots, Z_m$. The optimal procedure now is to form a composite instrumental variable by taking a weighted average of the Zs. The weights are chosen so as to maximise the correlation between this composite variable and X^*. The weighted average is obtained simply by using OLS to regress X^* on all the Zs. That is we compute

$$\hat{X}^* = \hat{\gamma}_1 Z_1 + \hat{\gamma}_2 Z_2 + \cdots + \hat{\gamma}_m Z_m$$

The required weights are simply the OLS estimates – that is the $\hat{\gamma}$s. This is the case because OLS minimises the sum of squared residuals and hence maximises the correlation between X^* and $\hat{X}^*$. It is $\hat{X}^*$ that is the required composite instrumental variable – that is the predicted value of X^* from the above regression. Notice that since the Zs are, by definition, uncorrelated with the disturbance in [5.5] (otherwise they could not be suitable instruments), $\hat{X}^*$ which is an exact linear function of the Zs must also be uncorrelated with this disturbance. Hence it is a suitable instrumental variable and deviations from its mean can be used as the z_is in the instrumental variable estimators [5.9]. To distinguish this procedure from that where a single original instrument is used, the resultant estimators are referred to as *generalised instrumental variable estimators* (GIVEs).

Instrumental variable estimation can also be used in the multiple regression case. To compute simple IV estimators, analogous to [5.9], it is necessary to find instruments for each explanatory variable that is correlated with the disturbance. Such instruments must, in each case, be correlated with the relevant explanatory variable but uncorrelated with the disturbance.[5]

Provided the number of potential instruments exceeds the number of explanatory variables, it is also possible to obtain GIVEs in multiple regression. Composite instrumental variables then have to be found for all explanatory variables by regressing each in turn on all the instruments.[6]

Despite the difficulties of finding suitable instruments, instrumental variable estimation is virtually the only available method of dealing with a contemporaneous correlation which arises from an errors-in-variables problem. We shall deal in Chapter 8 with the alternative estimation procedures that can be used when the contemporaneous correlation arises because of simultaneity in economic relationships. We merely note at this stage that one of these procedures – two stage least squares, is in fact a generalised instrumental variable method.

The Wu–Hausman test
Obviously, we would not adopt IV estimation if all regressors were uncorrelated with the disturbance. It is therefore useful to be able to test for such lack of correlation and Wu (1973) and Hausman (1978) have developed an appropriate procedure for doing so. Suppose we have to estimate the equation

$$Y = \beta_0 + \beta_1 X_1 + \beta_2 X_2 + \beta_3 X_3 + \varepsilon \qquad [5.10]$$

and suspect that the variables X_2 and X_3 are correlated with the disturbance ε. The Wu–Hausman test proceeds as follows. Given a set of suitable instruments $Z_1, Z_2, Z_3, \ldots, Z_m$, instrumental variables $\hat{X}_2$ and $\hat{X}_3$ are then constructed in the usual way. That is X_2 and X_3 are regressed on the Zs and the predicted values from these regressions retained. Equation [5.10] is estimated by OLS and then a further OLS regression is computed with the instrumental variables $\hat{X}_2$ and $\hat{X}_3$ added to the right-hand side variables in [5.10]. Note that X_2 and X_3 *and* $\hat{X}_2$ *and* $\hat{X}_3$ are included in this second regression. The F-statistic [4.45] is then computed to test the validity of omitting the instrumental variables from [5.10]. If this statistic exceeds the relevant critical value, taken from F-tables, then the hypothesis of non-correlation between X_2 and X_3 and the disturbance is rejected. That is the use of an IV estimation method is justified.

5.2 Breakdowns in assumptions concerning the disturbances

We shall now consider the effects on the OLS estimators of breakdowns in assumptions 2–5 of the classical model. In the present chapter we mainly consider the consequences of single breakdowns in the classical assumptions rather than the simultaneous breakdown of two or more of these assumptions. However, since assumption 1 – that of non-stochastic X variables – is so obviously a non-starter in econometric work, it would be somewhat unreal to consider breakdowns in the assumptions concerning the disturbances while still retaining assumption 1 intact. However, as we saw in the previous section, even if assumption 1 is relaxed then, provided we are prepared to assume the explanatory X variables are independent of the disturbances, we do not need to alter our interpretation of assumptions 2–5. Thus much of the following discussion of the consequences of breakdowns in assumptions concerning the disturbances can be regarded as occurring either in the context of non-stochastic explanatory variables or in the context of stochastic explanatory variables that are independent of the disturbances.

Suppose we wish to estimate a population regression equation, which for given values of two explanatory variables X_2 and X_3 has the form

$$EY = \beta_1 + \beta_2 X_2 + \beta_3 X_3 \qquad [5.11]$$

If the sample size is n then we have

$$Y_i = EY_i + \varepsilon_i$$
$$= \beta_1 + \beta_2 X_{2i} + \beta_3 X_{3i} + \varepsilon_i \qquad i = 1, 2, 3, \ldots, n \qquad [5.12]$$

All of what follows in this section can easily be generalised to the case of more than two explanatory variables.

The second assumption in the classical model stated that the means or expected values of the disturbances associated with each sample observation were all zero, i.e. $E\varepsilon_i = 0$ for all i. The breakdown of this assumption always has undesirable consequences for the OLS estimator of the intercept β_1 in equation [5.11]. However, it may not necessarily have such consequences for the OLS estimators of the regression slopes β_2 and β_3. Suppose all the classical assumptions except for assumption 2 hold but, for each sample observation, the associated disturbance now has a non-zero mean or expected value equal to some constant μ. That is, we replace the assumption $E\varepsilon_i = 0$ by $E\varepsilon_i = \mu =$ constant. If we now take expectations over equation [5.12] we obtain, for given values of X_2 and X_3,

$$EY_i = \beta_1 + \mu + \beta_2 X_{2i} + \beta_3 X_{3i}$$
$$= \beta_1^* + \beta_2 X_{2i} + \beta_3 X_{3i} \qquad i = 1, 2, 3, \ldots, n$$

The form of this relationship is identical to that arising from the population regression line [5.11] when $E\varepsilon_i = 0$, except for the fact that the intercept is now $\beta_1^* = \beta_1 + \mu$ instead of β_1. Thus OLS will yield estimators of the regression slopes β_2 and β_3 possessing all the desirable small and large sample properties. However, since μ is unknown, there is no way in which we can obtain either unbiased or even consistent estimators of the intercept β_1. Clearly, the OLS estimator of β_1^* will be a biased estimator of β_1.

Suppose now that, instead of $E\varepsilon_i = \mu$, we had $E\varepsilon_i = \mu_i \neq$ const, i.e. the expected values of the disturbances were not all equal. This would imply that the mean value of the dependent variable, Y, depended on other factors apart from the values of X_2 and X_3. This would suggest that the population regression line [5.11] had been mis-specified in some way – maybe by the omission of one or more further important explanatory variables. However, we will leave problems associated with such mis-specifications until Chapter 7. We merely point out at this stage that in such circumstances the application of OLS would be unlikely to provide unbiased or consistent estimators of β_2 and β_3 let alone β_1.

5.2.1 Heteroscedasticity

The third assumption in the classical model stated that all disturbances had a common variance, i.e. var $\varepsilon_i = \sigma^2 =$ const for all i. In section 2.4 we saw that this assumption of *homoscedastic disturbances* was most likely to break down when there was a large variation in the size of the explanatory variables. This typically occurs either with cross-sectional data or when a long span of time series data is available. The disturbances are then said to be *heteroscedastic* and we have the case of heteroscedasticity.

We saw in our discussion of the properties of the OLS estimators that only the classical assumptions 1 and 2 were necessary for these estimators to possess the properties of unbiasedness and consistency. Obviously, then, the breakdown of assumption 3 does not affect these properties. However, the assumption of homoscedasticity was necessary if the OLS estimators were to possess the properties of best-linear unbiasedness and asymptotic efficiency. Thus under heteroscedasticity the OLS estimators *remain unbiased and consistent but are no longer BLUE or asymptotically efficient.*[7] This has two implications. First, the loss of the small sample property of BLUEness means that there must now be some other linear unbiased estimators which have smaller sampling variances than the OLS estimators. Clearly, whatever the size of the sample such estimators are to be preferred. Secondly, the loss of the large sample property of asymptotic efficiency means that there now exist consistent estimators possessing sampling distributions that, as the sample size increases, collapse more quickly on to the regression parameters being estimated than do the OLS estimators. While there is little point in seeking for such estimators if the sample size is small, they are obviously to be preferred when large samples are available.

Unfortunately, heteroscedasticity has consequences which are not limited to the OLS estimators themselves. When the assumption of homoscedasticity fails it can be shown that the usual expressions, $s^2 x^{jj}$, used to estimate the sampling variances of the OLS estimators (see section 2.4 on making inferences), no longer provide unbiased estimates of the true values of these quantities. This has potentially an even more serious consequence. It means that we can no longer rely on usual inferential procedures – i.e. we can no longer rely on any confidence intervals computed for the regression parameters, the β_is, and neither can we rely on the usual procedures for testing hypotheses about them. For example, if the expressions $s^2 x^{jj}$ tend to underestimate the true variances of the $\hat{\beta}_i$s, then confidence intervals are likely to be narrower than they should be, giving a false impression as to the precision of the point estimates obtained. Also we are likely to find ourselves incorrectly regarding explanatory variables as 'statistically significant' when they are not.[8] In fact, it can be shown that precisely this sort of situation arises when the variance of the disturbance tends to increase the further are the sample values of explanatory variables from their mean (see, for example, Kmenta 1986: 276–8).

The seriousness of the consequences of heteroscedasticity means that an investigator clearly needs to know whether it is present or not. If necessary, he can then follow suitable corrective procedures. There is, in fact, no universally accepted procedure for 'testing' for heteroscedasticity but a number of tests have been proposed. Since heteroscedasticity is a property of the disturbances and in practice these disturbances remain unknown, all such tests proceed by examining the known residuals, i.e. the e_is obtained in the OLS estimation procedure. These may be treated as estimates of the ε_is – the unknown disturbances. We saw in section 2.4 that for many economic relationships the pattern of heteroscedasticity, when present, is such that the variance of *disturbances* increases as the sizes of the explanatory variables increase. One procedure followed is therefore to look for any increase in the variability in the least squares *residuals* as the sizes of the X-variables increase. For example, suppose in a two-variable regression problem we obtained a scatter diagram similar to that shown in Fig. 5.3.

The line shown in Fig. 5.3 is the estimated *sample* regression line so that the residuals, the e_is, represent the vertical distances of the (known) points in the scatter from this (known) line. Since in this scatter the spread of the residuals about the sample regression clearly seems to increase as X increases, we would conclude that the disturbances associated with the underlying population regression line are likely to be heteroscedastic.

It is, however, possible that scatters such as that in Fig. 5.3 could occur purely by chance. Remember that the OLS residuals are subject to sampling variability just as are the estimators themselves so that such a scatter could arise even when the unknown disturbances are in fact homoscedastic. Some form of inferential statistical testing procedure is therefore necessary.

A test that has been frequently used in the past is the Goldfeld–Quant test. This test is, strictly speaking, only applicable when heteroscedasticity takes the form var $\varepsilon_i = \sigma^2 X_i^2$ where σ^2 = const – i.e. when the variance of the disturbances increases with the square of the explanatory variable. The test procedure is to first rank the sample observations according to the size of the explanatory variable and then run separate OLS regressions for the 'high' X values and the 'low' X values.[9] The variances of the residuals are then calculated for each regression. If heteroscedasticity is present the residual variance for the 'high-X' regression is likely to be greater than that for the 'low-X' regression. In fact,

5.3 Residual pattern suggestive of heteroscedasticity.

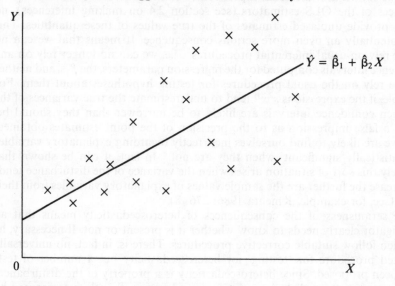

the null hypothesis of homoscedasticity is rejected if the ratio of the two variances is sufficiently greater than unity.

Although we have described the above test in the context of two-variable regression it can also be applied in multiple regression. In the multiple regression case, however, it is necessary to specify which explanatory variable the disturbance variance is related to. The ranking required for the test is then applied merely to this explanatory variable.

In multiple regression, if there is no obvious candidate among the explanatory variables to which we can link the disturbance variance, then more general tests are possible using the Lagrange multiplier approach outlined in section 4.7. For example, suppose again that we wish to estimate equation [5.11] but suspect that

$$\text{var } \varepsilon_i = \sigma^2 + \gamma(EY_i)^2 = \sigma^2 + \gamma(\beta_1 + \beta_2 X_{2i} + \beta_3 X_{3i})^2 \quad i = 1, 2, 3, ..., n \quad [5.13]$$

This case is sometimes referred to as *dependent variable heteroscedasticity* since it implies that the variance of the dependent variable depends on its expected value. Notice that if $\gamma = 0$ in [5.13] then the disturbances are homoscedastic so that a rejection of the null hypothesis implies the presence of heteroscedasticity.

In this case the required *LM* statistic cannot be computed along the lines suggested on page 79, although its value can still be found from a suitable auxiliary *LM* regression. In this case, however, the auxiliary regression is of the form

$$e_i^2 = \alpha + \beta \hat{Y}_i^2 + v_i \quad i = 1, 2, 3, ..., n \quad [5.14]$$

where the e_is and $\hat{Y}_i$s are the residuals and predicted values from the OLS estimation of equation [5.11] and v is a disturbance. Under the null hypothesis of homoscedasticity, ($\gamma = 0$ in [5.13]), the quantity nR^2 obtained from the estimation of [5.14] has a χ^2 distribution with one degree of freedom.

Notice the intuitive idea behind this test. Since var $\varepsilon_i = E\varepsilon_i^2$, $\gamma \neq 0$ in [5.13] implies that $E\varepsilon_i^2$ is related to $(EY_i)^2$. We search for such a relationship by regressing the e_i^2s on $\hat{Y}_i$s and reject the hypothesis $\gamma = 0$ if the relationship is sufficiently strong.

It is also possible to see intuitively why nR^2 is a suitable test statistic. Regard the auxiliary equation [5.14] as an unrestricted equation with residual sum of squares SSR_U. The null hypothesis of homoscedasticity implies $\beta = 0$ in [5.14] and hence a restricted equation

$$e_i^2 = \alpha + v_i \qquad i = 1, 2, 3, \ldots, n \qquad\qquad [5.15]$$

Both [5.14] and [5.15] have the same total sum of squares, SST, but, since the restricted equation [5.15] has no explanatory variables, its total and residual sums of squares are the same, i.e. $\text{SSR}_R = \text{SST}$. Hence, if we use the test statistic [4.50] to test the restriction $\beta = 0$, then in terms of the auxiliary regression [5.14],

$$\frac{\text{SSR}_R - \text{SSR}_U}{\text{SSR}_R / n} = \frac{\text{SST} - \text{SSR}_U}{\text{SST} / n} = nR^2$$

The above is only an intuitive derivation of the *LM* statistic because to apply [4.50] we really need to be able to estimate equations involving $E\varepsilon_i^2$ and $(EY_i)^2$. However, since these are unknown, we are forced to use e_i^2 and $\hat{Y}_i^2$, obtained by a method of estimation (OLS) which should not be used if heteroscedasticity is present. However, it can be shown that application of the *LM* principle also results in the above test statistic.

Similar Lagrange multiplier tests may be constructed for the case of *multiplicative heteroscedasticity* where, again considering [5.11], we test for

$$\text{var } \varepsilon_i = \sigma^2 X_{2i}^{\gamma_2} X_{3i}^{\gamma_3} \qquad i = 1, 2, 3, \ldots, n \qquad\qquad [5.16]$$

The null hypothesis of homoscedasticity is in this case $\gamma_2 = \gamma_3 = 0$.

Notice that *LM* tests are more general than the Goldfeld–Quandt test because the disturbance variance is not related specifically to a particular explanatory variable.

Dealing with heteroscedasticity

When heteroscedasticity is believed to be present the standard procedure is to 'transform' the equation being estimated so that its disturbance becomes homoscedastic rather than heteroscedastic and still obeys all the other classical assumptions. Ordinary least squares can then be applied to the transformed equation. In practice this normally means making some assumption about the form of the heteroscedasticity. Suppose, for example, we wish to estimate equation [5.11] and suspect that the heteroscedasticity takes the form var $\varepsilon_i = \sigma^2 X_{2i}^2$, i.e. variances are proportional to the square of the value of the first explanatory variable. In this case the disturbances can be transformed into the homoscedastic kind by dividing by X_{2i} for all i, since

$$\text{var}(\varepsilon_i / X_{2i}) = (1 / X_{2i})^2 \text{ var } \varepsilon_i = \sigma^2$$

However, to preserve the validity of the model this transformation must be applied to all terms in equation [5.12] which then becomes

$$\frac{Y_i}{X_{2i}} = \beta_1\left(\frac{1}{X_{2i}}\right) + \beta_2 + \beta_3\left(\frac{X_{3i}}{X_{2i}}\right) + \frac{\varepsilon_i}{X_{2i}} \qquad i = 1, 2, 3, \ldots, n \qquad [5.17]$$

We may rewrite this as

$$Y_i^* = \beta_2 + \beta_1 X_{2i}^* + \beta_3 X_{3i}^* + \varepsilon_i^* \qquad i = 1, 2, 3, \ldots, n \qquad [5.18]$$

where $Y_i^* = Y_i/X_{2i}$, $X_{2i}^* = 1/X_{2i}$, $X_{3i}^* = X_{3i}/X_{2i}$ and $\varepsilon_i^* = \varepsilon_i/X_{2i}$. Equation [5.18] is an equation in values of the 'transformed' variables Y^*, X_2^* and X_3^* and more importantly has a *homoscedastic* disturbance. Hence, we can obtain BLUE estimators of the parameters β_2, β_1 and β_3 (which appear in the original equations [5.11] and [5.12]), by using the OLS method to regress the *transformed* variable Y^* on the two *transformed* explanatory variables X_2^* and X_3^*. Moreover, our estimates of the variances and standard errors of these estimators will no longer be biased as they would be if we applied OLS directly to equation [5.12]. Notice, however, that now it will be the *intercept* in the sample regression equation which yields the estimate of β_2 (the coefficient of X_2 in the original equation) and the *coefficient on X_2^** in the sample regression equation which yields the estimate of β_1 (the intercept in the original equation).

The transformation required to overcome the problem of heteroscedasticity depends on the precise form of the heteroscedasticity present. For example, if it were believed that var $\varepsilon_i = \sigma^2 X_{3i}$, i.e. the variance of the disturbances was proportional to the size of the explanatory variable X_3, then equation [5.12] has to be divided throughout by $\sqrt{X_{3i}}$ to yield

$$\frac{Y_i}{\sqrt{X_{3i}}} = \beta_1\left(\frac{1}{\sqrt{X_{3i}}}\right) + \beta_2\left(\frac{X_{2i}}{\sqrt{X_{3i}}}\right) + \beta_3\sqrt{X_{3i}} + \frac{\varepsilon_i}{\sqrt{X_{3i}}} \qquad [5.19]$$

The disturbance in equation [5.19] is homoscedastic since

$$\text{var}(\varepsilon_i/\sqrt{(X_3)}) = (1/X_3)\,\text{var}\,\varepsilon_i = \sigma^2 = \text{const}$$

Hence, OLS may be applied to [5.19] to obtain BLUEs of β_1, β_2 and β_3. There is a minor problem here in that [5.19] does not contain an intercept. However, the OLS method can easily be adapted to accommodate this and many computer programs are available that minimise the residual sum of squares subject to the constraint that the regression equation passes through the origin.

It should be clear that the above procedures can be generalised to take account of any form of heteroscedasticity. In general, if var $\varepsilon_i = \sigma^2 \lambda_i$ where λ_i is *any* function of the sizes of one or more of the explanatory variables, then we can always transform our equation into one containing a homoscedastic disturbance by dividing throughout by $\sqrt{\lambda_i}$. Ordinary least squares can then be applied to the transformed equation. Notice that, although the expressions used to obtain the estimates of β_1, β_2 and β_3 will be the normal OLS estimators when expressed in terms of values of the transformed variables, they will not be the OLS estimators when expressed in terms of the original variables. For this reason they are referred to as *generalised least squares (GLS) estimators*, generalised in this case because, for the special case $\lambda_i = 1$ for all i, they reduce to the OLS estimators.

The reader should have noticed that if the above procedures are to be applied, it is necessary to assume something about the form of the heteroscedasticity before estimation is undertaken. The most convenient assumption to make is that the variance of the disturbances is proportional to the square of the size of one of the explanatory variables. While there is little empirical evidence in favour of such a formulation, its popularity presumably arose from the fact that the transformed equation does contain an intercept.

One situation where a form of GLS estimator is used occurs when variables refer to the group means of classified data. For example, expenditure surveys are often published with households classified according to income or total expenditure levels and the only published data refer to the mean expenditures of such groups. As we shall see in Chapter 9, when we discuss the estimation of Engel curves from cross-sectional data, regression equations fitted to such group means are likely to be subject to heteroscedastic disturbances and a GLS estimation procedure is necessary.

*Maximum likelihood estimation
When it is suspected that heteroscedasticity is present but we are unclear of the precise form it takes, maximum likelihood methods can be used to estimate, simultaneously, both the regression equation parameters and the heteroscedasticity parameter(s). For example, suppose again that [5.11] and [5.12] hold and we suspect that

$$\text{var } \varepsilon_i = \sigma_i^2 = \sigma^2 X_{2i}^\gamma \qquad [5.20]$$

but are unclear as to the value of the heteroscedasticity parameter γ.

The density function for the sample observations is now

$$f(Y_i) = \frac{1}{2\Pi\sigma_i^2} e^{-(Y_i - EY_i)^2/2\sigma_i^2} \qquad i = 1, 2, 3, \ldots, n \qquad [5.21]$$

since each observation now has a different variance. EY_i in [5.21] is given by equation [5.11]. Since

$$\log f(Y_i) = -\log 2\Pi - \log \sigma_i^2 - \frac{1}{2\sigma_i^2}(Y_i - EY_i)^2$$

$$= -\log 2\Pi - \log \sigma^2 - \gamma \log X_{2i} - \frac{1}{2\sigma^2}\frac{(Y_i - EY_i)^2}{X_{2i}^\gamma} \qquad [5.22]$$

the log-likelihood function for n sample observations is

$$l = \log L(\beta_1, \beta_2, \beta_3, \sigma^2, \gamma)$$

$$= \sum \log f(Y_i)$$

$$= -\frac{n}{2}\log 2\Pi - \frac{n}{2}\log \sigma^2 - \gamma \sum \log X_{2i} - \frac{1}{2\sigma^2}\sum \frac{(Y_i - EY_i)^2}{X_{2i}^\gamma} \qquad [5.23]$$

[5.23] can be maximised to provide MLEs of the β_js in equation [5.11] *and* the parameters σ^2 and γ in [5.20]. This maximisation problem is highly non-linear but can be solved by the methods referred to at the end of Chapter 3. Notice, however, that, if γ in [5.20] were known beforehand to equal 2, then the maximisation of [5.23] would involve selection of the β_js in [5.11] and

[5.12] that minimise the sum of squares

$$\sum \frac{(Y_i - EY_i)^2}{X_{2i}^2} = \sum \left[\frac{Y_i}{X_{2i}} - E \frac{Y_i}{X_{2i}} \right]^2$$

This is most easily done by applying OLS to equation [5.18]. Thus, in this case, the ML and GLS estimators of the β_js are identical. In fact, it should be clear that if γ is known then such ML and GLS estimators will always be the same. Under these circumstances the MLEs will therefore have all the desired small sample properties. However, if γ is unknown and has to be estimated along with the other parameters, then the MLEs will possess only the large sample properties of consistency and asymptotic efficiency.

5.2.2 Autocorrelated disturbances

The fourth assumption in the classical model specifies that the covariance, and hence the correlation, between any two disturbances is zero, i.e.

$$\text{cov}(\varepsilon_i, \varepsilon_j) = 0 \qquad \text{for all } i \neq j$$

When this assumption breaks down we have *autocorrelated disturbances*. We suggested in section 2.4 that autocorrelation was most likely to occur with time series data and when this happens it is also referred to as *serial correlation*. The problem with time series data is that all the random and independent factors which the disturbance term is supposed to represent are, if operating in a particular manner during any one period, likely to operate in a similar manner during the next and maybe following periods. The disturbance in any one period tends to 'spill over' into subsequent periods. For example, suppose the dependent variable is the output of a firm and that output is pushed below 'normal' during one month as a result of industrial action. Then, since there is a likelihood that such industrial action or at least its effects may persist into the following month, output is likely to be depressed during this period too. In this example if the disturbance is negative in one month it is likely to be negative in the following month as well. Note, however, that the longer the period of observation the less serious are such effects likely to be. Thus serial correlation is less likely to be a problem with annual data than it is, for example, with monthly data.

The consequences of autocorrelated disturbances are generally similar to those of heteroscedasticity. Assumption 4 in the classical model (like assumption 3) is necessary if the OLS estimators are to be BLUEs and asymptotically efficient estimators. However, it is not necessary for unbiasedness or consistency. Thus under autocorrelation (as under heteroscedasticity) the OLS estimators *remain unbiased and consistent but are no longer BLUE or asymptotically efficient*. The similarity with the consequences of heteroscedasticity extends to the usual OLS expressions for estimated standard errors. These are again biased estimators of the true standard errors so that under autocorrelation *we cannot rely on the normal confidence intervals for regression parameters or on the standard test procedures*.

Many attempts to handle the problem of autocorrelation have proceeded under the assumption that disturbances follow *a first-order autoregressive scheme*.[10] This involves replacing all the normal classical assumptions about the generation of the disturbances by the specification

$$\varepsilon_t = \rho\varepsilon_{t-1} + u_t \qquad -1 < \rho < 1 \qquad t = 1, 2, 3, \ldots, n \qquad [5.24]$$

where u is a further 'disturbance' or random variable. Thus the value of the disturbance in the present period t is determined partly by the value of the disturbance in the previous period $t - 1$ and partly by the value of u in the present period. ρ is a parameter in the relationship. Notice that when discussing autocorrelation it is customary to use t subscripts rather than i subscripts, since this problem typically arises with time series data. The random variable, u, is assumed to possess all the properties attributed to ε in the normal classical model.[11] Given these assumptions it is not difficult to show that ε itself will also satisfy assumptions 2, 3 and 5 in the classical model – i.e. $E\varepsilon_t = 0$, var $\varepsilon_t = \sigma^2 = $ const. and each ε_t is normally distributed. However, the ε_ts do not satisfy assumption 4. In fact, it can be shown (see, for example Kmenta 1986: 300–01) that

$$\text{cov}(\varepsilon_t, \varepsilon_s) = \rho^{t-s}\sigma^2 \neq 0 \qquad \text{for all } t \neq s \qquad [5.25]$$

Thus equation [5.24] represents a specification for the ε_t's that satisfies all the classical assumptions concerning the disturbances except that of non-auto-correlation. Notice two points about equations [5.24] and [5.25]. First, the nature of the autocorrelation present will depend on the sign of the parameter ρ. This parameter is restricted to be within the range plus and minus unity.[12] If ρ is positive then equation [5.24] implies that (since $Eu_t = 0$) a positive disturbance value in one period will *tend* to be followed by a positive disturbance value in the next period. Similarly, negative disturbance values will *tend* to follow negative disturbance values. Thus we can expect sequences of positive disturbance values broken only because of sufficiently negative *actual* values for u, followed by sequences of negative disturbance values broken only by sufficiently positive *actual* values for u. This form of autocorrelation is known as *positive autocorrelation*. It is obviously very much in tune with the economic interpretation of serial correlation given above where disturbing factors tend to 'spill over' from one period to another. If ρ is negative then we have *negative autocorrelation* and there is a tendency for positive disturbance values to follow negative disturbance values and vice versa. It is obviously more difficult to think of economic circumstances which would give rise to this sort of behaviour and for this reason we expect to encounter positive autocorrelation more frequently than negative autocorrelation in most econometric work.

The second point about the first-order autoregressive scheme follows from equation [5.25]. Since $\sigma^2 = $ const and $-1 < \rho < 1$, the covariance and hence the correlation between disturbances associated with any two periods declines as the interval between the two periods, $t - s$, increases. This is also in line with our economic interpretation since it implies that disturbing factors in any period are less likely to spill over into periods in the more distant future than they are into periods in the near future.

When the disturbance in a regression equation follows the first order scheme [5.24] it is possible to say something about the direction of the bias in the OLS expressions for estimated standard errors. If ρ in [5.24] is positive, then if the explanatory variables in the regression equation follow a definite trend over the sample period, it can be shown that the normal OLS expressions for standard errors underestimate the true standard errors of the OLS estimators (see, for example, Kmenta 1986: 310). Since positive rather than negative autocorrelation is to be expected with economic data, and since many economic variables possess a definite trend, either upwards or downwards, we can therefore frequently expect such downward bias. This means that confidence intervals will be narrower than they should be and we will tend to treat explanatory variables as 'statistically significant' when they are not.[13]

Obviously there is no reason to believe that equation [5.24] will always be an adequate representation of serial correlation when it occurs. For example, when using non-seasonally adjusted quarterly data, disturbances in any one quarter are likely to be akin to those in the same quarter in previous years (e.g. fuel and light expenditure is always highest during the winter quarter). Hence a 'fourth order scheme' of the kind

$$\varepsilon_t = \rho \varepsilon_{t-4} + u_t$$

may be more appropriate. Also, more complicated schemes of, for example, the kind

$$\varepsilon_t = \rho_1 \varepsilon_{t-1} + \rho_2 \varepsilon_{t-2} + u_t$$

where the disturbance in period t is directly related to more than just the previous period's disturbance, are possible. Another type of disturbance that we shall encounter several times in later chapters is the *first-order moving average disturbance*

$$\varepsilon_t = u_t + \theta u_{t-1}$$

where θ is a constant and u_t again obeys the normal classical assumptions. However, when some specific assumption has to be made regarding ε_t, the first-order autoregressive scheme is often likely to be a good approximation for economic data.

Testing for autocorrelation

Since the values of the disturbances are unknown, tests for autocorrelation, like those for heteroscedasticity, involve treating the known residuals as estimates of the ε_ts. Easily the best-known such test is that devised by Durbin and Watson (1950 and 1951). Consider the expression

$$\frac{\sum_{t=2}^{n} (\varepsilon_t - \varepsilon_{t-1})^2}{\sum_{t=1}^{n} \varepsilon_t^2}$$

[5.26]

Suppose autocorrelation follows the first-order scheme [5.24]. For positive autocorrelation ($\rho > 0$), successive disturbance values will tend to have the same sign and the quantities $(\varepsilon_t - \varepsilon_{t-1})^2$ will tend to be small relative to the squares of the actual values of the disturbances. We can therefore expect the value of the expression [5.26] to be low. Indeed, for the extreme case $\rho = 1$, it is possible that $\varepsilon_t = \varepsilon_{t-1}$ for all t so that the minimum possible value of [5.26] is zero. However, for negative autocorrelation, since positive disturbance values now tend to be followed by negative ones and vice versa, the quantities $(\varepsilon_t - \varepsilon_{t-1})^2$ will tend to be large relative to the squares of the ε_ts. Hence, the value of [5.26] now tends to be 'high'. The extreme case here is when $\rho = -1$ when it is possible that $\varepsilon_t = -\varepsilon_{t-1}$ for all t, in which case [5.26] takes its maximum value of 4.

These upper and lower limits for [5.26] suggest that when $\rho = 0$ we should expect the expression [5.26] to take a value in the neighbourhood of 2. Notice, however, that when $\rho = 0$, equation [5.24] reduces to $\varepsilon_t = u_t$ for all t, so that ε takes on all the properties of u – in particular it is no longer autocorrelated. Thus in the absence of autocorrelation we can expect [5.26] to take a value close to 2, when negative autocorrelation is present a value in excess of 2 and maybe as high as 4, and when positive autocorrelation is present a value lower than 2 and maybe close to zero.

Unfortunately, it is not in practice possible to compute the expression [5.26] since, as we have repeatedly stressed, the ε_ts are not observable. The Durbin–Watson statistic is calculated by replacing the ε_ts in [5.26] by the observable residuals, the e_ts. That is, we compute

$$d = \frac{\sum_{t=2}^{n}(e_t - e_{t-1})^2}{\sum_{t=1}^{n} e_t^2} \qquad [5.27]$$

Illustrative calculations by Durbin and Watson show that, assuming equation [5.24] holds, then if $\rho = 0$ the 'd-statistic', like the expression [5.26] ranges around the value 2. However, it must be remembered that both [5.26] and [5.27] are merely sample statistics and are hence subject to sampling variability. Thus, even when no autocorrelation is present and $\rho = 0$, a range of values is possible for d and it is feasible that we obtain an actual value some distance from 2. Such a problem is, of course, quite usual in statistical inference but there is an additional difficulty in this case. Given a null hypothesis of $\rho = 0$, the sampling distribution for the d-statistic depends on the sample size n, the number of explanatory variables k' and also *on the actual sample values of the explanatory variables*. Thus the critical values at which we might, for example, 'reject the null hypothesis of no autocorrelation at the 5 per cent level of significance', depend very much on the sample we have chosen. It is impracticable to tabulate critical values for all possible sets of sample values. What is possible, however, is, for given values of n and k', to find *upper and lower bounds* such that the actual critical values for *any* set of sample values will fall within these known limits. Tables are available which give these upper and lower bounds for various levels of n and k' and for specified levels of significance.

Suppose we wish to test the null hypothesis $\rho = 0$ against the alternative hypothesis of positive autocorrelation. The Durbin–Watson test procedure is illustrated in Fig. 5.4. Under the null hypothesis the actual sampling distribution of d, for the given n and k' and for the given sample X values, is shown by the unbroken curve. It is such that 5 per cent of the area beneath it lies to the left of the point d^*, i.e. $P_r(d < d^*) = 0.05$. If d^* were known, we would reject the null hypothesis at the 5 per cent level of significance if for our sample $d < d^*$. Unfortunately, for the reason given above, d^* is unknown. The broken curves labelled d_L and d_U represent, for given values of n and k', the upper and lower limits to the sampling distribution of d within which the actual sampling distribution must lie *whatever the sample X-values*. The point d_U^* and d_L^* are such that the areas under the respective d_U and d_L curves to the left of these points are in each case 5 per cent of the total area, i.e. $P_r(d_l < d_L^*) = P_r(d_u < d_U^*) = 0.05$. It is the points d_U^* and d_L^*, representing the upper and lower bounds to

5.4 The Durban–Watson test procedure.

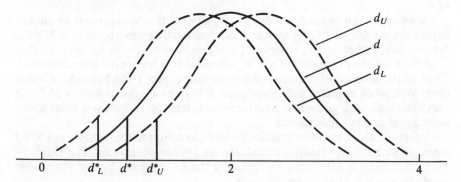

the unknown d^*, that are tabulated for varying values of n and k'. Clearly, if the sample value of the Durbin–Watson statistic lies to the left of d_L^* it must also lie to the left of d^*, while if it lies to the right of d_U^* it must also lie to the right of d^*. However, there is an 'inconclusive region', since if d lies between d_L^* and d_U^* we cannot know whether it lies to the left or right of d^*. The decision criterion for the Durbin–Watson test is therefore of the following form:

for $d < d_L^*$ reject the null hypothesis of no autocorrelation in favour of positive autocorrelation;

for $d > d_U^*$ do not reject null hypothesis, i.e. insufficient evidence to suggest positive autocorrelation;

for $d_L^* < d < d_U^*$ test inconclusive.

Because of the symmetry of the distributions illustrated in Fig. 5.4 it is also possible to use the tables for d_L^* and d_U^* to test the null hypothesis of no autocorrelation against the alternative hypothesis of negative autocorrelation, i.e. $\rho < 0$. The decision criterion then takes the form:

for $d > 4 - d_L^*$ reject the null hypothesis of no autocorrelation in favour of negative autocorrelation;

for $d < 4 - d_U^*$ do not reject null hypothesis, i.e. insufficient evidence to suggest negative autocorrelation.

for $4 - d_L^* > d > 4 - d_U^*$ test inconclusive.

Note that tables for d_U^* and d_L^* are constructed to facilitate the use of 'one-tail' rather than 'two-tail' tests, i.e. the alternative hypothesis is either $\rho > 0$ or $\rho < 0$ but rarely $\rho \neq 0$. We shall not provide a numerical example of the Durbin–Watson test here but such examples may be found in the empirical exercises in the appendices to Chapters 9 to 12.

Problems obviously arise with the Durbin–Watson test if the value of the d-statistic turns out to lie in the inconclusive region. However, for large samples this region becomes smaller and in fact it can be shown that d is asymptotically normally distributed with a mean of 2 and a variance of $4/n$ for *any* set of sample X-values. Hence, provided the sample size n is large enough critical values for d can be taken from standard normal tables. For small samples it is possible to find the exact critical value for any given set of X-values using methods suggested in Durbin and Watson (1971).

Important limitations on the use of the Durbin–Watson statistic must be stressed. First, the test is, strictly speaking, only a test for *first-order auto-correlation*. There is no reason why it should successfully detect, for example, fourth-order schemes of the type

$$\varepsilon_t = \rho\varepsilon_{t-4} + u_t$$

Secondly, and this point applies equally to any test for autocorrelation, a poor value for the Durbin–Watson statistic may be an indication not of 'genuine' autocorrelation but of something entirely different. We shall see in section 7.1 that any mis-specification of the population regression equation, such as for example the omission of an important explanatory variable, can lead to sequences of residuals which can be mistakenly regarded as indicative of autocorrelation in the disturbances. The Durbin–Watson test should therefore not be applied mechanically but should be accompanied by an *examination of the individual residuals themselves*. Such a visual examination of the time series of residuals is a valuable source of information in its own right and should be an automatic part of any form of regression analysis. The examination may not only help to identify any form of autocorrelation that may be present but can also sometimes help to reveal the source of the 'autocorrelation'. We shall return to this point in section 7.1.

The Box–Pierce Portmanteau test
If the presence of higher order autoregressive schemes is suspected then it becomes necessary to examine the *autocorrelations* between a disturbance in period t and the disturbance k periods previous. The autocorrelation of order k is the simple correlation between ε_t and ε_{t-k}, i.e.

$$\rho_{kt} = \frac{E\varepsilon_t\varepsilon_{t-k}}{\sqrt{E\varepsilon_t^2\, E\varepsilon_{t-k}^2}} \qquad \text{for all} \quad k \neq 0 \text{ and all } t$$

If we assume homoscedasticity (which implies $E\varepsilon_t^2 = E\varepsilon_{t-k}^2$), and in addition assume that all covariances $E\varepsilon_t\varepsilon_{t-k}$ remain constant over time,[14] then the process generating the disturbances is said to be *stationary* and we can rewrite ρ_{kt} as independent of time

$$\rho_k = \frac{E\varepsilon_t\varepsilon_{t-k}}{E\varepsilon_t^2} \qquad \text{for all} \quad k \neq 0$$

and approximate each such ρ_k by the *sample autocorrelation*

$$r_k = \frac{\sum_{t=k+1}^{n}\varepsilon_t\varepsilon_{t-k}}{\sum_{t=1}^{n}\varepsilon_t^2} \qquad \text{for all} \quad k \neq 0$$

Since the sample ε_t values are unknown we have to examine the *residual autocorrelation*

$$\hat{r}_k = \frac{\sum_{t=k+1}^{n}e_t e_{t-k}}{\sum_{t=1}^{n}e_t^2} \qquad \text{for all} \quad k \neq 0 \qquad\qquad [5.28]$$

If a value for any $\hat{r}_k$ is obtained which is significantly different from zero, then the null hypothesis $\rho_k = 0$ is rejected and kth order autocorrelation is accepted as present.[15]

It is possible to consider all the r_k simultaneously by computing the portmanteau statistic of Box and Pierce (1970)

$$Q_m = n \sum_{k=1}^{m} \hat{r}_k^2 \qquad [5.29]$$

Under the null hypothesis of no autocorrelation (i.e. $\rho_k = 0$ for all k), this statistic has an approximate χ^2 distribution with m degrees of freedom, m being the number of residual autocorrelations we wish to consider. In fact, it can be shown that Q_m in [5.29] is the appropriate LM statistic for testing both for an mth order autoregressive scheme of the kind

$$\varepsilon_t = \rho_1 \varepsilon_{t-1} + \rho_2 \varepsilon_{t-2} + \rho_3 \varepsilon_{t-3} + \cdots + \rho_m \varepsilon_{t-m} + u_t$$

and for mth order moving average disturbances of the type

$$\varepsilon_t = u_t + \theta_1 u_{t-1} + \theta_2 u_{t-2} + \cdots + \theta_m u_{t-m}$$

There is, however, a problem with the test. Q_m in [5.29] only has an approximate χ^2 distribution when m is small relative to the sample size n. However, if m is kept small, higher orders of autocorrelation are not being tested for and therefore may be missed. Also, there is some evidence that 'small' values of Q_m do not necessarily mean the absence of autocorrelation so that in such cases it is wise to examine each $\hat{r}_k$ individually.

A modified version of the Box–Pierce test, designed to improve small sample performance, is based on

$$Q'_m = n(n+2) \sum_{k=1}^{m} \frac{r_k^2}{n-k}$$

Under the null hypothesis of no autocorrelation up to order m, this statistic also has a χ^2 distribution with m degrees of freedom.

Testing for autocorrelation in the presence of a lagged dependent variable
A crucial limitation of both the Durbin–Watson and the Box–Pierce tests is that they are invalid when applied to a regression equation which includes a lagged dependent variable among its regressors. Suppose, for example, that ε_t in equation [5.2] follows the first-order autoregressive scheme given by [5.24]. Equation [5.2] can now be rewritten in the form

$$Y_t = \beta_1 + \beta_2 X_{2t} + \beta_3 X_{3t} + \beta_4 Y_{t-1} + \rho \varepsilon_{t-1} + u_t \quad t = 1, 2, 3, \ldots, n \quad [5.2A]$$

Lagging [5.2] by one period we see that ε_{t-1} and Y_{t-1} are correlated. Hence, considering [5.2A], some part of the effect of ε_{t-1} on Y_t will be attributed to the effect of Y_{t-1} (thus causing the bias in the OLS estimator of β_4) and less will appear in the residuals. The residuals will therefore mainly reflect the influence of the u_t in equation [5.2A]. Hence, since u is non-autocorrelated by assumption, we will tend to underestimate the extent of serial correlation in equation [5.2] when we examine the OLS residuals. For this reason the Durbin–Watson statistic is biased towards 2 under such circumstances, i.e. it is no longer a reliable guide to the presence of serial correlation.

It is important to have a valid test for autocorrelation in the presence of a lagged dependent variable because of the serious consequences for the OLS estimation procedure when autocorrelation is present under such circumstances.

106

We have already seen that the application of OLS to equations such as [5.2] leads to biased (but consistent) estimators because of the relationship between Y_{t-1} and ε_{t-1}. If, in addition, ε_t in equation [5.2] follows, for example, the first-order scheme [5.24], then ε_t also becomes dependent on ε_{t-1}. Hence, ε_t and Y_{t-1} will be related and we have a case of contemporaneous correlation between the disturbance and one of the explanatory variables. Under such conditions we know that OLS estimators are not merely biased but inconsistent as well. Notice that, although the presence of a first-order scheme alone leads to neither bias nor inconsistency and the presence of a lagged dependent variable alone leads to bias but not inconsistency, *the combination of autocorrelation and a lagged dependent variable results in the OLS estimators being both biased and inconsistent.*

We have already observed that equations such as [5.2] arise frequently when use is made of the so-called 'partial adjustment' and 'adaptive expectations' models. Unfortunately, these models also tend to yield estimating equations with autocorrelated disturbance terms. Thus the combination of lagged dependent variable and autocorrelated disturbance is by no means uncommon in econometrics. For example, we shall see the partial adjustment model generating such an awkward combination in section 6.3 and adaptive expectations model yielding it in section 6.2.

Durbin (1970) has developed an alternative test for first order autoregressive schemes when a lagged dependent variable appears among the explanatory variables. He shows that in the absence of serial correlation the statistic

$$h = (1 - 0.5d)\sqrt{\frac{n}{1 - ns_{\beta_i}^2}} \qquad [5.30]$$

where d is the normal Durbin–Watson statistic and $s_{\beta_i}^2$ is the estimated variance of the OLS estimator of the coefficient on Y_{t-1}, is normally distributed for large samples. It may therefore be used to test the null hypothesis $\rho = 0$ in these circumstances. For example, at the 0.05 level of significance, the null hypothesis of no autocorrelation is rejected if the absolute value of h exceeds 1.96.

Tests for first and higher-order autoregressive schemes, that are valid in the presence of a lagged dependent variable, can be derived using the Lagrangian multiplier approach. The form of the required auxiliary regressions can be obtained by using the procedure outlined at the end of section 4.7, but we shall adopt a more intuitive approach. For example, consider the estimation of equation [5.11] but suppose we suspect a second-order autoregressive scheme

$$\varepsilon_t = \rho_1 \varepsilon_{t-1} + \rho_2 \varepsilon_{t-2} + u_t \qquad [5.31]$$

Replacing i subscripts by t subscripts in [5.12], because we are dealing with time series data, substituting for ε_t yields

$$Y_t = \beta_1 + \beta_2 X_{2t} + \beta_3 X_{3t} + \rho_1 \varepsilon_{t-1} + \rho_2 \varepsilon_{t-2} + u_t \quad t = 1, 2, 3, \dots, n \quad [5.32]$$

Let us assume for the moment that ε_{t-1} and ε_{t-2} are known so that [5.32] can be estimated. Under the null hypothesis of no autocorrelation, $\rho_1 = \rho_2 = 0$ and [5.32] becomes

$$Y_t = \beta_1 + \beta_2 X_{2t} + \beta_3 X_{3t} + u_t \qquad t = 1, 2, 3, \dots, n \qquad [5.33]$$

Treating [5.32] and [5.33] as unrestricted and restricted equations respectively, we can now apply the F and χ^2 tests of section 4.4, to test the validity of the restrictions $\rho_1 = \rho_2 = 0$. In particular, if we first estimate [5.33] and then take the residuals, e_t, from this equation to form the auxiliary equation

$$e_t = \beta_1 + \beta_2 X_{2t} + \beta_3 X_{3t} + \rho_1 \varepsilon_{t-1} + \rho_2 \varepsilon_{t-2} + u_t \qquad t = 1, 2, 3, \ldots, n \qquad [5.34]$$

then, using [4.50A], we can say that, under the null hypothesis of no autocorrelation, nR^2 taken from the estimation of [5.34] will have a χ^2 distribution with $h = 2$ degrees of freedom. Hence we reject the null hypothesis of no autocorrelation if nR^2 exceeds the relevant critical value taken from χ^2 tables.

Unfortunately, of course, ε_{t-1} and ε_{t-2} in [5.34] are not known. In practice therefore we have to replace them by e_{t-1} and e_{t-2}, taken from the estimation of the restricted equation [5.33]. However, using the procedure at the end of section 4.7, it can be shown that the LM principle also leads to the above nR^2 test statistic. Note that the test would be equally valid if, for example, the regressor X_{3t} had been the lagged dependent variable Y_{t-1}. Unlike, for example, the Box–Pierce test, LM tests are valid in the presence of a lagged dependent variable.

LM tests for higher order autoregressive schemes are directly analogous to the above. For a third-order scheme, one simply adds ε_{t-3} (proxied by e_{t-3}) to the regressors in the auxiliary equation [5.34], for a fourth order scheme ε_{t-4}, and so on. In the mth order case nR^2 has a χ^2 distribution with m degrees of freedom. In fact it can easily be shown that the LM test for an mth order moving average disturbance is identical to that for an mth order autoregressive disturbance.

In the next subsection we shall consider some of the procedures that can be followed when it is believed that autocorrelation is present in the disturbances of a regression equation. However, we first repeat a warning made earlier. All the tests in this sub-section examine the residuals for evidence of autocorrelation. However, as we shall stress in section 7.1, autocorrelation in the residuals can be the result of a mis-specified estimating equation rather than of 'genuine' autocorrelation in the disturbances. If this is the case, then the procedures described in the next subsection are totally inappropriate and should not be used. The procedures should only be adopted when all attempts to solve the 'autocorrelation' problem by respecifying the population regression equation have been exhausted.

Dealing with autocorrelation

When autocorrelation is believed to be present, the alternative estimation procedure is akin to that for heteroscedasticity in that the idea is to transform the regression equation so as to remove the autocorrelation from the disturbances. Suppose, again, that we wish to estimate equation [5.11] but that on this occasion the disturbances follow the first-order autoregressive scheme given by equation [5.24]. Multiplying equation [5.12] throughout by ρ, replacing the i subscripts by t subscripts and lagging the equation by one period yields

$$\rho Y_{t-1} = \rho \beta_1 + \rho \beta_2 X_{2t-1} + \rho \beta_3 X_{3t-1} + \rho \varepsilon_{t-1} \qquad [5.35]$$

Subtracting [5.35] from [5.12] then yields

$$Y_t - \rho Y_{t-1} = \beta_1(1 - \rho) + \beta_2(X_{2t} - \rho X_{2t-1}) + \beta_3(X_{3t} - \rho X_{3t-1})$$
$$+ \varepsilon_t - \rho\varepsilon_{t-1} \qquad t = 2, 3, 4, \ldots, n \qquad\qquad [5.36]$$

We may rewrite this as

$$Y_t^* = \beta_1(1 - \rho) + \beta_2 X_{2t}^* + \beta_3 X_{3t}^* + u_t \qquad t = 2, 3, 4, \ldots, n \qquad [5.37]$$

using equation [5.24] and where $Y_t^* = Y_t - \rho Y_{t-1}$, $X_{2t}^* = X_{2t} - \rho X_{2t-1}$ and $X_{3t}^* = X_{3t} - \rho X_{3t-1}$. Equation [5.37] is an equation in values of the transformed variables Y^*, X_2^* and X_3^*. It contains a disturbance u that, by assumption, has all the normal classical properties *including that of non-autocorrelation*. We can therefore safely apply OLS to [5.37] in the knowledge that the estimators obtained together with the usual formulae for their estimated standard errors will have all the desirable properties.[16] These estimators are another example of Generalised Least Squares estimators since again they are only OLS estimators when expressed in terms of the transformed variables.

Notice that [5.37] can only be estimated for observations $t = 2, 3, 4, \ldots, n$. This is because $Y_1^* = Y_1 - \rho Y_0$ and Y_0 is unknown.

There is one rather severe snag in the above procedure. It requires a knowledge of ρ, the 'autoregressive parameter' in equation [5.24]. This is required, firstly to construct the transformed variables Y^*, X_2^* and X_3^*, and secondly to 'unscramble' an estimate of β_1, the intercept in the original equation, from the estimate obtained for $\beta_1(1 - \rho)$ when OLS is applied to the transformed equation [5.37]. Unfortunately, of course, ρ is generally unknown and has to be estimated. One method of estimating ρ, suggested by Durbin (1960) is to rewrite equation [5.36] as

$$Y_t = \beta_1(1 - \rho) + \rho Y_{t-1} + \beta_2 X_{2t} - \beta_2 \rho X_{2t-1} + \beta_3 X_{3t} - \beta_3 \rho X_{3t-1} + u_t$$
$$[5.38]$$

OLS estimation of [5.38] then yields a consistent estimate of ρ as the estimated coefficient of Y_{t-1}.

The most common method of estimating ρ is to take equation [5.24], replace the disturbance values, ε_t, by the OLS residuals, e_t, obtained from the straightforward regression of Y on X_2 and X_3, and use OLS to regress e_t on e_{t-1}. The OLS estimator $\hat{\rho}$ obtained in this way is known as the *Cochrane–Orcutt coefficient*.[17]

The transformed variables Y^*, X_2^* and X_3^* can now be constructed using the estimated $\hat{\rho}$ instead of the true ρ and OLS can then be applied to the transformed equation [5.37]. This procedure is usually referred to as the Cochrane–Orcutt two-stage procedure.

A problem with the above method is that the properties of the final estimators of the β_js will depend very much on the estimated $\hat{\rho}$. Under autocorrelation, there are more efficient estimators of the β_js than the OLS estimators. There are therefore better ways of estimating the disturbances than using the OLS residuals and hence better ways of estimating ρ than from these residuals. For this reason the so-called *Cochrane–Orcutt iterative procedure* is sometimes used (Cochrane and Orcutt 1949). This involves treating the above $\hat{\rho}$ as merely a 'first round' estimate of ρ. The regression coefficients obtained by the application of OLS to equation [5.37], when Y^*, X_2^* and X_3^* are constructed using $\hat{\rho}$, are then regarded as merely 'first round' estimates, $\hat{\beta}_1$, $\hat{\beta}_2$ and $\hat{\beta}_3$. A 'second round' estimate of ρ is then obtained by applying OLS to residuals calculated as $Y_t - \hat{\beta}_1 - \hat{\beta}_2 X_{2t} - \hat{\beta}_3 X_{3t}$. This second-round estimate of ρ can then be used to reconstruct the variables Y^*, X_2^* and X_3^* and hence to obtain second-round estimates of β_1, β_2 and β_3 by applying OLS to [5.37] using these reconstructed variables. This procedure may be continued to yield 'third round' and 'fourth round' estimates, and so on until the estimates 'converge', i.e. until successive estimates of the β_js and ρ are approximately the same. The estimators obtained by this procedure have been shown to be maximum-likelihood estimators and to be consistent and asymptotically equivalent to best linear unbiased estimators.

An alternative approach to dealing with a first-order scheme is that of Hildreth and Lu (1960). A grid or range of values for ρ (e.g. 0.1, 0.2, 0.3, ..., 1.0), is selected and separate series for the variables Y^*, X_2^* and X_3^* constructed using *each* value of ρ on the grid. Ordinary least squares is then used to estimate a version of [5.37] for each value of ρ and the estimated equation giving the lowest residual sum of squares selected. The value of ρ giving the best equation is taken as the estimate, $\hat{\rho}$, and the coefficients of the best equation provide estimates of β_1, β_2 and β_3. The estimators obtained by this procedure are asymptotically equivalent to MLEs.

Finally, note that the Durbin, Cochrane–Orcutt and Hildreth–Lu procedures can all be adopted to handle autoregressive schemes other than those of the first order.

5.2.3 Non-normally distributed disturbances

Assumption 5 in the classical model stated that each disturbance was normally distributed. Since only assumptions 1–4 were necessary for the OLS estimators to possess the properties of BLUEness and consistency, the breakdown of assumption 5 is not too serious as far as the properties of these estimators are concerned. They do, however, lose the property of efficiency. That is, if assumption 5 does not hold, there will be other *non-linear* unbiased estimators of the regression equation parameters which have smaller sampling variances. Also, the OLS estimators will no longer be maximum-likelihood estimators and while remaining consistent they will no longer be asymptotically efficient.

The major importance of assumption 5 in the classical model was that it ensured that the OLS estimators were normally distributed. This enabled us, by switching to the t-distribution to allow for the fact that σ^2 is unknown and has to be estimated, to compute confidence intervals for, and test hypotheses about, the population regression parameters. Thus, if the disturbances are non-normally distributed, then the hypothesis-testing procedures described in section 2.4 are no longer strictly valid.

It can, however, be shown that, as the sample size n approaches infinity, the sampling distributions of the OLS estimators approach the normal distribution regardless of the form of the distribution of the disturbances. That is, the larger the sample size the more closely can the distributions of the OLS estimators be approximated by normal distributions. It follows that for 'large' samples ($n > 50$ to be on the safe side) we can still rely on our standard testing procedures and confidence intervals even when assumption five breaks down. There are however two problems.

First, there is the question of small samples. If disturbances are non-normally distributed, there is no reason why we should expect the OLS estimators to have a normal distribution when the sample size is small. In these circumstances investigators tend to carry on regardless, applying the standard test procedures in the hope that any departures from normality are not sufficiently severe to totally invalidate results obtained. However, it is possible to test for non-normality in the disturbances. The OLS residuals are again treated as estimates of the disturbance values and tests can be performed to check whether the distribution of residuals is approximately normal (see, for example, Jarque and Bera 1980).

Secondly, problems also arise in large samples when the condition [5.1] is not valid. As we saw earlier, [5.1] breaks down for trending non-stationary regressors and when this happens we can no longer rely on the OLS estimators being consistent. The conventional demonstration that OLS estimators are approximately normally distributed in large samples, even in the presence of non-normal disturbances, also relies on the condition [5.1]. Consequently, this is a further reason why, even for large samples, we can have no faith in standard inferential procedures when our regressors are trending and the condition [5.1] breaks down.

5.3 Factors resulting in a lack of precision in the OLS estimators

Assumption 6 in the classical model requires that the number of observations, n, should exceed the number of parameters being estimated, k. If this assumption does not hold then the OLS estimating method breaks down. In the case of two-variable regression (i.e. $k = 2$) the reason for this breakdown is intuitively clear. If $n = 1$ then we have only one point in the two-dimensional scatter diagram through which an infinite number of sample regression lines may pass. With two points in the scatter there will be a single sample regression line passing through both points with, hence, a zero residual sum of squares. The OLS estimator of σ^2 now yields $\sum e_i^2 /(n - 2) = 0/0$ which is indeterminate so that in this case no inferences about the population parameters are possible. Analogous situations arise in multiple regression.

Even when $n > k$, but the number of 'degrees of freedom', $n - k$, is not large, difficulties arise because the OLS estimators will lack 'precision', i.e. confidence intervals for population parameters will be wide. For example, with two explanatory variables the sampling variances of the OLS estimators, $\hat{\beta}_2$ and $\hat{\beta}_3$, can be shown to be (see, for example, Kmenta 1986: 402)

$$\sigma_{\hat{\beta}_2}^2 = \frac{\sigma^2}{\sum x_2^2(1 - r^2)} \quad \text{and} \quad \sigma_{\hat{\beta}_3}^2 = \frac{\sigma^2}{\sum x_3^2(1 - r^2)} \qquad [5.39]$$

where r is the simple correlation between X_2 and X_3. Since the smaller is n, the smaller are the quantities $\sum x_2^2$ and $\sum x_3^2$ likely to be, one consequence of a 'lack of sufficient degrees of freedom' is that the standard errors of the OLS estimators tend to be large. Moreover, confidence intervals for β_2 and β_3 depend not only on the standard errors but also on the relevant critical values from the student's t-distribution.[18] The lower is $n - k$, the larger are these t-values and this is an additional factor leading to wide confidence intervals under these circumstances. A parallel consequence of high standard errors and high critical t-values is that, since we test hypotheses of the kind $\beta_j = 0$ by comparing the test statistic $\hat{\beta}_j/s_{\hat{\beta}_j}$ with the relevant t-value, we are rarely going to be in a position to reject such hypotheses. Hence, explanatory variables are rarely going to appear as 'significant'.

At this point it is worth pointing out that the quantities

$$\sum x_2^2 = \sum (X_2 - \bar{X}_2)^2 \quad \text{and} \quad \sum x_3^2 = \sum (X_3 - \bar{X}_3)^2$$

may be small even when the sample size n is large. This will occur when there is *little variation in the sample values of* X_2 *and/or* X_3. Again this will result in a reduction in the precision of the OLS estimators, this time reflecting the fact that if an X variable shows little variation we can hardly expect to assess accurately its effect on the dependent Y variable.

We shall encounter both the problem of insufficient degrees of freedom and that of a lack of variation in explanatory variables when we consider the estimation of the demand equation for a single good in sections 9.1 and 9.3. In theory, the demand for a good depends not only on its own price but on the price of *all* other goods. However, the 'degrees of freedom problem' precludes the inclusion of all such prices in a demand equation. In practice, investigators are usually restricted to including only a general price index or the price of a close substitute, in addition to income and 'own-price' variables. Theory also tells us that demand depends not on absolute but on relative prices. However, since prices tend to move together over time, price ratios or relative prices show little variation. For this reason we shall see that demand equations estimated with income and relative price ratios as the explanatory variables tend to provide useful information about the influence of consumers' income on demand, but much less information about the effect of relative price changes.

5.3.1 Multicollinearity

The final assumption in the classical model states that no exact linear relationship exists between the sample values of any two or more of the explanatory variables. When this assumption fails the OLS estimating procedure itself breaks down. To obtain an intuitive idea of why this is so suppose, again, that we are attempting to estimate the population regression equation [5.11]. Suppose, also, that our sample data is such that $X_{2i} = 2 + 3X_{3i}$ in equation [5.12] i.e. the sample values of X_2 are exactly linearly related to the sample values of X_3.

Suppose that a sample regression equation that 'minimises' the residual sum of squares, $\sum e_i^2 = \sum (Y_i - \hat{Y}_i)^2$, is given by

$$\hat{Y} = 10 + 20X_2 + 5X_3 \qquad [5.40]$$

It may appear at first sight that the numbers 10, 20 and 5 in equation [5.40] must represent the OLS estimates of β_1, β_2 and β_3 in equation [5.11]. However, since for all sample observations we have $X_2 = 2 + 3X_3$, we can rewrite equation [5.40] as

$$\hat{Y} = 10 + 10X_2 + 10(2 + 3X_3) + 5X_3$$

or

$$\hat{Y} = 30 + 10X_2 + 35X_3 \qquad [5.41]$$

Since $X_2 = 2 + 3X_3$, the predicted values of Y_i, i.e. the $\hat{Y}_i$s, obtained from

112

equation [5.41] by substituting the sample values of X_2 and X_3, must be identical to the $\hat{Y}_i$s obtained using equation [5.40]. Since the sample values of Y, the Y_is, also remain unchanged (we are still referring to the same sample), it follows that the residual sum of squares, $\sum e_i^2$, obtained from the sample regression equations [5.41] and [5.40] will be the same. Hence, if [5.40] 'minimises' $\sum e_i^2$ then so, too, must [5.41]. Clearly, we need not stop here. It is possible to construct under these circumstances any number of sample regression lines all yielding the same 'minimum' $\sum e_i^2$. One further example would be

$$\hat{Y} = 10 + 40X_2 - 20(2 + 3X_3) + 5X_3$$

or

$$\hat{Y} = -30 + 40X_2 - 55X_3 \qquad [5.42]$$

What this means is that there are an infinite number of sets of values for the estimators of β_1, β_2 and β_3 in equation [5.11], all yielding the same 'minimum' $\sum e_i^2$.[19] Obviously then, there are no unique OLS estimates so that the OLS estimating procedure breaks down.

When an *exact* linear relationship exists between explanatory variables as above, the situation is often referred to as one of *complete multicollinearity*. Complete multicollinearity means that we are in a situation of 'complete uncertainty' concerning the unknown parameters β_1, β_2 and β_3 in the population regression equation. We can have no idea whether to estimate β_1, β_2 and β_3 by, for example, the 10, 20 and 5 appearing in [5.40], the 30, 10 and 35 in [5.41] or the -30, 40 and -55 in [5.42], and so on.

Complete multicollinearity very rarely occurs in practice. However, a situation which does frequently arise, particularly for time series data, is one in which two or more of the explanatory variables are approximately linearly related. This situation also causes estimation difficulties and the closer the approximation to a linear relationship the more severe these difficulties tend to become.

Considering again the estimation of equation [5.11], suppose that the relationship $X_2 = 2 + 3X_3$ holds merely approximately rather than exactly for all sample observations. In such a situation there will be unique estimates of β_1, β_2 and β_3, i.e. a unique sample regression equation, which minimises $\sum e_i^2$. The OLS method therefore no longer breaks down completely. The problem now is that there will be many other sets of estimates for β_1, β_2 and β_3, i.e. many other sample regression lines, all with residual sums of squares not equal to but 'very close' to the minimum $\sum e_i^2$ yielded by the OLS sample regression line. Under these circumstances we will lack confidence and be uncertain about the precision of the actual OLS estimates since there are so many other sets of estimates which appear 'almost as good'. The higher the 'degree' of multi-collinearity in the sample data the greater, other things being equal, will be the degree of our uncertainty about the true values of β_1, β_2 and β_3.

In statistical terms the precision of an estimate is reflected in the size of its standard error (from which confidence intervals are constructed). High collinearity between X_2 and X_3, when it leads to considerable uncertainty about the true values of β_1, β_2 and β_3, is therefore reflected in *large standard errors and sampling variances* for the OLS estimators of these parameters. As an example, suppose we were attempting to assess the influence on consumer expenditure, C, of two explanatory variables – personal disposable income, Y, and the net liquid asset

113

holdings of consumers, L. The following OLS regression equations are obtained from postwar time series data:

$$\hat{C} = 153 + 0.93Y \qquad\qquad R^2 = 0.93 \qquad\qquad\qquad [5.43]$$
$$\phantom{\hat{C} = } (16) \quad (0.06)$$

$$\hat{C} = 246 + 0.64L \qquad\qquad R^2 = 0.81 \qquad\qquad\qquad [5.44]$$
$$\phantom{\hat{C} = } (28) \quad (0.05)$$

$$\hat{C} = \ 84 \ + 0.78Y + \ 0.43L \quad\ R^2 = 0.95 \qquad\qquad\qquad [5.45]$$
$$\phantom{\hat{C} = } (61) \quad (0.53) \quad (0.37)$$

Equations [5.43] and [5.44] illustrate that the variables Y and L, when included alone as explanatory variables, can explain 93 per cent and 81 per cent respectively of variations in C and in each case appear highly significant. However, when both variables are included together as explanatory variables, there is a distinct 'mushrooming' of the standard errors attached to each coefficient in equation [5.45]. As a result, although Y and L can jointly explain 95 per cent of the variation in C, neither of their coefficients appears significantly different from zero in the multiple regression equation. Equation [5.45], in fact, suggests high collinearity between Y and L during the sample period – not surprisingly since both disposable income and net liquid assets will have exhibited strong upward trends during the post-war era. Our uncertainty as to the true importance of each explanatory variable (caused by the multicollinearity problem) is reflected in the size of the standard errors in equation [5.45].[20] These would result in any confidence intervals for parameters of the underlying population regression line being very wide indeed.

We shall encounter examples of multicollinearity problems in each of the applied chapters of this book. For example in Chapter 9 we shall find that in the demand equation for any good the two most important explanatory variables – income and own-price are, typically, highly correlated over time. Similarly, in Chapter 11, when estimating production functions we shall find that capital and labour inputs tend to be highly correlated in both cross-sectional and time series data. In Chapter 12 we shall see that the uncertainty resulting from multicollinearity has prevented any firm conclusion being reached as to what is the most appropriate 'scale' variable in demand for money functions. All three possible scale variables – income, permanent income and non-human wealth tend to move together over time. Similarly, the high correlation between different interest rate variables has made it impossible to decide which such variable is best included in demand for money functions as a proxy for the opportunity cost of holding money.

When considering the consequences of multicollinearity it must be remembered that (except in the case of complete multicollinearity when the OLS estimating procedure breaks down) multicollinearity itself does not involve the violation of any of the assumptions of the classical regression model. The OLS estimators will still possess *all* the desirable properties of BLUEness, etc. Also, the usual formulae will still provide us with unbiased estimators of the standard errors of the OLS estimators. Provided all the classical assumptions hold, the OLS estimation procedure is still 'the best available' – the problem is that when multicollinearity is severe the best available is not very good. It is not that we cannot trust our usual hypothesis-testing procedures – unlike under autocorrelation or heteroscedasticity these are still valid. Unfortunately when multicollinearity is present they may not tell us very much.

We have already noted that one consequence of multicollinearity is the likelihood of large standard errors on the regression coefficients leading to *imprecision in our estimates of population regression line parameters* (the β_js). A further consequence of large sampling variances for the OLS estimators is that *specific estimates of the β_js may have large errors.* The fact that the OLS estimators remain unbiased or even BLUE simply means that, if we were to take many samples, the estimates obtained would be 'on average' equal to the parameters being estimated. Since in practice we take but a single sample, unbiasedness is of cold comfort if the 'spread' of estimates obtained over many samples is very wide – as it may be when multicollinearity is severe. It may well be the case that, for the single sample we take, estimates obtained will be a considerable distance away from the true values of the parameters we are estimating. Such 'instability' in the OLS estimates also tends to manifest itself in drastic changes in the values of the OLS estimators when merely a few extra observations are added to the available sample. This is yet another illustration of the basic uncertainty that exists about the true values of the β_j parameters when serious multicollinearity is present.

A further typical consequence of collinear explanatory variables is that *it may become impossible to disentangle their individual influences on the dependent variable.* This is well illustrated by equations [5.43–5.45]. The first two of these equations, taken separately, suggest that either disposable income or liquid assets could be regarded as an important determinant of consumer expenditure. However, despite the fact that taken together in equation [5.45] Y and L can explain 95 per cent of the variation in C, it is not possible to deduce which is the more important. This, of course, is because of the large standard errors in [5.45]. These make it impossible on the basis of [5.45] to reject either the null hypothesis that disposable income has no influence on consumer expenditure or the null hypothesis that liquid assets have no influence. Since we never accept the null hypothesis when making statistical tests,[21] if we are unable to reject either, this leaves us in the position of having nothing useful to say about the separate importance of either income or liquid assets. The difficulty arises because of the common upward movement in the three variables, C, Y and L during the post-war period. The upward movement in C could be attributed either to the upward movement in disposable income or to the upward movement in liquid asset holdings. However, on the basis of the sample evidence we cannot tell which of the upward movements in Y and L is the determining factor.

· When faced with a regression equation such as [5.45] there is a strong temptation to drop the 'least significant variable', in this case L. It is particularly tempting to do this if, as in [5.43] and [5.45], it leads to little deterioration in the goodness of fit of the equation. The danger now is that we may be omitting an explanatory variable which is an important determinant of the dependent variable but whose importance has been obscured by the multicollinearity that is present. As we shall see in section 7.1, such 'specification errors' have serious consequences for our estimates of the coefficients attached to other variable(s) in the equation.

The possibility that variables may be incorrectly dropped from an estimating equation becomes even more likely when the investigator is faced with equations containing more than two explanatory variables. Remember that assumption 7 of the classical model states that there should be no linear relationship between the sample values of any two *or more* of the explanatory X variables. For example, with four explanatory variables X_2, X_3, X_4 and X_5, exact linear relationships of the form

$$X_2 = 5 + 4X_3 + 7X_5 \quad \text{or} \quad X_3 = 3X_2 + X_4 - 5X_5$$

will lead to a complete breakdown in the OLS estimation method just as surely as more simple relationships such as $X_2 = 2 + 3X_3$. Similarly, when such relationships hold only approximately, the consequences are likely to be very similar to those of an approximate relationship $X_2 \approx 2 + 3X_3$. There will be uncertainty about the true values of underlying parameters, manifesting itself in high standard errors for the OLS estimators. Unfortunately, while linear relationships between just two explanatory variables are not difficult to detect, more complicated relationships such as those above may be easily 'missed' by the investigator.

In our discussion of autocorrelation and heteroscedasticity we spent considerable time on test procedures for determining whether these were present in the population of disturbances under study. If they were present alternative estimating procedures were necessary. The situation is somewhat different in the case of multicollinearity. First, when testing for autocorrelation or heteroscedasticity we were able to formulate hypotheses concerning population parameters (e.g. the first-order autoregressive parameter ρ). Such standard inferential procedures are not possible for multicollinearity. This is because multicollinearity is an attribute of the sample observations rather than of the population from which the observations have been drawn.[22] Secondly, for heteroscedasticity or autocorrelation a clear distinction can be drawn between cases where they are present (e.g. $\rho \neq 0$) and corrective procedures are necessary, and cases where they are not present (e.g. $\rho = 0$). No such clear distinction exists in the case of multicollinearity. Suppose we rule out the theoretically possible but in practice highly unlikely cases of complete multicollinearity and 'total absence' of multicollinearity (where each and every explanatory variable is completely uncorrelated with all other explanatory variables). What we are then concerned with is the 'degree' of multicollinearity or the 'extent' to which linear relationships appear among the explanatory variables. The closer the approximation to a linear relationship the higher the degree of multicollinearity. The problem, however, is that a given degree of multicollinearity does not always have the same consequences.

Consider again the case where we are attempting to estimate the population regression equation [5.11]. In such a case, we see from equation [5.39] that the variances of the OLS estimators of β_2 and β_3 will be estimated as

$$s_{\hat{\beta}_2}^2 = \frac{s^2}{\sum x_2^2(1 - r^2)} \quad \text{and} \quad s_{\hat{\beta}_3}^2 = \frac{s^2}{\sum x_3^2(1 - r^2)} \qquad [5.46]$$

where s^2 is the residual variance. r is again the simple correlation between the sample values of X_2 and X_3 by which we may measure the degree of multicollinearity. Clearly, as r increases the estimated variances (which are unbiased estimators of the true variances), and hence the standard errors of $\hat{\beta}_2$

and $\hat{\beta}_3$ will increase in size. As $r \to 1$ and we approach the case of complete multicollinearity, the rate of increase will become rapid. However, for a given degree of multicollinearity (i.e. a given r), the size of the standard errors also depends on the residual variance s^2 (measuring the 'overall fit' of the equation) and on $\sum x_2^2$ and $\sum x_3^2$ which measure the variability in the sample values of X_2 and X_3. Thus it is possible to obtain relatively 'low' standard errors and well-determined regression coefficients even when multicollinearity as measured by r is 'high', provided the overall fit of the equation is good and/or there is a sufficiently wide variation in the sample values of X_2 and X_3.

The upshot of the above is that, when we have an estimated equation with relatively well-determined coefficients and low standard errors, we need not be particularly concerned by the extent of multicollinearity among the explanatory variables. Remember that the OLS estimators retain all their desirable properties regardless of any multicollinearity present. Also, in contrast to the situation under heteroscedasticity or autocorrelation, the estimated standard errors remain unbiased estimates of the true standard errors. Hence, if the estimated standard errors are small the extent of multicollinearity (unlike, for example, the possible presence of serial correlation) is of no real consequence.

It is when the estimated standard errors are large that we begin to suspect that the presence of multicollinearity may be having a detrimental effect on the precision of our estimating procedure. For example, high standard errors combined with a very good 'overall fit' (as measured, for example, by R^2) is a virtually certain indicator of multicollinearity. Verification of its presence, however, may not necessarily be an easy matter. Approximate linear relationships between any *two* variables can be picked up by the examination of the simple 'zero order' correlations between each pair of explanatory variables. However, these will not indicate the presence of more complex relationships involving more than two explanatory variables. To cover such cases Farrar and Glauber (1967) have suggested that a more reliable guide is to compute the coefficient of multiple determination, R^2, between each X variable and the $k-1$ remaining X variables. If any of these R^2s is close to unity then the extent of multicollinearity must be severe.

At this point a strong warning must be given against the temptation invariably to attribute large standard errors and insignificant regression coefficients to the presence of multicollinearity. It is obvious that large standard errors can occur in an equation such as [5.45] even in the absence of any severe multicollinearity if neither of the explanatory variables is an important determinant of the dependent variable. This situation will be signalled by a low coefficient of multiple determination R^2 and a high residual variance for the estimated equation. Hence, it is easy to spot in practice. The most dangerous temptation arises when high standard errors occur on some or all of the explanatory variables in an equation with a good overall fit and when some degree of multicollinearity is clearly present. It is very tempting under these circumstances to blame any insignificance in the regression coefficients on the multicollinearity that is present. However, *there can be no guarantee that in the absence of multicollinearity these coefficients would have appeared significant*. High standard errors *may* simply reflect multicollinearity but can also arise because the relevant variable is genuinely unimportant. Of course, since the overall fit is a good one, we must expect some of the explanatory variables to become significant in the absence of multicollinearity. But there can be no guarantee that they all will.

117

For example, in equation [5.45] Y and L between them explain 95 per cent of the variation in C, so one at least of these variables appears to be important. Hence, in the absence of multicollinearity at least one of the two variables Y and L is likely to appear highly significant. However, it is by no means necessarily the case that both will.[23]

Summarising the last few paragraphs, if the coefficients of a regression equation are well determined with low standard errors we need not be over-concerned with any multicollinearity that is present. When standard errors are high, multicollinearity may well be present (particularly when R^2 is high) but we should be wary of regarding all such high standard errors as simply the consequence of multicollinearity. Multicollinearity does, frequently, result in high standard errors but it is not the only such cause.

When it is apparent that multicollinearity is handicapping the precise estimation of population regression parameters, it is sometimes possible to improve matters by an appropriate 'reparameterisation'. For example, equation [5.12] may be rewritten as

$$Y_t = \beta_1 + \beta_2(X_{2t} - X_{3t}) + \beta^* X_{3t} + \varepsilon_t \qquad [5.47]$$

where $\beta^* = \beta_2 + \beta_3$. While X_2 and X_3 may be highly correlated, this will not necessarily be the case for $X_2 - X_3$ and X_3. If not, the estimation of [5.41] will yield more precise estimates of β_2 and β_2^* although not of β_3.

If reparameterisation is of no help, then there is very little that can be done apart from the seeking of *new* information. Additional sample observations, for which the approximate linear relationships present in the original data no longer hold, will obviously help resolve the problem. While extra observations with this property are likely to be difficult to obtain, increasing the sample size, even if it leaves the extent of the multicollinearity unchanged, may of itself be of assistance. For example, consider the case of two explanatory variables. The expressions [5.46] indicate that even if r remains unchanged, since an increased sample size leads to larger values of $\sum x_1^2$ and $\sum x_2^2$, it must also result in smaller standard errors provided the overall fit of the equation does not worsen.

Extra information may also take the form of 'extraneous' estimates of some of the regression parameters. Suppose, again, that we are attempting to estimate the population regression line [5.11] under conditions where the sample values of X_2 and X_3 are highly correlated. If an extraneous estimate of, for example, the parameter β_2 is already available from some source other than the available sample, the multicollinearity problem can be circumvented. If β_2^* is the extraneous estimate, then we can use the sample data to form the variable $Y - \beta_2^* X_2$ and estimate the regression equation

$$\widehat{Y - \beta_2^* X_2} = \hat{\beta}_1 + \hat{\beta}_3 X_3 \qquad [5.48]$$

$\hat{\beta}_1$ and $\hat{\beta}_3$ provide the estimates of β_1 and β_3. This approach has been much used in demand equations when estimation is handicapped by the high time series correlation between the explanatory variables income and prices. Extraneous estimates of the coefficient on the income variable are obtained from cross-sectional data. We shall discuss this approach more fully in section 9.3.

Further reading

Breakdowns in the classical assumptions are covered in all the introductory textbooks mentioned in the Further Reading at the ends of Chapters 2 and 4. Non-matrix treatment is given by Kmenta (1986) and Kelejian and Oates (1989). The problems of errors in measurement and instrumental variables are well covered in Kmenta and at a more advanced level in Johnston (1984). Autocorrelation and heteroscedasticity are thoroughly covered in Stewart and Wallis (1981) and in Kmenta, while formal matrix-algebra treatments of generalised least squares can be found in Johnston (1984) and Stewart (1991). Multicollinearity is most clearly treated in Kmenta.

Notes

1. Remember that if X, Y, $Z = X + Y$ and u are random variables, then if u is uncorrelated with both X and Y, $EZu = E(X + Y)u = EXEu + EYEu = 0$ provided $Eu = 0$. Notice that contemporaneous non-correlation alone between X_{ji}s and ε_is is insufficient for unbiasedness since each C_{ji} depends on all X_{ji}s.
2. See also the section on non-normally distributed disturbances on page 110.
3. In fact, the covariance between explanatory variable and disturbance in [5.5] is given by $-\beta_2 \sigma_\omega^2$ where σ_ω^2 is the variance of ω. Thus, if β_2 is positive, the contemporaneous correlation will be negative and we have a situation similar to Fig. 5.2, with OLS tending to underestimate β_2 and overestimate β_1.
4. The covariance between explanatory variable and disturbance is again $-\beta_2 \sigma_\omega^2$ so that, for positive β_2, OLS again tends to underestimate β_2 and overestimate β_1.
5. In the multiple regression case some of the regressors may be uncorrelated with the disturbance. These regressors then serve as their own instruments.
6. Any regressors which are uncorrelated with the disturbance are included in the set of instruments.
7. Also, if they are no longer BLUE then, of course, they can no longer be efficient in small samples.
8. Since we test null hypotheses of the form $\beta_j = 0$ by examining the t-ratios $\hat{\beta}_j / s\sqrt{x^{jj}}$ then, if $s\sqrt{x^{jj}}$ tends to underestimate the true standard error of β_j, we may find ourselves rejecting null at a given level of significance when we should not do so.
9. A number of central observations, C, are, normally, omitted before the separate regressions are run. The ratio of residual variances then has an F distribution with degrees of freedom dependent on C and on the sample size. There are various rules of thumb for deciding on C.
10. Autocorrelated disturbances are sometimes referred to as autoregressive disturbances.
11. That is, $Eu_t = 0$, var $u_t = $ const for all t, $\text{cov}(u_t, u_s) = 0$ for all $t \neq s$ and u_t is normally distributed.
12. A value of ρ outside these limits would imply ε values of ever-increasing absolute size which is economically unrealistic.
13. See note 8.
14. That is, for each k, $E\varepsilon_t \varepsilon_{t-k} = $ const for all t. Hence, for example, the covariance between ε_3 and ε_7 is the same as that between ε_4 and ε_8 which is also the same as that between ε_7 and ε_{11}.
15. Since, when $\rho_k = 0$, r_k can be shown to be asymptotically normally distributed with mean $-1/n$ and variance $1/n$, in practice for large values of n and k $\hat{r}_k$ is regarded as significantly different from zero at the 5 per cent level if $\hat{r}_k > 2/\sqrt{n}$ or $< -2/\sqrt{n}$.
16. Since by carrying out the transformation we have 'lost an observation' this is not strictly correct and the application of OLS to [5.37] will not yield *best* linear unbiased estimators.

17. The intercept term has to be suppressed in this regression. The resulting OLS estimator is $\hat{\rho} = \sum e_t e_{t-1} / \sum e_t^2$.

18. Remember that, for example, 95 per cent confidence intervals for β_2 are given by $\hat{\beta}_2 \pm t_{0.025} s_{\hat{\beta}_2}$ where $s_{\hat{\beta}_2}$ is the estimate of $\hat{\sigma}_{\beta_2}$.

19. There are, in fact, an infinite number of sample regression equations all equally successful in explaining sample variations in Y.

20. The effect of high multicollinearity on standard errors can also be seen by considering the equations [5.39]. The higher is r, the correlation between X_2 and X_3, the larger are the sampling variances $\sigma_{\beta_2}^2$ and $\sigma_{\beta_3}^2$.

21. Because the probability of a type II error (i.e. the probability of accepting a false null hypothesis) is unknown.

22. If an exact or approximate linear relationship between explanatory variables exists in the *population* then this means that we have ignored an important feature of reality and the model needs to be respecified to take account of such a relationship.

23. Since C, Y and L are all trending upwards over time, the R^2 in equation [5.45] must also be treated with scepticism. There is a clear likelihood of spurious correlation.

6 Lagged Variables

It is often the case in economics that the current value of a dependent variable, Y, depends not only on the current value of some explanatory variable, X, but also on past or 'lagged' values of that variable. For example, in a simple consumption function, consumption may depend not only on current income but, for reasons of habit or inertia, also on past levels of income. We may therefore often need to write

$$Y_t = \alpha + \beta_0 X_t + \beta_1 X_{t-1} + \beta_2 X_{t-2} + \cdots + \beta_m X_{t-m} + \varepsilon_t \quad \text{for all } t \quad [6.1]$$

Equation [6.1] is known as a *distributed lag formulation* because the effect of the X-variable is distributed over a number of periods. The *maximum lag length*, m, can be finite or infinite. ε is a disturbance.

Notice that equations such as [6.1] mean that the long-run response of Y to a once-and-for-all change in X is different from the short-run immediate response. For example, suppose X has remained constant at the level Z for at least m periods. Assuming $E\varepsilon = 0$, Y will then take the constant *equilibrium* expected value of

$$EY = \alpha + \beta_0 Z + \beta_1 Z + \beta_2 Z + \cdots + \beta_m Z = \alpha + (\textstyle\sum \beta_j) Z \quad [6.2]$$

Suppose that at period t the value of X rises to $X_t = Z + 1$ and remains at this level. The expected value of Y at period t will then be

$$EY_t = \alpha + \beta_0(Z + 1) + \beta_1 Z + \beta_2 Z + \cdots + \beta_m Z = \alpha + \beta_0 + (\textstyle\sum \beta_j) Z \quad [6.3]$$

Notice that the rise of one unit in X has led to an immediate rise of β_0 units in the expected value of Y. Hence β_0, the coefficient on X_t in equation [6.1] measures the immediate or *short run* or *impact* effect on EY of a change in X. This is not the final effect however. By period $t + 1$, X has been at its new level for 2 periods and the expected value of Y becomes

$$EY_{t+1} = \alpha + \beta_0(Z + 1) + \beta_1(Z + 1) + \beta_2 Z + \cdots + \beta_m Z$$

$$= \alpha + \beta_0 + \beta_1 + (\textstyle\sum \beta_j) Z \quad [6.4]$$

Similarly,

$$EY_{t+2} = \alpha + \beta_0 + \beta_1 + \beta_2 + (\textstyle\sum \beta_j) Z \quad [6.5]$$

and so on.

Eventually, when X has been at its new level for m periods, the expected value of Y reaches a new equilibrium level of

$$EY = \alpha + \textstyle\sum \beta_j + (\textstyle\sum \beta_j) Z \quad [6.6]$$

and remains at this level until there is a further change in X. Comparing [6.2] and [6.6] we see that the unit change in X leads eventually, after the whole process has worked itself out, to a rise of $\sum \beta_j$ units in the expected value of Y. Thus the *sum of the β_j coefficients* in equation [6.1] measures the eventual, overall or *long run* effect on EY of a change in X.

Notice that when we talk about 'long run effects' in this context we are comparing equilibrium positions. The long run *does not necessarily involve a large number of periods be these days or years*. A new equilibrium may be reached very quickly or alternatively very slowly. For example, if $m = 2$ in equation [6.1] then equilibrium and 'the long run' is reached after only two periods. On the other hand, if m is infinite then a new equilibrium is never reached.

Even if m is infinite in equation [6.1], it is normally assumed that as $j \to \infty$, $\beta_j \to 0$. Hence the sum of the β_js is finite even if m is infinite. We shall encounter an example of such a scheme in the next section.

Provided all the β_j in [6.1] are non-negative the *mean* or *average lag* is defined as

$$\text{Mean lag} = \frac{\sum j\beta_j}{\sum \beta_j} \qquad [6.7]$$

The mean lag is a useful summary measure of the extent of the delay before the full impact of a change in X is felt by Y in equation [6.1]. For example, if

$$Y_t = 15 + 0.6X_t + 0.9X_{t-1} + 0.5X_{t-2} + \varepsilon_t$$

then

$$\text{Mean lag} = \frac{0(0.6) + 1(0.9) + 2(0.5)}{2.0} = 0.95 \text{ periods}$$

Notice that following a change in X it is possible, using equations such as [6.4] and [6.5], to trace the movement of EY_t over time as it moves from the old equilibrium to the new. Because of this, equation [6.1] is referred to as a *dynamic* model.

The estimation of equations such as [6.1] is not straightforward. Assuming non-stochastic X and that ε obeys all the usual assumptions, OLS will yield BLUE and consistent estimators of the parameters of equation [6.1]. Unfortunately, if the maximum lag length m (and hence the number of parameters to be estimated) is large relative to the sample size, we run into the 'degrees of freedom problems' mentioned in section 5.3. Even if the sample size is relatively large, we may still experience difficulties in obtaining precise well-determined estimates of the β_js because the various 'lagged' values of X are likely to be multicollinear. This could be particularly serious if we hoped to determine the length of the lag, i.e. the value of m, by examining the statistical significance of the coefficients on the lagged variables.

Because of these difficulties it is rare for a distributed lag model to be estimated in as general a form as [6.1]. Rather, some *a priori* restriction is frequently placed on the form of the β_js so as to reduce the number of independent parameters that have to be estimated.

122

6.1 Geometric lag distributions

One of the simplest restrictions that can be placed on the β_js is that they should decline in a geometric progression

$$Y_t = \alpha + \beta_0(X_t + \theta X_{t-1} + \theta^2 X_{t-2}, \ldots) + \varepsilon_t \qquad 0 < \theta < 1 \qquad [6.8]$$

In this case the maximum lag length m is infinite and the influence of X extends indefinitely into the past. However, successive lagged values of X have a declining effect on Y since θ lies between 0 and 1. The mean lag in this case is given by

$$\frac{\sum j\beta_0\theta^j}{\sum \beta_0\theta^j} = \frac{\sum j\theta^j}{\sum \theta^j} = \frac{\theta}{1-\theta}$$

Estimation of [6.8] can be simplified by applying the *Koyck transformation*. Multiplying [6.8] by θ and lagging by one period yields

$$\theta Y_{t-1} = \theta\alpha + \beta_0(\theta X_{t-1} + \theta^2 X_{t-2} + \theta^3 X_{t-3}, \ldots) + \theta\varepsilon_{t-1} \qquad [6.9]$$

Subtracting [6.9] from [6.8] then yields

$$Y_t - \theta Y_{t-1} = \alpha - \theta\alpha + \beta_0 X_t + \varepsilon_t - \theta\varepsilon_{t-1}$$

or

$$Y_t = \alpha(1-\theta) + \beta_0 X_t + \theta Y_{t-1} + v_t \quad \text{where} \quad v_t = \varepsilon_t - \theta\varepsilon_{t-1} \qquad [6.10]$$

Compared with [6.1], there are only three parameters to be estimated in [6.10] and the number of regressors has been reduced to two thus alleviating any multicollinearity problem. Hence if, for example, we estimate an equation

$$\hat{Y}_t = 64 + 0.3X_t + 0.6Y_{t-1} \qquad [6.11]$$

we would estimate $\hat{\beta}_0 = 0.3$, $\hat{\theta} = 0.6$ and $\hat{\alpha} = 64/(1 - \hat{\theta}) = 160$. Estimates of the coefficients in the original equation [6.8] can then be obtained using $\hat{\beta}_0$ and $\hat{\theta}$. That is

$$\hat{Y}_t = 160 + 0.3X_t + 0.18X_{t-1} + 0.108X_{t-2}, \ldots \qquad [6.12]$$

There are, however, major problems in the estimation of equation [6.10]. The disturbance term $v_t = \varepsilon_t - \theta\varepsilon_{t-1}$ is of first order moving average form and is almost certain to be autocorrelated. Since $v_{t-1} = \varepsilon_{t-1} - \theta\varepsilon_{t-2}$, we can see that both v_t and v_{t-1} have a term in common, i.e. ε_{t-1}, and hence will not normally be independent. In fact, only when ε_t in equation [6.8] follows a first-order autoregressive scheme with parameter $\rho = \theta$, will v_t in equation [6.10] be non-autocorrelated. Then we have (see section 5.2.2) $\varepsilon_t = \theta\varepsilon_{t-1} + u_t$, so that $v_t = u_t$ which is non-autocorrelated by assumption. Since there is no obvious reason why the values of θ and ρ should coincide, we can normally rule this case out and expect v_t in [6.10] to be autocorrelated.

Unfortunately, autocorrelation is not the only problem with [6.10]. Even if X is non-stochastic the other regressor in [6.10], Y_{t-1}, is not. Y_{t-1} clearly depends on the disturbance v_{t-1} and hence is stochastic. If v_t had been non-autocorrelated, the appearance of Y_{t-1} as a stochastic regressor in [6.10] would not have mattered too much. We know, from our discussion in section 5.1, that OLS estimators retain their desirable large sample properties in such circumstances. However, we also know from section 5.2.2 that the combination of autocorrelated disturbance and lagged dependent variable results in a case of contemporaneous correlation between disturbance and lagged variable. This means that application of OLS to [6.10] will in fact lead to both biased and inconsistent estimators.

If consistent estimates of α, β_0 and θ are to be obtained from the estimation of [6.10] then the simplest method is that of instrumental variables. We saw in section 5.1 that this is one possible method of dealing with a problem of contemporaneous correlation between disturbance and explanatory variable. The obvious procedure here is to use X_t as its own instrument and to use X_{t-1} as the instrument for Y_{t-1}. X_t is by assumption uncorrelated with ε_t and perfectly correlated with itself, while X_{t-1} is also uncorrelated with ε_t but likely to be highly correlated with Y_{t-1}. X_t and X_{t-1} are therefore suitable instruments. Unfortunately, however, X_t and X_{t-1} are likely to be highly correlated themselves so these estimators, although consistent, may be very inefficient.

Another possibility is to use a version of the GLS procedure, described in section 5.2.1 as a possible solution to heteroscedasticity and the first-order autoregressive scheme. The idea is to transform equation [6.10] in such a way that the disturbance obeys all the classical assumptions. Such a transformation can be found but its application requires prior knowledge of θ. The required estimate of θ can be obtained using the instrumental variable method just described. Alternatively, it is possible to estimate α, β_0 and θ simultaneously using the maximum likelihood methods described in chapter 3. However, the procedure in this case is very complicated and beyond the scope of this book.[1]

The question of stability

In our discussion of the geometric lag distribution [6.8] we assumed that the parameter θ lay between zero and unity. A value for $\theta > 1$ makes little sense in most economic models as a brief inspection of [6.8] will make clear. It would imply that successively lagged values of X had an increasingly large influence on Y. We can, however, give a sensible interpretation to the case where $\theta = 1$. It is then possible to rewrite equation [6.10] as

$$\Delta Y_t = Y_t - Y_{t-1} = \beta_0 X_t + v_t \qquad [6.13]$$

Equation [6.13] implies that it is the *change* in Y that depends on X. It is not difficult to think of situations where we might wish to specify such an equation in economics. For example, if Y was the price of a good and X the excess demand for that good, then [6.13] would simply imply, for $\beta_0 > 0$, that the rate at which price changed depended on the extent of excess demand.

What, however, does $\theta = 1$ imply for the time path of the 'level' variable Y? For a given value of $X_t = Z = $ constant, [6.13] implies, if we disregard the disturbance,

$$Y_t = Y_0 + \beta_0 Zt \qquad \text{for all } t \qquad [6.14]$$

where t is time and Y_0 is the value of Y at time $t = 0$. Hence, if $\beta_0 > 0$, Y increases linearly with time and does not tend to an equilibrium value as time passes. The time path of Y is therefore said to be unstable.

There is no reason why economic variables should not exhibit such instability.

Indeed, we have already pointed out that many economic variables do show regular upward trends through time. However, such instability has consequences for the process of estimation. Suppose that, instead of estimating [6.13], we attempt, without realising $\theta = 1$, to estimate [6.10]. Lagging [6.14] one period gives

$$Y_{t-1} = Y_0 + \beta_0 Z(t-1) \qquad \text{for all } t \qquad [6.15]$$

Again ignoring the disturbance, it is clear that Y_{t-1} also increases at a constant linear rate with time. Thus, not only the dependent variable, but also one of the regressors in [6.10], displays an upward trend. We saw, in Chapter 5, that in these circumstances the condition [5.1] cannot hold,[2] so that, consequently, we cannot make use of conventional large sample theory when estimating equation [6.10].

Notice that this problem is entirely separate from the difficulties that arose because v_t in equation [6.10] was autocorrelated. Normally, in the absence of autocorrelation, OLS, when applied to equations such as [6.10], will provide estimators that are consistent and normally distributed in large samples.[3] However, even with a non-autocorrelated v_t, if the condition [5.1] breaks down, we can no longer rely on the OLS estimators having these properties. The standard classical inferential procedures cannot be trusted even in large samples.

Similarly, although at the end of the last subsection we listed a number of estimators that could be employed on [6.10] in the presence of autocorrelation, the large sample properties of these estimators also change radically in the unstable case $\theta = 1$. The large sample theory available applies only to the case $\theta < 1$ and, consequently, we are again in the position where we cannot make reliable inferences.

In estimating equations such as [6.10] the value of θ is clearly of crucial importance. It is therefore highly desirable to be able to test the hypothesis $\theta = 1$ against the alternative $\theta < 1$. The natural way to do this is to use the normal t-statistic $(\hat{\theta} - 1)/s_{\hat{\theta}}$, where $\hat{\theta}$ is the OLS estimator of θ and $s_{\hat{\theta}}$ is its estimated standard error. Unfortunately, as we have stressed, normal large sample theory breaks down under the null hypothesis $\theta = 1$, so the standard t-test is inapplicable even in large samples. However, as we shall see in the next chapter, much recent work has been devoted to the problem of devising a valid test under these circumstances.

Equation [6.10] is of simple form. However, similar problems can arise with any dynamic equation that contains lagged values of the dependent variable among its regressors. Regardless of the properties of the disturbance in the equation, if the implied time path for the dependent variable is unstable, then conventional large sample theory will be inapplicable.

6.2 The formation of expectations

We next consider a very well-known economic model which leads to a distributed lag formulation virtually identical to equation [6.8]. Consider a situation where Y_t depends not on the actual value of X but on its expected or 'permanent' value X^*

$$Y_t = \alpha + \beta X_t^* + \varepsilon_t \qquad [6.16]$$

125

The most common interpretation of X_t^* is that it represents permanent income in the Friedman sense. We shall encounter such an interpretation both in Chapter 10 on the consumption function and in Chapter 12 on the demand for money. Since X_t^* is unobservable we need to specify how it is determined. Consider the following scheme for determining X_t^*

$$X_t^* - X_{t-1}^* = \lambda(X_t - X_{t-1}^*) \qquad 0 \leqslant \lambda \leqslant 1 \qquad \text{[6.17A]}$$

or

$$X_t^* = \lambda X_t + (1 - \lambda)X_{t-1}^* \qquad \text{[6.17B]}$$

Equations [6.17] are an example of what is known as an *adaptive expectations hypothesis* and λ in this context is known as an *adjustment coefficient*. From [6.17A] we see that if actual 'income' in period t, X_t, exceeds expected 'income' in the previous period, X_{t-1}^*, ideas about expected 'income' are revised upwards so that expected 'income' in period t, X_t^*, exceeds that of the previous period. The extent of the adjustment depends on the size of λ which lies between zero and unity. For the extreme case, $\lambda = 1$, adjustment is complete because then $X_t^* = X_t$ so that actual and expected 'income' are identical. For the other extreme, $\lambda = 0$, no adjustment at all takes place and expected 'income' remains unchanged being uninfluenced by actual 'income' whatever its magnitude. In general, the larger is λ the greater the extent of the adjustment.

Notice that successive substitution is [6.17B] for X_{t-1}^*, X_{t-2}^*, etc. leads to

$$\begin{aligned} X_t^* &= \lambda X_t + (1 - \lambda)\lambda X_{t-1} + (1 - \lambda)^2 X_{t-2}^* \\ &= \lambda X_t + (1 - \lambda)\lambda X_{t-1} + (1 - \lambda)^2\lambda X_{t-2} + (1 - \lambda)^3 X_{t-3}^* \\ &= \lambda X_t + (1 - \lambda)\lambda X_{t-1} + (1 - \lambda)^2 \lambda X_{t-2} + (1 - \lambda)^3\lambda X_{t-3} \\ &\quad + (1 - \lambda)^4\lambda X_{t-4}\ldots \end{aligned} \qquad \text{[6.18]}$$

Thus, in determining expected 'income' most weight is given to current 'income', X_t, and successively declining weights to past levels of 'income', X_{t-1}, X_{t-2}, X_{t-3},….

Substitution of [6.18] into [6.16] then yields

$$Y_t = \alpha + \beta\lambda[X_t + (1 - \lambda)X_{t-1} + (1 - \lambda)^2 X_{t-2},\ldots] + \varepsilon_t \qquad \text{[6.19]}$$

Equation [6.19] is identical to the geometric lag equation [6.8] except that $\beta_0 = \beta\lambda$ and $\theta = 1 - \lambda$. By applying the Koyck transformation as before, i.e. lagging [6.19] by one period, multiplying throughout by $1 - \lambda$ and subtracting the result from [6.19], we obtain

$$Y_t = \alpha\lambda + \beta\lambda X_t + (1 - \lambda)Y_{t-1} + \varepsilon_t - (1 - \lambda)\varepsilon_{t-1} \qquad \text{[6.20]}$$

which is identical to [6.10] except that again, of course, $\beta_0 = \beta\lambda$ and $\theta = 1 - \lambda$. Therefore if we were to accept the underlying adaptive expectations hypothesis, our estimated equation [6.11] would suggest $1 - \hat{\lambda} = 0.6$ so that $\hat{\lambda} = 0.4$, $\hat{\beta} = 0.3/\hat{\lambda} = 0.75$ and $\hat{\alpha} = 64/\hat{\lambda} = 160$. Thus we would estimate the behavioural relationship [6.16] as

$$\hat{Y}_t = 160 + 0.75 X_t^* \qquad \text{[6.21]}$$

and the adjustment coefficient in the adaptive expectations equation [6.17A] as 0.4. This value of 0.4 would imply that 40 per cent of any difference between actual and expected 'income' is reflected in the revised estimate of expected 'income'.

In estimating the adaptive expectations model we must, of course, remember that the disturbance in [6.20] like that in [6.10] is almost certain to be autocorrelated. Thus, the presence of Y_{t-1} in equation [6.20] means that the straightforward application of OLS will again yield biased and inconsistent estimators. Hence, it is necessary to employ one of the alternative methods of estimation mentioned above for the general geometric lag.[4]

During the twenty years after the Second World War, the adaptive expectations hypothesis enjoyed considerable popularity among econometricians as a simple and apparently sensible model of how economic agents formed expectations. However its deficiencies gradually became more apparent. For example, it was pointed out that to model expectations of a variable adaptively implies irrational behaviour on the part of economic agents, if that variable grows at a constant rate over time. Suppose, for example, X in equations [6.17] grows at a constant exponential rate g. This implies

$$X_{t+1} = (1 + g)X_t \quad \text{for all } t, \quad g > 0 \tag{6.22}$$

Hence

$$X_t = \frac{X_{t+1}}{1 + g}, \quad X_{t-1} = \frac{X_{t+1}}{(1 + g)^2}, \quad X_{t-2} = \frac{X_{t+1}}{(1 + g)^3}, \quad \text{etc, etc.}$$

Substituting in [6.18] we obtain

$$X_t^* = \frac{\lambda}{1 + g}X_{t+1} + \frac{(1 - \lambda)\lambda}{(1 + g)^2}X_{t+1} + \frac{(1 - \lambda)^2\lambda}{(1 + g)^3}X_{t+1} + \cdots$$

$$= \frac{\lambda}{1 + g}X_{t+1}\left[1 + \frac{1 - \lambda}{1 + g} + \left(\frac{1 - \lambda}{1 + g}\right)^2 + \cdots\right] \tag{6.23}$$

Since $(1 - \lambda)/(1 + g) < 1$, the term in square brackets in [6.23] is a convergent geometric series which may be summed to give

$$X_t^* = \frac{\lambda}{1 + g}X_{t+1}\left[\frac{1}{1 - (1 - \lambda)/(1 + g)}\right] = \frac{\lambda}{g + \lambda}X_{t+1} \tag{6.24}$$

Hence, since $g > 0$,

$$X_t^* < X_{t+1} \quad \text{for all } t \tag{6.25}$$

X_t^*, the expected value of X, can be interpreted as the economic agent's prediction of the value of X in the next period, i.e. period $t + 1$. That is

$$X_t^* = E_t(X_{t+1}) \tag{6.26}$$

where the t subscript on the expected value sign indicates that the expectation is that held at period t. Equation [6.25] therefore implies

$$X_{t+1} > E_t(X_{t+1}) \quad \text{for all } t \tag{6.27}$$

That is, the actual value of X in period $t + 1$ always turns out to be higher than the value predicted or forecast in period t. The agents *forecast error* is always positive.

A moment's reflection should make clear that for an agent to continue forming expectations adaptively under these circumstances is not rational. The agent will soon realise he is consistently underpredicting X and a rational individual will start taking this into account when he makes his predictions.

A far wider attack on equations such as [6.20] was made by Lucas in his 1975 critique of economic policy evaluation. Lucas argued that the structure of many estimated equations could not survive changes in government policy regimes. Such relationships, while they might be adequate for short-term forecasting under unchanging policies, were therefore of little use in assessing the likely impact of policy changes. Economic agents are aware of government policy and, clearly, are likely to adjust the way they form their expectations in the light of changes in such policies. To the extent that the structure of an estimated equation reflects the process of expectation formation, its parameters are therefore likely to change when government policy changes.

The problem with equations such as [6.10], and the implied geometric lag structure [6.8], is that they imply unchanged expectations even in the face of a government policy change. The same can be said of any other model in which expectations concerning a variable are based rigidly on past values of that variable. Agents are being irrational if they do not incorporate into their expectations formation any knowledge they may have about policy changes and their intended effect.

Rational expectations

The theory of *rational expectations* had a profound effect on theoretical macroeconomics and it was inevitably introduced into applied econometric work. In simple terms rational expectations implies that agents have access to all relevant information and make the best possible use of it when forming expectations regarding any variable. Relevant information, of course, includes knowledge of government policy aims. Algebraically, suppose agents, on the basis of past experience and current knowledge, believe that a variable X is determined as follows.

$$X_t = a_1 + a_2 X_{t-1} + a_3 Z_{t-1} + u_t \qquad \text{for all } t \qquad [6.28]$$

where Z is an exogenous variable that agents believe has an influence on X and u_t is a disturbance with $Eu_t = 0$. Notice that only lagged values of X and Z are included on the right hand side of [6.28] because, at time t, the agent is assumed to have no information on current values of X and Z.

At time $t - 1$ the agent forms his expectation about the value of X at period t on the basis of [6.28]. Taking expectations over [6.28]

$$E_{t-1}(X_t) = a_1 + a_2 X_{t-1} + a_3 Z_{t-1} \qquad [6.29]$$

where the expectation is that made at time $t - 1$. [6.29] is the *rational expectation* of X_t under the present assumptions. Subtracting [6.29] from [6.28] yields

$$X_t - E_{t-1}(X_t) = u_t \qquad [6.30]$$

We see from [6.30] that u_t is in fact the forecast error made by the agent. Under rational expectations the forecast error must not only have zero mean but must be totally unpredictable. For example the u_ts cannot be serially correlated. If the errors were predictable, this would constitute available and relevant information that economic agents were not making use of when forming their expectations. The existence of such information is contrary to the rational expectations hypothesis. If in practice forecast errors proved predictable then agents would simply reformulate equation [6.28] and continue to reformulate it until errors became unpredictable.

Nowadays, rational expectations are used frequently as a preferable alternative to adaptive expectations in applied work. For example, suppose a variable Y is determined by equation [6.16]. Instead of using equations [6.17] to model X_t^* we can use a rational expectation such as [6.29]. Thus, substituting in [6.16] we attempt the estimation of

$$Y_t = \alpha + \beta E_{t-1}(X_t) + \varepsilon_t \qquad [6.31]$$

The problem is that we do not have data on $E_{t-1}(X_t)$. The solution is a two stage procedure pioneered by McCullum (1976). In the first stage we obtain a proxy for $E_{t-1}(X_t)$ by taking the predicted value of X_t, $\hat{X}_t$, obtained by computing the OLS regression

$$\hat{X}_t = \hat{a}_1 + \hat{a}_2 X_{t-1} + \hat{a}_3 Z_{t-1} \qquad [6.32]$$

The second stage then involves replacing $E_{t-1}(X_t)$ by $\hat{X}_t$ in [6.31] and applying OLS to the resulting equation to obtain the required estimates of α and β.

Notice that the McCullum procedure is directly equivalent to a GIVE estimation of

$$Y_t = \alpha + \beta X_t + \varepsilon_t \qquad [6.33]$$

$\hat{X}_t$ is the instrumental variable used for X_t and is constructed by regressing X_t on the two instruments X_{t-1} and Z_{t-1}. We shall encounter this approach to the modelling of expectations when reviewing recent work on both consumption (section 10.6) and the demand for money (section 12.7).

6.3 Lags of adjustment

A second model that leads to the geometric lag equation [6.8] is the *partial adjustment model*. Suppose the desired level of Y at time t, Y_t^*, depends on some explanatory variable, X, plus a disturbance obeying the usual assumptions

$$Y_t^* = \alpha + \beta X_t + \varepsilon_t \qquad [6.34]$$

For example, the desired level of a firm's capital stock may depend on its output, or a household's optimal level of consumption expenditure may depend on its income. However, time may be necessary before actual Y can be adjusted to its optimal or desired level so that Y and Y^* are not normally the same. That is, the adjustment of actual Y to a change in X does not occur instantaneously. Such lagged adjustment might be the result of inertia or the persistence of habit in a household's demand for consumer goods, for example. Suppose that the relationship between actual and desired Y is as follows

$$Y_t - Y_{t-1} = \mu(Y_t^* - Y_{t-1}) \qquad 0 \leqslant \mu \leqslant 1 \qquad [6.35A]$$

or

$$Y_t = \mu Y_t^* + (1 - \mu) Y_{t-1} \qquad [6.35B]$$

That is, if desired Y in period t exceeds actual Y in the previous period, then actual Y in period t is increased above its level of the previous period but not by the full extent of the difference between Y_t^* and Y_{t-1}. The adjustment in Y is only partial and the extent of the movement in actual Y towards its desired level depends on the size of μ. At one extreme μ is unity and adjustment is complete since then $Y_t = Y_t^*$. At the other extreme $\mu = 0$ so that $Y_t = Y_{t-1}$ and no adjustment at all takes place. In general, the extent of the adjustment and hence the speed with which Y adjusts to X over time will depend on the size of μ. The larger μ the more rapid the adjustment. μ is again known as an adjustment coefficient but notice that its interpretation is totally different to that of λ in equation [6.17A].

Substitution of [6.34] into [6.35] now yields

$$Y_t = \alpha\mu + \beta\mu X_t + (1 - \mu) Y_{t-1} + \mu\varepsilon_t \qquad [6.36]$$

Apart from the disturbance, [6.36] is of identical form to equation [6.20] with μ now replacing λ. Notice, however, that in this case the disturbance is not autocorrelated (provided ε_t in equation [6.34] is non-autocorrelated). Hence *the application of* OLS *to equation* [6.36] *will yield consistent estimators*, although the presence of Y_{t-1} means they will not be unbiased. The estimation of a partial adjustment model therefore presents fewer problems than that of an adaptive expectations model.[5]

Finally, notice that successive substitution for Y_{t-1}, Y_{t-2}, etc. in [6.36] leads to

$$Y_t = \alpha + \beta\mu[X_t + (1 - \mu)X_{t-1} + (1 - \mu)^2 X_{t-2}, \ldots] + \xi_t \qquad [6.37]$$

where

$$\xi_t = \mu\varepsilon_t + \mu(1 - \mu)\varepsilon_{t-1} + \mu(1 - \mu)^2 \varepsilon_{t-2}, \ldots$$

Equation [6.37] is identical to equation [6.8] with $\beta_0 = \beta\mu$ and $\theta = 1 - \mu$ so that the partial adjustment model, like the adaptive expectations model, also implies a geometric lag.

Suppose, again, that we had obtained an estimated equation such as [6.11]. We have already seen that we could interpret such an equation in terms of an adaptive expectations model with adjustment parameter $\lambda = 0.4$. However, we could equally well interpret [6.11] in terms of equation [6.36] and conclude that it arose out of a partial adjustment process in which μ in equation [6.35A] was 0.4. The point is that, without prior knowledge of which model is appropriate, we cannot know whether the importance of the lagged dependent variable, Y_{t-1}, in equation [6.11] arises because of an adaptive expectations mechanism or because of lagged adjustment of actual Y to its desired level. This is a consequence of the fact that both equations [6.16] and [6.34] involve unobservable variables—expected X in equation [6.16] and desired Y in equation [6.34]. In transforming these equations into relationships between the observable actual X and Y variables, we lose the ability to discriminate between the two competing models.

This problem of discrimination is eased somewhat if an extra explanatory variable appears in equations [6.16] and [6.34]. For example, if [6.16] becomes

$$Y_t = \alpha + \beta X_t^* + \gamma Z_t + \varepsilon_t \qquad [6.38]$$

where X_t^* is again determined by [6.17] then, applying the Koyck transformation, the final estimating equation for the adaptive expectations model becomes

$$Y_t = \alpha\lambda + \beta\lambda X_t + \gamma Z_t - \gamma(1 - \lambda)Z_{t-1} + (1 - \lambda)Y_{t-1} + \varepsilon_t - (1 - \lambda)\varepsilon_{t-1} \qquad [6.39]$$

rather than [6.20]. However, if [6.34] becomes

$$Y_t^* = \alpha + \beta X_t + \gamma Z + \varepsilon_t \qquad [6.40]$$

where Y_t is again determined by [6.35], then the final estimating equation for the partial adjustment model becomes

$$Y_t = \alpha\mu + \beta\mu X_t + \lambda\mu Z_t + (1 - \mu)Y_{t-1} + \mu\varepsilon_t \qquad [6.41]$$

rather than [6.36].

Notice that equations [6.39] and [6.41] differ not only in their disturbances but also because the lagged explanatory variable Z_{t-1} appears in [6.39] but not [6.41]. In principle this should help to discriminate between the two models because if Z_{t-1} were to prove significant in the determination of Y_t this would constitute evidence in favour of the adaptive expectations model. Unfortunately, Z_t and Z_{t-1} are likely to be highly correlated with most time series data and hence have large standard errors. Thus neither variable is likely to prove significant even if [6.39] is the correct model.

There is in fact a further problem concerning the estimation of [6.39] in that its parameters are *over-identified*. That is, its estimation will provide five estimated coefficients from which we have to find just four parameters, α, β, γ and λ. That is, if our estimated equation is

$$\hat{Y}_t = \hat{a}_0 + \hat{a}_1 X_t + \hat{a}_2 Z_t + \hat{a}_3 Z_{t-1} + \hat{a}_4 Y_{t-1} \qquad [6.42]$$

where the $\hat{a}$'s are the estimated and hence *known* coefficients, then to estimate the underlying parameters we have to solve the equations

$$\hat{a}_0 = \alpha\lambda \qquad\qquad \hat{a}_1 = \beta\lambda \qquad\qquad \hat{a}_2 = \gamma$$

$$\hat{a}_3 = -\gamma(1 - \lambda) \qquad\quad \hat{a}_4 = 1 - \lambda$$

The above equations are obtained by comparing [6.42] with [6.39]. The problem is that these equations yield *two* estimates of each parameter. For example, the coefficient on Y_{t-1} in [6.42] yields an estimate of λ given by $\hat{\lambda}_1 = 1 - \hat{a}_4$, while the ratio of the coefficients on Z_t and Z_{t-1} yields another given by $\hat{\lambda}_2 = 1 + \hat{a}_3/\hat{a}_2$. The two estimates $\hat{\lambda}_1$ and $\hat{\lambda}_2$ will not coincide so, to obtain unique estimates of the parameters, [6.42] has to be estimated subject to the *non-linear* restriction $\hat{a}_3 + \hat{a}_2\hat{a}_4 = 0$. This is possible, using the non-linear maximum likelihood methods described at the end of Chapter 3, but at the same time taking into account the autocorrelated disturbance.

We have seen that the importance of lagged dependent variables could arise, either because of 'expectational lags' as in equations [6.20] and [6.39], or because of 'adjustment lags' as in equations [6.36] and [6.41], or even possibly because of both types of lag. This suggests that, in any attempt to discover the relative importance of the two types of lag, we should combine them into a single model in which desired Y depends on expected X. That is

$$Y_t^* = \alpha + \beta X_t^* + \varepsilon_t \qquad\qquad [6.43]$$

where X^* is determined by the adaptive expectations mechanism [6.17A] and Y adjusts to Y^* through the partial adjustment mechanism [6.35A]. The estimated sizes of λ and μ would then help us decide on the relative importance of expectational and adjustment-type lags. However, we shall delay considering such a model in detail until we study the adjustment process in demand for money equations in section 12.3.

However it arises, one of the problems with the geometric distributed lag formulation [6.8] is that it may not be appropriate for the weights in the lag structure to decline immediately as we move from the present value of the explanatory variable further into the past. Sometimes it may be the case that a change in the X variable has little effect on the Y variable for the first few periods. The β's in equation [6.1] might follow an 'inverted V' distribution as illustrated in Fig. 6.1, first rising to a peak but declining thereafter. For example, such a distribution could describe the adjustment of a firm's capital stock to a sustained increase in its output. Capacity constraints in the capital goods industry and the long and variable gestation period for many capital goods means that the effect of an output change does not make its maximum impact until some periods later. However, before considering how the geometric lag can be generalised to yield such an inverted V-shape we require some knowledge of lag operators.

Lag operators

The lag operator L is defined by

$$LX_t = X_{t-1} \qquad\qquad [6.44]$$

6.1 An inverted V-type lag distribution.

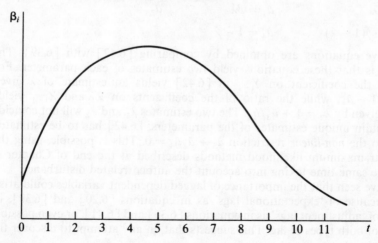

The lag operator may be applied more than once so that

$$L(LX_t) = L^2 X_t = X_{t-2}, \qquad L(L^2 X_t) = L^3 X_t = X_{t-3}, \text{ etc., etc.} \qquad [6.45]$$

It may also be handled algebraically like an ordinary variable. For example

$$L^4 L^6 X_t = L^{10} X_t = X_{t-10} \qquad [6.46]$$

Similarly

$$L^5(3X_t + 7X_{t-1} + 5Y_t) = 3X_{t-5} + 7X_{t-6} + 5Y_{t-5} \qquad [6.47]$$

We can therefore write the distributed lag equation [6.1], generalised to the case $m = \infty$, as

$$Y_t = \alpha + \beta_0 X_t + \beta_1 LX_t + \beta_2 L^2 X_t + \beta_3 L^3 X_t + \cdots + \varepsilon_t$$

$$= \alpha + \beta(L)X_t + \varepsilon_t \qquad [6.48]$$

where $\beta(L)$ is a polynomial in L. That is

$$\beta(L) = \beta_0 + \beta_1 L + \beta_2 L^2 + \beta_3 L^3, \ldots \qquad [6.49]$$

It is also possible to divide by L and to divide by functions of L. For example $(1/L)X_t$ simply means that variable which yields X_t when the lag operator is applied. Hence

$$\left(\frac{1}{L}\right) X_t = X_{t+1} \qquad [6.50]$$

Similarly, $(1/\beta(L))Y_t$ means that variable which yields Y_t when $\beta(L)$ is applied. For example, if

$$Y_t = 3X_t + 4X_{t-1} + 2X_{t-2}$$

$$= (3 + 4L + 2L^2)X_t$$

then

$$\left(\frac{1}{3 + 4L + 2L^2}\right) Y_t = X_t \qquad [6.51]$$

It is instructive to handle the geometric lag structure and the Koyck transformation using the lag operator notation. We may write [6.8] as

$$Y_t = \alpha + \beta_0(1 + \theta L + \theta^2 L^2 + \theta^3 L^3, \ldots)X_t + \varepsilon_t$$

$$= \alpha + \left(\frac{\beta_0}{1 - \theta L}\right)X_t + \varepsilon_t \qquad [6.52]$$

using the expression for the sum to infinity of a convergent geometric series. Hence, multiplying throughout by $1 - \theta L$,

$$(1 - \theta L)Y_t = (1 - \theta L)\alpha + \beta_0 X_t + (1 - \theta L)\varepsilon_t$$

or

$$Y_t = \alpha(1 - \theta) + \beta_0 X_t + \theta Y_{t-1} + \varepsilon_t - \theta\varepsilon_{t-1} \qquad [6.53]$$

which is identical to equation [6.10].[6]

6.4 Rational lags

A technique sometimes used in econometrics is to approximate the general *infinite* distributed lag, $\beta(L)$, in equation [6.49] by the ratio of two finite polynomials. That is

$$\beta(L) = \frac{\gamma(L)}{w(L)} = \frac{\gamma_0 + \gamma_1 L + \gamma_2 L^2, \ldots, \gamma_k L^k}{1 + w_1 L + w_2 L^2, \ldots, w_l L^l} \qquad [6.54]$$

Any lag function of the form [6.49] can be approximated by this so-called *rational lag function* provided l and k are chosen appropriately. In fact, l and k have to be chosen prior to the estimating process. For example, if $l = 2$ and $k = 2$ then [6.48] becomes

$$Y_t = \alpha + \left(\frac{\gamma_0 + \gamma_1 L + \gamma_2 L^2}{1 + w_1 L + w_2 L^2} \right) X_t + \varepsilon_t \qquad [6.55]$$

Multiplying throughout by $w(L) = 1 + w_1 L + w_2 L^2$, we obtain

$$(1 + w_1 L + w_2 L^2) Y_t = (1 + w_1 L + w_2 L^2)\alpha + (\gamma_0 + \gamma_1 L + \gamma_2 L^2) X_t$$
$$+ (1 + w_1 L + w_2 L^2)\varepsilon_t \qquad [6.56]$$

so that the equation actually estimated is

$$Y_t = \alpha(1 + w_1 + w_2) + \gamma_0 X_t + \gamma_1 X_{t-1} + \gamma_2 X_{t-2}$$
$$- w_1 Y_{t-1} - w_2 Y_{t-2} + u_t \qquad [6.57]$$

where

$$u_t = \varepsilon_t + w_1 \varepsilon_{t-1} + w_2 \varepsilon_{t-2}$$

Notice, however, that the disturbance, u_t, in equation [6.57] is of second-order moving average form and will be autocorrelated if ε_t obeys the classical assumptions. Hence, since the equation contains two lagged values of the dependent variable, OLS will yield biased and inconsistent estimators of its parameters.

As can be seen from [6.52], the geometric lag is a special case of [6.54] with $\gamma(L) = \beta_0$ and $w(L) = 1 - \theta L$, i.e. $k = 0$ and $l = 1$.

Given estimates of all the parameters in equations such as [6.57], it is possible to deduce all the implied values for the β's in equation [6.49] and hence the precise manner in which Y reacts over time to a change in X. For example, if we obtain

$$Y_t = 5.1 + 0.4 X_t + 0.8 X_{t-1} + 1.1 X_{t-2} + 1.1 Y_{t-1} - 0.4 Y_{t-2} \qquad [6.58]$$

then this implies

$$\gamma(L) = 0.4 + 0.8L + 1.1L^2$$
$$w(L) = 1 - 1.1L + 0.4L^2$$

From [6.54] we have

$$\beta(L)w(L) = \gamma(L)$$

134

or
$$(\beta_0 + \beta_1 L + \beta_2 L^2 + \beta_3 L^3, \ldots)(1 - 1.1L + 0.4L^2) = 0.4 + 0.8L + 1.1L^2$$
$$[6.59]$$

By comparing coefficients of the various powers of L in equation [6.59] we obtain

$$\beta_0(1) = 0.4$$
$$\beta_0(-1.1) + \beta_1(1) = 0.8$$
$$\beta_0(0.4) + \beta_1(-1.1) + \beta_2(1) = 1.1$$
$$\beta_0(0) + \beta_1(0.4) + \beta_2(-1.1) + \beta_3(1) = 0$$
$$\beta_0(0) + \beta_1(0) + \beta_2(0.4) + \beta_3(-1.1) + \beta_4(1) = 0$$

etc, etc.

These equations may now be solved recursively for the βs yielding $\beta_0 = 0.4$, $\beta_1 = 1.24$, $\beta_2 = 2.30$, $\beta_3 = 2.04$, $\beta_4 = 1.32$, etc, etc.

Hence, since $1 + w_1 + w_2 = 0.3$ so that $\alpha = 17$, the estimated version of [6.48] is

$$Y_t = 17 + 0.4X_t + 1.24X_{t-1} + 2.30X_{t-2} + 2.04X_{t-3} + 1.32X_{t-4}, \ldots,$$
$$[6.60]$$

Thus in this case we happen to obtain a typical inverted V lag distribution. Since *any* distributed lag function $\beta(L)$ can be approximated by the ratio of two finite polynomials, $\gamma(L)$ and $w(L)$, provided l and k are sufficiently large, the usefulness of the technique for estimating inverted V-type distributions is clear.

Consider again the general distributed lag equations [6.1] and [6.48]. The *long-run effect* of a change in X is the change in the *equilibrium* value of Y resulting from a unit sustained change in X. This was given by the sum of the β coefficients. However, it can be calculated directly from equations such as [6.57] by using [6.54]. Since

$$\beta_1 + \beta_2 + \beta_3 \cdots = \beta(1) = \frac{\gamma(1)}{w(1)} = \frac{\gamma_1 + \gamma_2 + \gamma_3, \ldots, \gamma_k}{1 + w_2 + w_3, \ldots, w_1}$$

the required multiplier can be obtained by taking the ratio of the γ coefficients to the w coefficients in the estimated equation. For example, for [6.58] we have

$$\sum \beta_j = \frac{\sum \gamma_j}{\sum w_j} = \frac{0.4 + 0.8 + 1.1}{1 - 1.1 + 0.4} = 7.67$$

Alternatively, of course, using [6.60]

$$\sum \beta_j = 0.4 + 1.24 + 2.30 + 2.04 + 1.32 \cdots = 7.67$$

Thus equation [6.58] implies that a unit sustained increase in X will lead in the long run to an increase of 7.67 units in Y.

It is possible to find the mean lag for a rational lag distribution as follows. Differentiating [6.49] with respect to L yields

$$\beta'(L) = \beta_1 + 2\beta_2 L + 3\beta_3 L^2 \cdots \qquad [6.61]$$

Setting $L = 1$ in [6.61] we have

$$\beta'(1) = \beta_1 + 2\beta_2 + 3\beta_3 + 4\beta_4 \cdots = \sum_j j\beta_j \qquad [6.62]$$

135

Hence, using [6.7]

$$\text{Mean lag} = \frac{\sum_j \beta_j}{\sum \beta_j} = \frac{\beta'(1)}{\beta(1)} \qquad [6.63]$$

Since, from [6.54], $\beta(1) = \gamma(1)/w(1)$, we have, using the quotient rule for differentiation

$$\beta'(1) = \frac{w(1)\gamma'(1) - \gamma(1)w'(1)}{[w(1)]^2} \qquad [6.64]$$

Substituting in [6.63] we finally obtain

$$\text{Mean lag} = \frac{\gamma'(1)}{\gamma(1)} - \frac{w'(1)}{w(1)} \qquad [6.65]$$

For example, for equation [6.58]

$$\gamma'(L) = 0.8 + 2.2L \quad \text{and} \quad w'(L) = -1.1 + 0.8L$$

Hence $\gamma'(1) = 3.0$, $\gamma(1) = 2.3$, $w'(1) = -0.3$, $w(1) = 0.3$ and the mean lag is therefore 2.3 periods.

Instability in the general case

We saw earlier that estimation of equations such as [6.10] became even more problematic when the time path of the dependent variable, Y, was unstable so that the condition [5.1] broke down. When this was the case we were unable to make use of conventional large sample theory, regardless of whether v_t in [6.10] was autocorrelated or not. Similar problems arise with equations such as [6.57]. Consider the general equation

$$Y_t = k + \alpha_0 X_t + \alpha_1 X_{t-1} + \alpha_2 X_{t-2} + \cdots + \alpha_m X_{t-m}$$
$$+ \varphi_1 Y_{t-1} + \varphi_2 Y_{t-2} + \cdots + \varphi_p Y_{t-p} + \varepsilon_t \qquad [6.66]$$

where ε_t is a disturbance obeying the usual classical assumptions.

For given values of X_t, X_{t-1}, X_{t-2}, etc., the time path of Y is determined by a non-homogeneous mth order difference equation with characteristic equation[7]

$$\lambda^p - \varphi_1 \lambda^{p-1} - \varphi_2 \lambda^{p-2} - \cdots - \phi_{p-1}\lambda - \varphi_p = 0 \qquad [6.67]$$

The time path of Y will be unstable if any of the roots, λ_i ($i = 1, 2, \ldots, p$), of the characteristic equation are greater than or equal to one in absolute value. If the time path of Y is unstable then, as in the first order case, when we attempt to estimate [6.66] conventional large sample theory cannot be applied. Thus our normal OLS inferential procedures *may become invalid even for large samples*. Similar difficulties occur with any other estimation procedures that might be adopted to deal with possible autocorrelation in ε_t.

6.5 Polynomial or Almon lags

The lag structures considered so far involve infinite lags. An alternative is to assume that the influence of a change in X on the Y variable is complete after a finite number of periods, i.e. there is a finite maximum lag. Such an assumption is built into the technique developed by Almon (1965). Consider again the general distributed lag equation [6.1] which assumes a maximum lag of m periods.

$$Y_t = \alpha + \beta_0 X_t + \beta_1 X_{t-1} + \beta_2 X_{t-2}, \ldots, \beta_m X_{t-m} + \varepsilon_t \qquad [6.68]$$

The Almon technique, unlike, for example, the Koyck approach, does not assume a rigid relationship between the β's. All that is assumed is that the relationship between the β's can be approximated by some polynomial. For example, if the β's describe some form of inverted V distribution with $m = 8$ as in Fig. 6.2, then a curve drawn through the points in this figure may be approximated by a second-order polynomial, i.e.

$$\beta_i = a_0 + a_1 i + a_2 i^2 \qquad [6.69]$$

The general rule is that the degree of the polynomial should be at least one more than the number of turning points in the curve. Notice that if it is possible to approximate all the β's in [6.68] by equation [6.69], then we must have

$$\beta_0 = a_0$$
$$\beta_1 = a_0 + a_1 + a_2$$
$$\beta_2 = a_0 + 2a_1 + 4a_2 \qquad [6.69A]$$
$$\vdots$$
$$\beta_m = a_0 + ma_1 + m^2 a_2$$

so that equation [6.68] becomes

$$Y_t = \alpha + a_0 X_t + (a_0 + a_1 + a_2)X_{t-1}$$
$$+ (a_0 + 2a_1 + 4a_2)X_{t-2}, \ldots, (a_0 + ma_1 + m^2 a_2)X_{t-m} + \varepsilon_t \qquad [6.70]$$

6.2 Points that can be approximated by a second-order polynomial.

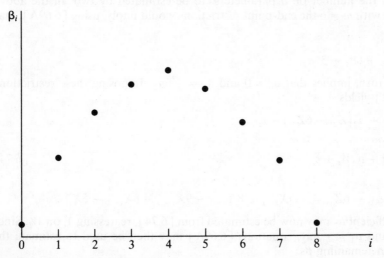

We can arrange [6.70] to give

$$Y_t = \alpha + a_0 \sum_{i=0}^{m} X_{t-i} + a_1 \sum_{i=0}^{m} i X_{t-i} + a_2 \sum_{i=0}^{m} i^2 X_{t-i} + \varepsilon_t \qquad [6.71]$$

It is now possible to define three new variables

$$Z_{0t} = \sum_{i=0}^{m} X_{t-i}, \qquad Z_{1t} = \sum_{i=0}^{m} i X_{t-i}, \qquad Z_{2t} = \sum_{i=0}^{m} i^2 X_{t-i}$$

so that [6.70] can be rewritten as

$$Y_t = \alpha + a_0 Z_{0t} + a_1 Z_{1t} + a_2 Z_{2t} + \varepsilon_t \qquad [6.72]$$

The parameters in [6.72] may now be estimated by normal OLS methods provided we can specify an appropriate value for m, the maximum lag length. For example, if $m = 6$, the Z variables would be constructed from the original X variable as

$$Z_{0t} = X_t + X_{t-1} + X_{t-2} + X_{t-3} + X_{t-4} + X_{t-5} + X_{t-6}$$

$$Z_{1t} = X_{t-1} + 2X_{t-2} + 3X_{t-3} + 4X_{t-4} + 5X_{t-5} + 6X_{t-6} \qquad [6.73]$$

$$Z_{2t} = X_{t-1} + 4X_{t-2} + 9X_{t-3} + 16X_{t-4} + 25X_{t-5} + 36X_{t-6}$$

Once estimates of a_0, a_1 and a_2 are obtained, estimates of the parameters β_0, $\beta_1, \beta_2, \ldots, \beta_m$ in the original equation [6.68] may be computed using [6.69A]. Moreover, it can be shown that, provided the maximum lag length, m, exceeds the order of the polynomial used (in the above case the order is 2), the estimators of the β's obtained using the Almon technique are more efficient (i.e. have smaller variances) than those obtained by the direct application of OLS to [6.68].

Notice that the polynomial [6.69] is used only to determine the parameters for values of i from zero to m. Outside this range the lag coefficients are specified to be zero. An additional possibility is to 'tie down' the lag distribution by imposing the 'end-point restrictions' that $\beta_0 = \beta_m = 0$. This has the effect of reducing the number of 'a parameters' to be estimated by two. In the above example with $m = 6$ the end-point restrictions would imply, using [6.69A], that

$$0 = a_0$$

$$0 = a_0 + 6a_1 + 36a_2$$

This, in turn, implies that $a_0 = 0$ and $a_1 = -6a_2$. Imposing these restrictions on [6.72] yields

$$Y_t = \alpha + a_2(Z_{2t} - 6Z_{1t}) + \varepsilon_t$$

or

$$Y_t = \alpha + a_2 W_t + \varepsilon_t \qquad [6.74]$$

where

$$W_t = Z_{2t} - 6Z_{1t} = -5X_{t-1} - 8X_{t-2} - 9X_{t-3} - 8X_{t-4} - 5X_{t-5}$$

The coefficient a_2 may now be estimated from [6.74], regressing Y_t on W_t. Since $a_0 = 0$ and $a_1 = -6a_2$, equations [6.69A] may then be used to estimate the unknown remaining βs.

Early users of the Almon lag technique typically made use of end-point restrictions either for *a priori* reasons or simply because of the reduction in the number of parameters involved. Unfortunately, the use of such restrictions will lead to biased estimates of the remaining non-zero β parameters unless the polynomial equation [6.69] does indeed yield values of zero for $i = 0$ and $i = m$. Nowadays, therefore, the tendency is to refrain from the use of end-point restrictions. Rather, if restrictions such as $\beta_m = 0$ are required then the maximum lag length is reduced to $m - 1$ and X_{t-m} omitted from equation [6.68].

The advantages of the Almon technique are the variety of the lag distributions that can be generated and the fact that, unlike the rational lag procedure, it does not involve transformations which lead to a violation of the classical assumptions. If the disturbance term in equation [6.68] obeys these assumptions then so does that in equations [6.72] and [6.74]. The disadvantages of the technique are that in practice we will not know the maximum lag length or the order of the most appropriate polynomial before estimation. In practice, the degree of the polynomial has to be high enough for the lag distributions obtainable to accommodate any likely pattern for the βs. However, it must be kept lower than m if the technique is to fulfil its purpose, which is to reduce the number of parameters that have to be estimated. The maximum lag length is best found by varying m so as to maximise, for example, the $\bar{R}^2$ statistic. Unfortunately, since the X variables are likely to be highly multicollinear, variations in $\bar{R}^2$ are likely to be small. However, by combining goodness-of-fit criteria with *a priori* criteria concerning the pattern of the βs (e.g. that they should all be non-zero) it is often possible to arrive at some 'best' value for m.

Further reading

The early development of the geometric lag was by Koyck (1954). An excellent survey is that by Griliches (1967). A good and understandable introduction to the *ML* estimation of distributed lag models is contained in Kmenta (1986). Johnston (1984) also has a section on the estimation of such models. Some further material on rational expectations can be found in Maddala (1989).

Notes

1. However see, for example, Klein (1958) and Zellner and Geisal (1970).
2. One of the diagonal elements in $(1/n)X'X$ is $(1/n)\sum Y_{t-1}$. If Y_{t-1} increases with time, then $(1/n)\sum Y_{t-1}$ increases without limit as $n \to \infty$. Note that we have assumed $X_t = $ constant in equation [6.10]. If instead X_t possessed a trend, then even if $\theta < 1$ assumption [5.1] would still break down.
3. See section 6.3 for a model which results in an estimating equation similar to [6.10] but in which the disturbance is non-autocorrelated.
4. Since the adaptive expectations model specifies $0 < \lambda < 1$, it follows that $(1 - \lambda)$ in equation [6.20] must lie between zero and unity, so we need not concern ourselves with the estimation problems that would arise if the time path of Y were unstable.
5. As with the adaptive expectations model, we need not be concerned about any problems of instability in the time path of Y. The model implies that $(1 - \mu)$ in equation [6.36] must lie between zero and unity.
6. Since α is a constant, $L^2\alpha = L\alpha = \alpha$.
7. For the method of solving non-homogeneous difference equations see, for example, Chiang (1984), Ch. 17.

7 The specification and selection of models

In this chapter, we address the very important question of how an econometrician should decide on which model or estimated equation to select as best representing the underlying process he is investigating. We begin by considering the often serious consequences of specifying an incorrect model.

7.1 Specification errors

In Chapter 5 we considered the consequences of breakdowns in the classical assumptions under the 'maintained hypothesis' that the population regression equation [2.12] (page 12) has been correctly specified. However, [2.12] is as much a part of the classical regression model as are the assumptions 1–7, so we begin this chapter by considering the effect on the OLS estimators of an incorrectly specified population regression equation. There are basically two ways in which equation [2.12] could be misspecified. First, we might include too many or too few explanatory variables or regressors. Secondly, we might assume that the population regression equation is of linear form, (as implied by [2.12]), when it is not. We consider, first, cases where the number of explanatory variables has been incorrectly specified.

The case where we include explanatory variables in [2.12], when they do not, in fact, have any influence on the dependent Y variable, is relatively easily disposed of. Such a mis-specification simply implies that some of the β_j parameters in equation [2.12] take the value zero. Provided assumptions 1–7 hold, the OLS estimators of all the β_js will still be unbiased and consistent although, of course, for those variables incorrectly included in the population regression equation, we will have 'unbiased estimators of zero'. The OLS estimators of the non-zero β_js, however, are unlikely to remain BLUE or efficient. Suppose an 'irrelevant' explanatory variable is correlated with any of the other explanatory variables. It follows from our discussion of multicollinearity that this will lead to an unnecessary increase in the sampling variances and standard errors of all explanatory variables, including the 'relevant' ones.[1] Only when the irrelevant variables are completely uncorrelated with the other variables will the OLS estimators of the non-zero β_j remain efficient.

The omission of a 'relevant' explanatory variable has even more serious consequences. The disturbance in the classical regression model is supposed to encapsulate the influence on the dependent Y variable of all factors other than those represented by the explanatory X-variables. It is therefore possible to regard an omitted relevant explanatory variable as being represented by the disturbance. However, if the omitted variable is correlated with any of the other explanatory variables, then *we will have a case of contemporaneous correlation between these variables and the disturbance*. We know from section 5.1 that under these circumstances the OLS estimators become *biased and inconsistent*. The direction of the biases involved will depend: (a) on the directions of the correlations between the omitted and the remaining explanatory variables, and (b) on the signs of the β_js associated with the omitted variables.

For example, consider again the case where the population relationships are given by [5.11] and [5.12] but where we apply OLS to

$$Y_i = \beta_1 + \beta_2 X_{2i} + \varepsilon_i^* \qquad i = 1, 2, 3, \dots, n \qquad [7.1]$$

where in fact $\varepsilon_i^* = \beta_3 X_{3i} + \varepsilon_i$. If $\beta_3 > 0$, then if the correlation between the X_{2i}s and the X_{3i}s, r, is positive, this will lead to positive correlation between the ε_i^*s and X_{2i}s. We then have a situation, equivalent to that illustrated in Fig. 5.1, with OLS tending to overestimate β_2 and underestimate β_1. However, if $\beta_3 > 0$ and $r < 0$, then the correlation between the ε_i^*s and the X_{2i}s will be negative and the situation will be as in Fig. 5.2. On the other hand, if $\beta_3 < 0$, then the directions of the correlations between the ε_i^*s and the X_{2i}s will be reversed.

Readers may object at this point that we have not considered what could be regarded as the most serious specification error of all – including the 'wrong' variable instead of another 'correct' variable. However, this is easily seen to be simply a combination of the two cases already considered. For example, suppose the 'correct' specification is given by [5.11] but instead we assume

$$EY_i = \beta_1 + \beta_2 X_{2i} + \beta_4 X_{4i} \qquad i = 1, 2, 3, \dots, n \qquad [7.2]$$

In this case we have both included an irrelevant explanatory variable (X_4) and excluded a relevant one (X_3). It is the latter error, as we have seen, that is the more serious. Note, however, that if X_4 happened to be correlated with the 'correct' X_3, then the estimate of β_4 obtained in the OLS estimation of [7.2] may well be significantly different from zero in this case.

The second most common form of specification error is where the population regression equation is of non-linear form. Economic relationships are frequently of a non-linear kind so the standard equation [2.12] is often likely to be inappropriate. When it is suspected that the population regression equation is non-linear, there are a number of simple non-linear functions by which we may attempt to approximate it. For example, three such functions were suggested at the beginning of Chapter 4 – that is equations [4.1], [4.2] and [4.3].

When an attempt is made to estimate a non-linear population regression equation by a linear sample regression equation, we cannot expect the OLS estimators to be unbiased or consistent. It is possible using Taylor's theorem[2] to approximate any of equations [4.1] to [4.3] by an equation of the form

$$EY_i = \beta_1 + \beta_2 X_{2i} + \beta_3 X_{2i}^2 + \beta_4 X_{2i}^3 \dots \qquad i = 1, 2, 3, \dots, n \qquad [7.3]$$

where the β_js in equation (7.3) depend on the mean of X_2. Attempting to estimate non-linear population regression equations by linear estimating equations can therefore be seen to be analogous to omitting relevant explanatory variables. Moreover, the omitted variables (in this case X_2^2, X_2^3, X_2^4, etc.) are clearly correlated with X_2 and in this situation we already know that the OLS estimators lose the properties of unbiasedness and consistency.

Specification errors relating either to an inappropriate choice of explanatory variables or an incorrect functional form are best spotted by a careful

7.1a A positive time trend in the residuals.   **7.1b A cyclical pattern in the residuals.**

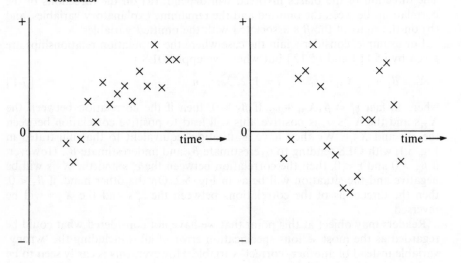

examination of the residuals obtained from fitted equations. For example, in Fig. 7.1a and 7.1b time is measured on the horizontal axis with positive residuals plotted above and negative residuals below this axis. In Fig. 7.1a the residuals exhibit a strong positive time trend, suggesting the omission of an explanatory variable or regressor itself containing a strong trend element. The residual plot in Fig. 7.1b again suggests an important variable has been omitted – this time one exhibiting a definite cyclical pattern.

Both of the above patterns of residuals would be reflected in a low value for the Durbin–Watson statistic so that this situation well illustrates the need for a visual examination of the residuals. Without such an examination, there would be a strong temptation to treat incorrectly the problem as one arising solely because of serial correlation in the disturbances. As we shall see later, low Durbin–Watson statistics frequently arise in practice because of '*dynamic mis-specifications*' of the population regression equation, when the omitted regressors consist of lagged values of the dependent variable.

An incorrectly specified form for the population regression equation is also best spotted by an examination of the residuals. For example, if we attempted to estimate a population relationship such as [4.2] (as illustrated in Fig. 4.1b), by a linear regression line then we are likely to observe a residual pattern as in Fig. 7.2.

In Fig. 7.2 a sequence of negative residuals is followed by a positive sequence and then another negative sequence. This suggests an incorrectly specified regression equation. If such sequences occur over time, they will be picked up by, for example, the Durbin–Watson statistic. Again, without a close visual examination of the residuals, the temptation will be to regard the problem as one arising solely out of serial correlation rather than resulting from a mis-specification.

The fact that low-values of the Durbin–Watson statistic are as likely to

7.2 Residual pattern suggestive of a mis-specification.

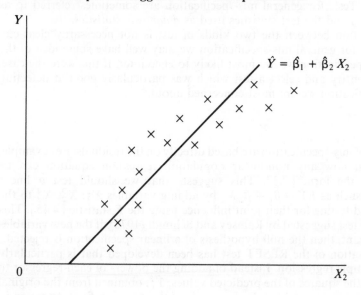

indicate specification errors as they are autocorrelation, has led in recent years to a reinterpretation of the Durbin–Watson test procedure. Nowadays this procedure is often regarded as a test of mis-specification rather than a test for autocorrelation. The other autocorrelation tests described in Chapter 5 – the portmanteau test, the h test and the LM test – are also frequently regarded in this way. Similarly, the various tests for heteroscedasticity can also be given a mis-specification test interpretation. The fact that the variance of the residuals from an estimated equation appears to vary in a systematic manner may be indicative not so much of heteroscedasticity but of a badly specified regression equation.

Tests of specification and mis-specification

At this point it is useful to distinguish between *tests of specification* and *tests of mis-specification*. Consider a case where we have a null hypothesis that the population regression line is correctly specified and the disturbance obeys all the classical assumptions. In a test of specification we have a very clear idea of what the alternative hypothesis is. For example, the alternative hypothesis might be that the disturbances follow a first-order autoregressive scheme. If we used the Durbin–Watson test under these circumstances, we would be carrying out a test of specification. We would in fact be trying to choose between two clear specifications. In a test of mis-specification, however, we have no clear view as to what the alternative hypothesis is. For example, we might be concerned both about various forms of autocorrelation and about the possibility of omitted variables. When using the Durbin–Watson statistic in these circumstances, we are really carrying out a test of mis-specification since we are unable to specify clearly what the problem is. Similarly, other tests for autocorrelation and for

143

heteroscedasticity can be regarded as tests either of specification or of mis-specification. Tests for general mis-specification are sometimes referred to as *diagnostic tests* and the test statistics used as *diagnostic statistics*.

The distinction between the two kinds of test is not necessarily clear-cut. When testing for general mis-specification we may well have some idea of the type of mis-specification we are most likely to encounter. If this were the case, we would then try and select a test which was particularly good at detecting the mis-specification we are most concerned about.[3]

Reset tests

Not all tests of mis-specification are based directly on the residuals. For example, we have seen how any non-linear population regression equation can be expressed in the form [7.3]. This suggests that we should test a linear specification such as $EY = \beta_1 + \beta_2 X_2$ by adding variables X_2^2, X_2^3, X_2^4 to the regression and testing for their joint influence using the F statistic [4.45]. This is the RESET test suggested by Ramsey and Schmidt (1976). If the new variables prove significant, then the null hypothesis of a linear specification is rejected.

A generalisation of the RESET test has been developed that is particularly useful in multiple regression. Instead of adding the powers of each regressor to an equation, the squares of the predicted values, $\hat{Y}_i^2$, obtained from the original estimated equation, are added. For example, if the equation first computed is

$$\hat{Y}_i = \hat{\beta}_1 + \hat{\beta}_2 X_{2i} + \hat{\beta}_3 X_{3i} \qquad i = 1, 2, 3, \ldots, n$$

then the RESET test proceeds by estimating

$$Y_i = \beta'_1 + \beta'_2 X_{2i} + \beta'_3 X_{3i} + \gamma \hat{Y}_i^2 + \varepsilon_i \qquad i = 1, 2, 3, \ldots, n$$

Clearly, $\hat{Y}^2$ depends on the squares of both X_2 and X_3 and also on their product. Further powers of $\hat{Y}$ can also be added to the equation. The joint significance of the $\hat{Y}$ variables can then be assessed by the usual F-test. Significance implies that we reject the null hypothesis of a linear specification. Notice that since we do not specify the precise form of non-linearity expected and the RESET statistic, even if significant, gives no indication, the test is a test of general mis-specification in the sense discussed earlier. We shall make use of the RESET test in the empirical exercises in the appendices to the applied chapters in this book.

7.2 Model selection

In the previous section we outlined the consequences of specification error. These consequences are so serious that it is clearly of the greatest importance that econometricians should select and estimate the appropriate or 'correct' model. It is to the problem of model selection that we now turn.

Two approaches to model selection

When estimating economic relationships the 'traditional' approach has been as follows. Economic theory or everyday *a priori* experience is used to specify the appropriate variables in the population regression equation. This equation

144

is then estimated, possibly by OLS, and assessed using the normal t-statistics, R^2 and the usual tests for autocorrelation and heteroscedasticity. The response to unsatisfactory test results is to modify or 'improve' the equation in some way. If R^2 is low, extra variables may be tried and those that prove to have significant coefficients added to the model. If the residuals from the equation appear autocorrelated, then a first-order autocorrelated scheme may be tacked on to the model, estimation now involving use of the Cochrane–Orcutt technique of section 5.2.2 Such a procedure is sometimes referred to as a *specific to general* methodology, since it normally results in the investigator eventually selecting a model that is more complicated or general than the one he or she started with.

The problem with the specific to general approach is that the investigator rarely totally abandons the original ideas and hypotheses embodied in the equation he started with. These are regarded as almost axiomatically correct and the search, often via various kinds of the data mining described in Chapter 1, is for 'results' which are consistent with them. Indeed it is perfectly possible for two different investigators, tackling the same problem and having available the same set of data, to come to totally different 'conclusions', purely because they began with different initial equations and preconceptions.

During the past 10 to 15 years, a school of British econometricians led by Professor D. F. Hendry has been pioneering a new approach to econometric research. One aspect of this is the conscious abandonment of the above, specific to general, line of investigation in favour of what is often described as a *general to specific* approach. This is best described by way of an example.

Suppose we are concerned with the behaviour of an economic variable Y. There are two main economic 'theories' regarding the determination of Y. One suggests that variable W is the main determining factor, while the other suggests that variable X has a big influence on Y. However, there may be some truth in both theories. Regardless of which theory best describes the real world, it is felt that variable Y may respond to W and/or X with a lag. This might be a short lag of up to one period or it might involve a partial adjustment process of the kind described by equation [6.36].

Adapting the general to specific approach to this problem, we might begin by estimating, from time series data an equation of the following form,

$$Y_t = \alpha + \beta_0 W_t + \beta_1 W_{t-1} + \gamma_0 X_t + \gamma_1 X_{t-1} + \delta Y_{t-1} + \varepsilon_t \qquad [7.4]$$

Notice, first, that the competing explanations of the behaviour of Y can all be written as special cases of equation [7.4]. For example

$$Y_t = \alpha + \beta_0 W_t + \delta Y_{t-1} + \varepsilon_t \qquad [7.5]$$

implies that W is the sole long run determinant of Y but that responses of Y to changes in W can be described by the partial adjustment model.

Alternatively,

$$Y_t = \alpha + \beta_0 W_t + \gamma_0 X_t + \gamma_1 X_{t-1} + \varepsilon_t \qquad [7.6]$$

implies that both W and X influence Y, the influence of changes in W being instantaneous, while X affects Y with a very short distributed lag. Clearly we could construct several other special cases of [7.4].

When equations such as [7.5] and [7.6] are special cases of a general equation such as [7.4], the special case models are said to be *nested* within the general

145

model. It is possible for a model to be nested within a second model which is itself nested within a third more general model. For example, considering equation [7.6], if the variables were in logarithms then theory might suggest that $\gamma_0 + \gamma_1 = 1$. This would imply that the long-run elasticity of Y with respect to X was unity. Imposing such a restriction on [7.6], in the manner of section 4.4, implies estimating

$$Y_t - X_{t-1} = \alpha + \beta_0 W_t + \gamma_0(X_t - X_{t-1}) \qquad [7.7]$$

Obviously [7.7] is nested within [7.6] which in turn is nested within [7.4]. Of course all models are not nested within one another. For example, equations [7.5] and [7.6] are *non-nested* models since neither is a special case of the other.

The general to specific approach to estimation, advocated by Professor Hendry, in this case would commence with the estimation of equation [7.4]. In general, the initial equation estimated should, if possible, have nested within it as special cases *all* the competing theories that require consideration. The Hendry approach then involves a *simplification search* whereby, provided the F-tests for restrictions described in section 4.4 are satisfied, we move from the general equation [7.4] to one of the many specific special cases of which equations [7.5] to [7.7] are but three possibilities. The estimated general equation may well itself suggest suitable simplifications. For example, estimates of the coefficients γ_0 and γ_1 in equation [7.4] may prove insignificantly different from zero, suggesting that X_t and X_{t-1} should be omitted from the model. Alternatively, the estimate of δ might have an incorrect negative sign suggesting that Y_{t-1} should be dropped. Another possibility is that two estimated coefficients might sum to something very close to unity, suggesting a model of the type [7.7].

Notice that in this so-called *testing down* procedure, F-tests such as [4.45] can be employed both to test the effect of omitting one or more variables from an equation and to test linear restrictions of the kind implied by equation [7.7]. However, if the restriction to be tested is non-linear, then the Wald or *LM* statistics of Chapter 4 can be used.

The testing down procedure should ideally involve a systematic and sequential testing procedure, proceeding step by step from the general model to simpler and simpler special cases. The procedure only ends when the restrictions implied by a particular model are rejected by the data. For example, if the restrictions on the general model [7.4] implied by equation [7.6], that is $\beta_1 = \delta = 0$, are rejected by the data, then we would *not* proceed to estimate equation [7.7] and test the restriction $\gamma_0 + \gamma_1 = 1$. To do so under such circumstances would involve a serious specification error because, if either β_1 or δ are non-zero, then we would be omitting a relevant variable from the estimating equation. However, if the restrictions implied by [7.6] were found to be consistent with the data, then we would proceed to estimate equation [7.7].

Unfortunately, some of the special cases of a general model will inevitably be non-nested and we are likely to be faced with having to make a choice between equations such as [7.5] and [7.6]. There is a problem in that none of the tests described in Chapter 4 can be used for discriminating between non-nested hypotheses.

A choice between non-nested models can either be made on the basis of goodness of fit or by adopting a hypothesis testing approach. If choice is made on a goodness of fit basis, then some allowance has to be made for the number of parameters estimated. It is clearly easier to obtain a good fit with an equation containing, for example, ten regressors rather than two regressors. A number of measures have been suggested, the simplest being the $\bar{R}^2$ statistic given by [2.40].[4]

If an hypothesis testing approach is adopted, one possibility is to nest the competing models in a suitable artificial general model. This may be less general than the equation first estimated. For example, [7.5] and [7.6] could be nested in

$$Y_t = \alpha + \beta_0 W_t + \gamma_0 X_t + \gamma_1 X_{t-1} + \delta Y_{t-1} + \varepsilon_t$$

which is a special case of [7.4]. Equations such as [7.5] and [7.6] may then be F-tested against the artificial model in the usual way. Such tests are known as encompassing F-tests and have been further developed by Mizon and Richard (1986). For examples of other non-nested tests see, for example, McAleer and Peseran (1986).

The problem with the hypothesis testing approach is that it can result either in both non-nested models proving to be consistent with the data, or both models being rejected by the data. If the former result is obtained, this simply means that we have insufficient information to choose between the two models. If both models are rejected then we have to revert to the general model from which they were obtained.

Advantages of the Hendry approach

A major advantage of the general to specific methodology is that, in the terminology of the last section, specification errors are hopefully limited to those occurring because of the inclusion of irrelevant variables rather than the omission of relevant ones. Recall that omitted variable error is the more serious problem because it leads to bias and inconsistency. Provided the initial general equation covers all competing theories to be considered, there should be no omitted variable bias in the estimators. Moreover, the problem of a lack of efficiency in estimators, arising from the inclusion of irrelevant explanatory variables, becomes less and less serious as the testing down process proceeds and such variables are gradually dropped from the equation.

In contrast, an investigator following the specific to general approach is almost certain to encounter omitted variable bias early on in his research and it is possible that this will lead to him making invalid generalisations of his original equation. For example, if omission of a relevant variable leads to a low Durbin–Watson statistic, then this can lead to a quite inappropriate use of the Cochrane–Orcutt iterative procedure.

It may seem, when models or theories differ only in terms of the variable or variables to be included in an equation, that the general to specific approach is so obviously the correct one that no sensible investigator would consider proceeding any differently. However, the fact remains that much applied econometric work has been and is carried out using the specific to general procedure. This is possibly because many so-called researchers have been concerned, to quote Gilbert (1986), merely to 'illustrate' the theories that they believe independently and are determined to support, come what may. It is also the case that the Hendry methodology is especially useful for choosing not so much between different theories but between models, all consistent with the same theory, but differing empirically in their lag structure. We shall return to this point later.

While the Hendry methodology is nowadays frequently adopted by British and other econometricians, it should not be thought that it is the only modern approach to applied work. For example E. E. Leamer (1978 and 1983) is equally scathing about the unrecognised influence of prior belief on much applied econometric work. However, his prescription is somewhat different from Hendry's. Leamer regards as inevitable the fact that an investigator's prior beliefs will tend to influence his research strategy and maintains that this should be explicitly recognised. In the Leamer methodology a researcher should identify the parameters of interest early in his study. The sensitivity of conclusions regarding these parameters to alternative specifications of an estimating equation should then be made clear. For example, is the statistical significance of the coefficient on a variable affected by including other variables in the equation or is it relatively robust to their inclusion? Leamer regards what he terms the 'fragility' of inferences about parameters as a matter that should be rigorously investigated in any research study.

A third approach, which also has its advocates is that of C. Sims (see, for example, 1980). In the Sims methodology the data is almost all-important and can be allowed to determine even causality, sometimes in the face of recognised theory. However, regardless of the attractions of the Leamer and Sims approaches, the fact remains that studies adopting the Hendry approach are far more common, particularly in the UK, than research work using either of the other methodologies.

The criteria for accepting models

Even if an investigator adopts the general to specific testing down procedure just outlined, it is still likely that he will eventually face a choice between competing models that cannot be made on the basis of any of the tests described above. In this subsection, we list some of the criteria that a satisfactory model should satisfy. Much of the material in this subsection is based on Hendry and Richard (1983).

Some of the criteria for a satisfactory model are straightforward and relatively obvious. For example, a model should be *consistent with theory* or at least with one of any competing theories. It would hardly be satisfactory if our preferred model of consumer behaviour implied a long-run average propensity to consume of 1.6! Indeed statistical criteria might conflict with common sense here. The restrictions imposed to obtain a consumer expenditure equation with an implied long run APC of 1.6 might even be consistent with the data on the usual F-tests. However, we would still reject such a model because of its inherent implausibility.

Another fairly obvious criteria is that of *data admissibility*. It should not be possible for models to predict values for variables which are inadmissible. For example, if the dependent variable is the price of bread then we have no interest in a model that is capable of predicting negative values of this price when the explanatory variables are given plausible values.

One highly important criterion that a model should satisfy is what is termed *data coherency*. Clearly a model should be able to explain adequately existing data. Data coherency is the goodness of fit criterion. However, there is more to goodness of fit in this context than simply obtaining high values of measures such as R^2. If a model is an adequate representation of the underlying data generating process, then the residuals from fitted versions of the model should be entirely random in the sense that they are totally unpredictable. For example, the residuals should not be autocorrelated since this would imply that there was some systematic part of reality that was not adequately represented by the model.

The real world is a complex and changing place and we cannot expect our models to provide an exact description of it. The aim of model building is to reproduce the main systematic parts of the process we wish to represent. On Hendry's view a model cannot have achieved this if the residuals it generates are non-random. Recall from the first section of this chapter, for example, that a clear sign of an omitted variable is often autocorrelated residuals which can be detected from the Durbin–Watson statistic.

The importance given to data coherency means that preferred models that arise out of the testing down process must always be rigorously checked for mis-specification. As we have seen many of the procedures, introduced in Chapter 5 as tests for breakdowns in the classical assumptions, can be re-interpreted as tests of mis-specification. The main difference here is that, whereas in Chapter 5 we have clear alternative hypotheses in mind when we perform the tests, now the alternative hypothesis is no longer precisely specified. For example, a low d-statistic may lead us to reject the null hypothesis of a correctly specified model but we might be unclear whether this is because of an omitted variable or an incorrect functional form.

Although ideally an investigator should take account of all relevant hypotheses when formulating his most general equation, he may well be unaware of certain possibilities or only become aware of them during the testing down process. Tests of mis-specification are therefore appropriate right from the outset of the investigation and should normally be carried out side by side with the F-tests, etc., used in the testing down process.

A fourth requirement for a satisfactory model is *parsimony*. This relates to a principle first put forward by the fourteenth-century philosopher, William of Occam. 'Occam's Razor' states that the simple explanation should always be preferred to the complex. In an econometric context this means that, for example, if two equations have similar explanatory power (as measured maybe by R^2), but one contains five explanatory variables and the other only two, then we should prefer the latter equation. As was pointed out earlier, reality is complex and we seek to represent in our models only its most relevant and important aspects. We lose little if unimportant aspects are consigned to the disturbance term in our models. Our models, then, should contain as few explicit variables as possible. To quote Milton Friedman (1953) – 'A hypothesis is important if it explains much by little'.

A practical advantage of parsimony is that it means we are unlikely to run up against the degrees of freedom problems, discussed at the beginning of section 5.3. The number of observations available in time series is rarely large, so that a lack of parsimony frequently results in imprecise estimation procedures.

Ideally a preferred model should also *encompass* all or at least most of the models presented by previous researchers in the field. One model is said to encompass another if it can explain all the results of that other model. A satisfactory model must therefore not only explain existing data but also be able to explain why alternative models can also do so. Moreover, if a model encompasses other models, it should be able to explain any different conclusions that previous researchers using different models may have come to.

Note that the criterion of encompassing need not conflict with that of parsimony. One model may be simpler than another and yet encompass it. Indeed, if new models are not both parsimonious and encompassing, then the progress of research in any field becomes totally haphazard and the systematic advancement of knowledge impossible.

Another requirement for satisfactory models listed by Hendry and Richard is that of *parameter constancy*. A model is of little use if it cannot forecast adequately *outside the sample period* used to estimate it. For a model to do this its parameters must obviously remain constant over time. To check parameter constancy, it is now becoming customary for investigators to estimate their models using only the earlier observations from their data and to 'save' maybe the last few observations for 'post-sample' tests. For example, the second of the Chow tests described in section 4.3 is frequently used for this purpose.

When the nature of the testing down procedure described earlier is reflected upon, the need for post-sample testing of a preferred model becomes even more apparent. If the initial equation estimated is very general and, consequently, the testing down procedure lengthy, then any preferred model eventually arrived at must inevitably be partly the result of a data mining process akin to that described in Chapter 1. The data has been used more to construct the model than to test it. Since this is almost always the case, it becomes imperative to test a model using *data that was not available when it was constructed.*

We have stressed the words 'not available when it was constructed' in the last paragraph because this has relevance for the use of the Chow test mentioned above when the last few observations of the data set have been 'saved'. Frequently the last few observations are not only available when the preferred model is selected but will have been used in its selection! If the first model derived from the testing down process fails the Chow test for the last few observations then it is fairly certain that the investigator will try another slightly different model. Moreover, he will continue to try until, unless he is unlucky, he finds a model which passes the Chow test and is otherwise satisfactory! Consequently, many preferred models are, as already argued, selected by a process at least akin to data mining. Obviously it is desirable that models should exhibit parameter constancy over the sample period and pass the Chow test. But true 'post-sample' testing must involve confronting a model with an entirely new set of data.

A final criterion for a satisfactory model is that the explanatory variables should be *exogenous* – that is they should not be contemporaneously correlated with the disturbance in the equation estimated. As we shall see in the next chapter, a major cause of contemporaneous correlation is the simultaneity of many economic relationships. Regressors may be *endogenous* rather than exogenous – that is they and the dependent variable may be jointly determined by the simultaneous system in which our equation is embedded.

Even if the testing down process of the general to specific approach proves 'successful' and a model is arrived at that satisfies all the above criteria, one must guard against regarding it as the 'correct' model. The models we select or build cannot be a perfect representation of a complex reality and are inevitably a simplification in some sense. Moreover, reality can change over time. Hence, it may always become necessary to improve or adapt our models. In Hendry's words a preferred model is merely a *tentatively adequate conditional data characterisation.* Such a model is only *congruent* with that data which is at present available. New data may well mean that we will have to revise and improve the model.

7.3 Error-correction models

The error-correction model (ECM) was first applied in economics by Sargan (1964) but in more recent years has been inextricably associated with the Hendry approach to econometrics described in previous sections of this chapter. As we shall see the ECM has a number of advantages, one of which is that it goes some way towards providing an answer to a problem that has plagued economists since the beginning of the century – the problem of *spurious* correlation.

Spurious correlation

One of the criteria most commonly used to assess the adequacy or otherwise of estimated equations or models is that of goodness-of-fit – as measured by, for example, the coefficient of multiple determination, R^2, or standard t-ratios. However, as we stressed in earlier chapters, it must always be remembered that such measures as R^2 do not necessarily reflect any *causal* relationship between dependent and explanatory variables. Correlations can be at least partly *spurious*, particularly when the variables involved exhibit consistent trends, either upwards or downwards, over time. For example, many macroeconomic variables, such as the general price level or the level of national output in most developed economies, have moved consistently upwards during the greater part of the postwar era. In addition, it is not always realised by beginners in econometrics that it is unnecessary for two variables to be trending in the same direction for a high but possibly spurious correlation to exist between them. Two variables, one trending strongly upwards and the other downwards, are bound to be highly correlated.

Since much econometric work is concerned with 'time series' data, it is therefore wise not to be too impressed (as many beginners tend to be) with high values of R^2. R^2s for time series regression equations are typically very high compared with those obtained from 'cross-sectional' data for which the trending problem does not arise. For example, as we shall see in Chapter 10, it is a simple matter to obtain R^2s as high as 0.98 for consumption functions estimated from time series data, but a large proportion of this goodness of fit is entirely spurious.

Until recent years far too little attention was paid by applied econometricians to the spurious correlation problem. However, as we have seen, 'classical' regression techniques, such as those described in Chapter 2, *are invalid when applied to stochastic time series variables that exhibit the trends mentioned above.* 'Classical' statistical inference in general was specifically designed for variables which are stationary in the sense that their mean, variance and covariances remain constant over time. Clearly if a variable is trending then its mean, and very possibly its variance, will change over time.

In the classical regression models of Chapter 2 these problems did not arise

151

given the assumptions made. The explanatory variables were non-stochastic – fixed by the investigator in a controlled experiment which could ensure non-trending regressors. The dependent variable was stochastic but it derived its stochastic nature from a disturbance which was assumed to have zero mean, constant variance and zero covariances. The dependent variable then, though stochastic, obeyed all the assumptions necessary for stationarity.

Controlled experiments, however, are not possible in economics. Variables are stochastic and much data consists of non-stationary time series. Consequently, we cannot rely on the standard regression procedures. As we have seen, if variables are non-stationary, *the OLS estimators have sampling distributions with properties very different from those described in Chapter 2*, and regression coefficients tend to appear spuriously significant.

A popular past method of attempting to overcome the problem of spurious correlation has been to estimate relationships between the rates of change of variables rather than between their absolute levels. The effect of looking at the rate of change in a variable is typically to remove any trend element. That is, many non-stationary economic time series become stationary when they are first-differenced. For example, while output and prices in most post-war economies have trended steadily upwards, this is not generally true of rates of growth in output or of inflation rates. Unfortunately, when attention is concentrated on relationships between rates of change, there is a real danger that valuable information on the long-run relationship between the levels of the variables will be lost. For example, if

$$Y_t = \beta_0 + \beta_1 X_{1t} + \beta_2 X_{2t} + \varepsilon_t \qquad [7.8]$$

where ε_t is a disturbance, then

$$Y_t - Y_{t-1} = \beta_1(X_{1t} - X_{1t-1}) + \beta_2(X_{2t} - X_{2t-1}) + u_t \qquad [7.9]$$

where $u_t = \varepsilon_t - \varepsilon_{t-1}$. If we estimate [7.9] instead of [7.8], we can obtain no information about β_0. Equation [7.9] focuses purely on the short-run relationship between Y and X and, hence, is likely to provide poor forecasts for even a few periods ahead if a long-run relationship exists but is ignored.

There is a further problem with the first-differenced equation [7.9]. If a relationship such as [7.8] really exists and if its disturbance ε_t is non-autocorrelated, then the disturbance u_t in equation [7.9] is of simple moving average form and hence will be autocorrelated.

First differencing, then, is an unsatisfactory method of dealing with a spurious correlation problem. A major advantage of error-correction models is that they result in equations with first-differenced and hence stationary dependent variables but avoid the problems just discussed. In particular, unlike simple first-differenced equations they do not fail to make use of any long-run information in the data.

A simple ECM

Suppose that when in 'equilibrium' or 'steady state' two variables bear the following relationship to each other:

$$Y_t = KX_t^{\gamma_2}, \qquad \gamma_2 = \text{constant}, K = \text{constant} \qquad [7.10]$$

For example Y might be consumer expenditure and X the disposable income of consumers. Letting lower case letters denote natural logarithms of variables and $\gamma_1 = \log K$ we can rewrite [7.10] as

$$y_t = \gamma_1 + \gamma_2 x_t \qquad\qquad\qquad [7.11]$$

If Y and X were at all times in equilibrium then clearly $y_t - \gamma_1 - \gamma_2 x_t = 0$. However there are many times when Y will not be at its equilibrium value relative to X and, at such times, the quantity $y_t - \gamma_1 - \gamma_2 x_t$ will be non-zero and will measure the 'extent of disequilibrium' between X and Y. Quantities such as $y_t - \gamma_1 - \gamma_2 x_t$ are therefore known as *disequilibrium errors*.

Since Y and X are not always in equilibrium we cannot observe the *long-run* relationship [7.10] directly. All we can observe is a disequilibrium relationship involving lagged values of Y and X, which reduces to [7.10] whenever equilibrium happens to occur. We denote this disequilibrium relationship by

$$y_t = \beta_0 + \beta_1 x_t + \beta_2 x_{t-1} + \alpha y_{t-1} + u_t \qquad 0 < \alpha < 1 \qquad [7.12]$$

where u_t is a disturbance

The problem with [7.12] is that it is an equation in the levels of variables that are likely to be non-stationary. However [7.12] can be re-arranged and *reparameterised* as follows. Subtracting y_{t-1} from either side yields

$$\Delta y_t = \beta_0 + \beta_1 x_t + \beta_2 x_{t-1} - (1 - \alpha)y_{t-1} + u_t$$

or

$$\Delta y_t = \beta_0 + \beta_1 \Delta x_t + (\beta_1 + \beta_2)x_{t-1} - (1 - \alpha)y_{t-1} + u_t \qquad [7.13]$$

where $\Delta y_t = y_t - y_{t-1}$ and $\Delta x_t = x_t - x_{t-1}$.

We can reparameterise [7.13] as

$$\Delta y_t = \beta_0 + \beta_1 \Delta x_t - (1 - \alpha)[y_{t-1} - \gamma_2 x_{t-1}] + u_t \qquad [7.14]$$

where the new parameter $\gamma_2 = (\beta_1 + \beta_2)/(1 - \alpha)$. Equation [7.14] can be further reparameterised as

$$\Delta y_t = \beta_1 \Delta x_t - (1 - \alpha)[y_{t-1} - \gamma_1 - \gamma_2 x_{t-1}] + u_t \qquad [7.15]$$

where $\gamma_1 = \beta_0/1 - \alpha$.

Equation [7.15] is no more than another way of writing the disequilibrium relationship [7.12]. However it can be given a very appealing interpretation. Equation [7.15] can be regarded as stating that changes in y depend on changes in x and on the term in square brackets which is *the disequilibrium error from the previous period*. This makes sound sense since it implies that the lower (higher) is Y compared with its equilibrium value relative to X, the greater (smaller) will be the immediate rise in Y. The value of Y is being corrected for the previous disequilibrium error. Hence the term error correction model. Although [7.15] can be derived from [7.12] without referring to the long-run relationship [7.11], it clearly makes sense to give it an error correction interpretation and regard the new parameters γ_1 and γ_2 as parameters in a long-run relationship such as [7.11]. Notice that α and hence $1 - \alpha$ determine the extent to which the disequilibrium in period $t - 1$ is 'made up for' in period t. Since $0 < \alpha < 1$, only part of this disequilibrium is made up for in period t, causing a different Δy_t than would otherwise occur.

ECMs such as [7.15] are not always of logarithmic form but, when they are, note that

$$\Delta y_t = y_t - y_{t-1} = \log Y_t - \log Y_{t-1} = \log \frac{Y_t}{Y_{t-1}} \approx \frac{Y_t - Y_{t-1}}{Y_{t-1}} \qquad [7.16]$$

The approximation in [7.16] will hold provided growth rates are small so that $Y_t \approx Y_{t-1}$. Hence Δy_t is the *proportionate* change in Y and, similarly Δx_t is the proportionate change in X.

An interesting property of ECMs such as [7.15] is that they imply that the parameter γ_1 in the equilibrium relationship [7.11] depends on long-term growth rates. Suppose X grows at a constant long-run proportionate rate g. That is $\Delta x_t = g$ or

$$x_t = g + x_{t-1} \qquad [7.17]$$

Substituting [7.17] into [7.11] we have

$$y_t = \gamma_1 + \gamma_2 g + \gamma_2 x_{t-1} = \gamma_2 g + y_{t-1} \qquad [7.18]$$

so that

$$\Delta y_t = \gamma_2 g \qquad [7.19]$$

Hence, if X grows at the constant long-run rate g, then Y must grow at the long-run rate $\gamma_2 g$ where, from [7.10] we see that γ_2 is the elasticity of Y with respect to X.

Substituting $\Delta x_t = g$ and $\Delta y_t = \gamma_2 g$ in [7.14] now yields, disregarding the disturbance,

$$\gamma_2 g = \beta_0 + \beta_1 g - (1 - \alpha)[y_t - \gamma_2 g - \gamma_2 x_t + \gamma_2 g] \qquad [7.20]$$

Solving [7.20] for y_t gives the long-term relationship between y_t and x_t as

$$y_t = \frac{\beta_0 - g(\gamma_2 - \beta_1)}{1 - \alpha} + \gamma_2 x_t = \frac{\beta_0 - g(\beta_2 + \gamma_2 \alpha)}{1 - \alpha} + \gamma_2 x_t \qquad [7.21]$$

(using $\gamma_2 = (\beta_1 + \beta_2)/(1 - \alpha)$).

Comparing [7.21] with [7.11] we see that the error correction model implies

$$\gamma_1 = \frac{\beta_0 - g(\beta_2 + \gamma_2 \alpha)}{1 - \alpha} \qquad [7.22]$$

Hence, a change in the long-run growth rate g leads to a change in γ_1 and hence K in equation (7.10).[5] Notice that if the long-run elasticity $\gamma_2 = 1$ in equation [7.10] then $K = Y/Z$ so that, in these circumstances, a change in the growth rate leads to a change in the long-run equilibrium Y/X ratio.

Advantages of the ECM formulation

We have seen that the standard regression techniques are invalid when applied to non-stationary variables. Since many economic variables exhibit long-run trend movements and only become stationary after first-differencing, this suggests that we apply regression techniques not to the absolute levels of variables but to their first differences. The error-correction model [7.15] clearly involves the first differenced variables Δy_t and Δx_t and moreover, as we shall

154

see later, provided the model has been correctly specified, the disequilibrium error in square brackets will also be stationary. An ECM model *may therefore be estimated by standard classical regression techniques, provided the sample is large*. For example, since the dependent variable in [7.15] is Δy_t and not the typically trending y_t, we can safely refer to such measures as R^2 without being concerned about spurious correlation problems.

ECMs also avoid the problems normally associated with simple models in first differences outlined below equation [7.9]. Since the disequilibrium error term in [7.15] involves x_{t-1} and y_{t-1}, an ECM formulation makes use of any long-run information about the levels of variables that is contained in the data. Furthermore, unlike in equation [7.9], there is no reason to expect the disturbance term in an equation such as [7.15] to be autocorrelated. If the disturbance in [7.12] is non-autocorrelated, then it will also appear as such in equation [7.15].

An ECM such as [7.15] also involves a parameterisation which clearly distinguishes between long-run and short-run effects. The parameters γ_1 and γ_2, which appear in the disequilibrium error term, are the long-run parameters that appear in equation [7.11]. The coefficient of Δx_t, β_1, however, is clearly a short-run parameter measuring the immediate impact effect on y of a change in x. Similarly, as we have seen, α is a short-run parameter. Most economic theories involve hypotheses or predictions about the long-run relationship between values but have little or nothing to say about the short-run dynamics of models. The clear separation between long- and short-run parameters in an ECM therefore makes it an excellent vehicle for either assessing the validity of the long-run implications of theory or of incorporating them into the estimation process.

Another important advantage of the ECM is that it fits in well with the Hendry-type general-to-specific methodology described earlier. Recall that equation [7.15] can be obtained from [7.12] simply by reparameterisation. Similarly, consider the general second order version of [7.12]

$$y_t = \beta_0 + \beta_1 x_t + \beta_2 x_{t-1} + \beta_3 x_{t-2} + \alpha_1 y_{t-1} + \alpha_2 y_{t-2} + u_t \qquad [7.23]$$

Simple rearrangement of [7.23] yields

$$\Delta y_t = \beta_0 + (\alpha_1 - 1)\Delta y_{t-1} + \beta_1 \Delta x_t + (\beta_1 + \beta_2)\Delta x_{t-1} - (1 - \alpha_1 - \alpha_2)y_{t-2}$$
$$+ (\beta_1 + \beta_2 + \beta_3)x_{t-2} + u_t \qquad [7.24]$$

or, reparameterising,

$$\Delta y_t = (\alpha_1 - 1)\Delta y_{t-1} + \beta_1 \Delta x_t + (\beta_1 + \beta_2)\Delta x_{t-1}$$
$$- (1 - \alpha_1 - \alpha_2)[y_{t-2} - \gamma_1 - \gamma_2 x_{t-2}] + u_t \qquad [7.25]$$

where

$$\gamma_2 = (\beta_1 + \beta_2 + \beta_3)/(1 - \alpha_1 - \alpha_2) \quad \text{and} \quad \gamma_1 = \beta_0/(1 - \alpha_1 - \alpha_2) \quad [7.26]$$

Clearly [7.25] is an ECM since the term in square brackets is the disequilibrium error from two periods before. In fact, any mth order general distributed lag of the form

$$y_t = \beta_0 + \sum_{i=1}^{m+1} \beta_i x_{t-i+1} + \sum_{i=1}^{m} \alpha_i y_{t-i} + u_t \qquad [7.27]$$

can, by suitable reparameterisation, be given an ECM representation akin to equations [7.15] or [7.25].

The point is, however, that in the general to specific methodology investigators are permitted to eliminate, without concern, any of the differenced variables in for example [7.25], if this is justified by the F-testing procedure described in section [7.2]. However, elimination of any of the lagged levels variables contained in the dis-equilibrium error term is a more serious matter, since this effects the implied long-run relationship and may be a violation of theory. Notice that since the differenced variables simply reflect short-run dynamics, about which theory typically has nothing to say, their elimination does not involve such violations. Eliminating one of the differenced variables in [7.25] merely implies the imposition of a restriction on equation [7.23]. For example, omitting Δx_{t-1} would imply imposing the restriction $\beta_1 + \beta_2 = 0$ on [7.23].

Equation [7.25] is not the only ECM that can be obtained from [7.23]. Clearly if we impose the restrictions $\beta_3 = \alpha_2 = 0$ then [7.23] becomes [7.12] which is equivalent to the ECM [7.15]. This illustrates the point that any given general equation such as [7.27] will have more than one ECM nested within it as special cases. In the Hendry methodology the purpose of the testing down procedure could be regarded as determining which ECM best describes the data.

Since γ_1 and γ_2 are unknown, equation [7.25] cannot be estimated as it stands. One possibility is to begin by estimating equation [7.24] and use [7.26] to obtain estimates of γ_1 and γ_2. However, a further useful reparameterisation is possible. It is possible to rewrite the Δx_t and Δx_{t-1} terms in [7.24] as

$$\beta_1 \Delta x_t + (\beta_1 + \beta_2)\Delta x_{t-1} = (2\beta_1 + \beta_2)\Delta x_t - (\beta_1 + \beta_2)\Delta^2 x_t$$

where $\Delta^2 x_t = \Delta x_t - \Delta x_{t-1}$. Hence the variable Δx_{t-1} can be replaced by $\Delta^2 x_t$ in the estimation of [7.24]. We merely place a different interpretation on estimated coefficients. The advantage of this change is that while Δx_t and Δx_{t-1} might be highly correlated with some time series this is unlikely to be the case for Δx_t and $\Delta^2 x_t$.

This leads us to another major and valid advantage claimed by Hendry for an ECM representation of equations such as [7.23]. Clearly with typical time-series data the variables in [7.23] are likely to be highly correlated regardless of whether y_t and x_t are stationary or not. In estimating [7.23] we will face the usual consequence of multicollinearity – large standard errors. A testing down process beginning with [7.23] is therefore likely to be handicapped by this fact. However, the variables in the equivalent ECM representation will normally be far less highly correlated. In fact they tend to be almost *orthogonal* – that is, correlations between them are often close to zero. For example, for typical time series data the correlation between x_{t-1} and Δx_t is very low, as is the correlation between Δx_t and $\Delta^2 x_t$. This facilitates the testing down procedure because, with low standard errors, the normal t-statistics in an estimated ECM will provide a good guide to which differenced variables should be eliminated. Thus it becomes easier to arrive at a sufficiently parsimonious final preferred equation.

It should be clear from the above that error correction models have considerable advantages over the more traditional type of econometric model. However, there are still several important questions that we need to answer. For example, how can we be certain that the Hendry testing down procedure will lead us to an ECM? ECMs are based on an implied long-run relationship

156

between variables. But how can we be sure that such a long-run relationship exists? Even if it does, are we sure that the variables in the ECM we are estimating are stationary? We know that standard regression techniques cannot be applied to non-stationary variables. The next section is devoted to answering such questions.

7.4 Stationarity

We have used the term 'stationary' in an intuitive sense on a number of occasions in this chapter and at this point it is appropriate to give a more precise definition. Consider the following equations all giving different explanations of the determination of a random or stochastic variable Y.

$$Y_t = \varphi_1 Y_{t-1} + \varphi_2 Y_{t-2} + \cdots + \varphi_p Y_{t-p} + \varepsilon_t \qquad [7.28]$$

$$Y_t = \varepsilon_t + \theta_1 \varepsilon_{t-1} + \theta_2 \varepsilon_{t-2} + \cdots + \theta_q \varepsilon_{t-q} \qquad [7.29]$$

$$Y_t = \varphi_1 Y_{t-1} + \varphi_2 Y_{t-2} + \cdots + \varphi_p Y_{t-p} + \varepsilon_t + \theta_1 \varepsilon_{t-1} + \cdots + \theta_q \varepsilon_{t-q} \qquad [7.30]$$

where ε_t is a random disturbance with the properties $E\varepsilon_t = 0$, var $\varepsilon_t =$ constant for all t and covar$(\varepsilon_t, \varepsilon_s) = 0$ for all $t \neq s$. In this context ε_t is often referred to as a 'white noise' process.

Equations [7.28] to [7.30] are all examples of random or *stochastic processes* in that Y_t is determined in each case by the random disturbance ε_t, past values of itself and/or past values of ε_t. Equation [7.28] is known as an *autoregressive* (*AR*) *process* of order p. The simplest version of such a scheme is the first-order process

$$Y_t = \varphi Y_{t-1} + \varepsilon_t \qquad [7.31]$$

Equation [7.29] is known a *moving average (MA) process* of order q, the simplest version of which is the first-order process

$$Y_t = \varepsilon_t + \theta \varepsilon_{t-1} \qquad [7.32]$$

We have already encountered stochastic processes such as [7.31] and [7.32]. In our discussion of autocorrelation in section 5.2.2, we suggested that the disturbance in a regression equation might follow the scheme [5.24]. This is clearly analogous to [7.31]. In the adaptive expectations model of section 6.2, the disturbance in the final estimating equation [6.20] was

$$v_t = \varepsilon_t - (1 - \lambda)\varepsilon_{t-1}$$

This is clearly an MA process of order 1 with θ in [7.32] equal to $-(1 - \lambda)$.

Equation [7.30] is a mixture of autoregressive and moving average elements and is therefore referred to as an *autoregressive-moving average (ARMA) process* of order (p, q). For example

$$Y_t = \varphi_1 Y_{t-1} + \varepsilon_t + \theta_1 \varepsilon_{t-1} + \theta_2 \varepsilon_{t-2} \qquad [7.33]$$

is an ARMA process of order $(1, 2)$.

A stochastic process is said to be *stationary* if

1. $EY_t =$ constant for all t [7.34]
2. Var $Y_t =$ constant for all t [7.35]
3. Covar$(Y_t, Y_{t+s}) =$ constant for all $t \neq s$ [7.36]

Equations [7.34] and [7.35] simply imply that the mean and variance of Y_t remain constant over time. Equation [7.36] requires that the covariance and hence correlation between any two values of Y taken from different time periods depends only on the *difference apart in time* between the two values. That is, for example, although $\text{cov}(Y_t, Y_{t-3})$ may differ from $\text{cov}(Y_t, Y_{t-6})$ both these covariances remain constant over time. Hence, for example, $\text{cov}(Y_{10}, Y_{13})$ differs from $\text{cov}(Y_{10}, Y_{16})$ but is the same as $\text{cov}(Y_{11}, Y_{14})$, $\text{cov}(Y_{12}, Y_{15})$, $\text{cov}(Y_{13}, Y_{16})$, etc, etc.

Strictly speaking, the above is a definition of what is known as *weak* stationarity. However, since in this book we need not distinguish between different types of stationarity, we shall refer to any process or variable that satisfies the above definition as stationary.

Notice that a stationary time series as defined above is not necessarily the same as what, in everyday language, might be termed a non-trending series. If [7.34] were true but [7.35] and [7.36] did not hold, a time series would be non-stationary in the statistical sense but would be unlikely to display a regular upward or downward trend.

Testing for stationarity

Since standard regression analysis requires that data series be stationary, it is obviously important that we test this requirement before we estimate, for example, an ECM. It can in fact be shown that all MA processes such as [7.29] are stationary. However, this is not necessarily the case with AR processes.

One way of determining whether an AR process is stationary is to treat [7.28] as a pth order difference equation and examine the time path of Y for stability in the manner of section [6.4]. The characteristic equation is again given by [6.67] so that the time path of Y is stable provided that the roots of [6.67] are *less* than unity in absolute value. The condition for stationarity in [7.28] is identical to that just obtained for stability. Stability in the time path of Y implies stationarity.

In this chapter it will prove useful if we consider a rather different condition for stationarity which is equally valid. Using the lag operator notation introduced in Chapter 6, we can rewrite [7.28] as

$$(1 - \varphi_1 L - \varphi_2 L^2 - \varphi_3 L^3 - \cdots - \varphi_p L^{t-p}) Y_t = \varepsilon_t \qquad [7.37]$$

Now consider the equation

$$1 - \varphi_1 L - \varphi_2 L^2 - \varphi_3 L^3 - \cdots - \varphi_p L^{t-p} = 0 \qquad [7.38]$$

For given values of the φs [7.38] is an equation in the lag operator L. It can be shown that the associated AR process [7.28] will be stationary if and only if *all* the roots of [7.38] are *greater* than unity in absolute value. For example, if just one root lies between 1 and -1 or is equal to 1 or -1, the process will be non-stationary.

Consider for example the first-order AR process [7.31]. This can be written as

$$(1 - \varphi L) Y_t = \varepsilon_t \qquad [7.39]$$

and will therefore be stationary if the root of $1 - \varphi L = 0$ is greater than unity in absolute value. The root is clearly $L = 1/\varphi$. Hence [7.31] will be stationary provided $-1 < \varphi < 1$.[6]

As a further example, consider the second-order AR process

$$Y_t = 2.8Y_{t-1} - 1.6Y_{t-2} + \varepsilon_t \tag{7.40}$$

To check [7.40] for stationarity we therefore have to solve

$$1 - 2.8L + 1.6L^2 = 0 \tag{7.41}$$

Factorising yields

$$(1 - 0.8L)(1 - 2L) = 0 \tag{7.42}$$

Hence the roots are $L = 1.25$ and $L = 0.5$. Since one of these roots is less than unity the process [7.40] is not stationary.

The above procedure would be relatively straightforward if we knew the φ parameters in the AR process. In practice, however, all we have is a data series on say income or the money stock. To test such a series for stationarity we have to *fit* an appropriate AR process to it, *estimate* the φs and then *test* whether the roots imply stationarity or not.

For example, suppose we were quite confident that our data series could be approximated or 'modelled' by the first order AR process [7.31]. Recall that such a process is stationary provided $-1 < \varphi < 1$. For economic time series we can rule out the possibility that φ is negative[7] so for stationarity we require $0 < \varphi < 1$. The simplest way of estimating φ is to apply OLS to [7.31]. Unfortunately, the problem then is that if $\varphi = 1$, so that the process is non-stationary, standard distribution theory does not apply and the *OLS estimator of φ can be shown to be biased downwards, however large the sample.*[8] It is therefore possible that we might conclude that a process is stationary when it is not. The usual t-test of the null hypothesis $\varphi = 1$ is not reliable.

D. A. Dickey and W. F. Fuller have tackled the above problem. First, note that the AR process [7.31] can be rewritten as

$$\Delta Y_t = \varphi^* Y_{t-1} + \varepsilon_t \tag{7.43}$$

where $\varphi^* = \varphi - 1$. Hence testing the null hypothesis $\varphi = 1$ against $\varphi < 1$, that is testing for a so-called *unit root*, is equivalent to testing $\varphi^* = 0$ against $\varphi^* < 0$. The reason for the reformulation will become clear shortly. Note that the null hypothesis $\varphi^* = 0$ implies a non-stationary Y_t series. Hence, if we reject this in favour of $\varphi^* < 0$ or stationarity, then we can safely reject $\varphi^* > 0$ (i.e. $\varphi > 1$) as well. We need therefore only concern ourselves with possibilities $\varphi^* = 0$ and $\varphi^* < 0$. The problem is that, for the reasons given above, the OLS estimators of φ and hence φ^* and the usual t-test cannot be relied upon. Dickey and Fuller (1981), however, have tabulated the asymptotic distribution of the t-statistic under these circumstances. Under the null hypothesis $\varphi^* = 0$, this statistic is distributed not about zero but about a value less than zero. This reflects the fact that the OLS estimator $\hat{\phi}^*$ is biased downwards. However critical values for the t-statistic (normally referred to as τ under these circumstances) are shown on the left-hand side of Table 7.1. Notice that they are considerably larger in absolute value than standard critical t-values. Using these values it is possible to test the null hypothesis of non-stationarity despite the bias in the OLS estimator. For example, suppose estimation of [7.43] by OLS yielded

$$\Delta \hat{Y}_k = -0.315 Y_{t-1} \qquad n = 100 \tag{7.44}$$
$$(0.177)$$

Table 7.1

	Critical values for τ level of significance			Critical values for τ_τ level of significance		
Sample size	0.01	0.05	0.10	0.01	0.05	0.10
25	-2.66	-1.95	-1.60	-4.38	-3.60	-3.24
50	-2.62	-1.95	-1.61	-4.15	-3.50	-3.18
100	-2.60	-1.95	-1.61	-4.04	-3.45	-3.15

Source: Fuller (1976), Table 8.5.2

The t-ratio on the coefficient of Y_{t-1} is -1.78. If we adopt a 0.05 level of significance then, using standard t-tables, we would reject the hypothesis $\phi^* = 0$ and conclude that Y is stationary since $-t_{0.05} = -1.64$. However, because of the OLS bias, we cannot use standard t-tables but instead must take the critical value from the left-hand side of Table 7.1. Since $-\tau_{0.05} = -1.95$, for $n = 100$, we cannot in fact reject the hypothesis of non-stationarity. The test statistic is not negative enough. For obvious reasons the above test is known as a *Dickey–Fuller (DF) test*.

A difficulty is that a data series will not necessarily be well approximated by a first-order AR process. However, the advantage of the formulation [7.43] with the first difference as the dependent variable is that the general AR process [7.28] can also be reparameterised in this way. [7.28] can be written as

$$\Delta Y_t = \varphi^* Y_{t-1} + \varphi_1^* \Delta Y_{t-1} + \varphi_2^* \Delta Y_{t-2} + \cdots + \varphi_{p-1}^* \Delta Y_{t-p+1} + \varepsilon_t \qquad [7.45]$$

where

$$\varphi^* = \varphi_1 + \varphi_2 + \varphi_3 + \cdots + \varphi_p - 1$$

and the φ_j^*s are also functions of the original φs. For example, a third-order AR process of the form

$$Y_t = \varphi_1 Y_{t-1} + \varphi_2 Y_{t-2} + \varphi_3 Y_{t-3} + \varepsilon_t \qquad [7.46]$$

can be reparameterised as

$$\Delta Y_t = (\varphi_1 + \varphi_2 + \varphi_3 - 1) Y_{t-1} - (\varphi_2 + \varphi_3) \Delta Y_{t-1} - \varphi_3 \Delta Y_{t-2} + \varepsilon_t \qquad [7.47]$$

Notice that if $\varphi^* = 0$ then [7.45] becomes an equation in first differences. The point is however that, if we wish to test the general pth order AR process [7.28] for stationarity, we need to test whether the associated equation [7.38] has a unit root. But a unit root, as we shall see shortly, implies $\phi^* = 0$ in equation [7.45]. If we reject $\phi^* = 0$ in favour of $\phi^* < 0$ then this implies stationarity. Once more, as in the first-order case, if we reject $\phi^* = 0$ in favour of $\phi^* < 0$, we can safely reject $\phi^* > 0$ as well. Thus again we only need to consider the cases $\phi^* = 0$ and $\phi^* < 0$.

The obvious way to test for such a unit root is to apply OLS to equation [7.45] and examine the t-ratio on the estimate of φ^*. The distribution of the t-ratio is the same as that tabulated on the left-hand side of Table 7.1 for the first-order AR case. The test for a unit root in this general case is known as the *augmented Dickey–Fuller (ADF) test*.

To see why testing for a unit root is equivalent to testing for $\varphi^* = 0$ in equation [7.45] consider again the third-order case. We can rewrite [7.46] as

$$(1 - \varphi_1 L - \varphi_2 L^2 - \varphi_3 L^3) Y_t = \varepsilon_t \qquad [7.48]$$

If a unit root exists it must be possible to factorise [7.48] into

$$(1 + \alpha L + \beta L^2)(1 - L) Y_t = \varepsilon_t \qquad [7.49]$$

where α and β depend on the φs. However, since $(1 - L) Y_t = Y_t - Y_{t-1} = \Delta Y_t$, a unit root must therefore imply

$$(1 + \alpha L + \beta L^2) \Delta Y_t = \varepsilon_t \qquad [7.50]$$

or

$$\Delta Y_t = -\alpha \Delta Y_{t-1} - \beta \Delta Y_{t-2} + \varepsilon_t \qquad [7.51]$$

Comparison of [7.51] with [7.47] indicates that a unit root implies that the coefficient of Y_{t-1} in [7.47] is zero – that is $\phi_1 + \phi_2 + \phi_3 = 1$ so that $\phi^* = 0$. It should also be clear that if $\phi^* < 0$, that is if $\phi_1 + \phi_2 + \phi_3 < 1$, then [7.46] must be stationary.

Notice that if there is only one unit root associated with [7.48] then the roots of $1 + \alpha L + \beta L^2 = 0$ must both be greater than unity in absolute value. It follows from [7.50] that ΔY_t must then be a stationary process although, because of the unit root, Y_t is non-stationary. Identical results hold for AR processes of any order.

It is of course possible that two unit roots are present. For example, it may be possible to further factorise [7.49] into

$$(1 - \gamma L)(1 - L)(1 - L) Y_t = \varepsilon_t \qquad [7.52]$$

where γ depends on α and β. However, this implies

$$(1 - \gamma L) \Delta^2 Y_t = \varepsilon_t \qquad [7.53]$$

where $\Delta^2 Y_t = \Delta Y_t - \Delta Y_{t-1}$ is the second difference of Y_t.

If two roots are present then ΔY_t as well as Y_t is a non-stationary process. However, provided $\gamma > 1$, the second difference $\Delta^2 Y_t$ will be stationary. This implies that, having found a series Y_t to be non-stationary, rather than assume the first difference is stationary we must apply the Dickey–Fuller test to ΔY_t. Indeed, if we require a stationary series then we must continue testing the first difference, the second difference, etc., until the hypothesis of non-stationarity is rejected.

There remains the problem that we will not know beforehand what order of AR process best fits a given time series. The augmented Dickey–Fuller test therefore proceeds as follows. Equations such as [7.45] are estimated adding as many terms of differenced variables as are necessary to achieve residuals that are non-autocorrelated. We use the general *LM* test for autocorrelation of section 5.2.2 to check whether the value of p is large enough. The final estimated version of [7.45] is known as an *augmented Dickey–Fuller regression*.[8] We then use this regression to test $\varphi^* = 0$ against $\varphi^* < 0$. If $\varphi^* = 0$ is rejected then the Y_t series is stationary.

161

Two types of trend

Suppose a variable Y is determined as follows

$$Y_t = \alpha + \beta T + \phi Y_{t-1} + \varepsilon_t \qquad\qquad [7.54]$$

where T is a time trend and ε_t is white noise. Subtracting Y_{t-1} from either side, [7.54] can be rewritten as

$$\Delta Y_t = \alpha + \beta T + \phi^* Y_{t-1} + \varepsilon_t \qquad \phi^* = \phi - 1 \qquad\qquad [7.55]$$

Equations [7.54] and [7.55] encompass two different types of trend. First, if $\beta = 0$ and $\phi = 1$, then we see from [7.54] that $\Delta Y_t = \alpha + \varepsilon_t$. Y is clearly subject to a trend which is referred to as a *stochastic trend*. This type of trend can be removed by first differencing and, hence, Y is referred to as a *difference stationary process*. The Dickey–Fuller procedure of the last sub-section tests for just such a trend because when $\beta = 0$ [7.55] reduces to the AR(1) process [7.43], with a constant added.

Secondly, however, suppose $\beta > 0$ and $\phi < 1$ in equation [7.54]. Since $\phi < 1$ there is now no stochastic trend but since Y depends on T it is still a trending variable. This type of trend is referred to as a *deterministic trend* and Y is now said to be a *trend stationary process*. Note that T also appears in [7.55], so such a trend cannot be removed by first differencing. A deterministic trend has to be removed by regressing Y on time. The residuals from such a regression will not display any deterministic trend.

The point, however, is that spurious correlations can occur between variables that display deterministic trends just as they can occur between variables that display stochastic trends. But, as we just noted, the procedure outlined in the previous sub-section is designed to test merely for stochastic trends. For this reason the Dickey–Fuller test for stationarity is usually applied to equations such as [7.55] rather than [7.43]. However, in these circumstances the t-statistic, (now referred to as τ_r) has to be compared with the critical values on the *right-hand side* of Table 7.1. Notice that these values are even larger in absolute terms than those on the left-hand side. This is because the presence of constant and time trend in [7.55] increases the negative bias in the OLS estimator of ϕ^*.

It is customary when estimating [7.55] also to test the joint hypothesis $\beta = \phi^* = 0$. Failure to reject this joint hypothesis implies that Y *is subject to a stochastic but not a deterministic trend*.[9] Under such conditions, as we have seen, stationarity can be achieved by first differencing.

The joint hypothesis $\beta = \phi^* = 0$ is tested for using the usual F-statistic [4.45]. However, since under the null hypothesis of a stochastic trend conventional distribution theory does not hold, critical values for the statistic cannot be taken from standard F-tables. Dickey and Fuller in fact show that the F statistic in this case must be compared with the values in Table 7.2. Notice that the values in this table are considerably larger than the standard critical F-values.

As an example, suppose that as well as computing [7.44] we also obtain

$$\Delta \hat{Y}_t = \underset{(0.210)}{0.643} + \underset{(0.041)}{0.034T} - \underset{(0.203)}{0.461 Y_{t-1}} \qquad n = 100 \qquad\qquad [7.56]$$

and find that the F-statistic [4.45] for testing the joint significance of T and Y_{t-1} takes the value 3.73.

The t-ratio on the coefficient off Y_{t-1} now has a value $\tau_r = -2.27$. At the 0.05 level of significance, the critical value, now taken from the right-hand side

Table 7.2 Testing $\beta = \phi^* = 0$ in $\quad \Delta Y_t = \alpha + \beta T + \phi^* Y_{t-1}$

	Level of significance		
Sample size	0.01	0.05	0.10
25	10.61	7.24	5.91
50	9.31	6.73	5.61
100	8.73	6.49	5.47
$F(2, \infty)$	4.61	3.00	

Source: Dickey and Fuller (1981), p. 1063,   Table 6

of Table 7.1, is -3.45. So we are still unable to reject the hypothesis of nonstationarity. To be sure that Y_t displays a stochastic trend and not a deterministic trend we consider the F-value of 3.73. With $(2, 97)$ d.f., standard F-tables yield a value of $F_{0.05} = 3.10$, suggesting we reject the null hypothesis $\beta = \phi^* = 0$. However, we see from Table 7.2 that, for a sample size $n = 100$, with a 0.05 level of significance, the correct critical value is 6.49. Therefore the hypothesis $\beta = \phi^* = 0$ should not in fact be rejected. Thus Y follows a stochastic but not a deterministic trend.

Equation [7.55] can be generalised in the manner of the previous subsection to allow for the possibility of higher order AR processes. That is [7.45] is replaced by

$$\Delta Y_t = \alpha + \beta T + \phi^* Y_{t-1} + \phi_1^* \Delta Y_{t-1} + \phi_2^* \Delta Y_{t-2} + \cdots + \phi_{p-1}^* \Delta Y_{t-p+1} + \varepsilon_t$$
$$[7.57]$$

Again, sufficient terms in the differenced variable are added to ensure non-autocorrelated residuals.

We conclude this section with a note of caution. The Dickey–Fuller tests of stationarity lack power and should not be regarded as precise. The values in Tables 7.1 and 7.2 are only approximate guides. Moreover, it is not always clear how many differenced terms should be included in equations [7.45] and [7.57]. The number of such terms included can seriously affect the values of the various Dickey–Fuller statistics. In addition, it is sometimes unclear whether conclusions should be based on equation [7.45] or equation [7.57]. Consequently the tests need to be applied with great care. You will find detailed examples of the testing of time series for stationarity in the empirical appendices to Chapters 10, 11 and 12.

7.5   Co-integration

The Dickey–Fuller procedure enables us to test the variables in an error-correction model for stationarity. However the very concept of an ECM rests on the idea that there exists an equilibrium relationship between the relevant variables. We turn now to the question of how we should test for the existence of such an equilibrium relationship.

Consider, first, the disequilibrium error $y_t - \gamma_1 - \gamma_2 x_t$ taken from the equilibrium relationship [7.11]. If the equilibrium relationship is to have any real meaning at all then, as pointed out by Engle and Granger (1987), the disequilibrium errors observed over time (which measure the extent of 'departures' from equilibrium) should tend to fluctuate about zero, should rarely drift very far from zero and should fairly frequently 'cross the zero line'. A precise definition of such behaviour is provided by the statistical concept of *co-integration*.

A process or series is said to be *integrated* of order d, denoted as $I(d)$, if it has to be differenced d times before it becomes stationary. For example, many economic time series such as income or consumption become stationary after first differencing, (or at least their logarithms do), and are therefore said to be $I(1)$. If a series is stationary without having to be first differenced then it is said to be $I(0)$.

Two time series are said to be *co-integrated* of order d, b, denoted $CI(d, b)$ if (i) they are both integrated of order d; (ii) but there exists some linear combination of them that is integrated of order $b < d$. The definition can in fact be extended to several variables – see Engle and Granger (1987).

Of most interest to us is the case where we have two variables x and y which are $CI(1, 0)$. Then both x and y are non-stationary, only becoming stationary on first differencing (that is they are both $I(1)$), but there is some linear combination of the two series which is stationary. That is instead of being $I(1)$ the linear combination is $I(0)$. Notice that normally if both series were $I(1)$ or non-stationary, we would expect *any* linear combination also to be non-stationary. But for co-integrated variables there exists a linear combination which is stationary.

Co-integration is the statistical implication of the existence of a long-run relationship between economic variables. For example, suppose we have a long-run relationship

$$y_t = \gamma_1 + \gamma_2 x_t \qquad [7.58]$$

If x and y were integrated to different orders, for example if y were a trend variable and $I(1)$, whereas x had no trend and were $I(0)$, then there could be no parameters γ_1 and γ_2 such that [7.58] would hold even approximately over time. Thus *the existence of an equilibrium relationship between x and y requires them to be integrated to the same order and vice versa.* Furthermore, consider the disequilibrium errors that result from [7.58]

$$\varepsilon_t = y_t - \gamma_1 - \gamma_2 x_t \qquad [7.59]$$

As we have already observed, if an equilibrium relationship such as [7.58] actually exists, then the disequilibrium error [7.59] should fluctuate about zero. This means it must be stationary or $I(0)$. If it were non-stationary and trending upwards, for example, then x and y would be moving further and further away from each other – hardly behaviour consistent with a long-run equilibrium relationship. But, from [7.59], if ε_t is $I(0)$ then the linear combination of the two series, $y_t - \gamma_1 - \gamma_2 x_t$, must obviously also be $I(0)$. Hence *the existence of an equilibrium relationship between x and y also requires that a linear combination of the two series be $I(0)$ or stationary and vice-versa.*

Testing for co-integration

To establish the existence or non-existence of an equilibrium relationship between two economic time series x and y we must first test whether x and y are integrated to the same order. We can do this using the augmented Dickey–Fuller test for stationarity described in the last subsection. If we find that they are both $I(1)$ – that is they become stationary on first differencing, which is frequently the case with economic data – then we complete the test for co-integration in the following manner.

The hypothesised equilibrium relationship [7.58] is estimated by OLS. This is known as the *co-integrating regression* or sometimes as the *static regression*. The residuals from this regression are retained. That is we retain

$$e_t = y_t - \hat{\gamma}_1 - \hat{\gamma}_2 x_t \qquad \text{for all } t \qquad [7.60]$$

If we treat the e_t from [7.60] as estimates of the disequilibrium errors in [7.59], then the obvious way to test them for stationarity is to apply the Dickey–Fuller tests described earlier. That is, estimate an equation analogous to [7.45]:

$$\Delta e_t = \varphi^* e_{t-1} + \sum_{i=1}^{p-1} \varphi_i^* \Delta e_{t-i} + v_t \qquad [7.61]$$

and test $\phi^* = 0$ against $\phi^* < 0$ using Table 7,1. Notice that no intercept or time trend is included in [7.61], since the e_t must have a zero mean and we do not expect them to have a deterministic trend.

This would be a valid approach if we knew γ_1 and γ_2 and hence the ε_ts in [7.59]. Unfortunately, we only have OLS estimates of γ_1 and γ_2, and the e_ts from equation [7.60]. As Engle and Granger point out (1987), OLS minimises the residual sum of squares and, hence, chooses those values of γ_1 and γ_2 that are most likely to result in stationary residuals. The normal Dickey–Fuller procedure will therefore reject the null hypothesis of non-stationarity more often than it should. The t-ratio on the OLS estimate of ϕ^* in [7.61] therefore needs to be more negative than suggested by Table 7.1 before we can safely reject non-stationarity.

Engle and Granger consider seven possible statistics for testing the e_ts from [7.60] for stationarity. They eventually recommend the augmented Dickey–Fuller test based on [7.61] but with different critical values to those in Table 7.1. The relevant critical values are given in Table 7.3. Notice that they depend on the

Table 7.3   Critical values for the co-integration ADF test

Sample size	$m = 2$ significance level 0.01	0.05	0.10	$m = 3$ significance level 0.01	0.05	0.10	$m = 4$ significance level 0.01	0.05	0.10
50	4.12	3.29	2.90	4.45	3.75	3.36	4.61	3.98	3.67
100	3.73	3.17	2.91	4.22	3.62	3.32	4.61	4.02	3.71
200	3.78	3.25	2.98	4.34	3.78	3.51	4.72	4.13	3.83

Source: Engle and Yoo (1987), Table 3

number of explanatory variables, m, in the co-integrating regression. m has been assumed to be 2 in equation [7.58].

Thus, to test $\phi^* = 0$ against $\phi^* < 0$ in [7.61], we compare the t-ratio on ϕ^* with the relevant critical t-value in Table 7.3. If $\phi^* = 0$ is rejected then the e_ts are stationary. Such a result would imply that we had found a linear combination of x and y which was stationary. This in turn would imply that x and y were co-integrated.

One other of the test statistics considered by Engle and Granger is worth noting. If the differenced terms in [7.61] are omitted then, since $\phi^* = \phi - 1$, this equation can be rewritten as

$$e_t = \phi e_{t-1} + v_t \qquad\qquad [7.61A]$$

Testing $\phi^* = 0$ against $\phi^* < 0$ is now equivalent to testing $\phi = 1$ against $\phi < 1$ in [7.61A]. But [7.61A] implies that the residuals, e_t, from the co-integrating regression follow a first-order autoregressive scheme. The simplest way to tackle an AR(1) scheme is to use the Durbin–Watson statistic [5.27]. As we saw in section 5.2.2, when $\phi = 1$ in [7.61A] the Durbin–Watson statistic is likely to take a value very close to zero. If $\phi < 1$ we expect a value in excess of zero. Engle and Granger conclude that at the 0.05 level of significance the null hypothesis $\phi = 1$ (i.e. that the e_ts are non-stationary) should be rejected if the Durbin–Watson statistic exceeds a value of 0.386. This test for stationarity is known as the *co-integrating regression Durbin–Watson* (CRDW) test.

Unfortunately, while the CRDW test works well when the disturbances in the co-integrating regression follow a first-order scheme, it has very different critical values for alternative specifications. This is in contrast to the augmented Dickey–Fuller test statistic for which the critical values are little changed when higher order processes are present.

Examples of the use of the co-integration ADF test can be found in the empirical appendices to Chapters 10, 11 and 12. However, another word of caution is in order at this point. The critical values in Table 7.3 are only approximate and the value of the ADF statistic (the t-ratio on ϕ^*) will depend very much on the order of AR process assumed (that is on the number of differenced terms included in [7.61]). Since we have no prior knowledge of what order process we are dealing with, and because the tests lack power the Dickey–Fuller procedures have to be applied with great care, discrimination and judgement.

Superconsistency

We conclude this section by stating a rather remarkable result first obtained by Stock (1987). If the two series x and y are co-integrated, then OLS estimators of γ_1 and γ_2 in the equilibrium relationship [7.58] will be consistent *regardless of whether or not there is a correlation between the explanatory x variable and the disturbance* in that equation. Normally of course such correlation leads to bias and inconsistency. This result is important, since for most time series such a correlation is likely to exist. [7.58] is only a long-run relationship and if the short-run disequilibrium relationship is, for example, [7.12] we might appear to have an omitted variable problem. However Stock's result means that, provided x and y are co-integrated, we need not be concerned about this, if our sample is sufficiently large.

Furthermore, not only are the OLS estimators consistent but their asymptotic efficiency is very high. That is their sampling distributions collapse very rapidly on to the true parameters as the sample size increases. Because this convergence on the true parameter values is more rapid even than when all the classical assumptions of Chapter 2 hold, Stock refers to the OLS estimators as 'superconsistent' in this case.

It is possible to gain an intuitive understanding of the superconsistency result. Recall that OLS minimises the sum of the squared residuals in [7.60]. If x and y are $I(1)$ then any linear combination of the two will also be $I(1)$ except for that given by the long-term relationship [7.58]. Hence if we were to select values for $\hat{\gamma}_1$ and $\hat{\gamma}_2$ in [7.60] that differ from the true γ_1 and γ_2, the resulting e_ts will be non-stationary and hence trending either upwards or downwards. Thus as the sample size increases $\sum e_t^2$ will increase rapidly. However, if we select the true values of α and β, then the e_ts will be stationary and $\sum e_t^2$ will not increase so rapidly. Since OLS seeks the minimum $\sum e_t^2$ it is able to select the correct values for γ_1 and γ_2 *provided the sample is large enough*. Hence the OLS estimators have the large sample property of consistency provided x and y are co-integrated.

The estimation of error correction models

We have seen that an ECM implies an underlying equilibrium relationship. Engle and Granger (1987) prove that if two variables are co-integrated (i.e. if an equilibrium relationship exists) *then the short-run 'disequilibrium' relationship between the two variables can always be represented by an ECM*. This result is sometimes referred to as the *Granger representation theorem*. Not surprisingly, however, if no equilibrium relationship exists then we should not represent short-run behaviour by an ECM.

Clearly, then, the first step in any model-estimating procedure should be to test for co-integration in the manner of the last section. If x and y are co-integrated then we can expect a Hendry-type testing down procedure to lead eventually to some form of ECM. There are however two ways in which a final preferred ECM can be estimated. Consider again the ECM given by [7.15] reproduced here as [7.62]

$$\Delta y_t = \beta_1 \Delta x_t - (1 - \alpha)(y_{t-1} - \gamma_1 - \gamma_2 x_{t-1}) + u_t \qquad [7.62]$$

with the equilibrium relationship given, as usual, by [7.58].

Engle and Granger propose a two-step procedure for the estimation of [7.62]. Because of Stock's super-consistency result, they suggest that the long-run parameters γ_1 and γ_2 be obtained by the application of OLS to [7.58] – that is from the co-integrating regression. The residuals from this regression, the e_ts from [7.60], are then substituted into [7.62] in place of the disequilibrium errors. The second stage of the procedure is therefore to apply OLS to

$$\Delta y_t = \beta_1 \Delta x_t - (1 - \alpha)e_{t-1} + u_t \qquad [7.63]$$

and thus estimate the short-run parameters, β_1 and α. Notice that since x and y are co-integrated all the variables in [7.63] are stationary so that the standard OLS procedures are valid for large samples. Engle and Granger show that the estimators of the short-run parameters obtained in this way are both consistent and as *asymptotically efficient as they would have been had true rather than estimated values for the disequilibrium errors been used in the second stage*.

There is a problem with the two-stage procedure, however. Although the OLS estimators from the co-integrating regression possess the large sample property of consistency and are highly efficient, they are still biased in small samples and this bias can be substantial. In the second stage of the procedure this bias carries over into the disequilibrium errors and this can lead to serious small sample bias in the estimation of the short-run parameters.

An alternative to the Engle–Granger two-step procedure is to apply OLS to [7.62] directly and hence estimate both long- and short-run parameters together. [7.62] is first rewritten as

$$\Delta y_t = \beta_0 + \beta_1 \Delta x_t - (1 - \alpha)y_{t-1} + \gamma_2(1 - \alpha)x_{t-1} + u_t \qquad [7.64]$$

where $\beta_0 = \gamma_1(1 - \alpha)$ as in equations [7.14] and [7.15]. The estimate of the long-run parameter γ_2 can then be obtained from the ratio of the estimated coefficients of x_{t-1} and y_{t-1}. Similarly an estimate of γ_1 is obtained from the ratio of the constant term to the coefficient of y_{t-1}.

Wickens and Breusch (1988) have developed this approach. It turns out that, while the properties of the estimators of the short-run parameters are identical to those of the two-step estimators, this does not appear to be the case for the estimators of the long-run parameters. There is some evidence that the small sample bias is smaller for these latter estimators than it is with the two-step procedure.

7.6 An overall strategy for model selection

We have introduced a whole series of new concepts in this chapter and this final section will attempt to bring everything together into some sort of overall strategy for model selection.

Ideally an investigator needs to begin his search for an appropriate model by formulating a general equation which nests, as special cases, all competing hypotheses concerning the process he is modelling. The competing hypotheses may differ not merely because they reflect alternative long-run economic theories but also because they represent alternative short-run adjustment patterns. For example, two models may involve very different distributive lag structures but imply the same long-run behaviour.

Formulating a suitable general model has a number of advantages. It enables us, hopefully, to avoid the specification errors that result from the omission of relevant variables. In particular the possibility of dynamic mis-specifications resulting from incorrect lag structures is much reduced. The goodness of fit of such a model also provides us with a useful criterion for judging the various nested special cases. Clearly if we end up with a 'preferred' model that comes nowhere near to matching the 'fit' of the general model we will have serious misgivings.

Often we may not be aware of all possible hypotheses when we first attempt to formulate a general model. Also, we may not have any clear idea of what functional form to adopt – should we, for example, work with the natural logarithms of variables? For these reasons it is necessary to check rigorously even the most general of models for possible mis-specifications. Such checks will involve both a visual examination of the residuals from the fitted version of the model and the use of LM tests, for example, for autocorrelation and

168

heteroscedasticity in the residuals. Any suggestion of autocorrelation in the residuals should lead to a re-think about the form of the general model.

Side by side with the specifying of a general model, an investigator should use the techniques of co-integration analysis to search for possible long run equilibrium relationships between variables in the general equation. This analysis will provide valuable clues as to which explanatory variables are likely to be long run influences on the dependent variable of interest and which variables are likely to have effects, if any, which are purely short run or transistory. In particular, co-integration analysis will hopefully provide some information about what type of ECM is likely to prove a satisfactory special case of the general model. Recall the Engle–Granger result that, if variables are co-integrated, then the short-run or disequilibrium relationship between them can *always* be represented by an ECM. Note, however, that the co-integration analysis will tell us nothing about the precise form and lag-structure of the short-run relationship. It yields information on long-run properties only.

The lag-structure and appropriate short run responses are uncovered during the testing down procedure that the general model is now subjected to. If possible a sequential testing down procedure should be mapped out at the start, beginning with the most general hypothesis and with each successive model tested being nested in the previous model. A simple example of such a sequence of F-tests was given in section 7.2. However in practice the number of possible nested models can be very large indeed. For example with quarterly data we might begin with a general model of the form

$$Y_t = \alpha_0 + \sum_{i=1}^{4} \alpha_i Y_{t-i} + \sum_{i=0}^{4} \beta_i X_{t-i} + \sum_{i=0}^{4} \gamma_i Z_{t-i} + \varepsilon_t \qquad [7.65]$$

where the dependent variable Y is thought likely to be influenced by X and/or Z. Lagged variables up to four quarters previous have to be included because we wish to consider the possibility that Y is influenced not so much by events in the previous quarter but by events four quarters (i.e. one year) ago. The selection of maximum lag-length is inevitably arbitrary because it is often determined by degrees of freedom problems rather than anything else. It is this arbitrary selection of maximum lag length that is one of the reasons why it is essential to test even the general model for possible specification error.

Clearly with an equation such as [7.65] the number of nested special cases is large so that the testing down procedure is likely to be lengthy. It is also likely to require considerable judgement since the ideal sequential testing of hypotheses may not be possible. That is, as in the simple example of section [7.2] we may be faced with the problem of choosing between non-nested models. In such a situation it is quite possible that neither non-nested model will be rejected by the data. When this is the case a choice between models has to be made on non-statistical grounds. This is when judgement comes into play and we have to make use of the criteria described at the end of section 7.2.

Indeed criteria such as parsimony, theoretical consistency, and so on, must be borne in mind throughout the testing down procedure. For example, it would be silly to accept a model with coefficients which are highly implausible from a theoretical viewpoint, even if the restrictions imposed satisfied the relevant F-test. Judgement therefore has to be employed throughout.

Ideally the testing down procedure should lead ultimately to a model, probably an ECM, suitably parsimonious, with a goodness of fit at least approaching that of the general model, satisfying in fact all the criteria listed at the end of section 7.2. Unfortunately, it would be idle to pretend that things are always as simple as this in the real world with a typical set of time series data. There are a number of reasons for this.

First, we have already stressed the importance of judgement in the testing down procedures. Different investigators can come to different judgements and this means that it is perfectly possible for two such researchers to come up with different final preferred models, even when faced with an identical data set. This is particularly the case if one such investigator adopts the Engle–Granger two-step approach while another relies entirely on a Hendry-type testing down procedure.

Secondly, we have assumed above that any long run equilibrium relationships involve only two of the variables under study. This is obviously not always going to be so. The problem is that when more than two variables, all integrated to order 1, appear in the equilibrium relationship, it is possible that there will be more than one linear combination of these variables that is integrated to order zero. That is there may be more than one 'co-integrating vector'. It is not clear which of these linear combinations should then be treated as *the* equilibrium relationship and used to generate the residuals for the second step of the Engle–Granger procedure.

Johansen (1988) suggests a maximum likelihood approach be adopted both for determining the number of stationary linear combinations (co-integrating vectors) and for their estimation. However, the method is complex and lies outside the scope of this book. Moreover, it still leaves unclear which co-integrating vector should be treated as the equilibrium relationship. Because of this problem, few econometricians would regard the Engle–Granger two-step procedure as adequate for estimation on its own. Rather, co-integration analysis is considered a valuable guide to the nature of possible long-run relationships and, hence, to the structure of the ECMs that are likely to form the final preferred equations of a Hendry-type testing down process. Thus the Engle–Granger two-step procedure and the Wickens–Breusch approach (mentioned earlier as a method of estimating short- and long-run parameters together), are regarded, not as alternatives, but as complementary to each other.

Above all it is vital that post-sample prediction tests are carried out on any preferred final model. We stressed earlier how akin to data mining the testing down procedure is. Parameter stability tests are not enough if carried out on data that was available to an investigator when he selected his final model. True post-sample prediction tests can only be performed using new data.

In addition to the above procedural difficulties, the ECM approach to modelling has recently been criticised on more fundamental grounds. It is argued that too little attention is paid to be precise type of economic behaviour that underlies the data generating process. For example Alogoskonfis and Smith (1990) argue that, instead of simply modelling the time series relationships in the data and then interpreting the results in terms of economics, a better approach is to derive relationships directly from economic theory, next impose the error correction mechanism as a possible short-run adjustment hypothesis, and only then specify an appropriate dynamic equation to be estimated. Moreover, theory often has something to say about the expectations generating process which at least partly determines the short-run dynamics of any relationship.

We saw in Chapter 6 that lagged variables appear in econometric equations either because of lags in adjustment to desired levels or because of some expectations generating process. It is not difficult to derive an ECM as the outcome of an adjustment process. For example suppose optimal or desired y is given by

$$y_t^* = \gamma_1 + \gamma_2 x_t \qquad\qquad [7.66]$$

Assume that economic agents choose y_t so as to minimise the 'quadratic loss function'

$$C = w_1(y_t - y_t^*)^2 + w_2(y_t - y_{t-1})^2 \qquad w_1 + w_2 = 1 \qquad [7.67]$$

The first term in [7.67] measures the cost of being in disequilibrium and the second term the cost of changing y. w_1 and w_2 reflect the relative weights attached to these types of cost. Minimising C requires

$$\frac{dC}{dy_t} = 2w_1(y_t - y_t^*) + 2w_2(y_t - y_{t-1}) = 0 \qquad\qquad [7.68]$$

Rearranging [7.68] yields, using $w_1 + w_2 = 1$,

$$y_t - y_{t-1} = w_1(y_t^* - y_{t-1}) \qquad\qquad [7.69]$$

Equation [7.69] is no more than the simple partial adjustment equation [6.35] with $\mu = w_1$. Substituting from [7.66] gives

$$y_t = w_1\gamma_1 + w_1\gamma_2 x_t + (1 - w_1)y_{t-1} \qquad\qquad [7.70]$$

The point of relevance here, however, is that [7.70] can easily be reparameterised as

$$y_t - y_{t-1} = w_1\gamma_2(x_t - x_{t-1}) - w_1(y_{t-1} - \gamma_1 - \gamma_2 x_{t-1}) \qquad [7.71]$$

Equation [7.71] is clearly of ECM form. In fact it is easy to see that it is a special case of the general first order ECM [7.15] with $\beta_1 = \gamma_2(1 - \alpha)$. In [7.71] $w_1 = 1 - \alpha$.

ECMs can obviously be regarded as generalisations of simple partial adjustment models. That should be clear from the above. However, it is by no means as clear how lags arising out of the generation of expectations fit into the picture. Alogoskonfis and Smith provide a simple example where expectations about x are generated in such a way that it is no longer possible to interpret, for example, γ_2 in the ECM [7.15] as a purely long run parameter. Rather it reflects equilibrium, adjustment and expectations parameters.

Alogoskonfis and Smith also provide a number of models of wage inflation, all of which result in ECM type estimating equations. However, by carefully specifying the economic models beforehand, they demonstrate that different models can imply different *non-linear* restrictions on the parameters of ECMs. This supports the contention, mentioned earlier, that it is preferable to derive relationships from theory at the outset rather than to rely on a data based approach and then simply interpret results in terms of theory.

Co-integration analysis, its relationship to ECMs and its use in conjunction with the Hendry-type testing down procedure is a relatively new but exciting development in econometrics. Many issues are still to be settled. But despite difficulties with and criticisms of the approach, it remains one of the very few systematic methodologies econometricians have available to them for conducting research.

Further reading

Specification errors are very clearly treated in Kmenta (1986). For an excellent discussion of the approaches to model selection, the criteria for model acceptance and error correction models, see Gilbert (1986). For an appraisal of different econometric methodologies, including that of Hendry, see Pagan (1987). Stochastic processes are well covered in Pindyck and Rubinfeld (1991), Chapters 14–16. Few econometric textbooks pay much attention as yet to stationarity and co-integration but Stewart (1991) and Maddala (1989) contain short but readable sections on these topics. See also the surveys by Permon (1991) and Muscatelli and Hurn (1992).

Notes

1. For example, with one explanatory variable, X_2, we have var $\hat{\beta}_2 = \sigma^2 / \sum x_2^2$. If a second irrelevant explanatory variable, X_3, is added to the equation, then from [5.39] var $\hat{\beta}_2 = \sigma^2 / \sum x_2^2 (1 - r^2)$. The ratio of these two variances is $1/(1 - r^2)$. Thus, if the correlation, r, between X_2 and X_3 exceeds zero, the inclusion of X_3 will increase the variance of $\hat{\beta}_2$.
2. See, for example Chiang (1984: 256–60).
3. That is we would select the test with the greatest power against the alternative hypothesis we have in mind. Recall that the power of a test is the probability of rejecting the null hypothesis when it is false. Such a probability can only be evaluated if the alternative hypothesis is clearly specified.
4. A more sophisticated measure is the Akaike Information Criterion under which the maximised likelihoods of models are compared, with an allowance made for the number of parameters estimated. See, for example Harvey (1989: 177–8).
5. Notice that this implies that we should only interpret γ_1 in equation [7.15] as a long-run parameter when $g = 0$.
6. Notice that if we treat [7.31] as a first-order difference equation, then its characteristic equation is $\lambda - \phi = 0$, with the single root $\lambda = \phi$. Provided this root is less than unity in absolute value the process will be stationary. Thus again we arrive at the condition $-1 < \phi < 1$ for stationarity.
7. A negative ϕ in [7.31] implies that Y would tend to have alternative negative and positive values. Economic time series do not normally behave in this manner.
8. Even if [7.31] were stationary, the OLS estimator of ϕ would be biased in small samples. This is because of the presence of the lagged dependent variable as the regressor in [7.31]. However, for stationary Y the OLS estimator of ϕ would at least be consistent. The point is that, for non-stationary Y, the bias persists even in large samples. Moreover, the bias has been demonstrated to be a downward bias.
9. Nelson and Plosser (1982) provide evidence that, in fact, most economic time series do not display both deterministic and stochastic trends; that is, a significant time trend in [7.55] is most unlikely when a unit root is present.

8 Simultaneous equation systems

In this chapter we shall be concerned with the problems arising when attempts are made to estimate systems of simultaneous equations. It will be assumed that the reader is familiar with such distinctions as those between exogenous and endogenous variables and between the structural and reduced forms of a model.

In previous chapters we concentrated attention on the estimation of single equations in which it was assumed that the only endogenous variable was the dependent variable and that the explanatory variables were truly exogenous. It was implicitly assumed that the only relationship between the variables in an equation was that described by the equation itself. However, economic models typically involve a set of relationships designed to explain the behaviour of the endogenous variables in the model. This gives rise to the possibility that additional relationships between the dependent and explanatory variables in any single equation may exist and that the explanatory variables may themselves be endogenous. For example, in the simple consumption function introduced at the beginning of Chapter 2 causation was assumed to be from the income variable to the consumption expenditure variable. However, if we were estimating such a function for the aggregate economy, we would be unable to ignore the fact that consumption expenditure was an important determinant of national income. There would therefore be a reverse causation present from the consumption variable to the income variable. An additional relationship between income and consumption would exist, apart from the consumption function, and these two relationships together could be regarded as jointly determining the endogenous variables, income and consumption.

The question we now attempt to answer concerns the extent to which the existence of a set of simultaneous relationships, in which a given equation is embedded, affects the manner in which we should attempt to estimate that equation. In the next section we discuss the separate but related problems of identification and simultaneous equation bias. In sections 8.2 and 8.3 we consider some of the methods used to estimate simultaneous equation systems.

8.1 The problems of identification and simultaneous equation bias

Imagine that we wished to estimate the 'demand curve' for some typical non-durable household commodity and to this end collected time series data on the price, P, of the commodity and on the quantity bought and sold, Q. If we now proceeded, somewhat naively, to regress (by OLS) quantity Q on price P, we would probably soon realise that our simple regression equation bore little relation to the demand curve we were trying to estimate.

First, the demand curve of the elementary economics textbook is drawn up under what is usually referred to as the *ceteris paribus* assumption. That is, the demand curve sketches the relationship between price and demand that would hold if all other variables influencing demand were held constant. Just conceivably we might have been fortunate enough to have collected our data on P and Q at a time when all such variables did, in fact, remain unchanged. However, even if this were the case, we might eventually begin to wonder, that if this were the best method of estimating the demand curve for the commodity, how we would have proceeded if we had wished to estimate its supply curve instead. The supply curve, after all, also sketches out a relationship between P and Q given the *ceteris paribus* assumption.

At this stage we would probably pause and do some serious rethinking. Suppose, on reflection, we decided that the market we were observing could be described by the following two-equation model

$$Q = a_0 + a_1 P + a_2 P^s + a_3 Y + u \qquad \text{demand equation} \qquad [8.1]$$

$$Q = b_0 + b_1 P + b_2 P^s + v \qquad \text{supply equation} \qquad [8.2]$$

where the as and the bs are unknown parameters, Y is the income of purchasers of the commodity, P^s is the price of a close substitute and u and v are disturbances.

Equations [8.1] and [8.2] represent the *structural equations* of the model, P and Q are the *endogenous* variables, while P^s and Y are assumed to be *exogenous* variables. Notice that for simplicity we assume that the market always clears, i.e. that quantity demanded is always equal to quantity supplied, both being represented by the symbol Q.

Suppose, for the sake of argument, that during the time we observed Q and P the exogenous variables P^s and Y actually did remain constant. The structural equations could then be written as

$$Q = a'_0 + a_1 P + u \qquad \text{demand equation} \qquad [8.1A]$$

$$Q = b'_0 + b_1 P + v \qquad \text{supply equation} \qquad [8.2A]$$

where $a'_0 = a_0 + a_2 P^s + a_3 Y$ and $b'_0 = b_0 + b_2 P^s$ are constants.

Suppose, further, that the disturbances u and v were always identically zero. All we could ever observe under these conditions would be a single pair of values for P and Q, those at the intersection point of the curves $Q = a'_0 + a_1 P$ and $Q = b'_0 + b_1 P$. No 'scatter' of points would be generated since throughout our time series we would continue to observe this single point. Even if the disturbances u and v were non-zero and varied from period to period, during each such period we would still be observing merely the intersection point of two curves. Any scatter of points obtained over different periods would merely be a series of such intersection points generated by the continually shifting demand and supply curves. This is illustrated in Fig. 8.1 where D_1 and S_1 are the demand and supply curves, respectively, for period 1 and D_2 and S_2 are those for period 2, and so on.

If we attempted to fit a line to such a scatter of points, by OLS or any other means, we would obviously be estimating neither demand curve nor supply curve but rather what is sometimes called a 'mongrel' equation containing elements of both. This is the simplest case of the so-called *identification problem*. Identification of either curve can only be achieved provided it remains stationary

8.1 Shifting demand and supply curves.

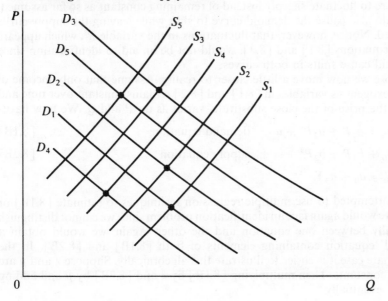

8.2 Shifting demand and stationary supply curve.

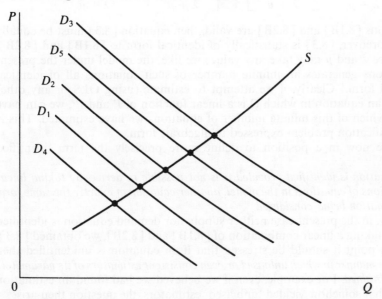

over time while the other curve shifts. For example, in Fig. 8.2 the supply curve S remains stationary while the demand curve shifts and the intersection points obtained trace out the supply curve. Such shifts in the demand curve might occur for two possible reasons. First, the demand disturbance, u, might vary sharply from period to period while the supply disturbance, v, remained very close to zero. Secondly, if the income variable in the demand equation [8.1] were to fluctuate sharply instead of remaining constant as so far assumed, this would also cause the demand curve to shift while leaving the supply curve unaffected. Notice, however, that fluctuations in the variable P^s, which appears in both equations [8.1] and [8.2], would not be an aid to identification since this would cause shifts in both curves.

Suppose we now move a little closer to reality. Assume that only income of the two exogenous variables in [8.1] and [8.2] remains constant over time and that P^s, the price of the close substitute, varies as do P and Q. We now have

$$Q = a_0'' + a_1 P + a_2 P^s + u \qquad \text{demand equation} \qquad [8.1B]$$

$$Q = b_0 + b_1 P + b_2 P^s + v \qquad \text{supply equation} \qquad [8.2B]$$

where $a_0'' = a_0 + a_3 Y$.

If we attempted to use multiple regression techniques to estimate [8.1B] or [8.2B] we would again face an identification problem since we cannot distinguish statistically between one equation and the other. Again, we would obtain a 'mongrel' equation containing elements of both [8.1B] and [8.2B]. In the multivariate case it is easier to illustrate this algebraically. Suppose λ and μ are *any* two constants. Then multiplying [8.1B] by λ and [8.2B] by μ and adding we have, eventually

$$Q = \frac{\lambda a_0'' + \mu b_0}{\lambda + \mu} + \left[\frac{\lambda a_1 + \mu b_1}{\lambda + \mu} \right] P + \left[\frac{\lambda a_2 + \mu b_2}{\lambda + \mu} \right] P^s + \frac{\lambda u + \mu v}{\lambda + \mu} \qquad [8.3]$$

If equations [8.1B] and [8.2B] are valid, then equation [8.3] must be equally valid. Moreover, [8.3] is statistically of identical form to [8.1B] and [8.2B]. Also, since λ and μ may take any values we like, the model under the present assumptions generates an infinite number of such equations all of identical statistical form.[1] Clearly, if we attempt to estimate (using OLS or any other method) an equation in which Q is a linear function of P and P^s, we can have no idea which of this infinite number of equations we have estimated. This is the identification problem expressed in algebraic form.

We are now in a position to define more precisely the term 'identified equation'.

An equation is identified provided it is not possible to derive, by taking linear combinations of equations in the model, another equation of exactly the same form as the equation being considered.

Clearly, in the present case neither supply nor demand equation is identified since, by taking a linear combination of [8.1B] and [8.2B], we obtained [8.3].

At this point it should be stressed that if an equation is unidentified then there is *no manner in which unbiased or even consistent estimators of its parameters may be obtained.* For example, even if we believed we had found an estimation method that somehow yielded 'unbiased' estimators, the question then arises – unbiased estimators of what? In the present example, do we have unbiased estimators for the demand equation, the supply equation or some version of equation [8.3]? We can have no idea which equation we are, in fact, estimating.

Let us now return to the original version of the model given by equations [8.1] and [8.2] in which both exogenous variables P^s and Y vary over time. If we take a linear combination of [8.1] and [8.2] in the same manner as we derived [8.3], the 'mongrel' equation now becomes

$$Q = \frac{\lambda a_0 + \mu b_0}{\lambda + \mu} + \left[\frac{\lambda a_1 + \mu b_1}{\lambda + \mu}\right]P + \left[\frac{\lambda a_2 + \mu b_2}{\lambda + \mu}\right]P^s + \left[\frac{\lambda a_3}{\lambda + \mu}\right]Y + \frac{\lambda u + \mu v}{\lambda + \mu}$$
[8.4]

There is clearly no way in which [8.4] can be confused with [8.2]. It contains the variable Y, whereas the supply equation does not. Thus, the supply equation is now identified since it is not possible to obtain an equation of similar form by taking linear combinations of equations [8.1] and [8.2]. However, the demand equation remains unidentified since it can obviously be confused with [8.4].

Observe that the supply equation becomes identified because of the appearance of the income variable Y *in the demand equation* – but not in the supply equation. However, it is instructive to regard this as a restriction on the form of the supply equation which we can regard as having the most general form

$$Q = b_0 + b_1 P + b_2 P^s + b_3 Y + v$$

Notice for future reference that the fact that Y does not appear in the supply equation can now be regarded as the imposition of the restriction $b_3 = 0$ on the form of this equation.

It should be stressed at this point that, so far, we have merely demonstrated that the supply equation [8.2] is *identified*. We have said nothing about the entirely separate problem of how this equation should be *estimated*. In fact, although under present assumptions the supply equation is identified, *the OLS method of estimation will still yield biased and inconsistent estimators of its parameters.* This can be best understood by considering the *reduced form* of equations [8.1] and [8.2]. Expressing the endogenous variables as functions of the exogenous variables and the disturbances we obtain the reduced form equations[2]

$$Q = \frac{a_0 b_1 - a_1 b_0}{b_1 - a_1} + \left[\frac{a_2 b_1 - a_1 b_2}{b_1 - a_1}\right]P^s + \left[\frac{a_3 b_1}{b_1 - a_1}\right]Y + \frac{b_1 u - a_1 v}{b_1 - a_1} \qquad [8.5]$$

$$P = \frac{a_0 - b_0}{b_1 - a_1} + \left[\frac{a_2 - b_2}{b_1 - a_1}\right]P^s + \left[\frac{a_3}{b_1 - a_1}\right]Y + \frac{u - v}{b_1 - a_1} \qquad [8.6]$$

From equation [8.6] it can be seen that the endogenous variable, P, is influenced by both disturbances u and v. However, it is the contemporaneous correlation between P and the disturbance v that is crucial because P is an endogenous variable on the right-hand side of the supply equation. The fact that it is correlated with the disturbance in that equation means, as we saw in section 5.1, that OLS will yield biased and inconsistent estimators of the supply equation parameters. This is the problem of *simultaneous equation bias*. It arises because of the simultaneous nature of equations [8.1] and [8.2]. Both these equations involve relationships between the endogenous variables Q and P and, given the values of the exogenous variables P^s and Y, they jointly determine the values of Q and P. The structural equations of simultaneous systems typically include endogenous variables on their right-hand sides and, as in the present case, these variables will typically be correlated with the corresponding disturbances. We stress again that this is a separate problem from that of identification. Even if an equation is identified, its estimation may, and probably will, involve the problem of simultaneous equation bias. We leave the question of how this problem can be dealt with until sections 8.2 and 8.3.

Moving from reduced form to structural form

The reduced-form equations [8.5] and [8.6] enable us to illustrate another aspect of the identification problem. These equations may be written as

$$Q = A_0 + A_1 P^s + A_2 Y + U \qquad [8.5A]$$

$$P = B_0 + B_1 P^s + B_2 Y + V \qquad [8.6A]$$

where

$$
\left.
\begin{aligned}
A_0 &= \frac{a_0 b_1 - a_1 b_0}{b_1 - a_1}, & A_1 &= \frac{a_2 b_1 - a_1 b_2}{b_1 - a_1}, & A_2 &= \frac{a_3 b_1}{b_1 - a_1} \\[2mm]
B_0 &= \frac{a_0 - b_0}{b_1 - a_1}, & B_1 &= \frac{a_2 - b_2}{b_1 - a_1}, & B_2 &= \frac{a_3}{b_1 - a_1}
\end{aligned}
\right\} \qquad [8.7]
$$

$$U = \frac{b_1 u - a_1 v}{b_1 - a_1}, \quad V = \frac{u - v}{b_1 - a_1}$$

The As and the Bs are known as the *reduced-form parameters* and U and V as reduced-form disturbances. Suppose the reduced-form parameters were known.[3] The interesting question now arises of whether, given such knowledge of the reduced-form parameters, it is possible to derive values for the structural parameters, i.e. the a's and the b's. In other words, can the system of equations [8.7] be solved for the structural parameters. This question is more easily tackled if we rearrange the system [8.7] into the two subsystems

$$A_0 - a_1 B_0 = a_0 \qquad\qquad\qquad A_0 - b_1 B_0 = b_0$$

$$A_1 - a_1 B_1 = a_2 \quad [8.8] \qquad\qquad A_1 - b_1 B_1 = b_2 \quad [8.9]$$

$$A_2 - a_1 B_2 = a_3 \qquad\qquad\qquad A_2 - b_1 B_2 = 0$$

The splitting of a system of equations such as [8.7] into two subsystems like [8.8] and [8.9] requires a knack which is not easily acquired. Indeed, such a split is not always possible. The reader is not expected to acquire this knack but merely to observe that solving the subsystems [8.8] and [8.9] will yield identical expressions for the as and the bs to those obtained by solving the combined system [8.7]. The advantage of the split is that subsystem [8.8] involves the demand equation parameters (i.e. the as) only, while subsystem [8.9] involves the supply equation parameters (i.e. the bs) only.

Consider subsystem [8.9] first. Since the As and Bs are known, this consists of three linear equations in the three unknowns b_0, b_1 and b_2. It may therefore be uniquely solved for these unknowns, the solution, in fact, being

$$b_1 = A_2/B_2, \quad b_2 = A_1 - [A_2/B_2]B_1 \quad \text{and} \quad b_0 = A_0 - [A_2/B_2]B_0$$
$$[8.10]$$

Thus, given knowledge of the reduced-form parameters, it *is* possible to derive the parameters of the identified supply equation.

Now consider subsystem [8.8]. This consists of *three* linear equations in the *four* unknowns a_0, a_1, a_2 and a_3 and hence will have more than one solution.[4] In fact, if α is any number, then *any* set of values for the as of the following form will satisfy subsystem [8.8]

$$a_1 = \alpha, \quad a_2 = A_1 - \alpha B_1, \quad a_3 = A_2 - \alpha B_2 \quad \text{and} \quad a_0 = A_0 - \alpha B_0$$

Thus, even given knowledge of the reduced-form parameters, it is *not* possible to derive unique values for the parameters of the unidentified demand equation. In fact, any demand equation of the form

$$Q = (A_0 - \alpha B_0) + \alpha P + (A_1 - \alpha B_1)P^s + (A_2 - \alpha B_2)Y + u$$

when combined with the unique supply equation [8.2], (with the bs given by [8.10]), will have a reduced form identical to [8.5A] and [8.6A].

It will probably be helpful if at this point we introduce some numbers into the above equations. Suppose that the reduced-form parameters in [8.5A] and [8.6A] were known to have the following values

$$A_0 = 0.3 \qquad A_1 = 0.2 \qquad A_2 = 0.1$$
$$B_0 = 0.2 \qquad B_1 = 0.1 \qquad B_2 = 0.3$$

We could then derive unique values for the supply equation parameters using [8.10]. That is, $b_1 = 0.333$, $b_2 = 0.167$ and $b_0 = 0.233$. The supply equation implied by the above reduced-form parameters is therefore

$$Q = 0.233 + 0.333P + 0.167P^s + v \qquad\qquad [8.11]$$

Subsystem [8.8], however, becomes

$$0.3 - 0.2a_1 = a_0$$
$$0.2 - 0.1a_1 = a_2$$
$$0.1 - 0.3a_1 = a_3$$

There are an infinite number of sets of values for the as which will satisfy this subsystem. We can assign any value α to a_1 and then use the equations to obtain a_0, a_2 and a_3. The resultant set of as will represent a solution. For example, if we let $a_1 = -0.2$ then $a_0 = 0.34$, $a_2 = 0.22$, and $a_3 = 0.16$. It is easily verified that these values satisfy the subsystem. The demand equation implied is

$$Q = 0.34 - 0.2P + 0.22P^s + 0.16Y + u$$

However, we can also set a_1 equal to, for example, -0.4. This would yield a solution $a_1 = -0.4$, $a_0 = 0.38$, $a_2 = 0.24$, $a_3 = 0.22$, and a demand equation

$$Q = 0.38 - 0.4P + 0.24P^s + 0.22Y + u$$

The reader should verify that either of these demand equations when combined with the supply equation [8.11] will yield reduced-form equations with values for the As and Bs as above. Similarly, by selecting different values for α we can generate an infinite number of such demand equations, all of which when combined with supply equation [8.11] yields this same reduced form. Hence, while such a reduced form implies an unique supply equation, it is consistent with an infinite number of possible demand equations.

It is no accident that, whereas we were able to obtain unique values for the parameters of the supply equation, which we know under the present assumptions to be identified, we were unable to do so for the unidentified demand equation. In general, while it is possible to move from the reduced-form parameters to the structural parameters of an identified equation, *it is impossible to do so when an equation is unidentified*.

To reinforce this point, suppose the income variable, Y, had not been present in the demand equation. That is, $a_3 = 0$ and demand equation [8.1] reduces to [8.1B]. We already know that under these assumptions not only the demand equation but also the supply equation is unidentified. In terms of the reduced-form equations, [8.5A] and [8.6A], the absence of the Y variable implies $A_2 = B_2 = 0$. The two subsystems [8.8] and [8.9] now reduce to

$$A_0 - a_1 B_0 = a_0 \quad \text{and} \quad A_0 - b_1 B_0 = b_0$$
$$A_1 - a_1 B_1 = a_2 \qquad \qquad A_1 - b_1 B_1 = b_2$$

Both the subsystems now consist of *two* linear equations in *three* unknowns. Hence, we can solve neither for the as nor the bs. This reflects the fact that when $a_3 = 0$ neither demand equation nor supply equation is identified.

Identification by the use of linear restrictions

Consider again the more general case where the demand and supply equations are given by [8.1] and [8.2] respectively. We have already seen that the supply equation may be regarded as being identified by the placing of a restriction on the values of its parameters. Specifically, this restriction was the simple one that $b_3 = 0$ in the equation

$$Q = b_0 + b_1 P + b_2 P^s + b_3 Y + v$$

Identification can sometimes be achieved by specifying more complicated linear restrictions on the values of structural parameters. For example, suppose all the variables in the present model had been defined in logarithmic form so that all the structural parameters could be interpreted as elasticities. Consumer theory suggests that in the demand equation the sum of such elasticities should be zero,[5] i.e. $a_1 + a_2 + a_3 = 0$. The true form of [8.1] then becomes

$$Q = a_0 + a_1 P + a_2 P^s - (a_1 + a_2)Y + u \qquad\qquad [8.1C]$$

The 'mongrel' equation that can be formed by taking linear combinations of [8.1C] and [8.2] is

$$Q = \frac{\lambda a_0 + \mu b_0}{\lambda + \mu} + \left[\frac{\lambda a_1 + \mu b_1}{\lambda + \mu}\right]P + \left[\frac{\lambda a_2 + \mu b_2}{\lambda + \mu}\right]P^s - \left[\frac{\lambda a_1 + \lambda a_2}{\lambda + \mu}\right]Y + \frac{\lambda u + \mu v}{\lambda + \mu}$$

This equation is no longer of the same form as the demand equation since it will not generally have the property that the sum of the coefficients on the variables P, P^s and Y equals zero. This property only holds when $\lambda = 1$ and $\mu = 0$, in which case the mongrel equation reduces to the demand equation. Thus the imposition of the linear restriction $a_1 + a_2 + a_3 = 0$ on the parameters of the demand equation serves to identify it.

The imposition of the above linear restriction also makes it possible to derive unique values for the structural parameters of the demand equation once the reduced-form parameters are known. Previously, this was not possible because we were unable to obtain a unique solution to subsystem [8.8]. However, we may now add the restriction $a_1 + a_2 + a_3 = 0$ to [8.8], making a new subsystem containing in all four equations in the four unknowns a_0, a_1, a_2, a_3. These may now be uniquely solved for the demand equation parameters. For example, in our previous numerical example the expanded subsystem [8.8] becomes

$$0.3 - 0.2a_1 = a_0$$

$$0.2 - 0.1a_1 = a_2$$

$$0.1 - 0.3a_1 = a_3$$

$$a_1 + a_2 + a_3 = 0$$

which now has the unique solution $a_0 = 0.4$, $a_1 = -0.5$, $a_2 = 0.25$, and $a_3 = 0.25$, implying the demand equation

$$Q = 0.4 - 0.5P + 0.25P^s + 0.25Y + u$$

At this point we stress again that the above merely demonstrates that the demand equation is identified. The question of how it should be estimated remains a separate matter.

We shall encounter the problems of identification and simultaneous equation bias many times in this book. They are not merely something to do with demand and supply curves! They will arise whenever we have a system of simultaneous economic relationships. For example, in Chapter 10 the simplest consumption function model we consider is the two-equation system

$$C = \alpha + \beta Y + w$$

$$Y = C + Z$$

[8.12]

where C, Y and Z are consumption, income and non-consumption expenditure respectively. C and Y are endogenous to the system and Z is exogenous. The first equation is a simple Keynesian consumption function containing a disturbance w, and the second is an equilibrium condition. The second equation does not require estimating because we know that the coefficients of the C and Z variables are both unity. We therefore consider the problem of estimating the first equation. The absence of Z from the consumption function clearly identifies it. Any mongrel equation formed from the two equations must obviously contain Z. We need therefore only be concerned with the problem of simultaneous equation bias. The reduced-form of the model is

$$C = \frac{\alpha}{1 - \beta} + \left[\frac{\beta}{1 - \beta}\right]Z + \frac{w}{1 - \beta}$$

$$Y = \frac{\alpha}{1 - \beta} + \left[\frac{1}{1 - \beta}\right]Z + \frac{w}{1 - \beta}$$

We see from the second reduced-form equation that Y is correlated with w, i.e. the explanatory variable in the consumption function is correlated with the disturbance in that equation. Hence, OLS will yield *biased and inconsistent*

181

estimators of the consumption function parameters *despite the fact that they are identified.* Some other method of estimation is therefore necessary. The direction of the OLS bias can easily be determined. The parameter β represents the marginal propensity to consume (MPC) and hence may be expected to lie between zero and unity. We can therefore see from the reduced form that Y will be positively correlated with w. This means we will have a situation similar to that illustrated in Fig. 5.1 (page 84) with the OLS estimators overestimating the MPC, β, and underestimating the intercept in the consumption function, α.

We shall come across simultaneous equation systems in all the applied chapters of this book. For example, in section 11.3 we shall see that production functions have to be viewed as but one equation in at least a three-equation system. These other relationships, normally involving the equating of marginal products to factor prices, have to be allowed for in the estimation of the production function. Similarly, in section 12.2, when estimating demand for money equations, we shall see that account must be taken of the possible existence of supply of money equations.

The general case

Economic models frequently consist of considerably more than the two relationships of the simple models we have so far been considering. When there are many equations in a model, deciding whether a particular equation is identified or not obviously becomes a more complicated affair. Fortunately 'general' conditions have been derived for such cases. The most frequently used of these is the so-called *order-condition for identification* which we state but do not derive:

A necessary (but not sufficient) condition for an equation in a model to be identified is that the total number of restrictions on its (structural) parameters should be at least as great as the number of equations in the model less one.

That is we must have $R \geqslant G - 1$ where R is the number of restrictions and G is the number of equations in the model.

This condition is 'necessary but not sufficient' because, although it must hold if an equation is to be identified, the mere fact that it does hold is not sufficient to guarantee identification. The restrictions referred to may be either of the more general kind of the last subsection, or the simple 'excluded variable' type used to identify the supply equation in our example.

A sufficient condition for identification known as the *rank-condition* also exists. However, it would be difficult to state or prove this condition given the level of mathematics used in this book. Equations which satisfy the rank condition necessarily satisfy the order condition but the reverse is not true. Fortunately, this latter possibility is relatively rare and in most cases the order condition alone may be used to determine the identification status of an equation. For example, in our original two-equation demand-and-supply model given by equations [8.1] and [8.2], $G - 1$ is obviously equal to 1. The demand equation has no restrictions on its parameters so that R is zero and equation [8.1] is unidentified. The supply equation, however, has one restriction – the absence of Y, so that $R = 1$ for this equation and hence it is identified.

At this point it should be noted that the general condition just introduced applies only to simultaneous systems that are linear in the endogenous variables. This was true of both the systems we have so far examined. However, many economic systems are non-linear in the endogenous variables. For example, suppose we replaced the system given by [8.1] and [8.2] by

$$Q = a_0 + a_1 P + a_2 P^s + a_3 Y + u \qquad \text{demand equation}$$

$$Q = b_0 + b_1 \sqrt{(P)} + b_2 P^s + v \qquad \text{supply equation}$$

The endogenous own-price variable, P, now appears non-linearly in the supply equation. Other less-contrived examples are not difficult to think of. For example, many models contain the money wage rate, w, and the general price level, p, as endogenous variables. If such a model also seeks to explain the real wage rate, w/p, then clearly the endogenous w/p is a non-linear function of the endogenous w and p. A similar problem would arise if a model contained as endogenous variables price, p, quantity sold, q, and total revenue $R = pq$.

The rules for linear systems cannot be applied to non-linear systems. For example, for the linear system given by equations [8.1] and [8.2], we have seen that the demand equation is unidentified. However, the replacement of [8.2] by the above non-linear supply curve does, in fact, serve to identify the demand equation. We shall not pursue the question of identification in non-linear systems here, but the interested reader is referred to Kelejian and Oates (1989: ch. 8) for an understandable introduction.

Identification by the use of restrictions on the disturbances

The order condition for identification in linear systems just discussed applies only when the sole means of identification is via linear restrictions on structural parameters. However, identification may also sometimes be achieved by specifying restrictions on the disturbances in the model. We have, in fact, already come across one such example. In the first case we considered, where the demand and supply equations were given by [8.1A] and [8.2A] respectively, we saw that the supply equation would become identified if it were possible to specify that the demand disturbance, u, varied more widely than the supply disturbance, v. Specifically the restrictions

$$\text{var } v = 0 \quad \text{and} \quad \text{var } u > 0$$

would serve to identify the supply equation.

These restrictions would also have served to identify the supply equation in the second case considered, where the demand and supply equations were given by [8.1B] and [8.2B] respectively. In this case the mongrel equation [8.3] could not be distinguished from either the demand or supply equations. However, it contained a disturbance term which we may write as

$$\varepsilon = \left[\frac{\lambda}{\lambda + \mu} \right] u + \left[\frac{\mu}{\lambda + \mu} \right] v \qquad [8.13]$$

If the above restrictions on u and v hold then, whereas the supply equation now contains a disturbance with zero variance, the mongrel equation contains a disturbance with a non-zero variance given by

$$\text{var } \varepsilon = \left[\frac{\lambda}{\lambda + \mu} \right]^2 \text{var } u$$

The supply equation is therefore no longer of the same form as the mongrel equation and is hence identified. The demand equation, however, still contains a disturbance with non-zero variance and therefore remains unidentified.

Finally, identification may also be achieved if it is possible to specify restrictions on the relationships between disturbances in different equations. Suppose in the model represented by [8.1B] and [8.2B] we specify that $\text{cov}(u, v) = 0$, i.e. that there is no contemporaneous correlation between demand disturbance, u, and supply disturbance, v. The demand equation [8.1B] now contains a disturbance, u, which is uncorrelated with v. However, the mongrel equation [8.3] contains a disturbance, given by [8.13], which is quite clearly correlated with v. It is therefore possible to distinguish between the demand equation and the mongrel equation and so the demand equation becomes identified.

Similarly, the supply equation [8.2B] now contains a disturbance, v, which is uncorrelated with u. It also becomes identified since it cannot now be confused with the mongrel equation which contains a disturbance which we see from [8.13] is correlated with u. Thus the restriction $\text{cov}(u, v) = 0$, if it could be imposed, would serve to identify both demand and supply equations.

While it should now be clear that it is possible to achieve identification by placing restrictions on disturbances, the reader may feel somewhat bemused as to how estimation should proceed under such circumstances. However, we have stressed throughout this section that the problem of estimation is a separate one and it is to this problem that we now proceed.

8.2 The estimation of simultaneous relationships

In the previous section we have seen, first, that if any single equation in a set of simultaneous equations is unidentified then it is impossible to obtain unbiased or even consistent estimates of its parameters. Secondly, even if such an equation were identified, the OLS estimators of its parameters will normally be subject to simultaneous equation bias. In this section we shall be concerned mainly with the various methods that have been devised for combating this bias. However, we begin by considering one rather special type of simultaneous system in which the OLS method of estimation is not, in fact, subject to it.

Recursive systems

Consider the following three-equation system in its structural form

$$Y_1 = a_0 + a_1 X_1 + a_2 X_2 + \varepsilon_1$$
$$Y_2 = b_0 + b_1 X_1 + b_2 X_2 + b_1' Y_1 + \varepsilon_2 \qquad\qquad [8.14]$$
$$Y_3 = c_0 + c_1 X_1 + c_2 X_2 + c_1' Y_1 + c_2' Y_2 + \varepsilon_3$$

The Y variables are endogenous, the X variables are exogenous, ε_1, ε_2 and ε_3 are disturbances and the as, bs and cs are structural parameters. Since the X variables are by definition determined outside the above model, we may assume that they are independent of the disturbances.

Considering only restrictions on the structural parameters and using the criteria developed in the previous section, the reader should be able to deduce that only the first of the equations in the above system is identified. Suppose, however, we add the restrictions that the three disturbances are contemporaneously uncorrelated with one another, i.e.

$$\text{cov}(\varepsilon_1, \varepsilon_2) = \text{cov}(\varepsilon_1, \varepsilon_2) = \text{cov}(\varepsilon_2, \varepsilon_3) = 0$$

Then, just as in the demand/supply model of the previous section, this serves to identify all the equations in the model.

In the first structural equation none of the explanatory variables are endogenous so that the problem of simultaneous equation bias does not arise. This equation is identified and the X variables are by assumption uncorrelated with ε_1. The OLS method of estimation may therefore be applied to the first structural equation to obtain unbiased and consistent estimators of its parameters. The problem of estimating the remaining two equations in the model is best illustrated by considering the reduced form, which in this case is particularly easy to derive.

The first reduced-form equation is identical to the first structural equation. The second reduced-form equation may be obtained by substituting the first reduced-form equation into the second structural equation. Finally, the third reduced-form equation may be obtained by substituting the first two reduced-form equations into the third structural equation. The reduced form obtained in this way has the following form

$$Y_1 = A_0 + A_1 X_1 + A_2 X_2 + \varepsilon_1$$
$$Y_2 = B_0 + B_1 X_1 + B_2 X_2 + b_1' \varepsilon_1 + \varepsilon_2 \qquad [8.15]$$
$$Y_3 = C_0 + C_1 X_1 + C_2 X_2 + (c_1' + b_1' c_2') \varepsilon_1 + c_2' \varepsilon_2 + \varepsilon_3$$

where the As, Bs and Cs are functions of the as, bs and cs but the precise form of these functions need not concern us.

What is significant about the reduced-form equations [8.15] is what they tell us about the relationships between the endogenous variables in the model and the disturbances. First, Y_1 is uninfluenced by either ε_2 or ε_3. In particular, Y_1 is independent of ε_2, the disturbance in the second equation, and is the only endogenous variable among the explanatory variables in that equation. This means that the OLS estimators of the parameters of this equation will not be subject to simultaneous equation bias. Secondly, Y_2 is uninfluenced by ε_3. Thus, both endogenous variables on the right-hand side of the third structural equation are independent of the disturbance in that equation. Hence, we may also apply OLS to the estimation of the third equation without worrying about the problem of bias.

The lack of dependence between the endogenous explanatory variables and the corresponding disturbances stems from the rather special shape of the structural form [8.14]. Notice that the first structural equation contains no endogenous explanatory variables, the second equation contains just the first endogenous variable on the right-hand side, while only the third equation contains both the first and second endogenous variables on the right-hand side. This structure, plus the assumption of contemporaneous non-correlation between the disturbances, means that the values of the endogenous variables are determined *recursively*. That is, firstly Y_1 is determined by the exogenous variables and ε_1. Secondly, once Y_1 is determined, the value of Y_2 is determined by Y_1, the exogenous variables and ε_2. Finally, and only after Y_1 and Y_2 are determined, Y_3 is determined by Y_1 and Y_2, the exogenous variables and ε_3. Thus the endogenous variables are determined recursively rather than simultaneously and, indeed, it could be argued that [8.14] is not a simultaneous system at all.

Summarising, the specification that the disturbances are uncorrelated across equations ensures that each equation in [8.14] is identified. The independence between right-hand side endogenous variables and the corresponding disturbances ensures the absence of simultaneous equation bias. Hence, since the X variables are independent of the disturbances by definition, the application of OLS to each equation of the model in turn will yield unbiased and consistent estimates of all the structural parameters.

When a model such as [8.14] is characterised, first by disturbances which are uncorrelated across equations, and secondly by the special structural form described above, it is known as a *recursive system*. These are the only types of simultaneous systems for which the OLS method of estimation will provide unbiased and consistent estimators.

In certain situations the X variables in a recursive model may not be all truly exogenous. Typically, some of them may be *lagged endogenous variables*. The expression '*predetermined variables*' is sometimes used to cover both exogenous and lagged endogenous variables. When any of the predetermined variables on the right-hand side of a structural equation in a recursive system are lagged endogenous, then OLS will yield consistent but not unbiased estimators. This follows from the discussion of stochastic explanatory variables in section 5.1.

For examples of simple recursive systems, see Wold's (1958) reformulation of the Suits (1955) water-melon market model in section 9.3 and models IIA and IIB in the subsection on simultaneity in section 12.2.

Indirect least squares

When a model is non-recursive, the most easily understood method of estimating its structural parameters is (if applicable) the method known as *indirect least squares* (ILS). Consider again the two-equation model represented by equations [8.1] and [8.2]. In the absence of any restrictions on the disturbances, the demand equation [8.1] is unidentified. However, the supply equation [8.2] is not and may be estimated by ILS. The method involves applying the OLS technique to the reduced-form equations of the model – in this case equations [8.5A] and [8.6A]. These equations contain, on the right-hand side, only exogenous variables which may be assumed to be independent of the reduced-form disturbances. Ordinary least squares may therefore be used to obtain unbiased and consistent estimates of the reduced-form parameters.[6] That

186

is, we compute the sample regression equations

$$\hat{Q} = \hat{A}_0 + \hat{A}_1 P^s + \hat{A}_2 Y$$
$$\hat{P} = \hat{B}_0 + \hat{B}_1 P^s + \hat{B}_2 Y \qquad\qquad [8.16]$$

where the $\hat{A}$s and $\hat{B}$s are the OLS estimates of the As and the Bs.

We have already seen that, if the reduced-form parameters were known, then by solving subsystem [8.9] it is possible to derive the values of the structural parameters of the identified supply equation. These values are given by [8.10]. This suggests that we use the *estimated* reduced-form parameters to obtain *estimates* of the structural parameters of the supply equation. The form of the estimators is given by [8.10]. We have

$$b_1^* = \hat{A}_2/\hat{B}_2, \quad b_2^* = \hat{A}_1 - [\hat{A}_2/\hat{B}_2]\hat{B}_1 \quad \text{and} \quad b_0^* = \hat{A}_0 - [\hat{A}_2/\hat{B}_2]\hat{B}_0$$

The estimators b_0^*, b_1^* and b_2^* of the structural parameters b_0, b_1 and b_2 are known as the *ILS estimators*. Since the As and Bs are consistent estimators of the reduced-form parameters, the b^*s are consistent estimators of the structural parameters of the supply equation. However, the b^*s are not unbiased despite the fact that the As and Bs have this property. This is because, as we have seen in section 2.3, while the property of consistency 'carries over' that of unbiasedness does not. Thus the ILS estimators have desirable *large sample* properties only.

Notice that the ILS method will not yield estimates of the structural parameters of the demand equation. This is obvious from the fact that the subsystem [8.8] does not have a unique solution, and reflects the unidentified status of the demand equation under the present assumptions.

As a further example of the ILS method of estimation, consider the simple consumption model [8.12]. The reduced form of this model, given below [8.12] can be written as

$$C = A_0 + A_1 Z + W$$
$$Y = B_0 + B_1 Z + W \qquad\qquad [8.17]$$

where

$$A_0 = B_0 = \frac{\alpha}{(1 - \beta)}, \quad A_1 = \frac{\beta}{(1 - \beta)}, \quad B_1 = \frac{1}{(1 - \beta)} \quad \text{and} \quad W = \frac{w}{(1 - \beta)}$$

To obtain ILS estimators of α and β in the consumption function we therefore apply OLS to the reduced-form equations [8.17] to obtain estimators, $\hat{A}$s and $\hat{B}$s, of the reduced-form parameters. The required ILS estimators are then given by

$$\beta^* = \hat{A}_1/\hat{B}_1 \quad \text{and} \quad \alpha^* = \hat{A}_0/\hat{B}_1 = \hat{B}_0/\hat{B}_1$$

Although the OLS estimators of the As and Bs above will be unbiased and consistent, the ILS estimators of α and β will again only retain the property of consistency.

It may seem that we obtain two separate estimators of α by the above procedure, $\hat{A}_0/\hat{B}_1$ and $\hat{B}_0/\hat{B}_1$. However, because the data used will satisfy the identity $Y = C + Z$, not only are A_0 and B_0 equal but so will be their OLS estimates, $\hat{A}_0$ and $\hat{B}_0$.[7]

The method of ILS appears to be a fairly straightforward method of overcoming the problem of simultaneous equation bias when estimating identified equations. Unfortunately, in practice, the method frequently breaks down and for this reason we shall encounter few examples of it in this book. Consider again the two-equation model given by [8.1] and [8.2] but suppose that a third exogenous variable, Z, appears in the demand equation. For example, Z might be an index of tastes. The model now becomes

$$Q = a_0 + a_1 P + a_2 P^s + a_3 Y + a_4 Z + u \qquad \text{demand equation} \qquad [8.18]$$

$$Q = b_0 + b_1 P + b_2 P^s + v \qquad \text{supply equation} \qquad [8.19]$$

The identification status of the equations appears to be unchanged but as we shall see it has now become impossible to estimate the supply equation by ILS. The reduced form now becomes

$$Q = A_0 + A_1 P^s + A_2 Y + A_3 Z + U$$

$$P = B_0 + B_1 P^s + B_2 Y + B_3 Z + V \qquad [8.20]$$

where

$$A_3 = \frac{a_4 b_1}{b_1 - a_1} \quad \text{and} \quad B_3 = \frac{a_4}{b_1 - a_1} \qquad [8.21]$$

The expressions for the remaining reduced-form parameters and the disturbances remain as in [8.7].

If the reduced-form parameters were known, then to derive the structural parameters we would now have to solve the subsystems

$$A_0 - a_1 B_0 = a_0 \qquad\qquad A_0 - b_1 B_0 = b_0$$

$$A_1 - a_1 B_1 = a_2 \qquad\qquad A_1 - b_1 B_1 = b_2$$

$$\qquad\qquad [8.22] \qquad\qquad\qquad\qquad\qquad [8.23]$$

$$A_2 - a_1 B_2 = a_3 \qquad\qquad A_2 - b_1 B_2 = 0$$

$$A_3 - a_1 B_3 = a_4 \qquad\qquad A_3 - b_1 B_3 = 0$$

Subsystem [8.22] consists of four linear equations in the five unknown as and hence has many solutions. This reflects the fact that the demand equation remains unidentified. Subsystem [8.23] now consists of four linear equations in three unknown bs. Apparently we have 'too many' equations and normally such a system would involve inconsistencies and have no solution. This appears to be the case here since the third and fourth equations yield seemingly contradictory values for b_1, i.e. $b_1 = A_2/B_2$ and $b_1 = A_3/B_3$. However, the two ratios A_2/B_2 and A_3/B_3 are, in fact, identical and both equal to b_1. This can be seen by considering [8.7] and [8.21]. The fact that these two ratios are the same means that the fourth equation in subsystem [8.23] is an exact multiple of the third. Hence, subsystem [8.23] contains only three independent equations, involves no inconsistencies and still yields the unique solution

$$b_1 = A_2/B_2, \quad b_2 = A_1 - [A_2/B_2]B_1 \quad \text{and} \quad b_0 = A_0 - [A_2/B_2]B_0 \quad [8.24]$$

Alternatively we could replace A_2/B_2 by A_3/B_3 in the above solution without affecting the value of the bs. Clearly, the supply equation remains identified. The difficulty in estimating its parameters arises *because we do not know the exact values of the reduced-form parameters but only have estimates of them.* Just because the 'true' ratios A_2/B_2 and A_3/B_3 are identical does not mean that the two estimated ratios $\hat{A}_2/\hat{B}_2$ and $\hat{A}_3/\hat{B}_3$ will be. Generally, the $\hat{A}$s and $\hat{B}$s will differ from the As and Bs so that we must expect the ratios $\hat{A}_2/\hat{B}_2$ and $\hat{A}_3/\hat{B}_3$ to differ.[8] This means that, in practice, when we replace the As and Bs in subsystem [8.23] by the estimated $\hat{A}$s and $\hat{B}$s, we do, unfortunately, end up with four independent equations in just three variables. That is, the subsystem will involve inconsistencies and have no solution. Thus the ILS method breaks down because we cannot obtain estimates of the bs from the estimates of the reduced form parameters.

When ILS breaks down in this manner, the equation concerned and its parameters are said to be *overidentified*. The term overidentified is used because only the presence in the demand equation of *one* of the variables Y and Z is necessary to achieve the identification of equation [8.19]. However [8.18] contains *both* Y and Z which is *more* than is necessary for straightforward identification.

Overidentification can only occur when an equation is identified in the sense of section 8.1 and hence only when the order condition stated there is satisfied. Recall that for a structural equation to be identified we must have $R \geqslant G - 1$, where R is the number of restrictions on its parameters and G is the total number of equations in the model. Overidentification can be detected by considering how this condition is satisfied. *Overidentification occurs whenever the order condition is satisfied as an inequality*, i.e. when $R > G - 1$ as it is for the supply equation [8.19]. When the order condition is satisfied as an equality, i.e. when $R = G - 1$, the equation concerned and its parameters are said to be *exactly identified* and the problems associated with overidentification do not arise.

Two-stage least squares

A method of estimation that has been frequently used in overcoming the problems of overidentification is that of *two-stage least squares* (TSLS). We shall illustrate this method by describing how it would be used to estimate the supply equation in the two-equation model given by [8.18] and [8.19].

When estimating the supply equation [8.19], simultaneous equation bias arises because of the appearance of the endogenous variable, P, as an explanatory variable in this equation. The basic idea of TSLS is that we 'purge' such variables of their troublesome correlation with the disturbance in the equation concerned. The *first stage* of the TSLS procedure for estimating an overidentified equation is therefore as follows. We take all endogenous explanatory variables in the equation and use OLS to regress *each* in turn on *all* the predetermined variables in the model. In the present example this involves regressing P on the exogenous variables P^s, Y and Z. We then have, for each observation in the available sample

$$P_i = \hat{B}_0 + \hat{B}_1 P_i^s + \hat{B}_2 Y_i + \hat{B}_3 Z_i + E_i \qquad [8.25]$$

where the $\hat{B}$'s are estimated OLS regression coefficients and the E_is are the residuals from the OLS regression performed.

Now since $P_i = \hat{P}_i + E_i$, where the $\hat{P}_i$s are the predicted values of P obtained from [8.25], we can write the supply equation which we wish to estimate as

$$Q = b_0 + b_1 P + b_2 P^s + v$$

$$= b_0 + b_1(\hat{P} + E) + b_2 P^s + v$$

or

$$Q = b_0 + b_1\hat{P} + b_2 P^s + b_1 E + v \qquad [8.26]$$

Equation [8.26] differs from the original supply equation [8.19] in that it has $\hat{P}$ as an 'explanatory' variable rather than P and $b_1 E + v$ as a 'disturbance' rather than v. It is possible to show that both $\hat{P}$ and P^s, the right-hand side variables in [8.26], are for large samples uncorrelated with the 'disturbance' $b_1 E + v$. Hence, for large samples, the problem of simultaneous equation bias is circumvented and the OLS estimation procedure when applied to [8.26] will provide estimators with the usual desirable large sample properties. In particular, they will be consistent but not, of course, unbiased.

The *second stage* of the TSLS procedure is therefore to replace any endogenous variables on the right-hand side of the equation being estimated by their predicted values obtained from the OLS regressions performed in the first stage. This effectively purges them of their correlation with the disturbance in the equation. Ordinary least squares may then be applied to the reconstituted structural equation to obtain consistent estimates of its parameters.

The TSLS procedure can also be used to estimate the parameters of an exactly identified equation. If this is done, then it can be shown that the estimates obtained are identical to those that would be obtained using the ILS estimation method described in the previous subsection. For this reason ILS is seldom used nowadays and TSLS is regarded as an estimation method suitable for any identified equation – whether exactly or overidentified.

If an attempt were made to estimate the parameters of an unidentified equation by TSLS then, not surprisingly, the procedure breaks down. We can illustrate this by considering the unidentified demand equation of the two-equation model [8.18] and [8.19]. The TSLS procedure would involve replacing the endogenous variable P in equation [8.18] by values of $\hat{P}$ obtained from equation [8.25]. However, $\hat{P}$ is an exact linear function of the variables P^s, Y and Z which all appear in the demand equation [8.18]. Thus, the second stage of the TSLS procedure would involve attempting to regress by OLS the variable Q on a set of explanatory variables which are exactly multicollinear. As we know from section 5.3.1, OLS breaks down in these circumstances.

Notice that TSLS is a method which can be used to estimate a single equation in a system. This contrasts with certain 'complete system' methods of estimation in which all the equations in a model have to be estimated simultaneously.

The application of TSLS to a single equation in a system of simultaneous relationships does not require complete knowledge of the structure of every relationship in the system. The only knowledge required is the precise specification of the single equation being estimated and a list of all the exogenous variables which influence the system. For example, in estimating the supply equation in the above model, no reference was made to the specification of the demand equation but we did require the knowledge that the three exogenous variables influencing the system were Y, P^s and Z.

Finally, note that TSLS is a form of the generalised instrumental variable type of estimation introduced at the end of section 5.1 as a way of dealing with contemporaneous correlations between explanatory variables and disturbances. The exogenous variables (which are uncorrelated with the disturbances in the structural equations), play the role of instruments and the predicted values of the endogenous variables, obtained from the first stage, are the instrumental variables.

We conclude this subsection with a further example of TSLS in action. Suppose we wish to estimate the following 'wage price model'

$$W = a_0 + a_1 P + a_2 U + a_3 S + u \qquad\qquad [8.27]$$

$$P = b_0 + b_1 W + b_2 X + b_3 M + v \qquad\qquad [8.28]$$

In this two-equation model the rate of wage inflation, W, and the rate of price inflation, P, are endogenous. There are four exogenous variables: U, the level of unemployment; S an index of strike activity; X the rate of increase in labour productivity, and M the rate of increase in import prices. Both equations are overidentified (verify this) and if the reduced form is derived it will be seen that P in the wage equation is correlated with u, and W in the price equation is correlated with v. Ordinary least squares will therefore yield biased and inconsistent estimates of the parameters of both equations.

To obtain TSLS estimates of all the parameters in the model, the first stage is to take the right-hand side endogenous variables, P and W, and use OLS to regress each in turn on all four exogenous variables, U, S, X and M. Estimates of the wage equation parameters are then obtained by replacing P in that equation by the predicted values, $\hat{P}$, obtained from the first stage and applying OLS to the resultant equation. Similarly, the TSLS estimates of the price equation parameters are obtained by replacing W in that equation by the $\hat{W}$ values obtained in the first stage.

*8.3 Maximum likelihood estimation of overidentified equations

The method of maximum likelihood estimation described in Chapter 3 can also be used to estimate the parameters of identified and overidentified equations. The reader is advised to re-read Chapter 3 thoroughly before tackling this section. The method may be used either to estimate a single equation in a set of simultaneous relationships or to estimate all such relationships at the same time. When attention is concentrated on a single equation the method adopted is known as *limited information maximum likelihood* (LIML) and we consider this procedure first. We shall illustrate its use in estimating the overidentified supply equation of the simple market model given by equations [8.18] and [8.19]. Suppose we have a sample, size n, from which we wish to obtain our estimates, i.e. we have

$$\left.\begin{aligned} Q_i &= a_0 + a_1 P_i + a_2 P_i^s + a_3 Y_i + a_4 Z_i + u_i \\ Q_i &= b_0 + b_1 P_i + b_2 P_i^s + v_i \end{aligned}\right\} \quad i = 1, 2, 3, \ldots, n$$

From the reduced form of this model given by equations [8.20] we also have

$$\left.\begin{array}{l} Q_i = A_0 + A_1 P_i^s + A_2 Y_i + A_3 Z_i + U_i \\ P_i = B_0 + B_1 P_i^s + B_2 Y_i + B_3 Z_i + V_i \end{array}\right\} \quad i = 1, 2, 3, \ldots, n$$

The values of the reduced-form disturbances are given by

$$U_i = \frac{b_1 u_i - a_1 v_i}{b_1 - a_1} \quad \text{and} \quad \left. V_i = \frac{u_i - v_i}{b_1 - a_1} \right\} \quad i = 1, 2, 3, \ldots, n$$

They are linear combinations of the structural form disturbances, the u_is and the v_is. Hence, provided the u_is and the v_is are all normally distributed with zero means, they will themselves be normally distributed with zero means and constant variances which we shall label σ_U^2 and σ_V^2 respectively. σ_U^2 and σ_V^2 will be dependent on the constant variances of the u_is and the v_is. Hence, for given values of the exogenous variables, if repeated samples were taken, then each sequence of Q_is obtained would be normally distributed with a mean

$$E(Q_i) = A_0 + A_1 P_i^s + A_2 Y_i + A_3 Z_i$$

and a variance of σ_U^2.[9] Similarly, each sequence of P_is obtained would be distributed normally with a mean

$$E(P_i) = B_0 + B_1 P_i^s + B_2 Y_i + B_3 Z_i$$

and a variance of σ_V^2. Knowing their distributions enables a likelihood function for the Q_is and P_is, similar to those of Chapter 3, to be formed. The procedure for deriving the exact form of this likelihood function is beyond the scope of this book, but it should be clear from the above that the sample likelihood will depend on:

1. the sample values of Q_i and P_i obtained, i.e. $Q_1, Q_2, \ldots, Q_n$ and $P_1, P_2, \ldots, P_n$;
2. the reduced-form parameters, since A_0, A_1, A_2 and A_3 determine $E(Q_i)$ and B_0, B_1, B_2 and B_3 determine $E(P_i)$;
3. the two variances σ_U^2 and σ_V^2;
4. the covariance σ_{UV} between the U_is and the V_is. This quantity appears because the U_is and the V_is are both dependent on the u_is and the v_is and hence are not independent of one another. It follows that P_i and Q_i are not independent and that the sample likelihood also depends on σ_{UV}.

Thus, denoting the sample likelihood by L as in Chapter 3, we have in this case

$$L = L(Q_1, Q_2, \ldots, Q_n, P_1, P_2, \ldots, P_n, A_0, A_1, A_2, A_3, B_0, B_1, B_2, B_3, \sigma_U^2, \sigma_V^2, \sigma_{UV})$$

[8.29]

We could now, for the given sample Q_is and P_is, maximise L as it stands to yield MLEs of the reduced-form parameters and also of σ_U^2, σ_V^2 and σ_{UV}. The problem with this procedure is that since the supply equation is overidentified, we would not be able to obtain unique estimators of its parameters from the MLEs of the reduced-form parameters. The likelihood function L is therefore maximised *subject to the restriction that the estimators of the reduced-form parameters obtained are such that they do yield unique values for the structural parameters we wish to estimate.* In the present case this would involve maximising L subject to the constraint $A_2/B_2 = A_3/B_3$. This ensures that the subsystem

[8.23], with the As and Bs replaced by their MLEs, will yield unique estimators of the bs, i.e. of the supply equation parameters. The estimators of the reduced-form parameters obtained in this way are known as *constrained* as opposed to *unconstrained* MLEs. These constrained estimators are consistent and hence, as the property of consistency 'carries over', the estimators of the supply equation parameters eventually obtained will also be consistent.

For an example of equations estimated by the LIML technique see the second and third equations of Suits' (1955) model of the US water-melon market described in section 9.3.

As with the method of TSLS, the LIML method can be applied to a single equation. It requires knowledge only of the structure of that equation and a list of the exogenous variables in the model. Hence, the prefix 'limited information'. However, an estimation method which estimates all equations in a model simultaneously, and hence requires knowledge of the structure of every equation in the model, is that known as *full information maximum likelihood* (FIML). We shall illustrate this method by again considering our simple two-equation market model. However, we introduce an extra variable, C, which might be an index of production costs, into the supply equation. Thus, for a sample of size n we have

$$\left. \begin{array}{l} Q_i = a_0 + a_1 P_i + a_2 P_i^s + a_3 Y_i + a_4 Z_i + u_i \\ Q_i = b_0 + b_1 P_i + b_2 P_i^s + b_3 C_i + v_i \end{array} \right\} \quad i = 1, 2, 3, \ldots, n \quad [8.30]$$

The appearance of the variable C in the supply equation means that both equations are now identified – the demand equation exactly identified and the supply equation overidentified.

The FIML method estimates *all* structural parameters in the model directly without, as in the case of LIML, first estimating any reduced-form parameters. If the u_i and the v_i are normally distributed with zero means, constant variances σ_u^2, σ_v^2 respectively and constant covariance σ_{uv}, it is possible to obtain for given σ_u^2, σ_v^2 and σ_{uv} the likelihood function for the u_is and the v_is. It is then possible to find, given the values of the exogenous variables, the likelihood function for the endogenous Q_is and P_is. This second step is somewhat complicated because, given values for the exogenous variables, the Q_is and P_is are jointly determined by the u_is and v_is. Thus, given values for the exogenous variables, the values of the Q_is and P_is will depend on all the structural parameters and on the values of the u_is and v_is. Hence, this second likelihood function when formed will depend on the values for the Q_is and P_is, on all the structural parameters and on the disturbance parameters σ_u^2, σ_v^2 and σ_{uv}. Again it is beyond the scope of this book to derive the exact form of this likelihood function but clearly we can now write

$$L = L(Q_1, Q_2, \ldots, Q_n, P_1, P_2, \ldots, P_n, a_0, a_1, a_2, a_3, a_4, b_0, b_1, b_2, b_3, \sigma_u^2, \sigma_v^2, \sigma_{uv})$$
$$[8.31]$$

For given sample values of the Q_is and P_is, the likelihood function [8.31] may now be maximised to yield the so-called full information MLEs of the structural parameters. These estimators are consistent and asymptotically efficient but will be generally biased for small samples. For an example of a system estimated by FIML see the estimates of the parameters of the Klein model I macroeconomic model presented in Table 13.1 (page 404). Not surprisingly, given what was stressed earlier in this chapter, the FIML method of estimation breaks down if attempts are made to apply it to an unidentified equation. Consider, for example, the two equation model given by equations [8.1B] and [8.2B]. Both equations are unidentified as they stand. If we form a likelihood function analogous to [8.31] we have

$$L = L(Q_1, Q_2, \ldots, Q_n, P_1, P_2, \ldots, P_n, a_0'', a_1, a_2, b_0, b_1, b_2, \sigma_u^2, \sigma_v^2, \sigma_{uv})$$
[8.32]

The problem now is that there turns out to be no unique set of values for the model parameters that will maximise [8.32]. There is in fact an infinite number of sets of values, all giving the same maximum value to L. Colloquially, all these different sets of values for the model's parameters are 'equally likely' to have generated the sample values of Q and P. Obviously, the investigator has no idea which set to choose and this reflects the unidentified status of equations [8.1B] and [8.2B].

We saw in section [8.1] that it was possible to identify equation [8.1A] and/or [8.1B] by placing restrictions on the disturbances u and v. For example, the restriction $\text{cov}(u, v) = 0$ served to identify both [8.1A] and [8.1B]. It is now possible to indicate one way by which estimation could proceed. $\text{Cov}(u, v) = 0$ obviously implies $\sigma_{uv} = 0$. If we set $\sigma_{uv} = 0$ in [8.32] it turns out that it *is* now possible to find an unique set of model parameters that maximise the likelihood function and this set of values form the FIML estimators of the as, the bs, σ_u^2 and σ_v^2.

We also saw, at the end of section [8.1] that the restriction $\text{var } v = \sigma_v^2 = 0$ on the supply disturbance enables the supply equation [8.2A] to be identified. In such a situation attempts at maximising [8.32] still yield an infinite number of possible sets of values for the structural parameters but the values for b_0, b_1. and b_2, the supply equation parameters, turn out to be the same in each such set. An unique set of values for the supply parameters can therefore now be found and these are the FIML estimators.

8.4 The choice of estimation technique

In deciding which technique should be employed for the estimation of equations in a non-recursive simultaneous system the first consideration is the identification status of the relevant equations. If an equation is unidentified *none of the techniques outlined in the previous two sections will provide consistent estimates of its parameters*. However, even if all the structural equations in a model are unidentified, it is still possible to obtain consistent and sometimes unbiased estimates of the parameters of the reduced-form of the model. This may well be a valuable exercise if the purpose of the model is simply the prediction or forecasting of values of the endogenous variables for given values of the predetermined variables. Such forecasting is most simply performed using the reduced-form and knowledge of the structural parameters is not required. The testing of most of the propositions of economic theory, however, requires the estimation of structural parameters and *this will only be possible when the relevant equation is identified*. Remember that the techniques described in this chapter are for overcoming the problem of simultaneous equation bias not that of non-identification.

If an equation is exactly identified, then all the estimating procedures described previously, with the exception of OLS, can be shown to provide identical estimates of its parameters. Since OLS provides inconsistent estimates, this method may be ruled out and a choice made between the remaining methods. Since they all yield identical estimates, the method adopted is generally either ILS or TSLS, since these methods are both the simplest and the cheapest in terms of computing time. When an equation is overidentified the ILS procedure breaks down and the remaining procedures no longer provide identical estimates of its structural parameters. The problem of choosing between the various estimators in this case will be discussed below.

The case of exact identification is rare in practice. Most applied econometricians assume that the equations they are trying to estimate are overidentified. However, one must beware that the apparent identified status of an equation is not spurious and simply the result of the convenient but unjustified exclusion of certain variables from the equation. An extreme view is, for example, taken by Liu (1960) who argues that, in the real world, relationships typically include many more variables than are normally included in estimated equations. Hence, underidentification is the normal state of affairs and under such conditions the only sensible procedure would be the estimation of reduced-form equations with many predetermined variables.

When an equation is overidentified, provided the available sample is a 'large' one, choice between estimation methods can fairly safely be made by balancing computing time and cost against the asymptotic efficiency of the various consistent estimators available. It is a general rule that the more relevant information used in an estimation procedure, the smaller the asymptotic variances of the estimators obtained, i.e. the more asymptotically efficient are these estimators. Thus, TSLS and LIML, which make use of the same information about the economic model concerned, provided estimators with the same asymptotic variance. Since both provide consistent estimators they are asymptotically equally efficient. While the availability of high speed computors, together with the requisite software, has increased the feasibility of LIML methods in recent years, the method invariably involves the solution of highly non-linear equations. For this reason TSLS estimators, which are so much easier to handle computationally, are often preferred.

Complete system estimation methods such as FIML and a method we have not discussed – three-stage least squares (which like TSLS is an instrumental variable method), make use of more information concerning the complete system and hence are asymptotically more efficient than TSLS and LIML. Three-stage least squares and FIML can be shown to have the same large sample properties. Hence, since FIML, like LIML, involves the solution of complicated non-linear equations, the computationally simpler three-stage least squares is still frequently the preferred full system method of estimation.

It must be remembered that the superiority of three-stage least squares and FIML over TSLS and LIML in terms of asymptotic efficiency, depends very much on the economic model under consideration being correctly specified. That is, the relevant equations must contain the correct variables and be of the right functional form while the disturbances must have all the properties they are assumed to have. Complete system estimation methods – i.e. FIML and three-stage least squares, since they involve making assumptions about all equations in the model, are the most sensitive to various specification errors.

In many situations, unfortunately, we will not have available the 'large' samples assumed in the preceding two paragraphs. When only 'small' samples are available the above ranking in terms of asymptotic properties is of little use. For example, all the estimators discussed are biased for small samples. Unfortunately, little is known about the small-sample properties of estimators usually adopted for simultaneous systems. However, such evidence that exists suggests that the large-sample superiority of the consistent estimators persists even for small samples. In the absence of specification errors complete system methods still appear best, although it is these methods that again seem most sensitive to such errors.

Further reading

For an understandable treatment, at a relatively simple mathematical level, of the order and rank conditions for identification, see Stewart and Wallis (1981). A rigorous matrix development of these conditions is contained in Johnston (1984). Kelejian and Oates (1989) consider the identification problem in non-linear simultaneous equation systems. The first section of Chapter 11 in Johnston (1984) is a good non-matrix introduction to the estimation of simultaneous systems. Two-stage least squares is thoroughly treated in Kelejian and Oates (1989). Non-matrix treatments of the limited and full information maximum likelihood methods of estimation are rare but standard matrix treatments of these methods plus that of three-stage least squares can be found in Kmenta (1986), with examples, and in Johnston.

Notes

1. That is, all such equations can be written in the form $Q = $ constant $+$ constant $(P) +$ constant $(P^s) +$ disturbance. The disturbance in [8.3] is the quantity $(\lambda u + \mu v)/(\lambda + \mu)$, which is a linear combination of u and v.
2. These are most easily derived by equating the right-hand sides of [8.1] and [8.2] and solving for P to yield [8.6]. Substitution for P in either [8.1] or [8.2] then yields [8.5].
3. The reduced-form parameters are not, of course, normally known but as we shall see in the next section it is generally possible to obtain consistent and often unbiased estimates of them.
4. It is assumed that the reader is familiar with the fact that a system of linear equations will normally have one and only one solution when the number of equations equals the number of unknowns. If the number of equations exceeds the number of unknowns then normally there will be no solution, while if the number of unknowns exceeds the number of equations there will be an infinite number of solutions. See, for example, Hadley (1965; ch. 5).
5. This is equivalent to saying that an equiproportionate change in money income and all prices leaves demand unchanged.
6. If the predetermined variables in a model include any lagged endogenous variables, then these will appear among the explanatory variables in the reduced form. The OLS estimators of reduced-form parameters will then still be consistent but no longer unbiased. This follows from the discussion in section 5.1.
7. To see this, apply the two-variables OLS formulae to show that $\hat{B}_1 - \hat{A}_1 = 1$. This means that $\bar{Y} = \bar{C} + (\hat{B}_1 - \hat{A}_1)\bar{Z}$. Now use the OLS formulae to show that $\hat{A}_0 = \hat{B}_0$.
8. Unlike in the previous consumption function example, there are no identities in the data to ensure they will be the same.
9. For example, if we treat the exogenous variables as non-stochastic, we have $Q_i = $ const $+ U_i$ so that var $Q_i = \sigma_U^2$.

9 Demand analysis

One of the first relationships encountered by the reader of any elementary economics textbook is that between the demand for a commodity and its price. It is therefore natural that we should begin the applied part of this text by considering the problems involved in estimating such a demand relationship. Indeed, the estimation of demand equations provides one of the earliest examples of the application of econometric techniques and dates back at least to the work of Moore in 1914. The importance of such empirical work should be obvious. At the micro-level any firm or industry benefits from accurate forecasts of the future level of demand for its products. Also, at the macro-level, forecasts of aggregate consumption expenditure may be insufficiently revealing since identical levels of such expenditure may have different impacts on the economy depending on their composition.

It should be noted at the outset that until very recently the vast majority of demand studies paid little or no attention to questions of spurious correlation and to whether variables could be treated as stationary time series. As was stressed in Chapter 7 standard regression techniques cannot be relied upon when variables are trending. Unfortunately, and certainly during the post-war period, the demand for many standard goods, together with such obvious explanatory variables as disposable income and prices, have shown regular and often steep upward movements. This however, has not prevented investigators and forecasters applying regression techniques to equations specified in terms of the *levels* of variables. Only occasionally were even token attempts (normally involving the simple first differencing of variables) made to tackle problems of common trends.

Similarly, again until recently, demand studies were performed using what we termed in Chapter 7 as the specific to general methodology, with all that this implied for specification errors during the early stages of the approach to finding a satisfactory equation.

From the above, it should be clear that many estimated demand equations should be treated with some scepticism. However, before examining any particular demand studies we consider some general problems that would arise even if it were possible to regard all variables in a demand equation as stationary time series.

9.1 Specification of the demand equation

Traditional consumer theory suggests that the demand of a utility-maximising consumer for any commodity depends on the prices of all commodities available to the consumer and on his total expenditure. Thus

$$q_i = q_i(p_1, p_2, \ldots, p_i, \ldots, p_n, x) \qquad i = 1, 2, 3, \ldots, n \qquad [9.1]$$

where q_i and p_i are the quantity demanded and price of the ith commodity, there are n commodities in all, and $x = \sum_i p_i q_i$ is total expenditure which for the moment we shall take as given.

Unfortunately, consumer theory has nothing to say about the precise functional form of equation [9.1] which is dependent on the consumer's (unspecified) preferences. Morever, there can be little satisfaction in knowing that in theory all prices should be included in a demand equation since in practice sample sizes are often relatively small. We are therefore likely to be confronted with the 'degree of freedom' problem described in section 5.3. Our estimates will lack precision unless we restrict ourselves to a limited number of explanatory variables. Theory does, however, provide us with some limited information about demand equations. For example, an equiproportionate change in all prices and total expenditure should leave demand unchanged, i.e. theory implies that [9.1] is homogeneous of degree zero in the p_is and x. Furthermore, the Slutsky equation implies that own-price substitution effects are negative (see, for example, Henderson and Quandt 1980: 25–8). This is the well-known law of demand and for consistency with theory the own-price and income derivatives of a demand equation should therefore always obey the restriction $\partial q_i / \partial p_i + q_i(\partial q_i / \partial x) < 0$.

By and large, however, theory is of little help in the specification of a demand equation and for this reason empirical versions of equation [9.1] are typically of an *ad hoc* nature. Functional forms are chosen for their ease of estimation and explanatory price variables normally restricted to own-price, the prices of close substitutes and complements and maybe the general price level. Common specifications are therefore

$$q_i = \alpha_0 + \alpha_1 p_i + \alpha_2 p_s + \alpha_3 \Pi + \alpha_4 x + \alpha_5 t + \varepsilon_i \qquad [9.2]$$

$$q_i = A p_i^{\alpha_1} p_s^{\alpha_2} \Pi^{\alpha_3} x^{\alpha_4} e^{\chi_5 t} \varepsilon_i \qquad [9.3]$$

where p_s is the price of a close substitute, Π is the general price level, t is a time trend and ε a disturbance. The time trend is frequently included as an additional variable in an attempt to capture the influence of changing tastes. Specification [9.2] has the advantage of being linear. Specification [9.3] is linear in the logarithms and has the additional property that the α parameters can be interpreted as elasticities which are the quantities frequently of most interest in demand studies.

One point concerning specifications [9.2] and [9.3] needs further explanation. Consumers in general will be intertemporal utility-maximisers so that current demand for any commodity depends on all current and future prices and on 'total lifetime resources' rather than merely on current prices and total current expenditure. However, provided we can regard the consumer as adopting a 'two-stage' approach to his intertemporal problem – first deciding on his total current expenditure, x, and, once x is determined, only then deciding its allocation between commodities on the basis of their current prices – it is possible to justify the above specification. Many demand studies, however, replace the total expenditure variable in [9.2] and [9.3] by a measure of the consumer's disposable income, only part of which is devoted to current expenditure. This procedure is much harder to justify theoretically and, indeed, most economists would consider the replacement of total lifetime resources by current income as a serious misspecification. The distinction between the two is, as we shall see in the next chapter, the basis of the life-cycle and permanent income hypotheses concerning aggregate consumption expenditure.

The homogeneity restriction may either be imposed prior to estimation or equations [9.2] and [9.3] can be estimated as they stand. Imposing homogeneity implies specifying that demand is a function of *relative* prices and *real* total expenditure so that [9.2] and [9.3] become

$$q_i = \alpha_0 + \alpha_1 \left(\frac{p_i}{\Pi} \right) + \alpha_2 \left(\frac{p_s}{\Pi} \right) + \alpha_4 \left(\frac{x}{\Pi} \right) + \alpha_5 t + \varepsilon_i \qquad [9.4]$$

$$q_i = A \left(\frac{p_i}{\Pi} \right)^{\alpha_1} \left(\frac{p_s}{\Pi} \right)^{\alpha_2} \left(\frac{x}{\Pi} \right)^{\alpha_4} e^{\alpha_5 t} \varepsilon_i \qquad [9.5]$$

Comparing [9.3] and [9.5] we see that, for the logarithmic specification, imposing homogeneity is equivalent to imposing the linear restriction

$$\alpha_1 + \alpha_2 + \alpha_3 + \alpha_4 = 0$$

on [9.3]. Hence, if both [9.3] and [9.5] are estimated, then it is possible to test for homogeneity by applying the F-statistic given by (4.45). If the residual sum of squares in an estimated version of [9.5] is sufficiently larger than that in [9.3], then the null hypothesis of homogeneity is rejected.

Most studies of the demand for a single good have, in fact, been concerned more with estimation than with the testing of economic theory. Working in terms of relative prices and real income reduces the multicollinearity between price and total expenditure variables that is frequently present in time series data. However, although homogeneity is typically imposed, little use has been made in estimation of the negativity restriction on the own-price substitution effect implied by the Slutsky equation. This is because of the difficulties of imposing an inequality-type restriction as opposed to the equality implied by homogeneity.

9.2 The aggregation problem

There are two broad sources of data normally available for the estimation of demand equations – time series data and cross-sectional data. Time series data normally refers to the purchases of large, sometimes economy-wide, groups of households over timespans of anything up to 100 years. Cross-sectional data comes from the so-called 'budget surveys' of the patterns of expenditure among individual households. The latter type of data is of particular use for focusing on the response of demands to changes in income or total expenditure. This is because of the typically large variation in income levels in a cross-section and because, since the surveys are normally completed within a brief time interval, it is legitimate to treat all households as facing almost identical prices.

Consumer theory refers to the *individual* consumer's demand for *individual* goods. However, available data tends to be aggregate in two senses. It typically refers not to individual goods but to broad classifications, e.g. 'food', 'clothing', etc. and almost always refers to large groups of, rather than individual, consumers. This is equally as true of much published cross-sectional data as it is of time series data. Budget surveys tend to provide information on broad categories of expenditure of all households within quite widely defined income classes.[1] Unfortunately, the fact that theory suggests a relationship between demand, total expenditure and prices for the individual consumer by no means guarantees that an identical or even similar relationship will hold at the aggregate level. The derivation of conditions under which 'micro-relationships' can be 'added together' to provide a 'macro-relationship' of the same form is known as *the aggregation problem*. Although we first approach this problem in the context of demand analysis, it should be clear that similar problems are likely to arise in the estimation of any aggregate or macro-relationship.

We shall pay particular attention here to the problem of *aggregating over consumers*. Although the theoretical conditions under which it is permissible to treat broad commodity groupings as a single good are quite restrictive, it appears that as long as goods are classified according to the different needs they satisfy (e.g. into 'clothing', 'entertainment', etc.) the errors involved are not large even when these conditions are not exactly met.

Suppose that household *j*s demand for a good is given by

$$q_j = \alpha_{0j} + \alpha_{1j}p + \alpha_{2j}p^s + \alpha_{3j}x_j + \varepsilon_j \qquad [9.6]$$

where p and p^s are own price and the price of a substitute good and x_j is household j's total expenditure. If necessary, the price and expenditure variables can be regarded as having been deflated by some general price index, and other variables could be added to [9.6] without affecting what follows. Notice, however, that only x_j of the explanatory variables has been subscripted so that we are assuming that all households face identical prices although their total expenditures will differ. ε_j is a disturbance relating to the jth household, obeying all the classical assumptions listed in section 2.4.

Given [9.6] for each individual household, we seek conditions under which a macro- or aggregate relationship will exist of the form

$$\bar{q} = \alpha_0 + \alpha_1 p + \alpha_2 p^s + \alpha_3 \bar{x} + \varepsilon \qquad [9.7]$$

where $\bar{q}$ and $\bar{x}$ are the arithmetic means of the demands and total expenditures of all households,[2] the α_i are constants and ε is a 'macro-disturbance' with the same properties as each ε_j.

If there are N households in all then, from [9.6]

$$\bar{q} = \frac{\sum q_j}{N} = \frac{\sum \alpha_{0j}}{N} + \left(\frac{\sum \alpha_{1j}}{N}\right)p + \left(\frac{\sum \alpha_{2j}}{N}\right)p^s + \left(\frac{\sum x_j \alpha_{3j}}{\sum x_j}\right)\bar{x} + \frac{\sum \varepsilon_j}{N} \qquad [9.8]$$

where the summations are over all households. Aggregation, therefore, leads to an equation similar to the required [9.7] with the macro-parameters α_0, α_1 and α_2 equal to the arithmetic means of the corresponding micro-parameters, i.e. $\alpha_0 = \sum \alpha_{0j}/N$, etc. However, α_3 is equal to a *weighted* mean of the micro α_{3j}s. That is, $\alpha_3 = \sum w_j \alpha_{3j}$ where each $w_j = x_j/\sum x_j$. The weights, the w_j's are equal to the proportion of aggregate total expenditure made by each household. The aggregate disturbance ε is simply the arithmetic mean of the ε_j and hence has the same properties as each individual ε_j.[3]

The problem with equations [9.7] and [9.8] is that α_3 remains constant over time only if the weights, the w_js, remain constant. This will only occur if the distribution of total expenditures across households remains unchanged over time. If this distribution changes, then α_3 varies and can no longer be regarded as a 'parameter' so that [9.7] is no longer a macro-equivalent of [9.6]. Only if all households have *identical marginal propensities to spend*, i.e. if $\alpha_{3j} = k = \text{constant}$ for all j, will α_3 and, hence, aggregate demand be independent of the distribution of total expenditures. In such a case

$$\alpha_3 = \frac{\sum x_j k}{\sum x_j} = \frac{k \sum x_j}{\sum x_j} = k = \text{constant}$$

Equal marginal propensities to spend is a very restrictive condition for 'exact aggregation'. However, less restrictive conditions are necessary if we adopt the so-called *convergence approach*. When aggregating over many households, provided that the x_j and the α_{3j} are distributed independently of one another (e.g. households do not tend to have *both* large total expenditures x_j *and* large marginal propensities α_{3j}) then the expenditure-weighted mean of the α_{3j} will be approximately equal to their arithmetic mean no matter what the distribution of expenditures.[4] Thus, we will have a close approximation to exact aggregation. The crucial requirement, however, is the independence of the x_js and the α_{3j}s. A positive correlation (as is likely in the case of 'luxury' goods) or a negative correlation (as is likely in the case of necessities) will lead to the expenditure-weighted mean overestimating or underestimating, respectively, the true arithmetic mean of the α_{3j}. Unfortunately, since all commodities are either luxuries or necessities, even this less restrictive condition for aggregation is unlikely to hold in practice. Thus, in many cases a macro-equation like [9.7] with constant αs will only exist when the distribution of total expenditures remains unchanged.

We have so far only considered the aggregation problem in the context of linear demand equations. Suppose, however, that household js demand equation is given by, for example,

$$q_j = A_0 p^{\alpha_1} p_s^{\alpha_2} x_j^{\alpha_3} \qquad [9.9]$$

Notice that the αs and A are not subscripted in [9.9] so we have simplified somewhat by assuming that these parameters are the same for all households. Equation [9.9] is linear in the logorithms

$$\log q_j = \alpha_0 + \alpha_1 \log p + \alpha_2 \log p_s + \alpha_3 \log x_j \qquad \alpha_0 = \log A \qquad [9.10]$$

so that an analysis similar to that for [9.6] is possible. Summing over all households and dividing by N yields

$$\frac{\sum \log q_j}{N} = \alpha_0 + \alpha_1 \log p + \alpha_2 \log p_s + \alpha_3 \left(\frac{\sum \log x_j}{N} \right)$$

since $\sum \alpha_0 = n\alpha_0$, etc. Thus, a macro-relationship of the same form as [9.10] can be derived provided we define the macro-variables $\bar{q}$ and $\bar{x}$ such that $\log \bar{q} = (\sum \log q_j)/N$ and $\log \bar{x} = (\sum \log x_j)/N$. However, this is equivalent to defining $\bar{q}$ and $\bar{x}$ as the *geometric* rather than the arithmetic means of the corresponding micro-variables.[5] Unfortunately, it is not possible to calculate geometric means from normal aggregate data although, occasionally, use can be made of known relationships between arithmetic and geometric means.

If a demand equation cannot, like [9.9], be transformed into a linear relationship then aggregation problems become even more complex and for this reason are frequently ignored by investigators. Hicks (1956: 55) provides an intuitive argument in support of this.

> To assume that the representative consumer acts like the ideal consumer is a hypothesis worth testing; to assume that an actual person, the Mr Brown or Mr Jones who lives round the corner does in fact act in such a way does not deserve a moment's consideration.

Thus, consumer theory can only be expected to apply to the representative consumer who may not, in fact, exist but who can be interpreted as a statistical average. So, to determine the demand equation for the representative consumer, we must consider the arithmetic averages of demands and total expenditures – the approach adopted in many studies.

9.3 Estimation from time series data

Early time series studies such as those of Schultz (1938) concentrated mainly on staple agricultural products, since the only available data at that time related to such homogeneous commodities. Studies for more heterogeneous manufactured goods were not possible until price indices and total expenditure series for such goods became generally available.

We have already considered in the previous chapter the problems of identification and simultaneity that may arise in the estimation of demand equations from time series data. We will merely stress one point here. In practice, it may seem a simple matter to find variables appearing in the supply equation and not the demand equation and vice versa which apparently serve to identify both equations. However, what really matters is *the extent to which these variables vary* during the sample period. If demand determining factors vary more over time than the supply determining factors then, no matter how many variables can justifiably be included in the supply equation, their lack of variation will mean that it is the supply rather than the demand equation which is 'traced out' by the data. Luckily, as we have noted, most early demand studies dealt with agricultural goods where, because of weather conditions, crop failures, etc. supply conditions were, in fact, extremely variable. For this reason it is probable that early demand studies did, indeed, deal with demand rather than supply relationships, although they paid little formal attention to identification problems. With manufactured commodities there is no reason why supply conditions should be more variable than demand conditions, so in such cases the identification problem requires more careful attention.

We saw in the last chapter that, because of the problem of simultaneity, the OLS estimation method will normally yield biased and inconsistent estimators for the demand equation parameters even when that equation is identified. There are, however, two not uncommon situations where the application of OLS is quite appropriate. The first such exception is when *own-price is a predetermined variable*. For example, this is the case for many public utilities such as gas and electricity where price tends to be set independently of market conditions by public regulation or government dictat. Since own-price is no longer endogenous, its presence on the right-hand side of the demand equation no longer gives rise to OLS bias. One of the first studies to make use of such conditions was that by Fisher and Kaysen (1962) of the demand for electricity in the US.

The second case where OLS may be more safely applied is where *supply itself is predetermined* and we can replace the supply equation by the simple statement

$$\bar{q} = \bar{q}_0 = \text{predetermined}$$

This might well be a valid specification for a perishable agricultural commodity. The supply of such commodities is subject to exogenous weather variations and is virtually totally inelastic with respect to current price because of time lags involved in planting and harvesting. Adding a demand equation such as [9.7] to the above supply statement and making the market clearing assumption (justified here by the perishable nature of the good) results in a model in which the only endogenous variable is own price, p. An obvious procedure is then to rewrite the demand equation [9.7] with the endogenous own-price as the dependent variable

$$p = -\frac{\alpha_0}{\alpha_1} + \left(\frac{1}{\alpha_1}\right)\bar{q}_0 - \left(\frac{\alpha_2}{\alpha_1}\right)p_s - \left(\frac{\alpha_3}{\alpha_1}\right)\bar{x} - \frac{\varepsilon}{\alpha_1} \qquad [9.7A]$$

Since all the explanatory variables in [9.7A] are either exogenous like p^s and $\bar{x}$ or predetermined like $\bar{q}_0$, they can be considered as independent of the disturbance, $-\varepsilon/\alpha_1$. Hence, the application of OLS to [9.7A] will yield unbiased and consistent estimators of its parameters. From these estimators it is then possible to obtain estimators of the α parameters in the original demand equation [9.7]. However, recalling section 2.3 and the appendix to Chapter 2, note that the α estimators will not be unbiased but merely consistent, since only the property of consistency 'carries over'. For example, although we can obtain an unbiased estimator of $1/\alpha_1$ by applying OLS to [9.7A], its reciprocal will not be an unbiased estimator of α_1. A well-known early example of the above procedure is that of Fox (1958) who, using US data for 1922–41, estimated demand elasticities for various food products.

Ordinary least squares, however, can only be used in the estimation of demand equations in such special cases as the above and normally resort has to be made to simultaneous equation estimating techniques. A well-known study which makes use of such techniques is that by Suits (1955) of the US water-melon market. This still provides an excellent illustration of the problems of constructing empirical simultaneous equation models.

Suits's model contains three equations: a crop-supply schedule, a harvest-supply schedule and a demand schedule. The crop-supply schedule is similar to that of Fox above in that decisions to plant are determined by last year's conditions and other predetermined factors. His crop-supply equation estimated by OLS is

$$Q = 769 + 34J - 155K + 0.587P_{-1} - 0.320C_{-1} - 0.141T_{-1} \qquad [9.11]$$
$$ (0.156) (0.095) (0.238)$$

Q is the total number of water-melons *available* for harvest, P_{-1} is the previous year's farm price of water-melons. C_{-1} and T_{-1} are the previous-year prices of cotton and other vegetables respectively and represent the opportunity cost of planting water-melons since these crops compete with water-melons for farm space. J and K are dummy variables representing government policy and the influence of the Second World War. The equation is estimated from US annual data for 1919–51 with the variables measured in logarithmic terms so that the

203

0.587 coefficient on P_{-1} is the own-price elasticity of crop supply. Since all the explanatory variables are predetermined, simultaneity problems do not arise in the estimation of this equation so the OLS method is, in fact, used.

However, decisions to harvest as distinct from decisions to plant are influenced by *current* prices. The model therefore contains a separate harvest supply equation which relates the number of water-melons actually *harvested*, X, to the current farm price of water-melons and the farm wage rate W. However, since X cannot exceed Q, this relationship only holds when $X < Q$ and has to be estimated ignoring all years when no unharvested crop is reported (i.e. when $X = Q$). Since data on X is only available in the later part of the period, the harvest supply equation has to be estimated using 1930–51 data, and to conserve degrees of freedom the price and wage variables are entered in ratio form

$$X = -118.04 + 0.237(P/W) + 1.205Q \qquad [9.12]$$
$$(0.110) \qquad (0.114)$$

Since the variables are in logarithmic form, coefficients again represent elasticities and we can write $0.237(P/W)$ as $0.237P - 0.237W$. Thus, the own-price elasticity of harvested supply is much smaller than that of crop supply. Also the elasticity of harvested supply with respect to crop supply is not significantly different from unity. This implies that, given P/W, a percentage change in crop supply leads to a roughly equal percentage change in harvested supply.

Finally, Suits's demand equation relates the farm price of water-melons to per capita disposable income Y/N, per capita market supply X/N and an index F of the cost of shipping water-melons from farm to market

$$P = -140.16 + 1.530(Y/N) - 1.110(X/N) - 0.682F \qquad [9.13]$$
$$(0.088) \qquad (0.246) \qquad (0.183)$$

The F variable is included since it is the market price of water-melons, that is determined by market forces, whereas the farm price P is less than the market price by a factor dependent on shipping costs. Equation [9.13] is also estimated in logarithmic form so that, rearranging to get X/N on the left-hand side, this equation yields estimates of -0.9 for the own-price elasticity of demand and 1.38 for the income elasticity. This equation also has to be estimated using the shorter 1930–51 period.

The endogenous variables in the above three-equation model are Q, P and X. All other variables are treated as exogenous or predetermined. Y and W are exogenous because the water-melon market represents a very small part of the US economy and also has little influence via the demand for farm labour on W. Notice, however, that equations [9.12] and [9.13] both contain endogenous variables on the right-hand side. Hence, OLS estimates of these equations would be subject to simultaneous equation bias and Suits's estimates, quoted above, were obtained by the LIML method described in section 8.3.

An interesting reformulation of the Suits' model is that of Wold (1958) who models the water-melon market as a recursive system similar to those described in section 8.2. The endogenous variables are again Q, P and X and they are determined recursively in that order. First, Q is determined by a crop-supply equation identical to that specified by Suits. Next P is determined by real income per capita and by the difference between demand and supply

$$P = \alpha_0 + \alpha_1 \left[\left(\frac{X^*}{N} \right)_{-1} - \frac{Q}{N} \right] + \alpha_2 \left(\frac{Y}{N} \right) \qquad [9.14]$$

Consumer demand, X^*, is given by the harvest X when part of the crop is left unharvested but is unknown for those years when the full crop is harvested. Since it is expected demand that influences the pricing decisions of merchants, last year's per capita demand $(X^*/N)_{-1}$ appears as a proxy for expected per capita demand in equation [9.14]. Real income per capita appears, since as real income increases there is more room for margins between price and production cost.

Given Q and P, per capita demand is then determined by price and real income per capita

$$\frac{X^*}{N} = \beta_0 + \beta_1 P + \beta_2 \left(\frac{Y}{N}\right) \qquad [9.15]$$

The recursive nature of Wold's system means that, provided the disturbances are not correlated across equations (otherwise an identification problem would arise) it can be estimated consistently simply by applying OLS to each equation in turn. However, L'Esperance (1964) subjected both Suits' original model and Wold's reformulated system to forecasting tests using post-1951 data. Suits's simultaneous system performed better than Wold's recursive system, hence suggesting that it was a better representation of the water-melon market.

Multicollinearity and extraneous estimators

Perhaps the greatest obstacle to obtaining precise estimates of both total expenditure and price elasticities from time series data alone is the multicollinearity frequently found between the expenditure and particularly the price variables which tend to move together over time. Its consequence, as we have seen in section 5.3.1, is to increase the standard errors associated with estimated coefficients, thus implying a lack of precision in these estimates. It is possible to reduce the multicollinearity that is present by 'imposing homogeneity' and using as explanatory variables *real* total expenditure and *relative* prices. However, since there is typically far greater variation in the real expenditure variable than in relative price variables, this procedure tends to yield fairly well-defined estimates of real expenditure elasticities but rather imprecise estimates of relative price elasticities. We are thus faced with another factor listed in section 5.3 as leading to lack of precision in the OLS estimators – insufficient variation in the values of explanatory variables. In addition, any multicollinearity remaining after the switch to real expenditure and relative prices may prevent use being made of any limited variation in relative prices that exists.

As we have already mentioned in section 5.3.1, investigators have tended to get round the multicollinearity problem by obtaining an extraneous estimator of the real expenditure elasticity from cross-sectional data. Cross-sectional data is often ideal for this purpose, first because it is generally reasonable to assume an absence of price variation over the cross-section and, secondly, because many cross-sections contain wide variations in the real-expenditure variable. Provided the extraneous estimator is unbiased then time series estimators of price elasticities obtained by estimating equations such as [5.48] (page 118) will also be unbiased. Moreover, as originally demonstrated by Durbin (1953), the sampling variability of the price-elasticity estimators obtained in this way will almost certainly be far less than that obtained in the normal time series regression of quantity demanded on both expenditure and price variables. In other words, the use of an extraneously estimated total expenditure elasticity results in far greater precision in the estimation of price elasticities.

Even if an unbiased estimate of the total expenditure elasticity can be obtained from cross-sectional data (and we shall consider the problems of obtaining such an estimate in the next section) serious interpretational difficulties may have to be considered before the estimate can be slotted into a time series equation. It is by no means obvious that the elasticity of total expenditure obtained from a cross-section of individual households *at a given point in time* is conceptually the same as that relevant to the behaviour of an aggregate of households or even an individual household *over a period of time*. Imagine two households of widely differing total expenditures in a cross-section. Suppose the circumstances of the 'poorer' household were changed suddenly in such a manner as to enable it to make, if it wishes, the same total expenditure as the other 'wealthier' household. In the *short run*, before the first household has adjusted to its new circumstances, habit may leave the pattern and maybe even the level of its total expenditure unchanged. However, in the *long run* the composition and level of its expenditures are likely to match those of the wealthy household. If it is reasonable to assume that most houses in a cross-section are well adjusted to their financial circumstances, we can therefore expect cross-sectional data to yield estimates of *long-run* total expenditure elasticities. However, when we consider the behaviour of one or more households over time, it may well be that the data does not conform to traditional static consumer theory. Time series data consists usually of annual or quarterly observations. However, because of habit or inertia, complete adjustments to changes in prices or total expenditure may take longer than one quarter and even longer than one year. For this reason it is often argued that it is predominantly *short-run* elasticities that tend to be estimated from time series data.

The above arguments do not mean that it is impossible to make use of extraneous estimates but that such estimates should be used with caution. When dealing with time series data, allowances must be made for lags in the process of adjustment to changes in total expenditure and prices if the two elasticity concepts are to be comparable. As we shall see, such allowances are particularly important in the cases of durable and 'habit-forming' goods and for this reason we shall later devote a separate section to this problem.

Spurious correlation and error correction models

During the years since the Second World War, variables typically included in demand equations – income, total expenditure, individual prices and the general price level, have all shown almost uninterrupted upward trends. This not only exacerbates the multicollinearity problem mentioned in the last subsection but also means that any demand equations estimated in terms of the levels of variables are likely to be subject to all the problems relating to non-stationary time series and spurious correlations described in Chapter 7. We saw in section 7.3 that almost the only serious attempt to deal successfully with such problems has involved the use of error correction models. In this subsection we consider how demand equations can be put into an error correction format.

All error correction models imply the existence of an equilibrium relationship. In the present context such an equilibrium relationship was in fact described in section 9.1. Demand equations such as [9.4] and [9.5] have to be reinterpreted as yielding long-run or equilibrium levels of demand. In fact, since these equations are based on static consumer theory, with its implicit assumption that consumers move immediately to a new optimal position following a change in either prices or total expenditure, such a reinterpretation is a necessary one.

Suppose then that we have a long-run or equilibrium relationship of the form

$$Q_t = A P_t^{\alpha_1} G_t^{\alpha_2} X_t^{\alpha_3} \qquad [9.16]$$

where Q is demand, P is own-price, G is a general price index and X is total expenditure. Using lower case letters in this case for natural logarithms this implies

$$q_t = \alpha_0 + \alpha_1 p_t + \alpha_2 g_t + \alpha_3 x_t \qquad [9.17]$$

where $\alpha_0 = \log A$.

A standard first-order error correction model would then take the form

$$\Delta q_t = \beta_1 \Delta p_t + \beta_2 \Delta g_t + \beta_3 \Delta x_t - \gamma \left(q_{t-1} - \alpha_0 - \alpha_1 p_{t-1} - \alpha_2 g_{t-1} - \alpha_3 x_{t-1} \right) + u_t$$

$$[9.18]$$

where u_t is a disturbance that, provided the ECM has been correctly specified, should obey all the usual classical assumptions. Note that [9.18] is simply a generalisation of equations such as [7.15] to the case of three long-run explanatory variables.

In [9.18] α_1, α_2 and α_3 represent the *long-run* elasticities of demand with respect to own-price, the general price level and total expenditure, while β_1, β_2 and β_3 represent *short-run* elasticities. The term in brackets is the disequilibrium error from the previous period, so the parameter γ measures the proportion of this error that is rectified in the current period.

Notice that [9.18] encorporates the adjustment lags mentioned at the end of the previous subsection. Indeed, always assuming that the ECM is correctly specified, the long-run total expenditure elasticity, α_3, obtained from an equation such as [9.18] could be regarded as akin to that obtained from cross-sectional data.

Of course, there can be no guarantee that an equilibrium relationship of the kind [9.16] exists or that the appropriate ECM will be of the first order. Determining whether an equilibrium relationship can be said to exist is a matter for co-integration analysis of the kind described in section 7.5. If such a relationship does appear to exist, then determining a correctly specified ECM is best achieved by using the testing down procedure described in section 7.2. We shall, in fact, present examples of the Hendry-type testing down procedure, as applied to demand equations, in the empirical appendix to this chapter.

9.4 The estimation of Engle curves

Cross-sectional relationships between expenditure on a specific good and the level of income or total expenditure are traditionally referred to as 'Engle curves'. This is in honour of E. Engle who, as the result of cross-sectional studies performed in the mid-nineteenth century, proposed his well-known 'law' that the income elasticity of the demand for food is always less than unity. We have already noted the great advantage of cross-sectional studies – that, apart from minor variations due to geographical and social factors, all prices facing households in the cross-section can be treated as constant. This, of course, enables investigators to concentrate on the relationship between household demands for particular commodities and household income or total expenditure.

The major problem in obtaining adequate cross-sectional estimates of total expenditure elasticities is that expenditure on any good will vary from household to household for reasons other than variations in household resources. The most important of these 'nuisance' variables are probably the size and composition of households, although such factors as age, social class, education, etc. will also be of relevance. While aggregate values of such variables will change only slowly over time and hence can be ignored in time series studies, it is clear that considerable variation is to be expected over a typical cross-section. Our analysis of section 7.1 suggests that, unless these nuisance variables happen to be completely uncorrelated with total expenditure over the cross-section, biased estimates of total expenditure elasticities are likely to be obtained if they are omitted from the estimating equation. There is therefore a danger of possibly serious specification error. Unfortunately, it is obviously likely that household size will be positively correlated with total expenditure. Hence, as our analysis in section 7.1 indicates, OLS estimators of total expenditure elasticities will be upward-biased if this variable is omitted. Similarly, correlations between any other nuisance variables and total expenditure will also lead to OLS bias.

Most attention has, in fact, been given to household size and composition variables. Other nuisance variables are normally dealt with either by using dummy variables to allow for, for example, differences in social class, or by dealing only with subsamples within the total cross-section. An obvious way of allowing for household size, S, is to include such a variable in the estimating equation. This, however, is likely to lead to problems of multicollinearity (S will usually be correlated with total expenditure). It also raises the question of how S is to be measured. Obviously, a household consisting of one adult and three children should not be regarded as the same 'size' as one consisting of four adults. Early investigators made much use of what are known as *equivalent adult scales*. These defined the size of a household as $S = \sum \lambda_j n_j$ where n_j was the number of individuals of the 'jth type' in the household and λ_j was the 'weight' attached to the jth type. λ_j was conventionally set equal to unity for an adult male and weights for other individuals were determined according to their nutritional requirements relative to adult males. For example, the so-called 'Amsterdam scale' assigned a weight of 0.9 to an adult female. There are two major problems with such scales. First, they are obviously inappropriate for non-food commodities and, secondly, they have a 'normative' aspect. Nutritional experts may believe that an adult female requires 0.9 times the food of an adult male but there can be no guarantee that households will plan their budgets on the basis of such an assumption.

An approach pioneered by Prais and Houthakker (1955) and Barten (1964) which attempts to deal with many of the above problems is to allow the *data* to determine the λ_j and to work in terms of expenditures 'per equivalent adult household'. Specific weights, in fact, have to be estimated for each commodity and general weights estimated to compute the household 'size' used to deflate consumer expenditure. However, there are problems. It is obviously desirable that the functional forms of Engle curves should be such that the sum of expenditures on all goods should equal a household's total expenditure. Unfortunately, if the Engle curves satisfy such an 'adding-up criterion', it can be shown (see, for example, Muellbauer, 1974 and 1980) that the specific weights are unidentified. The problem is that for n goods we have to estimate n specific weights from n Engle curves. However, if the Engle curves satisfy the adding-up criterion they can provide only $n - 1$ independent pieces of information – one too few to identify the specific weights. In fact, the ratios of the specific weights can then be estimated, but not their absolute sizes.

A further problem with cross-sectional data is that expenditure surveys often divide households into wide classifications based on income or total expenditure levels. Published data therefore tends to refer to the 'group means' of such classes, i.e. instead of having data on each household in a class, the only information we have refers to the mean expenditures of all households in the class. Equations must then be estimated using such group means as the basic observations and this causes problems.

Abstracting from problems of size and composition, suppose household j has the following Engle curve for a particular commodity

$$p_j q_j = \alpha + \beta x_j + \varepsilon_j$$

where ε_j is a disturbance obeying all the usual classical assumptions. In particular, var $\varepsilon_j = \sigma^2 = $ constant for all j.

If there are n households within a particular class, the mean expenditure on the commodity for the whole class will be

$$\overline{pq} = \alpha + \beta \bar{x} + \bar{\varepsilon} \qquad [9.19]$$

where $\bar{x}$ is mean total expenditure for the class and $\bar{\varepsilon} = (1/n)\sum \varepsilon_j$. It is group means such as $\overline{pq}$ and $\bar{x}$ which form the basic observations when estimating Engle curves from classified data. However, the variance of the disturbance in [9.19] is σ^2/n. Hence, if classes vary in size, so will the variance of the disturbance associated with them. Thus, an estimating equation based on [9.19] will have a *heteroscedastic disturbance* and the consequences described in section 5.2.1 will follow.

The solution to the problem is to adopt the GLS procedure also described in section 5.2.1. In this case, since var $\bar{\varepsilon} = \sigma^2/n$, we divide [9.19] throughout by $1/\sqrt{n}$ to obtain

$$(\sqrt{n})(\overline{qp}) = \alpha(\sqrt{n}) + \beta(\sqrt{n})(\bar{x}) + u$$

where $u = \bar{\varepsilon}(\sqrt{n})$. Since var $u = n$ var $\bar{\varepsilon} = \sigma^2$, this equation has a homoscedastic disturbance. Hence, OLS may be used to regress the variable $(\sqrt{n})(\overline{qp})$ on $(\sqrt{n})$ and $(\sqrt{n})(\bar{x})$ to obtain estimates of α and β. Notice that the intercept has to be suppressed in the manner of section 4.4 for this regression.

Much experimentation has been engaged in to determine the most appropriate *functional form* for Engle curves. Many goods, while luxuries at sufficiently low levels of income and total expenditure, become necessities as total expenditure increases. Hence, *a priori* considerations suggest that total expenditure elasticities will decline as total expenditure x rises. Values in excess of unity are possible for low values of x while at very high values of x, if 'satiation' sets in, elasticities

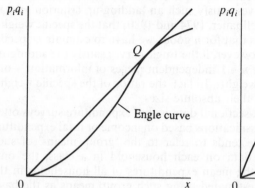

9.1a A sigmoid-shaped Engle curve.

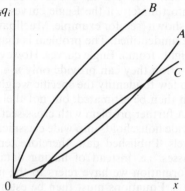

9.1b Logarithmic and semi-logarithmic Engle curves.

could fall to zero. The full shape of an Engle curve may therefore look something like the 'sigmoid'-shaped curve illustrated in Fig. 9.1a, with an elasticity of unity reached at the point Q. However, functional forms which yield this sigmoid shape are rather complex and in practice simpler, typically two-parameter, curves have commonly been fitted to cross-sectional data. Since variations in total expenditure are never large enough to reveal the full shape of an Engle curve, functional forms which approximate either the lower or the upper portion of the curve can be expected to fit such data reasonably well. A popular curve which can be used to approximate the lower part of the Engle curve, before the elasticity shows any definite tendency to fall, is the constant-elasticity or logarithmic curve. For commodity i

$$p_i q_i = A_1 x^{\beta_i} \qquad\qquad [9.20]$$

Such curves are illustrated in Fig. 9.1b. Curve A has an elasticity, β_i, in excess of unity and curve B an elasticity between zero and unity.

For cases where the elasticity is likely to decline as total expenditure rises, the 'semi-log' curve may be most appropriate.

$$p_i q_i = \alpha_i + \beta_i \log x \qquad\qquad [9.21]$$

This is illustrated by curve C in Fig. 9.1b and has an elasticity equal to $\beta_i / p_i q_i$. This curve has the additional advantage of intersecting the total expenditure axis at the point where $\log x = -\alpha_i / \beta_i$ and hence is useful in cases where a commodity is not purchased below a certain level of total expenditure.

Engle curves are typically estimated with expenditure rather than quantity as the dependent variable. However, since it is possible to treat price p_i as a constant over the cross-section, equations such as [9.20] and [9.21] can be converted into demand equations of the same functional form by the simple process of dividing throughout by p_i. The use of expenditure rather than quantity can cause confusion, however, when there is considerable variation in the quality of a good. For example, expenditure on coffee can be on good-quality 'genuine' coffee or on a poorer-quality 'instant' brand. Rises in total expenditure over the cross-section may coincide with a switching from the purchase of instant to the purchase of genuine coffee. If this occurs, then since instant coffee is the lower-priced, increases in expenditure on coffee will tend to exceed increases in the quantity (e.g. number of jars) purchased. There is therefore a danger that the 'true' total expenditure elasticity will be overestimated if expenditure is used as the dependent variable. Ideally, in such cases elasticities should be estimated only for homogeneous categories of commodities (e.g. both genuine *and* instant coffee), but data limitations frequently prevent this.

The explanatory variable used is normally total expenditure rather than income since answers to questions concerning a household's income are notoriously unreliable. We have seen that there are sound theoretical reasons for preferring total expenditure to income, but this choice sometimes causes problems when cross-sectionally estimated elasticities are used as extraneous estimates in time series equations. Investigators have tended to use income as the 'resource variable' in time series studies. To obtain extraneous estimates of income elasticities it is then necessary to multiply the extraneous total expenditure elasticity by some arbitrary estimate of the elasticity of total expenditure with respect to income.

Probably the most well-known work on Engle curves is the study of UK cross-sectional data by Prais and Houthakker (1955). They experimented with five functional forms but eventually rejected all but the logarithmic and semi-log forms [9.20] and [9.21]. The semi-log form proved especially suitable for food items which tend to become necessities at fairly low levels of total expenditure. However, estimates of total expenditure elasticities tended to be very similar no matter what non-linear functional form was fitted. Some examples of the elasticities found are given in Table 9.1. For the semi-log function (where the elasticity varies along the curve) the value given is that at the point of mean expenditure. The ranking by size of the elasticities is about what one would expect on *a priori* considerations.

Engle curves such as those fitted by Prais and Houthakker are sometimes criticised for not satisfying the so-called 'adding-up' criterion mentioned earlier (page 209). That is, if all Engle curves had either of these forms then the sum of all expenditures would not equal total expenditure, i.e. $\sum p_i q_i \neq x$. One of the few functional forms for Engle curves that satisfy this criterion is the linear form $p_i q_i = \alpha_i + \beta_i x$ which will do so provided $\sum \alpha_i = 0$ and $\sum \beta_i = 1$. In fact, it can be shown that this is the only functional form for which the OLS estimation method will yield estimated Engle curves which automatically satisfy the adding-up criterion. One of the earliest of modern studies using budget survey data, that of Allen and Bowley (1935), did, in fact, employ linear Engle curves. Unfortunately, linear Engle curves almost always provide inferior fits to the non-linear specifications and studies have been more concerned with finding adequate representations of the data than with satisfying the adding-up criterion.

Table 9.1 Food elasticities obtained using log and semi-log functions

Food	Farinaceous	Dairy	Vegetables	Fruit	Meat	Fish
Logarithmic	0.35	0.48	0.58	1.03	0.62	0.76
Semi-logarithmic	0.36	0.53	0.62	1.20	0.69	0.84

Source: Prais and Houthakker (1955)

However we shall return to the question of linear versus non-linear Engle curves in section 9.8.

9.5 The demand for durable goods

As we noted earlier, static consumer theory yields equilibrium values for quantities demanded for given configurations of prices and total expenditure. It also implies an instantaneous adjustment to new equilibrium values in response to any external change. Consumers, however, are likely to react only gradually to a change in prices or total expenditure and this will give rise to 'lags' in their adjustment to a new equilibrium. A major reason for such lags is that many goods are *durable goods*.

Since a durable good lasts for more than one 'period' this means that past purchases of such a good influence a consumer's present behaviour. Similarly, present purchases will influence his future behaviour. If a consumer purchases a new hi-fi set during one week and the following week the price of such sets declines then static theory would suggest an increase in his purchases of hi-fi sets. However, a far more likely response is that the consumer will delay purchasing another hi-fi set for some considerable time, thus holding expenditure *below its new 'equilibrium' level*.

The above example well illustrates a number of crucial points concerning durable goods. First, a durable good is a discrete indivisible quantity (unlike many non-durables which can be approximately regarded as almost infinitely divisible). Thus a consumer cannot purchase one-fiftieth of a hi-fi set. Secondly, we have to distinguish between *purchases* of a durable good and the consumption of the services which it yields. The flow of purchases adds to the *stock* of durable goods held by consumers while the consumption of services leads to depreciation, depletion or physical deterioration in the stock. Thirdly, a distinction can be made between purchases which represent a *replacement demand*, matching some depletion in the stock, and purchases representing a 'new demand' which results in a net increase in the stock.

The fact that adjustment to equilibrium levels of demand may not be instantaneous is the basis of the so-called *stock adjustment models* of the demand for durable goods. Ignoring any aggregation problems, suppose that the equilibrium or desired stock of the durable good, S_t^*, is a linear function of real total expenditure, x_t, and the relative price of the good, p_t. That is

$$S_t^* = \alpha_0 + \alpha_1 p_t + \alpha_2 x_t + \varepsilon_t \qquad [9.22]$$

where ε_t is a disturbance.[6]

Actual stock, S_t, however, does not normally equal desired stock, but is determined by partial adjustment model of the kind described in section 6.3.

$$S_t - S_{t-1} = \lambda(S_t^* - S_{t-1}) \qquad 0 < \lambda < 1 \qquad [9.23]$$

That is, the adjustment in actual stock equals only a fraction λ of the difference between desired and actual stock. In general, the longer the time period involved the greater will be the extent of the adjustment and the larger the adjustment coefficient λ.

Stocks of the durable good are normally assumed to depreciate at a constant rate, δ, per period and can therefore be related to quantities purchased of the good by the equation

$$S_t = (1 - \delta)S_{t-1} + q_t \qquad [9.24]$$

where q_t represents purchases per period. Using equations [9.22], [9.23] and [9.24], an equation for q_t can be derived which does not involve the unobservable desired stock variable and which hence may, hopefully, be estimated.

$$q_t = S_t - S_{t-1} + \delta S_{t-1} \qquad [9.25]$$
$$= \lambda(S_t^* - S_{t-1}) + \delta S_{t-1}$$

or

$$q_t = \lambda\alpha_0 + \lambda\alpha_1 p_t + \lambda\alpha_2 x_t + (\delta - \lambda)S_{t-1} + \lambda\varepsilon_t \qquad [9.26]$$

Purchases are therefore dependent not only on relative price and total expenditure, but also on the stock carried over from the previous period. Thus, as we have noted, past purchases influence present decisions. Notice that since δ can be interpreted as the proportion of beginning-period stock which becomes unusable during the period, equation [9.25] divides total purchases into net additions to stock and 'replacement' purchases. In the aggregate context, however, a 'replacement purchase' does not necessarily imply that a *given* consumer has replaced, for example, his hi-fi set with a new one. The first δS_{t-1} of total purchases are regarded as replacements whoever does the purchasing and if, in fact, total purchases are less than δS_{t-1}, then net additions to stock, $S_t - S_{t-1}$, will be negative.

The major problem in estimating [9.26] is that of finding data on S_t, the actual stock of the durable good. The stock will consist of goods of different ages or 'vintages' and, hence, an index number problem is involved. In an early study of the demand for automobiles in the US, Chow (1957; 1960) actually constructs a series for S_t taking a weighted sum of registrations at the end of each year with weights proportional to the prices of automobiles of different brands and ages. Measuring q_t as annual purchases of new cars per capita and p_t as the ratio of a car price index to a general price index, he estimated from US annual data for 1921–53

$$q_t = 0.08 - 0.020p_t + 0.012x_t - 0.23S_{t-1} \qquad R^2 = 0.858 \qquad [9.27]$$
$$\quad\;\; (0.003) \quad\;\; (0.001) \quad\;\; (0.047)$$

A disposable income variable was used for x_t rather than total expenditure. Notice that the parameters in [9.26] are unidentified since there are only four coefficients from which $\alpha_0, \alpha_1, \alpha_2, \lambda$ and δ have to be estimated. However, Chow obtains an extraneous estimate of the depreciation parameter $\delta = 0.25$ by comparing the prices of cars of different ages. Comparison of equation [9.27] with [9.26] then yields the parameter values

$$\lambda = 0.48, \quad \alpha_0 = 0.17, \quad \alpha_1 = -0.042 \quad \text{and} \quad \alpha_2 = 0.025$$

The value for the adjustment parameter λ suggests, from [9.23], that just under half of any difference between actual and desired stocks are made up during the year. Long-run elasticities of demand (i.e. those holding when actual stocks are completely adjusted to desired levels and $S_t = S_t^*$) can be evaluated at the point of sample means using the above values, and Chow obtains values of -0.63 for the long-run price elasticity and 1.7 for the long-run income elasticity.

Because of the value obtained for λ these are approximately twice as large as the short-run elasticities obtainable from equations [9.26] and [9.27].

Frequently data on stocks of durables are unobtainable, partly because of 'vintage' effects and the problem of obtaining an adequate external estimate of the depreciation parameter δ. An alternative approach, first adopted by Stone and Rowe (1957) for UK consumer durables, is as follows. Alternative series for S_t are constructed using equation [9.24], taking an arbitrary starting value, S_0, for S_{t-1}, and using actual data on purchases combined with various assumed values for δ. Thus, series are constructed as

$$S_t = q_t + (1 - \delta)q_{t-1} + (1 - \delta)^2 q_{t-2} + \cdots + (1 - \delta)^{t-1} q_1 + (1 - \delta)^t S_0$$

$$[9.28]$$

for different values of δ. When [9.28] is substituted into [9.26], the arbitrary S_0 is absorbed into the constant term and a value of δ is eventually selected which gives the best-fitting version of equation [9.26]. Thus δ is, in fact, estimated from the data as are λ and the αs. A method of estimation first suggested by Nerlove (1958) involves transforming equation [9.26] so as to eliminate the stock variable altogether. Lagging [9.26] by one period and multiplying throughout by $1 - \delta$ yields

$$(1 - \delta)q_{t-1} = (1 - \delta)\lambda\alpha_0 + (1 - \delta)\lambda\alpha_1 p_{t-1} + (1 - \delta)\lambda\alpha_2 x_{t-1}$$
$$+ (1 - \delta)(\delta - \lambda)S_{t-2} + (1 - \delta)\lambda\varepsilon_{t-1}$$

Subtracting this equation from [9.26] we have

$$q_t - (1 - \delta)q_{t-1} = \delta\lambda\alpha_0 + \lambda\alpha_1 p_t - (1 - \delta)\lambda\alpha_1 p_{t-1} + \lambda\alpha_2 x_t - (1 - \delta)\lambda\alpha_2 x_{t-1}$$
$$+ (\delta - \lambda)[S_{t-1} - (1 - \delta)S_{t-2}] + \lambda\varepsilon_t - (1 - \delta)\lambda\varepsilon_{t-1}$$

Moreover, since from equation [9.24] we have

$$S_{t-1} - (1 - \delta)S_{t-2} = q_{t-1}$$

we eventually obtain

$$q_t = \delta\lambda\alpha_0 + \lambda\alpha_1 p_t - (1 - \delta)\lambda\alpha_1 p_{t-1} + \lambda\alpha_2 x_t - (1 - \delta)\lambda\alpha_2 x_{t-1}$$
$$+ (1 - \lambda)q_{t-1} + \lambda\varepsilon_t - (1 - \delta)\lambda\varepsilon_{t-1}$$

$$[9.29]$$

Equation [9.29] expresses purchases as a function of price, total expenditure and lagged values of price, total expenditure and purchases. Despite the absence of the stock variable, however, equation [9.29] presents a number of estimation problems. First, the equation is 'overidentified' in the sense that it involves six coefficients from which we must obtain values for five parameters. For example, the ratio of the coefficients on p_t and p_{t-1} will provide one estimate of δ but the ratio of the coefficients on the expenditure variables will provide a second, almost certainly different, estimate. This means that a non-linear estimating procedure of the kind described in section 3.5 must be adopted which minimises the sum of squared residuals subject to constraints which ensure unique values for each estimated parameter.

Secondly, if the disturbance ε_t in equation [9.22] is non-autocorrelated, then the composite disturbance in equation [9.29], i.e.

$$u_t = \lambda\varepsilon_t - (1 - \delta)\lambda\varepsilon_{t-1}$$

214

will be autocorrelated since both u_t and u_{t-1} will be dependent on ε_{t-1}. This autocorrelation, when combined with the appearance of the lagged dependent variable q_{t-1} among the explanatory variables, means, as we saw in section 5.2.2, that normal OLS procedures will yield biased and inconsistent estimators of the parameters of [9.29]. Maximum likelihood procedures which explicitly take account of the autocorrelation are therefore necessary if consistent estimators are to be obtained.

Despite these estimation difficulties, the stock adjustment model has proved a popular vehicle for explaining the importance of lagged variables in demand equations for durable goods. However, other dynamic models can also give rise to estimating equations similar to [9.29] and it may in practice prove difficult to discriminate between competing models. For example, we turn next to a generalisation of the stock adjustment model first suggested by Houthakker and Taylor (1970).

The state adjustment model

We have already noted in our discussion of time series data that, because of habit and inertia, lagged adjustment to equilibrium values may be a characteristic of the demand for non-durable as well as durable goods. Houthakker and Taylor (1970) propose the following equation for *both* durable and non-durable goods

$$q_t = \beta_0 + \beta_1 p_t + \beta_2 x_t + \gamma S_{t-1} + \varepsilon_t \qquad [9.30]$$

S_t is now a 'state variable', to be interpreted in the case of durables simply as the beginning period stock of the good, but in the case of non-durables representing a psychological 'stock of habits' since in this case tastes and hence purchases are assumed to be influenced by past consumption. For durables [9.30] is identical to the stock adjustment equation [9.26] with $\gamma = \delta - \lambda$, while for non-durables it is simply assumed that $\gamma > 0$. Stocks of habit are determined by an equation identical to [9.24] except that δ is now interpreted as the rate (assumed constant) at which habits decay. Note that further purchases increase the stock of habits.[7] Also, [9.28] in the present context implies that habits depend on past purchases and an 'original' stock of habits S_0, but since $0 < \delta < 1$, recent past purchases are the most important in determining S_t.

Equations [9.30] and [9.24] can be manipulated in the same way as [9.22] and [9.24] to yield

$$q_t = \delta\beta_0 + \beta_1 p_t - (1 - \delta)\beta_1 p_{t-1} + \beta_2 x_t - (1 - \delta)\beta_2 x_{t-1}$$
$$+ (1 + \gamma - \delta)q_{t-1} + \varepsilon_t - (1 - \delta)\varepsilon_{t-1} \qquad [9.31]$$

Thus the stock variable is again eliminated, [9.31] being an identical estimating equation to [9.29] although it is given a different interpretation for habit-forming goods.

The advantage of the Houthakker–Taylor model is that it can be applied to any good – durable, habit-forming or *both*. The sign of γ in [9.30] depends on the properties of the relevant good. If $\gamma < 0$, then 'inventory effects' are held to outweigh 'habit-forming' effects while, if $\gamma > 0$, habit-forming effects pre-dominate.[8] More importantly, however, the sign of γ determines the relationship between short- and long-run elasticities. The long-run relationship

215

between purchases, prices and total expenditure can be obtained by setting

$$q_t = q_{t-1}, \quad p_t = p_{t-1} \quad \text{and} \quad x_t = x_{t-1}$$

in equation [9.31]. This yields

$$q_t = \frac{\delta\beta_0}{\delta - \gamma} + \frac{\delta\beta_1}{\delta - \gamma}p_t + \frac{\delta\beta_2}{\delta - \gamma}x_t \qquad [9.32]$$

The long-run effect of changes in p_t or x_t is therefore $\delta/(\delta - \gamma)$ times the short-run effect. Hence, if $\gamma < 0$, then short-run effects are greater than long-run effects, whereas if $\gamma > 0$ then (provided $\gamma < \delta$ as invariably found by Houthakker and Taylor) long-run effects are the more important. Any difference between short- and long-run elasticities has important implications for the effect of, for example, changes in indirect taxation on purchases and the marked differences found by Houthakker and Taylor were put forward as a clear justification for their model.

Houthakker and Taylor investigate eighty-one forms of consumer expenditure using annual US data over the period 1929–64. For sixty-five of their eighty-one categories the state adjustment model performs best and in forty-six of these cases the γ coefficient turns out to be positive, implying larger elasticities in the long run than in the short run.[9] These goods represented 61 per cent of total US consumer expenditure.

As an example, consider the following equation for 'clothing, including luggage' estimated by OLS. (Note, however, that the Durbin–Watson statistic is an invalid test for autocorrelation because of the presence of q_{t-1} among the explanatory variables. Autocorrelation is to be expected given the moving average disturbance in [9.31] and its presence together with q_{t-1} would make OLS inconsistent.)

$$q_t = 17.595 + 0.0763\Delta x_t + 0.0173x_{t-1} + 0.6243q_{t-1} \quad R^2 = 0.904 \, \text{d.w.} = 2.03$$
$$(8.905) \quad (0.0242) \qquad (0.0074) \qquad (0.1479)$$

Price variables turned out to be incorrectly signed for this category and were dropped from the equation. Since the terms in Δx_t and x_{t-1} can be rewritten as $0.0763x_t - 0.0590x_{t-1}$, the above equation implies the following values for the parameters in equation [9.31]

$$\beta_1 = 0, \quad \beta_2 = 0.0763, \quad \delta = 0.227 \quad \text{and} \quad \gamma = -0.149$$

Notice, first, that since $\gamma < 0$, inventory effects outweigh habit-forming effects for this category of good. The depreciation parameter is 0.227 although we cannot say to what extent this represents depreciation in stocks of goods or stocks of habit, β_2 measures the short-run effect of a total expenditure change and is positive as expected. The long-run effect is given by

$$\frac{\delta\beta_2}{(\delta - \gamma)} = 0.046$$

Thus, because $\gamma < 0$, the long-run effect of a total expenditure change is less than the short-run effect.

The model is also estimated for eleven much broader categories of expenditure. For example, for 'automobiles and parts', the short-run income elasticity is 5.06 falling to 1.07 in the long run. This reflects the high durability of automobiles

216

$(\gamma < 0)$ since, although initially purchases respond sharply to a change in income, such purchases raise future stocks of automobiles and this has the effect of reducing future purchases. On the other hand, 'food and beverages' have a short-run income elasticity of 0.72 rising to 0.85 in the long run. Here habit influences outweigh any inventory effects that may be present $(\gamma > 0)$ and initial purchases increase the 'stock' of habits which reinforces future demand.

The adjustment models outlined in this section are obviously a definite improvement on models in which all adjustments to equilibrium values are assumed to occur instantaneously. They do, however, fail to make allowance for a number of factors which may be of particular importance in the demand for durable goods. For example, no account is taken of expectations about the future price of durable goods, although such expectations might well affect demand, particularly as far as the timing of replacement demand is concerned. Indeed, replacement demand in these models is virtually defined to be a constant proportion of beginning-period stock, whereas in practice economic conditions could result in either an advancement or a delay in replacement purchases.

Another problem with adjustment models is that it is not clear how borrowing constraints such as government credit restrictions should be introduced into the analysis. One possibility is to add government policy variables to equation [9.22] and this is a method occasionally followed. However, such constraints are just as likely to affect the speed at which adjustment takes place. This confusion is partly the result of the *ad hoc* nature of the models – insufficient attention is paid to the reasons why adjustment is not instantaneous. The way forward may well involve the development of models in which partial adjustment arises *as a result* of utility-maximising behaviour, i.e. as a natural choice of the rational consumer.

An error correction approach

Lack of data on the stock of consumer durables has more recently led investigators to adopt a data-based approach to estimating demand equations for such goods. This has involved the Hendry general to specific methodology and the use of error correction models. It is not difficult to show that a proportionate relationship between the desired stock of durables, S^*, and disposable income, y, implies a proportionate relationship between equilibrium *expenditure* and income. Suppose $S^* = \alpha y$. A continuous version of [9.25] is

$$q = \dot{S} + \delta S \qquad [9.33]$$

where $\dot{S}$ is the change in the actual stock and δ is again the depreciation parameter. From [9.33] we have

$$\frac{q}{S} = \frac{\dot{S}}{S} + \delta \qquad [9.34]$$

In long-run equilibrium, actual stock $S = S^*$ and both y and S grow at the same constant rate g. Hence, since now $\dot{S}/S = g$, equation [9.34] can be rewritten as

$$q = (g + \delta)S = (g + \delta)\alpha y \qquad [9.35]$$

Equation [9.35] is a proportionate long-run relationship between q and y where the factor of proportionality depends on the long-run growth rate g. In the absence of data on the stock of durables [9.35] can be used as the equilibrium relationship underlying an error correction model.

Cuthbertson (1980) was one of the first to adopt this approach. He estimates demand equations for total expenditure on durable goods using quarterly UK data for 1964–76. The testing-down general to specific methodology is used to estimate error-correction models with the basic form

$$\Delta \log q = \alpha_0 + \sum_{j=1}^{n} \alpha_j \Delta \log q_{-j} + \sum_{j=0}^{n} \beta_j \Delta \log y_{-j} - \gamma_1 \log\left(\frac{q}{y}\right)_{-1}$$

$$- \gamma_2 \sum_{j=2}^{n} \log\left(\frac{q}{y}\right)_{-j} - \gamma_3 \sum_{j=1}^{n} \Delta \log\left(\frac{q}{y}\right)_{-j} \qquad [9.36]$$

Notice that more than one past value of the disequilibrium error $\log(q/y)$ is included in [9.36] and the equation also involves changes in $\log(q/y)$. This is because of the complex lag-structures necessary to capture adjustment patterns for durable goods. For example the change in purchases will be lower if purchases were above their equilibrium value in the previous period but even lower if purchases have been above their equilibrium value for some periods. In practice it proves possible to simplify [9.36] by imposing data-acceptable restrictions.

Cuthbertson expands his basic equations to allow for changes in higher purchase regulations, for variations in the flow and cost of credit and for changes in the liquid asset holdings of consumers represented by bank loans. The *flow* of credit to the personal sector is relevant when credit restrictions are in operation and there is an excess demand for credit. However, in the absence of such restrictions, Cuthbertson maintains that the relevant variable is the *cost* of credit represented by the interest rate on bank loans. Liquid assets variables are included on the grounds that if holdings of such assets exceed the desired level then such disequilibrium 'spills over' into purchases of consumer durables.

Cuthbertson concludes that a liquid asset model that also includes the real rate of interest on bank loans is the most acceptable model. The long run income elasticity of the demand for durables is estimated to be 1.9 (many durables are luxuries). Although liquid assets appear in the equation only in difference form and therefore have no long-run effect on demand, the short-run impact elasticity is about 1.5. The other 'monetary' variable, the real rate of interest, however, does have a long-run effect. A rise of 1 per cent in interest rates eventually leads to a decline of around $1\frac{1}{2}$ per cent in the demand for durable goods.

9.6 Estimating complete systems of demand equations

During the past three decades a second approach to the estimation of demand equations has developed, involving the estimation of complete systems of equations encompassing all current spending made by consumers. Traditional consumer theory leads to the system of n demand equations given by equation [9.1]. We have seen that, when attention is confined to just one of these equations, investigators are inevitably forced by degrees of freedom problems to adopt an *ad hoc* approach of dubious theoretical validity involving the suppression of most explanatory price variables. However, if the full system of demand equations [9.1] is considered, the degrees of freedom problem can be reduced and the number of independent parameters limited not by *ad hoc* methods but by making use of the series of restrictions on the parameters of equations [9.1] which are implied by consumer theory.

These restrictions arise partly because of the existence of the consumer's budget constraint and partly because of the assumption of utility maximisation.[10] The budget constraint is

$$p_1 q_1 + p_2 q_2 + p_3 q_3 + \cdots + p_n q_n = x$$

Partially differentiating the budget constraint with respect to x yields

$$p_1 \frac{\partial q_1}{\partial x} + p_2 \frac{\partial q_2}{\partial x} + p_3 \frac{\partial q_3}{\partial x} + \cdots + p_n \frac{\partial q_n}{\partial x} = 1 \qquad [9.37]$$

Partially differentiating with respect to $p_1, p_2, \ldots, p_n$ in turn yields the set of restrictions

$$p_1 \frac{\partial q_1}{\partial p_j} + p_2 \frac{\partial q_2}{\partial p_j} + p_3 \frac{\partial q_3}{\partial p_j} + \cdots + p_n \frac{\partial q_n}{\partial p_j} = -q_j \qquad j = 1, 2, 3, \ldots, n \qquad [9.38]$$

Equations [9.37] and [9.38] are sometimes referred to as the *aggregation* restrictions. *Homogeneity* has already been mentioned in the single equation context but applies, of course, to all n equations in [9.1]. Since homogeneity implies that the sum of all price elasticities plus the total expenditure elasticity equals zero, we can express these n restrictions as

$$\frac{p_1 \partial q_i}{q_i \partial p_1} + \frac{p_2 \partial q_i}{q_i \partial p_2} + \frac{p_3 \partial q_i}{q_i \partial p_3} + \cdots + \frac{p_n \partial q_i}{q_i \partial p_n} + \frac{x \partial q_i}{q_i \partial x} = 0 \qquad i = 1, 2, 3, \ldots, n$$

or, multiplying throughout by q_i

$$p_1 \frac{\partial q_i}{\partial p_1} + p_2 \frac{\partial q_i}{\partial p_2} + p_3 \frac{\partial q_i}{\partial p_3} + \cdots + p_n \frac{\partial q_i}{\partial p_n} = -x \frac{\partial q_i}{\partial x} \qquad i = 1, 2, 3, \ldots, n$$
$$[9.39]$$

We have already come across the Slutsky equation or 'law of demand' in the single equation context and it applies to all n equations in the system. That is

$$\frac{\partial q_i}{\partial p_i} + q_i \frac{\partial q_i}{\partial x} < 0 \qquad i = 1, 2, 3, \ldots, n \qquad [9.40]$$

The n equations [9.40] are known as the *negativity* restrictions and in fact follow from the assumption of utility maximisation. However, utility maximisation also implies $n(n-1)/2$ so-called *symmetry* restrictions involving more than just one equation

$$\frac{\partial q_i}{\partial p_j} + q_j \frac{\partial q_i}{\partial x} = \frac{\partial q_j}{\partial p_i} + q_i \frac{\partial q_j}{\partial x} \qquad \text{for all } i \neq j \qquad [9.41]$$

In the single-equation context the imposition of homogeneity reduced the number of independent parameters to be estimated by one. Similarly, imposition of any of the 'equality-type' restrictions [9.37–9.39] and [9.41] has the same effect on the number of independent parameters to be estimated in the system [9.1] whatever functional form is chosen. However, not all the restrictions listed above are independent of one another, since it can be shown that the aggregation and symmetry restrictions taken together imply homogeneity. There are therefore

$$\tfrac{1}{2}n(n+1)+1$$

independent equality-type restrictions in all. Notice, however, that the aggregation and symmetry restrictions are *cross-equation* restrictions, involving the parameters of *all* equations in [9.1]. Their imposition, therefore, requires the simultaneous estimation of all demand equations in the system.

In an n equation demand system there will, in the absence of restrictions, be n^2 price parameters and n total expenditure parameters to be estimated. Hence, ignoring the negativity restrictions (which, being inequalities, are more difficult to impose) the imposition of the theoretical restrictions reduces the total number of independent parameters to

$$n^2 + n - \tfrac{1}{2}n(n+1) - 1 = \tfrac{1}{2}n(n+1) - 1 \qquad [9.42]$$

Thus, in, for example, a twelve-equation system the number of parameters to be estimated falls from 156 to 77. In practice, limited sample sizes mean that this is still likely to be too many, so at first sight it may seem that the full system approach falls foul of degrees of freedom difficulties just as does the concentration on a single equation. Econometricians, however, have been reluctant to abandon this approach, first because of its sounder theoretical foundation, and secondly because the imposition of the theoretical restrictions should, provided they are valid, enable more precise estimates of demand equation parameters to be obtained. The most efficient estimators, i.e. those with the smallest sampling variances, are those that make use of all available valid information. Since many of the theoretical restrictions are cross-equation in nature, they cannot be imposed on each equation in isolation so that efficient estimation implies the estimation of the full system.

The way out of the 'degrees of freedom deadlock' has been to impose further restrictions on demand equations which are derived by making special assumptions about the consumer's utility function. In this way it is possible to reduce dramatically the number of independent parameters that have to be estimated. The most popular of these special assumptions is that known as *additivity* or 'want independence'. A consumer's preferences are said to be want-independent if they can be represented by a utility function which is additive in the sense that the marginal utility of any one good is independent of the quantities consumed of all other goods.[11] Advocates of the additivity assumption argue that it is acceptable provided 'goods' are defined in a sufficiently broad manner. For example, the marginal utility of 'entertainment' is unlikely to be much affected by the quantity of 'clothing' consumed. However, additivity is a somewhat extreme assumption, for it can be shown that it implies that goods cannot be inferior and neither can they be complements in the modern Hicksian sense. Its major advantage is that, *provided* it is a valid assumption, it reduces the number of independent parameters in a demand system from the $\tfrac{1}{2}n(n+1) - 1$ of equation [9.42] to as few as n. Many economists, however, would regard so few independent responses as, in itself, unrealistic. Fortunately, there are a number of assumptions, less restrictive than additivity, which increase the number of independent responses beyond n but still keep them well below that of equation [9.42].

In estimating demand systems two approaches are possible. First, the precise form of the utility function can be specified. Hence, a system of demand equations can be derived which are guaranteed to satisfy at least the general restrictions [9.37–9.41] implied by consumer theory. The advantage of such an approach is the increase in degrees of freedom available; the disadvantages that it cannot be used to *test* the restrictions of the theory and a loss in generality resulting from whatever precise form is given to the utility function. The second approach is to begin with a set of demand equations which are capable of satisfying theoretical restrictions but do not necessarily do so. With this approach it is possible to test theoretical restrictions, but the obvious disadvantage here is that since restrictions are not imposed we come up against the degrees of freedom problem. Furthermore, although properties of the utility function are not *explicitly* specified in this approach, there is a real danger that in deciding on particular functional forms for the demand equation we may be *implicitly* imposing restrictions on the underlying utility function which, for all we know, are totally unacceptable. In the next section we consider some of the first examples of the estimation of complete systems of demand equations, involving both the above approaches. In the following section we look at more recent developments.

9.7 Early complete system models

We consider, first, two systems which specify a precise form for the utility function in either its direct or indirect form. As we noted in the previous section, such systems cannot be used for testing consumer theory.

The linear expenditure system

The linear expenditure system (LES), first extensively used by Stone (1954), has an explicitly specified direct utility function of the form

$$U = \beta_1 \log(q_1 - \gamma_1) + \beta_2 \log(q_2 - \gamma_2) + \cdots + \beta_n \log(q_n - \gamma_n) \qquad [9.43]$$

where the β's and γ's are parameters and, if the logarithms are to be defined, it is necessary that $q_i > \gamma_i$ for all i. Maximisation of [9.43] subject to the usual budget constraint $\sum p_i q_i = x$ leads, after some manipulation, to the system of demand equations

$$p_i q_i = p_i \gamma_i + \beta_i \left[x - \sum_j p_j \gamma_j \right] \qquad i = 1, 2, 3, \ldots, n \qquad [9.44]$$

with $0 < \beta_i < 1$ for all i. The great advantage of this system is that it expresses q_i as a *linear* function of x/p_i (a measure of real total expenditure) and of relative prices p_j/p_i and this makes for ease of estimation. In fact, it can be shown that [9.44] is *the only linear demand equation which satisfies all the theoretical restrictions*.

221

An appealing way of interpreting equation [9.44] is to regard expenditure $p_i q_i$ on good i as made up of two parts. One part, $p_i \gamma_i$, is the minimum possible expenditure on good i so that γ_i is to be interpreted as the 'subsistence level' of consumption for good i. Hence, a portion of total expenditure, $\sum p_i \gamma_i$, is committed to unavoidable subsistence purchases. The remainder of total expenditure, $x - \sum p_i \gamma_i$, is sometimes referred to as 'supernumerary expenditure' and is spent on all goods in constant proportions. Thus, the second part of expenditure on good i is always some constant fraction, β_i, of supernumerary expenditure.

While ease of estimation is the obvious attraction of the LES, it should be clear from equation [9.43] that the underlying utility function is an additive one so that the system suffers from the limitations of additive systems mentioned above. Notwithstanding this, the LES proved a popular method of estimating the magnitude of consumer responses to expenditure and price changes. Estimated systems were then used for forecasting purposes. Stone and his associates used a system based on data going back to the beginning of the century to forecast UK demand up until 1970. Other well-known estimated LESSs are those of Pollock and Wales (1969) for the US, Goldberger and Gamaletsos (1970) for thirteen OEC countries and Deaton (1975) who estimated a thirty-seven-equation system for the UK.

The indirect addilog model

It is often useful in applied demand analysis to work not in terms of the normal 'direct' utility function but from the so-called *indirect utility function*. For example, in the simple two-good case if a consumer is assumed to maximise a utility function

$$U = U(q_1, q_2) \qquad [9.45]$$

subject to the budget constraint

$$p_1 q_1 + p_2 q_2 = x \qquad [9.46]$$

then we obtain the two demand equations

$$\begin{aligned} q_1 &= q_1(p_1, p_2, x) \\ q_2 &= q_2(p_1, p_2, x) \end{aligned} \qquad [9.47]$$

Substituting these expressions for q_1 and q_2 back into [9.45] we obtain the maximum utility obtainable for any given combination of p_1, p_2 and x. This yields the indirect utility function

$$U^* = U^*[q_1(p_1, p_2, x), \quad q_2(p_1, p_2, x)] \qquad [9.48]$$

Alternatively, we may *start* with the indirect utility function [9.48]. If we specify a precise functional form for [9.48] then functional forms for the demand equations [9.47] can easily be obtained by using *Roy's Identity* which states that[12]

$$q_i = -\frac{\partial U^*}{\partial p_i} \bigg/ \frac{\partial U^*}{\partial x} \qquad [9.49]$$

Houthakker (1960) suggested that, in the general case, [9.48] should be specified as

$$U^* = \alpha_1 \left(\frac{p_1}{x}\right)^{\beta_1} + \alpha_2 \left(\frac{p_2}{x}\right)^{\beta_2} + \cdots + \alpha_n \left(\frac{p_n}{x}\right)^{\beta_n} \tag{9.50}$$

This specification implies that the indirect utility function is homogeneous of degree zero in prices and total expenditure. This is a necessary requirement of theory since in [9.48] each q_i is homogeneous of degree zero in prices and x. Applying Roy's Identity to [9.50] and taking logarithms, now yields a system of demand equations known as the *indirect addilog model*.

$$\log q_i = \log \alpha_i \beta_i + (\beta_i + 1) \log\left(\frac{x}{p_i}\right) + \log\left\{ \sum_k \alpha_k \beta_k \left(\frac{x}{p_k}\right)^{\beta_k} \right\}$$

$$i = 1, 2, 3, \ldots, n \tag{9.51}$$

The indirect addilog model is akin to the LES in that, since it is derived using the assumption of utility maximisation, its equations must necessarily satisfy all the restrictions of consumer theory. However, the non-linearity of [9.51] makes estimation more complicated than for the LES. Moreover, when direct comparisons of the two models have been made, the indirect addilog model appears to fit data worse than the LES.

We turn next to two systems that involve the second of the two approaches described at the end of the last subsection. Demand equations in these systems do not necessarily obey the restrictions of theory and, hence, may be used for testing such restrictions.

The Rotterdam model

The Rotterdam model for some years proved the most popular method of attempting to 'test' the restrictions implied by consumer theory. The Rotterdam model, first developed by Theil (1965) and Barten (1966), employs as dependent variables, not quantities demanded, q_i, but variables of the form

$$w_i \left(\frac{dq_i}{q_i}\right) = w_i d \log q_i$$

where

$$w_i = \left(\frac{p_i q_i}{x}\right)$$

is the proportion of total expenditure allocated to good i. This may seem a strange choice unless it is remembered that consumer theory is concerned with the allocation of total expenditure between various goods. It therefore makes sense to consider the *budget shares*, w_i, rather than the q_i. Furthermore, a budget share w_i changes as total expenditure, x, and price, p_i, change both directly because it depends on x and p_i and indirectly because the consumer adjusts q_i

the quantity demanded. That is,

$$dw_i = \frac{\partial w}{\partial q_i} dq_i + \frac{\partial w}{\partial p_i} dp_i + \frac{\partial q_i}{\partial x} dx$$

$$= \frac{p_i}{x} dq_i + \frac{q_i}{x} dp_i - \frac{p_i q_i}{x^2} dx = w_i \frac{dq_i}{q_i} + w_i \frac{dp_i}{p_i} - w_i \frac{dx}{x}$$

or

$$dw_i = w_i d \log q_i + w_i d \log p_i - w_i d \log x \qquad [9.52]$$

Since changes in total expenditure and prices are taken as given by the consumer, only that part of dw_i represented by the first term on the right-hand side of [9.52] can be thought of as being endogenously determined. This makes $w_i d \log q_i$ a very appropriate choice as the dependent variable in a demand equation.

Demand equations with such a dependent variable can be obtained by taking the total differential of equation [9.1] and multiplying throughout by w_i/q_i. This eventually yields

$$w_i d \log q_i = \sum_j \Pi_{ij} d \log p_j + \mu_i \sum_j w_j d \log q_j \qquad i = 1, 2, 3, \ldots, n \qquad [9.53]$$

where $\mu_i = p_i(\partial q_i / \partial x)$ is the marginal propensity to consumer good i and Π_{ij} is the product of w_i and the 'income-compensated' elasticity of demand for good i with respect to the price of good j. Changes in expenditure are reflected in equation [9.53] by the $\sum w_j d \log q_j$ term which is a measure of real income. Notice that [9.53] as it stands is completely general, since it is derived from [9.1] without specifying any particular form for the demand equations. It is hence implied by *any* underlying utility function. The equations [9.53] represent a 'differential demand equation system' since they determine changes in demand rather than the demands themselves.

The μ_i and the Π_{ij} in equations [9.53] will normally be dependent on total expenditure, x, and on all prices. The Rotterdam model however, 'parameterises' the μ_i and the Π_{ij}, treating them as constants and ignoring their dependence on x and on prices. This may seem a somewhat drastic procedure but if estimation is to proceed at all then some quantities have to be parameterised.[13] The great advantage of treating the μ_i and Π_{ij} as constants is that it enables the theoretical restrictions [9.37–9.41] to be rewritten as equations which are *unchanged for all values of total expenditure and prices*. When the restrictions are formulated in terms of first derivatives, then, as an examination of [9.37–9.41] indicates, their precise form will be dependent on levels of x and prices. However, in terms of the μ_i and Π_{ij} it can be shown that they become

Aggregation $\begin{cases} \mu_1 + \mu_2 + \mu_3 + \cdots \mu_n = 1 & [9.37A] \\ \Pi_{1j} + \Pi_{2j} + \Pi_{3j} + \cdots \Pi_{nj} = 0 \qquad j = 1, 2, 3, \ldots, n & [9.38A] \end{cases}$

Homogeneity $\quad \Pi_{i1} + \Pi_{i2} + \Pi_{i3} + \cdots \Pi_{in} = 0 \qquad i = 1, 2, 3, \ldots, n \qquad [9.39A]$

Negativity $\qquad \Pi_{ii} < 0 \qquad i = 1, 2, 3, \ldots, n \qquad\qquad\qquad\qquad [9.40A]$

Symmetry $\qquad \Pi_{ij} = \Pi_{ji} \qquad$ for all $i \neq j$ $\qquad\qquad\qquad\qquad\qquad [9.41A]$

Notice that the 'strongest' of the restrictions, i.e. [9.37–9.39] and [9.41] are now of especially simple linear form and moreover retain exactly this form *for every observation in a sample* and this makes their imposition a relatively simple matter. By contrast, if the derivatives in [9.37–9.41] are parameterised then the restrictions to be imposed would vary in form from observation to observation.

It may now seem that the Rotterdam model presents a perfect method of either testing the restrictions of consumer theory or of enforcing them and reaping the benefits of more efficient estimation. However, the parameterisation of the μ_i and the Π_{ij} has implications which were not foreseen by the originators of the system. As first shown by D. McFadden in an unpublished paper, differential demand equations in which the μ_i and Π_{ij} are constants can only arise when the demands themselves are determined by a system of the following kind

$$q_i = \mu_i \left(\frac{x}{p_i} \right) \qquad i = 1, 2, 3, \ldots, n$$

This demand system implies that expenditure on any good, $p_i q_i$, is a constant proportion, μ_i, of total expenditure, x, no matter what the structure of relative prices. A moment's reflection should convince the reader that 'expenditure proportionality' is a clearly implausible description of consumer behaviour. In addition, the above demand system can easily be shown to arise from the maximization of the additive utility function $U = \sum \mu_i \log q_i$ and, hence, *must necessarily satisfy all the theoretical restrictions.*

These unexpected implications may seem to damage severely any claim the Rotterdam model has to be a completely general demand system. Moreover, if the Rotterdam model automatically satisfies the theoretical restrictions it can hardly be used to test them! However, empirical versions of the Rotterdam model, in which variables of the kind $w_i(\log q_{it} - \log q_{it-1})$ are used to approximate the log differentials of equation [9.53], certainly do not suggest expenditure proportionality. Moreover, Rotterdam theorists claim that their system can be regarded as a first-order approximation to any arbitrary demand system (see, for example, Theil 1975). However, McFadden's result well illustrates the unforeseen dangers of arbitrary parameterisation in this area of empirical research.

Typically, maximum likelihood methods were used to estimate Rotterdam systems. Well-known studies are those of Barten (1969) using Dutch data for 1921–63 and Deaton (1974) for UK data from 1900–70. The most interesting feature of this work was that the theoretical restriction of homogeneity, and also possibly that of symmetry, *appeared to be rejected by the data.* Equiproportionate changes in total expenditure and prices did *not* appear to leave quantities demanded unchanged. This apparent rejection of theory could be attributed to the fact that the Rotterdam model is at best an approximation. However, as we shall see in a moment, other investigators using different demand systems, involving different approximations, came up with similar results. Although research in this field is bedevilled by the need to find parameterisations which have no undesirable implications, and there is always the possibility that non-homogeneity may be a consequence of the model used rather than a property of the data, this unanimity was impressive.

The double logarithmic system

Of demand systems not necessarily satisfying the theoretical restrictions and which hence may be used for testing them, the simplest used in applied work has been the *double logarithmic system*

$$q_i = A p_1^{\alpha_{1i}} p_2^{\alpha_{2i}} p_3^{\alpha_{3i}}, \ldots, p_n^{\alpha_{ni}} x^{\beta_i} \qquad [9.54]$$

The parameters in this system are, of course, elasticities. Unfortunately, when the theoretical restrictions are expressed in terms of elasticities then, just as was the case when they were expressed in terms of first derivatives, they do not remain unchanged for all configurations of total expenditure and prices. The model cannot therefore satisfy fully these restrictions. Investigators generally test the restrictions at one particular combination of expenditure and prices. If the restrictions are satisfied for this combination of expenditure and prices it is assumed that they will be satisfied approximately for other combinations.

Results with this model were very similar to those for the Rotterdam model. For example, Byron (1970a and 1970b) and Lluch (1971) both found the homogeneity and symmetry restrictions to be rejected. However, like the Rotterdam model, the double-log model is at best an approximation and in this case the approximation has yielded some strange results. Byron found that despite the fact that his (Dutch) data satisfied the aggregation restrictions in that it obeyed the budget constraint for all observations, his tests rejected one of the aggregation restrictions. Such a result has to reflect the model used rather than any deficiency in consumer theory. This result highlights the necessity, noted at the end of our discussion of the Rotterdam model, of where possible making a clear distinction between findings which genuinely represent properties of the data under analysis and those which are simply a reflection of the model in use.

9.8 Some later developments

The deficiencies of both the above approaches to estimating complete systems of demand equations led to a number of significant developments in this area during the 1970s and early 1980s.

Flexible functional forms

The desire actually to test the restrictions of consumer theory led to attempts to approximate either the direct or the indirect utility function by some so-called 'flexible functional form' that contains sufficient parameters to be regarded as an adequate approximation to whatever the 'true' underlying utility function happens to be.[14] The earliest approach along these lines was that of Christensen, Jorgenson and Lau (1975). In the first of their two specifications, *the direct translog model*, they approximate the negative of the logarithm of the *direct* utility function by a function which is quadratic in the logarithms of the quantities consumed

$$-\log U = \alpha_0 + \sum_i \alpha_i \log q_i + \tfrac{1}{2} \sum_i \sum_j \beta_{ij} \log q_i \log q_j \qquad [9.55]$$

Maximisation of such a utility function subject to the usual budget constraint leads to a system of equations expressing the budget shares, w_i, of the n goods as functions of the logarithms of the quantities consumed. That is

$$w_i = \frac{\alpha_i + \sum_j \beta_{ij} \log q_j}{\alpha + \sum_j \beta_j \log q_j} \qquad i = 1, 2, 3, \ldots, n \qquad [9.56]$$

where

$$\alpha = \sum_i \alpha_i \quad \text{and} \quad \beta_j = \sum_i \beta_{ij}$$

In their second specification, the *indirect translog model*, Christensen, Jorgenson and Lau approximate the logarithm of the *indirect utility* function by a function quadratic in the logarithms of the ratios of prices to total expenditure

$$\log U^* = \alpha'_0 + \sum_i \alpha'_i \log\left(\frac{p_i}{x}\right) + \tfrac{1}{2} \sum_i \sum_j \beta'_{ij} \log\left(\frac{p_i}{x}\right) \log\left(\frac{p_j}{x}\right) \qquad [9.57]$$

Using Roy's Identity [9.49], a system of budget share equations is again obtained, this time expressing the w_i as functions of the logarithms of the price-expenditure ratios. That is

$$w_i = \frac{\alpha'_i + \sum_j \beta'_{ij} \log(p_j/x)}{\alpha' + \sum_j \beta'_j \log(p_j/x)} \qquad i = 1, 2, 3, \ldots, n \qquad [9.58]$$

where

$$\alpha' = \sum_i \alpha'_i \quad \text{and} \quad \beta'_j = \sum_i \beta'_{ij}$$

The authors argue that since [9.55] and [9.57] can be regarded as second-order Taylor approximations to *any* direct or indirect utility function, data should conform to the demand systems they have derived (together with the restrictions implied) if consumer theory is to be regarded as valid. They used maximum likelihood methods to estimate their system for US annual data for 1929–72 using three commodity groupings – non-durable consumption goods, services from durable consumption goods and other services. They concluded that their results implied a rejection of the theory of demand. However, [9.55] and [9.57] are merely approximations (whether good or bad) to the true utility functions, so that a rejection of consumer theory on the basis of the translog models is no more final than a rejection on the basis of the Rotterdam or double log models. What was more convincing, of course, was that *all* three models, each using different approximations, came up with exactly the same result – that the restrictions implied by consumer theory did not hold.

The aggregation problem again

In section 9.2 we discussed, in the context of individual demand equations, the question of whether it was possible to aggregate the micro equations of individual households into a macro equation of the same functional form. The conditions for perfect aggregation of a *system* of demand equations are the same as those for a single equation – all households must have demand equations which are linear functions of their total expenditures and the marginal propensities to spend on all goods must be identical for each household. The hth household's demand for the ith good must therefore take the form

$$q_i^h = a_i^h + b_i x^h \qquad [9.59]$$

where x^h is the total expenditure of the hth household and the a_i^h and the b_i are functions of all prices. It is assumed that all households face the same prices. Notice that the a_i^h functions vary across households in [9.59] but the b_i functions cannot as all households must have the same marginal propensities to spend.[15]

Provided the general theoretical restrictions are satisfied by the micro-equations [9.59], it can be shown that they will also be satisfied by the macro-equations obtained by aggregating the micro-equations. Thus not only does linearity in total expenditures and identical marginal propensities enable sensible aggregate equations to be constructed but it also justified the procedure of *using such aggregate equations to test theoretical restrictions which really only apply to the behaviour of the individual household.* Since this is what many estimators of demand systems seem to do, the aggregation problem is clearly of great importance.

Unfortunately the assumptions implied by [9.59] are very restrictive. Multiplying [9.59] throughout by the constant p_i makes clear that they imply that *all Engle curves are linear* and that *the Engle curves of different households all have the same slope.* But we have already seen in section 9.4 that the empirical evidence suggests strongly that Engle curves are non-linear. Moreover, with the exception of the LES, nearly all the demand systems that have been successfully fitted to data imply non-linear Engle curves.

The aggregation problem is of more than theoretical interest. As pointed out by Blundell (1988), if plausible forms for demand patterns can be found that can be sensibly aggregated, then not only can we deduce facts about individuals from aggregate data but we can expect aggregate models to make sensible predictions. Not surprisingly, then, considerable efforts were made by econometricians to devise demand systems that implied non-linear Engle curves but yet could, in some way, be sensibly aggregated.

We noted in section 9.2 the additional difficulties that arise when attempts are made to aggregate non-linear equations. However, Muellbauer (1975) and (1976) demonstrated that if consumer preference orderings are of a certain type then they imply non-linear Engle curves that can be satisfactorily aggregated, provided that the macro or aggregate demands are expressed as functions of *representative* expenditure (defined below) rather than mean expenditure. Full details of this aggregation procedure are beyond the scope of this book but an accessible introduction is provided by Thomas (1987).

An important special case of the preference orderings that permit Muellbauer type aggregation is the so called PIGLOG case.[16] If such aggregation is to be possible the Muellbauer analysis indicates that Engle curves for the individual household h have to take the form (for good i)

$$p_i q_i^h = a_i x^h + b_i x^h \log\left(\frac{x^h}{k^h}\right) \qquad [9.60]$$

where k^h is a parameter that varies from household to household. For example k^h could simply be the size of household h. Both a_i and b_i are functions of all prices. The Engle curves [9.60] can be aggregated to yield a macro Engle curve expressing aggregate expenditure in terms of a representative expenditure defined as a weighted geometric mean of the individual x^h/k^hs. Moreover, provided the x^hs always change equiproportionately, this representative expenditure will be proportionate to mean expenditure.

Engle curves of the kind [9.60] are clearly non-linear and are well known for providing close fits to cross-sectional data and date back to the study by Working (1943). The Muellbauer approach therefore provides a way of aggregating very plausible non-linear Engle curves.

The almost ideal demand system

Much recent work in the analysis of consumer demand makes use of the concept of *duality*. The consumer's problem is normally expressed as that of choosing quantities consumed so as to maximise utility subject to the budget constraint that total expenditure should not exceed a given level x. However, it may be reformulated as that of choosing quantities so as to minimise the total expenditure necessary to achieve a given utility level U.

Just as we obtained the indirect utility function of the previous section by substituting for quantities demanded into the direct utility function, so we can obtain the consumer's so-called *cost-function* by substituting the solutions to the expenditure-minimising problem into the expression for total expenditure. In the two-good case, the consumer minimises

$$x = p_1 q_1 + p_2 q_2 \tag{9.61}$$

subject to the constraint that he attains a given utility U^* where

$$U^* = U^*(q_1, q_2) \tag{9.62}$$

This yields cost-minimising values of q_1 and q_2 which depend on U^* and the given prices, p_1 and p_2

$$q_1 = f_1(p_1, p_2, U^*): \quad q_2 = f_2(p_1, p_2, U^*) \tag{9.63}$$

The equations [9.63] are normally referred to as *Hicksian compensated demand functions*. Substituting back into equation [9.61] for q_1 and q_2 yields the consumer's *cost function*

$$x^* = x(p_1, p_2, U^*) \tag{9.64}$$

The cost function yields the minimum expenditure necessary to obtain the utility level U^* at given prices, p_1 and p_2. It is directly analogous to a firm's cost function which gives the minimum cost of producing a given output at given factor prices. It is homogeneous of degree unity in prices because if, for example, prices double then the cost of obtaining a given utility level must also double.

The usefulness of the cost function is that differentiating with respect to p_1 and p_2 leads back to the equations [9.63].[17] The normal demand equations [9.47] can then be obtained by substituting for U^* in [9.63] using the indirect utility function [9.48] which expresses U^* as a function of p_1, p_2 and x. Thus, *any* function which obeys certain conditions such as homogeneity of degree unity can be used to generate a system of demand equations which satisfy the theoretical restrictions.

Deaton and Muellbauer (1980) in their Almost Ideal (AI) demand system adopt the following flexible functional form for the cost function of an individual household h.

$$\log x^h = \alpha_0 + \log k^h + \sum_i \alpha_i \log p_i + \tfrac{1}{2} \sum_i \sum_j \gamma_{ij}^* \log p_i \log p_j$$
$$+ U^h \beta_0 p_1^{\beta_1} p_2^{\beta_2} p_3^{\beta_3}, \dots, p_n^{\beta_n} \qquad [9.65]$$

where x^h and U^h are the total expenditure and utility of the hth household. k^h is a parameter that varies across households. Differentiating [9.65] with respect to each price in turn leads eventually to budget share equations

$$w_i^h = \alpha_i + \sum_j \gamma_{ij} \log p_j + \beta_i \log\left(\frac{x^h}{k^h P}\right) \qquad i = 1, 2, 3, \dots, n \qquad [9.66]$$

where P is an index of prices defined by

$$\log P = \alpha_0 + \sum \alpha_i \log p_i + \tfrac{1}{2} \sum_i \sum_j \gamma_{ij} \log p_i \log p_j \qquad [9.67]$$

and the γ_{ij} are defined as

$$\gamma_{ij} = \tfrac{1}{2}(\gamma_{ij}^* + \gamma_{ji}^*) = \gamma_{ji} \qquad [9.68]$$

The equations [9.66] constitute the AI demand system for household h. The system has a number of advantages.

1. The cost equation [9.65] contains sufficient parameters to be regarded as a close second-order approximation to any cost function and hence any underlying preference ordering.[18] The AI system is therefore as general as the translog models.
2. The budget share equations [9.66] contain sufficient parameters to be regarded as a first-order approximation to any demand system, whether that system is consistent with demand theory or not. The AI system is therefore as general as the Rotterdam model but does not have the restrictive implications of that model, mentioned earlier.
3. Like the Rotterdam model, it can be shown that for the AI system the general restrictions of theory, that is equations [9.37] to [9.41], are unchanged for all possible configurations of prices and total expenditure. They can be expressed entirely in terms of the parameters of the budget share equations [9.66]. For example, homogeneity simply implies $\sum_j \gamma_{ij} = 0$ for all i and symmetry $\gamma_{ij} = \gamma_{ji}$. This makes the AI system a good vehicle for testing the theoretical restrictions.
4. The budget share equations [9.66] imply non-linear Engle curves of the type [9.60]. (Recall that a_i and b_i in [9.60] are functions of prices.) This is because the cost function [9.65] belongs to the class of functions that correspond to the PIGLOG special case we mentioned when discussing Muellbauer type aggregation in the last subsection. Thus, despite the non-linearity of [9.66]

it is possible to formulate macro budget share equations of the form

$$\bar{w}_i = \alpha_i + \sum_j \gamma_{ij} \log p_j + \beta_i \log\left(\frac{x_0}{P}\right) \qquad i = 1, 2, 3, \ldots, n \qquad [9.69]$$

where x_0 is the representative expenditure referred to in the last subsection and P is the price index given by [9.67]. [9.69] can in fact be regarded as derived from the cost function of some 'representative' utility maximising consumer.

5. The AI demand system is easy to estimate. Since prices tend to move together over time, the rather complicated price index P, given by [9.67] can be closely approximated by $P^* = \sum w_i \log p_i$ for time series data. P^* can be calculated prior to the estimation process. Moreover, as we saw in the last subsection, provided there is little change in the distribution of household total expenditures, representative expenditure will be proportional to mean expenditure $\bar{x}$. That is, $x_0 = \bar{x}/k$ where $k \approx$ constant. [9.69] can thus be rewritten as

$$\bar{w}_i = (\alpha_i - \beta_i \log k) + \sum_j \gamma_{ij} \log p_j + \beta_i \log\left(\frac{\bar{x}}{P^*}\right) \qquad i = 1, 2, 3, \ldots, n$$
$$[9.70]$$

The equations [9.70] are linear in the parameters, which makes them far easier to estimate than for example the budget share equations [9.56] and [9.58] arising from the translog models.

Deaton and Muellbauer estimated their system using British data for 1954–74 involving eight non-durable commodity groups. They found that in four of these groups – food, clothing, housing and transport – the homogeneity restriction was rejected. The cross-equation symmetry restrictions were also rejected and, moreover, unlike in some previous studies (e.g. Deaton 1974) symmetry was rejected whether or not the maintained hypothesis includes homogeneity. Thus, yet again, we appear to arrive at the conclusion that available data is inconsistent with consumer theory. Of course, the AI demand system involves approximations, but we can now list four models – Rotterdam, log-linear, translog and AI – all making use of different approximations but which all led to the same result – an apparant rejection of consumer theory.

9.9 Outstanding issues

It would be most premature to reject the whole of consumer theory on the basis of the results quoted in the last section. Many applied demand studies have paid little or no attention to a whole range of problems which could, potentially, invalidate many of the results obtained.

First, in our discussion of the single-equation approach to demand analysis we paid attention in section 9.3 to the problems of identification and simultaneity. In the complete system approach these problems have often been totally ignored. This is presumably because estimation is sufficiently complex (especially when cross-equation restrictions are to be imposed) even without allowing for joint endogeneity in the determination of prices and quantities. Even if identification poses no problem, the likelihood of simultaneous equation bias can only be safely ignored if it can be assumed that prices are set exogenously and that quantities are in infinitely elastic supply. While this may not be an unreasonable assumption for many 'manufactured' goods in an industrial society, it is by no means clear that it will hold for many foodstuffs. One attempt to test the assumption of exogenous prices was that of Bronsard and Salvas Bronsard (1984). Their comparison of models with endogenous and models with exogenous prices suggests that the assumption of price exogeneity is 'not a dramatic one'. Results for both types of models turn out to be very similar. However, this problem is nowhere near resolved.

Secondly, consumption decisions involve intertemporal choices. As indicated earlier, most demand studies begin by assuming that total *current* expenditure is given. A consumer is regarded as first deciding what part of his 'total lifetime resources' is to be allocated to current expenditure, and only then to decide on the allocation of total current expenditure between various goods and services. But the conditions under which such 'two-stage budgeting' will be consistent with lifetime utility maximisation are rather restrictive. If such conditions do not hold even approximately then attention has to be given to the intertemporal aspects of demand. However, there are problems even with models of this kind. Intertemporal utility maximisation implies that the consumer is able to borrow using illiquid assets and future income as collateral and, in practice, this is often not possible. As we shall see in the next chapter when we consider the determinants of aggregate consumption, many consumers are subject to 'liquidity constraints' and are unable to spend much beyond their current income.

Thirdly, even the consumer's total lifetime resources cannot be regarded as given exogenously. A consumer can, to some extent, decide for himself how many hours of work he will put in during his life. For given present and future wage rates, the consumer therefore has some control over his lifetime resources. Neo-classical consumer theory allowed for this by including 'leisure', defined as the difference between hours worked and maximum time available for work, in the consumer's utility function. The budget constraint was then reformulated with the wage *rates* taken as given rather than total resources. However, there are obvious difficulties with this approach. Workers' choice of hours is often limited by the job specification – a more plausible choice is between working or not working. Furthermore, if wage rates are dependent on labour supply then the budget constraint will no longer be linear and such non-linearities will be accentuated by complex tax and social security systems.

Perhaps the greatest weaknesses of the complete system demand studies described in the previous section are their failure to take account either of the vastly differing characteristics of different households or of dynamic factors. A household's spending pattern depends not only on prices and total expenditure but on vital demographic and social factors. As far as dynamic factors are concerned, we have seen in the single equation context the importance of allowing for lagged adjustment, whether because of habit effects or because of the durable nature of many goods. Yet many system studies have ignored such problems. Still less have they paid attention to the possible non-stationarity of price and expenditure variables, despite the implications of this for estimation procedures.

Attempts have been made to introduce dynamic effects into the Deaton–Muellbauer AI system. For example, Blanciforti and Green (1983) introduce habit effects into such a model, while Anderson and Blundell use an error-correction generalisation in their 1983 and 1984 studies. The latter use the normal AI model to describe long-run behaviour but non-symmetric and non-homogeneous short-run behaviour is permitted. The symmetry and homogeneity restrictions are only expected to hold in steady state. Dynamic equations of the following type are estimated:

$$\Delta w_{it} = \sum_j c_{ij} d \log p_{jt} + b_i d \log\left(\frac{x}{P}\right)_t$$
$$- \lambda\left[w_{it-1} - \sum_j \gamma_{ij} \log p_{jt-1} - \beta_i \log\left(\frac{x}{P}\right)_{t-1} \right] \qquad [9.71]$$

Thus, current changes in budget shares depend not only on current changes in the normal AI system explanatory variables but also on the extent of consumer disequilibrium in the previous period. In steady state, however, equation [9.71] reduce to a normal AI demand system. Although Anderson and Blundell do not test for this, the use of differenced variables and an ECM means that estimating problems resulting from the use of non-stationary time series are much less likely to arise than is the case in a static AI demand model.

In their 1983 study, Anderson and Blundell apply their model to annual Canadian data on five categories of non-durable goods for 1947–79. The 1984 study deals with quarterly UK data on four categories of non-durables for 1955–81. Results are substantially the same in both cases. The static AI model is rejected in favour of the above dynamic version. Moreover, the dynamic model proves superior both to the static model with autocorrelated error term and to a simple habit persistence-partial adjustment type of dynamic model.

The results also indicate that the restrictions of symmetry and homogeneity are not rejected *when imposed on the long-run or steady-state structure of the model*. This suggested that previous rejections of symmetry and homogeneity may have been the result of mis-specifications that are inherent in purely static models.

Studies such as those of Anderson and Blundell led to a general feeling among econometricians that the tendency for empirical results to conflict with theoretical expectations was indeed a consequence of a failure to allow for dynamic factors. This belief was compounded by the fact that a number of the static demand systems previously estimated had suffered from autocorrelation problems which strongly suggested dynamic mis-specification (see for example Deaton and Muellbauer 1980). More recently, however, it has been suggested that the failure of tests for homogeneity and symmetry may instead reflect investigators failure to allow for the differing characteristics of households. For example, Stoker (1986) demonstrated that the failure to allow for demographic and other characteristics of households could well show up as an autocorrelation problem which could be mistaken for dynamic mis-specification.

Blundell, *et al.* (1987) investigate the question of differing household characteristics. In a massive study they estimate a seven-good AI demand

233

system from a pooled cross-section involving 65,000 non-pensioner households over fifteen annual observations. The data is drawn from the UK family expenditure survey. Demographic, social and locational characteristics of households are allowed to influence budget shares. It is clear that the price and income parameters vary widely with these characteristics. Of equal interest, however, is that, now varying household characteristics are allowed for, *both the homogeneity and the symmetry restrictions prove acceptable for all seven types of good*. This suggests that it may be the failure of previous studies to pay sufficient attention to household characteristics, rather than dynamic mis-specification, that was at the root of their apparent rejection of consumer theory.

Much empirical work continues on systems of demand equations. Recent attention has been given to the development of models allowing for the fact that many consumers, because of for example 'infrequency of purchase', simply do not purchase certain goods during certain data periods. Blundell (1988) has surveyed developments in this and other areas. As techniques are evolved for handling very large bodies of cross-sectional data (see for example Deaton 1990), it is from such data that future new insights may be most likely obtained.

Appendix: Empirical exercise

As our first empirical exercise we shall estimate demand equations for certain categories of non-durable consumers' expenditure. We shall adopt the Hendry-type general to simple methodology outlined in section 7.2. We do not in this exercise employ the techniques of co-integration but merely introduce the idea of the simplification search or testing down procedure, making use of the F-tests of section 4.4.

First, we will estimate demand equations for food using annual data for 1956–85. All data are taken from the Economic Trends Annual Supplement (ETAS) 1990. We define variables as follows.

Quantity demanded Q_t = expenditure on food in constant 1985 prices

Total expenditure X_t = total consumers' expenditure in current prices

Price of food P_t = implied deflator of expenditure on food

General price index G_t = implied deflator of total consumers' expenditure.

Q_t is taken from page 45 of the above publication and X_t from page 35. We use constant price data for Q_t because this is the nearest approximation to 'quantity' we have. P_t can be obtained by dividing figures for food expenditure in current prices (ETAS 1990: 42) by the corresponding constant prices figures. We can do this because constant price figures always equal current price figures divided by the relevant price index. Similarly, G_t can be obtained by taking the ratio of total consumers' expenditure in current prices to that in constant prices (ETAS 1990: 35). The basic data set used in the following regressions can be found at the end of this appendix, in Table A9.2.

The reader should attempt to duplicate all the regression results that follow using whatever OLS computer program is available to him. Examples of suitable programs were given in Chapter 1. Your program will contain transformation routines that will enable you to form the variables P_t and G_t without the necessity of computing them by hand.

The variable G_t will be used to represent 'all other prices' which consumer theory tells us should also influence the demand for food. Theory therefore suggests a long-run or equilibrium relationship of the form $Q = Q(P, G, X)$ although it says nothing about the functional form of this relationship. Our data of course refers to some short-run relationship involving lags of the above variables. We shall therefore use as our general model an equation involving current and first-order lagged values of all variables, adopting a logarithmic functional form for convenience. Hopefully, since we are dealing with annual data, first-order lags should be sufficient to capture adequately the dynamics of the short-run equation. Our general model is therefore

$$q_t = k + \phi q_{t-1} + b_0 p_t + b_1 p_{t-1} + c_0 g_t + c_1 g_{t-1} + d_0 x_t + d_1 x_{t-1} + \varepsilon_t$$
[A9.1]

where lower case letters denote the natural logarithms of variables. Estimating such a general equation yields, for the years 1956–85

$$\hat{q}_t = 1.997 + 0.679 q_{t-1} - 0.205 p_t + 0.187 p_{t-1} - 0.184 g_t + 0.084 g_{t-1}$$
$$(0.846)\ (0.150) \qquad (0.111) \quad (0.119) \qquad (0.115) \quad (0.142)$$

$$+ 0.402 x_t - 0.294 x_{t-1}$$
[A9.2]
$$(0.102) \quad (0.129)$$

$$R^2 = 0.990, \quad \sum e^2 = 0.01139, \quad dw = 2.25, \quad Z1 = 1.007, \quad Z2 = 2.091$$

where numbers in parentheses are estimated standard errors.

Calculation of the standard t-ratios in [A9.2] indicates that both total expenditure variables, x_t and x_{t-1}, and the lagged demand variable, q_{t-1}, are significant at the 0.05 level of significance (with $n - k = 30 - 8 = 22$ d.f., the critical t-value is $t_{0.05} = 1.717$). However of the other explanatory variables only the current own-price variable p_t with a t-ratio of -1.85 is significant.

dw is the Durbin–Watson statistic used to test for first-order autocorrelation in the residuals. Its value is fairly close to 2, indicating no autocorrelation. However we have to remember that the presence of the lagged dependent variable q_{t-1} on the right-hand side of [9.2] means that the Durbin–Watson statistic is biased towards 2.

$Z1$ and $Z2$ are the Lagrange multiplier test statistics for first-order autocorrelation and heteroscedasticity outlined in section 5.2 pages 107–8 and 96–7 respectively. Both have χ^2 distributions with 1 d.f. under the null hypothesis. Since with 1 d.f., the critical value of χ^2 is $\chi^2_{0.05} = 3.84$, there is no evidence of either first-order autocorrelation or of heteroscedasticity in the residuals of equation [A9.2]. Your program should also enable you to compute the LM statistic for up to, for example, fourth-order autocorrelation. The value for this statistic should be 5.91. Since with 4 d.f. the critical value for χ^2 is $\chi^2_{0.05} = 9.49$, there appears to be no problem with autocorrelation. Recall, from Chapter 7, that the *LM* tests can also be regarded as tests for mis-specification. Hence, since equation [A9.2] passes these tests, we can hopefully assume that there is no need to include lags of higher than the first order in our general model.

Do not be too impressed by the high value for R^2, the coefficient of multiple determination, obtained for equation [A9.2]. All the variables in this equation were subject to strong upward trends during the period 1956–85. You can verify this by asking your computer to plot values for each variable against time. The high R^2 is obviously likely to be partly spurious. In fact it is probably the least useful statistic displayed above! In later exercises we shall treat the problem of spurious correlation more formally. For now, however, merely note that by subtracting q_{t-1} from each side of equation [A9.1] we obtain

$$\Delta q_t = k - \theta q_{t-1} + b_0 p_t + b_1 p_{t-1} + c_0 g_t + c_1 g_{t-1} + d_0 x_t + d_1 x_{t-1} + \varepsilon_t$$
[A9.3]

where $\Delta q_t = q_t - q_{t-1}$ and $\theta = 1 - \phi$.

If you estimate equation [A9.3] you will obtain

$$\widehat{\Delta q_t} = 1.997 - 0.321 q_{t-1} - 0.205 p_t + 0.187 p_{t-1} - 0.184 g_t + 0.084 g_{t-1}$$
$$(0.846)\ (0.150)\qquad (0.111)\qquad (0.119)\qquad (0.115)\qquad (0.142)$$

$$+\ 0.402 x_t - 0.294 x_{t-1}$$
$$(0.102)\qquad (0.129)$$
[A9.4]

$$R^2 = 0.634, \quad \sum e^2 = 0.001139, \quad dw = 2.25, \quad Z1 = 1.007, \quad Z2 = 0.228$$

Notice that [A9.4] is virtually identical to [A9.2]. The only difference is that the coefficient on q_{t-1} in [A9.4] is equal to the corresponding coefficient in [A9.2] minus one. This is as expected since $\theta = 1 - \phi$. All other coefficients and all standard errors are identical in the two equations. In fact equation [A9.2] can be rearranged to yield [A9.4]. This is not surprising because all we have really done is estimate the same equation twice! However, note the value of R^2 in equation [A9.4]. It is only 0.634 compared with 0.990 in [A9.2]. This is because, whereas in equation [A9.2] we were able to explain 99 per cent of variations in q, in [A9.4] we are attempting to explain variations in Δq. Since, unlike q, Δq is not a trend variable, (check its plot against time), this is not such an easy task. Hence we are able to explain only 63.4 per cent of the variation in Δq in equation [A9.4]. However, since now we need be less worried about spurious correlations between trends, the R^2 of 0.634 in [A9.4] means rather more than the R^2 of 0.990 in [A9.2].

Equation [A9.4] is obtained from [A9.2] by a simple 'reparameterisation'. By a more complicated reparameterisation we express [A9.2] and [A9.4] in error correction form. They can be rewritten as

$$\Delta q_t = b_0 \Delta p_t + c_0 \Delta g_t + d_0 \Delta x_t$$
$$-\ \theta [q_{t-1} - \alpha - \beta p_{t-1} - \gamma g_{t-1} - \delta x_{t-1}] + \varepsilon_t$$
[A9.5]

where $\alpha = k/\theta$, $\beta = (b_0 + b_1)/\theta$, $\gamma = (c_0 + c_1)/\theta$ and $\delta = (d_0 + d_1)/\theta$.

The term in square brackets in [A9.5] is the disequilibrium error, the implied long-term relationship being

$$q_t = \alpha + \beta p_t + \gamma g_t + \delta x_t$$
[A9.6]

236

To estimate [A9.5] we must first multiply out the term in square brackets. If we do this and then apply OLS we obtain

$$\widehat{\Delta q_t} = 1.997 - 0.205\Delta p_t - 0.184\Delta g_t + 0.402\Delta x_t - 0.321 q_{t-1}$$
$$(0.846)\ \ (0.111)\ \ \ \ \ (0.115)\ \ \ \ \ \ (0.102)\ \ \ \ \ \ (0.150)$$

$$ - 0.018 p_{t-1} - 0.100 g_{t-1} + 0.107 x_{t-1} \qquad\qquad\text{[A9.7]}$$
$$(0.084)\ \ \ \ \ \ (0.125)\ \ \ \ \ \ (0.075)$$

$$R^2 = 0.634, \quad \sum e^2 = 0.001139, \quad dw = 2.25, \quad Z1 = 1.007, \quad Z2 = 0.228$$

Notice that R^2, $\sum e^2$, etc. in [A9.7] are identical to their values in [A9.4]. In fact, just as [A9.4] can be obtained from [A9.2] simply by rearranging, so we can obtain [A9.7] from [A9.4] by rearranging. The three equations [A9.2], [A9.4] and [A9.7] are merely alternative 'parameterisations' of the same equation. The fact that in all essentials they are the same equation is signalled by the identical value taken by $\sum e^2$, the sum of the squared residuals, in each case.

If we cast [A9.7] in the form of [A9.5] we obtain

$$\widehat{\Delta q_t} = -0.205\Delta p_t - 0.184\Delta g_t + 0.402\Delta x_t$$

$$ - 0.321[q_{t-1} - 6.22 + 0.056 p_{t-1} + 0.312 g_{t-1} - 0.333 x_{t-1}] \qquad \text{[A9.8]}$$

You should now be able to read off estimates of the short- and long-run elasticities of demand for food with respect to own-price, the general price level and total expenditure. Do you regard them as reasonable? How would you interpret the coefficient -0.321 in front of the square brackets in [A9.8]?

Now we have estimated our general model in error correction form, we can begin the simplification search for a more parsimonious equation. In this case economic theory is of some help. As we saw in the first section of this chapter, theory suggests that the elacticities in a demand equation should sum to zero. In terms of equation [A9.5] this means that, for the long-run elasticities, $\beta + \gamma + \delta = 0$, while for the short-run elasticities $b_0 + c_0 + d_0 = 0$. For equation [A9.7] the long-run elasticities sum to 0.035, while the short-run elasticities sum to 0.013. These values are not quite zero but are the differences statistically significant? To find this out we can apply the F-test for linear restrictions described in section 4.4. Enforcing the restrictions implies estimating an equation in which absolute prices and nominal total expenditure are replaced by the relative price $P^* = P/G$ and real total expenditure $X^* = X/G$. That is equation [A9.5] becomes

$$\Delta q_t = b_0\Delta p^* + d_0\Delta x^* - \theta[q_{t-1} - \alpha - \beta p^*_{t-1} - \delta x^*_{t-1}] + \varepsilon_t \qquad \text{[A9.9]}$$

where $\Delta p^*_t = \Delta p_t - \Delta g_t$, $\Delta x^*_t = \Delta x_t - \Delta g_t$, $p^*_t = p_t - g_t$ and $x^*_t = x_t - g_t$. Remember that lower case letters denote logarithms. Multiplying out [A9.9] and estimating yields

$$\widehat{\Delta q_t} = 1.397 - 0.126\Delta p^*_t + 0.359\Delta x^*_t - 0.187 q_{t-1}$$
$$(0.645)\ \ (0.088)\ \ \ \ \ \ (0.078)\ \ \ \ \ \ (0.093)$$

$$ - 0.022 p^*_{t-1} + 0.043 x^*_{t-1} \qquad\qquad\qquad\text{[A9.10]}$$
$$(0.046)\ \ \ \ \ \ (0.028)$$

$$R^2 = 0.610, \quad \sum e^2 = 0.001213, \quad dw = 2.32, \quad Z1 = 1.397, \quad Z2 = 0.942$$

To apply the F-test of section 4.4 we require the residual sums of squares for the unrestricted equation [A9.7] and the restricted equation [A9.10]. Since we are testing two restrictions, the test statistic [4.45] in this case is therefore

$$\frac{(\text{SSR}_R - \text{SSR}_U)/2}{\text{SSR}_R/(n - k)} = \frac{(1213 - 1139)/2}{1139/(30 - 8)} = 0.71$$

With $(2, 22)$ d.f. the critical value for F is $F_{0.05} = 3.44$. It is therefore clear that the restrictions are 'data acceptable'. Moreover, as can be seen from the dw, $Z1$ and $Z2$ statistics, there does not appear to be any problem with the residuals in equation [A9.10]. Hence we can safely conclude that the enforcement of the restrictions does not lead to any mis-specification problems. Verify for yourself that the equation also satisfies LM tests for higher-order autocorrelation.

Since the homogeneity restrictions are acceptable, we adopt [A9.10] as a more parsimonious characterisation of the data than [A9.7]. However, a number of the variables in [A9.10] have t-ratios below the critical value which, with $n - k = 24$ d.f., is $t_{0.05} = 1.711$. The relative price variables, Δp_t^* and p_{t-1}^*, for example, have t-ratios of -1.43 and 0.48 respectively. Dropping the price variables from the equation yields

$$\widehat{\Delta q_t} = 1.649 + 0.317\Delta x_t^* - 0.219q_{t-1} + 0.049x_{t-1}^* \qquad [A9.11]$$
$$\phantom{\widehat{\Delta q_t} = }(0.576) \quad (0.072) \qquad (0.087) \qquad (0.028)$$

$$R^2 = 0.573, \quad \sum e^2 = 0.001327, \quad dw = 2.04, \quad Z1 = 0.056, \quad Z2 = 1.034$$

There is no noticable deterioration in our 'diagnostic' statistics dw, $Z1$ and $Z2$ and we can again use the F-test to see whether we are justified in dropping the price variables. This time [A9.10] is our unrestricted equation and [A9.11] our restricted version. The statistic [4.45] in this case takes the value 1.13, compared with a critical F-value with $(2, 24)$ d.f. of $F_{0.05} = 3.40$. Omitting the price variables is data acceptable.

Equation [A9.11] is our final preferred model. Compared with our original general model [A9.7], it contains (including the intercept) only four instead of eight variables and hence is suitably parsimonious. It is of course nested within the general model, so we can F-test whether the four restrictions needed to reduce [A9.7] to [A9.11] are acceptable when imposed simultaneously. The statistic this time takes a value of 0.91 whereas the critical F-value with $(4, 22)$ d.f. is $F_{0.05} = 2.82$.

Expressing [A9.11] in error correction form we obtain

$$\widehat{\Delta q_t} = 0.317\Delta x_t^* - 0.219[q_{t-1} - 7.53 - 0.226x_{t-1}^*] \qquad [A9.12]$$

From [A9.12] we observe that the demand for food appears to depend on real total expenditure only. Since food is obviously a necessity this is not unreasonable, although an alternative model might have included a short run relative price effect since the t-ratio on Δp_t^* in equation [A9.10] was as high as -1.43. The short- and long-run elasticities with respect to real expenditure are 0.317 and 0.226 respectively. These values are well below unity as is expected for a necessity. The long-run demand for food relationship, assuming zero long-run growth rates is

$$Q = 1894X^{*0.226}$$

Before leaving this data set, we will estimate two further equations. First, we estimate a partial adjustment model of the type given by equation [6.36]:

$$\hat{q}_t = 3.038 - 0.070p_t - 0.127g_t + 0.180x_t + 0.492q_{t-1} \qquad [A9.13]$$
$$(0.766) \ (0.050) \quad (0.070) \quad (0.060) \quad (0.138)$$

$$R^2 = 0.984, \quad \sum e^2 = 0.001688, \quad dw = 1.65, \quad Z1 = 1.435, \quad Z2 = 2.624$$

Superficially equation [A9.13] looks quite impressive. The t-values are all relatively high, R^2 is very high and the diagnostic statistics seem satisfactory, although the Durbin–Watson statistic is not valid in the presence of the lagged dependent variable. However, note that the dependent variable is now the trend dominated q so the R^2 value is suspect. Moreover [A9.13] is nested in our general model [A9.7] and is obtained by imposing the restrictions $b_1 = c_1 = d_1 = 0$. If we F-test these three restrictions we obtain a value for the test statistic of 3.535 compared with a critical F-value, with $(3, 22)$ d.f., of 3.05. Hence the partial adjustment model is rejected by the data.

Finally, we estimate an equation containing only current values of the variables:

$$\hat{q}_t = 5.632 - 0.142p_t - 0.278g_t + 0.384x_t \qquad [A9.14]$$
$$(0.297) \ (0.055) \quad (0.067) \quad (0.024)$$

$$R^2 = 0.977, \quad \sum e^2 = 0.002553, \quad dw = 0.674, \quad Z1 = 11.726, \quad Z2 = 3.093$$

Although all coefficients are statistically significant in [A9.14], we clearly have a problem with the autocorrelation statistics. For example, at the 0.05 level of significance, with $k' = 3$ explanatory variables, the lower limit for the Durbin-Watson statistic is $d_L = 1.21$. However, we know from what has gone before that the problem is not one of autocorrelation. Our earlier estimated equations indicated clearly that lagged variables need to be included in the demand for food equation. The low dw and high LM statistics are signalling this dynamic specification error. In fact, if the residuals from equation [A9.14] are examined, one can easily observe long sequences of positive residuals suggestive of autocorrelation. It is not surprising that the dw statistic is so low. But, as we saw in section 7.1, residual patterns such as this can as easily indicate a specification error as they can autocorrelation.

This first exercise well illustrates the advantages of the general to simple methodology. Suppose we had adopted the reverse simple to general approach. We would probably have begun by estimating equation [A9.14] and observed the dubious autocorrelation statistics. Assuming we were not rash enough to plunge immediately into a Cochrane–Orcutt routine, and recognised that we had a specification problem, we would next, very likely, have estimated the partial adjustment model [A9.13]. Noting the now satisfactory autocorrelation statistics, we would probably have been content with this model. Yet as we saw earlier the simple partial adjustment model is rejected by the data. It is only by starting with the general model [A9.2] and employing the general to specific testing down procedure that we arrive at the preferred model [A9.11].

For our second illustration of the general to specific methodology we use quarterly seasonally unadjusted data on the expenditure category 'drink and tobacco' for 1960(i) to 1970(iv). Variables are defined in a similar manner to the last exercise and the source of data is again ETAS 1990. The data set used is again presented at the end of this appendix in Table A9.3. With quarterly data we need to cater for a more complicated lag structure so we include up to fourth order lags in our general model

$$q_t = k_0 + \sum_{i=1}^{4} \theta_i q_{t-i} + \sum_{i=0}^{4} b_i p_{t-i} + \sum_{i=0}^{4} c_i g_{t-i} + \sum_{i=0}^{4} d_i x_{t-i}$$

$$+ k_1 D1_t + k_2 D2_t + k_3 D3_t + \varepsilon_t \qquad\qquad [A9.15]$$

In [A9.15], $D1$ is the first quarter dummy, taking the value unity in the first quarter and zero in all other quarters, $D2$ is the second quarter dummy and $D3$ the third quarter dummy. These dummies allow for seasonal variations in the data. No fourth quarter dummy is included (why?).

The coefficients in the estimated version of [A9.15] for 1961(i) to 1970(iv) are shown in Table A9.2 together with their estimated standard errors. The data for the 4 quarters in 1960 are needed for constructing the lagged variables. The following statistics also refer to this equation.

$$R^2 = 0.991, \sum e^2 = 0.00463, dw = 1.81, Z14 = 5.91, Z18 = 12.25, Z2 = 5.23$$

$Z14$ and $Z18$ are the LM statistics for up to fourth- and eighth-order autocorrelation respectively. We test for up to fourth- and eighth-order autocorrelation because we are now dealing with quarterly data. $Z14$ is distributed as χ^2 with 4 d.f. under the null hypothesis of no autocorrelation and the critical value in this case is $\chi^2_{0.05} = 9.49$. So at the 0.05 level of significance there is no evidence of autocorrelation. The $Z18$ statistic is also satisfactory and the reader should verify that the LM statistic for first-order autocorrelation is also well inside its critical value.

$Z2$ is again the LM statistic for heteroscedasticity, distributed as χ^2 with one degree of freedom. Since the critical values here are $\chi^2_{0.05} = 3.84$ and $\chi^2_{0.01} = 6.64$, we have a slight problem with this statistic at present.

Table A9.1 Estimated version of equation [A9.15]

i	θ_i	b_i	c_i	d_i	k_i
0		−0.532	0.156	1.025	2.561
		(0.274)	(0.852)	(0.292)	(2.827)
1	0.326	0.143	0.761	−0.840	−0.119
	(0.226)	(0.345)	(1.116)	(0.442)	(0.063)
2	−0.430	0.190	−1.970	0.148	0.007
	(0.271)	(0.338)	(1.215)	(0.430)	(0.053)
3	−0.191	−0.561	0.648	0.239	−0.050
	(0.269)	(0.365)	(1.096)	(0.471)	(0.057)
4	−0.012	0.145	0.354	0.266	
	(0.248)	(0.284)	(0.941)	(0.377)	

Note: Values in parentheses are estimated standard errors

Unsatisfactory diagnostic statistics are frequently an indication not of autocorrelation or heteroscedasticity but of mis-specification, possibly resulting from an incorrect functional form or an inappropriate lag structure. To check for functional form mis-specification we can use the RESET test described at the end of section 7.1. If your program computes the required statistic you should confirm that, with just $\hat{q}^2$ included in the auxiliary regression, its value is 0.399 compared with a critical value of $\chi^2_{0.05} = 3.84$, with 1 degree of freedom. We can therefore detect no mis-specification of functional form.

We can also check the appropriateness of the lag structure in our general model [A9.15] by testing to see whether the inclusion of fifth-order lags improves matters. You should verify that reestimation with such lags included causes the autocorrelation statistics to deteriorate, and use the F-test to demonstrate that the addition of fifth-order lags does not significantly improve the fit of the equation.

We now estimate two error correction models, both nested within the general model [A9.15]. Since we are dealing with quarterly data, we estimate a fourth-order model as well as a first-order model. The estimated first-order model is

$$\widehat{\Delta q_t} = 0.479 - 0.718\Delta p_t - 0.127\Delta g_t + 1.035\Delta x_t - 0.768q_{t-1} - 0.475p_{t-1}$$
$$(1.607)\ (0.191)\quad (0.676)\quad (0.201)\quad (0.186)\quad (0.165)$$

$$- 0.054g_{t-1} + 0.585x_{t-1} - 0.165D1_t - 0.050D2_t - 0.023D3_t \quad [A9.16]$$
$$(0.226)\quad (0.194)\quad (0.022)\quad (0.028)\quad (0.013)$$

$R^2 = 0.993,\ \sum e^2 = 0.00657,\ dw = 1.72,\ Z14 = 5.45,\ Z18 = 10.38,\ Z2 = 2.92$

and the fourth-order model

$$\widehat{\Delta_4 q_t} = -0.959 - 0.682\Delta_4 p_t - 0.169\Delta_4 g_t + 0.771\Delta_4 x_t$$
$$(2.108)\ (0.156)\quad (0.388)\quad (0.198)$$

$$- 0.943q_{t-4} - 0.746p_{t-4} - 0.088g_{t-4} + 0.859x_{t-4}$$
$$(0.186)\quad (0.187)\quad (0.280)\quad (0.228)$$

$$- 0.167D1_t - 0.070D2_t - 0.033D3_t \quad\quad\quad [A9.17]$$
$$(0.038)\quad (0.017)\quad (0.011)$$

$R^2 = 0.824,\ \sum e^2 = 0.00705,\ dw = 1.48,\ Z14 = 11.00,\ Z18 = 16.17,\ Z2 = 0.096$

where $\Delta_4 q = q_t - q_{t-4}$, etc.

Both [A9.16] and [A9.17] involve the placing of twelve linear restrictions on the general model. Can you list them? The placing of each linear restriction on the parameters of an equation always reduces the number of variables in that equation by one. Since the general model contained 23 variables (including the intercept) and both [A9.16] and [A9.17] have 11 variables, we have 12 restrictions in each case. We can test the validity of each set of restrictions by using our F-test. The unrestricted equation is the general model and the restricted equations are the two-error correction models. For [A9.16] the value of the F-statistic is 0.59 and for [A9.17] it is 0.74. The critical F-value (with 12, 17 d.f.) is $F_{0.05} = 2.38$. Hence both models are data acceptable in in this sense. The R^2s in the equations are not comparable since in [A9.16] we are seeking to explain variations in Δq, whereas in [A9.17] $\Delta_4 q$ is the dependent variable. $\sum e^2$ however is lower for [A9.16] and this is reflected in the above F-values.

Although both equations [A9.16] and [A9.17] pass the F-test, notice that, whereas imposition of the restrictions has little effect on the autocorrelation statistics in the 1st order case, there is a distinct deterioration in these statistics for the fourth-order ECM. For equation [A9.17] both $Z14$ and $Z18$ now exceed their critical values at the 0.05 level of significance and there has been a sharp fall in the Durbin–Watson statistic. Notice, also that the LM statistic for heteroscedasticity now takes an acceptable value in both ECMs.

The reader should now verify that more complex first- and fourth-order ECMs, although still special cases of our general model, represent no improvement on equations [A9.16] and [A9.17]. For example, if lagged values of Δp, Δg and Δx are added to [A9.16], they prove insignificant and lead to a deterioration in the autocorrelation statistics. Similarly, the addition of $\Delta_4 p_{t-4}$, $\Delta_4 g_{t-4}$ and $\Delta_4 x_{t-4}$ to equation [A9.17] leads to no improvement.

Of the two ECMs [A9.16] and [A9.17] the former first-order equation appears preferable. As noted above, the residual sum of squares is slightly smaller for this equation and, more importantly, the satisfactory diagnostic statistics suggest that we have no obvious problems of mis-specification. We shall therefore examine this equation for further possible simplification.

Theory suggests that, in both the long and the short run, demand should depend on relative prices and real total expenditure. Imposing these homogeneity restrictions on [A9.16], our first-order model yields

$$\widehat{\Delta q_t} = -0.617 - 0.711\Delta p_t^* + 1.085\Delta x_t^* - 0.735 q_{t-1} - 0.467 p_{t-1}^*$$
$$\phantom{\widehat{\Delta q_t} = } (0.501) \quad (0.175) \qquad (0.182) \qquad (0.176) \qquad (0.159)$$

$$+ 0.653 x_{t-1}^* - 0.164 D1_t - 0.041 D2_t - 0.022 D3_t \qquad\qquad \text{[A9.18]}$$
$$ (0.164) \qquad (0.021) \qquad (0.025) \qquad (0.011)$$

$R^2 = 0.993$, $\sum e^2 = 0.00669$, $dw = 1.69$, $Z14 = 6.10$, $Z18 = 11.79$, $Z2 = 2.89$

The two long run homogeneity restrictions prove acceptable with an F-value of 0.26 compared with a critical value of $F_{0.05} = 3.33$, (2, 29 d.f.), and the diagnostic statistics remain within their critical values. This is not a surprising result because the sums of both the short-run and the long-run elasticities in equation [A9.16] are close to zero, as implied by theory.

Notice that the coefficients on both the general price variables, Δg_t and g_{t-1}, in equation [A9.16] were statistically insignificant from zero with t-ratios of just -0.19 and -0.24 respectively. An alternative way of proceeding would therefore have been to drop these variables from the equation. However, the reader should verify that this leads to non-homogeneous equations which are inconsistent with theory. A better procedure is to impose the data-acceptable restriction of homogeneity on [A9.16] immediately, thus maintaining consistency with theory. This was the procedure adopted above.

Our testing down procedure or simplification search has led us from the general model with 23 variables to the far more parsimonious equation [A9.18] which has only nine variables including the intercept and three seasonal dummies. But are there any further simplifications that are data acceptable that we can make? The estimated long-run elasticity of demand with respect to real expenditure is given by the ratio of the coefficients on the variables q_{t-1} and x_{t-1}^* in equation [A9.18]. This gives a value of 0.888, which suggests it might just be possible to impose a value of unity for this elasticity. Imposition of such a restriction implies replacing the variables q_{t-1} and x^*_{t-1} in [A9.18] by the composite variable $(q_{t-1} - x^*_{t-1})$. This results in

$$\widehat{\Delta q_t} = -1.246 - 0.721\Delta p^*_t + 1.153\Delta x^*_t - 0.623(q_{t-1} - x^*_{t-1})$$
$$\quad (0.340) \ (0.180) \qquad (0.182) \qquad (0.167)$$

$$- 0.512p^*_{t-1} - 0.161D1_t - 0.023D2_t - 0.016D3_t \qquad\qquad \text{[A9.19]}$$
$$\quad (0.162) \qquad (0.021) \qquad (0.023) \qquad (0.010)$$

$R^2 = 0.992$, $\sum e^2 = 0.00729$, $dw = 1.70$, $Z14 = 6.84$, $Z18 = 16.72$, $Z2 = 3.42$

We can test the additional restriction imposed in the usual manner. This yields an F-value of 2.78 compared with a critical value (with 1, 31 degrees of freedom) of $F_{0.05} = 4.16$. Hence the restriction is data-acceptable on the F-test but notice that there has been some deterioration in the autocorrelation statistics compared with equation [A9.18]. The $Z18$ statistic now exceeds its critical value of $\chi^2_{0.05} = 15.51$. There is therefore some doubt as to whether this restriction should be imposed. Remember that there is no *a priori* reason why the elasticity of demand with respect to total expenditure should be unity.

We shall therefore take [A9.18] as our final preferred equation. As noted it can be obtained from our general model [A9.15] by the imposition of fourteen restrictions in total. We can check the overall data-acceptability of these restrictions by using our F-test. Treating the general model as the unrestricted equation and [A9.18] as the restricted equation yields an F-value of only 0.54 compared with a critical value, with (14, 17) d.f. of $F_{0.05} = 2.33$.

If we express [A9.18] in error correction form we obtain, setting the dummy variables equal to zero for the moment,

$$\Delta q_t = -0.617 - 0.711\Delta p^*_t + 1.085\Delta x^*_t$$
$$\quad - 0.735[q_{t-1} + 0.635p^*_{t-1} - 0.888x^*_{t-1}] \qquad\qquad \text{[A9.20]}$$

Assuming a long run growth rate in real expenditure of λ, the long-run elasticity of 0.888 implies a long-run growth rate in demand of 0.888λ. That is

$$\Delta x^*_t = \lambda \quad \text{so that} \quad x^*_{t-1} = x^*_t - \lambda$$

$$\Delta q_t = 0.888\lambda \quad \text{so that} \quad q_{t-1} = q_t - 0.888\lambda$$

If in addition we assume that in the long-run relative prices are constant, substituting for Δx^*_t, Δq_t, x^*_{t-1} and q_{t-1} in [A9.20] now enables us to derive the long-run demand relationship.

$$0.888\lambda = -0.617 + 1.085\lambda - 0.735[q_t + 0.635p^*_t - 0.888x^*_t]$$

Hence

$$q_t = -0.839 + 0.268\lambda - 0.635p^*_t + 0.888x^*_t$$

or

$$Q_t = KP^{*-0.635}_t X^{*0.888}_t \quad \text{where} \quad K = e^{-0.839+0.268\lambda} \qquad\qquad \text{[A9.21]}$$

[A9.21] is the long-run demand relationship. Notice that, as is usual for ECMs, the long-run relationship is dependent on growth rates. For example if $\lambda = 0.005$

Table A9.2 Annual demand data set

	X	Q	P	G		X	Q	P	G
1954	12 210	23 550	0.1399	0.1180	1970	32 114	29 107	0.2209	0.2053
1955	13 172	24 384	0.1470	0.1222	1971	36 010	29 203	0.2433	0.2230
1956	13 882	24 776	0.1528	0.1276	1972	40 750	29 247	0.2603	0.2375
1957	14 652	25 148	0.1562	0.1320	1973	46 428	29 629	0.2954	0.2578
1958	15 464	25 452	0.1583	0.1360	1974	53 491	29 121	0.3444	0.3014
1959	16 296	25 939	0.1603	0.1374	1975	65 864	29 126	0.4227	0.3727
1960	17 114	26 496	0.1595	0.1389	1976	76 560	29 436	0.4912	0.4314
1961	18 008	26 935	0.1621	0.1430	1977	87 530	29 175	0.5688	0.4952
1962	19 097	27 205	0.1676	0.1483	1978	100 847	29 714	0.6183	0.5400
1963	20 354	27 348	0.1715	0.1512	1979	119 516	30 380	0.6908	0.6132
1964	21 733	27 689	0.1766	0.1566	1980	139 016	30 419	0.7776	0.7127
1965	23 154	27 673	0.1828	0.1643	1981	154 701	30 217	0.8256	0.7926
1966	24 505	27 978	0.1893	0.1709	1982	169 816	30 299	0.8743	0.8618
1967	25 761	28 440	0.1929	0.1753	1983	185 895	30 658	0.9152	0.9047
1968	27 751	28 587	0.1993	0.1837	1984	198 895	30 171	0.9713	0.9507
1969	29 466	28 700	0.2103	0.1939	1985	217 023	30 726	1.0000	1.0000

Table A9.3 Quarterly demand data set

	Q	X	P	G		Q	X	P	G
59Q4	4346	4414	0.1289	0.1393	65Q3	4501	5899	0.1717	0.1647
60Q1	3454	4000	0.1271	0.1374	65Q4	4840	6114	0.1719	0.1668
60Q2	4038	4299	0.1305	0.1387	66Q1	3870	5732	0.1721	0.1676
60Q3	4202	4287	0.1302	0.1386	66Q2	4540	6196	0.1727	0.1704
60Q4	4442	4528	0.1328	0.1409	66Q3	4639	6190	0.1755	0.1715
61Q1	3634	4174	0.1313	0.1403	66Q4	4879	6387	0.1775	0.1737
61Q2	4290	4499	0.1310	0.1421	67Q1	3948	5958	0.1765	0.1741
61Q3	4367	4558	0.1379	0.1437	67Q2	4564	6380	0.1768	0.1750
61Q4	4538	4777	0.1435	0.1458	67Q3	4766	6554	0.1773	0.1751
62Q1	3503	4407	0.1439	0.1460	67Q4	5079	6869	0.1776	0.1769
62Q2	4147	4846	0.1466	0.1490	68Q1	4212	6570	0.1781	0.1791
62Q3	4325	4802	0.1431	0.1486	68Q2	4589	6749	0.1826	0.1830
62Q4	4594	5042	0.1463	0.1495	68Q3	4791	7015	0.1835	0.1847
63Q1	3498	4658	0.1452	0.1498	68Q4	5255	7417	0.1867	0.1877
63Q2	4378	5126	0.1457	0.1515	69Q1	4007	6853	0.1952	0.1911
63Q3	4550	5180	0.1457	0.1504	69Q2	4647	7264	0.1956	0.1928
63Q4	4835	5390	0.1466	0.1529	69Q3	4933	7429	0.1960	0.1941
64Q1	3777	5006	0.1467	0.1534	69Q4	5358	7920	0.1988	0.1972
64Q2	4344	5427	0.1531	0.1563	70Q1	4007	7315	0.2029	0.2005
64Q3	4605	5518	0.1574	0.1568	70Q2	4809	7862	0.2036	0.2034
64Q4	4977	5782	0.1585	0.1596	70Q3	5255	8200	0.2036	0.2059
65Q1	3757	5370	0.1602	0.1611	70Q4	5598	8737	0.2069	0.2107
65Q2	4207	5771	0.1711	0.1645					

(i.e., a growth rate in total expenditure of 0.5 per cent per quarter) then $K = 0.43$ in [A9.21]. Since we have set the dummy variables equal to zero, [A9.21] is in fact the long-run relationship holding in the first quarter. It is left to the reader to derive the corresponding relationships for the second, third and fourth quarters and to see what a growth rate of $\lambda = 0.005$ implies for them.

The reader should now use the annual and quarterly data in ETAS (1990) to estimate further demand equations for the various categories of consumer expenditure. Use the general to specific/error correction approach adopted in this appendix. Notice though that some of these categories refer to durable goods so that the lag structures that are appropriate may turn out to be rather more complicated than the ones used above. This will be especially the case when quarterly data is used.

Notes

1. This has become less of a problem. Now that full details of family expenditure surveys in the US and the UK are available on microfilm, researchers need no longer rely on standard published sources.
2. Working in terms of simple arithmetic means implies that we are ignoring for the moment the fact that households are likely to vary in their size and composition.
3. ε will, in fact, be non-autocorrelated and normally distributed with zero mean and, provided all the ε_j can be treated as independent variables, variance equal to $\sigma^2/n = $ constant where $\sigma^2 = \text{var } \varepsilon_j$.
4. We can write the relevant term in [9.8] as

$$\left(\frac{\sum x_j \alpha_{3j}}{\sum x_j} \right) \bar{x} = \frac{\sum x_j \alpha_{3j}}{N}$$

If x_j and α_{3j} are independently distributed, then

$$E x_j \alpha_{3j} = E x_j E \alpha_{3j}$$

Thus, for large N

$$\frac{\sum x_j \alpha_{3j}}{N} \simeq \left(\frac{\sum x_j}{N} \right) \left(\frac{\sum \alpha_{3j}}{N} \right) = \left(\frac{\sum \alpha_{3j}}{N} \right) \bar{x}$$

Thus the coefficient of $\bar{x}$ in [9.8] becomes approximately equal to $\sum \alpha_{3j}/N$.
5. The geometric mean of a set of n numbers, $x_1, x_2, x_3, \ldots, x_n$ is defined as

$$\tilde{x} = (x_1 x_2 x_3, \ldots, x_n)^{1/n}$$

i.e. the nth root of the product of the n numbers. Hence, the log of such a mean is

$$\log \tilde{x} = \frac{1}{n} \log(x_1 x_2 \ldots \ldots x_n) = \frac{1}{n} \sum \log x_j$$

6. Consumer theory would suggest that the desired flow of *services* from the good depends (given homogeneity) on real total expenditure and relative prices. However, if we assume that services yielded are proportional to stock held and represent all relative prices by p_t, the ratio of own price to a general index of prices, an equation such as [9.22] can be obtained.
7. The unit of measurement for S_t is chosen so as to make the coefficient of q_t in equation [9.24] equal to unity.

8. Unfortunately this flexibility means that it is often possible to rationalise away unlikely values for underlying parameters. For example, in the stock adjustment model an unacceptably high value for the depreciation parameter δ or a value for the adjustment parameter λ which is in excess of unity can both be explained away by claiming that habit effects are present.

9. The authors, in fact, originally formulate their model in continuous terms and derive a discrete approximation for estimating purposes. They use an estimation method which allows for any autocorrelation that may be present. For details of this method, referred to as 'three pass least squares' readers should consult Houthakker and Taylor (1970).

10. In the empirical literature on demand systems the restrictions that follow are normally derived in matrix terms. However, for a traditional but rather more tedious derivation see Henderson and Quandt (1980: 18–33).

11. An additive utility function has to take the form

$$U = f_1(q_1) + f_2(q_2) + \cdots + f_n(q_n)$$

if it is to possess this property. Hence the name 'additive'.

12. See, for example, Henderson and Quandt (1980: 41–2).

13. In a demand system which is linear in the logarithms, for example, it is the elasticities which are parameterised and whose dependence on x and all prices is ignored.

14. Consider, for example, the utility function [9.55]. For any given values of q_i and q_j this function contains sufficient parameters for it to be possible to make its first- and second-order derivatives equal to those of *any* arbitrary utility function. Also, for any values of the q_i and q_j in the neighbourhood of the selected values, we will still have a good 'local' second-order approximation of the arbitrary utility function. Since this is so for any arbitrary utility function, it must be so for the true underlying utility function, whatever that may be.

15. Equation [9.59] is analogous to [9.6] except that a different notation is being used. However, [9.59] differs from [9.6] in that the b_i (α_{3j} in [9.6]) are here assumed to be the same for each household and to be a function of all prices.

16. Muellbauer refers to the special case where representative expenditure is independent of prices, and dependent only on the distribution of household expenditures, as that of *price independent, generalised linearity* (PIGL). A logarithmic version of PIGL is the PIGLOG case.

17. This property is often referred to as Shephard's Lemma – see, for example, Henderson and Quandt (1980: 44–5).

18. See note 14 for the meaning of 'second-order approximation'.

10 Consumption functions

In the previous chapter we considered, first, the estimation of demand equations for individual commodities and, secondly, the estimation of the sets of demand equations which arise when an individual consumer allocates a given total expenditure amongst the many commodities available to him. In this chapter we concentrate on the factors which determine the way a consumer divides his total disposable income between total consumption and saving. We shall be concerned, however, with consumption as theoretically defined – i.e. with the sum of consumer expenditures on *non-durable* goods and services plus the value of the flow of services obtained by consumers from durable goods. While total consumer expenditure might be a more relevant aggregate from the economic policy point of view, we dealt with expenditure on consumer durables in the last chapter. Furthermore, non-durable consumption represents a large proportion (between 85 and 90 per cent in the UK for example) of total spending in any economy so that its determination is of considerable importance in its own right.

We begin by considering some of the early empirical work on the consumption function.

10.1 General problems and early empirical work

The term 'consumption function' originates in Keynes's *The General Theory of Employment, Interest and Money* where Keynes put forward his 'fundamental psychological law' that consumption increases as income increases but that the increase in consumption is less than the increase in income. That is

$$C = F(Y) \qquad 0 < \partial C / \partial Y < 1 \qquad [10.1]$$

where C and Y are the real consumption and real income respectively of an individual consumer and the marginal propensity to consume (MPC) lies between zero and unity. Much of the analysis in the General Theory requires that the function (10.1) be 'fairly stable' (Keynes 1936: 95), indicating that while other factors such as interest rates and windfall changes in capital values might also affect real consumption, it was real income that was the dominant force in the Keynesian scheme of things.

Equation [10.1] is sometimes referred to as the *absolute income hypothesis* (AIH) although nowadays other variables tend to be added to ensure that the function fits available data.[1]

Keynes's ideas concerning the consumption function led quite naturally to a series of attempts to test the validity of the above propositions. However, the estimation of consumption functions involves a number of general problems, although at most scant attention was paid to them in early work.

An obvious problem is choice of appropriate data series, although there is little difficulty as far as income data is concerned. The variable referred to by Keynes can be fairly closely identified with real personal disposable income, i.e. income in constant price terms net of taxes on income and insurance contributions, etc. Unfortunately, deciding on the relevant consumption variable is not so easy. Theoretically, consumption may be regarded as the sum of expenditures on 'non-durable' consumer goods and the value of the flow of services on 'durable' consumer goods. However, in practice there are obvious difficulties in drawing a precise line between those goods which are durable and those which are non-durable. For example, clothing is usually classed as a non-durable but clearly possesses many of the attributes of a durable good. Hopefully, acceptance of the standard data classifications for such items does not seriously affect empirical results. A more serious difficulty is the flow of services from what are obviously durable goods. The value of this flow is an important element in consumption and should also be included in a consumer's income. Unfortunately, data concerning it is very rarely available. The majority of empirical studies have therefore defined consumption as either consumption expenditure on non-durables or the sum of expenditures on durable and non-durables.[2]

A further problem arises when attempts are made to estimate consumption functions from aggregate time series data. The Keynesian consumption function is formulated in terms of the individual consumer, so in using economy-wide data we face an aggregation problem similar in nature to that for demand equations discussed in section 9.2. For example, suppose the ith individual's consumption function in real terms is given by

$$C_i = \alpha_i + \beta_i Y_i + \varepsilon_i \qquad [10.2]$$

For meaningful aggregation we must assume either that the parameter β_i is constant for all individuals or, appealing to the 'convergence approach', that it is distributed across individuals in a manner which is independent of income. In either case the aggregate function obtained expresses *per capita real consumption* as a function of *per capita real income*.

A third problem is that OLS estimators of consumption function parameters are likely to be subject to simultaneous equation bias. We have seen in Chapter 8 that in a simple model such as that given by equations [8.12], the OLS estimator of the MPC, β, will be biased upwards.

Finally, estimated consumption functions obtained from time series data will frequently suffer from the problems of non-stationary regressors and spurious correlation described in earlier chapters. As an example, consider the function estimated by Davis (1952), using annual US data in per capita constant price terms for 1929–40:

$$C = 11.45 + 0.78Y \qquad R^2 = 0.986 \qquad [10.3]$$
$$(0.02)$$

A large part of the high R^2 is simply due to common trends in the data series for C and Y – both variables were rising steadily for much of the sample period.

Early empirical studies of the consumption function involved either cross-sectional data, i.e. budget survey data for individual households in a given year, or aggregate time series data for the relatively short time span of the 1930s. First impressions appeared to confirm the Keynesian predictions. In particular, real consumption did, indeed, appear to be a stable function of real income and the MPC was invariably found to lie between zero and unity. A typical early consumption function is illustrated in Fig. 10.1a. Note that it possesses an intercept, implying positive consumption (i.e. dis-saving) even at low levels of income. Since Keynes had suggested that such an intercept might exist, the function in Fig. 10.1a is often referred to as a typical 'Keynesian consumption function'.

Doubts were first cast on the simple Keynesian consumption function in the early post-war years. It was found that functions fitted to prewar US data, when used for forecasting purposes, seriously underpredicted postwar consumption expenditure in the US. Such underpredictions were well illustrated by Davis's equation [10.3] above. Despite the extremely good 'fit' for 1929–40, forecasts for 1946–50 using this equation resulted in underpredictions for aggregate consumption as high as US $12 bn. Such results were clearly inconsistent with a stable relationship between consumption and income – the consumption function appeared to have shifted 'upwards'. They illustrate the dangers of placing too much faith in a model simply because high sample R^2s have been obtained – very high R^2s are typical, and easy to obtain, when dealing with time series data on income and consumption.

Other evidence at about this time was also suggesting that the simple Keynesian consumption function was shifting upwards. The work of Brady and Friedman (1947) suggested that, while cross-sectional budget studies for any given year tended to confirm the shape illustrated in Fig. 10.1a, the evidence from successive budget studies taken over a period of years was that although the MPC remained relatively constant the intercept was shifting upwards.

The most important findings, however, were those of Kuznets (1942). Examining US data over the period 1879–1938, he found that over long periods the average propensity to consume (APC), measured as the ratio of consumption to national income, had remained relatively constant at about 0.9. The long-run constancy of the APC was later confirmed by Goldsmith (1955) using data for personal income rather than national income. Long-run time series data therefore yielded consumption functions of the form shown in Fig. 10.1b. They possessed no intercept and implied an MPC identical to the APC.

10.1a A Keynesian consumption function.

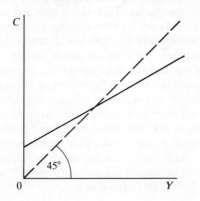

10.1b A long-run time series consumption function.

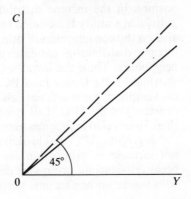

10.2 Long- and short-run consumption functions.

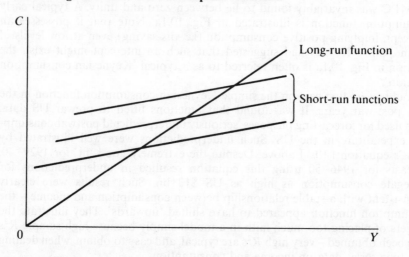

By the late 1940s a clear contradiction appeared to have arisen. Long-run time series data suggested a consumption function with a constant APC, i.e. a linear function with no intercept. However, cross-sectional budget studies consistently suggested a function of typical Keynesian shape, and similar functions tended to be estimated from short-run (ten to twenty years) time series data. These differences could be reconciled empirically by postulating a 'short-run' consumption function of Keynesian shape which shifted upwards over time, as illustrated in Fig. 10.2. However, economic reasons for the upward movement were unclear. Most of the theoretical and empirical work concerning the consumption function performed during the next twenty years was aimed directly or indirectly at reconciling these apparent contradictions.

The relative income hypothesis

The first serious attempt at explaining both time series and cross-sectional data was provided by the so-called *relative income hypothesis* (RIH) developed independently by Duesenberry (1949) and Modigliani (1949).

According to Duesenberry, an individual's APC depends on his percentile position in the income distribution of his associates. This is so because an individual's utility is assumed to depend not only on his own consumption but also on the consumption of others. Those individuals who are low down in the income distribution emulate the consumption patterns of their wealthier neighbours. Thus, the lower an individual's percentile position in the income distribution the higher his APC. This explains the shape of the cross-sectional consumption function but also provides an explanation of the long-run constancy in the APC. If all incomes increased over time by the same proportion then, since relative incomes remain unchanged the individual APCs and hence the aggregate APC would remain unchanged. Even if individual incomes do not increase in proportion the *aggregate* APC still remains constant since, because the income groups are defined in terms of percentiles, for every individual who moves up one income percentile another must move down.

250

In reconciling the findings from long-run and short-run time series data both Duesenberry and Modigliani resorted to a rather different concept of relative income. They argued that habit and a desire to maintain living standards meant that an individual's consumption depended not only on the size of his income but also on its size relative to previous highest or peak values of income and/or consumption. Thus during times of recession individuals would offset temporary reductions in income by consuming a larger proportion of their incomes.

Brown (1952) generalised this approach with his *habit persistence model*. He argued that the influence of past consumption is continuous and not limited to situations where current consumption levels are below their previous peak. Thus consumption in any one period is always influenced by consumption in the previous period because of habit persistence, and we may write

$$C_t = \beta_0 Y_t + \beta_1 C_{t-1} \qquad\qquad [10.4]$$

Thus, in time series data, if C_{t-1} is omitted from a simple regression of C_t on Y_t then the estimated consumption function will exhibit an intercept, (representing the absent C_{t-1}), that will increase in size over time as C_{t-1} increases. However if consumption grows at a constant rate g then, since $C_t = (1 + g)C_{t-1}$, a long-run consumption function with a constant APC is obtained. Substituting for C_{t-1} in [10.4] we have

$$C_t = \beta_0 Y_t + \beta_1 \left(\frac{C_t}{1+g} \right) \qquad\qquad [10.5]$$

Hence, solving for C_t, the long-run consumption function is

$$C_t = \left(\frac{\beta_0}{1 - (\beta_1/1 + g)} \right) Y_t \qquad\qquad [10.6]$$

An interesting point arises from the above explanation of time series data. Equation [10.6] implies that the greater the long-run rate of growth in real income the lower is the APC, i.e. the larger the proportion of income that is saved. This was in accordance with observations on saving ratios for different countries over periods of time. Countries with the highest income-growth rates do tend to have the highest average propensities to save (APS).

Notice that in Brown's model the single equation to be estimated is [10.4]. This is the short-run consumption function. The long-run consumption function is simply deduced from the short-run function by substituting into [10.5], first, the long-run growth rate and, secondly, the estimated values of β_0 and β_1 obtained from the estimation of [10.4]. Quite generally, it is not the case that the short-run function is obtained from a data span of, for example, fifteen to twenty years, and the long-run function from perhaps 100 years. No matter what the length of the sample period the same estimating equation is fitted. This point will become even more relevant towards the end of this chapter when we come to consider recent work on consumption but, for the moment consider, as an example, the equation estimated by Evans (1969) using US annual data for 1929–62,

$$\hat{C}_t = 0.280 Y_t + 0.676 C_{t-1} \qquad\qquad [10.4A]$$
$$\quad (0.041) \quad\ (0.052)$$

Equation [10.4A] is the short-run consumption function, yielding estimates $\hat{\beta}_0 = 0.280$ and $\hat{\beta}_1 = 0.676$. Assuming an annual growth rate of $g = 0.04$ (i.e. 4 per cent) in US consumption over this period, the implied long-run consumption function obtained from substitution in [10.6] is $C_t = 0.80Y_t$. Alternatively, for a zero growth rate the long-run function is $C_t = 0.86Y_t$.

10.2 The life-cycle hypothesis

Duesenberry's explanation of the pattern of income-consumption data, with its assumption that an individual's utility depends not only on the goods he consumes but also on the consumption of others, involves a microeconomic theory totally different from the traditional Hicksian demand analysis. Other attempts at reconciling the apparently conflicting evidence have been based on a more orthodox micro-foundation.

Consider, for example, the special case of a consumer faced with the problem of maximising utility over just two periods. That is, he must allocate his resources between consumption in the first period, C_1, and that in the second period, C_2. The consumer's preferences may be summarised by the system of indifference curves shown in Fig. 10.3 which are concave for the usual reasons. Suppose the consumer's total receipts or income in the first period is Y_1 and in the second period Y_2, and let r be the interest rate. The maximum the consumer can spend on consumption during the first period is $Y_1 + Y_2/(1 + r)$ – his income during the first period plus the maximum loan he can repay with his income of the second period. If he consumed this quantity in the first period, he would have nothing to spend in the second period so this possibility is represented by the point A in Fig. 10.3. Alternatively, if the consumer spent nothing in the first period his maximum consumption level in the second period would be $Y_1(1 + r) + Y_2$ – his first-period income, plus interest earned on it, plus his second-period income. This possibility is represented by the point B. The line

10.3 Utility maximisation over two periods.

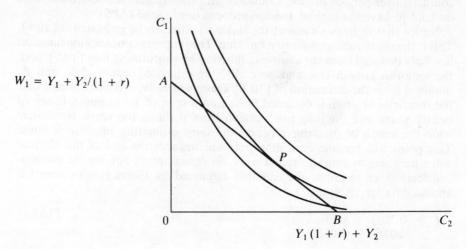

252

AB represents the consumer's budget constraint, i.e. it defines all possible combinations of C_1 and C_2 that may be chosen by the consumer, assuming he wishes to have no resources remaining at the end of the second period.

The consumer's optimal combination of C_1 and C_2 is where the budget line is tangential to an indifference curve, i.e. the point P in Fig. 10.3. What is interesting about P is that, given the set of indifference curves, its position and hence first-period consumption, C_1, depends on income in *both* periods and on the interest rate. *There is no way in which we can derive the AIH from a traditional microeconomic analysis.* Specifically, the position of point P depends on the height and slope of the budget constraint. The height of the line AB clearly depends on the quantity $Y_1 + Y_2/(1 + r)$ which is normally referred to as the consumer's total wealth, W_1, in the first period. The slope of the line is given by $-1/(1 + r)$ and is hence dependent on the interest rate. Thus, optimal consumption in either period is a function of W_1 and r.

Algebraically, the consumer maximises a utility function $U = U(C_1, C_2)$ subject to the condition that C_1 and C_2 satisfy the budget constraint[3]

$$Y_1 + \frac{Y_2}{1 + r} = C_1 + \frac{C_2}{1 + r}$$

The solution to this constrained optimisation problem is given by $C_1 = f_1(W_1, r)$ and $C_2 = f_2(W_1, r)$. The precise shape of the functions f_1 and f_2 will depend on the consumer's indifference map, but it is clear from Fig. 10.3 that the greater W_1, i.e. the greater OA, the larger will be C_1 and C_2. Also, as the rate of interest rises with W_1 constant, the budget line becomes less steep and we have a pure substitution effect with first-period consumption falling while second-period consumption rises. Thus, as r rises the consumer substitutes future consumption for present consumption.

An interesting and not too implausible special case arises if we assume that the consumer's utility function is *homothetic*. Graphically, this means that the slopes of the indifference curves are the same along any straight line drawn through the origin.[4] Thus, for a given rate of interest, as W_1 increases and the budget line is shifted outwards parallel to itself, the optimal ratio C_1/C_2 remains unchanged regardless of the magnitude of W_1. The ratio C_1/C_2 will, however, depend on the tastes of the consumer, as represented by the precise form of his indifference map, and on the rate of interest. The constancy of the optimal ratio C_1/C_2 when combined with the above budget constraint means that C_1 and C_2 are, in fact, constant proportions of W_1. That is, $C_1 = \gamma_1 W_1$ and $C_2 = \gamma_2 W_1$ where the γ's are again dependent on consumer preferences and the rate of interest.[5]

Consider finally the situation where the consumer exhibits an absence of 'time preference proper' and where the rate of interest is zero. The absence of such time preference implies that each indifference curve is symmetrical about a line through the origin at an angle of $45°$ to each axis. This is illustrated in Fig. 10.4 and means that the consumer is indifferent between, for example, $C_1 = 100, C_2 = 30$ and $C_1 = 30, C_2 = 100$. A zero interest rate implies that the budget constraint has a slope of -1 and hence its point of tangency with any indifference curve is always on the $45°$ line. Thus, $C_1 = C_2$, i.e. under these very special conditions the consumer plans to consume at exactly the same rate in

10.4 Absence of 'time preference proper'.

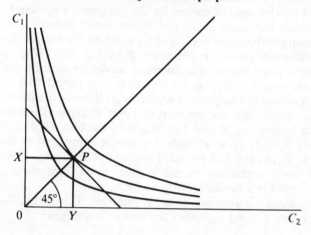

each period. In Fig. 10.4

$$C_1 = OX \quad \text{and} \quad C_2 = OY$$

We shall refer back to this particular case later.

The above analysis was not new and indeed the early part of it was identical to that of Fisher (1907). It was adopted and generalised by Modigliani and Brumberg (1954) in their *life-cycle hypothesis* (LCH). Modigliani and Brumberg assumed that a household plans its lifetime consumption pattern so as to maximise the total utility it obtains from consumption during its lifetime. In the empirical version of their hypothesis it is assumed that households do not plan to leave assets to their heirs so that a household of age T maximises a utility function of the form

$$U = U(C_T, C_{T+1}, C_{T+2}, \ldots, C_L) \tag{10.7}$$

where C_i ($i = T, T + 1, T + 2, \ldots, L$) is planned consumption at age i and L is the household's expected age at 'death'. Since the household plans to exactly exhaust its resources during its lifetime, [10.7] is maximised subject to the lifetime budget constraint

$$A_{T-1} + Y_T + \sum_{i=T+1}^{N} \frac{Y_i^e}{(1+r)^{i-T}} = \sum_{i=T}^{L} \frac{C_i}{(1+r)^{i-T}} \tag{10.8}$$

A_{T-1} is non-human wealth (i.e. physical and financial assets) carried over from the households $(T - 1)$th year, Y_T is the household's earned or non-property income at age T, Y_i^e is its expected non-property income at age i and N is the household's age at retirement. Note that it is non-property income that enters the budget constraint. For the reader who is uncertain why this should be so, the constraint is derived for the three-period case in Appendix B to this chapter.

Modigliani and Brumberg now adopt the simplifying assumption that the utility function [10.7] is homothetic. As we might expect from our simple two-period example this implies that planned current consumption is given by

$$C_T = \gamma_T W_T \tag{10.9}$$

254

where W_T is the household's total expected lifetime resources at age T. That is, it is the sum of all terms on the left-hand side of the budget constraint [10.8]

$$W_T = A_{T-1} + Y_T + \sum_{i=T+1}^{N} \frac{Y_i^e}{(1+r)^{i-T}}$$ [10.10]

Similarly planned consumption in future years is given by

$$C_i = \gamma_i W_T \qquad i = T + 1, T + 2, \ldots, L$$ [10.11]

The γ_is in equations [10.9] and [10.11] will be dependent on the rate of interest and on the household's tastes and preferences as in the simple two-period case. however, they will also depend on the age of the household. Because resources are to be completely exhausted during its lifetime, the nearer the household is to 'death' the larger the proportion of its resources it plans to expend during any given year. The important aspect of [10.9] and [10.11] is that the γ_is are independent of the magnitude of W_T. Thus, the household keeps the ratios of its planned consumption expenditures in any two future years unchanged no matter what the size of its lifetime resources.[6]

Two points need to be stressed concerning, in particular, equation [10.9].

First, *a change in current income Y_T will influence current consumption C_T only to the extent that it changes W_T*, the household's expected lifetime resources. Normally, changes in Y_T, unless they lead to revisions in expectations concerning future income, i.e. to changes in the Y_i^es, can be expected to have little influence on current consumption unless the household is near 'death'. This is perhaps the main conclusion of the LCH.

Secondly, equation [10.9] implies that current consumption is a constant proportion of total lifetime resources. This is the famous 'proportionality postulate'. It follows from the assumption made above of a homothetic utility function. However, the implications of the LCH remain largely unchanged if this convenient assumption is dropped. We can see from the simple two-period case discussed earlier that current consumption would remain a function of total lifetime resources, although the relationship would no longer be one of strict proportionality. Thus a change in current income would still only influence current consumption via its normally small effect on total lifetime resources. The proportionality postulate is not therefore a necessarily vital part of the LCH.

To sample the true flavour of the LCH it is instructive to consider, as we did for the two-period case, a situation where there is an absence of 'time preference proper' and where the interest rate is zero. The household then plans to consume its wealth at a constant rate throughout its lifetime. Since the income of a typical household varies throughout its lifespan, it is interesting to compare the time profiles of expected income and planned consumption for a household of 'average' size under the above assumptions. Such a household might expect its real income to rise steadily until somewhere near its anticipated retirement age and to decline thereafter. Such a profile is illustrated in Fig. 10.5 for the case where consumption proceeds at a constant rate.

It is apparent from Fig. 10.5 that even in the absence of time preference and with a zero rate of interest a household will still borrow and save. A major motive for saving in the life-cycle model is therefore the desire to flatten out the lifetime stream of consumption expenditures. Without dis-saving during the later part of its life and saving in the middle section the household would be

10.5 Time profile of average household.

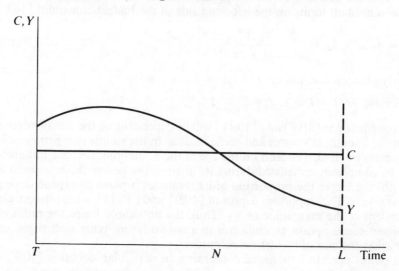

forced to spend its whole income (no more and no less) during each of its future years.

The above analysis has important implications for the aggregate saving ratio in an economy. Recall that the time series version of the RIH provided a reason why there should be a positive relationship between the rate of growth in real income and the APS. The LCH provides a possibly more fundamental reason. Consider first a static, no-growth economy with a constant population and age distribution and an absence of technical change. Such an economy in cross-section could be likened to a series of households at different points in their life-span. Aggregate saving would therefore be zero since, provided there was no saving for heirs, the saving of the working population would just be counterbalanced by the dis-saving of the retired. If the economy were growing because of an increase in population, then clearly the greater number of younger households would mean that saving would exceed dis-saving and the aggregate saving ratio would be positive. However, even with a constant population, if technical change results in rising income and output per head, then those currently in employment will have higher incomes and expected incomes than did currently retired consumers when they were earning. Those currently employed plan to consume more per head in retirement than do the currently retired. Thus, saving will again exceed dis-saving and, moreover, the greater the rate of growth in real income per head the greater will be the aggregate saving ratio. This relationship was, in fact, first put forward by Harrod (1948) but was further developed by Modigliani (1966).

Ando and Modigliani (1963) adopted equation [10.9] for estimation from aggregate time series data. Problems in estimating the expected non-property income of consumers meant that their final equation simply involved regressing aggregate consumption, C_t, on aggregate current non-property income, Y_t, and the aggregate net wealth of consumers, A_{t-1}. Their most important finding was that, for annual US data for 1929–59, A_{t-1} was a significant determinant of

C_t. The MPC out of net worth was estimated to be in the region 0.07–0.10. If the aggregate consumption function is, in fact, of the form

$$C_t = \alpha A_{t-1} + \beta Y_t$$

then this provides another explanation of the upward shifts in the short-run consumption function, If A_{t-1} is omitted from the regression of C_t on Y_t, then the estimated short-run consumption function will have a positive intercept and shift upwards over time as positive saving increases A_{t-1}.

10.3 The permanent income hypothesis

Although it has many close similarities with the LCH, the *permanent income hypothesis* (PIH) was developed independently and found its first definitive form in the work of Friedman (1957). Recall from the simple two-period model of the previous section that first-period consumption depended on first-period total wealth and the rate of interest, i.e.

$$C_1 = f_1(W_1, r)$$

Friedman, like the life-cycle theorists, generalises the two-period case but generalises to an 'indefinitely long horizon' rather than to a remaining lifespan. Present period planned or *permanent consumption*, C^P, is therefore a function of present period total wealth, W, and the rate of interest

$$C^P = q(W, r) \qquad [10.12]$$

Total wealth in the Friedman formulation is defined as the discounted sum of *all* future receipts including income from non-human assets. That is, wealth in period t is given by

$$W_t = Y_t + \frac{Y_{t+1}}{1+r} + \frac{Y_{t+2}}{(1+r)^2} + \frac{Y_{t+3}}{(1+r)^3} \cdots \qquad [10.13]$$

where Y_t is total expected receipts in period t. Note that in a perfectly competitive world with complete certainty the Modigliani–Brumberg and the Friedman measures of wealth would be identical. In such a world the value of non-human assets would be exactly equal to the discounted sum of future income from them.

Friedman now makes use of the simplifying assumption that the consumer's utility function is homothetic and equation [10.12] becomes

$$C^P = qW \qquad [10.14]$$

where the factor of proportionality, q, is dependent on the consumer's tastes and on the rate of interest.

Friedman next introduces the concept of *permanent income*, Y^P. This is defined, theoretically, as the maximum amount a consumer could consume while maintaining his wealth intact. It is, in fact, the rate of return on wealth, i.e. $Y^P = rW$. To see this, consider again the two-period model of the previous section. Initial wealth is W_1. If the individual consumed nothing during the first period, his wealth would have grown to $W_1(1 + r)$ by the start of the second period. However, if he consumed a quantity rW_1 in the first period his wealth at the start of the second period would be W_1, i.e. he would have maintained his wealth intact. This argument extends, of course, to the multiperiod case.

We can now rewrite equation [10.14] as

$$C^P = q\left(\frac{Y^P}{r}\right) = kY^P \qquad [10.15]$$

where $q = rk$.

Note that consumption is now related to a flow concept (permanent income) rather than a stock concept (wealth). Friedman, in fact, has annuitised W since permanent income can be regarded as that level of income which, if received in perpetuity, would have a discounted present value equal to W. This can be seen by solving the following equation for Y^P

$$W = \frac{Y^P}{1 + r} + \frac{Y^P}{(1 + r)^2} + \frac{Y^P}{(1 + r)^3} \cdots \qquad [10.16]$$

The right-hand side is a convergent geometric series with common ratio $1/(1 + r)$. Summing this to infinity yields Y^P/r so that we obtain $Y^P = rW$ as before.

The replacement of a stock concept (W) by the flow concept (Y^P) does, however, raise one awkward inconsistency. If an individual consumes an amount exactly equal to his permanent income, then by definition his wealth remains unchanged. However, equation [10.15] implies that a consumer will normally consume less than his permanent income (empirical estimates of k tends to be in the range 0.8–0.9) and, hence, that wealth will be perpetually increasing. While the annuitisation of wealth and the switch to an implied infinite lifespan can be justified by maintaining that a household attaches as much importance to consumption by its heirs as to its own consumption, it is difficult to see why it should plan for an ever-increasing level of wealth.

The quantity k in equation [10.15] depends on the tastes of the household and on the rate of interest. However, under conditions of uncertainty Friedman introduces an additional motive for saving – the need to accumulate a reserve of wealth for emergencies. Since human wealth makes a less satisfactory reserve than non-human wealth, the proportion of permanent income consumed, k, is made to depend, also, on the proportion of total wealth which is held as non-human wealth. For a given rate of interest this ratio is directly proportional to the ratio of non-human wealth to permanent income for which Friedman uses the symbol w. Thus we have

$$C^P = k(r, w, u)Y^P \qquad [10.17]$$

where u is a portmanteau variable reflecting the consumer's tastes.

Notice the basic similarities between the PIH and the LCH. In Friedman's model an increase in current income influences current consumption only to the extent that it changes W and, hence, permanent income. Moreover, although equation [10.15] implies a proportionate relationship between C^P and Y^P, the 'proportionality postulate' is again not vital to the model. Even if the homotheticity assumption is dropped, C^P remains a function of W and hence, of permanent income rather than current income.

There are, however, clear if relatively minor, differences between the models. The annuitisation of total wealth means that the stock of non-human assets does not appear explicitly in Friedman's consumption function. However, Friedman does distinguish between the different influences of human and non-human wealth on consumption. The factor of proportionality, k, i.e. the APC out of permanent income, is dependent on the ratio of the two. In the Modigliani–Brumberg formulation, as can be seen from equations [10.10] and [10.9], the effect on planned consumption of an extra £1 of resources is identical whether that £1 is an addition to non-human assets or an addition to the present value of future income. Finally, in the life-cycle model the household merely looks ahead to the end of its life. Friedman's annuitisation of total wealth suggests that his household has an infinite life or at any rate attaches as much importance to the consumption of its heirs as it does to its own consumption.

Permanent income and measured income

When we attempt to relate the PIH to actual data we face obvious problems. Current or 'measured' income is clearly different from the theoretical concept of permanent income and even if we had adequate 'flow of services' data on current or 'measured' consumption this would still differ from planned or permanent consumption. Friedman regards measured income, Y, as being made up of two components – a permanent component, Y^P, and a *transistory* component, Y^t. Measured consumption, C, is similarly divided into *permanent consumption*, C^P, and *transistory consumption*, C^t. Thus we have

$$Y = Y^P + Y^t \quad \text{and} \quad C = C^P + C^t \qquad [10.18]$$

The empirical definition of Y^P is that it is the normal or expected or unfortuitous income of the consumer. This roughly corresponds to the theoretical definition but is purposely left vague by Friedman since 'the precise line to be drawn between permanent and transistory components is best left to the data themselves, to be whatever seems to correspond to consumer behaviour' (Friedman 1957: 23). In other words, since, theoretically, planned or permanent consumption depends on permanent income, then, empirically, permanent income must be whatever quantity that in practice the consumer regards as determining his planned consumption. The transitory component of income is to be regarded as that which arises from accidental or chance occurrences, while permanent and transitory consumption may be interpreted as planned and 'unplanned' consumption respectively.

To give his model operational content, i.e. to make it capable of being contradicted by observed data. Friedman makes the following assumptions:

$$Y^P \text{ is uncorrelated with } Y^t \text{ and } C^P \text{ is uncorrelated with } C^t \qquad [10.19]$$

$$Y^t \text{ is uncorrelated with } C^t \qquad [10.20]$$

The lack of correlation assumed between permanent and transitory components is uncontroversial and indeed virtually follows from the definition of a transitory component. However, a zero correlation between transitory income and transitory consumption implies that any unforeseen increment in income does not result in unplanned consumption. This is obviously more open to debate. Friedman justifies it, firstly, by pointing out that actual, as opposed to planned, saving is commonly regarded as a residual, i.e. even if income is other than as expected the consumer tends to stick to his consumption plan but to adjust his asset holdings. Also, when it is remembered that consumption theoretically includes only the flow of services from durable goods rather than actual expenditure on such goods, the assumption begins to look more reasonable. If a receipt of transitory income is spent on the purchase of durable goods then this expenditure may be largely classified as saving.

Friedman's model as specified above is formally almost exactly equivalent to the 'errors in variables' model described in section 5.1.1. The 'true' variables are C^P and Y^P and are linked by the underlying deterministic relationship $C^P = kY^P$. However, C^P and Y^P are observed with measurement errors C^t and Y^t respectively, so that we, in fact, observe C and Y. Moreover, as in section 5.1.1 the errors of measurement are uncorrelated with each other and are also uncorrelated with the true values of the variables concerned. The only minor difference from the model of section 5.1.1 is that the basic relationship $C^P = kY^P$ does not contain an intercept. Substituting for C^P and Y^P in $C^P = kY^P$ we obtain

$$C = kY + (C^t - kY^t) \qquad [10.21]$$

If [10.21] is regarded as a relationship expressing measured consumption, C, as a function of measured income, Y, then it contains a 'disturbance', $C^t - kY^t$, which is negatively correlated with the explanatory variable which is $Y = Y^P + Y^t$. Thus, if we regress measured C on measured Y, then, as the model of section 5.1 suggests, the OLS estimator of the slope coefficient (in this case k) will be downward-biased. Similarly, the OLS estimator of the intercept (in this case zero) will be upward-biased. Moreover, these biases will persist however large is the sample. Friedman, in fact, shows that for the OLS regression $\hat{C} = \hat{\alpha} + \hat{\beta}Y$, for large samples

$$\hat{\beta} = kP_y \qquad \text{where } P_y = \frac{\text{var } Y^P}{\text{var } Y^t + \text{var } Y^P} = \frac{\text{var } Y^P}{\text{var } Y} \leqslant 1 \qquad [10.22]$$

Also, provided the mean transitory components of income and consumption are zero then

$$\hat{\alpha} = k(1 - P_y)\bar{Y}^P \qquad [10.23]$$

where $\bar{Y}^P$ is the mean value of permanent income. P_y is the proportion of the variation in measured income which results from variations in the permanent component of income. Thus, if $P_y < 1$, i.e. if variations in Y are in any part due to a transitory component, then $\alpha > 0$ and $\hat{\beta} < k$. That is, we will observe a consumption function with an intercept and with a shallower slope than the underlying function $C^P = kY^P$.

It is now possible to use the PIH to reconcile, firstly, the findings from short-run and long-run aggregate time series data.

Figure 10.6a illustrates the time path of aggregate income for a typical Western economy since, say, the turn of the century. The dotted line indicates the secular trend rate of growth in income whereas actual income exhibits cyclical fluctuations about this trend. The trend line may be interpreted as reflecting the growth in permanent income. Had actual income followed the trend line this would have implied that *aggregate* transitory income was always zero (although it may have been positive or negative for *individual* households). Hence, all the variation in aggregate income would be due to variations in the permanent component. Hence, $P_y = 1$ and the observed consumption function

10.6a The relationship between measured and permanent income in the long run.

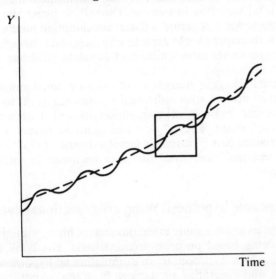

10.6b The relationship between measured and permanent income in the short run.

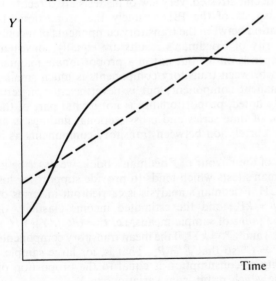

would have the form $C = kY$. Even if income follows the cyclical pattern of Fig. 10.6a over the long term the variations in income are still dominated by variations in the permanent component so that P_y is still close to unity. Thus we still observe a function of roughly the form $C = kY$.

Suppose, however, we consider, for example, merely a ten-year period. Such a period is illustrated in Fig. 10.6b which is actually a 'blown-up' version of

261

the boxed area in Fig. 10.6a. For this period the secular trend no longer dominates the path of actual income so that transitory movements account for a considerable part of the total variation in income. Thus, $P_y < 1$ and hence $\hat{\alpha} > 0$ and $\hat{\beta} < k$, and we observe for this period a flatter consumption function with an intercept. The PIH is therefore able to explain why long-run time series data yield a function of proportionate form while short-run data yield one of typical Keynesian form.

For cross-sectional data the PIH again predicts a consumption function with an intercept. Since we are now dealing with individual households, transitory components are certainly not zero and will make an important contribution to the cross-sectional variation in income. Thus, $P_y < 1$ and again we have $\hat{\alpha} > 0$ and $\hat{\beta} < k$. We shall not reproduce here Friedman's famous diagram (1957: 34) which illustrates the cross-sectional case, since this may be found in many standard macroeconomic texts.

Tests of the permanent income hypothesis using cross-sectional data

Friedman (1957) presents a series of often quite ingenious tests of his hypothesis, the majority of these tests being based on cross-sectional data. His book is deservedly recognised as a classic in its procedure of formulating an hypothesis on the basis of existing data, and generating predictions from that hypothesis which can be tested against further data. However, many of his predictions can also be derived, even if sometimes with a little more difficulty, from the RIH. Also, as Mayer (1972) in particular stressed, very few of his tests are direct tests of the more controversial aspects of the PIH, namely the proportionality postulate and the zero correlation between the transitory components of income and consumption. The majority of Friedman's results are equally consistent with a model in which C^P depends on Y^P but not in a proportionate manner, and in which the correlation between transitory components is much smaller than that between the permanent components but is nevertheless non-zero. However, as we have already noted, proportionality is not a vital part of the PIH. Also, the reconciliation of time series and cross-sectional findings is as equally possible with a 'low' correlation between transitory components as it is with a zero correlation.

To give readers some idea of the flavour of Friedman's book, we describe in this subsection one of Friedman's tests which tends to provide support for his hypothesis but not for the RIH. Friedman's analysis is carried out in terms of both the estimated MPC, $\hat{\beta} = kP_y$, and the estimated income elasticity of consumption measured at the point of sample means, i.e. $\hat{E} = (dC/dY)(\bar{Y}/\bar{C})$. Since $\hat{E} = \hat{\beta}(\bar{Y}/\bar{C}) = kP_y(\bar{Y}/\bar{C})$ and $C^P = kY^P$, if the mean transitory components are zero then $\bar{Y} = \bar{Y}^P$ and $C = \bar{C}^P$ so that $\hat{E} = P_y$. That is, for large samples, the estimated income elasticity of consumption is equal to the proportion of the total variations in income which result from variations in Y^P.

In a series of tests, Friedman compares cross-sections in which the variations in transitory incomes can be presumed to be unimportant, i.e. P_y is close to unity, with cross-sections where variations in Y^t make large contributions to variations in Y, i.e. P_y is much less than unity. As predicted by the PIH, both $\hat{\beta}$ and $\hat{E}$ tend to be larger for the first type of cross-section. For example, of four cross-sections of urban and non-farm households in the US taken between 1941 and 1950,[7] three 'non-wartime' cross-sections have $\hat{\beta}$s in the range

0.73–0.79. But the wartime cross-section, 1944, for which transitory income variations are likely to have been most important, had a $\hat{\beta}$ as low as 0.57. However, since $\hat{\beta} = kP_y$, this lower value for $\hat{\beta}$ could be the result of a lower k, i.e. a lower APC, resulting from higher precautionary savings during unsettled wartime conditions. Thus a more impressive comparison is between the respective income elasticities of consumption, since $\hat{E}$ is not dependent on k. For the non-wartime years the $\hat{E}$s range from 0.80 to 0.87 whereas for 1944 $\hat{E} = 0.70$. Such findings provide impressive support for PIH yet it is hard to explain them on the basis of either the AIH or the RIH.

We do not have the space here to do justice to Friedman's book but readers are encouraged to examine it for themselves. Especially striking are the tests concerning 'year on year income changes' (pp. 101–102) and 'income correlations' (pp. 104–105).

Time series estimation under the permanent income hypothesis

A major problem that arises when attempts are made to estimate equations concerning the PIH is that normal data refers to measured income, Y_t, rather than permanent income Y_t^p. Friedman suggests that, for aggregate time series data, permanent income in period t may be estimated by

$$Y_t^p = \lambda Y_t + \lambda(1 - \lambda)Y_{t-1} + \lambda(1 - \lambda)^2 Y_{t-2}\ldots \qquad 0 < \lambda < 1 \qquad [10.24]$$

That is, he adopts what is known as a *distributed lag* formulation with geometrically declining weights.[8] The argument is that consumers will give most weight to their current income in assessing their permanent income and successively declining weights to whatever income has been in the past. This formulation clearly stresses the 'expected' nature of permanent income. Also, as reference to section 6.2 should make clear, equation [10.24] implies that permanent income is determined by what we referred to as an *adaptive expectations hypothesis*. In this case, that is

$$Y_t^p - Y_{t-1}^p = \lambda(Y_t - Y_{t-1}^p) \qquad 0 < \lambda < 1 \qquad [10.25]$$

Thus, differences between permanent and measured income lead to an adjustment in the perceived level of permanent income. The extent of the adjustment depends on the size of λ which we can therefore expect to be larger for annual data than, for example, for quarterly data.

Friedman's time series work was, however, based on versions of equation [10.24]. He computed various time series for Y_t^p using a different value for λ in each case, truncating [10.24] after sixteen terms. Using annual real per capita US data for 1905–51 he then ran regressions of the form[9]

$$\hat{C}_t = \hat{\alpha} + \hat{\beta}Y_t^p \qquad [10.26]$$

for each Y_t^p series and chose that value of λ which provided the closest fit. The highest R^2 was obtained for $\lambda = 0.33$. For this equation the intercept term was insignificant with a very low t-ratio and the estimate of k was $\hat{\beta} = 0.88$. This supported the hypothesis that the relationship between C^p and Y^p was one of proportionality. Also the value obtained for $\hat{\beta}$ was close to the observed APC for the period.

Perhaps of greatest interest in these results was the relatively low weight attached to current income in the determination of permanent income. In fact, a value for λ of 0.33 suggests that incomes of three or more years previous are assigned as much as 30 per cent of the total weight used to assess permanent income. These results, if correct, suggest that the AIH (where $\lambda = 1$ and all the weight is assigned to current income so that Y^p and Y are identical) is a serious mis-specification of the true consumption function.

Since, from the basic relationship $C^p = kY^p$ and equation [10.24], the MPC current measured income is $k\lambda$, the practical importance of a low λ is that it implies a low MPC. Hence, the various Keynesian multipliers will have low 'impact' values and this has obvious policy implications. For example, the short-run or impact effect of an exogenous change in non-consumption expenditure will be much smaller than the long-run effect. However, Friedman's time series conclusions are not universally accepted. For example, Wright (1969), reworking Friedman's data, with only a minor modification for wartime years, obtained a value for λ as high as 0.8. Similarly, other investigators have presented results that imply, for annual data, a value of λ closer to unity. A value of λ near unity would imply that the distinction between permanent and measured income is by no means clear-cut so that the AIH becomes a much less serious mis-specification.

Friedman's estimating procedure can, of course, be simplified by application of the Koyck transformation. Adding a disturbance term ε_t to the basic relationship $C_t^p = kY_t^p$, and applying the same procedure as in section 6.2 yields in this case

$$C_t^p = k\lambda Y_t + (1 - \lambda)C_{t-1}^p + \varepsilon_t - (1 - \lambda)\varepsilon_{t-1} \qquad [10.27]$$

Equation [10.27] no longer includes the unobservable permanent income variable but still involves present period and lagged permanent consumption. However, on substituting

$$C_t^p = C_t - C_t^t$$

the equation becomes

$$C_t = k\lambda Y_t + (1 - \lambda)C_{t-1} + C_t^t - (1 - \lambda)C_{t-1}^t + \varepsilon_t - (1 - \lambda)\varepsilon_{t-1} \qquad [10.28]$$

Equation [10.28] can be regarded as expressing measured consumption, C_t, as a function of measured income Y_t, C_{t-1} and a composite disturbance given by u_t where

$$u_t = C_t^t - (1 - \lambda)C_{t-1}^t + \varepsilon_t - (1 - \lambda)\varepsilon_{t-1} \qquad [10.29]$$

For example, as we noted earlier, Evans (1969) estimated, using US annual data for 1929–62, the equation

$$\hat{C}_t = \underset{(0.041)}{0.280Y_t} + \underset{(0.052)}{0.676C_{t-1}} \qquad [10.30]$$

Interpreting [10.30] in terms of Friedman's hypothesis yields

$$\lambda = 1 - 0.676 = 0.324$$

and a value for

$$k = \frac{0.280}{\lambda} = 0.86.$$

Both these estimates are obviously very close to those obtained by Friedman.

However, as we already know from our discussion in section 6.2, there are severe problems when OLS is applied to equations such as [10.28]. The combination of autocorrelated disturbance term and lagged dependent variable means the OLS estimators will be both biased and inconsistent. The Friedman approach at least yields MLEs of k and λ.

Notwithstanding the technical difficulties of estimating equation [10.28], there is a more fundamental problem. Notice first that, disregarding the disturbance, this equation has exactly the same specification as that for equation [10.4], i.e. for Brown's habit-persistence model. That is, C_t is dependent on Y_t and C_{t-1}. Indeed, consider the following model where *optimal* or *desired* consumption, C_t^*, depends on measured income and a disturbance

$$C_t^* = kY_t + \varepsilon_t \qquad\qquad [10.31]$$

Suppose, also, that *actual* consumption is determined by a *partial adjustment* process as described in section 6.3. That is

$$C_t - C_{t-1} = \lambda(C_t^* - C_{t-1}) \qquad 0 < \lambda < 1 \qquad\qquad [10.32]$$

Thus differences between desired and actual consumption are not immediately eliminated because of 'habit persistence'. The speed with which they are eliminated depends on the size of λ which now, of course, has a totally different interpretation to that in equation [10.25]. Substituting for C_t^* in [10.32] yields

$$C_t = k\lambda Y_t + (1 - \lambda)C_{t-1} + \lambda\varepsilon_t \qquad\qquad [10.33]$$

Equation [10.33], apart from the specification of the disturbance, has exactly the same form as equation [10.28], the estimating equation obtained from the PIH.

It can be seen that, since both hypotheses are formulated initially in terms of 'unobservable' variables such as permanent income and optimal consumption, it becomes extremely difficult to discriminate, from time series data, between the PIH and the habit-persistence version of the RIH. When expressed in terms of 'measurable' variables both yield, apart from the disturbance specification, identical estimating equations, the only difference being the interpretation one places on the coefficients. That interpretation depends crucially on which of the underlying hypotheses is valid – the PIH or the habit-persistence version of the RIH.

10.4   Prices, inflation and wealth effects

In recent years much attention has been paid to the possible influences of the price level and the rate of inflation on consumer expenditure. In the models of the previous sections it was implicitly assumed that any changes in the price level could be ignored. For example, suppose we added a price variable to a simple LCH estimating equation and obtained

$$C_t = \alpha + \beta Y_t + \gamma W_t + \delta P_t + \varepsilon_t \qquad\qquad [10.34]$$

where C_t, Y_t and W_t are real per capita consumption, income and wealth respectively and P_t is an index of consumer prices which has also been used to deflate the other variables. Economic theory suggests that the price coefficient,

δ, in equation [10.34] should be zero. A rise in the price level, with real income and real wealth remaining constant, must imply an equiproportionate rise in money income and in money wealth and hence should lead to no change in consumption expenditure. If δ was positive in equation [10.34] then this would imply that consumers were exhibiting the phenomenon commonly known as 'money illusion'. A positive δ means that a rise in P_t, with Y_t and W_t constant, results in a rise in consumption. Consumers must therefore be treating the equiproportionate rise in money income and money wealth as if it were a rise in real income and real wealth and 'not noticing' the rise in prices. A negative δ, however, implies some sort of reverse illusion. In the face of equiproportionate changes in the price level, money income and money wealth, consumers reduce consumption. This suggests that they believe their real income and wealth have fallen when in fact they have not. In some way they are 'noticing' the rise in prices but not the equiproportionate rises in money income and money wealth.

As early as 1969, Branson and Klevorick estimated a consumption function basically similar to [10.34] although it contained fairly complex lags on the income and price variables. Using quarterly US data for 1955–65 they found their equivalent of δ to be significantly greater than zero and concluded that a significant degree of money illusion existed in the US consumption function.

The rapid inflation experienced by many Western economies during the 1970s led to a number of attempts to establish a link between, not the price level, but the inflation rate and consumption. For example Juster and Wachtel (1972) found that high inflation rates tended to *reduce* US consumption expenditure. They argued that this was because high inflation rates are historically associated with variable inflation rates. Hence, if consumers do not expect a similar variability in money income, future real income will be subject to greater uncertainty during times of high inflation and this will lead to greater precautionary savings.

Deaton (1978) also considers inflation rates but argues that it is *accelerating* inflation that reduces consumer expenditure. For example, suppose that past inflation has been of 5 per cent per annum, that consumers expect this inflation rate to continue but that the inflation rate has, in fact, accelerated to 10 per cent. A consumer, purchasing a specific good, will find its price higher than expected but, because his expectations are still based on the past inflation rate, he will not realise that the prices of all goods have risen to the same extent. An absolute rise in the price of all goods is therefore confused with a relative price rise for the good that the consumer is considering buying. The consumer may therefore decide to revise, temporarily, his expenditure plans and refrain from buying the good. Since all consumers are in the same position (although not all buying the same good) the aggregate APS declines whenever inflation accelerates, i.e. whenever the actual exceeds the expected inflation rate.

The underlying consumption function in Deaton's model is of the Friedman type and the model is estimated using quarterly US data for 1954–74 and quarterly UK data for 1955–74. The expected inflation rate is, in fact, assumed to be constant so that changes in the APS are made to depend on the actual rate of inflation. Deaton does, indeed, find that, for both countries, changes in the APS are positively related to the inflation rate.

Deaton's results for the US are consistent with those of Juster and Wachtel for a similar period but it is difficult to reconcile them with those of Branson and Klevorick. If the rate of *change* in the APS rises as the rate of price *change* rises, then consumption *levels* must fall as the price *level* rises. This implies a negative δ in equation [10.34] in contrast to the positive value found by Branson and Klevorick. For the UK, similar results concerning the inflation rate were obtained by Townend (1976), although his consumption function also included a liquid assets variable.

The possibility that there may be a link between the rate of inflation and the level of consumer expenditure provides one feasible explanation of a striking feature of consumer behaviour. Many Western economies experienced sharp variations in their saving/income ratios during the 1970s. For example, in the UK the APS (defined as personal saving as a proportion of personal disposable income) had *risen* from approximately 8 per cent during the 1960s to around 14 per cent at the end of the 1970s. However, during the 1980s the APS in the UK steadily *declined* until by 1990 it had fallen as low as 5 per cent.

It is obviously tempting to attribute these variations in the APS to the fact that the UK experienced high and generally accelerating inflation rates during the 1970s but lower and mostly decelerating inflation rates during the 1980s. However, it is by no means clear that there is a direct link. Rather it may be an indirect but no less powerful effect operating via consumer wealth.

The LCH implies that a household's expenditure depends not only on its income but on its total wealth both human and non-human. A household's non-human wealth – that is its financial and physical assets, is held either in assets that are fixed in money terms, such as building society deposits, or as non-money-fixed assets such as stocks and shares. Rapid inflation seriously erodes the real value of that part of a household's wealth that is money-fixed.

During the 1970s, not only did the UK experience rapid inflation but, since this was a decade during which stock market prices generally failed to keep pace with inflation, non-money-fixed assets in household portfolios also tended to decline in real value. Such a decline in real wealth could, then, explain the rising propensity to save during the 1970s.

In contrast, the 1980s was a decade of generally less rapid inflation so that erosion of the value of money-fixed assets was less severe. In addition, share price rises far outstripped rises in the general price level, so that the real value of non-money-fixed assets rose steadily. These factors could, therefore, at least partly explain the falling APS in the UK during the 1980s.

Some early studies of wealth effects

The idea that variables relating to the consumer's stock of non-human wealth should be included in the consumption function can be traced right back to Keynes's *General Theory*. Also, as we have seen, such a variable is assigned an important role in time series estimating equations based on the LCH. Frequently, however, a lack of adequate data on total non-human wealth meant that earlier researchers have had to rely either on the liquid asset component of such wealth or to construct their own series from past data on saving. For example, Townend (1976), using quarterly post-war UK data, found that a liquid assets variable was a significant determinant of non-durable consumption. Stone (e.g. 1964; 1973) constructed wealth data for the UK using the relationship

$$W_t = W_0 + \sum_{i=1}^{t} S_i$$

where W_0 refers to wealth in some 'bench-mark' year for which data is available and S_i is saving in year i. Although data constructed in this way will not reflect changes in wealth arising from 'revaluations' (i.e. capital gains), Stone interpreted his variable as 'permanent wealth' and invariably found it to be significant in his consumer expenditure equations.

A well-known early US time series study of the influence of liquid assets was that of Zellner, Huang and Chau (1965). Basically, they specified a consumption function of the following form

$$C_t = kY_t^p + \alpha(L_{t-1} - L_t^d) + u_t \qquad [10.35]$$

where L_{t-1} stood for liquid asset holdings at the beginning of the current period and L_t^d the desired level of such assets during the current period. If $\alpha > 0$, an asset adjustment process therefore leads to a reduction in consumption when the desired asset stock exceeds the actual asset stock and an increase in consumption if L_t^d is less than L_{t-1}. Y_t^p is permanent income and u_t is a disturbance. Y_t^p was assumed to be determined by an adaptive expectations process identical to equation [10.25] and the desired stock of liquid assets was assumed to be proportional to permanent income, i.e. $L_t^d = \eta Y_t^p$.

Few of the above studies paid much attention to the precise type of consumer behavior that might cause wealth variables to be important. An exception was the model developed by Ball and Drake (1964). Similar ideas had been put forward by Spiro (1962) and were further developed by Clower and Johnson (1968).

In the Ball–Drake model individuals are assumed to be short-sighted in the face of uncertainty and their basic motive for saving is a broad precautionary one. The arguments in the consumer's utility function are current real consumption and current real non-human wealth. That is

$$U_t = U(C_t, W_t) \qquad [10.36]$$

where W_t is wealth at the end of the (short planning) period over which utility is maximised and C_t is consumption during that period. Thus, the consumer does not ignore the future but safeguards against its uncertainties by accumulating wealth. The more wealth he accumulates the more secure he feels and, given his rate of consumption, the more utility he derives. The future is therefore allowed for without making the possibly unrealistic assumption of a rigorous intertemporal utility maximisation required by the LCH and the PIH.

The utility function is maximised subject to the budget constraint

$$W_{t-1} + Y_t = C_t + W_t \qquad [10.37]$$

where W_{t-1} is real wealth at the beginning of the period and Y_t is real income during the period. W_{t-1} and Y_t are taken as given during the maximising process. If [10.36] is assumed to be homothetic then the optimal relationship between C_t and W_t is one of proportionality, i.e. $W_t = hC_t$. Substituting in [10.37] then yields the consumption function

$$C_t = \frac{1}{1+h} Y_t + \frac{1}{1+h} W_{t-1} \qquad [10.38A]$$

or

$$C_t = \frac{1}{1+h} Y_t + \frac{h}{1+h} C_{t-1} \qquad\qquad [10.38B]$$

Aggregating over all consumers, it can be seen that the wealth hypothesis has led to an identical estimating equation for time series data to that obtained both from the PIH and the habit-persistence version of the RIH. C_t is again dependent on Y_t and C_{t-1}. However, in this case an extra prediction is derived – the coefficients in [10.38B] should sum to unity if the wealth hypothesis is valid.

Empirical testing of models such as Ball and Drake's was handicapped, firstly, by the fact that the budget constraint [10.37] makes no allowance for capital gains on the original wealth W_{t-1} made during the planning interval and, secondly, because the lag in equations [10.38A] and [10.38B] is required to be one planning period. The planning period is of course unknown, whereas data is normally either annual or quarterly. Obviously there is no reason why the planning period should be exactly one year or one quarter.

These conceptual difficulties do not represent a fundamental criticism of the Ball–Drake hypothesis. The idea of including current consumption only, together with current wealth, in the utility function remains an attractive one and, for example, Thomas (1981) has attempted to adopt the model to allow for the above difficulties.

10.5 Error correction models of consumption

The argument over whether price changes have a direct effect on consumption or work indirectly via wealth effects is well illustrated by considering the studies of Davidson, Hendry, Srba and Yeo (1978) (henceforth DHSY) and Hendry and Ungern-Sternberg (1980). The DHSY study, in particular, has been on especially influential paper since it represented the first explicit use in this area of the Hendry-type general to specific type methodology described in section 7.2. Also as we noted, early in this chapter, studies of consumer expenditure are frequently plagued by problems of non-stationary regressions and of spurious correlation. In the post-war period particularly, common upward trends in real income and consumption make it impossible to rely on any of the conventional testing procedures when equations are estimated in the levels of these variables. *This criticism applies to virtually all of the empirical studies referred to so far in this chapter.* The DHSY study, however, through its use of error correction models similar to those of Chapter 7, was the first serious study of consumption that attempted to deal with the spurious correlation problem.

DHSY were perplexed that previous investigators of the UK relationship between income and non-durable consumption had come to widely different conclusions regarding, for example, lag structures and short-run marginal propensities to consume. To highlight the issues involved they concentrate on three previous studies – those of Hendry (1974), Ball, *et al.* (1975) and Wall, *et al.* (1975). They aim not only to resolve the conflicts in the three studies but also to discover why the research methods of the three papers led to such different conclusions.

DHSY find that, even when a common sample period of identical non-seasonally adjusted data is used, with identical functional forms and data transformations, the three models still seem to lead to different conclusions. Remaining possible reasons for this are the varying lag structures employed in the three studies and the different estimating methods and test statistics used.

The above standardisation by sample period, etc., enables DHSY to 'nest' the three competing hypotheses as special cases of a general hypothesis or estimating equation. This enables them to test, on purely statistical grounds, which provides the best description of the UK relationship between income and consumption. On the basis of standard statistical criteria such as goodness of fit, the best of the three models appears to be that of Wall, *et al.* which is of the form

$$\Delta C_t = \alpha_0 + \alpha_1 \Delta Y_t + \alpha_2 \Delta Y_{t-1} \qquad \alpha_0 > 0 \qquad [10.39]$$

where ΔC_t and ΔY_t are the quarterly changes in consumption and income.

Unfortunately, the statistically preferred equation [10.39] has some rather strange economic properties. For example, it implies that even if the level of income were to remain constant indefinitely, in which case

$$\Delta Y_t = \Delta Y_{t-1} = 0$$

consumption would continue to rise without limit since under such conditions $\Delta C_t = \alpha_0 > 0$. In other words, equation [10.39] has no static equilibrium solution. Also, the equation implies that the adjustment of consumption to any change in income is complete after just two quarters and, moreover, is apparently independent of any disequilibrium in the previous levels of the variables C_t and Y_t. Normally, when consumption is, for example, 'well above' its equilibrium level relative to income, the increase in C_t accompanying an increase in Y_t can be expected to be much smaller than would have been the case if C_t and Y_t had previously been well adjusted to each other.

The way to resolve the last of the above problems is, of course, to adopt an error correction approach, and, with the aim of reconciling the conflict between statistical and economic criteria DHSY present an error correction model. The equilibrium or steady-state relationship is assumed to be

$$C_t = KY_t \qquad [10.40]$$

or, using lower case letters for natural logarithms

$$c_t = k_t + y_t \qquad [10.41]$$

However, consumption and income are not usually equal to their equilibrium values and we normally observe a 'disequilibrium relationship' involving lagged values of c_t and y_t. DHSY represent this disequilibrium relationship by

$$c_t = k^* + \beta_1 y_t + \beta_2 y_{t-1} + \alpha c_{t-1} \qquad [10.42]$$

The equilibrium or steady state relationship *implied by* [10.42] can be obtained for a constant growth rate g in both consumption and income, by setting

$$c_t = c_{t-1} + g \quad \text{and} \quad y_t = y_{t-1} + g \qquad [10.43]$$

Substituting for y_{t-1} and c_{t-1} in [10.42] we obtain

$$(1 - \alpha)c_t = k^* - g(\beta_2 + \alpha) + (\beta_1 + \beta_2)y_t$$

or

$$c_t = \frac{k^* - g(\beta_2 + \alpha)}{1 - \alpha} + \left(\frac{\beta_1 + \beta_2}{1 - \alpha}\right)y_t \qquad [10.44]$$

For the model to be internally consistent, it is necessary that the equilibrium relationship [10.44] implied by [10.42] should be identical with [10.41]. For this to be so, it is necessary that

$$k = \frac{k^* - g(\beta_2 + \alpha)}{1 - \alpha} \qquad [10.45]$$

and

$$\beta_1 + \beta_2 = 1 - \alpha \qquad [10.46]$$

Equation [10.45] implies that the long run APC, K, is a function of the growth rate g. We noted in section 7.3 that ECM's had the property that long-run parameters were dependent on growth rates. This is particularly appropriate in the present case since, as we have already observed in this chapter, economic growth rates *do* appear, empirically to influence aggregate saving and consumption ratios.

Clearly, if the model is to be consistent, the disequilibrium relationship [10.42] must also satisfy the restriction [10.46]. Imposing this restriction on [10.42] yields

$$c_t = k^* + \beta_1 y_t + \beta_2 y_{t-1} + (1 - \beta_1 - \beta_2)c_{t-1}$$

or

$$c_t - c_{t-1} = k^* + \beta_1(y_t - y_{t-1}) - \gamma[c_{t-1} - y_{t-1}] \quad \text{where } \gamma = 1 - \alpha \quad [10.47]$$

or

$$c_t - c_{t-1} = k^* - k\gamma + \beta_1(y_t - y_{t-1}) - \gamma[c_{t-1} - k - y_{t-1}] \qquad [10.48]$$

Equation [10.48] is a relationship which in equilibrium reduces to [10.41]. Notice, however, that the last term in this equation, $c_{t-1} - k - y_{t-1}$, represents *the extent of disequilibrium* between the levels of consumption and income in the previous period. Equation [10.48] therefore relates changes in consumption not merely to changes in income, as does Wall, *et al.*'s equation [10.39], but also includes, in the terminology of Chapter 7, a disequilibrium error. That is, if previous levels of c_t and y_t satisfy the equilibrium relationship [10.41], then $c_{t-1} = k + y_{t-1}$ and the change in consumption depends only on the change in income. Otherwise it depends also on the extent to which previous levels of c_t and y_t depart from their equilibrium relationship.

Although k in equation [10.41] depends on the long-run growth rate, this growth rate remained relatively constant during Wall, *et al.*'s sample period so that $k \approx$ constant and hence $c_{t-1} - y_{t-1} \approx$ constant. Hence the good statistical performance of Wall, *et al.*'s equation can be explained if it is regarded as an approximation to an equation similar to [10.48]. The constant term in the Wall, *et al.* equation was, for their sample period, able to undertake the role of the required but absent disequilibrium error. Again, using the terminology of Chapter 7, the DHSY model is able to *encompass* Wall, *et al.*'s findings.

Since DHSY use non-seasonally adjusted data, it makes more sense to relate c_t to c_{t-4}, i.e. consumption in the same quarter last year, than to c_{t-1} consumption in the last quarter. Hence, the appropriate lag length in equation [10.48] is four quarters rather than one quarter and for estimating purposes the equation can be rewritten as

$$c_t - c_{t-4} = k^* + \beta_1(y_t - y_{t-4}) - \gamma(c_{t-4} - y_{t-4}) \qquad [10.49]$$

DHSY, in fact, estimate a slightly generalised version of [10.49] with a constant term suppressed

$$c_t - c_{t-4} = \underset{(0.04)}{0.49}(y_t - y_{t-4}) - \underset{(0.05)}{0.17}\Delta_1(y_t - {}^y_{t-4}) - \underset{(0.01)}{0.06}(c_{t-4} - y_{t-4}) + \underset{(0.004)}{0.01}D_t$$

$$R^2 = 0.71 \quad s = 0.0067 \quad d = 1.6 \quad z = 23 \qquad [10.50]$$

where $\Delta_1(y_t - y_{t-4})$ is the quarterly change in $y_t - y_{t-4}$ and D_t is a dummy variable introduced to account for advance warning of purchase tax increases in the second quarter of 1968. s is the standard error of the residuals and z is the Box–Pierce portmanteau autocorrelation statistic described in section 5.2.

DHSY interpret [10.50] in terms of a simple 'feed-back' model whereby consumers plan to spend in any quarter what they spent in the same quarter of the previous year, (i.e. $c_t = c_{t-4}$), but where this quantity is modified by, firstly, a proportion of the annual change in income that has occurred $(0.49[y_t - y_{t-4}])$, secondly, whether that change is itself increasing or decreasing $(-0.17\Delta_1[y_t - y_{t-4}])$, and finally a feedback from the previous C/Y ratio $(-0.06[c_{t-4} - y_{t-4}])$ which ensures coherence with the long-run target outcome $C_t = KY_t$.

Equation [10.50] was estimated for 1958–70. Although data for 1971–75 was available it is used merely for 'post-sample' predictions. Unfortunately, [10.50] consistently overpredicts consumption during this period when, as we noted earlier there was a steady increase in the UK propensity to save. To get round this problem DHSY are forced to invoke the Deaton hypothesis described above and to add price variables to the equation. Their final preferred equation is

$$c_t - c_{t-4} = \underset{(0.04)}{0.47}(y_t - y_{t-4}) - \underset{(0.05)}{0.21}\Delta_1(y_t - y_{t-4}) - \underset{(0.02)}{0.10}(c_{t-4} - y_{t-4})$$

$$+ \underset{(0.003)}{0.01}D_t - \underset{(0.07)}{0.13}(p_t - p_{t-4}) - \underset{(0.15)}{0.28}\Delta_1(p_t - p_{t-4})$$

$$R^2 = 0.77 \quad s = 0.0061 \quad d = 1.8 \quad z = 19 \qquad [10.51]$$

where p_t is the log of the implied consumption deflator (i.e. an index of consumer prices). Equation [10.51] satisfactorily predicts consumption during 1971–75 so DHSY are eventually able to resolve their forecasting problem.

The underlying long-run consumption function implied by [10.51] is easily derived. Assuming a long-run annual growth rate of g in income and consumption and zero long-run inflation we have, using the technique of section 7.3

$$g = 0.47g - 0.10(c_t - y_t)$$

Hence

$$c_t - y_t = -5.3g$$

or

$$C_t = K Y_t \quad \text{where } K = e^{-5.3g} \tag{10.52}$$

Thus a zero-growth or stationary economy has a long-run APC, $K = 1$. That is consistent with the implications of the LCH as outlined at the end of section 10.2. However, the UK economy had a long-run growth rate of about $g = 0.025$ per annum during the 1960s and early 1970s. The long-run function implied by such a growth rate is $C_t = 0.88 Y_t$.

There were, however, some slightly worrying aspects concerning the DHSY study. Firstly, while their basic equation [10.49] is rigorously derived by the addition of disequilibrium effects to underlying theory, the inflation effects are rather awkwardly tagged-on at the end in an *ad hoc* attempt to resolve the forecasting problem. Secondly, it appears that when data for 1958–70 only was available, DHSY felt no need to consider inflation effects. Only when 1971–75 data became available and the forecasting problem emerged were they led to introduce price variables into their equation. We have already pointed out, in Chapter 7, the danger of using *existing* data for checking the adequacy of a model. Proper assessment of any model must necessarily wait until it can be tested against data that was not made use of in its formulation.

Finally, it is possible to show that the importance of the variables $p_t - p_{t-4}$ and $c_{t-4} - y_{t-4}$ in equation [10.51] can be explained in terms of a wealth effect. Intuitively, it can be seen that $c_{t-4} - y_{t-4}$ can be regarded as reflecting changes in wealth that arise from saving, while $p_t - p_{t-4}$ could represent reductions in the real value of money fixed assets resulting from a rise in prices. Indeed, Bean (1978) demonstrated that the size of the coefficients in [10.51] is perfectly consistent with such an interpretation.

The paper by Hendry and Ungern-Sternberg (1980), henceforth HUS, went some way to resolving the above issues. They begin by noting that equations such as [10.47] have a major flaw as a complete account of the dynamic behaviour of flow variables. Since c_t and y_t are rarely equal this means that some latent asset stock must be changing and changes in this stock may itself affect the change in c_t. This, of course, is merely another way of saying that wealth effects may be an influence on consumption.

Wealth or 'culmulative saving' effects are introduced into the model by assuming that consumers seek to maintain constant ratios not only between consumption and income but also between the latent asset stock and income. Thus as well as [10.40] and [10.41] we have another 'equilibrium relationship'

$$A_t = B Y_t \quad \text{or} \quad a_t = b + y_t \tag{10.53}$$

where A_t is the latent asset stock or wealth variable and lower-case letters again represent natural logarithms.

In disequilibrium 'costs' or 'losses' are incurred if c_t or a_t differ from their equilibrium values. The consumer is assumed to minimise a quadratic function of these losses subject to a budget constraint. This eventually leads to an equation of the form

$$c_t - c_{t-1} = \theta_0 + \theta_1(y_t - y_{t-1}) + \theta_2(c_{t-1} - y_{t-1}) + \theta_3(a_{t-1} - y_{t-1}) \tag{10.54}$$

where $\theta_2 < 0$ and $\theta_3 > 0$.

Equation [10.54] is a generalisation of [10.47] since it contains two

273

disequilibrium errors, $c_{t-1} - y_{t-1}$ and $a_{t-1} - y_{t-1}$, the latter reflecting the extent of previous period disequilibrium between the asset stock and income.[10]

Another important aspect of the HUS work is their redefinition of the personal disposable income variable, Y. The normal definition includes interest receipts which, since the personal sector is a substantial net creditor, comprise a not insubstantial proportion of Y. During times of high inflation nominal interest rates rise, thus increasing the interest component of Y. However, such increases are offset by inflation-induced capital losses on monetary assets and such losses are not reflected in Y. Since it seems illogical to include only one but not both of these inflation-induced effects, HUS redefine Y to reflect capital losses on monetary assets. A new income variable $Y^\dagger$ is defined as

$$Y^\dagger = Y - h\dot{p}L \qquad [10.55]$$

In equation [10.55], L is the real stock of liquid assets, used to proxy the stock of monetary assets and $\dot{p}$ is the inflation rate. Thus, $\dot{p}L$ is the capital loss on liquid assets. The parameter, h, is introduced to account for possible scale effects arising from wrongly chosen measures for $\dot{p}$ and L. When disposable income is redefined in this way the apparent fall in the APC during the 1970s becomes much less marked.

HUS begin their empirical work by re-estimating DHSY's equation [10.51] for the period 1962–72 and testing its predictions for 1973–77. The predictions are much less impressive than over the DHSY period and re-estimation over HUS's full sample period confirmed an apparent change in parameter values particularly for the $\Delta_1(p_t - p_{t-4})$ price variable. HUS therefore seek to improve on the DHSY specification by estimating variants of equation [10.54] with liquid assets used to proxy a_{t-1} and income redefined as $Y^\dagger$ as in [10.55]. The value of h is estimated to be in the region of 0.5.

The HUS equation proves superior to the original DHSY specification and also passes the Chow test for predictive failure described in section 4.3. Both disequilibrium variables are significant and the coefficient on $c_{t-4} - y^\dagger_{t-4}$ is nearly twice as large as in the original DHSY specification. The steady state solution to the model is

$$C/Y^\dagger = K_i\left(\frac{L}{Y^\dagger}\right)^{0.44} \quad \text{where } Y^\dagger = Y - \tfrac{1}{2}\dot{p}L$$

and where K_i varies seasonally and also depends on the growth rate.

The significance of the HUS work is that it suggests that inflation rates do not influence the conventionally measured APC directly in the Deaton manner but rather do so via wealth effects and through a mismeasurement of real income. In particular, the importance of a real balance or wealth effect is strongly supported.

10.6 Rational expectations and consumption

Recall that, in its simplest form, time series estimation under the PIH involved estimation of equations such as [10.28] under the implicit assumption that permanent income could be regarded as determined by an adaptive expectations process. We noted in section 6.2 that adaptive expectations implied irrationality on the part of the consumer under circumstances where income was rising continuously over time. The dubious nature and likely instability of 'consumption functions' such as [10.28] was further stressed by Lucas (1976) in his famous critique of econometric policy evaluation. Since a rational consumer is forward looking, changes in government policy that are expected to influence future events will be incorporated into his or her expectations. Under such circumstances defining permanent income in terms of past income levels, whether via the standard adaptive expectations hypothesis or any other method, cannot be successful. The stability of parameters in equations such as [10.28] is highly unlikely to survive changes in government policy. While such consumption equations might prove excellent for short-term forecasting under unchanged policies, they are of little use for evaluating the outcomes of alternative policies.

The Lucas critique heralded a whole series of empirical papers applying the theory of rational expectations to the consumer. Since a stable consumption function was held not to exist, attention was focused on the time profile of consumption alone. Recall that under the LCH the consumer is held to maximise the utility function [10.7] subject to the budget constraint [10.8]. Hall (1978) assumes that [10.7] can be represented by an intertemporally separable function

$$U = u(C_t) + \frac{u(C_{t+1})}{1 + \delta} + \frac{u(C_{t+2})}{(1 + \delta)^2} + \frac{u(C_{t+3})}{(1 + \delta)^3} + \cdots \qquad [10.56]$$

where δ is the subjective rate of discount.

The consumer maximises, subject to the budget constraint [10.8], the expected value of U in [10.56] where the expectation is based solely on the information available at period t which includes knowledge of current consumption, c_T. If expected lifetime utility EU is to be maximised, then it is necessary that

$$\frac{E \, \partial U / \partial C_t}{E \, \partial U / \partial C_{t+i}} = (1 + r)^i \qquad i = 1, 2, 3, \ldots, \qquad [10.57]$$

where E is the expectations operator. Since C_t is known, then for the case $i = 1$ we have using [10.56]

$$\frac{\partial u / \partial C_t}{E \, \partial u / \partial C_{t+1}} = \frac{1 + r}{1 + \delta} \qquad [10.58]$$

Equation [10.58] is sometimes referred to as an *Euler equation*. If we assume

$$u(C_t) = -\tfrac{1}{2}(\bar{C} - C_t)^2 \quad \text{and} \quad u(C_{t+1}) = -\tfrac{1}{2}(\bar{C} - C_{t+1})^2 \qquad [10.59]$$

where $\bar{C}$ is the 'bliss' level of consumption, then marginal utilities are linear and, in particular, $\partial u / \partial C_{t+1} = \bar{C} - C_{t+1}$, so that

$$E \, \partial u / \partial C_{t+1} = \bar{C} - EC_{t+1} \qquad [10.60]$$

The Euler equation [10.58] therefore becomes

$$EC_{t+1} = \frac{(1 + \delta)}{(1 + r)} C_t + \frac{(r - \delta)}{(1 + r)} \bar{C} \qquad [10.61]$$

Actual consumption in period $t + 1$ is

$$C_{t+1} = \frac{(1 + \delta)}{(1 + r)} C_t + \frac{(r - \delta)}{(1 + r)} \bar{C} + \varepsilon_t \qquad [10.62]$$

275

Where ε_t is the consumer's forecast error, $C_{t+1} - EC_{t+1}$. Under rational expectations ε_t must be unpredictable. If the error were predictable given the information available at period t, the consumer would simply revise the forecast. Equation [10.61] implies that all the information available at period t that is necessary for efficient forecasting is encapsuled in the value of current consumption, C_t. If $\delta \approx r$, then we have

$$C_{t+1} - C_t = \varepsilon_t \qquad\qquad [10.63]$$

Equation [10.63] implies that the change is consumption is entirely random and hence cannot be predicted or forecast.[11] This implication of the rational expectations version of the life-cycle/permanent income hypothesis can be tested by regressing the change in consumption on *lagged* variables to see whether it can in fact be forecast. The lagged and not the current values of variables must be used because their values are the only information available at the beginning of the current period.

Hall in his 1978 paper, however, bases his tests on equation [10.62] which, lagging by one period, can be rewritten as

$$C_t = \beta_0 + \beta_1 C_{t-1} + \varepsilon_t \qquad \beta_0 = \frac{(r-\delta)}{(1+r)}\bar{C}, \qquad \beta_1 = \frac{1+\delta}{1+r} \qquad [10.64]$$

The explanatory power of [10.64] is compared with that of equations of the form

$$C_t = \beta_0 + \beta_1 C_{t-1} + \beta_2 C_{t-2} + \beta_3 C_{t-3} + \cdots + u_t \qquad\qquad [10.65]$$

$$C_t = \beta_0 + \beta_1 C_{t-1} + \beta_2 Y_{t-1} + \beta_3 Y_{t-2} + \beta_4 Y_{t-3} + \cdots + v_t \qquad\qquad [10.66]$$

$$C_t = \beta_0 + \beta_1 C_{t-1} + \beta_2 S_{t-1} + \beta_3 S_{t-2} + \beta_4 S_{t-3} + \cdots + w_t \qquad\qquad [10.67]$$

where Y_t is non-property income and S_t is an index of stock market prices used as a proxy for consumer wealth.

If the life-cycle/permanent income hypothesis is valid, then equations [10.65] to [10.67] should have no greater explanatory power than [10.64], since all the information necessary and available to forecast C_t is summed up in the value of C_{t-1}. Remember that, under rational expectations, the consumer has access to all such relevant information and is assumed to make the best use of it. If any of [10.65], [10.66] and [10.67] prove superior to [10.64] then ε_t in [10.64] can be forecast. Hall found that, for quarterly US data for 1948–77, neither the additional variables in [10.65] nor those in [10.66] were significant according to the standard F-test. However, the extra explanation provided by the stock price variables in [10.67] was significant. Moreover, all the coefficients on the stock price variables he included were individually significant according to standard t-tests.

Although Hall's results were a rejection of the pure LCH, he maintained that they were consistent with a slightly modified version of the hypothesis under which part of consumption takes a little time to adjust to permanent income. Most of the extra explanation provided by the stock price variables was due to S_{t-1} and S_{t-2} which Hall claims were correlated with lagged values of permanent income. Hall also stressed, in particular, the non-sensitivity of consumption to lagged income as evidence consistent with the basic idea of the life-cycle/permanent income hypothesis.

276

One of the assumptions underlying Hall's analysis was that the real rate of interest, r can be treated as a constant. However, equation [10.62] clearly indicates that C_{t+1} is influenced not only by C_t but also by the real interest rate. If r is varying and uncertain then the standard LCH suggests that a rise in its value will induce the consumer to substitute future consumption for current consumption. C_{t+1} rises relative to C_t hence the change in consumption becomes larger. Related work using US data (e.g. Hansen and Singleton 1983; Mankiw, Rotemberg and Summers 1985) appeared to suggest significant intertemporal substitution. However, in a later paper, Hall (1988) found no evidence of any relationship between growth rates in consumption and real interest rates and concluded that the intertemporal elasticity of substitution was close to zero.

Hall's conclusions were soon disputed. For example, Flavin (1981), examining the sensitivity of consumption to income, rejected the Hall model, finding consumption 'excessively volatile' relative to the theoretical prediction. In her results the parameter measuring this excess response of consumption to unlagged changes in income was found to have a value of 0.36. Although Flavin's original work has been criticised for its use of detrended data, it is now generally accepted that, for US data at least, the Hall model cannot provide a complete description of consumer behaviour. For example, more recently Campbell and Mankiw (1989) concluded that US data was best regarded as generated by two types of consumer. The first type have their consumption determined by permanent income as in the Hall model, while the second type are 'rule of thumb' consumers whose consumption is determined by their current income. Campbell and Mankiw, however, support the Hall finding that forward-looking consumers engage in practically no intertemporal substitution in response to interest rate changes. They maintain that their model is consistent with three observed empirical regularities – the sensitivity of current consumption to current income, the lack of sensitivity of consumption to real interest rates, and the fact that periods when the APC is high are typically followed by periods of rapid growth in income. This last empirical observation suggests that at least some consumers are forward-looking, increasing consumption in anticipation of increased income.

As far as UK data is concerned, the Hall findings regarding the predictability of current consumption were rejected as early as 1981 in a paper by Daly and Hadjimatheou. Later studies by, for example, Muellbauer (1983) confirmed this rejection. In addition there is some evidence (see, for example, Wickens and Molana 1984) that, in the UK at least, some intertemporal substitution of consumption in response to interest rate changes does occur.

We have seen that for the rational consumer, the forecast error, ε_t, in equation [10.63] should be entirely random and unpredictable. This implies that changes in consumption cannot be forecast and hence are only influenced by *unanticipated* changes in variables such as income or wealth. Under rational expectations the change in consumption cannot be influenced by *anticipated* changes or it would be forecastable. If the consumer realised that his forecast errors were non-random and related to the anticipated value of some variable then he would revise his forecasting procedure until errors were no longer predictable. All this suggests that a test of the rational expectations version of the LCH can be based on a division of actual changes in, for example, income or wealth into anticipated and unanticipated components. If ε_t or changes in consumption are influenced by the anticipated component then this is contrary to the hypothesis.

The obvious problem with this approach is the finding of adequate values for anticipated changes. Suppose we require data on anticipated and unanticipated changes in income. The procedure normally adopted in such cases was outlined at the end of section 6.2 and in this case is as follows. OLS is used to regress actual changes in income on various 'instruments' in an attempt to model the process whereby the consumer actually forms his expectations. Since, under rational expectations, consumers are assumed to have a clear idea of the actual process by which income is determined, the instruments usually reflect underlying theory about this process. Since expectations are formed on the basis of information available in the *current* period, only *lagged* values of the instruments are included in this first-stage regression. The fitted or predicted values from this regression are then taken as the anticipated component of income changes and the residuals as the unanticipated component. The procedure can, of course, be adopted for variables other than income.

Once anticipated and unanticipated components have been obtained, consumption equations are estimated, as the second stage of the procedure, with any contemporaneously dated variables replaced by their two components.[12] Under the rational expectations hypothesis only the unanticipated or 'surprise' components should have coefficients which are statistically significant. Such equations are sometimes referred to as *surprise consumption functions*. Generally speaking, anticipated values have proved to have significant coefficients in such consumption functions, contrary to the rational expectation hypothesis – see, for example, Muellbauer (1983), Blinder and Deaton (1985), Curry, Holly and Scott (1989). However, as Blinder and Deaton point out, there does seem to be some empirical gain from splitting income and wealth variables into anticipated and unanticipated components rather than treating both components as identical in effect.

The fact that the Hall version of the life cycle/permanent income hypothesis appears to be rejected by UK data and, at most, only partially supported by US data has provoked much discussion. It seems agreed that the existence of *liquidity constraints* is a major cause of any breakdown in the hypothesis. Underlying the LCH is the implicit assumption that the consumer can borrow using his financial assets and future income as collateral. However, illiquid assets such as housing wealth and pension fund liabilities are not generally regarded as suitable collateral for loans, and few consumers can borrow to any significant extent simply on the strength of their future earning capability. Consequently, many households find that current consumption is constrained by their current income. The consumption spreading implied by the LCH is not always possible.

The theoretical implications for consumption of the existence of liquidity constraints were first stressed by Pissarides (1978). One method of incorporating them into empirical models is that of Hall and Mishkin (1982) who in their US cross-sectional study, divide the population into two classes of consumer – those whose consumption behaviour is determined by an Euler equation such as [10.58] and those whose consumption, because of liquidity constraints, must increase in line with income. This approach, of course, anticipates that of Campbell and Mankiw mentioned earlier, although these later investigators do not necessarily identify their 'rule of thumb' consumers with those who are liquidity constrained.

An alternative method of allowing for liquidity constraints is actually to include them in the utility maximising process. A consumer then maximises utility subject both to the lifetime budget constant and to the restriction that current consumption cannot (because of liquidity constraints) exceed some given multiple of current income. The Euler equation [10.58] then has to be generalised and the resultant optimality condition involves a Lagrange multiplier, μ_t, corresponding to the liquidity constraint for period t. Only when the liquidity constraint is redundant ($\mu_t = 0$) does the original Euler equation hold. Muellbauer and Bover (1986) adopt this approach. What is most interesting about their work is that after making various approximations and making use of certain proxy variables they are able to arrive at an empirical equation *which is of error-correction form*. This then provides an important link between Hall type permanent income models and the data-based approach discussed in the previous subsection. Such evidence as exists suggests that ECMs are able empirically to out-perform equations based on the Hall specification. The existence of liquidity constraints provides a possible explanation of why this should be so.

10.7   Recent work on UK consumption

As noted earlier, the rise in the UK average propensity to save during the 1970s was steadily reversed during the following decade and at the height of the consumer boom at the end of the 1980s the APS had declined to a value as low as 5 per cent. It became increasingly clear that consumption equations that had forecasted relatively well during the early 1980s had broken down when faced with this unpredicted surge in consumer expenditure. The problem is well illustrated by the work of Carruth and Henley (1990a).

Carruth and Henley estimate alternative consumption equations, using quarterly data for 1969(ii) to 1984(iv), and use them to predict changes in consumption during 1985(i) to 1987(iv). First, they estimate a DHSY specification similar to equation [10.51] except that the $\Delta(p_t - p_{t-4})$ variable proves to have an insignificant coefficient and is therefore omitted. The other coefficients in the equation are very similar to those obtained by DHSY for their earlier sample period, yet the equation badly underpredicts consumption changes for 1985–7. It also fails the Chow test for predictive failure, described in section 4.3.

Secondly, a HUS specification is estimated. This is based on equation [10.54] except that a real interest rate variable is added and total net financial assets are used instead of merely liquid assets. The HUS equation performs better than the DHSY equation but still underpredicts and also fails the Chow test.

Finally, the London Business School version of the HUS equation is tried. This version uses total consumer expenditure (including durables) instead of non-durable consumption and is normally estimated using seasonally adjusted rather than unadjusted data. The HUS wealth variable is also further redefined to include housing wealth as well as net financial assets. This version of HUS works better and passes the Chow test, although there is still some underprediction of consumption change during 1985–7.

Aggregate equations for both durable and non-durable goods are unusual – as we saw in the last chapter, the factors determining the demand for durable goods may differ from those affecting expenditure on non-durables. However, Carruth and Henley's success in redefining wealth to include private housing wealth gives a clue to identifying an important possible factor behind the decline in the APS – that of *housing equity withdrawal* (HEW).

House prices rose rapidly throughout most of the 1970s and 1980s in the UK. However, until recently most owner occupiers were unable to benefit from the paper gains resulting from rising prices. Housing wealth was therefore the most illiquid of assets. The financial liberalisation of the 1980s and, most importantly, the increased availability of new and second mortgages on property already owned, has enabled the owner occupier to realise more easily any capital gain on the house that he owns. It has become increasingly less difficult to 'withdraw equity' from housing wealth.

Curry, Holly and Scott (CHS) in a 1989 paper were among the first to attempt to take account explicitly of HEW. They include in a DHSY type equation the real value of the personal sector housing stock. Another factor they allow for is demographic change. The proportion of the UK population in the age range 45–65 fell steadily from around 25 per cent in 1960 to about 21 per cent in 1988. Since this is the only segment of the population with a positive saving ratio (all others dis-save), its declining importance can be expected to influence aggregate consumption. Hence the proportion of 45–65 year olds is added to the estimating equation.

CHS use quarterly data from 1956(ii)–1985(iv) for original estimation and use 1986–87 data for prediction. The overall fit and predictions of the DHSY equation improve markedly when the HEW and demographic variables are included. A role is also found for nominal interest rate changes. In fact the demographic effect can be detected only when the interest rate variable is included. CHS are therefore able to attribute the fact that previous investigations were unable to uncover a demographic effect to a failure to allow for nominal interest rate changes.

Carruth and Henley (1990b) also draw attention to housing equity withdrawal as a possible cause of increased consumer expenditure. They concentrate on the HEW that is possible when houses are sold. A series for 'liquid housing wealth' is constructed as TW_h where W_h is the real value of the privately owned housing stock and T is the proportion of this housing stock that is bought and sold during the relevant period. Housing is thus treated as a liquid asset only at the point of sale. HEW is defined as some constant proportion of liquid housing wealth. That is

$$HEW = \delta TW_h \qquad 0 < \delta < 1 \qquad\qquad [10.68]$$

Carruth and Henley then proceed to estimate an HUS equation of the type [10.54] in which disposable income *is further redefined to include HEW*. However, HEW is assumed only to occur during housing market upswings when house prices are rising. The HUS definition [10.55] therefore becomes

$$Y^\dagger = Y - h\dot{P}W + \delta DTW_h \qquad\qquad [10.69]$$

where D is a dummy variable taking the value unity during market upswings but zero during downswings. W in equation [10.69] refers to total real personal wealth as opposed to liquid assets in the original HUS specification.

The equation is estimated from quarterly data for 1971(iv) to 1986(i) and is able successfully to predict changes in consumption during 1986(ii) to 1989(i). It also passes the Chow test for predictive failure. The estimate of δ in [10.69]

280

obtained by the maximum likelihood method is around 0.1, implying that 10 per cent of housing equity tends to be withdrawn and spent when a house is sold.

Carruth and Henley's equation relates to total consumer expenditure on both non-durable and durable goods as did their final equation in their other paper mentioned earlier. Furthermore, many economists would also consider as strange their treatment of the gains from house price rises as an addition to consumer income rather than an addition to consumer wealth.

At the time of writing, one of the most thorough investigations of the factors behind the UK consumer boom of the late 1980s is the 1989 study of Muellbauer and Murphy (MM). MM attribute the decline in the APS at this time to three main factors.

1. Consumers experienced big increases in the ratios of financial assets and physical assets to disposable income. The LCH implies that this must lead to a decline in the APS.
2. The 1980s was a decade of increasing financial liberalisation, marked by the gradual elimination of credit rationing. This had two effects. First, the number of households whose expenditure was constrained by an inability to acquire credit steadily declined throughout the decade. Secondly, financial liberalisation and factors such as HEW led to a gradual increase in the 'fungibility' of illiquid assets such as housing and land. That is, the distinction between liquid and illiquid assets became less clear-cut with more opportunity arising to reduce net holdings of the latter in order to finance consumption.
3. The 1980s were years of reduced uncertainty following the sharp economic fluctuations of the 1970s and the 1980–1 recession. This reduction in uncertainty reduced the need for precautionary saving.

The basic structure of the MM model is as follows. It contains separate equations for consumers whose expenditure is constrained by the amount of credit they obtain and for consumers who are not constrained in this way. A weighted average of these equations is in fact estimated, that is the change in total expenditure on non-durable goods and services is given by

$$\Delta \log C_t = \Pi \Delta \log C_t^c + (1 - \Pi) \Delta \log C_t^u \qquad [10.70]$$

where $\Delta \log C_t^c$ and $\Delta \log C_t^u$ are the changes in consumption of constrained and unconstrained consumers respectively and Π is the proportion of consumers constrained by credit.

Π in equation [10.70] is allowed to fall during the 1980s as financial liberalisation proceeds. MM introduce a financial liberalisation dummy, FLIB, taking the value zero up until 1981 but then rising in irregular steps to unity by 1989. Π is then determined by

$$\Pi_t = \Pi_0 - \Pi_1(\text{FLIB})_t \qquad 0 < \Pi_0 < 1, \qquad 0 < \Pi_1 < 1 \qquad [10.71]$$

Thus the proposition of constrained households falls from Π_0 in 1981 to $\Pi_0 - \Pi_1$ by 1989. Π_1 is left to be determined by the data.

In equation [10.70] the change in consumption of unconstrained consumers, $\Delta \ln C_t^u$, is assumed to be determined by a first-order ECM – first order because the data used is annual. The equilibrium or long-run relationship in this ECM is based on a generalised LCH equation. As noted in the last subsection, a basic assumption of the LCH is that consumers are free to borrow up to the limit of their future expected income, paying off their debts in future years. For unconstrained consumers this assumption is, by definition, valid.

The LCH variables in the equilibrium relationship for unconstrained consumers include the real rate of interest and the ratios of liquid assets to income and illiquid assets to income. However, *the size of the coefficient on illiquid assets is allowed to increase over time* to reflect the increasing fungibility of these assets during the 1980s. The FLIB dummy described above is employed for this purpose.

The LCH cannot apply to consumers who are constrained by credit restrictions – if it did then such consumers could not be regarded as constrained. For contrained consumers the life-cycle variables are therefore replaced by k = ratio of debt to income that is permitted by lending institutions. Since data on k is unavailable, it is proxied by the nominal interest rate. The larger is the nominal interest rate, the smaller is k and hence the tighter is credit. The change in the consumption of constrained consumers, $\Delta \ln C_t^c$ in equation [10.70] is assumed to depend on the change in their income and the change in the nominal interest rate. Note that an error correction model is not used for constrained consumers, since their consumption is regarded as always being at its target level – they are fully adjusted to their credit constraint.

MM estimate a generalised version of [10.70] by an instrumental variable method with further variables, representing demographic change, the incidence of long-term strikes, the relative price of non-durable goods (compared with durables) and real income uncertainty added. Real income uncertainty is proxied by the standard deviation of real income change during the past four years. Annual data for 1957–88 is used, partly because of inadequate quarterly wealth data prior to 1966, and partly because MM believe that the limited additional information content in quarterly as opposed to annual data means that a longer annual data set is preferable to a shorter quarterly one. An interesting aspect of the estimation process is that to conserve degrees of freedom, MM impose *a priori* values on certain parameters. For example, Π_0 the consumption share of constrained households between 1957 and 1981 is set equal to 0.2 and the long-run income elasticity is set equal to 0.95. Also since MM could find no significant real interest rate effects, they eventually set both short and long-run real interest rate elasticities equal to zero.

The MM model fits the data extremely well for 1957–81 and is also able to explain the rise in consumption during 1982–8 *once the consumption share of credit constrained consumers and the size of the coefficient on illiquid assets are allowed to vary over time.* MM in fact deduce that, while long run total consumption rose by 14 per cent during 1982–88 because of a 15 per cent rise in real income, it rose by 22 per cent because of a rise in the ratio of illiquid assets to income. This 22 per cent rise is the result of three factors:

1. the rise from 3.6 to 5.7 in the illiquid assets to income ratio (the result of, for example, rapid rises in house prices), compounded by
2. an increase of 43 per cent in the size of the long-run coefficient on the illiquid assets to income ratio during 1982–8. This reflects the increasing importance of illiquid assets in determining the consumption of unconstrained consumers;
3. although the illiquid assets to income ratio affects only unconstrained consumers, the proportion, $1-\Pi$, of such households was estimated to have increased from 80 to 96 per cent during 1982–8.

MM also deduce from their estimated model that consumption increased 3.5 per cent during 1982–8 because of reduced real income uncertainty, but actually fell 3.2 per cent because of a substitution effect caused by a rise in the price of non-durable relative to durable goods. Demographic changes are found to have a minor but statistically significant effect. MM are able to detect no significant direct effect on consumption for either real or nominal interest rates. However, they conjecture that indirect effects via illiquid asset prices must be large. For example, sharp rises in interest rates have an important, if lagged, effect on the rate of house price inflation.

In a follow up to their (1989) paper, Curry, Holly and Scott (1990) apply the co-integration technique described in section 7.5 to the analysis of UK consumption expenditure. Using quarterly data for 1957(i) to 1988(iv), they demonstrate that, allowing for a changing seasonal pattern in consumption, consumption, personal disposable income and consumer wealth are all integrated of order unity, that is they all become stationary on first differencing. A co-integrating vector is then obtained between consumption, income and three components of consumer wealth – liquid assets, illiquid financial assets and net housing wealth. This vector is then treated as the long-run consumption function and used to form the error correction term in a short-run relationship. Thus the dynamics of the consumption function are estimated by what, in essence, is the two-stage Engle–Granger procedure described in section 7.5.

The ECM estimated by CHS successfully explains the consumption boom of the late 1980s. Nearly half the surge in consumption is explained by the rise in income, 20 per cent by the increase in liquid asset holdings, 17 per cent by increased illiquid assets and 8 per cent by increased housing wealth. The fall in inflation accounts for 8 per cent of the rise in consumption and the changing age structure of the population a further 3 per cent. However, CHS find that the effect of financial liberation has been, not so much to increase the fungibility of illiquid assets as suggested by MM, but rather to allow illiquid assets to be more readily converted into liquid assets. They find no evidence that the MPC illiquid assets increased during the 1980s. Experiments with MM's FLIB dummy prove to be unsuccessful. This CHS study differs from that of MM in two further ways. First, as in the 1989 CHS study, nominal interest rates are found to influence consumption directly, and, secondly, no role can be found for the measures of income uncertainty used by MM.

CHS conclude that the major explanation for the 1980s consumer boom was the acceleration in the growth of wealth, particularly illiquid wealth. Combined with increased opportunities for switching from illiquid to liquid wealth, this surge in wealth led to the rapid increase in consumption.

10.8 Conclusions

There are a number of competing hypotheses concerning the consumption function, all to a greater or lesser extent, intuitively appealing on *a priori* grounds. However, given all the empirical evidence that has been accumulated over the past forty years, most economists would probably support some version of the PIH or LCH, albeit qualified by the existence of liquidity constraints on some consumers, as being the most likely explanation of observed consumer behaviour. It is certainly generally accepted that consumption cannot be explained by either current income alone, as suggested by the original AIH, or by permanent income alone.

US data appears best explained by a model in which the majority of consumers behave as the LCH predicts but a sizeable minority have their consumption constrained by *current* income. The existence of liquidity constraints is the most favoured explanation for this. In the UK too, the Muellbauer–Murphy results suggest that liquidity constraints are important, although the proportion of consumers who are constrained in this way appears to have declined during the 1980s.

Certainly as far as the UK is concerned, it now seems accepted that non-human wealth should be included explicitly in consumption equations as in the LCH, rather than be included in total wealth and annuitised as in the PIH. Real wealth effects are seen as an important channel whereby the inflation rate influences consumer expenditure. What is not yet clear is the appropriate definition for the non-human wealth variable that is to be included in consumption equations – for example should physical wealth such as housing be included? It is also not yet clear whether inflation has any additional effect on consumption over and above that operating via real wealth.

Another issue over which there is still much argument is the responsiveness of consumption to interest rate changes. Even economists who claim that interest rate effects are significant are divided over whether they have a direct effect on consumption or an indirect effect via asset prices.

Perhaps the most worrying aspect of empirical work on aggregate consumption is the regularity with which apparently established equations break down when faced with new data. This has happened repeatedly in the UK since the 1970s. As stressed by Hendry, there may be no such thing as a perfect model and we must expect existing models always to be capable of empirical improvement. But the reader can be forgiven for wondering whether econometricians will ever reach the stage where even in the short run their consumption equations survive the confrontation with new data.

Appendix A: Empirical exercise

In this exercise we shall examine the relationship between consumer expenditure, disposable income and the rate of inflation. However, before attempting to model any short-term relationship between these variables, we use the co-integration techniques described in section 7.5. to determine whether a stable long-term relationship exists. We use annual time series data for 1956 to 1985, defining the following variables

Consumption C = consumer expenditure on non-durable goods and services in 1985 prices
Income Y = disposable income in 1985 prices
Price level P = implied deflator of consumption
Inflation rate = $\Delta \ln P_t = \ln P_t - \ln P_{t-1}$.

Remember that the log-change of a variable is a close approximation to the proportionate change. We use the symbol ln to denote a natural logarithm

All data is taken from ETAS 1990. C can be obtained by subtracting the figures for durable-good expenditure from those for total expenditure using the series on page 45. A similar series for non-durable expenditure in current prices can be constructed using the data on page 42. P can then be constructed by dividing consumption in current prices by consumption in 1985 prices. Remember, the data transformation routines in your programme will do these calculations for you once you have inputted the basic data. Disposable income, Y, can be found on page 35. The final data set used for the exercise can be found at the end of this appendix.

Working throughout in natural logarithms, we first attempt to determine the 'order of integration' of our basic time series, $\ln C$, $\ln Y$ and $\ln P$. That is, we test whether these series are stationary in their levels, or whether they have to be differenced once or maybe even twice before they can be regarded as stationary. Let us deal first with the income series.

To test $\ln Y$ for stationarity we compute an augmented Dickey–Fuller regression of the type [7.57]. The idea is to include as many Δy terms as are necessary to ensure that the residuals from the regression are non-autocorrelated. However, in practice it is often difficult to decide how many terms to include. Consequently, it is best to calculate the augmented Dickey–Fuller (ADF) statistic for a number of such regressions. As noted in Chapter 7, these tests are not precise and must be used with care and scepticism, particularly since in this case we have a sample of just 25 observations. In the present case typical ADF regressions are

$$\Delta y_t = 3.73 + 0.007T - 0.31y_{t-1} + 0.22\Delta y_{t-1} - 0.30\Delta y_{t-2} - 0.37\Delta y_{t-3}$$
$$\quad (2.43) \quad (0.005) \quad (0.21) \quad (0.20) \quad (0.23) \quad (0.21)$$

$$R^2 = 0.45, \quad Z11 = 0.58, \quad Z14 = 3.20 \quad (1961\text{--}85) \qquad [A10.1]$$

and

$$\Delta y_t = 6.10 + 0.012T - 0.52y_{t-1} + 0.38\Delta y_{t-1}$$
$$\quad (1.97) \quad (0.004) \quad (0.17) \quad (0.19)$$

$$R^2 = 0.35, \quad Z11 = 0.15, \quad Z14 = 3.78 \quad (1961\text{--}85) \qquad [A10.2]$$

where lower case letters as usual denote the natural logarithms of variables. The equations are estimated for 1961–85 because the 1956–61 data is needed to compute the required lagged values.

$Z11$ and $Z14$ represent the LM statistics for first and up to fourth order autocorrelation in the residuals. Since the 0.05 critical levels for χ^2 (with 1 and 4 d.f. respectively) are 3.84 and 9.49, there is no evidence of autocorrelation problems in either [A10.1] or [A10.2].

The idea of the Dickey–Fuller tests is to reject the null hypothesis that y is non-stationary if the coefficients on y_{t-1} in the above equations are significantly less than zero. The 't-ratios' on these coefficients (that is the ADF statistics) are -1.5 in [A10.1] and -3.1 in [A10.2]. Remember, however, that we cannot compare these numbers with the critical values from normal t-tables but must compare them with the values given on the right-hand side of Table 7.1. Clearly, the absolute values of these ADF statistics are not large enough to justify rejecting the hypothesis of non-stationarity even at the 10 per cent level. The income variable, y, does not appear to be stationary. It is normal at this point to test the joint hypothesis that the coefficients on T and y_{t-1} in the above equations are both zero. If we fail to reject this hypothesis then we are justified in regarding Δy as being determined only by lagged values of itself and a disturbance. That is, it is not subject to a 'deterministic trend'. The normal F-test for this joint hypothesis yields values of 3.3 in [A10.1] and 5.0 in [A10.2]. These figures, however, must be compared with the critical values in Table 7.2 rather than those in normal F-tables. Clearly, we cannot reject the joint null hypothesis. ΔY appears to be determined solely by past values of itself.

Even if Δy depends only on its own past values and a disturbance, it may still be non-stationary. To test this we estimate Dickey–Fuller equations of the types [7.44], [7.56] and [7.57] for $\Delta^2 y_t = \Delta y_t - \Delta y_{t-1}$, the second difference in income. This results in, for example,

$$\Delta^2 y_t = \underset{(0.02)}{0.04} - \underset{(0.001)}{0.001T} - \underset{(0.26)}{1.12\Delta y_{t-1}} + \underset{(0.20)}{0.35\Delta^2 y_{t-1}}$$

$$R^2 = 0.51, \qquad Z11 = 1.22, \qquad Z14 = 7.89 \qquad (1961–85) \qquad \text{[A10.3]}$$

and

$$\Delta^2 y_t = - \underset{(0.16)}{0.45\Delta y_{t-1}}$$

$$\underset{}{\qquad} Z11 = 0.12, \qquad Z14 = 2.22 \qquad (1961–85) \qquad \text{[A10.4]}$$

No R^2 value is given for [A10.4] because the intercept has been dropped.

The 't-ratios' for the coefficients on Δy_{t-1}, that is the ADF and DF statistics, are -4.3 in [A10.3] and -2.8 in [A10.4]. Comparison with the values in Table 7.1, (the right-hand side values in the table for [A10.3] but left-hand side values for [A10.4] because of the absence of constant and time trend), indicates that we can reject the hypothesis that Δy is non-stationary.

The above tests suggest that, although our income data series is non-stationary, it becomes stationary after first differencing once only. The series is therefore said to be integrated of order one. That is y is I(1). You should now apply the augmented Dickey–Fuller test to the data series for consumption and the first difference of consumption. If you work again in logarithms you should have no difficulty in demonstrating that, although c is non-stationary, Δc, its first difference, appears to be stationary. That is, like y, the series c is I(1), integrated of order one.

We now consider the inflation rate. However, since this is defined as Δp, that is the first difference of the log of the price level, you should first test p for stationarity. You will find that you cannot reject the null hypothesis of non-stationarity of p. The ADF statistics for equations of type [7.57] are between -2 and -3.

To test the inflation rate itself for stationarity, we estimate augmented Dickey–Fuller equations for $\Delta^2 p = \Delta p_t - \Delta p_{t-1}$, that is the first difference of the inflation rate. This yields, for example,

$$\Delta^2 p_t = \underset{(0.017)}{0.015} + \underset{(0.0012)}{0.0005T} - \underset{(0.18)}{0.30\Delta p_{t-1}} + \underset{(0.23)}{0.21\Delta^2 p_{t-1}}$$

$$R^2 = 0.16, \qquad Z11 = 0.12, \qquad Z14 = 2.21 \qquad (1961–85) \qquad \text{[A10.5]}$$

and

$$\Delta^2 p_t = 0.019 + 0.000T - 0.22\Delta p_{t-1}$$
$$ (0.017) \quad (0.001) \quad (0.15)$$

$$R^2 = 0.13, \quad Z11 = 0.93, \quad Z14 = 2.02 \quad (1961-85) \qquad [A10.6]$$

The ADF statistics are the 't-ratios' on the coefficients of Δp_{t-1}, and take the values -1.7 in [A10.5] and -1.5 in [A10.6]. In absolute value these are clearly below the critical values in Table 7.1, so we cannot reject the hypothesis that the inflation rate is non-stationary. The F-statistics for the joint hypothesis that the coefficients of the time trend and Δp_{t-1} are both zero are 1.97 in [A10.5] and 1.62 in [A10.6]. The values in Table 7.2 indicate that the joint hypothesis cannot be rejected. It appears then that the change in the inflation rate depends only on past values of itself and a disturbance.

Finally, we test the first difference of the inflation rate, $\Delta^2 p_t = \Delta p_t - \Delta p_{t-1}$, which is the same as the second difference of the price level, for stationarity. To do this we compute augmented Dickey–Fuller regressions for $\Delta^3 p_t = \Delta^2 p_t - \Delta^2 p_{t-1}$. We obtain, for example,

$$\Delta^3 p_t = 0.02 - 0.001T - 0.98\Delta^2 p_{t-1}$$
$$ (0.02) \quad (0.001) \quad (0.21)$$

$$R^2 = 0.49, \quad Z11 = 0.23, \quad Z14 = 3.96 \quad (1961-85) \qquad [A10.7]$$

and

$$\Delta^3 p_t = -0.94\Delta^2 p_{t-1}$$
$$ (0.20)$$

$$\text{\underline{}} \quad Z11 = 0.95, \quad Z14 = 2.49 \quad (1961-85) \qquad [A10.8]$$

The DF statistics now refer to the variables $\Delta^2 p_{t-1}$ and take the values -4.7 in [A10.7] and -4.7 in [A10.8]. As the critical values in Table 7.1 confirm, we can reject the hypothesis that the first difference of the inflation rate is non-stationary.

Our results indicate that the first difference of the inflation rate, i.e. the second difference of p, is stationary. Hence p is integrated of order two and the inflation rate is integrated of order one. That is p is I(2) but Δp is I(1). In fact inspection of equation [A10.8] suggests that the inflation rate could be modelled by as simple a stochastic process as $\Delta^2 p_t = \varepsilon_t$ or $\Delta p_t = \Delta p_{t-1} + \varepsilon_t$, that is as a simple 'random walk'.

Although, as we have stressed before, the Dickey–Fuller tests for stationarity have to be applied with caution, we do now seem to have established that our income, consumption and inflation variables are all integrated of order one. Plots of the variables and their first differences against time should confirm this. This means that it is possible that two or maybe all three of these variables are co-integrated and that a long-run relationship exists between them. However, co-integration is not a certainty. To test for co-integration we need to compute static regressions, involving the three variables, and then check to determine whether the residuals from these regressions are stationary or not. Only if such residuals form a stationary series do we have co-integration.

We shall estimate two static regressions, one with just income as a regressor and the other with both income and the inflation rate as regressors. These equations are estimated for 1957–85. The 1956 value for price is required to calculate the 1957 value for the inflation rate. We obtain

$$c_t = 1.794 + 0.838y_t \qquad R^2 = 0.996 \qquad (1957\text{–}85) \qquad [\text{A}10.9]$$
$$(0.115) \quad (0.010)$$

$$c_t = 1.672 + 0.848y_t - 0.073\Delta p_t \qquad R^2 = 0.997 \qquad (1957\text{–}85) \quad [\text{A}10.10]$$
$$(0.142) \quad (0.012) \qquad (0.051)$$

No diagnostic statistics are quoted for the static regressions.[13] Firstly, they would not be valid and, secondly, the absence of any lagged terms in [A10.9] and [A10.10] means that the residuals in these equations are almost certain to be autocorrelated anyway. The point is that if these residuals form stationary autocorrelated series then the variables are co-integrated and OLS will still provide consistent estimates of long-run parameters.

To test the residuals, e, for stationarity we need to compute augmented Dickey–Fuller regressions of the form [7.61] (that is without intercept or time trend). We shall use Δe terms lagged up to four periods. We have available, for testing, residuals for 1957–85, so we shall estimate equations for 1962–85. The residuals for 1957–61 are needed to compute the lagged Δe terms. We consider first the residuals from equation [A10.9]. Again the Dickey–Fuller tests are not precise, lack power, and must be applied with discrimination. It is not always clear how many Δe terms should be included, so the tests should be applied to a number of equations. For the residuals of [A10.9] we obtain, for example,

$$\Delta e_t = -0.72e_{t-1} + 0.41\Delta e_{t-1} + 0.18\Delta e_{t-2} + 0.25\Delta e_{t-3} + 0.10\Delta e_{t-4}$$
$$(0.32) \qquad (0.29) \qquad (0.27) \qquad (0.24) \qquad (0.24)$$

$$\text{------} \quad Z11 = 0.43, \qquad Z14 = 4.75 \qquad (1962\text{–}85) \qquad [\text{A}10.11]$$

and

$$\Delta e_t = -0.48e_{t-1} + 0.22\Delta e_{t-1}$$
$$(0.19) \qquad (0.22)$$

$$\text{------} \quad Z11 = 0.08, \qquad Z14 = 0.34 \qquad (1962\text{–}85) \qquad [\text{A}10.12]$$

The LM statistics suggest no autocorrelation either of first order or of up to fourth order in either equation. The ADF statistic is computed as the 't-ratio' on the e_{t-1} variable and takes the value -2.3 in [A10.11] and the value -2.5 in [A10.12]. Remember that, when testing for co-integration, critical values for the ADF statistic are those given in Table 7.3 rather than those in Table 7.1. In this case the ADF statistic is not sufficiently negative for us to reject the hypothesis that the residuals from equation [A10.9] are non-stationary. Hence the variables c and y, although they are both I(1), cannot be shown to be cointegrated. It therefore appears that no long-run relationship necessarily exists between c and y alone.

We now test the residuals from the static regression [A10.10] for stationarity.

In this case augmented Dickey–Fuller regressions are, for example,

$$\Delta e_t = -0.71 e_{t-1} + 0.24 \Delta e_{t-1} + 0.17 \Delta e_{t-2} + 0.30 \Delta e_{t-3} + 0.08 \Delta e_{t-4}$$
$$(0.30)(0.27)(0.25)(0.23)(0.22)$$

$$\underline{}\quad Z11 = 0.86, \qquad Z14 = 6.71 \qquad (1962\text{–}85) \hspace{2cm} [A10.13]$$

and

$$\Delta e_t = -0.46 e_{t-1}$$
$$(0.17)$$

$$\underline{}\quad Z11 = 0.25, \qquad Z14 = 3.35 \qquad (1962\text{–}85) \hspace{2cm} [A10.14]$$

The *LM* statistics indicate no autocorrelation problems in the above equations even when no terms in Δe are included. However, the ADF statistics are again too small in absolute value to suggest co-integration. They take the values -2.4 in [A10.13] and -2.7 in [A10.14]. So the variables c, y and Δp cannot be shown to be co-integrated and hence no long-term relationship necessarily exists between them.

At this point we stress again that, especially in this case given the smallness of our sample, the Dickey–Fuller tests are imprecise and lack power. Thus our failure to reject non-stationarity of the residuals in [A10.9] and [A10.10] is by no means conclusive. A long-run relationship between c, y and Δp could still exist, we merely having failed to detect it on this occasion. Maybe, however, the fact that we were unable to show that income, consumption and the inflation rate were co-integrated should not surprise us. We know from our discussion in the main part of this chapter that wealth and/or interest rate variables are almost certain to enter into any long-run consumption function for the UK. We might well find a set of variables, expanded to include measures of consumer wealth and ability to borrow, to be co-integrated. You should try computing static regressions including, for example, a liquid assets variable, and testing the residuals obtained for stationarity. Liquid assets and other wealth series can be found in the CSO publication 'Financial Statistics'. Remember though to check first that your liquid assets series is I(1).

Although we suspect that there may be no long-run relationship between income, consumption and the inflation rate, it will nevertheless be interesting to adopt the general to specific approach to the estimation of a short-run equation for consumer expenditure. The Granger representation theorem discussed at the end of section 7.5 suggests that, since we were unable to show that our variables are co-integrated, the short-run consumption equation may not be of ECM form.

Since we are dealing with annual data, we adopt a general model with up to just second-order lags before starting our simplication search. Estimation of such a model yields

$$c_t = -0.279 + 0.907 c_{t-1} + 0.164 c_{t-2} + 0.513 y_t - 0.479 y_{t-1} + 0.079 y_{t-2}$$
$$(0.308)(0.283)(0.277)(0.070)(0.130)(0.150)$$

$$-0.107 \Delta p_t + 0.065 \Delta p_{t-1} + 0.059 \Delta p_{t-2} \qquad (1959\text{–}85)$$
$$(0.055)(0.078)(0.041)$$

$$R^2 = 0.999, \ \sum e^2 = 0.000\,556, \ dw = 1.94, \ Z11 = 0.002, \ Z14 = 4.45, \ Z2 = 0.47$$
$$\hspace{10cm} [A10.15]$$

Equation [A10.15] has to be estimated for 1959–85 because the data for 1956–58 is needed to construct the various lagged terms.

There are no problems with the autocorrelation statistics in the above equation. $Z2$ represents the LM statistic for heteroscedasticity covered in section 5.2 and is distributed as χ^2 with 1 d.f. It indicates that we cannot reject the hypothesis of homoscedastic residuals. If your program enables you to carry out the RESET test for functional form mis-specification, described at the end of Chapter 7.1, verify that with just $\hat{c}^2$ included among the regressors the RESET statistic comes to 1.03. Since this statistic is also distributed as χ^2 with 1 d.f. under the null hypothesis, there are clearly no problems of functional form.

Our diagnostic statistics suggests that [A10.15] is a satisfactory general model and that we do not, for example, need to include any higher order lagged terms. Remember that the LM statistics for autocorrelation can also be regarded as diagnostic statistics for possible dynamic mis-specification.

A number of coefficients in [A10.15] have low t-ratios, particularly c_{t-2}, y_{t-2} and Δp_{t-1}. An obvious way to start the testing down procedure or simplication search is therefore to drop c_{t-2}, y_{t-2} and Δp_{t-1} from the equation. This yields

$$c_t = -0.233 + 1.054c_{t-1} + 0.504y - 0.537y_{t-1} - 0.135\Delta p_t$$
$$\quad (0.233) \quad (0.128) \qquad (0.055) \quad (0.088) \qquad (0.029)$$

$$+ 0.034\Delta p_{t-2} \quad (1959\text{–}85)$$
$$\quad (0.029)$$

$$R^2 = 0.999, \ \sum e^2 = 0.000\,586, \ dw = 2.10, \ Z11 = 0.32, \ Z14 = 4.37, \ Z2 = 0.0055$$

$$[A10.16]$$

The LM statistics in [A10.16] still indicate no specification problems. We can use the residual sums of squares in [A10.15] and [A10.16] to F-test the dropping of the variables c_{t-2}, y_{t-2} and Δp_{t-1}. Since each variable omitted is equivalent to the imposing of one restriction on [A10.15] we have three restrictions to test in all. The test statistic [4.45] therefore takes the value

$$\frac{(\text{SSR}_R - \text{SSR}_u)/3}{\text{SSR}_u/(n-k)} = \frac{(586 - 556)/3}{556/(27-9)} = 0.32$$

Since the critical F-value with (3, 18) d.f. is $F_{0.05} = 3.16$, dropping the variables is clearly data acceptable. Examination of the t-ratios in equation [A10.16] suggests we can also drop the variable Δp_{t-2} from our equation. This yields

$$c_t = -0.249 + 1.031c_{t-1} + 0.512y_t - 0.520y_{t-1} + 0.124\Delta p_t$$
$$\quad (0.234) \quad (0.128) \qquad (0.056) \quad (0.088) \qquad (0.028)$$

$$R^2 = 0.999, \ \sum e^2 = 0.000\,624, \ dw = 2.10, \ Z11 = 0.19, \ Z14 = 7.12, \ Z2 = 0.13$$

$$[A10.17]$$

Notice, next, that the coefficient on c_{t-1} in equation [A10.17] is very close to unity and that the coefficients on y_t and y_{t-1} are very similar but of opposite sign. Firstly, this suggests strongly that we can replace the dependent variable c_t by Δc_t and eliminate c_{t-1} from the right-hand side of equation [A10.17].

Secondly, it suggests that we replace the variables y_t and y_{t-1} by a single regressor, Δy_t. Imposing these two restrictions yields

$$\Delta c_t = \underset{(0.003)}{0.015} + \underset{(0.049)}{0.505\Delta y_t} + \underset{(0.025)}{0.083\Delta p_t}$$

$$R^2 = 0.884, \ \sum e^2 = 0.000\,815, \ dw = 1.67, \ Z11 = 0.24, \ Z14 = 4.41, \ Z2 = 0.54$$

[A10.18]

Our diagnostic statistics show no real sign of deterioration and, although R^2 is lower in [A10.18] than in [A10.17], this is not surprising as now we are attempting to explain variations in Δc, whereas previously our dependent variable was c. A more important comparison is of the $\sum e^2$s which we can use to F-test whether the two latest restrictions imposed are data acceptable. Treating [A10.17] as the unrestricted and [A10.18] as the restricted equation, the F-statistic [4.45] yields a value of 3.21. Since the critical F-value, with $(2, 22)$ d.f., is $F_{0.05} = 3.44$, we do not reject the restrictions.

Since all the coefficients in [A10.18] have sufficiently high t-ratios (5.00, 10.31 and -3.32 respectively, whereas the critical value for t with 24 d.f. is $t_{0.05} = 1.711$), this is the final preferred equation we arrive at by the general to specific approach. We can check whether all six restrictions we have imposed are data acceptable, when considered together, by comparing the residual sums of squares for the general model [A10.15] with that for [A10.18]. The F-test this time yields a value of 1.40 compared with a critical value, with $(6, 18)$ d.f., of 2.66. All our restrictions thus appear to be data acceptable.

Our final preferred equation, however, is rather a strange one. It is certainly not an error correction model because it contains only differenced variables. Moreover it implies that, for zero inflation and zero income growth rate ($\Delta y = \Delta p = 0$), the growth rate in consumption is still positive. That is $\Delta c = 0.015$ or 1.5 per cent per annum. Consumption continues to rise indefinitely even when income is unchanging! What this means in technical terms is that [A10.18] has no long-run or stationary solution. But this is not altogether surprising given the findings of our earlier co-integration analysis. This cast doubt on whether a long-run or equilibrium relationship existed between the three variables income, consumption and inflation rate.

The reader may ask what might have happened if we had actually searched for an error correction representation of the short-run relationship between our variables. ECMs of course imply the existence of a long-run relationship. Our general model [A10.15] can in fact be reparameterised as a second-order ECM. If it is re-estimated in this form we obtain

$$\Delta c = \underset{(0.308)}{-0.279} + \underset{(0.283)}{0.093\Delta c_{t-1}} + \underset{(0.070)}{0.513\Delta y_t} + \underset{(0.152)}{0.035\Delta y_{t-1}} - \underset{(0.055)}{0.107\Delta^2 p_t}$$

$$\underset{(0.049)}{-0.172\Delta^2 p_{t-1}} + \underset{(0.167)}{0.070c_{t-2}} - \underset{(0.141)}{0.045y_{t-2}} - \underset{(0.042)}{0.113\Delta p_{t-2}}$$

$$R^2 = 0.921, \quad \sum e^2 = 0.000\,556, \quad dw = 1.94, \quad Z11 = 0.002,$$
$$Z14 = 4.45, \quad Z2 = 0.47$$

[A10.19]

Table A10.1 Consumption data set

	Y	C	P		Y	C	P
1956	115088.0	104592.0	0.1276	1971	174197.0	150215.0	0.2230
1957	116926.0	106355.0	0.1320	1972	188858.0	157907.0	0.2375
1958	118688.0	108275.0	0.1360	1973	200218.0	165673.0	0.2578
1959	124753.0	112165.0	0.1374	1974	198748.0	164829.0	0.3014
1960	132962.0	116546.0	0.1389	1975	199814.0	163866.0	0.3727
1961	138515.0	119525.0	0.1430	1976	199115.0	163976.0	0.4314
1962	140017.0	122063.0	0.1483	1977	195455.0	164227.0	0.4952
1963	146056.0	126860.0	0.1512	1978	210047.0	172422.0	0.5400
1964	152274.0	130363.0	0.1566	1979	221999.0	178726.0	0.6132
1965	155438.0	132534.0	0.1643	1980	225532.0	179643.0	0.7127
1966	158874.0	135194.0	0.1709	1981	223715.0	179466.0	0.7926
1967	161243.0	138201.0	0.1753	1982	222857.0	180547.0	0.8618
1968	164064.0	141705.0	0.1837	1983	227887.0	185928.0	0.9047
1969	165582.0	143218.0	0.1939	1984	232945.0	189795.0	0.9507
1970	171973.0	146930.0	0.2053	1985	239581.0	196787.0	1.0000

The identical sums of squared residuals and diagnostic statistics indicate that [A10.19] is indeed no more that a reparameterisation of [A10.15].

If we had began the testing down process with this version of the general model, our first step without doubt would have been to omit the insignificant rate of change variables Δc_{t-1} and Δy_{t-1} because of their very low t-ratios $(-0.33$ and $0.23)$. This yields

$$\Delta c_t = -0.281 + 0.501\Delta y_t - 0.118\Delta^2 p_t - 0.162\Delta^2 p_{t-1} + 0.077 c_{t-2}$$
$$\quad\quad (0.269) \quad (0.055) \quad\quad (0.043) \quad\quad\quad (0.039) \quad\quad\quad (0.137)$$

$$\quad -0.051 y_{t-2} - 0.106\Delta p_{t-2} \quad\quad (1959-85)$$
$$\quad\quad (0.114) \quad\quad\quad (0.035)$$

$$R^2 = 0.920, \quad \sum e^2 = 0.000\,560, \quad dw = 2.00, \quad Z11 = 0.06,$$
$$Z14 = 4.06, \, Z2 = 0.10 \quad\quad\quad\quad\quad\quad\quad\quad [A10.20]$$

The reader should verify that dropping the variables Δc_{t-1} and Δy_{t-1} is 'F-acceptable'. Unfortunately, the 'levels variables' in [A10.20], c_{t-2} and y_{t-2}, still have coefficients that are insignificantly different from zero, (t-ratios 0.56 and -0.45), so we are forced to drop them:

$$\Delta c_t = 0.014 + 0.507\Delta y_t - 0.096\Delta^2 p_t - 0.141\Delta^2 p_{t-1}$$
$$\quad\quad (0.003) \quad (0.046) \quad\quad (0.038) \quad\quad\quad (0.038)$$

$$\quad -0.061\Delta p_{t-2} \quad\quad (1959-85)$$
$$\quad\quad (0.025)$$

$$R^2 = 0.908, \quad \sum e^2 = 0.000\,647, \quad dw = 1.79, \quad Z11 = 0.005,$$
$$Z14 = 2.64, \, Z2 = 0.68 \quad\quad\quad\quad\quad\quad\quad\quad [A10.21]$$

All coefficients in [A10.21] have statistically significant t-ratios and, if we F-test this equation against the general models [A10.15] and [A10.19], all 4 restrictions imposed are found to be data acceptable. However [A10.21] like [A10.18] is a model without a long-run stationary equilibrium. This, again, is not inconsistent with our original co-integration analysis.

It may seem strange that, when starting with the [A10.15] version of the general model, we tested down to [A10.18] whereas, if we start with [A10.19], we end up with the seemingly different model [A10.21]. However [A10.18] is in fact nested within [A10.21]. It can in fact be obtained from [A10.21] by imposing the restriction that the coefficients on the variables $\Delta^2 p_t$, $\Delta^2 p_{t-1}$ and Δp_{t-2} should all be equal. To see this note that

$$a\Delta^2 p_t + b\Delta^2 p_{t-1} + c\Delta p_{t-2} = a(\Delta p_t - \Delta p_{t-1}) + b(\Delta p_{t-1} - \Delta p_{t-2}) + c\Delta p_{t-2}$$

$$= a\Delta p_t + (b - a)\Delta p_{t-1} + (c - b)\Delta p_{t-2}$$

Hence, if we impose the two restrictions $a = b = c$, the above expression reduces to $a\Delta p_t$.

To test these two restrictions we can compare the residual sums of squares for equations [A10.18] and [A10.21], which is treated as the unrestricted equation. The F-statistic gives a value of 2.86, compared with a critical value for $(2, 22)$ d.f. of 3.44. The restrictions are acceptable so we prefer [A10.18] to [A10.21]. The general to specific testing down procedure does lead eventually to the same preferred equation no matter where we start from!

Appendix B

We derive here the lifetime budget equation [10.8] for a three-period case. Suppose we have a household in its tenth year ($T = 10$) that intends to retire at the end of its eleventh year ($N = 11$) and expects to die (!) at the end of its twelfth year ($L = 12$). The lifetime budget constraint therefore becomes

$$A_9 + Y_{10} + \frac{Y_{11}^e}{1 + r} = C_{10} + \frac{C_{11}}{1 + r} + \frac{C_{12}}{(1 + r)^2} \qquad [\text{B10.1}]$$

To derive [B7.1] we make the simplifying assumption that interest on non-human wealth is always paid at the beginning of the year. The household's budget constraint for its *tenth year* is then given by

$$A_9(1 + r) + Y_{10} = C_{10} + A_{10} \qquad [\text{B10.2}]$$

where Y_{10} represents *earned or non-property income only*, since unearned income is already included in the constraint as $A_6 r$. Similarly, the household's budget constraints for its *eleventh and twelfth years* are given by

$$A_{10}(1 + r) + Y_{11}^e = C_{11} + A_{11} \qquad [\text{B10.3}]$$

and

$$A_{11}(1 + r) = C_{12} \qquad [\text{B10.4}]$$

where Y_{11}^e is expected earned income in the eleventh year, $Y_{12}^e = 0$ since the household has now retired and $A_{12} = 0$ because household plans to have no resources left at death.

From [B7.4] we have

$$A_{11} = \frac{C_{12}}{1 + r}$$

Substituting for A_{11} in [B7.3] yields

$$A_{10} = \frac{C_{11}}{1 + r} + \frac{C_{12}}{(1 + r)^2} - \frac{Y^e_{11}}{1 + r}$$

Substituting for A_{10} in [B7.2] yields

$$A_9(1 + r) + Y_{10} = C_{10} + \frac{C_{11}}{1 + r} + \frac{C_{12}}{(1 + r)^2} - \frac{Y^e_{11}}{1 + r}$$

which on rearrangement yields the three-year budget constraint [B7.1] provided we interpret A_9 in equation [B7.1] as *including* interest received during the household's tenth year. Thus, by combining the budget constraints for each separate year, we eventually obtain the lifetime budget constraint.

Notes

1. For example, a liquid assets variable is often included as an additional explanatory variable in post-war UK consumption functions.
2. For the US economy a data series does, in fact, exist for depreciation on consumer durables.
3. To see that this is the budget constraint equation, substitute the intercept and slope of the line AB into the general equation for a straight line $C_1 = $ (intercept) $+$ (slope)C_2.
4. The marginal rate of substitution of C_1 for C_2 thus depends only on the ratio C_1/C_2 and not on the absolute magnitudes of C_1 and C_2.
5. If the optimal ratio $C_1/C_2 = k$ then, since

$$W_1 = C_1 + \frac{C_2}{(1 + r)}$$

we have

$$\gamma_1 = \frac{k(1 + r)}{k + kr + 1} \quad \text{and} \quad \gamma_2 = \frac{1 + r}{k + kr + 1}$$

6. 'If the individual receives an additional dollar's worth of resources he will allocate it to consumption at different times in the same proportion in which he had allocated his total resources prior to the addition' (Ando and Modigliani 1963: 56).
7. See Friedman (1957: 44–5).
8. Readers actually consulting the relevant section (Friedman 1957: 142–52) may become somewhat confused at this point. Friedman originally formulates Y^p_t as a *continuous* function of past and present income with exponentially declining weights and also builds-in a factor reflecting secular long-run growth in Y^p_t. However, since his data is in annual form he has to use a discrete approximation of his continuous function when actually estimating his consumption function. This discrete approximation involves the geometrically declining weights of [10.24]. However, the λ of equation [10.24] is equal to $1 - e^{-\beta}$ in the continuous formulation where β is the weight attached to the current *instantaneous* rate of flow of income as opposed to

λ which is the weight attached to the current year's income in the discrete approximation. Friedman estimates β as 0.4 which yields $\lambda = 1 - e^{-0.4} = 0.33$. However, Friedman and others sometimes refer to the 0.4 as the weight attached to current income and this can cause confusion.

9. Strictly speaking, if $C_t^p = \alpha + \beta Y_t^p$ then $C_t = \alpha + \beta Y_t^p + C_t^t$ but transitory consumption C_t^t can be regarded simply as a disturbance.

10. Note that [10.54] may be rewritten as

$$c_t - c_{t-1} = \theta_0 - k\theta_2 + b\theta_3 + \theta_1(y_t - y_{t-1}) + \theta_2(k + y_{t-1} - c_{t-1})$$
$$- \theta_3(b + y_{t-1} - a_{t-1})$$

11. The intuitive rationale behind [10.63] rests on the fact that the current period perception of life-cycle/permanent income tends to be little different from that of the last period. Hence, since last period's consumption is determined by last period's perception of life cycle/permanent income, last period consumption should be a good predictor of current consumption. Current consumption will only differ from that of the previous period by a revision resulting from some change in the perception of life-cycle/permanent income. ε_t therefore depends on this 'new' information and in fact equals any 'surprise' change in life-cycle/permanent income.

12. Pagan (1984) considers the question of the efficiency of the second stage estimates and whether their standard errors can be used for making valid inferences. An alternative method of estimation, based on the work of Mishkin (1982), is to 'substitute in' for the anticipated components in the consumption function using the first-stage equations and then to estimate both equations jointly.

13. The CRDW statistic mentioned in section 7.5 takes the values 0.749 and 0.826 respectively in equations [A10.9] and [A10.10]. These exceed the critical value of 0.386 suggesting stationary residuals. However, since the CRDW test can only be relied upon as a test of non-stationarity when the residuals follow a first-order scheme, we have preferred to make use of the Dickey–Fuller tests that follow.

11 Production functions

The concept of a production function plays an important role in both micro- and macroeconomics. At the macro-level it has been combined with marginal productivity theory to explain the prices of the various factors of production and the extent to which these factors are utilised. It is therefore important in theories of economic growth and in theories of distribution. At the micro-level it is of interest because of its usefulness in the analysis of such problems as the degree to which substitution between the various factors of production is possible and the extent to which firms experience decreasing or increasing returns to scale as output expands. At both the macro- and micro-levels the production function has been used as a tool for assessing what proportion of any increase in output over time can be attributed to, firstly, increases in the inputs of factors of production; secondly, to the existence of increasing returns to scale; and thirdly, to what is commonly referred to as 'technical progress'.

We begin this chapter with a brief review of the neo-classical production function and its role in the theory of the firm and then introduce two examples of this type of production function which have been much used in empirical work.

11.1   The neo-classical production function

The production function in the traditional theory of the firm expresses output Q as a function of, typically, two inputs: capital, K, and labour, L

$$Q = Q(K, L) \tag{11.1}$$

The variables Q, K and L are flow variables so that [11.1] expresses a flow of output as a function of the flows of services provided by the two factor inputs. Thus K represents the flow of services provided by the existing capital stock rather than the capital stock itself. K therefore depends not only on the size of the capital stock but also on the extent of its utilisation. All the variables are assumed to be continuously variable and infinitely divisible. Moreover, the inputs are assumed to be continuously substitutable at all levels of production.[1] An important point to be noted at the outset is that, for given levels of K and L, equation [11.1] defines the maximum possible level of output Q. Thus the *technical* problem of how to achieve the greatest output from given inputs is assumed to be solved and we are not concerned with it. However, because of factor substitutability, a given output can be produced by many alternative combinations of inputs. The problem of deciding which input combination provides the given output at minimum cost is an economic problem which we *are* concerned with. Equation [11.1] is not then confined to least-cost combinations of capital and labour.

The production function is assumed to be such that the marginal products of capital, $\partial Q/\partial K$, and labour $\partial Q/\partial L$, are both always positive but 'diminishing'. Thus, for example, *if capital inputs remain constant*, the relationship between output and labour input is as shown in Fig. 11.1. This illustrates the so-called 'law of diminishing marginal productivity'. Similarly, if labour inputs are fixed, then as capital inputs increase the marginal product of capital declines.

Diminishing marginal productivity must not be confused with 'decreasing returns to scale'. The returns to scale implied by a production function depend on the response of output to an equiproportionate change in *both inputs*. If equation [11.1] is homogeneous of degree n, then depending on whether n is less than, equal to, or greater than, unity, equiproportionate increases in inputs will lead to less than proportionate, equiproportionate, or more than proportionate increases in output. That is, we have decreasing, constant, or increasing returns to scale respectively. In terms of equation [11.1]

$$Q(\lambda K, \lambda L) = \lambda^n Q(K, L)$$

where λ is the given equiproportionate change in factor inputs. Thus for $n > 1$ a production function may exhibit both diminishing marginal productivity and increasing returns to scale. It must be remembered, however, that all production functions are not homogeneous and that some, while exhibiting increasing returns to scale at, for example, low levels of K and L, may show decreasing returns to scale at higher input and output levels.

The fact that K and L are assumed to be continuously substitutable means that there are an infinite number of possible combinations of factor inputs (implying a wide variety of alternative techniques) which may be used to produce a given output. Such possible combinations trace out a constant-product curve or isoquant similar to those shown in Fig. 11.2. The higher the given level of output the further from the origin is the corresponding isoquant. The slope of an isoquant yields the rate at which one factor can be substituted for another

11.1 Diminishing marginal productivity of labour.

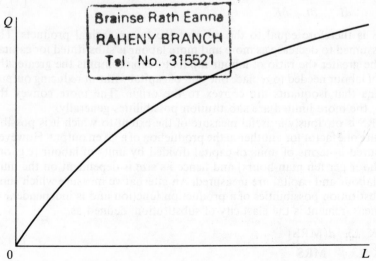

11.2 Isoquants convex to the origin.

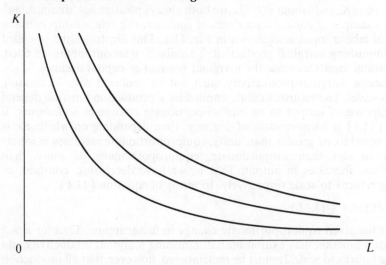

without altering the level of output. The absolute value of this slope is known as the marginal rate of substitution (MRS)

$$\text{MRS} = -\frac{dK}{dL} \qquad [11.2]$$

Also, taking the total derivative of [11.1] we have

$$dQ = \frac{\partial Q}{\partial K}dK + \frac{\partial Q}{\partial L}dL = 0$$

since output is assumed constant along the isoquant. Thus

$$\text{MRS} = -\frac{dK}{dL} = \frac{\partial Q}{\partial L} \bigg/ \frac{\partial Q}{\partial K} \qquad [11.3]$$

The MRS is therefore equal to the ratio of the two marginal products. The MRS is assumed to decrease as more and more labour is substituted for capital. That is, the greater the ratio of labour inputs to capital inputs the greater the quantity of labour needed to replace one unit of capital without reducing output. This means that isoquants are convex to the origin. The more convex the isoquants, the more limited are substitution possibilities generally.

The MRS is obviously a useful measure of the extent to which it is possible to substitute one factor for another in the production of a given output. However, it is measured in terms of units of capital divided by units of labour (e.g. one machine hour per ten man-hours) and hence its size is dependent on the units in which labour and capital are measured. An alternative measure which sums up the substitution possibilities of a production function and is independent of units of measurement is the elasticity of substitution, defined as

$$\sigma = \frac{d(K/L)}{K/L} \bigg/ \frac{d(\text{MRS})}{\text{MRS}} \qquad [11.4]$$

298

It is therefore the proportionate change in the capital/labour ratio occurring, as we move along an isoquant, divided by the accompanying proportionate change in the MRS. Thus, if the isoquants are relatively flat (i.e. substitution is relatively easy), then movements along an isoquant (i.e. changes in the K/L ratio) are accompanied by little change in the MRS and hence the elasticity of substitution is high. However, if the isoquants have a pronounced curvature, implying that substitution possibilities are more limited, then σ will be low. The meaning of this concept will become clearer once factor prices are introduced into the analysis.

Nothing yet has been said about what determines the proportions in which factor inputs are combined. This is an economic as opposed to technical problem and, at the micro-level, the production function is usually set in a model of firm behaviour in which the firm maximises profits, π, where

$$\pi = pQ - mK - wL \qquad [11.5]$$

and p, m and w are the prices of output, capital and labour flows respectively. Assuming perfect competition in the product and factor markets, the firm is a price-taker and p, m and w may be treated as given. The firm then maximises [11.5] subject to the constraints that inputs and outputs should satisfy the production function [11.1]. Forming the Lagrangean

$$H = pQ - mK - wL - \lambda[Q - Q(K, L)]$$

the first-order conditions for a maximum are

$$\frac{\partial H}{\partial Q} = p - \lambda = 0, \quad \frac{\partial H}{\partial K} = -m + \lambda \frac{\partial Q}{\partial K} = 0, \quad \frac{\partial H}{\partial L} = -w + \lambda \frac{\partial Q}{\partial L} = 0$$

Eliminating the Lagrangean multiplier, λ, we thus obtain the so-called *marginal productivity conditions*

$$\frac{\partial Q}{\partial K} = \frac{m}{p} \quad \text{and} \quad \frac{\partial Q}{\partial L} = \frac{w}{p} \qquad [11.6]$$

Thus each factor is utilised up to the point where its marginal product equals its real price (in terms of output produced). Provided the required second-order conditions are satisfied, solving [11.6] together with [11.1] yields the profit-maximising values of Q, K and L.[2]

In this context the production function must be seen as merely one relationship in a three-equation system (comprised of [11.1] and [11.6]) which *jointly determines the values of the endogenous variables Q, K and L* and in which the exogenous variables are m/p and w/p. Thus, given the above simple economic model, we see that the factor inputs, K and L, cannot be regarded as exogenous variables determining Q as the original single equation [11.1] might superficially suggest.

An alternative economic model which has important empirical applications is that in which output Q is assumed to be predetermined. The firm's aim is then to minimise costs subject to the constraint on its level of output. Retaining the assumption that the firm is a price-taker, costs

$$C = mK + wL \qquad [11.7]$$

are therefore minimised subject to the output constraint

$$Q^0 = Q(K, L)$$ [11.8]

where Q^0 is the predetermined level of output. Forming the Lagrangean

$$H = mK + wL - \lambda[Q^0 - Q(K, L)]$$

the first-order conditions for a minimum are

$$\frac{\partial H}{\partial K} = m + \lambda\frac{\partial Q}{\partial K} = 0, \quad \frac{\partial H}{\partial L} = w + \lambda\frac{\partial Q}{\partial L} = 0$$

which together yield the cost-minimising condition

$$\text{MRS} = \frac{\partial Q}{\partial L}\bigg/\frac{\partial Q}{\partial K} = \frac{w}{m}$$ [11.9]

Thus factor inputs should be combined in such a way that the MRS equals the factor price ratio. Solving equations [11.8] and [11.9] then yields the cost-minimising levels of K and L. Notice that we now have a *two*-equation system which jointly determines the endogenous variables K and L and in which the exogenous variables are now Q, w and m.

The introduction of the factor prices m and w into the analysis yields further insight into the concept of the elasticity of substitution. Notice from [11.6] that the profit-maximisation model as well as the cost-minimisation model also implies that factors will be combined so as to equate the MRS with the ratio of factor prices. Indeed, even if the assumption that the firm is a price-taker in the product market is dropped, profit maximisation still implies equation [11.9]. This means that we can rewrite equation [11.4], our definition of the elasticity of substitution as

$$\sigma = \frac{d(K/L)}{K/L}\bigg/\frac{d(w/m)}{w/m}$$ [11.10]

Thus σ is given by the proportionate change in the capital/labour ratio divided by the proportionate change in the factor price ratio. When the price of labour rises relative to that of capital, firms will attempt to substitute capital for labour and increase the K/L ratio. When such substitution is possible only to a limited extent, a given proportionate change in w/m will lead to only small changes in K/L and the elasticity of substitution will be small. However, when considerable substitution is possible, σ will be large.

The Cobb–Douglas production function

The production function most frequently employed in early empirical work was the Cobb–Douglas production function. Douglas, working in the late 1920s, observed that the share of total US national output going to labour had remained approximately constant over time. That is, in aggregate terms

$$wL = \beta pQ$$ [11.11]

where β is a constant between zero and unity.

As we shall see presently, the underlying production function which gives rise to the empirical observation [11.11] is

$$Q = AK^\alpha L^\beta \qquad\qquad [11.12]$$

The Cobb–Douglas production function [11.12] has a number of convenient properties. The parameters, α and β, measure the *elasticities* (assumed constant and between zero and unity) of output with respect to capital and labour respectively. The parameter, A, may be regarded as an *efficiency* parameter, since for fixed inputs K and L, the larger is A, the greater is the maximum output Q obtainable from such inputs.

The marginal products of capital and labour are given by

$$\frac{\partial Q}{\partial K} = \alpha AK^{\alpha-1}L^\beta = \alpha\frac{Q}{K}, \qquad \frac{\partial Q}{\partial L} = \beta AK^\alpha L^{\beta-1} = \beta\frac{Q}{L}$$

Both 'diminish' as the relevant factor input increases since both $(\alpha - 1)$ and $(\beta - 1)$ are negative quantities. Assuming the firm is a price-taker and a profit-maximiser, equations [11.6] imply that the marginal productivity conditions for this production function are

$$\alpha\frac{Q}{K} = \frac{m}{p}, \qquad \beta\frac{Q}{L} = \frac{w}{p} \qquad\qquad [11.13]$$

Notice that the equations [11.13] can be rewritten as $\alpha = mK/pQ$ and $\beta = wL/pQ$. Thus, if the marginal productivity conditions hold, the exponents α and β in the Cobb–Douglas function are equal to the respective shares of capital and labour in the value of total output.[3] It is, in fact, the second of the equations [11.13] which leads to Douglas's empirically observed equation [11.11].

For the Cobb–Douglas case, the three-equation simultaneous system determining the endogenous Q, K and L in the profit-maximising model is given by equations [11.12] and [11.13]. For the two-equation cost-minimising model with predetermined output, the cost-minimising condition is given by

$$\text{MRS} = \frac{\partial Q}{\partial L}\bigg/\frac{\partial Q}{\partial K} = \frac{\beta K}{\alpha L} = \frac{w}{m} \qquad\qquad [11.14]$$

and this together with equation [11.12] yields the simultaneous system in the two endogenous variables K and L, with Q, m and w being in this case exogenous.

Note that for both models the optimising conditions imply that

$$\frac{K}{L} = \left(\frac{\alpha}{\beta}\right)\left(\frac{w}{m}\right) \qquad\qquad [11.15]$$

Thus, for a given factor price ratio, the greater is α/β the greater is the optimal capital/labour ratio. Thus the size of the exponent α, relative to that of β, determines the 'capital-intensity' of the productive processes represented by a Cobb–Douglas function.

The Cobb–Douglas function is homogeneous of degree $\alpha + \beta$ since

$$Q(\lambda K, \lambda L) = A(\lambda K)^\alpha(\lambda L)^\beta = \lambda^{\alpha+\beta}AK^\alpha L^\beta = \lambda^{\alpha+\beta}Q(K, L) \qquad [11.16]$$

Thus if $\alpha + \beta > 1$ we have increasing returns to scale, if $\alpha + \beta = 1$ we have constant returns to scale and if $\alpha + \beta < 1$ we have decreasing returns. Note, however, that the returns to scale property is the same at all levels of output. For example, the Cobb–Douglas function cannot exhibit increasing returns at low Q and decreasing returns for high Q.

The Cobb–Douglas function is also restricted in that it implies an elasticity of substitution which is constant and always equal to unity. This is probably best understood if we accept either the profit-maximisation or cost-minimisation models, although it is a property of the Cobb–Douglas function itself and is not dependent on market conditions or firm behaviour. It then follows from equation [11.14] that, since α/β is constant, a 1 per cent increase in the ratio of factor prices, w/m, must lead to a 1 per cent increase in the capital labour ratio, K/L. From the alternative definition of σ given by equation [11.10] we see that this implies an elasticity of substitution equal to unity for the Cobb–Douglas function.

One awkward problem with the profit-maximising model, introduced above, concerns the question of whether a three-equation system such as that formed by equations [11.12] and [11.13] yields a single determinate solution corresponding to a point of maximum profit. This will depend on whether the second-order conditions as well as the first-order conditions for a maximum are met. Wallis (1979), for example, shows that in the Cobb–Douglas case the condition is that $\alpha + \beta < 1$, i.e. that there should be decreasing returns to scale.[4]

Suppose the second-order conditions for a maximum are *not* met and we have $\alpha + \beta \geqslant 1$, i.e. constant or increasing returns to scale. If, for example, $\alpha + \beta = 1$ then three outcomes are possible. If product and factor prices are such that there is some given combination of inputs which yield a positive profit, then profit can always be increased by expanding the scale of output and there is no finite maximum level of profits. If prices are such that any given input combination yields a negative profit then any scale of output will yield a negative profit and the firm cannot stay in business. Finally, if profits are zero for any given output combination, then they are zero at all levels of output and the size of the firm is indeterminate. Similar strange results occur if $\alpha + \beta > 1$, i.e. if there are increasing returns to scale.

In practice we cannot just rule out the possibility of constant or increasing returns to scale – certainly not without estimating α and β first. Obviously, there are no *a priori* reasons why firms should not operate under conditions of non-decreasing returns to scale. When they do so it is obvious that in practice the value of Q is determined in some manner or other – firms *do* have a definite size, whether it be large or small. The answer to this apparently baffling problem is to relax the assumptions of perfect competition where all prices are given and Q, K and L can be varied at will. However, this involves making prices endogenous to the system and, hence, necessitates the addition of extra equations to the model, namely, demand for product and supply of factor relationships.

The constant elasticity of substitution production function

As already noted, the Cobb–Douglas production function has an elasticity of substitution, σ, which is always equal to unity. This is a particularly restrictive property. One of the purposes of production function analysis is to examine the extent to which factor substitution is possible and such substitution may obviously vary between firms and industries. For example, if we wished to compare the substitution possibilities in two different industries, the estimation of Cobb–Douglas functions for each industry could tell us nothing of value. An improvement would be some form of production function in which σ, although still, maybe, a constant, could take alternative values other than unity. *The constant elasticity of substitution* (CES) production function has such a form.

The CES function was first introduced by Arrow, Chenery, Minhas and Solow (SMAC) in 1961, who estimated cross-sectional equations of the form

$$\frac{Q}{L} = \frac{1}{\beta}\left(\frac{w}{p}\right)^{\chi} \qquad [11.17]$$

Notice, from [11.11] or [11.13] that a Cobb–Douglas function, given profit-maximisation under perfect competition, implies that χ in equation [11.17] should be unity. SMAC however, obtained estimated values for χ which were consistently less than unity and deduced, assuming profit-maximisation, perfect competition and constant returns to scale, that the production function giving rise to [11.17] must have the form

$$Q = \gamma[\partial K^{-\theta} + (1 - \delta)L^{-\theta}]^{-1/\theta} \qquad [11.18]$$

where γ, δ and θ are parameters to be interpreted shortly. Equation [11.18] specifies the CES production function.

The parameter γ is to be interpreted as an *efficiency parameter* akin to the A in the Cobb–Douglas function, since for given δ and θ, the larger is γ the greater is the maximum output Q obtainable from given inputs K and L.

The marginal products of capital and labour are given by

$$\frac{\partial Q}{\partial K} = \frac{\delta\gamma}{K^{1+\theta}}[\delta K^{-\theta} + (1 - \delta)L^{-\theta}]^{-(1+\theta)/\theta} = \frac{\delta}{\gamma^{\theta}}\left(\frac{Q}{K}\right)^{1+\theta}$$

$$\frac{\partial Q}{\partial L} = \frac{(1 - \delta)\gamma}{L^{1+\theta}}[\delta K^{-\theta} + (1 - \delta)L^{-\theta}]^{-(1+\theta)/\theta} = \frac{(1 - \delta)}{\gamma^{\theta}}\left(\frac{Q}{L}\right)^{1+\theta} \qquad [11.19]$$

Assuming profit maximisation under perfect competition the marginal productivity equations corresponding to [11.6] are

$$\frac{\delta}{\gamma^{\theta}}\left(\frac{Q}{K}\right)^{1+\theta} = \frac{m}{p}, \qquad \frac{(1 - \delta)}{\gamma^{\theta}}\left(\frac{Q}{L}\right)^{1+\theta} = \frac{w}{p} \qquad [11.20]$$

The second of these conditions leads to SMAC's estimating equation [11.17] with $\chi = 1/1 + \theta$ and $1/\beta = (\gamma^{\theta}/1 - \delta)^{1/1+\theta}$.

The MRS is

$$\left(\frac{1 - \delta}{\delta}\right)\left(\frac{K}{L}\right)^{1+\theta}$$

so that cost minimisation subject to a predetermined output, implies

$$\left(\frac{1 - \delta}{\delta}\right)\left(\frac{K}{L}\right)^{1+\theta} = \frac{w}{m} \qquad [11.21]$$

Equation [11.21] also holds for the profit-maximisation model since it may be

303

derived from [11.20]. It is instructive to rewrite [11.21] as

$$\frac{K}{L} = \left(\frac{\delta}{1-\delta}\right)^{1/1+\theta} \left(\frac{w}{m}\right)^{1/1+\theta}$$

Since the quantity $(\delta/1-\delta)^{1/1+\theta}$ is a constant, it follows that a 1 per cent rise in the factor price ratio w/m leads to a $(1/1+\theta)$ per cent rise in the capital–labour ratio. From equation [11.10] this implies that the CES function has an elasticity of substitution $\sigma = 1/1+\theta$.[5] Because of its relationship with σ, θ is known as the *substitution parameter*

$$\theta = \frac{1}{\sigma} - 1 \qquad\qquad [11.22]$$

Possible values for θ range from $\theta = \infty$ (when $\sigma = 0$ and substitution is impossible) to $\theta = -1$ (when $\sigma = \infty$, the isoquants are straight lines and substitution possibilities are greatest). When $\theta = 0$, $\sigma = 1$ as for the Cobb–Douglas function, and it can be shown that for this value of θ the CES function, in fact, reduces to the Cobb–Douglas function.[6] The fact that σ can take different values means that the CES function, unlike the Cobb–Douglas function, is a suitable tool for investigating the varying substitution possibilities between, for example, different industries.

Equation [11.21] may also be rewritten as

$$\frac{wL}{mK} = \frac{(1-\delta)}{\delta}\left(\frac{K}{L}\right)^{\theta} \qquad\qquad [11.23]$$

so that, for a given capital/labour ratio and a given value of θ, we see that as δ rises the ratio of labour's share in total output to capital's share declines. For this reason δ is known as the *distribution parameter*. In contrast, for the Cobb–Douglas function the ratio of factor shares is a constant.

The CES function [11.18] implies constant returns to scale and may be generalised to

$$Q = \gamma[\delta K^{-\theta} + (1-\delta)L^{-\theta}]^{-v/\theta} \qquad\qquad [11.24]$$

The function [11.24] is homogeneous of degree v since

$$Q(\lambda K, \lambda L) = \gamma[\delta(\lambda K)^{-\theta} + (1-\delta)(\lambda L)^{-\theta}]^{-v/\theta}$$
$$= \lambda^v \gamma[\delta K^{-\theta} + (1-\delta)L^{-\theta}]^{-v/\theta} = \lambda^v Q$$

Hence, v is a returns-to-scale parameter since for $v > 1$, $v = 1$ and $v < 1$ we have increasing returns, constant returns and decreasing returns to scale respectively. The parameters γ, θ and δ in equation [11.24] have exactly the same interpretation as those in [11.18].

11.2 Matching the models to the real world – some conceptual problems

It takes little thought to realise that, regardless of the precise form adopted for the production function, the simple economic models of the firm described in the previous section are a far cry from the firms of a modern industrial economy.

A firm typically produces more than one output and employs more than two separate factors of production. Raw material and intermediate-good inputs are frequently as important as capital and labour inputs and, furthermore, no inputs can be treated as completely homogeneous in quality. There are many different types of labour inputs – skilled and unskilled is an obvious and often too simple classification – whereas capital equipment clearly varies even more considerably both in its form and up-to-dateness.

However, even if data on all such variables was accessible and sufficient observations were available, potential multicollinearity problems are so severe that some form of aggregation is inevitably necessary. A frequent first step is to work in terms of the real output actually originating in the firm, i.e. in terms of 'value added'. Value added is defined in this context as

$$V = \bar{Q} - \bar{M} \qquad [11.25]$$

where

$$\bar{Q} = \sum_{i=1}^{n} p_i Q_i \quad \text{and} \quad \bar{M} = \sum_{i=1}^{s} v_i M_i \qquad [11.26]$$

p_i and v_i are the prices, in some base year, of the ith output Q_i and ith intermediate input M_i respectively. Base year prices are used because we wish $\bar{Q}$, a weighted measure of total output, and $\bar{M}$, a weighted measure of total intermediate input, to be in 'real' or 'constant price' terms. Value added, V, is then expressed as a function of single indices $\bar{K}$ and $\bar{L}$ of capital and labour, which may themselves simply be weighted averages of the individual capital and labour inputs

$$V = V(\bar{L}, \bar{K}) \qquad [11.27]$$

Equation [11.27] is clearly akin to the production functions of the theoretical models in the previous section. Unfortunately, the conditions under which this vast simplification is legitimate are very restrictive. They have been derived by Green (1964) and we shall not discuss them here except to say that they are rather unlikely to be met in practice. However, one implication of adopting a value-added formulation is relatively clear. Equation [11.27] implies that

$$\bar{Q} = \bar{M} + V(\bar{K}, \bar{L}) \qquad [11.28]$$

Such a formulation implies that the 'marginal product' of intermediate-good inputs is constant and equal to unity. It is not at all clear that such a rigid and fixed relationship between output and, for example, raw material inputs is likely to provide an adequate approximation of reality.

When dealing with the individual firm, aggregation need not necessarily be as complete as that above. It is often still possible to retain maybe two or three separate types of input for both capital and labour. However, some degree of aggregation is always necessary and this invariably causes theoretical problems.

Aggregate production functions

In practice, production functions are not only estimated for individual firms but often for entire industries or industrial sectors and even for the economy as a whole. Just as it is possible to aggregate individual demand curves to obtain a market demand curve, so it may seem possible to aggregate micro-production functions to obtain an 'aggregate production function'. However, there are serious conceptual problems involved with the idea of a macro-production function. We consider, first, the problems which arise when aggregation is performed over firms all within the same industry.

First, there are the more or less standard aggregation problems that we have already met in demand analysis. Suppose the individual firms have production functions of Cobb–Douglas type. Since we are dealing with a single industry, the range of available productive techniques is likely to be similar for each firm. Hence, it may not be unreasonable to assume that the exponents α and β in the Cobb–Douglas function are the same for all firms and this simplifies the aggregation problems involved. However, since the Cobb–Douglas function is merely linear in the logarithms this means, as we saw in section 9.2, that sensible aggregation now requires macro-variables to be defined as the geometric rather than the arithmetic means of the corresponding micro-variables.

Secondly, there are less obvious but more deep-seated difficulties. Since the production function is only one of a system of three simultaneous equations, the marginal productivity conditions need to be aggregated too. Even if such aggregation is possible, there is no guarantee that the macro-marginal productivity conditions obtained by differentiating the macro-production function will be of the same form as those obtained by aggregating the micro-marginal productivity conditions.

There are also problems created by the possible presence of external economies of scale. For example, if each individual firm were operating under constant returns to scale but the inputs and outputs of all firms expand, external economies would mean that aggregate output expands at a proportionately greater rate than do aggregate inputs. Hence, the aggregate production function would exhibit increasing returns to scale although the micro-functions did not. The whole is greater than the sum of its parts.

Aggregation is also frequently performed over firms or industries with widely different types of output and this creates even greater problems. Available techniques of production are now likely to vary considerably from industry to industry and it is no longer remotely realistic to suggest that, for example, the exponents α and β in a Cobb–Douglas function are the same in all industries. The capital intensity of the productive process will vary. The convergency approach to aggregation, outlined in section 9.2, indicates that, under these conditions, sensible aggregation requires the parameters α and β to be distributed independently, across firms, of the input variables K and L. However, given competitive markets it is easy to see that this condition is unlikely to be met. From equation [11.15] we see that, since the factor price ratio w/m can be considered to be constant across industries under competitive conditions, high values of K are likely to be associated with high values of α. Similarly, high values of L are associated with high values of β. In economic terms capital inputs are greatest in capital-intensive industries and labour inputs greatest in labour-intensive industries.

All this might not matter too much if the correlations between K and α and between L and β remained similar over time, i.e. if both labour-intensive and capital-intensive industries always expanded at the same rate. A fixed relationship between aggregate output and aggregate inputs could then exist, although it would not be possible to interpret the aggregate α and β as simple means of the corresponding micro-parameters. However, different industries generally expand at different rates. When this is the case, the expansion of aggregate outputs will depend on how the increased inputs are distributed across industries. For example, increases in aggregate output will be greater if the extra labour inputs go to labour-intensive industries rather than capital-intensive industries. However, which industries new factor inputs will flow to depends on factor prices, which in the *non-competitive* conditions generally prevailing are likely to vary from industry to industry. Hence, in general, the increase in aggregate output will depend on these relative prices. Thus, aggregate output is not only dependent on aggregate inputs but also on relative factor prices and hence on market conditions. The idea of the production function as a purely *technical* relationship, independent of economic decision-making, has been lost.

It should be clear from the above discussion that the very concept of an aggregate production function is a nebulous one. The question naturally arises of whether there is any point in trying to estimate such a 'hazy' relationship. However, it is an attractive proposition to attempt to find some simple relationship which sums up the whole technology under which an economy operates. Although such an estimated relationship cannot be a 'pure' technical one it may still prove a useful statistical description of the relationships between aggregate Q, K and L. The attractiveness of the production function approach has meant that investigators have not been deterred by the conceptual problems involved.

Measuring the inputs and outputs – aggregation in practice

Whether one is dealing with a single firm, an industry or the entire manufacturing sector, the measurement of either inputs or outputs almost invariably involves the aggregation of heterogeneous quantities and should therefore involve the construction of index numbers or weighted averages.

The most easily measured of the variables involved is probably the flow of labour inputs which can generally be measured in terms of man-hours. However, there are many types of labour input – male and female, skilled and unskilled, etc. – and ideally some weighted measure of total labour input should be derived. Appropriate weights would be base-period hourly wage rates for the different types of labour, provided that these wage rates adequately measure the relative usefulness of the various labour flows in the productive process. Base-year wage rates need to be used since we wish to measure labour input in physical or 'constant price' terms and abstract from any changes in the value of labour inputs which arise simply because of changes in its price. However, difficulties will still arise if the quality of the various labour inputs changes much over time and there is the obvious problem of which year should be selected as the base year. In practice, the procedure just described is often approximated by aggregating the money values of inputs in current price terms and deflating by any available index of labour input prices. However, unweighted measures of labour flows are also frequently used, e.g. total man-hours, and on occasion even stock measures such as the total number of employees.

As we have seen, even for the individual firm, total output is generally heterogeneous, so that its measurement also involves problems of aggregation. When different output flows have to be aggregated, market prices are generally used as weights on the assumption that these best represent the relative values of different outputs to society. Market prices in some base year should be used since again we wish our aggregate measure to be in real or constant-price terms. However, as with labour inputs, changes in quality cause obvious problems. Again, in practice, the procedure frequently used is to measure total output in current prices and then to deflate by the most appropriate available index of output prices.

When dealing with an individual firm either net output (i.e. value-added) or gross output data may be available. If the value-added formulation is adopted the normal procedure is to aggregate gross output in current prices and deflate by an appropriate index, aggregate intermediate-good inputs in current prices and deflate by an appropriate index, and then to subtract the latter measure from the former. If a gross output measure is used then the aggregate measure of intermediate-good inputs becomes an additional argument on the right-hand side of the production function. When production functions are estimated for an industry or industrial sector, indices of industrial production are generally used as measures of output. These are value-added measures so that in such cases it is not necessary to construct indices for intermediate-good inputs.

The greatest difficulties arise in the measurement of capital inputs. The index number problems caused by variations in quality are far more serious than in the case of outputs and labour inputs because of the existence of technical progress and innovation over time. Old machines become obsolete and provide inferior services to new up-to-date machines. Furthermore, while we require a measure of the flow of capital services, existing data is almost invariably concerned with the stock of capital equipment. If such data is used, variations in the utilisation of the capital stock become important because if utilisation varies then a given capital stock will provide varying rates of flow of capital services. In practice, the money value of capital stock measured in terms of its replacement cost in some base year is generally used as the capital input variable. Such figures may be either in gross terms or net of depreciation estimates. Attempts are sometimes made to adjust such figures for varying utilisation by using the available data on the percentage of the labour force that is unemployed or 'unutilised'. However, this implies making the assumption that the percentage utilisation of capital is identical to the percentage employment of labour.

Occasionally, use is made of the assumption that all revenue accrues to either labour or capital in an attempt to estimate capital inputs. Given knowledge of Q, p, L, w and m, the accounting identity, $pQ = wL + mK$, which this assumption implies, may be used to estimate K. Notice, however, that in the context of the models of the previous section, this method implies that 'profits' are always zero. Furthermore, as we shall see in the next section, there are serious difficulties in the interpretation of estimated production functions when this accounting identity holds.

Estimation of K via the above accounting identity requires data on the price of capital, m. We shall also see in the following sections that data on factor prices is frequently necessary if consistent estimators of the production function parameters are to be obtained. Since the input variables are flow variables, m is the rental price of capital, i.e. it is the price of hiring capital for a given period of time. However, since under perfect competition a firm will be indifferent between hiring or purchasing and then selling a machine, m is usually calculated as the total cost of actually owing fixed capital. These costs involve the opportunity cost of having funds tied up in fixed capital, depreciaton costs, and any capital losses/gains resulting from changes in the price of capital goods. If

r is the rate of interest, δ the depreciation rate and q the price of capital goods, then the sum of opportunity costs and depreciation costs will be $q(r + \delta)$. It is measures such as this, sometimes adjusted for capital losses/gains, that are normally used as estimates of m, the rental price of capital. Measures of wage costs per unit of time are, of course, more readily available.

11.3   Estimating the micro-production function

In this section we consider some of the problems that arise when attempts are made to estimate a micro-production function from data on individual firms. Discussion is, for the moment, restricted to the Cobb–Douglas function, since many of the major problems can be adequately discussed in this context. We consider, first, cross-sectional data and then time series data and in each case describe some of the efforts that have been made to overcome the various problems.

Estimation from cross-sectional data

Suppose we have data on a cross-section of firms all within the same industry, so that all firms are producing essentially similar outputs. Suppose each firm has a Cobb–Douglas production function [11.12]. Since we are dealing with a single industry, it is not unreasonable to assume that the parameters α and β are the same for all firms because feasible production techniques are unlikely to vary to any great extent. Equation [11.12] is deterministic and we therefore need to introduce a disturbance term to account for random or unexplained variations in output. This is most easily done if a disturbance, ε, is introduced in multiplicative form. That is, for the ith firm, we have

$$Q_i = AK_i^\alpha L_i^\beta \varepsilon_i \tag{11.29}$$

This formulation is convenient since [11.29] is then linear in the logarithms and this facilitates estimation

$$\log Q_i = \log A + \alpha \log K_i + \beta \log L_i + \log \varepsilon_i \tag{11.30}$$

The disturbance in equation [11.30] may be assumed to have a mean of zero, in which case ε_i in [11.29] has a mean of unity. Also ε_i must always be positive, otherwise [11.29] could yield negative outputs and furthermore $\log \varepsilon_i$ would not be defined.

It is possible in this case to give a meaningful interpretation to the disturbance. It measures the *technical efficiency* of the ith firm's entrepreneur since, the larger is ε_i, the greater the maximum output this firm can achieve from a given quantity of inputs. Equation [11.29] could be written as $Q_i = A_i K_i^\alpha L_i^\beta$ where $A_i = A\varepsilon_i$ so that the introduction of ε_i can be regarded as making the efficiency parameter, A, in equation [11.12] vary from firm to firm.

The multiplicative introduction of ε_i is convenient for another reason. It means that the marginal products of capital and labour for the ith firm can still be written as $\alpha(Q_i/K_i)$ and $\beta(Q_i/L_i)$ which do not depend on the disturbance in the production function.[7] Thus if all firms are profit-maximisers and price-takers, the marginal productivity conditions for the ith firm are, from

[11.13]

$$\alpha\left(\frac{Q_i}{K_i}\right) = \frac{m_i}{p_i}, \quad \beta\left(\frac{Q_i}{L_i}\right) = \frac{w_i}{p_i} \qquad [11.31]$$

Random disturbances u_i and v_i may also be introduced multiplicatively into the marginal productivity equations

$$\alpha\left(\frac{Q_i}{K_i}\right) = \left(\frac{m_i}{p_i}\right)u_i, \quad \beta\left(\frac{Q_i}{L_i}\right) = \left(\frac{w_i}{p_i}\right)v_i \qquad [11.32]$$

If u_i and v_i are assumed to be always positive and each to have a mean of unity, then departures of u_i and v_i from their mean values imply that the firm's entrepreneur is failing to maximise profits. These disturbances are therefore measures of the firm's *economic efficiency*, i.e. its ability correctly to combine its factor inputs. Taking logarithms we have, from [11.32]

$$\log Q_i = -\log \alpha + \log\left(\frac{m_i}{p_i}\right) + \log K_i + \log u_i \qquad [11.33]$$

$$\log Q_i = -\log \beta + \log\left(\frac{w_i}{p_i}\right) + \log L_i + \log v_i \qquad [11.34]$$

Equations [11.33] and [11.34] are, of course, as convenient for estimation purposes as is equation [11.30]. These equations taken together represent, for each firm, the three-equation simultaneous system in the endogenous Q_i, K_i and L_i with all prices being exogenous. Hence, if we wish to attempt estimation of the production function we must immediately consider the problems both of identification and of simultaneous equation bias. Although the system is non-linear, it is linear in the logarithms so we may apply the normal rules for linear systems.

At first glance there may seem to be no identification problem, since the other equations in the system both contain variables, $\log(m_i/p_i)$ and $\log(w_i/p_i)$, which do not appear in the production function. Recalling the arguments in section 8.1, it appears impossible to obtain, by taking linear combinations of the equations in the system, an equation of similar form to the production function equation [11.30]. However, we are considering a cross-section of firms, in the same industry at the same point in time and under such conditions it is very likely that each firm will be faced with similar or identical prices. That is, p_i, m_i and w_i are the same for all firms and do not vary through the cross-section. Indeed, the marginal productivity conditions [11.32] imply perfect competition, and at a given moment under perfect competition all firms must be facing the same prices. This means that in the present case [11.33] and [11.34] may be written as

$$\log Q_i = \alpha^* + \log K_i + \log u_i \qquad [11.35]$$

$$\log Q_i = \beta^* + \log L_i + \log v_i \qquad [11.36]$$

where α^* and β^* are constants.

It should now be clear that we *do* have an identification problem, since the production function equation [11.30] could be confused, for example, with a linear combination of the marginal productivity equations [11.35] and [11.36].

310

To obtain an intuitive grasp of the problem suppose that ε_i, u_i and v_i are unity for all firms, i.e. the disturbances in equations [11.30], [11.35] and [11.36] are always zero. The three-equation system would now be identical for all firms (e.g. they would all have the same production function), and hence all would be producing the same levels of output with identical levels of inputs. In effect, they would all be at the same point on the same isoquant and we cannot hope to estimate a production function from knowledge of just a single point. If, more realistically, the disturbances ε_i, u_i and v_i vary randomly about unity, then all we observe are random departures from this single point.

It is instructive to consider the case where, of the three disturbances, only ε_i varies about unity. That is, the disturbance in the production function equation [11.30] varies about zero but those in the marginal productivity equations [11.35] and [11.36] are identically zero. Under these conditions the shifting production function 'traces out' the marginal productivity conditions. Any attempt to relate output, Q, to K and L will only yield an estimate of some linear combination of equations [11.35] and [11.36] such as

$$\log Q_i = \frac{\lambda\alpha^* + \mu\beta^*}{\lambda + \mu} + \left(\frac{\lambda}{\lambda + \mu}\right)\log K_i + \left(\frac{\mu}{\lambda + \mu}\right)\log L_i \qquad [11.37]$$

where λ and μ are any two constants. Notice that the coefficients of $\log K_i$ and $\log L_i$ in any such linear combination will invariably sum to unity. Hence attempts to estimate a production function equation like [11.30] will, under these conditions, be *likely to lead to the conclusion that there are constant returns to scale regardless of the true values of α and β*. Economically, this is the result of the fact that, since the marginal productivity conditions are satisfied exactly and are identical for all firms, Q, K and L vary across the cross-section in direct proportion to each other. Thus, equiproportionate changes in inputs appear to cause equiproportionate changes in output. Each firm has an identical factor input ratio and firms vary in size only because of varying technical efficiency. That is, a varying ε_i means that different firms obtain different quantities of output from given inputs. This special case well illustrates the dangers of the 'unthinking' estimation of production functions from cross-sectional data.

Although when prices do not vary over the cross-section the production function is unidentified, it should be noted at this point that the marginal productivity equations [11.35] and [11.36] *are* identified. A variable in the model is missing from each of these equations – the labour variable, L, in the case of equation [11.35] and the capital variable, K, in the case of equation [11.3⟩]. Moreover, the coefficient of $\log K_i$ in [11.35] is unity as is that of $\log L_i$ in [11.36]. Neither of these equations can therefore be confused with linear combinations of other equations in the model.

There is a further problem, very much akin to the above, concerning the production function. Suppose the data used in estimation obeys the accounting identity

$$p_i Q_i = m_i K_i + w_i L_i \qquad [11.38]$$

This may artificially be so if, as we saw in the previous section to be sometimes the case, the capital variable K is calculated by using such an identity.

Equation [11.38] may be rewritten as

$$Q_i = \left(\frac{m_i}{p_i}\right)K_i + \left(\frac{w_i}{p_i}\right)L_i \qquad [11.39]$$

Since p_i, m_i and w_i are constant over the cross-section, the identity [11.39] expresses Q_i simply as a function of K_i and L_i, just as does the production function [11.29]. Hence, in attempting to estimate [11.29] we may in fact be confusing it with [11.39]. A 'good fit' may merely mean that we have rediscovered the identity that was artificially enforced on the data.

How might these problems be overcome? One obvious possibility is to obtain data in which the prices p_i, m_i and w_i do, in fact, vary over the cross-section. If this were so, the marginal productivity equations [11.33] and [11.34] would contain variables, namely m_i/p_i and w_i/p_i, that do not appear in the production function. Hence, there would be no question of confusing the production function with the marginal productivity equations and neither could it be confused with any accounting identity.

Prices would vary over the cross-section if the assumption that firms are price-takers no longer held, i.e. if market conditions were imperfectly competitive. Adopting such a model would, however, involve the treating of all prices as endogenous and hence require the introduction of additional demand for output and supply of input equations. An alternative is to use an 'inter-state' cross-section where each observation comes from a similar industry but from a different country or national economy. Since there is no reason why p_i, m_i and w_i should be identical in different countries, this would overcome the identification problem.

One further possible way by which the production function might be identified concerns the disturbances. As we saw in section 8.1, if the disturbances in equations of a simultaneous model are uncorrelated then all equations in the model are identified. The problem here is that ε_i, the disturbance in the production function, represents technical efficiency, while the marginal productivity disturbances u_i and v_i represent economic efficiency. Since the technically efficient firm is also likely to be economically efficient, ε_i is likely to be correlated with u_i and v_i so that this route to identification is unlikely to be feasible.

Even if prices vary over the cross-section and we are confident that the production function is identified, the problem of simultaneous equation bias must still be considered. The production function equation is, as we have already noted, only one equation in the simultaneous system consisting of [11.30], [11.33] and [11.34] which jointly determine Q, K and L. The reduced form of this system is

$$\log Q_i = \text{const} - h\alpha \log\left(\frac{m_i}{p_i}\right) - h\beta \log\left(\frac{w_i}{p_i}\right) + h\alpha \log u_i$$
$$+ h\beta \log v_i + h \log \varepsilon_i \qquad [11.40]$$

$$\log K_i = \text{const} - h(1-\beta) \log\left(\frac{m_i}{p_i}\right) - h\beta \log\left(\frac{w_i}{p_i}\right) - h(1-\beta) \log u_i$$
$$+ h\beta \log v_i + h \log \varepsilon_i \qquad [11.41]$$

$$\log L_i = \text{const} - h\alpha \log\left(\frac{m_i}{p_i}\right) - h(1-\alpha) \log\left(\frac{w_i}{p_i}\right) + h\alpha \log u_i$$

$$- h(1-\alpha) \log v_i + h \log \varepsilon_i \qquad [11.42]$$

where the constants are functions of A, α and β and need not concern us and $h = (1 - \alpha - \beta)^{-1}$. We see from equations [11.41] and [11.42], that $\log K_i$ and $\log L_i$, the explanatory variables in the production function equation [11.30], are correlated with ε_i, the disturbance in that equation. This is the source of the simultaneous equation bias. Thus the OLS estimators of the parameters of equation [11.30] will be biased and inconsistent *even if that equation is identified*.

Provided prices vary over the cross-section this problem can be tackled by using normal simultaneous equation estimating methods. The production function is exactly identified since the number of variables omitted from it $-\log(m_i/p_i)$ and $\log(w_i/p_i)$, is one less than the total number of equations in the system. It may therefore be estimated by, for example, ILS, TSLS, or any other instrumental variable method. However, if prices are constant over the cross-section then not only is the production function unidentified but there are effectively no exogenous variables in the model. This means that the above methods cannot even be used to estimate the identified marginal productivity equations.

However, even with constant prices there is one method, pioneered by Klein (1953), by which the parameters α and β may be consistently estimated. This makes use of the identified marginal productivity equations [11.33] and [11.34]. For example, equation [11.34] may be rewritten as

$$\log \beta = \log L_i - \log Q_i + \log\left(\frac{w_i}{p_i}\right) + \log v_i$$

$$= \log\left(\frac{w_i L_i}{p_i Q_i}\right) + \log v_i \qquad [11.43]$$

This suggests that, given n observations in the cross-section, we should estimate $\log \beta$ by

$$\widehat{\log \beta} = \frac{1}{n} \sum_{i=1}^{n} \log\left(\frac{w_i L_i}{p_i Q_i}\right) \qquad [11.44]$$

Provided $\log v_i$ has a mean of zero, $\widehat{\log \beta}$ is easily shown to be an unbiased and consistent estimator of $\log \beta$. For example, using [11.43]

$$E \widehat{\log \beta} = \frac{1}{n} \sum_{i=1}^{n} E \log\left(\frac{w_i L_i}{p_i Q_i}\right)$$

$$= \frac{1}{n} \sum_{i=1}^{n} E(\log \beta - \log v_i) = \log \beta \qquad [11.45]$$

Given that [11.44] provides an estimator of $\log \beta$, an estimator of β is given by the sample geometric mean of labour's share in total output. Similarly, an estimator of α is provided by the geometric mean of capital's share. That is

$$\hat{\beta} = \sqrt[n]{\prod_{i=1}^{n} \left(\frac{w_i L_i}{p_i Q_i} \right)} \qquad \hat{\alpha} = \sqrt[n]{\prod_{i=1}^{n} \left(\frac{m_i K_i}{p_i Q_i} \right)} \qquad [11.46]$$

For obvious reasons this method is known as *the method of factor shares*. It provides consistent but not unbiased estimates of α and β. This is because, although $\widehat{\log} \beta$, for example, is an unbiased estimator of $\log \beta$, the property of unbiasedness, unlike that of consistency, does not 'carry over'.

Note that the method of factor shares enables us to estimate two of the parameters of the production function, α and β, via the identified marginal productivity equations. The validity of the method, however, requires the assumption that marginal products are indeed equated to factor prices and all that this implies about market conditions.

Nerlove's study of electricity supply

Nerlove's (1963) cross-sectional study of the US electricity supply industry remains a classic example of how the problems of identification and simultaneous equation bias may sometimes be overcome. Conditions in this privately owned but publicly regulated industry are such that power must be supplied on demand. Output Q can therefore be regarded as a predetermined variable. Since prices are set by a public commission total revenue is also predetermined, so that the problem of firms within the industry may be regarded as that of minimising total cost. The two-equation model of section 11.1 therefore becomes relevant, although Nerlove uses a slightly generalised version of this model in which there are three factor inputs – labour, capital and fuel. His production function is of Cobb–Douglas form:

$$Q = A x_1^{\alpha_1} x_2^{\alpha_2} x_3^{\alpha_3} \varepsilon \qquad [11.47]$$

where x_1, x_2 and x_3 are the inputs of labour, capital and fuel respectively and ε is a 'technical efficiency'-type disturbance.

Although the factor markets cannot all be regarded as perfectly competitive it is possible to treat each firm as a price-taker. The capital market is highly competitive while wages and fuel prices are set by long-term contracts so that firms are price-takers in the short run in the labour and fuel markets. Total costs are therefore given by

$$C = p_1 x_1 + p_2 x_2 + p_3 x_3 \qquad [11.48]$$

where p_1, p_2 and p_3, the prices of labour, capital and fuel may be regarded as given. Minimising [11.48] subject to the constraint [11.47] on output, means that firms must equate ratios of marginal products to ratios of factor prices. That is

$$\frac{\partial Q}{\partial x_1} \bigg/ \frac{\partial Q}{\partial x_2} = \frac{\alpha_1 x_2}{\alpha_2 x_1} = \frac{p_1}{p_2}, \qquad \frac{\partial Q}{\partial x_1} \bigg/ \frac{\partial Q}{\partial x_3} = \frac{\alpha_1 x_3}{\alpha_3 x_1} = \frac{p_1}{p_3} \qquad [11.49]$$

Equations [11.47] and [11.49] form a three-equation system in which the endogenous variables are the three factor inputs x_1, x_2 and x_3. The exogenous variables are output, Q, and the factor prices. If prices did not vary over the cross-section, the production function [11.47] would not be identified. However,

314

because of the manner in which labour and fuel prices are determined, there is sufficient variation in these variables to remove this problem. There remains the problem of simultaneous equation bias which Nerlove circumvents by estimating via the reduced form.

The reduced form of the system consists of three equations expressing each of the endogenous variables, x_1, x_2 and x_3, as functions of the exogenous variables and the disturbance ε.[8] Note that Nerlove does not introduce disturbances into the marginal productivity equations [11.49]. These are assumed to be satisfied exactly.

Nerlove, however, does not estimate each reduced-form equation separately. Since his data concerns total costs, he estimates a linear combination of the reduced-form equations, which is, in fact, the total cost function. That is, he substitutes the reduced-form expressions for x_1, x_2 and x_3 into [11.48] and obtains

$$C = kQ^{1/r}p_1^{\alpha_1/r}p_2^{\alpha_2/r}p_3^{\alpha_3/r}\varepsilon^{-1/r} \qquad [11.50]$$

where

$$r = \alpha_1 + \alpha_2 + \alpha_3$$

is a returns-to-scale parameter and the constant

$$k = r(A\alpha_1^{\alpha_1}\alpha_2^{\alpha_2}\alpha_3^{\alpha_3})^{-1/r}$$

The cost function [11.50] expresses the endogenous total costs as a function of the exogenous Q and the exogenous factor prices. It may be expressed in logarithmic form as

$$\log C = \log k + \left(\frac{1}{r}\right)\log Q + \left(\frac{\alpha_1}{r}\right)\log p_1 + \left(\frac{\alpha_2}{r}\right)\log p_2$$

$$+ \left(\frac{\alpha_3}{r}\right)\log p_3 - \left(\frac{1}{r}\right)\log \varepsilon \qquad [11.51]$$

Provided $-(1/r)\log \varepsilon$ obeys all the classical assumptions (it may be assumed independent of the explanatory variables, since these are all exogenous), then the application of OLS to [11.51] will yield unbiased and consistent estimates of its coefficients. There is a problem, however. The *five* coefficients of [11.51] which are to be estimated are functions of only *four* production function parameters, α_1, α_2, α_3 and r. Thus, the αs and r are overidentified. This problem can be overcome by using the fact that, since $\alpha_1 + \alpha_2 + \alpha_3 = r$, the coefficients on $\log p_1$, $\log p_2$ and $\log p_3$ in equation [11.51] must sum to unity. The equation can therefore be rewritten as

$$\log C - \log p_3 = \log k + \left(\frac{1}{r}\right)\log Q + \left(\frac{\alpha_1}{r}\right)(\log p_1 - \log p_3)$$

$$+ \left(\frac{\alpha_2}{r}\right)(\log p_2 - \log p_3) - \left(\frac{1}{r}\right)\log \varepsilon \qquad [11.51A]$$

Nerlove applies OLS to [11.51A] (i.e. he regresses $\log C - \log p_3$ on $\log Q$,

$\log p_1 - \log p_3$ and $\log p_2 - \log p_3$) and obtains

$$\log C - \log p_3 = \text{const} + \underset{(0.175)}{0.721} \log Q + \underset{(0.198)}{0.562}(\log p_1 - \log p_3)$$

$$- \underset{(0.192)}{0.003}(\log p_2 - \log p_3) \qquad R^2 = 0.92$$

This yields a value $r = 1/0.721 = 1.39$, suggesting *increasing returns* to scale. Notice that the coefficient on $\log p_2 - \log p_3$ has an incorrect sign – Nerlove attributes this to deficiencies in his data series for the price of capital. The coefficient on $\log p_1 - \log p_3$ yields an estimate of the elasticity of output with respect to labour input of $\alpha_1 = 1.39 \times 0.562 = 0.78$.[9]

An examination of the OLS residuals suggests problems, however. When firms are ordered by the size of their output it is found that long runs of positive residuals at low levels of output are followed by long runs of negative residuals at higher levels of output. A possible explanation of this is provided by the fact that, as noted in section 11.1, the Cobb–Douglas function is restricted in that the returns to scale implied are the same at all levels of output. If, in fact, there were increasing returns to scale at lower levels of output but decreasing returns at higher levels, the true total-cost curve would look like the heavy line in Fig. 11.3. However, by adapting the cost curve [11.51] an attempt is being made to represent the true curve by one similar to the dashed line in Fig. 11.3. This could explain the pattern of residuals observed.

To investigate this possibility, Nerlove divides his sample into five groups of twenty-nine firms each, ordered by the size of their outputs, and runs separate OLS regressions for each such group. In this way five separate segments of the true cost curve are estimated and their returns to scale properties analysed. Not

11.3 True and estimated cost curves.

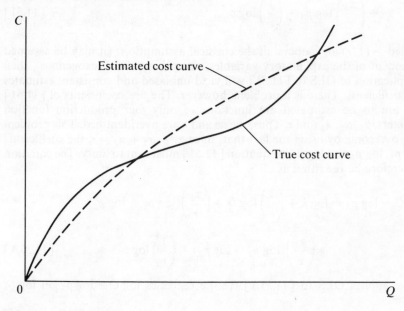

unexpectedly, returns to scale are much greater at low levels of output. For the twenty-nine smallest firmst $\hat{r} > 2.5$, but $\hat{r}$ declines as output rises, being less than unity (although not significantly so) for the largest group of firms. Nerlove therefore concludes that, while there are definite increasing returns to scale at the firm level, their extent decreases as output rises.

More recently the Nerlove study has been updated by Christensen and Greene (1976), using fresh 1970 data. However, since this study makes use of a more general cost function than Cobb–Douglas, we delay consideration of it until section 11.6.

Estimation from time series data

Time series studies of the production function at the level of the individual firm are relatively rare – mainly because investigators have been more concerned with the 'representative firm' or the industry as a whole. However, it is worth examining the problems of estimating micro-functions from time series data because, in doing so, we can abstract from some of the more difficult conceptual problems that arise when aggregates of firms or industries are considered.

The problems with cross-sectional data that arose because of the constancy of product and factor prices disappear to some extent in time series. Prices facing the individual firm are likely to vary over time so that the possibility of confusing the production function with either the marginal productivity equations or any accounting identity is less. However, notice that in equations [11.33] and [11.34], it is the price ratios m_i/p_i and w_i/p_i which appear in the marginal productivity equations. Thus, identification problems will still arise if product and factor prices show any marked tendency to change at similar rates over time, since this would still leave the price *ratios* constant. The problem of simultaneous equation bias is, of course, present with time series data as with cross-sectional data.

There is, however, a more serious problem with time series data – that of technical progress or innovation over time. In a cross-section, taken at a given point in time, the technology available to each firm can be regarded as given, but this is clearly not the case when we consider a single firm over a period of time. The firm's production function will shift as new and more efficient techniques of production come into existence and are put into practice. A major problem with time series data is therefore that of distinguishing between increases in output resulting from movements along the production function (i.e. from increased inputs), and increases in output which occur because of shifts in the production function resulting from technical progress.

Consider equation [11.29], the production function for the ith firm in a cross-section. The disturbance, ε_i, in this equation represented the technical efficiency of the ith firm. While ε_i could be regarded as a 'random' factor in a cross-section, varying from firm to firm with a mean of unity, when we consider a *single* firm over time it obviously cannot be given this interpretation. A firm which is technically efficient in one year is likely to remain so in the next. Recall that equation [11.29] could be rewritten as

$$Q_i = A_i K_i^{\alpha} L_i^{\beta}$$

so that variations in ε_i represented variations in the maximum output that could be obtained from given inputs. When we consider the ith firm only, such maximum output is likely to increase over time because of technical progress. This suggests that one way of handling technical progress is to make the efficiency parameter in a Cobb–Douglas function vary over time and write the individual firm's production function as

$$Q_t = A(t)K_t^\alpha L_t^\beta \varepsilon_t \qquad [11.52]$$

Q_t, K_t and L_t are the output and factor inputs during period t, $A(t)$ is some function of t and ε_t is now a genuinely random disturbance reflecting such factors as strikes, weather conditions, etc.

Before an equation such as [11.52] can be estimated from time series data, some form has to be given to the function $A(t)$. The form most frequently used in practice has been

$$A(t) = Ae^{gt}$$

where A and g are constants, so that [11.52] becomes

$$Q_t = Ae^{gt}K_t^\alpha L_t^\beta \varepsilon_t \qquad [11.53]$$

The interpretation of A and g is straightforward. A is simply the value of $A(t)$ at time $t = 0$. Partially differentiating [11.53] with respect to t yields

$$\frac{\partial Q_t}{\partial t} = gQ_t$$

Hence

$$\frac{\partial Q_t}{\partial t} \Big/ Q_t = g$$

Thus g measures the proportionate change in output per time period when input levels are held constant. It is therefore the proportionate change in output that occurs because of technical progress. Equation [11.53] is convenient from the estimating point of view since, taking logarithms, we have

$$\log Q_t = \log A + gt + \alpha \log K_t + \beta \log L_t + \log \varepsilon_t \qquad [11.54]$$

Thus the estimation of [11.53] simply requires the inclusion of a time trend in the usual Cobb–Douglas estimating equation.

The limitations of the above representation of technical progress should be made clear. Obviously the constancy of g and its implication that technical progress occurs at a constant rate may not be realistic. However, there are more serious difficulties. Firstly, the above type of technical progress is that generally known as *neutral* technical progress. That is, it has no effect on the MRS of capital for labour[10] and hence for a given ratio of factor prices does not influence the proportions in which capital and labour inputs are combined.[11] Thus, such technical progress does not affect the capital or labour intensity of the productive process. Unfortunately, it is not difficult to think of technical innovations which have been either labour-saving or capital-saving, so that the assumption of neutral technical progress is obviously restrictive. If non-neutral technical change is to be introduced into [11.53] then it is necessary to permit the ratio α/β to vary over time.

318

A possibly even more serious limitation of equations like [11.52] is that they represent technical progress that is firstly 'exogenous' and secondly 'disembodied'. Technical progress in this case is exogenous because it has been superimposed on the system (A is simply assumed to grow over time for no stated reason). In practice, techniques become more efficient because of, for example, 'learning by doing' (Arrow 1962), or by the occurrence of research and development expenditure generated by pressures endogenous to the system.

Disembodied technical progress is a form of exogenous technical progress which has been likened to 'manna from heaven', since when it occurs it transforms all existing factors of production no matter how long these factors have been in existence. This is clearly unrealistic, certainly as far as capital inputs are concerned. The occurrence of some new invention does not normally mean that all existing capital machinery, no matter of what age, can now be fully adapted to take advantage of the new technique. Rather, a firm, if it wishes to make full use of new innovations must normally purchase new machinery which 'embodies' the new technique. It is easy to see that equation [11.52] represents technical progress of the disembodied type. As we have noted, [11.52] implies that for given input levels the maximum output obtainable increased over time. However, [11.52] also implies that the given input levels could consist of exactly the same units of capital and labour. These units must therefore be the recipients of disembodied 'manna from heaven' if the maximum output they can produce is to continually increase.

Notwithstanding the limited nature of the representation of technical progress in [11.52], this is the formulation that has most frequently been employed in empirical work. Only recently have attempts to introduce non-neutral or embodied technical change into econometric-type models become more common.

There is an additional difficulty which may arise with either cross-sectional or time series data. This concerns the likelihood of a high degree of multicollinearity amongst the explanatory input variables in the production function. In a cross-section, it is obvious that large firms will tend to have high levels of both capital and labour inputs and small firms low levels of such inputs. Thus, capital inputs may well be highly correlated with labour inputs. For time series data on an individual firm, capital and labour inputs are again likely to be highly collinear.

As we saw in section 5.3.1, the consequence of high multicollinearity is likely to be a lack of precision in the estimation of the production function parameters. This lack of precision would be reflected in high standard errors for the estimators of these parameters. The extent to which multicollinearity has this effect will depend on the overall ability of the explanatory variables to explain variations in the dependent output variable. As we noted in section 5.3.1, if the overall 'fit' is good, then the estimates of parameters of the production function may still be well determined even when the input variables are highly correlated. However, when the effects of multicollinearity are severe, there is little that can be done apart from obtaining additional information to break the 'deadlock'. One possibility, which in some cases may be acceptable, is to impose before estimation the restriction that there are constant returns to scale, i.e. that

$$\alpha + \beta = 1$$

Equation [11.29] is then replaced by

$$Q_i = AK_i^\alpha L_i^{1-\alpha}\varepsilon_i = A\left(\frac{K_i}{L_i}\right)^\alpha L_i\varepsilon_i$$

or

$$\frac{Q_i}{L_i} = A\left(\frac{K_i}{L_i}\right)^\alpha \varepsilon_i \qquad\qquad [11.29A]$$

Hence, estimates of A and α may be obtained by regressing $\log(Q_i/L_i)$ on $\log(K_i/L_i)$ and since we now have only one explanatory variable, the problem of multicollinearity has been circumvented.

One further problem frequently arises when estimation is from time series data, whether that data refers to a single firm, an industry or the whole economy. During periods of economic growth, both output and factor inputs are likely to increase steadily over time. There is, therefore, a real danger that relationships estimated from such data will be at least partly spurious and strongly influenced by the common trends in the data. Many past time series studies of the production function have totally ignored such problems. Since classical regression procedures can no longer be relied upon when applied to non-stationary variables, such work has to be viewed with some scepticism. Certainly the nature of the data used needs to be carefully considered.

Because of the problems that arise when variables are non-stationary, results can be even harder to interpret if, in addition, a time trend representing technical progress is included in the production function. If the output and factor input variables are difference stationary, but equations are estimated in levels, it is possible that a time trend will prove significant even in the absence of technical progress. However, its significance will be spurious and merely a reflection of the common trends in the data.[12] Given this problem, it is by no means clear how the significant time trends found in many past studies should be interpreted.

Fortunately, it is possible to make use of the co-integration analysis, described in section 7.5, to detect the existence or otherwise of long-run relationships in trending data. Furthermore, as we shall see at the end of this chapter, these techniques are also now being applied to the problem of assessing the importance of technical progress.

11.4 Estimating aggregate production functions

As we have already observed, production functions are not only estimated for individual firms but also for entire industries and sometimes for large industrial sectors. We begin this section by considering the problems involved in estimating 'industrial production functions' and then move on to cases where the aggregation process has been carried even further. In each case we discuss the problems in the context of the Cobb–Douglas function.

Industrial production functions

We consider cross-sectional data first. In such studies *each* observation consists of measurements of aggregate inputs and output for an entire industry. A series of observations on the relevant industries is obtained by considering *inter-state* cross-sections. That is, if we were attempting to estimate the production function for the steel industry, one observation might consist of aggregate inputs and output for the US steel industry, another of inputs and output for the UK steel industry, and so on.

There are obvious problems with this approach. We have already drawn attention to the conceptual difficulties involved in attempting to aggregate the individual production functions of firms even when they are all within the same industry. Also, the classification of the relevant industry may vary from country to country – what constitutes 'the steel industry' in the UK may differ slightly from what is classified as 'the steel industry' in the US. A more serious problem concerns variations in the 'state of technology' from country to country. Whereas for a cross-section of firms within a single industry it may be not unreasonable to regard the technological knowledge available as varying little from firm to firm, this may not be plausible for an inter-state cross-section. To some extent such variations can be allowed for if we adopt, for example, equation [11.29] as our industrial production function and interpret the disturbance, ε_i, as reflecting differences in technical 'know-how' between countries. However, this implies that technology varies neutrally between countries[13] and there is no real reason why this should be so. If non-neutral technical change is to be introduced then this implies that the ratio of α to β in equation [11.29] should be permitted to vary across countries.

One important advantage of inter-state cross-sections is that product and factor prices do vary from country to country. Thus, considering the three-equation simultaneous model given by equations [11.30], [11.33] and [11.34], where the ith observation now refers to the ith country, we no longer have any problem in identifying the production function. Problems of simultaneous equation bias and multicollinearity of course, remain.

The first major use of an inter-state cross-section was by Arrow, *et al.* (1961) but, since this involved the CES production function, discussion of it is deferred until the next section. Another well-known early study is that of Hildebrand and Liu (1965). Although their cross-section is not truly interstate in the above sense – each observation relates to a particular state within the US – factors such as transport costs and labour immobility meant that there was sufficient variation in product and factor prices over the cross-section to remove any problems of identification.

Hildebrand and Liu adopt a production function of basically Cobb–Douglas form but with one major modification. The exponents α and β are permitted to vary over the cross-section and to depend on the quality of the capital and labour inputs. Thus technical differences between firms are allowed to be non-neutral, yet the basic simplicity of the Cobb–Douglas function is retained. The function estimated is of the kind

$$Q_i = A K_i^{\alpha(\log R_i)} L_i^{\beta(\log S_i)} \varepsilon_i \tag{11.55}$$

where R_i and S_i are measures of the quality of capital and labour respectively. One measure of R_i is inversely related to the 'average age' of the capital equipment in use, while S_i is based on the extent of the education of the labour force employed. The logarithmic transformation of [11.55] is

$$\log Q_i = \log A + \alpha \log R_i \log K_i + \beta \log S_i \log L_i + \log \varepsilon_i \tag{11.56}$$

Equation [11.56] could be estimated by OLS if $\log Q_i$ were regressed on the variables $(\log R_i \log K_i)$ and $(\log S_i \log L_i)$. However, there are obvious problems of simultaneity so other equations are introduced into the model. An unusual feature of the full model is that the assumption of perfect competition is dropped. Product price is allowed to vary with output and a demand for product equation is introduced.

Hildebrand and Liu estimate their production function for fifteen different industries using both OLS and TSLS. Their data was a 1957 cross-section of US states, with variables expressed in 'per-establishment' form. Their main conclusion is that there are generally increasing returns to scale at the industry level. Equiproportionate changes in capital and labour inputs lead to more than proportionate changes in output in twelve of the fifteen industries even if the quality indices for capital and labour are held constant. If the increasing capital inputs are accompanied by an increase in capital quality (as is likely with new investment) the increasing returns are even more marked and occur in all industries. The influence of technical change is therefore of great importance. Notice, that since the assumption of perfect competition has been relaxed, the conflict between profit maximisation and non-decreasing returns to scale discussed in section 11.1 no longer arises. Another interesting conclusion is that firms adjust labour inputs very slowly in response to changing conditions. As a result the authors maintain that US industry in general was seriously over-employing labour in the late 1950s.

An exceptional feature of the Hildebrand–Liu study is that, as noted above, the assumption of perfect competition in the product market is dropped. The introduction of a demand for product equation makes it possible to allow for a two-way relationship between output and the price of output. The possibility of such a two-way relationship also occurs at the firm level in the estimation of micro-production functions. While it is not unreasonable to regard the individual firm as a price-taker in the factor markets, it may be less valid to assume that the firm can increase output without influencing product price.

When product price can no longer be regarded as exogenous, estimation methods which treat it as such will be subject to simultaneous equation bias. They allow only for the influence of product price on output but ignore the 'feedback' effect whereby any change in the firm's output has an effect on product price.

The problem of the endogeneity or otherwise of product price has generally been dodged at the firm level simply by assuming that firms are price-takers in the product market. For this reason we did not discuss it in section 11.3. However, once aggregation is taken beyond the firm level, the problem can no longer be ignored with any safety. Clearly, the feedback effect whereby output influences product price becomes much stronger when we consider the output of firms in aggregate rather than that of an individual firm. Furthermore, once we have aggregated to industry level it is no longer reasonable to regard factor prices as exogenous either. Each individual firm may be a price-taker in the factor markets and hence be able to vary its inputs without influencing their prices. However, variations in aggregate inputs for the entire industry are unlikely to leave factor prices unchanged. If simultaneity problems similar to those discussed above are to be allowed for, then the assumption of infinite elasticities of supply for the factor inputs must be relaxed. Additional supply of factor equations must be introduced into the model making factor prices as well as product price endogenous variables. Obviously, the greater the extent of the aggregation involved, the greater the need to consider the possible endogeneity of the price variables. Unfortunately, the estimators of aggregate production functions have generally been content to ignore such problems.

When attempts are made to estimate industrial production functions from time series data, we meet again all the problems discussed in the previous section concerning the estimation of micro-production functions from such data. In addition, of course, there is now the problem of aggregation over firms and such awkward difficulties as the existence of external economies of scale. These were discussed in section 11.2.

Technical progress over time is again a problem as it was in the estimation of micro-functions. However, there is now the additional difficulty that different firms within an industry may experience different rates of technical progress. That is, even if each firm has a production function like [11.53], g may vary from firm to firm. If g varies in this manner, then for sensible aggregation we require either that all firms grow at a constant rate over time, or that the input variables K and L should be distributed across firms independently of g. Unfortunately, neither of these conditions is likely to hold. Firms with the highest rate of technical progress are likely to be the most competitive and, hence, will tend to grow at the fastest rate and will also employ the largest inputs of capital and labour. This means that if an aggregate version of equation [11.53] is estimated from time series data then the estimate of g will represent more than just the 'average rate of technical progress'. It will also reflect increases in output resulting from a redistribution of inputs from the less efficient firms to the more efficient ones. It could be said to measure 'economic progress' as well as 'technical progress'.

Production functions for industrial sectors

Much of the empirical work on production functions has been concerned, not with the individual firm or even the industry, but with aggregates such as the entire manufacturing sector or even the whole of private industry. We have already discussed the aggregation problems involved in even the concept of such truly aggregate functions. In this subsection, discussion will be mainly limited to considering the extent to which empirical studies can be regarded as having provided estimates of such functions, nebulous in concept though they may be.

Cross-section studies of the aggregate production function use as observations aggregate data for different industries within the same economy. That is, one observation may consist of aggregate inputs and output for the textile industry, another of inputs and output for the iron and steel industry, and so on. The 'production function' estimated in this manner is then interpreted as being that for the industrial or manufacturing sector as a whole. However, one cannot help feeling that a scatter of points obtained in this way must represent not a single sectoral production function but a set of observations, each representing a point on an entirely different production function – one for each industry in the cross-section. This is particularly so if, as in many studies, no attempt is made to allow for the fact that productive techniques, e.g. the degree of capital intensity, are almost certain to vary between industries – far more so, for example, than they do within a cross-section of firms within the same industry.

Results obtained from inter-industry cross-sections are also likely to depend on the manner in which industries have been classified. Walters (1970) provides a neat example of this fact. Suppose the estimated production function suggested increasing returns to scale in the sense that 'larger' industries, while using more inputs than 'smaller' industries, succeeded in producing a more than proportionately higher output. This finding would be entirely the result of the manner in which industries had been classified. If, for example, a finer classification had been used for the 'larger' industries, splitting them up into smaller entities, the results obtained might be entirely reversed with what are now the 'smaller' industries appearing the more productive. A better way of determining the 'size' of an industry is to examine the average size of firms within each classification.

Time series studies of aggregate production functions use as observations aggregate data on, for example, the entire manufacturing sector, gathered over a period of time. The early studies of this nature were mainly carried out by Douglas using a Cobb–Douglas function and were summarised in his 1948 article. No allowance was made for technical progress in these studies, possible identification problems were not considered and the method of estimation was invariably OLS. Despite all this and the conceptual problems involved in the very idea of an aggregate production function, the results appeared uniformly good. A selection is presented in Table 11.1.

On the basis of his results, Douglas concluded that the Cobb–Douglas function represented a fairly general 'law of production' with constant returns to scale, and that the shares of output going to capital and labour were indeed equal to the α and β exponents in the Cobb–Douglas function. This latter finding was interpreted as strong support for the marginal productivity theory of distribution. Given all the problems that were not allowed for, it seems astonishing that these early results should have turned out so well. However it has to be remembered that all three variables in Table 11.1 will have been subject to strong upward trends during much of the sample periods employed.

Table 11.1 **Results obtained using the Cobb–Douglas production function**

Sample period	α	β	$\alpha + \beta$	Labour share
US, 1899–1922	0.30 (0.05)	0.63 (0.15)	0.93	0.61
Victoria, 1907–29	0.23 (0.17)	0.84 (0.34)	1.07	n.a.
New South Wales, 1901–27	0.20 (0.08)	0.78 (0.12)	0.98	n.a.
New Zealand, 1915–35	0.42 (0.11)	0.49 (0.03)	0.91	0.52

Source: Douglas (1948)

324

Hence, a number of the high correlations and good 'fits' obtained may have been at least partly spurious.

Another possible reason why such satisfactory results were obtained is provided by the fact that the relative prices m/p and w/p remained relatively constant over the periods considered. As we saw in the previous section, the production function is unidentified under such conditions and if in addition the data used happens to satisfy an accounting identity such as [11.38], then a good 'fit' may simply be a reflection of this identity.

Solow's study of US technical progress

The problem of technical progress bedevils the estimation of production functions from aggregate time series data just as it does with industry or firm data. Moreover, the problem of varying rates of technical progress mentioned in the context of industrial time series estimation is now more acute. Variations in g are likely to be even wider between industries than they are between firms within a single industry. An early, if relatively extreme, example of how technical progress might be handled and shifts in the aggregate production function separated from movements along it is provided by Solow (1957).

Solow does not specify the precise form of the production function but assumes that technical progress is both neutral and disembodied so that

$$Q_t = A(t)F(K_t, L_t) \tag{11.57}$$

Constant returns to scale are assumed so that [11.57] may be written as

$$\frac{Q_t}{L_t} = A(t)F\left(\frac{K_t}{L_t}, 1\right) = A(t)f\left(\frac{K_t}{L_t}\right) \tag{11.58}$$

or

$$q_t = A(t)f(k_t) \tag{11.59}$$

where q_t and k_t are output per head and capital per head respectively. Changes in output per head over time are therefore the result of either neutral technical progress or of increases in capital per head. Formally, by total differentiation of [11.59] with respect to time, we have, letting

$$\dot{q} = \frac{dq}{dt}, \quad \dot{k} = \frac{dk}{dt} \quad \text{and} \quad \dot{A} = \frac{dA}{dt},$$

$$\dot{q} = \dot{A}f(k_t) + \frac{\partial q_t}{\partial k_t}\dot{k} \tag{11.60}$$

Dividing [11.60] by q_t leads to an expression for the proportionate rate of change in output per head

$$\frac{\dot{q}}{q_t} = \frac{\dot{A}}{A(t)} + \frac{\partial q_t}{\partial k_t} \cdot \frac{\dot{k}}{q_t} \tag{11.61}$$

Solow assumes that factors are paid their marginal products so that

$$\frac{\partial q_t}{\partial k_t} = \frac{\partial Q_t}{\partial K_t} = \frac{m_t}{p_t} \tag{11.62}$$

Equation [11.61] can now be written as

$$\frac{\dot{q}}{q_t} = \frac{\dot{A}}{A(t)} + \left(\frac{m_t K_t}{p_t Q_t}\right)\frac{\dot{k}}{k_t} \qquad [11.63]$$

Using the relationship [11.63], US annual data on output per man-hour, capital per man-hour and on mK/pQ, the share of capital in total output, Solow is able to estimate, for each year of the period 1909–49, the quantity $\dot{A}/A(t)$. This is an index of technical change, measuring the proportionate change in output per man-hour that would have occurred if capital per man-hour had remained constant. Over the entire sample period the average rate of technical progress is estimated to be 1.5 per cent per annum. Of the total rise in output per man-hour during the forty-year period, Solow estimated that 90 per cent was the result of technical progress (i.e. of shifts in the production function), and only the remaining 10 per cent the result of increases in capital per man-hour (movements along the production function).

As Solow himself acknowledged there are obvious objections to such calculations. Technical progress when defined in this way is simply a name for any increase in output per head which is not the result of increased capital per head. These increases are the result not only of the disembodied neutral technical progress assumed above, but also of increasing returns to scale (both internal and external to the firm) as output expands, redistributive effects as factor inputs switch to more efficient industries, and embodied types of technical change caused by improvements in the quality of capital and in the education of the labour force.

11.5 Estimating the constant elasticity of substitution production function

Estimation of the CES production functions [11.18] and [11.24] is subject to all the problems of identification and simultaneity discussed in the context of the Cobb–Douglas function. We shall not repeat this discussion, but concentrate in this section on the additional difficulties that arise when attempts are made to estimate the CES function.

Such problems arise because, unlike the Cobb–Douglas function, the CES function cannot be linearised by a simple logarithmic transformation. Most investigators have approached its estimation via the marginal productivity conditions [11.20] or [11.21]. The first empirical study of the function was by SMAC (1961) who developed the constant returns to scale formulation [11.18]. As noted in section 11.1 they began their investigation by estimating [11.17] which may be derived from the second of the marginal productivity equations [11.20] in the form

$$\frac{Q}{L} = \left(\frac{\gamma^\theta}{1-\delta}\right)^{1/1+\theta}\left(\frac{w}{p}\right)^{1/1+\theta} \qquad [11.64]$$

Remembering that the elasticity of substitution $\sigma = 1/1 + \theta$, the logarithmic transformation of [11.64] is

$$\log\left(\frac{Q}{L}\right) = \sigma \log\left(\frac{\gamma^\theta}{1-\delta}\right) + \sigma \log\left(\frac{w}{p}\right) \qquad [11.65]$$

The coefficient of $\log(w/p)$ in the regression of $\log(Q/L)$ on $\log(w/p)$ therefore yields an estimate of σ. SMAC estimated [11.65] by OLS using an interstate cross-section. Estimates of σ were obtained for twenty-four separate industries using up to nineteen observations (countries) in each case. The values obtained for σ ranged from 0.721 to 1.011. Ten were significantly less than unity at the 5 per cent level and a further four at the 10 per cent level. Hence, SMAC were able to claim that the elasticity of substitution was typically less than unity and that their function was to be preferred to a Cobb–Douglas specification.

Doubts were first cast on the SMAC conclusions by Fuchs (1963) who noted a wide variation in the average wage over the nineteen countries in the cross-section. Fuchs therefore split the SMAC sample into more and less well-developed countries and found, when estimating [11.65], that there were significant differences in the intercept term between the two groups but no significant differences as far as the slope coefficient, σ, was concerned. Fuchs estimated the equation

$$\log\left(\frac{Q}{L}\right) = \beta_0 + \beta_0' D + \sigma \log\left(\frac{w}{p}\right) \qquad [11.66]$$

where D is a dummy variable of the kind described in section 4.2 taking the value unity for more developed and zero for less well-developed countries. Estimates of [11.66] for twenty-four industries yielded estimates of σ which were now evenly spread about unity with only two of them significantly different from unity at the 5 per cent level of significance. There were problems, however, with the estimate of β_0' which typically turned out to be about -0.2. This implied that the intercept term was smaller for more developed countries. This is contrary to what is to be expected from consideration of the intercept term in [11.65]. More developed countries may be expected to be more efficient (i.e. have a higher γ) and to have more capital-intensive techniques (i.e. have a higher δ). This suggests that the intercept term should have been larger for the more developed countries and Fuchs had difficulty explaining this contradiction.

In their 1961 article, SMAC also make use of the marginal productivity of labour equation to estimate a time series equation for aggregate non-farm US data. Equation [11.64] may be rearranged as

$$\frac{wL}{pQ} = (1 - \delta)^\sigma \gamma^{\sigma-1}\left(\frac{w}{p}\right)^{1-\sigma} \qquad [11.67]$$

Assuming neutral technical progress at a constant rate g, so that the efficiency parameter may be written as $\gamma = \gamma_0 e^{gt}$, a logarithmic transformation of [11.67] yields

$$\log\left(\frac{wL}{pQ}\right) = \sigma \log(1 - \delta) + (\sigma - 1)\log \gamma_0 + (1 - \sigma)\log\left(\frac{w}{p}\right) + (\sigma - 1)gt$$

$$= (\text{const}) + (1 - \sigma)\log\left(\frac{w}{p}\right) + (\sigma - 1)gt \qquad [11.68]$$

SMAC estimated [11.68] using Solow's 1909–49 data. This yielded estimates $\hat{\sigma} = 0.595$ and $\hat{g} = 0.018$ with an R^2 of 0.74. The low value obtained for $\hat{\sigma}$ was regarded as evidence against the hypothesis $\sigma = 1$ as was the relatively high R^2

327

since a Cobb–Douglas function implies $wL/pQ = \text{const}$. The value for g implies an annual rate of growth due to technical progress of 1.8 per cent, which was fairly close to Solow's estimate.

Estimating σ via the marginal productivity equation has the attraction that data is not required on either capital inputs or their price. However, this method does not provide estimates of the other parameters, γ and δ, in the SMAC version of the CES function. Moreover, its validity depends on the assumption that firms are price-takers so that the marginal product of labour is equated to the real wage rate. That is, an economic assumption has to be added to the technical production function relationship. In addition, equation [11.64] is derived under the assumption that there are constant returns to scale. If this assumption is relaxed and the marginal productivity equations derived from the more general equation [11.24], then it is not difficult to show that the estimating equation [11.65] should include $\log Q$ as an additional explanatory variable. In fact,

$$\log\left(\frac{Q}{L}\right) = \sigma \log\left(\frac{\gamma^{\theta/v}}{v(1-\delta)}\right) + \sigma \log\left(\frac{w}{p}\right) + \frac{(1-\sigma)(1-v)}{v}\log Q$$

If $v \neq 1$, so that the above equation holds, then our analysis of specification error in section 7.1 indicates that the regression of $\log(Q/L)$ on $\log(w/p)$ alone will yield a biased estimator of σ. Only if $\sigma = 1$, in which case $\log Q$ disappears from the equation, or if $\log(w/p)$ and $\log Q$ are uncorrelated, will this bias disappear.

A further problem concerns the exogeneity or otherwise of the real wage rate in equations [11.64] and [11.65]. Exogeneity may be a reasonable assumption at the firm level. But at any higher level of aggregation the adjustment of output and inputs is likely to have a 'feedback effect', via the labour market, on the real wage rate which will lead to simultaneous equation bias. Maddala and Kadane (1966), in fact, reversed the relationship between Q/L and w/p in equation [11.65], effectively treating w/p as the endogenous variable, and regressed $\log(w/p)$ on $\log(Q/L)$. Using the same cross-sectional data as SMAC they obtained very different results with only three of the twenty-four industries having a σ significantly different from unity.

The estimation of the other parameters of the CES function requires data on capital inputs and their price. Given such data, one method of proceeding is via equation [11.21] which equates the marginal rate of substitution to the ratio of factor prices. The logarithmic transformation of [11.21] can be rewritten as

$$\log\left(\frac{K}{L}\right) = \sigma \log\left(\frac{\delta}{1-\delta}\right) + \sigma \log\left(\frac{w}{m}\right) \qquad [11.69]$$

Provided the factor prices can be taken as exogenous, the application of OLS to [11.69] will yield consistent estimators of $\theta = (1/\sigma) - 1$ and of δ from the constant term.[14] Given such estimates, the CES function may then be written as

$$Q = \gamma Z^v \quad \text{where} \quad Z = (\delta K^{-\theta} + (1-\delta)L^{-\theta})^{-1/\theta} \qquad [11.70]$$

A set of observations for Z can then be constructed using the estimates of θ and δ and the available data on K and L. Estimates of γ and v may then be obtained by estimating the equation $\log Q = \log \gamma + v \log Z$.

After the initial investigation by SMAC a series of empirical studies of the CES function were carried out, mainly using US data – both cross-sectional and time series. Dhrymes (1965), for example, used a US interstate cross-section to estimate the elasticity of substitution for seventeen industries both by means of equation [11.65] and using a similar equation derived from the marginal productivity equation for capital

$$\log\left(\frac{Q}{K}\right) = \sigma \log\left(\frac{\gamma^{\theta}}{\delta}\right) + \sigma \log\left(\frac{m}{p}\right) \qquad [11.71]$$

The estimates of σ obtained from [11.65] and [11.71] should be similar. However, those obtained by Dhrymes using [11.65] – the SMAC method – were generally significantly less than unity, while those obtained using [11.71] were in all cases much higher. Dhrymes suggested that it was the SMAC estimator that was at fault, being downward biased because of the assumption of perfect competition in the labour market. If the labour market is imperfectly competitive then the marginal productivity of labour estimating equation [11.65] is no longer valid and should be replaced by

$$\log\left(\frac{Q}{L}\right) = \sigma \log\left(\frac{\gamma^{\theta}}{1 - \delta}\right) + \sigma \log\left(\frac{w}{p}\right) + \sigma \log \phi$$

where $\phi = 1 + 1/\eta$ and η is the elasticity of supply of labour.[15] Hence if ϕ and w/p are positively correlated then, since $\sigma > 0$, the standard specification error analysis of section 7.1 indicates that the normal estimator of σ will be downward biased.

Nerlove (1967), in surveying the results of CES studies, concluded that even slight variations in the period or concepts used tended to result in drastically different estimates of the elasticity of substitution. This is partly because, given the relatively small number of observations available, estimators of σ inevitably lack precision and are subject to considerable sampling variability. However, it is probably true that, despite the early conclusions of SMAC, investigations in general have failed to refute the Cobb–Douglas assumption of a unitary elasticity of substitution.

All the above procedures for estimating the parameters of the CES function involve the use in some form or other of the marginal productivity equations. Hence, behavioural and economic assumptions about how a firm or industry operates have to be made before the estimation can proceed. Kmenta (1967) suggested a more direct approach, considering the more general equation [11.24], the logarithmic transformation of which is

$$\log Q = \log \gamma - \left(\frac{v}{\theta}\right) \log[\delta K^{-\theta} + (1 - \delta)L^{-\theta}] \qquad [11.72]$$

By taking a Taylor series expansion about $\theta = 0$, Kmenta obtains a linear approximation of [11.72]

$$\log Q = \log \gamma + v\delta \log K + v(1 - \delta) \log L - \tfrac{1}{2}v\theta\delta(1 - \delta)[\log(K/L)]^2 \qquad [11.73]$$

Provided θ is near zero (i.e. provided the elasticity of substitution σ is near unity) [11.73] provides a close and convenient approximation to [11.72].

Hence, estimates of γ, v, δ and θ may be obtained directly by regressing $\log Q$ on $\log K$, $\log L$ and $(\log K/L)^2$. However, there are difficulties if the estimate of θ turns out to be much different from zero (i.e. if σ is much different from unity) because, if this is the case [11.73] no longer closely approximates the CES function.

The equivalent to [11.73] for the Cobb–Douglas function is simply its logarithmic transformation

$$\log Q = \log A + \alpha \log K + \beta \log L \tag{11.74}$$

If $\theta = 0$ and $\sigma = 1$ as it is for the Cobb–Douglas function then [11.73] reduces to the same form as [11.74]. Hence, when [11.73] is estimated, the significance of the coefficient on $(\log K/L)^2$ provides a test of whether the function is Cobb–Douglas or not. If it is Cobb–Douglas, the coefficient on $(\log K/L)^2$ should not be significant. However, if this estimated coefficient is significantly different from zero (i.e. $\theta \neq 0$), although this means that the Cobb–Douglas form should be rejected, it does not necessarily imply that the function is CES. As already noted, the approximation [11.73] may not then be valid.

There is also a further problem in that the coefficient of $(\log K/L)^2$ is likely, in any case, to be small for typical values of v, θ and δ. For example, suppose $v = 1$, $\delta = 0.5$ and $\theta = 0.5$ (implying $\sigma = 0.67$). The coefficient then has a true value of -0.0625. Given the high degree of multicollinearity probable between the variables $\log K$, $\log L$ and $(\log K/L)^2$, the standard error on the estimate of this coefficient is likely to be large so that the estimate will rarely appear significantly different from zero. In other words, the 'power' of the test is small.

An example of the use of this test and of the Kmenta approximation is provided by Griliches and Ringstad (1971) using cross-sectional interfirm data for different Norwegian industries. They rearrange [11.73] as

$$\log\left(\frac{Q}{L}\right) = \log \gamma + (v - 1)\log L + (v\delta)\log\left(\frac{K}{L}\right)$$
$$- \tfrac{1}{2}v\theta\delta(1 - \delta)\left[\log\left(\frac{K}{L}\right)\right]^2 \tag{11.75}$$

and, with 185 observations on the industry 'suits, coats and dresses', for example, estimate

$$\log\left(\frac{Q}{L}\right) = 1.431 + 0.142 \log L + 0.183 \log\left(\frac{K}{L}\right) + 0.008\left[\log\left(\frac{K}{L}\right)\right]^2$$
$$\phantom{\log\left(\frac{Q}{L}\right) = 1.431 +} (0.025) (0.055) \phantom{\log\left(\frac{K}{L}\right) +} (0.044)$$

Hence, we have $(\hat{v} - 1) = 0.142$, $(\hat{v}\hat{\delta}) = 0.183$ and $-0.5\hat{v}\hat{\theta}\hat{\delta}(1 - \hat{\delta}) = 0.008$. This implies $\hat{v} = 1.142$, i.e. slightly increasing returns to scale, $\delta = 0.160$, i.e. a relatively labour-intensive production function, and $\hat{\theta} = -0.104$, i.e. an elasticity of substitution $\sigma = 1.12$. The closeness of $\hat{\theta}$ to zero suggests the Kmenta approximation to the CES function is valid. However, the coefficient on $(\log K/L)^2$ is not significantly different from zero so the Cobb–Douglas form cannot be rejected. Note, though, that as expected this coefficient is very small so that its insignificance may be due to collinearity among the explanatory variables.

330

11.6 Further developments

The translog functions

Once the assumption of a unitary elasticity of substitution, σ, implicit in the Cobb–Douglas function, had been superseded by the merely constant σ of the more general CES function, it was clear that the next stage would be the development of variable elasticity of substitution (VES) production functions. Reasons why the elasticity of substitution should vary are not hard to find. For example, σ might be expected to vary with the capital/labour ratio K/L. The greater is the ratio, i.e. the greater the capital intensity of production, the harder it is likely to be to substitute further capital for labour and the lower σ is likely to be. Alternatively, even with a constant K/L ratio, the elasticity of substitution may simply change over time if technical progress affects the ease with which factors may be substituted for each other.

Variable elasticity of substitution production functions were indeed developed. Early notable examples were those of Revankar (1971), who developed a model in which σ was a linear function of the capital/labour ratio, and Sato and Hoffman (1968) who presented a series of forms – one similar to Revankar's and another in which σ varied over time. However, a general form for VES functions was finally presented by Christensen, Jorgenson and Lau (1973). The problem had always been that of finding a functional form that not only allowed for a variable elasticity of substitution but was easily estimatable and could be considered a sufficiently close approximation to whatever the underlying productive process actually was. The 'transcendental logarithmic' or *translog production function* of Christensen, Jorgenson and Lau approximates the logarithm of output by a quadratic in the logarithms of the inputs

$$\log Q = \beta_0 + \beta_K \log K + \beta_L \log L + \beta_{KK}(\log K)^2$$
$$+ \beta_{LL}(\log L)^2 + \beta_{LK} \log K \log L \qquad [11.76]$$

The big advantage of [11.76] is the ease with which it may be estimated. Also, since it can be regarded as a second-order Taylor approximation[16] to *any* production function, VES or otherwise, it can be used to *test* whether the elasticity of substitution is, in fact, constant or not. If we set $\beta_{KK} = \beta_{LL} = -\frac{1}{2}\beta_{LK}$ in [11.76] then the equation becomes

$$\log Q = \beta_0 + \beta_K \log K + \beta_L \log L - \frac{1}{2}\beta_{LK}(\log K - \log L)^2 \qquad [11.77]$$

which is of the same form as [11.73], Kmenta's Taylor approximation to the CES function. Hence, if [11.76] is estimated, the hypothesis of a CES may be tested by checking whether the estimated coefficients of [11.76] obey the restrictions

$$\beta_{KK} = \beta_{LL} = -\frac{1}{2}\beta_{LK}$$

Griliches and Ringstad (1971) in fact performed such a test for Norwegian manufacturing industry and found a variable elasticity of substitution (i.e. the restrictions did not hold).

The production function [11.76] also has the interesting property that the nature of the returns to scale implied is not the same for all values of the inputs. Griliches and Ringstad, in fact, found increasing returns to scale when firms were small but something very close to constant returns to scale for larger firms. The property of non-varying returns to scale is, of course, one of the limitations of the more restrictive Cobb–Douglas and CES functions.

Christensen, Jorgenson and Lau (1973) also proposed the transcendental logartithmic cost function which has the form

$$\log C = \alpha_0 + \alpha_Q \log Q + \alpha_Q \log w + \alpha_m \log m + \alpha_{QQ}(\log Q)^2$$
$$+ \alpha_{ww}(\log w)^2 + \alpha_{mm}(\log m)^2 + \alpha_{Qw} \log Q \log w$$
$$+ \alpha_{Qm} \log Q \log m + \alpha_{wm} \log w \log m \qquad [11.78]$$

where w and m are the prices of labour and capital respectively. Since a doubling of input prices must double costs for a given level of output, a restriction has to be placed on the α parameters to ensure that the cost function [11.78] is homogeneous of degree one in w and m.

The translog cost function can be regarded as a second-order approximation to any arbitrary cost function and, like the translog production function, permits the nature of the returns to scale implied to vary with the levels of inputs and output. This last property was made use of by Christensen and Greene (1976) to re-examine the Nerlove (1963) findings regarding returns to scale in the US electricity supply industry.

Recall from section 11.3 that Nerlove, adopting a Cobb–Douglas formulation, found that cost functions estimated for the smallest firms in the industry indicated extensive economies of scale but that *separate* equations for the largest firms suggested constant or even decreasing returns to scale. Christensen and Greene update Nerlove's 1955 data base with new 1970 data. Estimating a *single* translog cost equation, they find that in 1955 substantial economies of scale had been available, thus confirming the Nerlove findings. However they also find that by 1970 such economies had largely been exploited and most firms by then were operating on the flat portion of their average cost curve.

The cost function [11.78] can be generalised to include other factors of production such as fuel and energy. One of its advantages is that differentiation of [11.78] with respect to factor prices yields derived demand equations for each factor of production in terms of their prices and output. This fact was exploited by Pindyck (1979) in an international study of the industrial demand for energy and the possibility of substitution between various fuels. Pindyck found that energy and capital were strongly complementary as factor inputs. That is a fall in the price of energy/capital leads to a rise in the demand for capital/energy.

The translog cost function approach has been extended by Pollack, Sickles and Wales (1984) to include a CES type cost function. In a study of US and Dutch manufacturing industry they conclude, using likelihood ratio tests of the kind described in section 4.5 that the CES translog cost function is empirically superior to the original formulation. A similar approach is used by Daughety and Nelson (1988) in a study of the US trucking industry.

Frontier production functions

As we noted at the beginning of section 11.1, the production function of theory is a technical relationship defining the *maximum* output obtainable from given inputs. However, the statistical model, first introduced as equations [11.29] and [11.30], incorporates a disturbance term which is permitted to take positive or negative values. This implies that empirical studies provides estimates of production functions that yield the *average* output obtainable from given inputs rather than the maximum output. To estimate the production function of theory we need to estimate α and β, in, for example, a Cobb–Douglas function, such that

$$\log Q_i \leqslant \log Q_i^* \tag{11.79}$$

where

$$\log Q_i^* = \log A + \alpha \log K_i + \beta \log L_i$$

for all observations in the sample. Equation [11.79] implies that actual output, Q_i, is always less than, or equal to, but never greater than, maximum output Q_i^*. One possibility is to choose α and β so as to minimise

$$\sum (\log Q_i - \log A - \alpha \log K_i - \beta \log L_i)^2$$

subject to the set of constraints given by [11.79].

Production functions estimated in this way are referred to as *frontier production functions* and attempts have been made to estimate such functions. For example, Schmidt (1976) presented a statistical model for which the above procedure yields MLEs of α and β.

Alternative representations of technical progress

Another area that has seen much development has been the treatment of technical progress. Recall from section 11.3 that the representation of technical progress by a simple time trend has many deficiencies. This form of disembodied technical progress implies, firstly, that increases in efficiency are simply superimposed on the system, occurring for no clearly defined reason and, secondly, that such improvements always affect all 'machines' equally no matter what their age. Progress has however been made in the estimation of so-called vintage models of production.

In a vintage model the neo-classical assumption of a homogeneous capital stock is relaxed and all items of capital equipment are distinguished by their vintage, i.e. the data of their construction. Machines of a later vintage are more efficient than those constructed earlier but their efficiency is determined by the state of technical knowledge *at the moment of their construction*. They do *not* benefit from any improvements in technology occurring after that date. Old machines cannot be redesigned to accommodate new technology. Vintage models represent a major step towards reality in that new technology now has to be 'embodied' in new kinds of equipment in new machines. Thus a 'transmission mechanism' – the investment process – is provided whereby new ideas eventually influence the level of output.

The first rigorous attempt to formulate a model of embodied technical progress was that of Solow (1960). In the Solow model technical progress proceeds at a constant rate, g, but affects only newly produced capital goods. Separate production functions exist for machines of different vintages. Thus, if Q_v is the output produced by machines of vintage v (i.e. constructed in year v), K_v is the number of machines of that vintage, and L_v is the labour employed on such machines, then (assuming a basic Cobb–Douglas form) the production function for machines of vintage v is

$$Q_v = Ae^{gv}K_v^{\alpha}L_v^{\beta} \qquad [11.80]$$

where g is the rate of technical progress. Capital stock of vintage, v, K_v, is dependent on investment in machines in the year v and the rate (assumed constant) at which such machines depreciate. Total output is the sum of all outputs obtained from machines of all vintages and Solow was able to derive an aggregate production function in which the normal capital stock variable was replaced by an index of 'effective capital stock'. This index was a weighted sum of all machines with weights declining with age.

One way in which vintage models can be developed further is to relax the neo-classical assumption that capital equipment is 'malleable' and, hence, can be automatically transformed so as to be capable of operation by any number of workers. Capital stock is not generally like 'putty' and cannot be moulded to accommodate any capital/labour ratio. A machine built to be operated by two workers cannot instantaneously be transformed so that it is capable of operation by twenty workers. Models which still retain the assumption of malleability, both at the time of a machine's construction and *throughout the remainder of its life*, are commonly known as 'putty–putty' models. While Solow's original model was of this kind, most empirical models abandon such assumptions. An alternative and probably more realistic assumption is that while machines can be *designed* to accommodate any required capital/labour ratio, once they are constructed the capital/labour ratio can no longer be varied and substitution between capital and labour becomes impossible. Early examples of the estimation of such 'putty-clay' models are the studies by King (1972), Ando, *et al.* (1974), and Mizon (1974). However, because data on the output from each vintage of machine are not generally available, the estimation of such models is a complicated affair, requiring assumptions about the optimal service life of machines. We shall not attempt, therefore, to describe these models in detail here.

Technical progress and cointegration

More recently, Budd and Hobbis (1989) have applied the co-integration analysis described in section 7.5 to the UK production function and in particular to the problem of how best to represent technical progress. They argue that there are two main sources of technological advance. First, it can come through domestic research effort which Budd and Hobbis proxy by the number of new patents taken out in the US by UK residents. Secondly, new technology can be imported from abroad and this flow is proxied by imports of new machinery and by royalty payments to foreign countries. These flows are converted into 'net stock of technology' variables by a simple cumulating process in which given depreciation rates are assumed.

Capital stock figures are adjusted to take into account that proportion which consists of recently imported machinery (which may be assumed to be technologically superior otherwise it would not have been imported). 'Quality-adjusted' capital stock, K is defined as

$$K^* = K(M/K)^{\gamma}$$

where M is the net stock of recently imported machinery and K is the unadjusted capital stock.

A technology index, T, is then defined as

$$T = aP^\theta R^\phi \qquad\qquad\qquad [11.81]$$

where P and R are the patents and royalties variables respectively.

A Cobb–Douglas production function of the kind

$$Q = A^* T L^\alpha K^{*\beta} \qquad\qquad\qquad [11.82]$$

is assumed which, after substitution from [11.80] and [11.81], becomes

$$Q = AL^\alpha [K(M/K)^\gamma]^\beta P^\theta R^\phi \qquad A = A^* a \qquad\qquad [11.83]$$

If the technology variables are unimportant then $\gamma = \theta = \phi = 0$ and the function [11.83] reduces to the standard Cobb–Douglas form

$$Q = AL^\alpha K^\beta \qquad\qquad\qquad [11.84]$$

Budd and Hobbis are not concerned with the short-run dynamics of the production function and therefore use quarterly data on UK manufacturing for 1968(i) to 1985(iv) to estimate long-run relationships using co-integration analysis. They find that all their variables – both the traditional factor inputs and the technology proxies are integrated of order one. That is they become stationary on first differencing. This means that it is possible for a co-integrating vector to be found and hence a long-run relationship to exist between some or all of these variables.

Relationships based both on the standard form [11.84] and on the technology modified form [11.83] are tested for co-integration using the Dickey–Fuller tests. Static or co-integrating regressions are computed with and without a time trend included to represent disembodied technical progress. The standard forms based on [11.84] invariably fail the co-integration tests and frequently have implausible coefficients. Only when the technology variables are added to the equations is it possible to find a co-integrating vector. Also when the technology variables are included there appears to be no need for the time trend. Hence Budd and Hobbis conclude that the long-run production function is of the form [11.83] rather than [11.84] and that technical progress is better represented by their proxy variables than by the traditional time trend.

Budd and Hobbis' long-run equations suggest that a very large and possibly implausible contribution to UK economic growth is made by machinery imports whereas growth due to their other technology variables is estimated to be small. This is a major problem with their model because the machinery imports variable increases throughout the sample period and may therefore be picking up other trend factors that are contributing to economic growth. However, they claim that their analysis implies that any long- or short-run relationship estimated from UK data is likely to be seriously mis-specified unless it includes technology variables of the kind they have constructed.

A vast number of production studies have been undertaken and published during the post-war era. Unfortunately, such have been the data and specification problems met with, that it is doubtful whether we are much nearer answering many of the questions posed at the beginning of this chapter. The general magnitude of elasticities of substitution, the extent of economies of scale and the quantitative importance of technical progress are not much clearer today than when Douglas undertook his pioneering studies. The principal finding of Nerlove's 1967 survey of CES functions, that even the slightest variation in the period or methods used tends to produce drastically different estimates, is probably as true today as it was a quarter of a century ago. It is to be hoped that some of the later developments described above, on which future work is likely to be concentrated, will shed more light on matters.

Appendix: Empirical exercise

In this exercise we shall attempt the estimation of Cobb–Douglas production functions, from annual data for 1960–79, for the industry groupings referred to as Food, Drink and Tobacco, and Paper, Printing and Publishing in the UK Standard Industrial Classification. We shall adopt an error correction model approach and, as in the last exercise, we make use of the co-integration techniques of section 7.5. We begin by defining the variables:

Output Q = Index of Industrial Production at constant factor cost.

Capital K = Gross Capital Stock at 1975 replacement cost.

Labour L = Employees in employment (June figures).

Q is taken from Table 2.4 in the National Income and Expenditure 1982 Blue Book (BB 1982). You will have more difficulty constructing the series for K and L. Data for K for 1971–81 can be found in Table 11.8 of BB 1982 and data for 1968–70 in the 1979 and 1980 editions. However the only pre-1968 data you will be able to find is not at 1975 replacement cost. Fortunately, in BB 1972 you will find data for 1960–71 at 1963 replacement cost. The fact that you have data series that overlap for the years 1968–71 will enable you to calculate the ratios of K at 1975 cost to K at 1963 cost. For example, for Food, Drink and Tobacco the ratio is about 2.45 to 1. Multiplying the K values for 1960–67 by this ratio will convert them into 1975 replacement cost. The final series you should obtain are shown in Table A11.1 at the end of this appendix.

You will have even greater difficulty constructing a consistent series for L. The June (i.e. mid-year) figures for employees in employment can be found in table 1.2 in the data section of the Department of Employment Gazette (Table 102 or 103 in earlier editions). Unfortunately, there were a whole series of changes in the way data on L was collected during these years. The major change was in 1971 (you will discover what happened as you construct the series) but there were a number of other minor changes as well. To construct consistent series you will therefore have to adopt similar procedures to those used in the construction of the capital stock series. Remember to use the latest available figures (footnotes to the tables will indicate whether data is provisional or in its final revised form). You should eventually obtain (in thousands) series very similar to those in Table A11.1 at the end of this appendix. However, do not rely on the series given there. You should attempt their construction yourself. Collecting data is rarely as easy as it was in the first two exercises (see Chapters 9 and 10). Usually considerable time and effort is necessary if consistent data series are to be obtained.

We now apply the techniques of section 7.5 to see whether the Q, K and L series are co-integrated. If so, then we can be assured that a long-run relationship (the production function) exists between them. At this point we should note that, in the paper discussed at the end of Chapter 11, Budd and Hobbis found that, for total manufacturing, although Q, L and K were all integrated of order unity, it was not possible to achieve co-integration unless proper account was taken of technical progress. We shall investigate whether a similar conclusion holds for individual industry groups.

We begin with the industry grouping Food, Drink and Tobacco. Considering the employment series first, you will note that, unlike any of the data series we have examined so far, the employment series trends gently downwards over our sample period. However, this necessitates no change in the tests for stationarity.

Working in natural logarithms, we begin by testing to see whether the employment series is stationary in the levels or whether it has to be differenced before becoming stationary. We compute a series of Dickey–Fuller regressions of the types [7.56] and [7.57], including as many differenced terms on the right-hand side as are necessary to produce non-autocorrelated residuals. Remember, though that the Dickey–Fuller tests are not precise, lack power and must be used with care, particularly as, in this case we only have 20 annual observations. Typical Dickey–Fuller regressions are

$$\Delta l_t = 2.85 - 0.0037T - 0.43l_{t-1}$$
$$ (1.08) \quad (0.0012) \quad (0.16)$$

$$R^2 = 0.39, \qquad Z11 = 0.04, \qquad Z12 = 3.65 \qquad (1961-79) \qquad [A11.1]$$

and

$$\Delta l_t = 2.59 - 0.0042T - 0.39l_{t-1} - 0.45\Delta l_{t-2}$$
$$ (1.35) \quad (0.0016) \quad (0.20) \quad\quad (0.21)$$

$$R^2 = 0.46, \qquad Z11 = 3.76, \qquad Z12 = 2.61 \qquad (1963-79) \qquad [A11.2]$$

Lower case letters as usual denote natural logarithms. The second regression is estimated only for 1963–79 because the 1960–62 data is needed to compute the necessary lagged values.

$Z11$ and $Z12$ represent the LM statistics for first and up to second order autocorrelation, respectively. Since critical 0.05 levels for χ^2 (with 1 and 2 d.f.) are 3.84 and 5.99 respectively, there appears no serious problem of autocorrelation in the residuals of [A11.1] or [A11.2].

The Dickey–Fuller tests imply stationarity if the coefficients on the variable l_{t-1} in the above equations are significantly less that zero. The Dickey–Fuller statistics are the 't-ratios' on these coefficients. These take the values -2.7 in [A11.1] and -1.9 in [A11.2]. They should be compared with the critical values on the right-hand side of Table 7.1 rather than those in normal t-tables. The absolute values of the statistics are clearly not large enough for us to reject the null hypothesis of non-stationarity. The employment series cannot be shown to be stationary in the levels.

We next test the joint hypothesis that the coefficients on T and l_{t-1} in the above equations are both zero. Failure to reject this joint hypothesis will mean that we are justified in ruling out the possibility that Δl_t is subject to a deterministic trend. The F-statistic [4.45] in this case yields the values 5.13 for [A11.1] and 3.57 for [A11.2]. These must be compared with the critical values in Table 7.2

rather than those in normal F-tables, and we see that we cannot reject the joint null hypothesis. Δl_t can be regarded as determined by a disturbance and maybe past values of itself.

We now test Δl_t the differenced value of employment for stationarity. To do this we estimate Dickey–Fuller equations of the types [7.44], [7.56] and [7.57] for $\Delta^2 l_t = \Delta l_t - \Delta l_{t-1}$. This results in, for example

$$\Delta^2 l_t = 0.005 - 0.001 T - 1.16 \Delta l_{t-1}$$
$$\quad (0.010) \ (0.001) \quad (0.25)$$

$$R^2 = 0.59, \qquad Z11 = 4.77, \qquad Z12 = 7.71 \qquad (1962\text{–}79) \qquad \text{[A11.3]}$$

and

$$\Delta^2 l_t = -0.94 \Delta l_{t-1}$$
$$\quad (0.23)$$

$$\rule{2cm}{0.4pt} \quad Z11 = 0.10, \qquad Z12 = 1.40 \qquad (1962\text{–}79) \qquad \text{[A11.4]}$$

No R^2 value is given for [A11.4] because this equation does not contain an intercept. The LM statistics for autocorrelation are too high in [A11.3] and the constant and the coefficient on T both appear to be insignificantly different from zero. Equation [A11.4] which is a version of equation [7.44] is therefore preferable. The Dickey–Fuller statistic for this equation is the 't-ratio' on Δl_{t-1} and takes the value -4.1. It must be compared with the values on the left-hand side of Table 7.1, (because of the absence of constant and time trend), and we see that, despite the fact that [A11.4] is based on only 18 observations, we can fairly confidently reject the hypothesis of non-stationarity. Thus, although the employment series itself is non-stationary, its first difference appears stationary. That is, the variable l is integrated of order unity or is $I(1)$.

The reader should now verify that the output and capital stock series for the industry grouping Food, Drink and Tobacco are also $I(1)$, that is these series become stationary on first differencing. Since all three series l, k and q are $I(1)$, it is possible that they are co-integrated and that a long-run relationship exists between them. However, co-integration is by no means certain. It may well be necessary to allow for technical progress in any long-run production function and we have no data to represent this factor. Remember that Budd and Hobbis, in the work mentioned earlier, failed to find a co-integrating vector using the output, capital stock and employment series for total UK manufacturing.

The first step in testing for co-integration is to compute the static or co-integrating regression for the three variables, q, k and l. Using the full sample period, we obtain

$$q = -0.036 + 0.579 k + 0.496 l \qquad R^2 = 0.992 \qquad \text{[A11.5]}$$
$$\quad (0.792) \ (0.020) \quad (0.114)$$

As in the last exercise, no diagnostic statistics are quoted for the co-integrating regression. The absence of any lagged variables in [A11.5] means that the residuals from this regression are almost certain to appear autocorrelated. The point is, however, whether the residuals form a stationary series. If so then q, k and l are co-integrated.

We therefore test the residuals, e, from [A11.5] for stationarity by estimating the following Dickey–Fuller and augmented Dickey–Fuller equations[17]

$$\Delta e_t = -0.88 e_{t-1}$$
$$\quad\;\; (0.23)$$

$$Z11 = 8.45, \qquad Z12 = 9.85 \qquad (1961\text{–}79) \tag{A11.6}$$

and

$$\Delta e_t = -1.36 e_{t-1} + 0.66 \Delta e_{t-1}$$
$$\quad\;\; (0.24) \qquad\;\; (0.18)$$

$$Z11 = 0.35, \qquad Z12 = 1.62 \qquad (1963\text{–}79) \tag{A11.7}$$

The Dickey–Fuller statistics in this case are the 't-ratios' on the coefficients of e_{t-1} of the above equations and take the values -3.8 in [A11.6] and -5.7 in [A11.7]. The absolute values of these statistics must be compared with the critical values in Table 7.3, and appear to be large enough for us to reject the null hypothesis that the residuals of [A11.5] are non-stationary. However, the conclusion in this case is not straightforward. Our sample is rather small for the co-integration test and, moreover, the LM statistics for [A11.6] clearly indicate autocorrelation problems, whereas in [A11.7] the coefficient on e_{t-1} is less than -1. It is clearly significantly less than zero on the usual augmented Dickey–Fuller test but its absolute size raises the possibility of a negative unit root. Note that if

$$e_t = -e_{t-1} \quad \text{then} \quad \Delta e_{t-1} = -2 e_{t-1}$$

The coefficient of e_{t-1} in [A11.7] is clearly closer to -2 than it is to zero. The possibility of a negative unit root throws considerable doubt on any finding that the residuals from the static regression [A11.5] are stationary.[18]

Despite the doubts as to whether q, k and l can be regarded as co-integrated we shall nevertheless proceed, for the moment, under the assumption that a long-term relationship between these variables exists. Hence we will now adopt the general to specific approach to estimating a short-run relationship between q, k and l. Since we are dealing with annual data we shall use, in our general model, up to second-order lags only. That is we first estimate the equation

$$q_t = \alpha_0 + \alpha_1 q_{t-1} + \alpha_2 q_{t-2} + \sum_{i=0}^{2} \beta_i k_{t-i} + \sum_{i=0}^{2} \gamma_i l_{t-i} \tag{A11.8}$$

Recall from section 7.3 that equations such as [A11.8] can be reparameterised as second order ECMs. We therefore present our estimated version of [A11.8] in its ECM form.

$$\Delta q_t = -0.184 - 0.294 \Delta q_{t-1} + 0.790 \Delta k_t + 0.321 \Delta k_{t-1} + 0.120 \Delta l_t - 0.104 \Delta l_{t-1}$$
$$\quad\;\; (0.839) \;\; (0.275) \qquad\quad (0.192) \qquad (0.197) \qquad\quad (0.209) \qquad (0.267)$$

$$\quad - 1.029 q_{t-2} + 0.597 k_{t-2} + 0.530 l_{t-2} \qquad (1962\text{–}79) \tag{A11.9}$$
$$\quad\;\; (0.309) \qquad\; (0.191) \qquad\; (0.221)$$

$$R^2 = 0.892, \qquad \sum e^2 = 0.000500, \qquad dw = 2.33, \qquad Z11 = 0.968,$$
$$Z12 = 2.58, \; Z2 = 0.003$$

There are no problems with the autocorrelation statistics in the above general model. $Z2$ represents the LM statistic for heteroscedasticity described in section

5.2.1 and is distributed as χ^2 with one degree of freedom. Its value suggests homoscedastic residuals. If possible, you should now compute the RESET test statistic for functional form mis-specification, described at the end of section 7.1. This should confirm that there appears to be no functional form mis-specification.

Our diagnostic statistics suggest that there are no specification problems with equation [A11.9], but is a simpler model equally data acceptable? Recall, from section 7.3, that a first-order ECM is a special case of second-order ECMs such as [A11.9]. Estimation of the appropriate first-order ECM results in

$$\Delta q_t = 0.273 + 0.903\Delta k_t + 0.658\Delta l_t - 1.042q_{t-1} + 0.614k_{t-1} + 0.464l_{t-1}$$
$$\qquad (1.171) \quad (0.309) \qquad (0.279) \qquad (0.365) \qquad (0.228) \qquad (0.285)$$
$$\qquad\qquad\qquad\qquad\qquad\qquad\qquad\qquad\qquad\qquad (1962\text{--}79) \qquad [A11.10]$$

$$R^2 = 0.617, \qquad \sum e^2 = 0.001775, \qquad dw = 1.82, \qquad Z11 = 0.92,$$
$$Z12 = 9.46, \qquad Z2 = 0.040$$

Although all the estimated coefficients in [A11.10] have respectable t-ratios, the *LM* statistic for up to second order autocorrelation is unsatisfactory, suggesting that the omission of second-order lags is a specification error. Also, since specification [A11.10] can be obtained from the general model [A11.8] by the imposition of three restrictions, (list them), we can test the validity of these restrictions by applying the F-test of section 4.4. The F-statistic [4.45] in fact takes the value

$$\frac{(SSR_R - SSR_u)/3}{SSR_u/9} = \frac{(1775 - 500)/3}{500/9} = 7.65$$

Since the critical F-value with $(3, 9)$ d.f. is $F_{0.05} = 3.85$, the restrictions imposed are clearly rejected by the data.

Our examination of [A11.10] suggested that the omission of all second-order lags from the general model is a serious mis-specification. However, both the variables Δl_t and Δl_{t-1} in [A11.9] have coefficients that are statistically insignificant from zero, with t-ratios of 0.57 and -0.39 respectively. Dropping Δl_{t-1} yields

$$\Delta q_t = -0.362 - 0.375\Delta q_{t-1} + 0.797\Delta k_t + 0.368\Delta k_{t-1} + 0.173\Delta l_t$$
$$\qquad (0.673) \quad (0.172) \qquad (0.182) \qquad (0.150) \qquad (0.152)$$
$$\qquad - 1.127q_{t-2} + 0.660k_{t-2} + 0.603l_{t-2} \qquad (1962\text{--}79) \qquad\qquad [A11.11]$$
$$\qquad (0.172) \qquad (0.097) \qquad (0.112)$$
$$R^2 = 0.890, \qquad \sum e^2 = 0.000509, \qquad dw = 2.31, \qquad Z11 = 0.83,$$
$$Z12 = 2.41, \qquad Z2 = 0.038$$

The coefficient on Δl_t remains statistically insignificant in [A11.11] but, since its t-ratio exceeds unity, we will retain this variable in the model. The specification [A11.11] appears satisfactory from a statistical point of view, but can any further simplification be achieved? One possibility is that the long-run production function for this industry grouping exhibits constant returns to scale. For a Cobb–Douglas production function such as we have here, constant returns to scale implies that the long-run output elasticities should sum to unity.

Imposing this restriction results in

$$\Delta q_t = 0.472 - 0.442\Delta q_{t-1} + 0.828\Delta k_t + 0.460\Delta k_{t-1} + 0.156\Delta l_t$$
$$\quad (0.079)\ (0.168) \qquad (0.185) \qquad (0.134) \qquad (0.156)$$

$$\quad - 1.160(q_{t-2} - l_{t-2}) + 0.663(k_{t-2} - l_{t-2}) \qquad (1962\text{--}79) \qquad [\text{A}11.12]$$
$$\quad (0.174) \qquad\qquad (0.100)$$

$$R^2 = 0.873, \qquad \sum e^2 = 0.000588, \qquad dw = 2.10, \qquad Z11 = 0.084,$$
$$Z12 = 0.084,\ Z2 = 1.13$$

There is no deterioration in the diagnostic statistics for [A11.12]. Also, if we test the restriction being imposed, the F-statistic [4.45] gives a value of only 1.55, compared with a critical F-value (with (1, 10) d.f.) of $F_{0.05} = 4.96$. The restriction is clearly not rejected by the data so we can adopt [A11.12] as our statistically preferred final equation. The long-run production function appears to exhibit constant returns to scale. It is left to the reader to try imposing constant returns to scale in the short-run as well.

We can deduce the implied long-run production function from [A11.12]. With a zero long-run growth rate, for example, we have $\Delta q_t = \Delta k_t = \Delta l_t = 0$ and also $q_t = q_{t-2}$, $k_t = k_{t-2}$, $l_t = l_{t-2}$, so that [A11.12] becomes

$$q_t = 0.407 + 0.572k_t + 0.428l_t \quad \text{or} \quad Q_t = 1.50K^{0.572}L^{0.428}$$

There is, however, one worrying aspect of equation [A11.12]. This can best be seen if we express [A11.12] in its full ECM form as

$$\Delta q_t = -0.442\Delta q_{t-1} + 0.828\Delta k_t + 0.460\Delta k_{t-1} + 0.156\Delta l_t$$
$$\quad - 1.162[q_{t-2} - 0.407 - 0.572k_{t-2} - 0.428l_{t-2}]$$

The coefficient on the disequilibrium error term in square brackets exceed unity in absolute value. Since our data is annual this coefficient measures the proportion of any disequilibrium two years previous that is compensated for in the current period. In our equation there appears to be overcompensation. Although the coefficient is not significantly different from unity, its size is highly implausible and suggests that error corrections are actually destabilising. We must, however, remember that our findings are based on a very small sample size which inevitably casts doubt on their reliability. In addition, recall that our test for co-integration of q, k and l was less than satisfactory – there was considerable doubt whether an equilibrium relationship between just these variables existed. If such a relationship did not exist then we could not expect to be able to estimate a sensible stable short run ECM involving just these variables.

One reason for our difficulties is not difficult to think of. As we have already noted, technical progress is likely to play at least some part in long-run production functions and we lack the data to represent it. Our failure to model technical progress may therefore be the cause of our estimation difficulty.

The reader should verify that the addition of a time trend either to the static regression equation [A11.5] or to the ECM [A11.12] has a minimal effect. Technical progress clearly cannot be represented in this simple manner.

There is another problem with our data set. We have used stocks as our input variables, whereas the true inputs are the flows of services obtained from the factors of production. Machine hours and man hours would have been more appropriate units of measurement. There is certainly a serious problem with our capital stock variable. Capital service flows are unlikely to be proportionate to capital stock because capacity utilisation is likely to vary so much over the business cycle. A less serious but similar problem arises with our employment series. Average hours worked also varies over the business cycle so labour utilisation is not constant. It is true that we have reduced utilisation problems by ending our sample period in 1979 before the deep recession of 1980–82, but this still leaves earlier less severe slowdowns in economic activity.

We now attempt the estimation of a Cobb–Douglas production function for the industry grouping Paper, Printing and Publishing, using the same procedures as those used for Food Drink and Tobacco. The data sources are identical to those above and the final series are again shown at the end of this appendix.

All three data series again appear to be integrated of order unity – that is they only become stationary on first differencing. For example, for the employment series

$$\Delta^2 l_t = 0.005 - 0.0008T - 0.85\Delta l_{t-1}$$
$$(0.014) \quad (0.0012) \quad (0.27)$$

$$R^2 = 0.41 \qquad Z11 = 0.89 \qquad Z12 = 4.00 \qquad (1962–79) \qquad [A11.13]$$

and

$$\Delta^2 l_t = -0.73\Delta l_{t-1}$$
$$(0.23)$$

$$\text{———} \quad Z11 = 0.65, \qquad Z12 = 1.97 \qquad (1962–79) \qquad [A11.14]$$

The time trend and intercept can be dropped from [A11.13] and the Dickey–Fuller statistic of -3.2 in [A11.14] must be compared with values in the left-hand side of Table 7.1. It suggests that Δl is stationary. The reader should again verify that Δq and Δk are also stationary variables.

The co-integrating regression for Paper, Printing and Publishing is

$$q_t = -0.802 + 0.655k_t + 0.678l_t \qquad (1960–79) \quad R^2 = 0.872 \qquad [A11.15]$$
$$(1.770) \quad (0.069) \quad (0.266)$$

Testing the residuals from [A11.15] for stationarity yields

$$\Delta e_t = -0.78e_{t-1}$$
$$(0.22)$$

$$Z11 = 6.21, \qquad Z12 = 8.27 \qquad (1961–79) \qquad [A11.16]$$

and

$$\Delta e_t = -1.21e_{t-1} + 0.64\Delta e_{t-1}$$
$$(0.22) \qquad (0.17)$$

$$Z11 = 0.23, \qquad Z12 = 1.00 \qquad (1962–79) \qquad [A11.17]$$

Equations [A11.16] and [A11.17] are very similar to the equations [A11.6] and [A11.7] obtained for Food, Drink and Tobacco. While at first sight the Dickey–Fuller statistics of -3.5 and -5.5 appear satisfactory, the auto-correlation statistics are well above their critical values in [A11.16], and in [A11.17] the coefficient on e_{t-1} exceeds unity in absolute value.[19] As for

Table A11.1 Production function data sets

	Food, Drink and Tobacco			Paper, Printing and Publishing		
	Q	K	L	Q	K	L
1960	72.8	6.1	748	82.4	3.7	574
1961	75.1	6.1	763	81.1	3.9	589
1962	76.5	6.4	772	80.9	4.0	597
1963	78.9	6.9	764	83.4	4.2	596
1964	80.7	7.1	761	91.1	4.3	597
1965	82.6	7.4	766	93.0	4.4	607
1966	85.0	7.8	768	95.5	4.6	614
1967	86.5	8.1	760	95.1	4.8	604
1968	90.1	8.6	744	98.9	5.0	605
1969	93.0	9.0	755	102.2	5.1	611
1970	94.4	9.4	765	102.8	5.4	618
1971	95.0	9.8	744	100.0	5.5	589
1972	99.0	10.2	730	105.6	5.7	573
1973	103.1	10.7	728	115.2	5.8	568
1974	102.5	11.1	740	115.2	6.0	582
1975	100.0	11.4	701	100.0	6.2	559
1976	102.5	11.7	691	102.4	6.3	536
1977	104.0	12.1	689	106.7	6.4	531
1978	106.2	12.5	682	109.1	6.6	534
1979	107.6	12.8	680	112.4	6.8	543

Food, Drink and Tobacco, this casts doubt on the properties of the residuals from [A11.15].

Despite these doubts we shall again attempt the estimation of error correction models. For Paper, Printing and Publishing, the ECM form of the general equation [A11.8] is

$$\Delta q_t = -1.137 - 0.369\Delta q_{t-1} + 0.469\Delta k_t + 1.473\Delta k_{t-1} + 1.330\Delta l_t$$
$$\quad\;\;(1.974)\;\;(0.251)\qquad\;(0.825)\qquad(0.805)\qquad\;\;(0.494)$$

$$\quad\; - 1.073\Delta l_{t-1} - 0.741 q_{t-2} + 0.478 k_{t-2} + 0.584 l_{t-2}\qquad (1962\text{–}79)$$
$$\qquad(0.718)\qquad(0.264)\qquad(0.227)\qquad(0.388)\qquad\qquad [\text{A11.18}]$$

$$R^2 = 0.869, \qquad \sum e^2 = 0.00545, \qquad dw = 2.26, \qquad Z11 = 0.97,$$
$$Z12 = 6.52, \qquad Z2 = 0.63$$

In [A11.18] the variable Δk_t has a coefficient with a t-ratio of only 0.57 and the LM statistic for up to second-order autocorrelation exceeds its critical value. However, the reader should verify that if Δk_t is dropped from the equation, this LM statistic falls to a satisfactory value.

The reader should also verify that if a standard first-order ECM similar to [A11.10] is estimated, then it has to be rejected against [A11.18] on the usual F-test. Also, as with Food, Drink and Tobacco, the omission of second-order lags leads to a serious deterioration in the autocorrelation statistics.

Imposing constant returns to scale in this case yields

$$\Delta q_t = 0.321 - 0.241\Delta q_{t-1} + 1.098\Delta k_{t-1} + 1.109\Delta l_t - 1.385\Delta l_{t-1}$$
$$(0.304)\ \ (0.178)(0.593)(0.388)(0.398)$$
$$- 0.551(q_{t-2} - l_{t-2}) + 0.279(k_{t-2} - l_{t-2})(1962\text{--}79)[\text{A11.19}]$$
$$(0.202)(0.134)$$

$$R^2 = 0.843, \qquad \sum e^2 = 0.00651, \qquad dw = 2.22, \qquad Z11 = 1.46,$$
$$Z12 = 8.88, \qquad Z2 = 0.87$$

Although it is easily verified that the returns to scale restriction is data acceptable on the usual F-test, in [A11.19] the $Z12$ statistic has again risen above its critical value.

It is difficult to choose between the ECMs [A11.18] and [A11.19]. However the long-run production functions for both equations are very similar. For example, for [A11.19] we have in the long run, with zero growth rates,

$$q = 0.583 + 0.506k + 0.494l \qquad \text{or} \qquad Q = 1.79K^{0.506}L^{0.494}$$

Unlike equation [A11.12] for Food, Drink and Tobacco, the coefficient on q_{t-2} in equation [A11.19] is less than unity in absolute value, implying a stable error correction mechanism with eventual convergence to long-run values. However, the short-run coefficients on the capital and labour variables are large and this, together with the opposite signs on the labour change variables, suggests a somewhat bumpy and implausible ride to long-run equilibrium.

The defects of our estimated equations for Paper, Printing and Publishing can again be attributed to data deficiencies. We were unable to make any allowance for technical progress (the reader should verify that, as with Food, Drink and Tobacco, it is not possible to employ a time trend to adequately represent technical progress). Also, we again represented input flows by stock measures of capital and labour. The lesson of this exercise is that it is very hard to obtain sensible time series estimates of production function relationships in the absence of adequate data series on technical progress.

Notes

1. We are therefore not concerned with so-called 'fixed coefficient' models of the productive process and will not consider either, for example, input–output or linear-programming models.
2. Notice that if the production function is homogeneous of degree unity, i.e. if there are constant returns to scale, then by Euler's theorem we have

$$Q = L(\partial Q/\partial L) + K(\partial Q/\partial K)$$

Hence, if equations [11.6] hold we have

$$pQ = wL + mK$$

in which case $\pi = 0$ and the total payments to labour and capital just 'exhaust' the value of total output.

3. Only in the case of constant returns to scale, of course, will these shares exactly equal the value of total output.
4. The requirement of decreasing returns to scale is, in fact, perfectly general and does not depend on the production function having the Cobb–Douglas form.

5. Notice that this implies that the χ parameter in equation [11.17] should also be interpreted as the elasticity of substitution.
6. See, for example, Heathfield (1971: 53–4).
7. For [11.29]

$$\frac{\partial Q_i}{\partial K_i} = A\alpha K_i^{\alpha-1} L_i^{\beta} \varepsilon_i = \alpha \frac{Q_i}{K_i}$$

However, if [11.29] were replaced by

$$Q_i = A K_i^{\alpha} L_i^{\beta} + \varepsilon_i$$

then we would have

$$\frac{\partial Q_i}{\partial K_i} = A\alpha K_i^{\alpha-1} L_i^{\beta} = \frac{\alpha(Q_i - \varepsilon_i)}{K_i}$$

8. For example, the reduced-form equation for labour inputs is

$$x_1 = \left(\frac{Q}{A}\right)^{1/r} \left(\frac{\alpha_2 p_2 \alpha_3 p_3}{\alpha_1 p_1}\right)^{\alpha_1/r} \varepsilon^{-1/r} \quad \text{where } r = \alpha_1 + \alpha_2 + \alpha_3$$

9. Since the price of capital varies little over the cross-section, Nerlove in a second model treats it as a constant. This reduces the number of explanatory variables in [11.51] to four again, resolving the identification problem, and results in a virtually identical estimate of r.
10. For [11.53] we still have $\partial Q_t/\partial K_t = \alpha(Q_t/K_t)$ and $\partial Q_t/\partial L_t = \beta(Q_t/L_t)$ so that

$$\text{MRS} = \left(\frac{\beta}{\alpha}\right)\left(\frac{K_t}{L_t}\right)$$

Since for any K/L ratio the MRS remains constant, we have what is known as Hicks neutral technical progress. It is also Harrod neutral, since for any Q/K ratio, the marginal product of capital is left unchanged. For an excellent introduction to the various kinds of technical progress see Jones (1975: Chs 7 and 8).
11. This form of technical progress means that the isoquants are all shifted towards the origin, but their slopes at the point where they meet *any* ray from the origin (i.e. for any K/L ratio) remain unchanged.
12. On the other hand, if the output/input variables are trend stationary, then an appropriate procedure would be to estimate equations in the levels of variables but with a time trend included to allow for trend. Under these circumstances, this procedure should be followed even in the absence of technical progress.
13. In the sense that it leaves both the MRS between capital and labour unchanged for any K/L ratio and the marginal product of capital unchanged for any Q/K ratio.
14. The OLS estimators of the constant term and of σ are unbiased as well as consistent. However, the resultant estimators of θ and δ are merely consistent because the property of unbiasedness, unlike that of consistency, does not 'carry over'.
15. If the assumption of perfect competition in the labour market is relaxed, the marginal productivity of labour equation becomes $\partial Q/\partial L = (1 - \delta)/\gamma^{\theta} \times (Q/L)^{1+\theta} = \varphi(w/p)$.
16. See Note 9.14 for the meaning of second-order Taylor approximation.
17. The CRDW statistic takes the value 1.74 in equation [A11.5], suggesting stationary residuals. However, as in the last exercise, we prefer to rely on the Dickey–Fuller tests for non-stationarity.
18. It is possible to test the hypothesis of a negative unit root, using the test statistic $(\hat{\phi}^* + 2)/s_{\hat{\phi}^*}$ where ϕ^* is the estimated coefficient on e_{t-1} and $s_{\hat{\phi}^*}$ is its estimated standard error. This yields a value of 2.7 for equation [A11.7], somewhat below the values in Table 7.3.
19. Testing for a negative unit root, using the test statistic given in note 18, yields a value of 3.6 for equation [A11.17]. A negative unit root is therefore less likely than for equation [A11.7].

12 The demand for money

Empirical interest in demand for money functions arises because the stability and interest elasticity of such functions are of crucial importance for the relative effectiveness of monetary and fiscal policy. The smaller is the interest elasticity of the demand for money the greater are the sizes of monetary multipliers relative to fiscal multipliers. Monetarists also claim that monetary multipliers are far more stable than fiscal multipliers. That is, it is much easier to predict the effect on aggregate money income of a given increase in the money supply than of a given increase in government expenditure. A necessary condition for a stable money multiplier is a stable demand for money function. An unstable (shifting) demand for money function would make it impossible to predict the effect on interest rates and, hence, on aggregate expenditure, of a given increase in the money supply. Notice, however, that for a stable money multiplier, a stable relationship between interest rates and aggregate expenditure is also necessary although we are not concerned with such relationships here.

It is important, at this point, to consider in detail what is meant by a 'stable' demand for money function. Suppose the function is given by

$$M_D = \alpha + \beta R + \gamma Y + \varepsilon \qquad [12.1]$$

where M_D, R and Y are suitably defined measures of the 'real demand for money', 'the rate of interest' and 'real income' – we shall consider the question of appropriate measures and definitions later. ε is a disturbance with zero mean and constant variance. Stability in the function [12.1] implies that given values of R and Y always result in the same, or at least very similar, values for M_D, the demand for money. This requires, firstly, that the 'parameters' α, β, and γ should remain constant over time. It also requires that the variance of the disturbance ε should be small. Otherwise, large changes in ε could lead to large changes in M_D even for constant values of R and Y. Note that this second requirement implies that no other variables apart from R and Y have important influences on the demand for money. If no other variables are specifically included in [12.1] then their influence must be represented by the disturbance. But since the variance of ε is small this rules out the possibility of other variables seriously affecting the demand for money. Of course, if a third variable (maybe the expected rate of price change) were important in the determination of M_D, then it is possible that a stable relationship might exist between M_D, R, Y and this third variable. However, when we refer to a stable demand for money function, we normally mean a stable relationship between the demand for money and just a few, typically two or three, explanatory variables. If a large number of variables seriously influence M_D then a stable function, in our sense, does not exist.

Empirically, two findings are necessary if it is to be maintained that a stable demand for money function has been found. Firstly, the constancy of α, β and γ

cver time requires that versions of [12.1] estimated over different time periods should yield non-significantly different estimates of these parameters. Secondly, a low variance for ε should be reflected in small residuals from fitted equations and, hence, high values for the coefficient of multiple determination.[1] If these conditions are met, then equations such as [12.1] should yield accurate predictions for the demand for money. Alternatively, the forecasting performance of such equations can be assessed directly by using them to predict the demand for money over data periods not available when the equations were estimated.

12.1 Alternative specifications of the demand for money function

The Keynesian view of the demand for money function split the demand for real balances into two parts – a demand for transactionary and precautionary balances, assumed to be proportional to the level of real income, Y, and a demand for speculative balances assumed to vary inversely with the rate of interest, R. However, it was always clear that such a split was little more than a convenient simplication. Later, for example, Baumol (1952) and Tobin (1956) suggested that the transactionary demand for money may also depend on, at least, short-run interest rates since firms can earn interest by holding transactions balances in the form of short-term liquid assets other than money. Their 'inventory-theoretic' approach leads to the following demand function for transactionary balances

$$\frac{M_{DT}}{P} = \frac{1}{2}\sqrt{\frac{2bY}{R}} \qquad [12.2]$$

where M_{DT} is the demand for nominal transactionary balances, P is the price level and b is a 'brokerage' fee payable every time a firm converts short-term interest-bearing assets into cash. Notice that equation [12.2] implies that transactionary demand is negatively related to the interest rate with an elasticity of -0.5 and positively related to real income with an elasticity of only $+0.5$. This implied income elasticity contrasted with the proportional relationships previously suggested. It has the important policy implication that a given increase in the money supply might have a more than proportionate rather than a proportionate effect on money income. When the income elasticity is less than unity, there are said to be '*economies of scale*' in the holding of money since a proportionate change in income requires a less than proportionate change in money balances to sustain it. Equation [12.2] also suggests that another variable 'the brokerage fee' may be of relevance in the determination of transactionary demand.[2]

The possibility that the demand for transactionary as well as speculative balances might be interest-elastic, plus the fact that with most data sources it is virtually impossible to distinguish one type of balance from the other, meant that demand for money functions began to be formulated simply as

$$\frac{M_D}{P} = AR^\beta Y^\gamma \qquad [12.3]$$

where M_D is now the *total* demand for nominal balances.

The logarithmic formulation was adopted not from any theoretical considerations but simply for convenience since it is then possible to interpret β and γ as elasticities. Some empirical studies (for example, Bronfenbrenner and Mayer 1960) restricted γ to unity, implying a demand for real balances that is exactly proportional to the level of real income at a given interest rate.[3] Such a formulation, of course, ruled out the possibility of 'economics of scale' in moneyholding as implied by the Baumol–Tobin approach, while the omission of any variable representing the brokerage fee provides a possible reason for instability arising in a relationship such as [12.3].

The Keynesian analysis of the speculative demand for money laid greatest stress on the asset holder who has definite ideas about what constitutes a 'normal' rate of interest. Provided different asset holders have different ideas about the level of such a normal rate, this analysis leads, for the *aggregate* of the asset holders, to a negative relationship between the current interest rate and the demand for money. However, it also implies that the *individual* asset holder holds either 'all bonds' or 'all money'. This is at variance with the commonly observed phenomenon of 'portfolio diversification – individuals typically hold both 'bonds' and money. Tobin (1958) hypothesised that while utility derived by the individual from his portfolio of assets depends positively on the expected return from the portfolio, it also varies inversely with the risk (resulting from possible capital loss) attached to the portfolio.[4] This yielded the result that the proportion of the *individual's* non-human wealth held in the form of money varies inversely with the rate of interest but increases as the 'riskiness' of bonds increases. Thus Tobin was able to explain the phenomenon of portfolio diversification. Such analysis implied a demand for money function of the form

$$\frac{M_D}{P} = f(R, \sigma)W \qquad [12.4]$$

where W is the individual's real non-human wealth and σ is a measure of the riskiness of bonds. Equation [12.4] led to empirical specifications (see, for example, Meltzer 1963) of the form

$$\frac{M_D}{P} = AR^\beta W^\gamma \qquad [12.5]$$

Notice that the Tobin analysis suggests the wealth-elasticity of the demand for money, γ, should be unity. Equation [12.5] also differs from equation [12.3] in that a different 'scale variable' is included – the Tobin analysis suggests that it is real non-human wealth rather than real income that influences the demand for money. Finally, [12.4] suggests that the riskiness of bonds may be an additional determinant of M_D/P so that changes in such a variable may make it impossible to isolate stable functions of the form [12.5] unless this variable is taken into account.

Friedman (1956), in his restatement of the quantity theory of money, regards money as being held because an individual receives services from it as he would from any other durable good. A diminishing MRS is assumed between the services yielded by money and those by other assets. The demand for money therefore depends on the rates of return on all assets (including money) and also on the individual's wealth which limits the total value of the portfolio.

Friedman's wealth variable, however, includes both human and non-human wealth since an individual may borrow on the strength of his expected future earned income and hold such extra assets as money. Friedman's demand for money function takes the form

$$\frac{M_D}{P} = f(R_b, R_e, \dot{P}^e, W, h) \qquad [12.6]$$

where R_b and R_e are the expected rates of return on bonds and equities (including durable goods), $\dot{P}^e$ is the expected rate of change in the price level, W is Friedman's wealth concept and h is the ratio of human to non-human wealth. R_b and R_e are defined so as to include any expected capital gain or loss on bonds or equities. $\dot{P}^e$ is included because the expected change in prices is an obvious determinant of the expected *future* real value of money balances and, hence, of the services likely to be yielded. $\dot{P}^e$ is therefore to be regarded as an important determinant of the expected rate of return on money itself. The variable h is included to allow for the fact that, because of the non-marketability of human wealth, the greater is the proportion of total wealth held in human form the greater is the demand for money. Equation [12.6] determines the demand for real rather than nominal balances (i.e. the demand for nominal balances is homogeneous of degree unity in the price level), because it is holdings of *real* balances which determine the magnitude of the flow of services from which the assetholder derives utility.

Since R_b and R_e tend to move together over time, they are generally replaced by a single interest rate variable, R, in empirical versions of Friedman's equation. Measurement problems have led to total wealth, W, being replaced by permanent income Y^p, to which it is directly proportional provided the rate at which future income is discounted remains constant over time. Finally, the ratio of human to non-human wealth, h, is generally also taken as constant over time so that empirical versions of equation [12.6] take the form

$$\frac{M_D}{P} = f(R, Y^p, \dot{P}^e) \qquad [12.7]$$

Notice, however, that if [12.7] is cast in the form of [12.3] and [12.5]

$$\frac{M_D}{P} = AR^\beta (Y^p)^\gamma \qquad [12.8]$$

then we have another possible choice for the 'scale variable' in the demand for money function – permanent income as opposed to measured income or non-human wealth. Furthermore, in so far as the expected rate of price change influences the demand for real balances, this is a further reason for expecting instability in functions such as [12.8] involving only a scale variable and an interest rate variable.

12.2　Some problems of estimation

Before we turn to specific empirical studies of the demand for money function, it will be helpful to consider, in a general way, some of the problems that are likely to be met once an attempt is made at estimation.

Data problems and the definition of variables

While at a theoretical level it may be quite appropriate to talk about 'money' in a very general sense, for empirical work a precise definition is obviously necessary if required data series are to be obtained. Unfortunately, in practice it is unclear which assets should be classified as money and which not. A spectrum of assets exists, of varying acceptability as a medium of exchange and of varying suitability as a store of value. These range from currency in circulation, through various types of bank and saving deposits, to highly illiquid securities unacceptable as a medium of exchange and on which there would be a considerable risk of capital loss if they were sold. If it were possible to concentrate on transactionary or speculative balances alone, it might be clearer which assets should be classified as money, but in practice functions often have to be estimated for the total demand for money, so that any division of the spectrum of assets between 'money' and 'non-money' becomes essentially arbitrary. A procedure frequently adopted is to 'let the data decide'. Alternative definitions of money are tried – the most common being a 'narrow' definition, normally referred to as M_1 including just currency in circulation and current accounts or 'demand deposits' at commercial banks, and a 'broad' definition termed M_2 or M_3, including also deposit accounts or 'time deposits' and maybe certain other saving accounts. That definition which results in the most stable demand for money function may then be regarded as the most appropriate. Fortunately, a number of the properties of estimated demand for money functions (e.g. their interest elasticity) seems not to depend on the precise definition of money adopted.

A further problem is whether money should be measured in nominal terms, in real or constant price terms or in real per capita terms. As already noted, theoretical considerations suggest that at the individual level it is the demand for real money balances which we should be concerned with although, as we shall see (page 360) it is possible to test this proposition. For aggregate data, dealing in per capita quantities at least represents a token attempt to deal with aggregation problems. Unfortunately, most demand for money functions are formulated in logarithmic terms and, as we have seen in Chapters 9 and 11 proper handling of the aggregation problem would require at least dealing in terms of geometric rather than arithmetic means. However, during periods of large population change, working with per capita variables (i.e. arithmetic means) is probably an advance on the use of simple aggregates.

Just as problems arise in *a priori* attempts to decide on an appropriate definition of money, there are difficulties in selecting which interest rate variables should be included in a demand for money function. While the speculative motive suggests that a long-term rate should be included, if the transactionary motive predominates then a short-term rate may be the more appropriate. On the other hand, Friedman's analysis suggests that rates of return on *all* alternative assets are relevant. However, since all rates are likely to move together closely over time, multicollinearity problems normally make the inclusion of more than one interest rate variable impractical. Investigators have usually adopted a pragmatic approach, experimenting with either a long-term rate of interest or a short-term rate, occasionally trying both together. For example, in the UK the yield on 2.5 per cent consolidated government stock and the three-month local authority rate are often used as long-term and short-term rates. In the US, favourites are the yield on twenty-year corporate bonds for the long-term rate and that on four- to six-month commercial bills for the short. Such measures have the advantage that they are calculated so as to allow for any capital gain or loss on the assets concerned.

In most theoretical work money is regarded as yielding a zero return. However, in practice, the deposit account or time deposit component of 'broad money' is clearly interest-bearing and even narrowly defined money is implicitly interest-bearing in the sense that banks may give preferential treatment or reduce service charges to large depositors. The Friedman approach clearly specifies that the own rate of return on money should be a variable in the demand for money function. Also, in all the other approaches to the demand for money, the interest rate of theory is to be interpreted as the opportunity cost of holding money. The own rate of return on money is an important determinant of this opportunity cost. For example, in a two-asset world of money and 'bonds' the true opportunity cost of holding money is not simply the yield on bonds but the difference between that yield and the own rate of return on money. It is therefore clear that the rate of return on money itself may be a relevant variable as far as the demand for money is concerned. Unfortunately, calculating such implicit interest rates is not a straightforward matter.

Another factor relevant to the own rate of return on money is the expected rate of inflation. In particular, this needs to be considered during times of rapid and highly variable rates of inflation since it is then that expectations are likely to change most quickly. Since Cagan (1956), the most common way of representing this variable has been by an adaptive-expectations hypothesis of the kind described in section 6.2. This implies that expected inflation is measured by a distributed lag function of current and past inflation rates, similar to equation [6.19], with geometrically declining weights. However, adaptive expectations and the backward looking approach it implies is subject to all the criticisms listed in section 6.2. More recently, therefore, the rational expectations approach outlined in Chapter 6 has been used to generate expected inflation rates.

For selection of the most appropriate scale variable to be included in a demand for money function, we have seen that there are three main candidates – income, non-human wealth and permanent income. A priori arguments can be put forward in favour of each of these variables. Indeed, in so far as all the motives for holding money discussed above are relevant, a case can be made for including at least two, and may be all three, in an estimating equation. However, since all these potential scale variables tend to move together over time, multicollinearity problems have generally resulted in their being tried one at a time with the selection of the most appropriate again being regarded as mainly an empirical matter. Only if it were believed that one motive for holding money predominates, would theory be of much help here. For example, with a very narrow definition of money, it could be argued that the transactions motive was predominant and that, hence, income was the appropriate scale variable.

In empirical work, 'income' is generally defined as net or gross national product in real constant price terms, and is expressed in per capita terms if there has been substantial variation in population during the sample period. Non-human wealth is most appropriately measured by the aggregate net worth of the private sector.[5]

Permanent income variables have been constructed using the adaptive expectations hypothesis exactly as in empirical work on the consumption function, except that in this case variables are frequently defined in logarithmic terms. Unfortunately, estimation problems now arise, essentially similar to those encountered in PIH versions of the consumption function. Letting lower-case letters represent the logarithms of variables, and letting $\bar{M}_D$ refer to real balances as opposed to nominal balances, M_D, suppose the demand for money function is given by

$$\bar{m}_{Dt} = \alpha + \beta r_t + \gamma y_t^P + \varepsilon_t \qquad [12.9]$$

where ε_t is a disturbance. The logarithmic equivalent of the adaptive expectations equation [10.25] is

$$y_t^P = \lambda y_t + (1 - \lambda) y_{t-1}^P \qquad [12.10]$$

Substituting [12.10] into [12.9] and applying the Koyck transformation then yields

$$\bar{m}_{Dt} = \lambda\alpha + \beta r_t - (1 - \lambda)\beta r_{t-1} + \lambda\gamma y_t + (1 - \lambda)\bar{m}_{Dt-1} + \varepsilon_t - (1 - \lambda)\varepsilon_{t-1}$$

$$[12.11]$$

Notice, first, that [12.11] is overidentified since four parameters have to be obtained from five estimated coefficients – the estimate of λ obtained from the coefficient on the $\bar{m}_{Dt-1}$ variable is unlikely to coincide with that obtained from the ratio of coefficients on the interest rate variables.

Secondly, just as in the PIH time series estimating equation [10.28], if ε_t is non-autocorrelated then [12.11] presents the combination of an autocorrelated disturbance term plus a lagged dependent variable among the explanatory variables. We know from section 5.2.2 that under such conditions, OLS estimators will be biased and inconsistent.

Finally, we must note again the backward looking nature of the adaptive expectations hypothesis. Its use implies that equations such as [12.11] are as much subject to the Lucas (1976) critique as are consumption equations based on adaptive expectations. The stability of such equations is unlikely to survive major changes in policy regimes. Thus the possibility exists that apparent instability in estimated demand for money functions may be the result of inappropriate assumptions concerning the determination of permanent income rather than any fundamental instability in the underlying long-run function. Consequently, as we shall see in section 12.7, some investigators nowadays prefer to model expectations in a separate equation that allows for changes in policy regime.

Non-stationary and spurious correlation

The vast majority of empirical studies of the demand for money function involve time series data, much early work making use of annual data stretching back to the beginning of the century. A number of the variables in money demand functions have been subject to long-run upward trends over this period. This has been the case for any potential scale variable whether it be an income measure or a wealth measure. It is also true of virtually all measures of the money stock. Certainly the nominal money stock in any economy tends to rise sharply over time and real money stocks have also moved consistently upwards. Only potential opportunity cost variables, that is rates of interest and measures of the expected rate of inflation are likely to exhibit stationarity over any typical sample period.

The presence of upward trends in so many of the data series means that any attempt to estimate simple demand for money equations such as [12.3], [12.5] or [12.8] is almost certain to run into the problems of non-stationarity and spurious correlation described in Chapter 7. The problem is likely to be particularly severe if the nominal money stock is used as the dependent variable with the price variable included among the explanatory variables. Like the nominal money stock, the price level is likely to be trending sharply upwards. Unfortunately, very few of the earlier studies paid much attention to the possibility of non-stationary regressors, spurious correlation and the resultant problems. As we shall see in section 12.6, it is only during the past 10–15 years that investigators have began to make use of the co-integration techniques and error correction models, described in Chapter 7, in the demand for money field.

The simultaneity problem

So far we have treated the demand for money function as if it were an isolated relationship, paying no attention to which variables in the function are endogenous and which can be treated as predetermined. In reality any demand for money function can only be one of a set of simultaneous relationships, also containing at least a simple supply of money function and some equation describing how quickly and in what manner the money market is cleared. What estimation procedures should be used to estimate a demand for money function will depend very much on the characteristics of the simultaneous system in which the function is embedded.

To illustrate the problems involved, we consider two simple stylistic models of the market for money. The price level is assumed constant so that we need not distinguish between real and nominal money balances. Both models have a simple and more general version. In both models the level of income is treated as exogenous, whereas in an economy-wide model account would have to be taken of the influence of the money supply both directly and via interest rates, on income.

The simplest version of the first model, which we shall call model IA, has the following three equations (lower case letters as usual denoting the logarithms of variables).

$$m_D = \alpha + \beta r + \gamma y + \varepsilon_1 \qquad\qquad [12.12]$$

$$m_S = \lambda + h \qquad \text{where } \lambda = \log \theta \qquad [12.13]$$

$$m_S = m_D \qquad\qquad [12.14]$$

Equation [12.12] is a normal demand for money function, although a scale variable other than income could have been selected without affecting the following arguments. Equation [12.13] is a very simple supply of money function in logarithmic form, giving the money supply in non-logarithmic form as

$$M_S = \theta H \qquad [12.15]$$

where H is the stock of 'high powered' money or eligible reserve assets. The multiplier θ, assumed constant, will depend on the reserve asset ratio adhered to by commercial banks and on the proportion of their money holdings that the public wish to hold in the form of currency. Equation [12.14] is a simple market-clearing assumption. Since income is assumed exogenous, the implicit assumption is that the rate of interest adjusts instantaneously to bring the demand and supply of money into equilibrium. M_S and M_D are therefore always identical to M, the actual stock of money in existence.

In model IA the endogenous variables are assumed to be M_S, M_D and the rate of interest, R. In addition to income, the stock of high-powered money, H, controlled by the monetary authorities, is also assumed to be exogenous. Given these assumptions the reduced form of the model is given by

$$m_D = \lambda + h$$

$$m_S = \lambda + h$$

$$r = \frac{1}{\beta}(\lambda - \alpha) - \frac{\gamma}{\beta}y + \frac{1}{\beta}h - \frac{\varepsilon_1}{\beta} \qquad [12.16]$$

Notice from equation [12.16] that the rate of interest variable, r, is positively correlated (since $\beta < 0$) with the disturbance ε_1. Thus, in attempting to estimate the demand for money function [12.12], we are faced with the familiar consequence of simultaneity – correlation between an explanatory variable (r in this case) and the disturbance. We know from our discussion in section 5.1 that the application of OLS to equation [12.12] therefore yields, *under the present assumptions*, biased and inconsistent estimators of demand for money elasticities.

For model IA the solution to the estimating problem is relatively simple. Ordinary least squares can be directly applied to the reduced-form equation [12.16]. Moreover, since $\lambda + h = m$, the log of the actual money stock, [12.16], can be rewritten as

$$r = -(\alpha/\beta) - (\gamma/\beta)y + (1/\beta)m - (\varepsilon_1/\beta) \qquad [12.17]$$

Ordinary least squares may therefore also be used to regress r on y and m to yield unbiased and consistent estimators of the coefficients in equation [12.17]. Estimators of α, β and γ, the parameters in the demand for money function [12.12] may then be obtained but these will retain only the property of consistency. Notice that this procedure merely involves 'turning round' the demand for money function [12.12], expressing r as a function of y and m.

The simple solution to the estimating problem in model IA stems from the very simple supply of money function assumed. Since the supply of money is assumed to be a constant multiple of the exogenously determined high-powered money stock, h, we have effectively assumed that the money supply itself is exogenous. In model IB we generalise this situation by making the money supply, as well as the demand for money, dependent on the rate of interest. The higher are interest rates the more inclined are the banks to make advances and loans so that the multiplier in equation [12.15] is likely to be a positive function of the rate of interest. Thus we have

$$M_S = \theta R^\mu H \tag{12.18}$$

rather than [12.15].

In logarithmic terms this involves replacing equation [12.13] in model IA by

$$m_S = \lambda + \mu r + h + \varepsilon_2 \tag{12.19}$$

where ε_2 is a disturbance introduced into the supply function.

Model IB is given by equations [12.12], [12.19] and [12.14]. The level of income and the high-powered money stock are still assumed exogenous. Notice that there is still no *identification* problem despite the fact that the rate of interest now appears in both the demand and the supply functions. A variable, income, appears in the demand function but not in the supply function, while another variable – high-powered money – appears in the supply function but not in the demand function. The consequences of *simultaneity*, however, must still be considered and for this we turn to the reduced form which for model IB is

$$r = \frac{\lambda - \alpha}{\beta - \mu} - \left(\frac{\gamma}{\beta - \mu}\right)y + \left(\frac{1}{\beta - \mu}\right)h + \frac{\varepsilon_2 - \varepsilon_1}{\beta - \mu} \tag{12.20}$$

$$m_D = \frac{\lambda\beta - \mu\alpha}{\beta - \mu} - \left(\frac{\mu\gamma}{\beta - \mu}\right)y + \left(\frac{\beta}{\beta - \mu}\right)h + \frac{\beta\varepsilon_2 - \mu\varepsilon_1}{\beta - \mu} \tag{12.21}$$

Because $m_S = m_D$, the reduced-form equation for m_S is identical to that for m_D. Since $\beta < 0$ and $\mu > 0$ the rate-of-interest variable is again positively correlated with ε_1, so that the application of OLS to the demand for money function [12.12] will again result in biased and inconsistent estimators. Now, however, no simple solution to the problem of simultaneous equation bias is available since it is no longer possible to make the simple substitution for h in equation [12.20] as was done in equation [12.16]. Neither is it possible to turn the demand for money function round as in equation [12.17] and regress the rate of interest on income and the money stock. Since m_S, m_D and m are, by assumption, identical, equation [12.21] implies that the money stock is also correlated with ε_1. Thus, under the assumptions of model IB, the application of OLS to equation [12.17] will also yield inconsistent estimators.

Obtaining consistent estimates of the demand for money function in model IB requires a fully-fledged simultaneous estimating procedure. Under the present assumptions, the demand for money function is exactly identified so that the simplest methods are ILS and TSLS. In the TSLS procedure, for example, the first stage would involve regressing r on y and h, the two exogenous variables in the model. That is, the reduced form equation [12.20] would be estimated. The second stage of the procedure would then be to apply OLS to equation [12.12] but with the r values replaced by the predicted r values obtained from the first stage.

In the second type of money market model we abandon the assumption of an exogenous stock of high-powered money. Instead, it is the rate of interest that is treated as exogenous together with the level of income. The assumption, implicit in the model, is that the authorities decide on an appropriate rate of interest and are able to adjust the high-powered money stock, and hence the total money supply, so as to attain this desired interest rate. The high-powered

355

money stock thus becomes an endogenous variable together with the demand for, and supply of, money.

In model IIA the structural equations are identical to model IA, that is equations [12.12–12.14]. The difference, of course, is that the exogenous variables are now y and r rather than y and h. Under these conditions the problem of estimation becomes straightforward. Since y and r are exogenous they can be regarded as independent of the disturbance in equation [12.12]. Thus we can obtain unbiased and consistent estimators of α, β and γ, the demand for money parameters, by simply applying OLS to equation [12.12]. Equation [12.12] is, in fact, the first equation in a very simple recursive system of the type discussed in section 8.2.

In the more general model IIB the structural equations are identical to those of model IB, i.e. equations [12.12], [12.19] and [12.14]. Again, the exogenous variables are r and y rather than y and h. Fortunately, the replacement of equation [12.13] by [12.19] does not complicate the estimation problem. As in model IB, the appearance of the rate of interest in both demand and supply functions causes no identification problem so that, since y and r are again independent of ε_1, the application of OLS to the demand for money function will yield unbiased and consistent estimators of its parameters. Models IIA and IIB are sometimes referred to as models in which the money stock is 'demand-determined'. That is, predetermined values of the exogenous variables (r and y in model II) determine the demand for money. The stock of money then adjusts passively (with the acquiescence of the monetary authorities), so as to satisfy the ongoing demand. This adjustment may either occur instantaneously as is implied by models IIA and IIB or, more realistically, via some form of partial adjustment process which we shall consider in the next sub-section. In either case, however, the long-run or equilibrium value of the money stock is essentially determined by demand factors.

Apart from the adjustment process just mentioned, the lessons of this section may appear straightforward. Provided we can decide on the correct variables to treat as exogenous then the appropriate estimation procedure can be selected. Unfortunately, matters are never as simple as this in practice. Firstly, it is highly unlikely that we will ever find, for estimating purposes, a data period of sufficient length in which the monetary authorities consistently followed a policy of controlling the same policy variable, whether that variable be the money supply or the rate of interest. Rather, we are likely to find periods of a few years when attention was focused on money supply targets followed by similarly short periods when attempts were made to control interest rates. Indeed, there are very likely to be some years when the aim of the monetary authorities was unclear or ambivalent so that we would be uncertain as to which of our two models represented the closest approximation to reality.

Secondly, it may well be the case that variables which we might like to treat as exogenous are not truly under the control of the monetary authorities. For example, in the UK during the 1970s the stock of high-powered money, which in the UK context is to be interpreted as the stock of eligible reserve assets, was partly outside the control of the Bank of England. Thus during this period, even if some version of model I was deemed most appropriate, the money supply can best be regarded as being only partly exogenous. Similarly, in model IIB it is not necessarily the case that the monetary authorities will be able to select the correct stock of high-powered money so precisely as to obtain, exactly, the desired rate of interest. This would require a very accurate knowledge of the demand for, and supply of, money functions and no unforeseen variations in the level of income. Under such circumstances it is debatable whether it is the rate of interest that could be regarded as exogenous.

Finally, even if it were true that the authorities are able to control either H or R, these variables may be no more than policy instruments and still not genuinely exogenous. That is, the level at which the authorities wish to fix their policy instruments may itself be influenced by economic variables and even by variables within the monetary sector. For example, although the authorities may be controlling H, an increase in the stock of high-powered money might be made *in response to* a rise in income which would otherwise result in rising interest rates. Similar considerations apply when it is the rate of interest which is the chosen policy instrument. When the setting of policy instruments is influenced by economic conditions in this way, there is a limit to the extent to which they can be regarded as exogenous variables.

The implication of the above discussion is that the selection of an appropriate method of estimation for a demand for money function is rarely likely to be a clear-cut matter. However, a few rough-and-ready guidelines may be discerned. As a crude approximation it is probably true to say that, prior to 1970 in both the UK and the US, it was the rate of interest rather than the supply of money which was generally the policy target. To the extent that this was the case, the estimation of demand for money functions as in model II appears to be most appropriate for pre-1970 data. That is, OLS may be applied directly to the demand for money function. This, in fact, was how most pre-1970 demand for money functions were estimated – although not necessarily because any thought had been given to simultaneity problems.

An an equally rough generalisation it might be said that since the early 1970s, in both the UK and the US, it is money supply aggregates rather than interest rates that have been the main policy target. Given such an assumption, the best way to estimate demand for money elasticities from post-1970 data may well be as in model I. In particular, suppose it is believed that interest rates have little influence on the *supply* of money and that model IA is a reasonable approximation to reality. It is then probably better to reverse the causation in the demand for money function and apply OLS to equations such as [12.16] rather than apply OLS directly to demand for money functions such as equation [12.12].

12.3 The adjustment process

For our discussion in the previous section we assumed that the money market always cleared, so that we could treat M_D and M_S as always equal to M, the actual stock of money in existence. In reality however, the market will not always be in such an equilibrium and, although it may still be legitimate to treat M_S and M as identical, the demand for money M_D will not always be equal to M, the stock in existence. Only if the market is given sufficient time to adjust in some way will equilibrium be achieved and $M_D = M$. Relationships such as [12.2] to [12.8] in section 12.1 *are therefore best regarded as long run or equilibrium demand for money functions.* For example, we could only replace

[12.3] by

$$\frac{M}{P} = AR^\beta Y^\gamma \qquad\qquad [12.22]$$

and estimate [12.22] if it were always the case that the market were in equilibrium and $M_D = M$. In disequilibrium we cannot estimate [12.3] because, although we have data on M, the actual money stock, we have none on M_D.

How does the adjustment from disequilibrium to eventual equilibrium take place and how can it be modelled? This will depend very much on whether we can treat the money supply as endogenous or 'demand determined' as in models IIA and IIB of the last subsection, or whether the money supply is essentially exogenous as in models IA and IB. We consider each situation in turn.

Adjustment when the money supply is demand determined

Consider a situation where pre-determined values of the explanatory variables in functions such as [12.3] determine the demand for money. If the stock of money then gradually adjusts (with the approval of the monetary authorities) until it satisfies this demand, then the partial adjustment model of section 6.3 can be used to model the process. Again using lower case letters to represent the logarithms of variables, suppose the demand for money or *desired real balances* is determined by

$$\bar{m}_{Dt} = \alpha + \beta r_t + \gamma y_t + \varepsilon_t \qquad\qquad [12.23]$$

Actual real balances, however defined, necessarily refer to balances actually in existence rather than balances which individuals in aggregate would like to hold. There can be no guarantee that the two quantities are the same and, certainly with quarterly data, it is doubtful whether assetholders have time to adjust actual balances to the desired level within such a short interval. Feige (1967) suggested a model in which the individual assetholder seeks to minimise the sum of 'adjustment costs' and 'disequilibrium costs'. Adjustment costs are assumed to vary with the square of the change in *actual* real balances held, $\bar{m}_t - \bar{m}_{t-1}$ while disequilibrium costs are assumed proportional to the square of the difference between *actual* real balances $\bar{m}_t$ and *desired* real balances $\bar{m}_{Dt}$. This type model has in fact already been described at the end of Chapter 7 and leads to an equation of the form

$$\bar{m}_t - \bar{m}_{t-1} = \mu(\bar{m}_{DT} - \bar{m}_{t-1}) \qquad 0 < \mu < 1 \qquad\qquad [12.24]$$

Equation [12.24] is an example of the partial adjustment hypothesis. Since $0 < \mu < 1$, only a proportion of any difference between actual and desired balances is made up during any one period.

Substituting [12.23] into [12.24] yields, for actual real balances

$$\bar{m}_t = \mu m_{Dt} + (1 - \mu)\bar{m}_{t-1} \qquad\qquad [12.25]$$

or

$$\bar{m}_t = \mu\alpha + \mu\beta r_t + \mu\gamma y_t + (1 - \mu)\bar{m}_{t-1} + \mu\varepsilon_t \qquad\qquad [12.26]$$

Under present assumptions the monetary authorities automatically make available the money stock required by [12.25] and [12.26]. Hence the money supply is 'demand determined'.

Notice that, apart from the disturbance term, equation [12.26] is of very similar form to the estimating equation [12.11] which arose from combining a permanent income scale variable with the assumption that actual money balances are always fully adjusted to their desired level. Both types of equation contain the lagged money stock as an explanatory variable. The only difference is that the lagged rate of interest, r_{t-1}, appears as an additional explanatory variable in equation [12.11]. In practice, however, r_t and r_{t-1} are likely to be highly correlated so it may be difficult to determine statistically whether or not r_{t-1} should be included in estimating equations. This is a potentially serious matter since equation [12.26] arises from a totally different idea about factors underlying demand for money equations than that implied by [12.11]. The practical importance of this is that the two approaches imply a clearly different response for $\bar{m}_t$ over time to changes in real income and the rate of interest. For example, successive substitution for $\bar{m}_{t-1}$ in equation [12.26] leads, ignoring disturbance terms to

$$\bar{m}_t = \alpha + \beta[\mu r_t + \mu(1 - \mu)r_{t-1} + \mu(1 - \mu)^2 r_{t-2}\cdots]$$
$$+ \gamma[\mu y_t + \mu(1 - \mu)y_{t-1} + \mu(1 - \mu)^2 y_{t-2}\cdots] \qquad [12.27]$$

On the other hand, substituting for permanent income in equation [12.9] yields

$$\bar{m}_t = \alpha + \beta r_t + \gamma[\lambda y_t + \lambda(1 - \lambda)y_{t-1} + \lambda(1 - \lambda)^2 y_{t-2}\cdots] \qquad [12.28]$$

Thus the partial adjustment approach implies an *identical* geometric distributed lag for *all* explanatory variables whereas the permanent income hypothesis implies such a lag *only* for the income variable. In the latter case responses to changes in the rate of interest are completed within one period.

As we shall see, many investigators have found the lagged money stock $\bar{m}_{t-1}$ to be a significant variable in demand for money functions. Unfortunately, the above problems make it very difficult to tell whether its importance is the result of permanent income being the correct scale variable or the result of a non-instantaneous adjustment of actual to desired balances. This difficulty stems from our inability to measure directly such concepts as 'permanent income' and 'desired balances'. Assumptions therefore have to be made which lead to essentially similar estimating equations.

Feige (1967) was the first to suggest a model of the demand for money involving *both* lagged adjustment and the use of permanent income as the scale variable. The desired level of balances is given by [12.9], permanent income again being determined by the adaptive equation [12.10]. Partial adjustment of actual to desired balances is also introduced via equation [12.24].

Substituting [12.9] and [12.10] into [12.24] yields first

$$\bar{m}_t = \mu\alpha + \mu\beta r_t + \mu\gamma y_t^P + (1 - \mu)\bar{m}_{t-1} + \mu\varepsilon_t \qquad [12.29]$$

and then

$$\bar{m}_t = \mu\alpha + \mu\beta r_t + \mu\lambda\gamma y_t + \mu(1 - \lambda)\gamma y_{t-1}^P + (1 - \mu)\bar{m}_{t-1} + \mu\varepsilon_t \qquad [12.30]$$

Multiplying [12.30] by $1 - \lambda$ and lagging by one period gives

$$(1 - \lambda)\bar{m}_{t-1} = \mu(1 - \lambda)\alpha + \mu(1 - \lambda)\beta r_{t-1} + \mu(1 - \lambda)\gamma y_{t-1}^P$$
$$+ (1 - \mu)(1 - \lambda)\bar{m}_{t-2} + \mu(1 - \lambda)\varepsilon_{t-1} \qquad [12.31]$$

Finally, subtracting [12.31] from [12.30], we eventually obtain an equation which does not involve the unobservable permanent income variable

$$\bar{m}_t = \mu\lambda\alpha + \mu\beta r_t - \mu(1-\lambda)\beta r_{t-1} + \mu\lambda\gamma y_t + (2 - \mu - \lambda)\bar{m}_{t-1}$$
$$- (1-\mu)(1-\lambda)\bar{m}_{t-2} + \mu\varepsilon_t - \mu(1-\lambda)\varepsilon_{t-1} \qquad [12.32]$$

Straightforward estimation of [12.32] by OLS is not feasible however, firstly because of the familiar problem of an autocorrelated disturbance term combined with lagged dependent variables on the right-hand side, and secondly, because, as with equation [12.11], its parameters are overidentified. However, provided appropriate estimation techniques are used, the model does, in theory, seem to provide a way of distinguishing the relative importance of general adjustment-type lags and expectational lags which are specific to the income variable. In practice, however, multicollinearity between r_t and r_{t-1}, and between m_{t-1} and m_{t-2} is likely to lead to some imprecision in estimators of the parameters of [12.32]. Since the relative importance of the types of lags is assessed by comparing the estimates of μ and λ, such imprecision may make it difficult to reach any firm conclusion on this matter.

Real versus nominal balances

It has been implicitly assumed in the above discussion that, as theory suggests, the appropriate dependent variable was the demand for real rather than nominal balances, i.e. that, at least in the long run, the demand for nominal balances was unit-elastic with respect to the price level. However, if it is felt necessary to test this assumption, then equations such as [12.23] must be rewritten as

$$m_{Dt} = \alpha + \beta r_t + \gamma y_t + \delta p_t + \varepsilon_t \qquad [12.23A]$$

with m_{Dt} referring to nominal balances and equation [12.24] also re-interpreted in nominal terms. Substitution of [12.23A] into [12.24] then yields

$$m_t = \mu\alpha + \mu\beta r_t + \mu\gamma y_t + \mu\delta p_t + (1-\mu)m_{t-1} + \mu\varepsilon_t \qquad [12.26A]$$

Notice that, if we restrict δ to unity in [12.26A], rearrangement gives

$$m_t - p_t = \mu\alpha + \mu\beta r_t + \mu\gamma y_t + (1-\mu)(m_{t-1} - p_t) + \mu\varepsilon_t \qquad [12.26B]$$

This is not quite the same as [12.26] since in that equation $\bar{m}_{t-1}$ represents lagged nominal balances deflated by the *lagged* price level, whereas in [12.26B] deflation is by the current price level.

Hence, deflation of lagged nominal balances by the lagged price level as in [12.26] implies an instantaneous adjustment of the demand for nominal balances to changes in the price level. However, deflation by the current price level as in [12.26B] implies a lagged adjustment to price level changes identical to the response to changes in y_t or r_t.

Adjustment when the money supply is exogenous

In the previous subsection, the assumption throughout was that the supply of money was demand determined. Once the demand for money was determined by its arguments, the monetary authorities permitted supply to adjust passively to bring about eventual equilibrium. The partial adjustment mechanism introduced fits relatively easily into this framework. Suppose, however, the aggregate money supply is exogenous (its value fixed by the monetary authorities). It cannot then be treated as determined by demand factors: it is outside the control of asset holders. Under such circumstances it is still possible to regard an individual asset holder as gradually, and over time, adjusting his actual money balances until they equal a desired level determined by demand factors such as r and y. However, it is not reasonable to treat the economy as a whole (i.e. the aggregate of asset holders) as adjusting the aggregate money supply to some desired level. The aggregate money supply is, by assumption, outside the control of the aggregate of asset holders. Clearly, under such conditions, the process of adjustment to equilibrium must be totally different from that implied by equations [12.26] or [12.26A].

If the money supply is fixed exogenously, equilibrium can only be brought about if the demand for money adjusts to that exogenous supply. This can only occur through changes in one or more of the arguments in the demand for money function – that is the price level, the interest rate or the level of real income. Suppose, for example, the demand for money function is given by [12.23] which, since $\bar{m}_{Dt} = m_{Dt} - p_t$, we may write as

$$m_{Dt} = \alpha + \beta r_t + \gamma y_t + p_t + \varepsilon_t \qquad [12.33]$$

Suppose the authorities set a value for the nominal money supply m_t that is not equal to the demand for nominal balances determined by [12.33]. Clearly, variations in one or more of r_t, y_t and p_t can change m_{Dt} so as to restore equilibrium at $m_{Dt} = m_t$. Since few economists would argue that the long-run level of real income, y is determined in the money market, most investigators have concentrated on the effect of disequilibrium on r and p.

Laidler (1982) considers the possibility of adjustment via changes in the price level. If the given money supply exceeds demand, then the excess supply spills over into increased spending on goods, thereby increasing the price level and hence the demand for money via [12.33]. Given real income and the interest rate, the price level required for equilibrium can be obtained by setting $m_{Dt} = m_t$ in [12.33] and solving for p_t to yield

$$p_t^* = -\alpha + m_t - \beta r_t - \gamma y_t - \varepsilon_t \qquad [12.34]$$

where p_t^* is the equilibrium price level.

Adjustment via the price level is possible because, while the monetary authorities can control the nominal money supply, the real supply can still vary if the price level changes. In fact we could still regard the adjustment just described as a process in which the demand for *real* balances is predetermined and the *real* money supply adjusts to it via price level changes.

In Laidler's model prices are 'sticky' and adjust only gradually to the equilibrium level given by [12.34]. The process is described by the partial adjustment mechanism

$$p_t - p_{t-1} = \mu(p_t^* - p_{t-1}) \qquad 0 < \mu < 1 \qquad [12.35]$$

Substituting for p_t^* in [12.35] yields

$$p_t = -\mu\alpha + \mu m_t - \mu\beta r_t - \mu\gamma y_t + (1 - \mu)p_{t-1} - \mu\varepsilon_t \qquad [12.36]$$

Laidler points out that by manipulating equations such as [12.36] it is possible to obtain an equation very similar to the more usual partial adjustment equation [12.26]. In fact, multiplying [12.36] throughout by -1 and adding m_t to either side yields

$$m_t - p_t = \mu\alpha + \mu\beta r_t + \mu\gamma y_t + (1-\mu)(m_t - p_{t-1}) + \mu\varepsilon_t \qquad [12.37]$$

or

$$m_t - p_t = \mu\alpha + \mu\beta r_t + \mu\gamma y_t + (1-\mu)(m_{t-1} - p_{t-1}) + (1-\mu)(m_t - m_{t-1}) + \mu\varepsilon_t$$

$$[12.38]$$

Noting that $\bar{m}_t = m_t - p_t$, we see that [12.38] is identical to [12.26] apart from the term $(1-\mu)(m_t - m_{t-1})$. Yet the adjustment process underlying [12.38] is totally different to that underlying [12.26]. The parameter μ has a completely different interpretation and is likely to take a very different value. Laidler therefore argued that, in situations where the money supply should be regarded as exogenous, the significance of lagged real balances in estimated versions of equation [12.26] is the result, not of the gradual adjustment of actual money balances to a desired level, but of a gradual adjustment of the price level to its equilibrium value. He suggested that the low values obtained for the parameter μ by many investigators indicate not an implausibly slow adjustment rate in money balances but the expected slow adjustment of a 'sticky' price level.

Artis and Lewis (1976) have suggested rather different adjustment mechanisms for the case of an exogenous money supply. One possibility they put forward is that in equation [12.33] it is the rate of interest that adjusts to restore equilibrium. An excess supply of money in this case makes itself felt in the financial asset market, driving down interest rates until the demand for money increases sufficiently to match the predetermined supply. The interest rate necessary for equilibrium can be obtained by inverting [12.33] to obtain

$$r_t^* = -\frac{\alpha}{\beta} + \frac{1}{\beta}m_t - \frac{\gamma}{\beta}y_t - \frac{1}{\beta}p_t - \frac{\varepsilon_t}{\beta}$$

$$= -\frac{\alpha}{\beta} + \frac{1}{\beta}\bar{m}_t - \frac{\gamma}{\beta}y_t - \frac{\varepsilon_t}{\beta} \qquad [12.39]$$

where r_t^* is the equilibrium interest rate.

Artis and Lewis suggest that the actual interest rate adjusts gradually to r_t^* via the partial adjustment mechanism

$$r_t - r_{t-1} = \lambda(r_t^* - r_{t-1}) \qquad [12.40]$$

Substituting for r_t^* in [12.40] then leads to

$$r_t = -\frac{\lambda\alpha}{\beta} + \frac{\lambda}{\beta}\bar{m}_t - \frac{\lambda\gamma}{\beta}y_t + (1-\lambda)r_{t-1} - \frac{\lambda\varepsilon_t}{\beta} \qquad [12.41]$$

Estimation of [12.41] enables estimates of the underlying demand for money parameters α, β and γ, together with the adjustment parameter λ to be obtained.

An alternative adjustment process suggested by Artis and Lewis involves the adjustment of the aggregate money-income ratio to some desired level. Adjustment is via a simple quantity theory mechanism. Rewriting [12.33] this time as

$$(m_D - y - p)_t = \alpha + \beta r_t + (\gamma - 1)y_t + \varepsilon_t \qquad [12.42]$$

362

notice that the left-hand-side variable in [12.42] is the logarithm of M_D/PY the money-income ratio desired by asset holders. If the actual money-income ratio exceeds this, then the excess spills over into spending on goods and this increases the price level and maybe, in the short run, the level of real income. This leads to a decline in the actual money-income ratio, eventually to its desired level given by [12.42]. Adjustment is again gradual and Artis and Lewis suggest the standard partial adjustment mechanism

$$(m - y - p)_t - (m - y - p)_{t-1} = \theta[(m_D - y - p)_t - (m - y - p)_{t-1}] \quad 0 < \theta < 1$$

$$[12.43]$$

Substituting for $(m_D - y - p)_t$ in [12.43] then yields the estimating equation

$$(m - p - y)_t = \theta\alpha + \theta\beta r_t + \theta(\gamma - 1)y_t + (1 - \theta)(m - p - y)_{t-1} + u_t \quad [12.44]$$

where $u_t = \theta\varepsilon_t$.

Artis and Lewis's second adjustment model is similar to that of Laidler because it relies, at least partly, on price level movements. However, it has an advantage over the Laidler model in that it can more easily be generalised to handle factors that cause changes in actual money holdings independently of the adjustment process. Suppose there is a sudden large increase in the money supply resulting from, for example, an unexpected large government borrowing requirement. This disturbs the process [12.43] whereby the actual money-income ratio is adjusting to the desired level and leads to a sudden rise in this ratio. Artis and Lewis suggested that such happenings can be allowed for by rewriting [12.43] as

$$(m - y - p)_t - (m - y - p)_{t-1} = \theta[(m_D - y - p)_t - (m - y - p)_{t-1}] + \phi C_t$$

$$[12.43A]$$

where C_t represents any factor influencing the money-income ratio independently of the normal adjustment process. Equation [12.44] then becomes

$$(m - p - y)_t = \theta\alpha + \theta\beta r_t + \theta(\gamma - 1)y_t + \phi C_t + (1 - \theta)(m - p - y)_{t-1} + u_t$$

$$[12.44A]$$

The notion inherent in equations [12.43A] and [12.44A] is that asset holders may find themselves with money balance levels in excess of that planned but yet not start immediately to spend them on goods or financial assets in accordance with the usual transmission mechanisms. This has given rise to the idea of money being the 'shock absorber' or *buffer stock* in asset holders' portfolios. Large unexpected rises in money balances are initially held as 'transitory balances' before, eventually, long-run adjustment takes place. However, we shall delay discussion of so-called buffer stock models until section 12.7.

It would be a mistake to regard the various adjustment processes described in this subsection as in any way mutually exclusive. When the money supply is exogenous, adjustment is likely to occur via all the processes outlined here working simultaneously. In the short run, the burden of adjustment will be most likely borne by interest rates and possibly real income, with price adjustments occurring mainly in the long run. However, the fact that the various adjustment processes almost certainly work together makes their adequate modelling a more complicated procedure. It is unlikely that any single equation out of [12.36], [12.41] or [12.44] can alone provide a satisfactory representation of the process.

There is a further problem with the partial adjustment equations of this and the last subsection. In estimating equations such as [12.26] or [12.41], for example, the specification of a standard partial adjustment process, means that the lag structure has been imposed *a priori* with disturbance terms in effect just 'tagged' on at the end. In reality *short-run* adjustment processes may be far more intricate than those of the standard partial adjustment model and the required lag structure of estimating equations consequently more complicated. A preferable approach may be therefore to begin with a very general equation specifying long lags for all the explanatory variables, and then determine the appropriate lag structure by 'testing down' in the Hendry 'general to specific' manner described in section 7.2. Immediate estimation of standard partial adjustment equations is likely to result in serious dynamic specification errors. As we saw in section 7.1, this is likely to be reflected in the autocorrelation statistics for such equations. Indeed, a number of researchers, for example Hamburger (1977) and Laidler (1980), have estimated partial adjustment equations and interpreted low Durbin–Watson statistics as evidence of autocorrelation rather than mis-specification. This has led to the probably totally unjustified use of the Cochrane–Orcutt procedures described in section 5.2.2 for tackling autocorrelation problems.

12.4   Empirical findings on the demand for money

We saw at the outset that two of the major reasons for interest in the demand for money function were the questions of its stability and its elasticity with respect to its various arguments, particularly the rate of interest. We shall look at the evidence for stability in the next section. First, we look at empirical findings on elasticities and at the related questions of which variables should be included as arguments in demand for money equations.

A word of caution is, however, in order at this point. Much of the evidence quoted in this section has been obtained from long-run time series data for which, as we saw in the last section, many variables exhibited strong upward trends. It follows that, because of possible spurious correlation problems, such simple statistics as *t*-ratios and coefficients of multiple determination may be artificially inflated in the quoted studies. The conclusions reached are therefore perhaps not as firm as once claimed.

The interest elasticity of the demand for money

Of all the above issues, the question of the interest elasticity of the demand for money is the one on which empirical studies have led to the greatest agreement. Almost without exception investigators have found a non-zero interest elasticity, although the absolute size of this estimated elasticity is virtually always less than unity. Moreover, a non-zero elasticity is found no matter what definition of money is used, whatever the scale variable included in the function, and whether elasticity is measured with respect to short-term interest rates or long-term interest rates. For example, Meltzer (1963), in one of the most comprehensive of earlier studies, fitted logarithmic functions of the kind [12.3],

[12.5] and [12.8] to annual US data for the period 1900–58, using three alternative definitions of the money stock – M1 including currency and demand deposits, M2 including, as well, time deposits, and M3 including also deposits at mutual savings banks. In all cases he found a significant negative elasticity with respect to the long-term rate of interest (defined as the yield on twenty-year corporate bonds). While the absolute size of the interest elasticity varied with the definition of money used, all estimates were in the range 0.5–0.95 and the evidence suggested that the size of the elasticities remained relatively constant decade by decade. The following result based on equation [12.5] for Meltzer's full sample period is fairly typical of results obtained for the US at that time. Figures in parentheses are t-statistics.

$$\bar{m}_{2t} = -1.98 - 0.50r_t + 1.32w_t \qquad \bar{R}^2 = 0.994 \qquad [12.45]$$
$$\phantom{\bar{m}_{2t} = -1.98} (10.8) \quad (53.2)$$

The coefficient on the rate of interest variable clearly appears highly significant in the statistical sense. Notice, however, the very high value for $\bar{R}^2$. This is clearly the result of common upward trends in m_2 and y. Much of the correlation is therefore likely to have been spurious so that the high t-ratios obtained have to be taken with a pinch of salt.

The interest elasticity of the UK demand for money was first confirmed by Kavanagh and Walters (1966) using annual data for 1877–1961. During the decade after this, non-zero interest elasticities for either short-term or long-term rates were confirmed for a wide variety of economies. For a summary of some of these results, see Fase and Kune (1975) and for a more detailed discussion than there is room for here, see Laidler (1977: 122–30).

In general the size of estimated interest elasticities has depended on whether a short- or long-run interest rate variable has been included and to a lesser extent on the definition of money used. For example, in the US, when a narrow definition of money is used, the elasticity with respect to the long-term rate has been found to be about -0.7 but for a short-term rate only -0.2. The figures are slightly less for broader definitions of money. Similar values are found for most other countries. These variations are not difficult to explain. Long-term rates vary less than short-term rates although the two tend to be highly correlated. Hence, for a given degree of variation in a money stock series, the long-term rate is always likely to yield the higher elasticity. Also, when a broad definition of money is used, part of the substitution effects caused by changes in the rate of interest are hidden within the composition of money itself. Hence, a smaller elasticity is obtained than when a narrower definition is employed.

All the studies referred to above based their conclusions on the straightforward application of OLS to the demand for money function, making no attempt to allow for the presence of supply of money relationships. However, as we noted in the last section, this is in fact the most appropriate procedure provided it is reasonable to regard the rate of interest as an exogenous variable. If this is not the case then both versions of model I suggest that the rate of interest will be positively correlated with the disturbance in a demand for money function. Under such circumstances OLS is likely to *underestimate* rather than over-estimate the absolute size of interest rate elasticities. Hence, any bias due to simultaneity in the estimates described above is in a downwards direction, with true elasticities if anything being larger than those estimated. In the rare cases where simultaneous equation estimating methods have been employed, estimates of interest elasticities have generally confirmed estimates obtained by OLS. For example, Teigen (1964) constructed a structural model of the US monetary sector which contained not only a supply of money function but also an income relationship. Thus both the rate of interest and the level of income were treated as endogenous variables. Two-stage least squares estimation of the model yielded a short-term interest elasticity in steady state of about -0.15 – very similar to most OLS estimates.[6]

Although empirical work has established the interest elasticity of money demand beyond much doubt it has not generally suggested the existence of a Keynesian liquidity trap. Studies from Laidler (1966) onwards have found no evidence of higher, let alone infinite, elasticities when attention is confined to periods of low interest rates. It should be remembered that the idea of a trap arose because of a belief that some 'normal' rate of interest might be important in the demand for money function. Keynes suggested that, if the rate of interest was sufficiently low, all asset holders would expect it to rise and, hence, the demand for money would be unlimited. Attempts dating back to Starleaf and Reimer (1967) to find a role for such a normal rate in demand for money functions have proved largely unsuccessful. For this reason, plus the general lack of evidence in its support, the majority of econometricians would nowadays doubt the existence of a 'liquidity trap'.

Price and scale variable elasticities

Theory predicts that the demand for real balances is homogeneous of degree zero in the price level. This implies that demand for money functions should be formulated in terms of real rather than nominal balances. Early studies of annual data, particularly for the US, did, in fact, suggest homogeneity of degree zero or, what amounts to the same thing, that the demand for nominal balances has unit elasticity with respect to the price level. However, most of these early studies failed to distinguish between short- and long-run elasticities. This is, of course, particularly important for dealing with quarterly data. As we have seen, a more appropriate procedure is to attempt the estimation of equations such as [12.23A] and to test whether the *long-run* price elasticity, δ, is significantly different from unity.

Some evidence on price elasticities is available for UK quarterly data. Hacche (1974) specified an equation of the form [12.26A] but arbitrarily set the long-run price elasticity, δ, equal to unity, thus actually estimating equation [12.26B]. While such *a priori* restriction may appear to be in accordance with theory, as Courakis (1978) pointed out we can have no way of knowing which is the precise measure of prices to which unitary elasticity is expected to refer. Hacche used the current value of the implicit deflator for final expenditure in his equation concerning personal sector M3 holdings, but there is no reason why this should be the appropriate price variable. Indeed, Courakis, using identical data to Hacche found that a unitary price elasticity was at variance with the data. It is also notable that both Coghlan (1978), using a more flexible lag structure, and Rowan and Miller (1979), adopting a simpler lag specification, obtain an unrestricted estimate for the same long-run price elasticity in the neighbourhood of 0.7 for narrow money. However, as we shall see in section 12.6, studies during the 1980s using the general to specific methodology have found no reason to reject a unitary price elasticity.

Evidence for countries other than the UK is less plentiful. However, in a recent study of money demand in large industrial countries, which we discuss in greater detail later, Boughton (1991) finds that long-run price elasticities appear significantly less than unity in the US, the UK, Japan, Germany and France. Such evidence certainly suggests that a unitary long-run elasticity is something that should be tested for rather than imposed *a priori*.

Interest in the elasticity of money demand with respect to income or any other scale variable arises because of the possibility of economies of scale in money holding. Recall that the Baumol–Tobin inventory theoretic approach implies such economies of scale with an interest elasticity as low as 0.5, at least for transactionary balances.

Early studies for both the UK and the US tended to produce elasticities in excess of unity, although there was some evidence that elasticities were smaller for narrow as opposed to broad money aggregates. However, it was noticed by Laidler as early as 1971 that elasticities have tended to decline over time. This is possibly the result of long-run institutional factors involving better access to banking facilities, particularly in the post-war period. Such findings appear to hold no matter what scale variable is used. However, it has to be remembered that they are obtained from long-run time series in which both money stock and scale variables exhibit common upward trends.

By and large, scale variable elasticities have varied from study to study, depending on the sample period used and the economy concerned. The general to specific UK studies of the 1980s have generally supported an elasticity of unity. However, it cannot be said that the existence of economies of scale has either been confirmed or rejected. There is, though, very little evidence of elasticities as low as the 0.5 suggested by the Baumol–Tobin analysis, even for transactionary balances.

The definition of money and the choice of scale variable

At one time it was hoped that empirical work on the demand for money would provide some help in determining the appropriate definition of money – for example, whether it should be defined in narrow or broad terms. It was felt that if demand for money functions with given arguments proved more stable for one certain definition rather than for others, then that definition would have some claim to be the appropriate one. It has turned out, maybe not surprisingly, that empirical work has been of little assistance on this question. By the 1970s it appeared possible to isolate stable demand functions for *both* narrow and broad definitions of money. Moreover, as we shall see in the next section, since that time instability appears to have arisen in the broad money aggregate for the UK and in the narrow money aggregate for the US.

The consensus now appears to be that different behavioural relationships must be expected to hold for different components of the money stock. This approach was first stressed in the UK by Coghlan, who argued that 'there is no general theory of the demand for money which is applicable regardless of the definition of money adopted' (Coghlan 1978: 48). If this is so, we cannot expect to isolate stable demand functions for broad money aggregates involving components as different as, for example, currency and time deposits.

This approach was advanced even earlier in the US particularly by Goldfeld (1973) who, having modelled the demand for both narrow and broad money, argued strongly that it was advisable to disaggregate the broad money aggregate.

The choice of scale variable in demand for money functions is obviously closely linked to the definition of money employed. For narrow definitions of money, believed mainly to serve the transactionary motive, it can be argued that current measured income is the appropriate scale variable. However, for broader definitions of money some measure of wealth, either non-human wealth only or total wealth (proxied by permanent income) is likely to be more appropriate.

The likely superiority of wealth measures as scale variables was demonstrated as early as 1963 by Meltzer who, using US annual data for 1900–58, compared the stability over different decades of equations similar to [12.5] but containing alternative scale variables: non-human wealth, permanent income and measured income. He found that the wealth variables produced stabler demand for money functions than the income variable no matter what definition was used for money. Such a conclusion was supported by Brunner and Meltzer (1963), Chow (1966) and Laidler (1966).

Until recently, lack of data on private sector financial wealth for most economies apart from the US meant that in many cases the choice of scale variable in practice lay between measured and permanent income. Choice was most frequently made on the basis of equations such as [12.11], the underlying implication being that permanent income can be regarded as the usual distributed lag function of present and past measured income levels. Estimated versions of [12.11] almost invariably confirmed the importance of lagged as well as current income levels as determinants of the demand for money. While it is tempting to interpret this as support for permanent income as the appropriate scale variable, we have already observed in section 12.3 that the issue is not as simple as that. Equation [12.26], obtained by using measured income as the scale variable and postulating only a gradual adjustment of actual to desired balances, is very similar to [12.11]. Thus, the importance of past income values may arise from adjustment rather than expectational lags, so that measured income rather than permanent income could still be the appropriate scale variable.

The first serious attempt to resolve this problem was by Feige (1967) who attempted the estimation of an equation similar to [12.32], using US data for 1915–63. Feige found that estimates of the partial adjustment parameter, μ, in [12.32] were not significantly different from unity, whereas estimates for λ, the permanent income or expectational parameter, were 0.37 for narrow money and 0.30 for broad money. These results suggested that, at least for annual data, the adjustment of actual to desired balances could be treated as instantaneous. Thus, the importance of lagged income variables indeed appeared to be the result of permanent income being the appropriate scale variable. Moreover, the estimates of λ were close to those obtained by Friedman in his time series work on the consumption function (see section 10.3).

While with annual data there may appear no place for adjustment lags once the scale variable has been properly specified as permanent income, it is still conceivable that such lags could have a role to play over shorter time periods. A natural extension of Feige's work was therefore to estimate equations such as [12.32] from quarterly data. Laidler and Parkin (1970) attempted this using

UK quarterly data for 1955–67 and, although the results were less conclusive, they also concluded that the importance of past values of income on the demand for money was a reflection not so much of lags of adjustment, but of permanent income being the appropriate scale variable.

Since the early 1970s estimated versions of equations such as [12.11] and [12.26] have continued to demonstrate the importance of past income levels on money demand. At one time it seemed fairly well established that the lags observed were expectational in nature. Results implied an implausibly low rate of portfolio adjustment that could only be rationalised by reinterpreting them as reflecting expectational lags. These results appeared to confirm the earlier findings of Feige and of Laidler and Parkin. However, this consensus has had to be revised in the light of the fact that, as pointed out in the last section, the conventional partial adjustment equation [12.26] cannot adequately portray short-run dynamics when the money supply is exogenous. As noted earlier, Laidler (1982) has pointed out that, once alternative adjustment processes are envisaged, it becomes possible to attribute low values of adjustment parameters to, for example, slow adjustments in the price level to an excess of money supply over demand.

The more recent availability of reliable data on private sector wealth for some economies has led to more direct attempts at assessing the importance of at least non-human wealth as a scale variable. For example, Grice and Bennett (1984), in a study of the UK demand for the broad money aggregate M3, include the gross financial wealth of the non-bank private sector in their equations as well as an income variable. A distinction is drawn between changes in wealth that arise because of asset-price changes and those that are the result of new saving. Using quarterly data and a general to specific approach, they conclude that the influence of financial wealth on money demand cannot be ignored and that demand reacts more slowly to wealth created by asset price changes than to that created by new savings, although the long-run effect of asset price changes may be slightly the greater. The long-run wealth elasticities are well in excess of unity. Despite the importance of wealth, income still has a role to play, although its long-run elasticity is only 0.32. The study is therefore unusual in that it finds a significant role for *two* scale variables.

A number of recent studies have concentrated on determining the appropriate lag structure for money demand equations without concern over whether the lags are adjustment lags or expectational lags. This procedure involves the specification of an initial short-run equation involving longish lags in both the dependent variable and the explanatory variables. The general to specific testing process is then employed to determine a final preferred lag structure. We shall consider studies adopting this approach in section 12.6.

Opportunity cost and other variables

A priori preferences as to the appropriate opportunity cost variables to be included in demand for money functions have depended on investigators' theoretical persuasions. 'Neo-Keynesian' research workers tend to regard short-term interest rates as most relevant for narrow definitions for money when transactionary motives are dominant, and only consider longer-term rates in the context of broad money aggregates. Monetarists, however, have always maintained that rates of return on all alternative assets are relevant even for

narrow money. For the monetarist, money is an effective substitute for all assets
– both financial and physical.

Empirical clarification of which are the most appropriate interest rate
variables is bedevilled by multicollinearity problems since most rates tend to
move together over time. For example, Laidler, in his 1980 paper experimented
with alternative interest rates using narrow money for US quarterly data
(1953–78). Some of his estimates of versions of the partial adjustment equation
[12.26] are shown in Table 12.1. Figures in parentheses are t-ratios, r_1 is a
short-term and r_2 a long-term interest rate.

The typical multicollinearity problem is well illustrated by the fact that the
estimates of both interest rate elasticities lose precision when r_1 and r_2 are
included together. Notice also that, when r_1 is added to the equation already
containing r_2, its coefficient proves insignificantly different from zero despite
the fact that s, the standard error of the residuals, falls, i.e. despite the fact that
the 'fit' of the equation is improved.

Laidler also found that there was 'room' in his equation for either r_1 or r_2
plus a dividend/price ratio variable, first used by Hamburger (1977), as a
measure of the 'real rate' on all equities including durable goods. There is, in
fact, increasing evidence, particularly for the US economy, that rates of return
on equities as well as more traditional interest rate variables are important
determinants of the demand for money even when a narrow definition of money
is adopted.

There is also evidence that, in more open economies, interest rates ruling in
international capital markets should be regarded as relevant opportunity-cost
variables. For example, Hamburger and Wood (1978) found the uncovered
three-month rate on Eurodollar deposits to be a significant variable in the UK
demand for money function. Hamburger (1977) had similar success with
such a variable, thus confirming the openness of the UK economy and the
close substitutability between UK domestic money and Eurodollar deposits.
Hamburger also provides evidence that the Eurodollar rate may be important
in the West German demand for money function.

Investigators using interest rates as opportunity cost variables have usually
proceeded as if expected capital gains on non-monetary assets were zero.
However Grice and Bennett (1984), in the paper referred to earlier, include
estimates of expected gains in their opportunity cost measures. Their augmented
variables prove significant in their demand for money equations.

Table 12.1 Demand functions for US narrow money

Constant	r_1	r_2	y	$\bar{m}_{-1}$	s
−0.148	−0.011		0.030	0.949	0.0097
(3.01)	(3.13)		(3.25)	(29.6)	
−0.320		−0.043	0.067	0.913	0.0095
(3.69)		(3.60)	(3.95)	(28.3)	
−0.307	−0.006	−0.031	0.062	0.928	0.0092
(3.67)	(1.57)	(2.29)	(3.73)	(28.9)	

Source: Laidler (1980), Table 1

In recent years attention has been paid to the own rate of return on money, including this as a variable in demand function in addition to opportunity cost variables. In the UK, Hacche (1974), in a study to be discussed in the next section, used a measure based on the three-month certificate of deposit rate. Artis and Lewis (1976) and Grice and Bennett in the study already mentioned form measures constructed as weighted averages of the rates of return on various components of the broad money stock. Also Taylor (1987) in a broad money equation includes an own-rate variable constructed from the rate on interest bearing cheque accounts and the seven-day deposit rate. Own-rate variables have, of course, a positive relationship with money demand, in contrast to rates reflecting opportunity cost which appear with a negative sign. The successful inclusion of own-rate measures suggests that broad money at least should not be treated as an asset bearing a zero return.

Many economists would regard the expected rate of inflation as an important determinant of the opportunity cost of holding money. While theoretically one might expect its influence to be reflected in the nominal rates of interest usually included in demand for money functions, the evidence does suggest that expected inflation rates affect the demand for money directly in a manner over and above their indirect influence via nominal interest rates. That this is so during periods of rapid inflation has been established reasonably clearly in a series of studies dating back to Cagan's (1956) work on European hyperinflations and Vogel's (1974) study of sixteen Latin American republics. Since the studies of US data, by Shapiro (1973) and Goldfeld (1973), it has also been accepted that even more moderate inflation rates can have an effect on money demand in that economy. In the UK Budd and Holly (1986) fitted a dynamic demand function for M3 to annual data for 1878–1984 and found strong evidence of inflation effects.

Other investigators such as Hendry (1985) and Taylor (1987), using the general to specific/error correction approach, also detect long run inflation effects on the UK demand for money. There is, however, a problem in distinguishing non-zero long run inflation elasticities from non-zero short run price elasticities. For example, consider the following two models. In the first model the long-run demand for money function is

$$\bar{m}_t = a + by_t + c\Delta p_t \qquad\qquad [12.46]$$

where Δp_t is the change in the logarithm of the price level and hence equal to the inflation rate. Since $\bar{m}_t$ refers to real balances, [12.46] implies that the demand for nominal balances has a long-run price elasticity of unity as predicted by theory. A standard error correction model based on [12.46] would be

$$\Delta\bar{m}_t = \beta\Delta y_t + \gamma\Delta^2 p_t - \lambda[\bar{m}_{t-1} - a - by_{t-1} - c\Delta p_{t-1}] \qquad\qquad [12.47]$$

where $\Delta^2 p_t = \Delta p_t - \Delta p_{t-1}$ and $0 < \lambda < 1$.

In the second model there are no inflation effects and the long-run function expressed in terms of the demand for nominal balances is

$$m_t = a + by_t + dp_t \qquad\qquad [12.48]$$

A standard error correction model based on [12.48] would be

$$\Delta m_t = \beta\Delta y_t + \delta\Delta p_t - \lambda[m_{t-1} - a - by_{t-1} - dp_{t-1}] \qquad\qquad [12.49]$$

where δ is the short-run price elasticity. Assuming a long-run price elasticity $d = 1$, as predicted by theory, [12.49] can be rewritten as

$$\Delta m_t - \Delta p_t = \beta \Delta y_t + (\delta - 1)\Delta p_t - \lambda[m_{t-1} - p_{t-1} - a - by_{t-1}] \qquad [12.50]$$

Since $\Delta m_t - \Delta p_t = \Delta \bar{m}_t$ and using $\Delta p_t = \Delta^2 p_t + \Delta p_{t-1}$, [12.50] can be further rearranged as

$$\Delta \bar{m}_t = \beta \Delta y_t + (\delta - 1)\Delta^2 p_t - \lambda\left[\bar{m}_{t-1} - a - by_{t-1} - \left(\frac{\delta - 1}{\lambda}\right)\Delta p_{t-1}\right] \qquad [12.51]$$

Clearly, [12.47] and [12.51] are virtually identical, yet [12.47] arises because of a long-run inflation effect while [12.51] arises because $\delta \neq 1$, that is because the short-run price elasticity of the demand for nominal balances is not equal to unity. The similarity between [12.47] and [12.51] makes it impossible to distinguish between a short-run price effect on real balances and a long-run inflation effect arising because of opportunity cost factors.

Less work has been done on other possible factors influencing the demand for money. The possible importance of the 'riskiness' of bonds was emphasised by Tobin as early as 1958 but has received virtually no attention in empirical work, although Slovin and Sushka (1983) find a role for interest rate variability in their US study. Finally, both the inventory-theoretical approach to the demand for transactionary balances and later work on the precautionary motive draw attention to the 'brokerage fee' involved in selling bonds. Proxied by the real wage rate, such a fee has been successfully included in US demand for money functions by, for example, Dutton and Gramm (1973) and Karni (1974). However, the general importance of such variables is as yet unclear and the chain of theoretical arguments leading to the inclusion of the real wage rate does seem somewhat tenuous.

12.5   The stability of demand for money functions

Until the early 1970s the general consensus of opinion concerning stability was that, since the beginning of the century, demand for money functions had been stable in the sense described at the start of this chapter. To quote Laidler (1971: 99), 'For the United States, the evidence is overwhelming and for Britain it is at the very least highly suggestive'. Little attempt had been made at that time to test rigorously for stability, and this conclusion was based mainly on rough comparisons of scale variable and interest rate elasticities obtained from equations estimated for various subperiods within full sample periods of from thirty to seventy years. Such comparisons (see, for example, Laidler 1966; 1971) suggested fairly constant interest rate elasticities but provided some evidence that scale variable elasticities were declining over time. However, it was felt that these changes were gradual and predictable, reflecting long-run institutional changes rather than short-run unpredictable shifts in income velocity that might offset any changes in the money supply.

During the next ten years the stability of demand for money functions was subjected to more rigorous statistical tests. We lack the space to describe the theoretical basis of these tests but their application by, for example, Kahn (1974), Laumas and Mehra (1976) and Laumas (1978) tended to confirm previous findings for pre-1970 data.

By the mid-1970s, however, doubts began to be cast on the stability of both the UK and the US demand for money functions. In the UK, Hacche (1974) found that equations estimated from quarterly data for 1964–71 severely under-estimated M3, the UK broad money aggregate during 1972–74. This was especially the case for that portion of M3 held by the company sector. Hacche argued that the major reform of the UK monetary system in 1971 (the new Competition and Credit Control system) had led to competition by the clearing banks for large wholesale deposits in parallel money markets that had previously been dominated by the secondary banking system. The clearing banks also began issuing their own certificates of deposit at this time. These developments increased the attractiveness of M3 (which includes wholesale time deposits and certificates of deposit) to asset holders and hence led to an upward shift in the demand for M3 function.

Hacche's work was rather severely criticised by Courakis (1978) and Hendry and Mizon (1978) (see section 12.6). However, it appeared fairly clear that the type of demand for money equations normally estimated prior to 1971 (i.e. those with the money stock as the dependent variable) were not capable of satisfactorily explaining post-1971 data. Rather than any general instability there appeared to be a distinct shift in the relationship occurring in the early 1970s. For example, Artis and Lewis (1974), using the Chow tests described in section 4.3 found evidence of a definite shift in demand for money functions for *both* M3 *and* M1 at the time of the introduction of the new Competition and Credit Control system.

Artis and Lewis (1976) suggested a very different reason from that of Hacche for the apparent breakdown in previous relationships. They argued that it was no longer reasonable, during the post-1971 period, to treat the supply of money as endogenous or 'demand-determined'. Roughly, this is equivalent to saying that model I of section 9.2 was a closer approximation to reality than was model II. The gradually increasing influence of 'monetarism' on successive UK governments meant that it had become more and more appropriate to treat the money supply rather than the rate of interest as the exogenous variable. Artis and Lewis went further, however, and argued that there was at least some ground for doubting the endogeneity of the money supply even before 1971. They argued that the money supply cannot be fully endogenous in an open economy with fixed exchange rates and that, although interest rates may have appeared to be administered in the earlier period, this did not mean that rates were set without regard for market conditions. There was, at least, sufficient doubt about the endogeneity of the money supply in the 1960s to justify experimenting with something akin to model I for the whole sample period 1963(ii)–1973(i).

As we saw in section 12.3, if the money supply is regarded as exogenously determined, then it makes no sense to adapt the standard partial adjustment model [12.26]. Rather alternative adjustment processes must be considered. Artis and Lewis in fact experimented with versions of [12.44A], in which adjustment is through the money-income ratio, and of [12.41], where adjustment occurs via changes in the rate of interest.

Their version of [12.44A] was estimated from quarterly UK data for 1963–73 using M1 and M3, the yield on $2\frac{1}{2}$ per cent consols for r and GDP as the income variable. C_t was represented by the domestic borrowing requirement, an index of Bank of England restraint on bank lending and the high-powered money stock. The first two of these measures proved to be important influences on the M1 ratio and the third on the M3 ratio. When post-Competition and Credit Control data were included in the sample, not only were these influences most marked but equation [10.44A] exhibited much greater parameter stability than did normal demand for money equations excluding constraint variables. Unlike Hacche, Artis and Lewis do not claim that the demand for money function shifted; rather the economy had been pushed off a stable demand for money function because the supply of money expanded too rapidly for demand to adjust to it.

When Artis and Lewis estimated equation [12.41] over the same sample period, this equation exhibited even greater coefficient stability than [12.44A]. The speed of adjustment implied by [12.41] was noticeably faster than that suggested by the money-income ratio equation [12.44A]. This is consistent with a sequence whereby in the short run the market clearing function is borne by the interest rate but where income adjustments make their presence felt in the longer run.

The belief that there had been a general breakdown in all UK demand for money functions was first seriously questioned by Coghlan (1978). Coghlan started from the very reasonable proposition that no general theory of the demand for money could be applicable regardless of the definition of money applied. Factors influencing the demand for M1 are likely to differ from those determining the demand for M3. Since the demand for M1 is primarily a transactions demand, its most likely determinants are the level of income (rather than a wealth variable) and short- (rather than long-term) rates of interest. Furthermore, there is a much greater likelihood that M1 balances (unlike M3 balances) were demand-determined even during the post-1971 period. It is certainly true that the supply of currency is determined by the public's demand for it, and demand deposits can also be regarded as largely determined in this way since individuals can switch, relatively easily, between these and interest-bearing time deposits.

Since M1 could be regarded as demand-determined throughout the 1960s and 1970s, Coghlan retained money stock as the dependent variable throughout his empirical work. Equations incorporating both adjustment and expectational lags were estimated from quarterly data for 1964–76. The results revealed that when data for the 1970s was included the overall fit of the equations deteriorated badly.

The deterioration in explanatory power as the sample period was lengthened, plus the fact that it appeared unreasonable to impose, a priori, an identical lag pattern of adjustment on all explanatory variables, led Coghlan to experiment with rational distributed lags of the kind described in section 6.4. In this case

$$P(L)m_t = Q(L)y_t + R(L)r_t + u_t \qquad [12.52]$$

where $P(L), Q(L)$ and $R(L)$ are polynomials in the lag operator L. The best-fitting equation for the full sample period proved to be (figures in parentheses are t-statistics)

$$m_t = \text{const} + 0.405y_t - 0.233y_{t-1} + 1.430p_{t-1} - 2.282p_{t-2} + 1.813p_{t-3}$$
$$(3.95) \quad (2.16) \quad (6.00) \quad (5.81) \quad (4.60)$$

$$- 0.836p_{t-4} - 0.053r_t + 0.830m_{t-1} \qquad\qquad [12.53]$$
$$(3.37) \quad (5.29) \quad (14.41)$$

$$\bar{R}^2 = 0.998 \qquad d = 2.142 \qquad s = 0.0131$$

This time, there was no deterioration in the fit of the equation as the sample period was lengthened. The estimated coefficients became very stable once data for later years was included. This reflected the greater variability in the 1970s data which enabled parameters to be more precisely estimated. The lag structure of the equation is quite complex and is *not the same for each explanatory variable.* While adjustment to real income and prices is rapid, being complete in less than a year, there appears to be a geometric lag on the rate of interest variable with little more than half of the adjustment complete within a year.

Coghlan used both the more traditional type of equation and equations such as the above to forecast the money stock during 1976 and 1977. His preferred equations forecast considerably the better and, in particular, correctly predicted the rapid growth of M1 during 1977.

Coghlan's finding that it was still possible to isolate a stable UK demand for M1 function, provided sufficiently complex lag structures were allowed for, was supported during the 1980s by investigators using the general to specific approach described in section 7.2. Such investigators also claim that it is possible to find a stable M3 function using their approach. Others, however, while accepting these findings as far as M1 is concerned, would argue that the breakdown of the original partial adjustment type demand for M3 equations is not just due to a failure to correctly specify the lag structure. Rather, it is still argued, the breakdown has occurred for the reasons originally advanced by Artis and Lewis which we discussed earlier. The Artis–Lewis notion of 'disequilibrium money' has led to the so-called 'buffer stock' models of money demand. However we defer discussion of these models and of the general to specific approach until the next two sections.

Doubts about stability in the UK context coincided with similar doubts about the stability of the US demand for money function. However, the problem with US functions was that, in contrast to UK findings, instability occurred in the demand for narrow rather than for broad money. Also, the tendancy, at least at first, was to overpredict rather than underpredict the actual money stock.

Instability in the US function was first observed by Goldfeld (1976) and Enzler, Johnson and Paulus (1976) who found that standard partial adjustment models of the demand for money, estimated from 1955–1972 data, seriously overpredicted the M1 money stock in the mid to late 1970s. This finding led to the concept of the 'missing money'.

Overprediction of the M1 stock was confirmed by Laidler (1981) in an extensive study. Laidler also drew attention to the fact that estimates of the adjustment parameter μ in estimated versions of [12.26] were as low as 0.05, suggesting an implausibly low rate of adjustment of actual money balances to desired levels. This led Laidler to consider alternative adjustment processes. He experimented with an Artis-Lewis type model akin to equations [12.39] to

[12.41] in which the brunt of short-run adjustment is borne by interests rates, and also with a real income adjustment model. However, he ultimately opted for a price adjustment model not dissimilar to his 1982 model which was described in section 12.3. It was thus possible to attribute low values for the adjustment parameter μ, not to implausibly slow portfolio adjustment, but to a very gradual price level adjustment.

As in the UK, work on the US demand for money function during the 1980s was dominated by two approaches. First, the general to specific methodology was employed in an effort to tackle the instability problem and, secondly, buffer stock models were extensively estimated. These two approaches are the subjects of the next sections.

12.6 The ECM approach to the demand for money function

We begin this section by recalling a major controversy over the UK demand for money function that occurred during the 1970s. We have already referred to the Hacche (1974) paper in section 12.5. While Hacche's findings concerning the instability of UK broad money functions estimated at that time is now in dispute, his methodology also came under considerable criticism in two papers by Courakis (1978) and Hendry and Mizon (1978). Hacche's model is as specified in equation [12.26B] – a partial adjustment-type equation in which the long-run price elasticity is restricted to unity. However, the model actually estimated by Hacche is somewhat different. First, equation [12.26B] is 'first differenced' to remove any possibility of 'spurious correlations' caused by common trends in the data. It therefore becomes

$$m_t - p_t - (m_{t-1} - p_{t-1}) = b_1(r_t - r_{t-1}) + c_1(y_t - y_{t-1})$$
$$+ e_1[m_{t-1} - p_t - (m_{t-2} - p_{t-1})] + v_t \quad [12.54]$$

where $b_1 = \mu\beta, c_1 = \mu\gamma, e_1 = 1 - \mu$ and $v_t = \mu(\varepsilon_t - \varepsilon_{t-1})$. Next, the disturbance, v_t, is assumed to follow a first-order autoregressive scheme $v_t = \rho v_{t-1} + u_t$ so that, before estimation, [12.54] is further transformed in the manner described in section 5.2.2 for dealing with such schemes. Since [12.54] can be rearranged as

$$m_t = b_1 r_t - b_1 r_{t-1} + c_1 y_t - c_1 y_{t-1} + (1 - e_1)p_t - (1 - e_1)p_{t-1}$$
$$+ (1 + e_1)m_{t-1} - e_1 m_{t-2} + v_t \quad [12.55]$$

this second transformation means that the equation eventually estimated by Hacche is[7]

$$m_t = b_1 r_t - b_1(1 - \rho)r_{t-1} + b_1\rho r_{t-2} + c_1 y_t - c_1(1 + \rho)y_{t-1}$$
$$+ c_1\rho y_{t-2} + (1 - e_1)p_t - (1 - e_1)(1 + \rho)p_{t-1} + (1 - e_1)\rho p_{t-2}$$
$$+ (1 + e_1 + \rho)m_{t-1} - (\rho + e_1 + e_1\rho)m_{t-2} + e_1\rho m_{t-3} + u_t \quad [12.56]$$

As pointed out by both Courakis and Hendry–Mizon, equation [12.56] implies a whole series of restrictions on the lag structure of the demand for money equation which are, in principle, testable hypotheses which may well not be valid. For example, [12.56] implies that the ratios of the coefficients on r_t and r_{t-1}, on y_t and y_{t-1} and on p_t and p_{t-1} are all equal to $-(1 + \rho)$. Such restrictions arise because Hacche assumes that first differencing is an appropriate procedure and then assumes that the disturbance in the first-differenced equation [12.54] follows a first-order autoregressive scheme. However, while differencing may remove any spurious correlation problem, as we saw in section 7.3, it will also, almost certainly, lead to an autocorrelation problem. Clearly, if a non-autocorrelated disturbance is present in equation [12.26B], then v_t in the first-differenced equation [12.54] will be of the first-order moving average type. Moreover, residual autocorrelation may reflect no more than a mis-specification of the lag structure in the equation, (for example Hacche specifies no expectational lags but takes first differences), and its approximation by a first-order scheme may be quite inadequate[8] and can lead to considerable biases in estimated coefficients and implied long-run elasticities. For this reason it becomes important specifically to *test* the assumptions made by Hacche and to consider the effect on estimated elasticities of alternative specifications.

Courakis used maximum likelihood methods to estimate a sequence of nested equations, i.e. the earlier equations may be derived from the later ones by the imposition of restrictions on the coefficients of the latter. Courakis's estimation method enabled him, by comparing these equations, to test whether any of the restrictions necessary to move from one such equation to another were rejected by the data.

We have already noted, in a previous section, that Courakis found a unit long-run price elasticity to be rejected by the data. In addition, it could also be seen that a model in the *levels* of the variables such as [12.26B] with an autocorrelated disturbance term was preferable to a model in *differences* with an autocorrelated disturbance term such as that estimated by Hacche. In fact, the restrictions implicitly imposed by Hacche were rejected by the data.

Courakis's most striking result was the clear rejection of Hacche's specification, but even the alternative equations considered perform with only varying degrees of success for different sample periods. Since no alternative was clearly to be preferred, Courakis considered the effects on estimated elasticities of varying specifications of the demand for money function. He presents results obtained for three such specifications. Such was the alarming variation in the elasticities obtained that Courakis questioned whether it was possible to obtain sufficiently reliable estimates of demand for money parameters to resolve any of the main issues in this area.

The study by Hendry and Mizon (1978) represents one of the very first published examples of the use of the general to specific methodology described in section 7.2. They estimated, first, a general equation of the form

$$m_t = a + \sum_{j=1}^{5} b_j r_{t-j+1} + \sum_{j=1}^{5} c_j y_{t-j+1} + \sum_{j=1}^{5} d_j p_{t-j+1} + \sum_{j=1}^{5} e_j m_{t-j} \qquad [12.57]$$

The maximum lag is increased to four quarters in [12.57] compared with [12.56] because quarterly data is being used. To derive Hacche's equation [12.56] it is necessary to impose, in all, sixteen restrictions (we shall not list them) on the coefficients of [12.57]. Unrestricted estimation of [12.57] for the period 1963(i)–1975(ii) yields the values shown in Table 12.2. Figures in parentheses are standard errors.

While, in part because of multicollinearity, few of the individual coefficients in Table 12.2 are significantly different from zero, it is still the case that some of Hacche's restrictions are rejected by the data. In particular, Hacche's first differencing transformation is rejected. In fact when Hacche's equation [12.56]

Table 12.2   Unrestricted estimation of equation [12.57]

j	b_j	c_j	d_j	e_j	$a = 2.40\ R^2 = 0.9995$ $s = 0.0096(3.63)$
1	0.90	0.22	0.59	0.92	
	(0.39)	(0.13)	(0.25)	(0.22)	
2	−0.82	0.05	−0.71	−0.05	
	(0.66)	(0.15)	(0.42)	(0.28)	
3	−0.99	0.14	0.94	−0.17	
	(0.76)	(0.15)	(0.59)	(0.28)	
4	1.28	0.01	−0.99	−0.22	
	(0.81)	(0.15)	(0.60)	(0.29)	
5	−0.63	0.20	0.24	0.30	
	(0.68)	(0.13)	(0.39)	(0.23)	

Source: Hendry and Mizon (1978)

is estimated with restrictions imposed the coefficients are as shown in Table 12.3. It can be seen that these numbers differ considerably from those in Table 12.2.

Hendry and Mizon are not surprised that an equation in *differences* alone should be rejected by the data, since, for reasons similar to those outlined in section 7.3, they believe that such equations must also allow for mechanisms by which previous disequilibria in the *levels* of the variables are permitted to affect their rate of change. As an analogue to the model used by DHSY (1978), which cannot be rejected against [12.57], they estimate the equation

$$m_t - p_t - (m_{t-1} - p_{t-1}) = 1.61 + 0.21(y_t - y_{t-1}) + 0.81(r_t - r_{t-1})$$
$$(0.65)\ (0.09) \qquad\qquad (0.31)$$

$$+\ 0.26[m_{t-1} - p_{t-1} - (m_{t-2} - p_{t-2})] - 0.40(p_t - p_{t-1}) -$$
$$(0.12) \qquad\qquad\qquad\qquad\qquad (0.15)$$

$$0.23(m_{t-1} - p_{t-1} - y_{t-1}) - 0.61r_{t-4} + 0.14y_{t-4}$$
$$(0.05) \qquad\qquad\qquad (0.21) \qquad (0.04)$$

$$R_2 = 0.69 \qquad s = 0.0091 \qquad\qquad\qquad [12.58]$$

The major difference between [12.58] and Hacche's specification is that [12.58] is an ECM that contains *both* levels *and* differences, providing the mechanisms mentioned above. Previous disequilibria in the relationship between the levels of 'real' money and 'real' income affect changes in real demand through the disequilibrium error term $(m_{t-1} - p_{t-1} - y_{t-1})$ which is the ratio of lagged real balances to lagged real income. Equation [12.58] can, in fact, be 'solved' for the resultant coefficients on lagged and unlagged values of r_t, y_t, p_t and m_{t-1}. These are shown in Table 12.4 and demonstrate that [12.58] in effect omits the unsuccessful variables in [12.57] and rearranges the remainder such that they represent 'separate decision variables with sensible economic interpretations' (Hendry and Mizon 1978: 561).

Table 12.3 Restricted estimation of equation [12.56]

j	b_j	c_j	d_j	e_j
1	0.89	0.13	0.67	1.53
2	−1.07	−0.16	−0.80	−0.46
3	0.18	0.03	0.13	−0.07

Source: Hendry and Mizon (1978)

Table 12.4 Solved version of equation [12.58]

j	b_j	c_j	d_j	e_j
1	0.81	0.21	0.60	1.03
2	−0.81	0.02	−0.63	−0.26
3	0	0	0.26	0
4	0	0	0	0
5	−0.61	0.14	0	0

Source: Hendry and Mizon (1978)

The above criticisms of Hacche well illustrate the dangers of the mechanical use of 'standard' econometric techniques. Much US work of that time (e.g. Laidler 1980; Hamburger 1977a) is equally free with the automatic use of 'OLS with Cochrane–Orcutt adjustment'. The work of Courakis in particular suggested that much greater attention needed to be paid to the dynamic structure and/or autocorrelation properties of demand for money equations. The ECM approach was also, of course, clearly the best known way of coping with any spurious correlation problems arising from common trends in the data.

Later work

The general to specific methodology continued to play a key role in attempts to model the UK demand for M3 throughout the 1980s. For example Grice and Bennett (1984), in the paper already mentioned, used such an approach and Taylor (1987) also adopts it.

Taylor begins with a general model, including four lags on all his variables, and tests down to a final equation which is then reestimated by the GIVE method described in section 5.1. Quarterly data for 1964(ii) to 1980(iv) are used in the specification search, with data for the next five years used for post-sample prediction. His final preferred equation is

$$\Delta(m-p)_t = \underset{(0.007)}{0.030} + \underset{(0.102)}{0.287\Delta(m-p)_{t-2}} - \underset{(0.183)}{0.415\Delta p_t} - \underset{(0.006)}{0.019(m-p-y)_{t-4}}$$

$$- \underset{(0.002)}{0.005(RTB_{t-1} - RM_t)} - \underset{(0.001)}{0.003\Delta^2(RLB)_{t-2}} + \text{seasonal}$$
$$\text{dummies}$$

$$R^2 = 0.76 \qquad\qquad\qquad\qquad\qquad\qquad\qquad\qquad [12.59]$$

where all variables are in logs except for the various interest rates. RTB is the three-month Treasury Bill rate, RLB is the yield on long-term government bonds and RM is the own-rate on money, defined as the larger of the 7-day deposit rate and the rate on high interest checking accounts. Such accounts did not exist before 1984, so the equation allows for financial innovation arising from their introduction. Y is real GDP and P the implied deflator of GDP.

Taylor's equation passes a battery of diagnostic tests, including an LM test for up to fifth-order autocorrelation and a test for post-sample predictive failure. It also passes the first Chow test for a structural break after 1971(iv). Taylor therefore claims that there is no sign of instability after the introduction of Competition and Credit Control in 1970. Furthermore, the new financial regime of the early 1980s also appears to leave coefficients unchanged. However, when the own rate on M3 is dropped from the equation, there is substantial evidence of omitted variable bias.

Taylor also derives the long-run demand for money function implied by his equation. Given a constant growth rate in real balances and GDP of g, a constant inflation rate of π and constant interest rates, equation [12.59] becomes

$$g = 0.030 + 0.287g - 0.019(m - p - y) - 0.005(RTB - RM) - 0.415\pi \quad [12.60]$$

Hence, in the long run

$$m = 1.579 + p + y - 37.52g - 21.84\pi - 0.263(RTB - RM)$$

Since g and π are in quarterly proportionate terms in [12.60], expressing them in annual percentage terms yields

$$m = 1.579 + p + y - 0.094g - 0.055\pi - 0.263(RTB - RM) \quad [12.61]$$

Notice that [12.61] reflects the fact that in the estimated equation [12.59] long-run homogeneity of degree unity of nominal balances with respect to real income and prices has been imposed. The ECM term in [12.59] is $(m - p - y)_{t-4}$ and there are no lagged terms in either y or p included in the equation. Notice also that it is the difference between the short-term rate of interest and the own-rate on M3, i.e. $(RTB - RM)$, that appears in both the short and the long-run functions. This is as expected since it is $(RTB - RM)$ that is now the true opportunity cost of holding M3.

The ECM general-to-specific approach has also been successfully applied to modelling the UK demand for the narrow money aggregate, M1, by Hendry (1979 and 1985). Using quarterly seasonally adjusted data for 1961(i) to 1982(iv) Hendry tests down to

$$\Delta(m - p)_t = 0.041 + 0.37\Delta y_{t-1} - 0.80\Delta p_t - 0.28\Delta(m - p)_{t-1} - 0.58\Delta R_t$$
$$(0.005) \quad (0.13) (0.12) (0.07) (0.07)$$

$$- 0.10(m - p - y)_{t-2} \quad R^2 = 0.71 \quad [12.62]$$
$$(0.02)$$

R_t in [12.62] is the three-month local authority rate. Hendry's equation passes the usual tests for autocorrelation and parameter stability. In fact the equation was first estimated for 1961(i) to 1977(i), but there was little change in coefficient values when the data for 1978–82 were added despite the 'Thatcher experiment' that began in the early 1980s.

380

The lag structures implied by equations [12.59] and [12.62] are quite complex but both have plausible long-run implications. For example, both equations suggest that, as predicted by theory, the long-run demand for real balances is independent of the price level. The success of such studies has led general-to-specific practitioners to claim that, provided sufficiently complex lag structures are allowed for, there is no real problem in estimating stable and robust UK demand for money functions for either M1 or M3.

The general-to-specific methodology has also been applied to the estimation of US demand for money functions. However, in this case attention has been mainly confined to M1, since in the US it is this money aggregate that has been posing most problems. For example, Baba, Hendry and Starr (1985) estimated a final preferred equation having the long-run solution

$$m - p = 0.5y + 4.6r^S + 7.2r^L \tag{12.63}$$

where r^S and r^L are short and long-term interest rates respectively. Notice that r^S has a positive sign, indicating that it is acting as the own rate of interest on M1. Initial estimates suggested a long-run income elasticity of 0.5 and a long-run price elasticity of unity for nominal balances, so these values were imposed on the eventually estimated equation.

More recently, Porter, Spindt and Lindsey (1989) used US data to estimate ECMs for both currency and demand deposits (the two components of M1). Their equations incorporated a trend variable to allow for financial innovations that helped agents to economise on money holdings. The trend proved significant with a negative coefficient over their 1961–86 data period and, when it was included, the real income elasticity of money demand was found to be close to unity. This result of course conflicts with that of Baba, Hendry and Starr and suggests that the low income elasticity found by the latter was the result of a failure to allow for financial innovation.

In recent years the techniques of co-integration described in section 7.5, have been applied to the estimation of demand for money equations. For example, Hall, Henry and Wilcox (1989) use these techniques to judge whether given sets of explanatory variables are sufficient to model adequately various UK monetary aggregates. If such a set does not co-integrate then there is little point in trying to estimate dynamic short-run error correction models since these will be subject to spurious correlation problems.

They find that it is indeed impossible to find co-integrating vectors for the variables (money stock, price level, real income, rate of interest) in standard textbook demand for money functions. For narrow money aggregates (M0 and M1), only when account is taken of innovations in cash management (e.g. introduction of cash dispensers, increased use of credit cards, introduction of interest bearing cheque accounts), is it possible to find a satisfactory co-integrating vector and hence a plausible long-run relationship. For the broader monetary aggregates (M3 and M4), it is necessary to introduce personal sector wealth as a scale variable and the inflation rate as an additional opportunity cost variable before a co-integrating vector can be found.

In a wide-ranging study Boughton (1991) examines the nature of the long-run demand for money in five large industrial countries – US, UK, Japan, Germany and France. His maintained hypothesis is that the long-run functions have remained stable but that dynamic adjustment processes and short-run behaviour are much more complex and variable than suggested by earlier and simpler partial adjustment models.

Boughton's analysis is complicated by the fact that the demand for money is a multivariate relationship. As we saw in section 7.6, this means that there is almost certainly more than one co-integrating vector linking the variables in the function. That is there are a number of static regressions having stationary error terms. There is therefore a problem in deciding which co-integrating vector should be regarded as the equilibrium relationship or long-run demand for money function. Despite this, Boughton's results suggest that it is possible to find co-integrating regressions with coefficients that satisfy a priori notions about long run demand for money functions. Hence, by the Engle–Granger representation theorem (see section 7.5) it must be possible to represent the short-run demand for money functions as error correction models.

Boughton estimates equations for all five countries using both narrow and broad money aggregates and adopting both a two-stage Engle–Granger approach and a single-stage general-to-specific strategy. Tests for choosing between non-nested equations have to be employed to determine the final preferred equations for each data set and broadly speaking these tests support the single-stage estimation procedure over the two-stage approach. However long-run elasticities found are generally very similar regardless of which approach is adopted.

Two of the long-run functions obtained by Boughton, for US narrow money and UK broad money, are as follows

$$US(M1) \quad m = \text{const} + 0.652p + 1.338y + 1.487r^S - 3.013r^L \qquad [12.64]$$

$$UK(M3) \quad m = \text{const} + 0.699p + 3.281y - 3.441r^L \qquad [12.65]$$

Notice that in both [12.64] and [12.65] price elasticities are less than unity while income elasticities exceed unity. These values are typical of Boughton's overall results. Contrary to theory the price elasticity of demand for nominal balances is found to be less than one. Also Boughton finds no evidence of economies of scale in the holding of money balances. Indeed the income elasticity in the UK demand for M3 equation is far higher than would be acceptable to most UK econometricians. However, Boughton finds no evidence of instability in the UK equation after 1973, although there are some problems with the US function. Finally, note that, as in the Baba–Hendry–Starr equation [12.63], the short-term interest variable in [12.65] has a positive coefficient, indicating that it is acting as the own rate of interest on money.

12.7 Buffer stock models

All the models of the previous section assume, implicitly, that the supply of money is demand determined. That is the monetary authorities automatically adjust the money supply to a level equal to the short run demand for it. This is the case whether that short-run demand be determined by a simple partial adjustment equation such as [12.26] or a complex equation such as [12.59]. While this is not unreasonable for narrow definitions of money, we saw in section 12.2 that, at least during the post-1970 period, it is more appropriate to regard the supply of broad money aggregates such as M3 as being exogenously determined. It was this belief that lay behind the Artis–Lewis idea, discussed in sections 12.3 and 12.5, that the breakdown in standard partial adjustment models in the UK was the result of the economy being pushed off an essentially stable demand function. This occurred because the exogenously determined money supply was expanding too rapidly for money holders to adjust in the normal fashion.

The notion that exogenous variations in the money supply can lead to disequilibrium in the money market is the basic idea behind the buffer stock models developed in the 1980s. These models assume that money is the residual or buffer asset in a portfolio, because asset holders permit money balances to fluctuate up and down in response to any unexpected or transitory changes in the overall size of the portfolio resulting from exogenous changes in the money supply. This is so because the cost of adjusting money balances is much smaller than that of adjusting other assets in the portfolio. Only when changes are regarded as permanent do individuals adjust their holdings of non-money assets. Hence the result of an exogenous change in the money supply depends crucially on whether the change is perceived as permanent or transitory. If the former, then asset holders will make permanent changes in their portfolio. If, however, the change is unexpected, regarded as transitory and expected to be reversed very shortly, then money holdings as the buffer asset take the main burden of the adjustment.

The best known buffer-stock model is that of Carr and Darby (1981) who make the above distinction between expected and unexpected changes. New classical monetary theory implies that an expected change in the money supply will result in an immediate and equiproportionate change in the price level, leaving all real variables unchanged. It is possible to capture such an adjustment process by a standard partial adjustment equation such as [12.25] reproduced below:

$$\bar{m}_t = \mu \bar{m}_{Dt} + (1 - \mu)\bar{m}_{t-1} \qquad\qquad [12.25]$$

where we recall that the logarithm of real balances $\bar{m}_t = m_t - p_t$. Clearly, $\bar{m}_{t-1}$ is uninfluenced by an expected change in the nominal money supply in period t but, since prices rise equiproportionately, $\bar{m}_t$ is uninfluenced also. In addition $\bar{m}_{Dt}$ depends only on, for example, real income and the interest rate and hence is unaffected too. Thus equation [12.25] is left unchanged by an expected increase in the nominal money supply.

As Carr and Darby pointed out, however, empirical evidence suggested strongly that unexpected increases in the nominal money supply had little immediate influence on the price level but mainly affected real income and interest rates. Hence such increases would cause the real money stock $\bar{m}_t$ to rise. They would also cause the long-run demand for real money, $\bar{m}_{Dt}$, to rise because of the changes in real income and interest rates. The problem was that empirical estimates of μ in [12.65] were so low that the rises in real income and/or falls in interests rates necessary for [12.65] to remain valid were implausibly great. Thus, while [12.65] could adequately capture the adjustment process in response to an expected rise in the nominal money supply, it could not represent the response to an unexpected rise.[9]

Because of this problem, Carr and Darby replaced [12.25] by

$$\bar{m}_t = \mu \bar{m}_{Dt} + (1 - \mu)\bar{m}_{t-1} + \beta y_t^t + \theta(m_t - m_t^*) + u_t \qquad\qquad [12.66]$$

where m_t^* is the expected nominal money supply so that $m_t - m_t^*$ is the 'unexpected' supply. Y_t^t represents transitory income. $\bar{m}_{Dt}$ in [12.66] is determined by

$$\bar{m}_{Dt} = \alpha + \alpha_1 y_t^p + \alpha_2 R_t$$

where Y_t^p is permanent income and R_t the interest rate.

If $\theta > 0$ in [12.66] then an unexpected change in the money supply pushes asset holders away from their short-run desired level of real balances given by [12.25]. If $\beta > 0$ then a receipt of transitory income has the same effect. Carr and Darby maintain that transitory income is absorbed into transitory money balances. If there is no unexpected change in money supply and no receipt of transitory income then [12.66] reduces to [12.25] which is able to capture the response to any expected money supply change.

In their empirical work Carr and Darby model the expected money supply m_t^* as a separate equation with previous actual money supply values as the dependent variables. Thus asset holders form their expectations about the money supply from what has happened in the past. There is a possibility of contemporaneous correlation between the disturbance u_t and $(m_t - m_t^*)$ in equation [12.66]. With quarterly data the monetary authorities may be aware of increases in u_t, (i.e. random rises in the short-run demand for money), and may increase $(m_t - m_t^*)$ to accommodate them. Carr and Darby therefore estimate [12.66] by an instrumental variable method. The equation is estimated for eight industrial countries, including the UK and the US, using quarterly data from 1957(i) to 1976(iv). The estimates of θ are always significantly different from zero and take values between 0.6 and 1.3. This is as predicted by the buffer stock hypothesis. The coefficient on transitory income turns out to be generally insignificant, however. Their result for the UK was

$$\bar{m}_t = \underset{(0.125)}{0.167} + \underset{(0.024)}{0.036} y_t^p - \underset{(0.146)}{0.571} R_t + \underset{(0.055)}{0.883} \bar{m}_{t-1} + \underset{(0.143)}{0.262} y_t^t + \underset{(0.165)}{0.690} (m_t - m_t^*)$$

$$\bar{R}^2 = 0.948 \quad h = 0.287 \tag{12.67}$$

The coefficient on $(m_t - m_t^*)$ in [12.67] indicates that 69 per cent of any unexpected increase in the money supply is absorbed into portfolios as transitory balances. Notice that the coefficients on both income variables are insignificant but that the coefficient on transitory income is much larger than that on permanent income.[10]

The buffer stock hypothesis has an important policy implication. We saw earlier that the simple partial adjustment equation [12.25] implied large fluctuations in real income, or more likely interest rates, during the adjustment to an unexpected increase in the money supply. However, if the buffer stock hypothesis is valid then the interest rate effects of a sudden increase in the money supply are much less severe, since much of the increase will be absorbed as transitory balances in the short run.[11] In the long-run price movements are then able to restore equilibrium in the money market.

The Carr–Darby findings were soon disputed by MacKinnon and Milbourne (1984). They argued first that a correlation between u_t and $(m_t - m_t^*)$ in equation [12.66] was not merely a possibility but inevitable. Dropping the transitory income variable from [12.66], it can be rewritten as

$$m_t - p_t = \mu \bar{m}_{Dt} + (1 - \mu)\bar{m}_{t-1} + \theta(m_t - m_t^*) + u_t \qquad [12.68]$$

MacKinnon and Milbourne argued that, for given p_t, [12.68] implies that u_t influences m_t. Hence for given m_t^* there must be a correlation between the explanatory variable $(m_t - m_t^*)$ and u_t.

Although Carr and Darby had attempted to allow for any correlation between u_t and $(m_t - m_t^*)$ in their estimation method, MacKinnon and Milbourne criticise their choice of instrumental variables and propose an alternative and apparently simpler estimation method based on a rearrangement of [12.68]. Solving [12.68] for m_t yields

$$m_t = \left(\frac{\mu}{1-\theta}\right)\bar{m}_{Dt} + \left(\frac{1-\mu}{1-\theta}\right)\bar{m}_{t-1} - \left(\frac{\theta}{1-\theta}\right)m_t^* + \left(\frac{1}{1-\theta}\right)p_t + \frac{u_t}{1-\theta}$$

Hence

$$m_t - p_t = \left(\frac{\mu}{1-\theta}\right)\bar{m}_{Dt} + \left(\frac{1-\mu}{1-\theta}\right)\bar{m}_{t-1} - \left(\frac{\theta}{1-\theta}\right)(m_t^* - p_t) + \frac{u_t}{1-\theta} \qquad [12.69]$$

Since m_t no longer appears on the right-hand side in [12.69], they suggest that the buffer stock hypothesis is better tested by the estimation of equations such as this. First, however, they add a term in the expected nominal money supply to [12.68]

$$m_t - p_t = \mu \bar{m}_{Dt} + (1 - \mu)\bar{m}_{t-1} + \theta(m_t - m_t^*) + \phi m_t^* + u_t \qquad [12.68A]$$

The estimating equation [12.69] then becomes

$$m_t - p_t = \left(\frac{\mu}{1-\theta}\right)\bar{m}_{Dt} + \left(\frac{1-\mu}{1-\theta}\right)\bar{m}_{t-1} - \left(\frac{\theta}{1-\theta}\right)(m_t^* - p_t) + \frac{\phi}{1-\theta}m_t^* + \frac{u_t}{1-\theta}$$

$$[12.69A]$$

The buffer stock hypothesis implies $1 < \theta < 0$ and $\phi = 0$ in [12.68A]. Hence the coefficient on $(m_t^* - p_t)$ in [12.69A] should be negative and that on m_t^* should be zero. For US quarterly data, however, MacKinnon and Milbourne find the coefficients on $(m_t^* - p_t)$ and m_t^* both to be significantly positive. This implied that ϕ in [12.68A] was positive and that the value of θ was as negative as -4.3. Since this suggested that unexpected increases in the money supply actually led to a reduction in real balances held, they maintained that their results completely refuted the buffer stock hypothesis.

Carr, *et al.* (1985) responded to the MacKinnon–Milbourne critique by pointing out that [12.69], with its dependent variable $m_t - p_t$, is an appropriate estimating equation only when the money supply can be assumed endogenous. But the buffer stock model was designed to cope with situations where the money stock is exogenous. If this is the case and it is the price level that is endogenous and eventually adjusts to bring money demand back into line with supply, then it is equation [12.69] rather than [12.68] that suffers from correlation between explanatory variable and disturbance. From [12.69] it can be seen that, under such circumstances, a rise in u_t will, given the exogenous m_t, lead to a fall in p_t. Hence a rise in u_t is associated with a rise in the explanatory variable $(m_t^* - p_t)$. Hence application of OLS to [12.69] will result in biased and inconsistent estimates.

Carr, *et al.* therefore estimate [12.68A] by their instrumental variable method, again using US data, and find that, while the coefficient on $(m_t - m_t^*)$ again proves positive and significant, that on m_t^* is insignificant. They also point out that the MacKinnon–Milbourne equation [12.69] implies that the coefficients on m_t^* and p_t should have equal and opposite signs. However, when they test this restriction using the F-statistic [4.45], they find it to be rejected by their data.

Cuthbertson (1986) estimates both equations [12.68A] and [12.69A] using UK quarterly data for the narrow money aggregate M1. He finds that, as with the US data, [12.68A] provides support for the buffer stock hypothesis but [12.69A] does not. General distributed lag versions of [12.68A] and [12.69A] are also estimated with similar results.

A rational expectations approach

Clearly the success or otherwise of equations such as [12.68A] or [12.69A] must depend partly on how well the investigator is able to model the expected money supply m^*. A number of investigators have adopted a rational expectations approach. Money holders are assumed to know the mechanism by which the monetary authorities decide on the money supply and to form expectations on this basis. The expectations generating process is modelled as

$$m_t = \gamma z_{t-1} + v_t \qquad [12.70]$$

where γ is a vector of coefficients and z_{t-1} is a vector of variables that money holders believe have a systematic influence on the money supply. For example, z_{t-1} might include lagged values of the money supply and of interest rates. Only lagged values are included because at time t money holders do not have information about period t values. If Equation [12.70] is estimated as

$$m_t = \hat{\gamma} z_{t-1} + \hat{v}_t$$
$$= \hat{m}_t + \hat{v}_t \qquad [12.71]$$

then predicted values from this equation, $\hat{m}_t$, can be used as a data series for the expected money supply and the residuals, $\hat{v}_t$, for the unexpected or unanticipated money supply. The buffer stock hypothesis can then be tested by estimating

$$\bar{m}_t = \mu \bar{m}_{Dt} + (1 - \mu)\bar{m}_{t-1} + \theta \hat{v}_t + \phi \hat{m}_t + u_t \qquad [12.72]$$

Cuthbertson and Taylor (1986) and (1988) point out that if money holders form their expectations on the basis of [12.70] then $m^* = \gamma z_{t-1}$ so that, substituting in [12.68A] we have

$$\bar{m}_t = \mu \bar{m}_{Dt} + (1 - \mu)\bar{m}_{t-1} + \theta(m_t - \gamma z_{t-1}) + \phi \gamma z_{t-1} + u_t \qquad [12.73]$$

If [12.70] and [12.73] are estimated jointly then it becomes possible to test whether the estimate of γ obtained from [12.73] is the same as that obtained from [12.70]. The two-stage process represented by equations [12.71] and [12.72] implicitly assumes that this is so. Testing whether the estimates are the same is equivalent to testing whether money holders do, in fact, form their

386

expectations rationally. Moreover, if the restriction is valid then joint estimation is the more efficient procedure.

Cuthbertson and Taylor adopt both the two-step and the joint estimation approaches using UK data on narrow money in an 1986 paper and US narrow money in an 1988 paper. The two-step approach is based on the method of Pagan (1984) and the joint estimation procedure is based on the methodology of Mishkin (1982) and (1983). A likelihood ratio test is used to test the rationality restriction concerning the γs. Results from the two-step approach seem to support the buffer stock hypothesis. When joint estimation is performed, however, although the coefficient, θ, on unanticipated money is positive and highly significant, the rationality restriction is rejected. It appears then that, while there is evidence in support of the buffer stock model, that model cannot be combined with the assumption that money holders form expectations rationally.

In their 1986 paper and also in a further 1987 article, Cuthbertson and Taylor experiment with alternative 'non-rational' mechanisms for generating expectations, one of which permits money holders to update forecasting parameters using the latest available data. Using narrow money for the UK, they again find that while anticipated money has no influence on holdings of real money, unanticipated money is strongly significant.

In a sequence of slightly later papers Cuthbertson and Taylor (1987C, 1989) and Cuthbertson (1988) adopt an alternative approach to the modelling of buffer stocks. Instead of forming expectations about future values of the money supply, it is assumed that money holders form expectations about future values of the arguments in the demand for money function. A 'forward looking' buffer stock model is developed in which money holders plan the future time path of their money balances on the basis of such expectations. The long-run demand for nominal money balances is given by

$$m_{Dt} = \alpha_0 + \alpha_1 y_t + \alpha_2 p_t + \alpha_3 R_t \qquad [12.74]$$

where Y is real income, P is the price level and R the interest rate.

The time path is chosen so as to minimise the discounted value of a quadratic function of future expected disequilibrium and adjustment costs. That is minimise

$$C = E \sum_{j=0}^{T} \delta^j [a_1(m_{t+j} - m_{Dt+j})^2 + a_2(m_{t+j} - m_{t+j-1})^2] \qquad [12.75]$$

where δ is a discount factor and expectations are those held at time $t - 1$. a_1 and a_2 reflect the relative weights placed on disequilibrium and adjustment costs. Equation [12.75] is in fact a multi-period generalisation of equation [7.67], the minimisation of which leads to simple partial adjustment models such as [12.26].

It can be shown that as a result of the minimisation of [12.75], planned current holdings of money, m_t^p, are given by

$$m_t^p = (1 - \lambda)\alpha_0 + \lambda m_{t-1} + (1 - \lambda)(1 - \lambda\delta) \left[\alpha_1 \sum_j (\lambda\delta)^j y_{t+j}^e \right.$$

$$\left. + \alpha_2 \sum_j (\lambda\delta)^j p_{t+j}^e + \alpha_3 \sum_j (\lambda\delta)^j R_{t+j}^e \right] \qquad [12.76]$$

where the superscript e denotes the expected value of a variable and λ is a parameter dependent on a_1 and a_2 in [12.75].[12] Notice that [12.76] implies what Cuthbertson and Taylor refer to as 'backward-forward restrictions' involving the coefficients on the backward-looking variable m_{t-1} and the forward-looking expected value variables. That is the coefficients on the expected values of each argument in the money demand function should decline geometrically and be related to the coefficient on m_{t-1}.

Actual current money balances are composed of the planned element [12.76] and a buffer element that is dependent on current unanticipated values of the money demand function arguments. Hence

$$m_t = m_t^p + \theta_1 (y - y^e)_t + \theta_2 (p - p^e)_t + \theta_3 (R - R^e)_t + \varepsilon_t \qquad [12.77]$$

where ε_t is a disturbance.

In the model an expected change in the future values of any of the variables y, R or p leads to only a small immediate change in money balances held because of the non-zero costs of adjustment, although the movement will continue in later periods. However an unanticipated change in y, R or p leads to an immediate increase in the buffer component of money holdings. Thus unanticipated increases in the money supply cause unanticipated changes in the long-run arguments of the demand for money function and hence lead to a rise in buffer stock holdings.

Empirical versions of [12.77] support the buffer stock hypothesis with a given increase in the expected values of y, R or p having a much smaller immediate effect on money holdings than a similar unanticipated increase in y, R or p.

Cuthbertson and Taylor compare their empirical model with a backward looking error correction type model similar to that of Hendry (1985), described in the last section. Forecasts with their model are only 'slightly worse' than those of the Hendry model. Although the Hendry type model fits the data slightly better, this is regarded as inevitable because the general to specific approach has the advantage of allowing lag structures to be determined by the data. In contrast, as noted earlier, the lag structure of [12.76] is determined prior to estimation by the backward-forward restrictions.

Cuthbertson and Taylor claim that their results support the inclusion of forward-looking variables in demand for money equations. In particular they claim that the separate modelling of expectations makes it easier to determine values for long-run demand for money parameters. The alternative single equation approach of Hendry and others fails to distinguish properly between adjustment, structural and expectational parameters. Moreover, such equations are likely to fall foul of the Lucas (1976) critique mentioned in section 6.2. Their incorporation of expectational elements make it unlikely that such equations will survive major changes of policy regime.

Criticisms of the buffer stock models

The claims of the buffer stock modellers have been strongly disputed. The assumption of the Carr–Darby model, that it is the price level that is endogenous and adjusts to bring about money market equilibrium, has been examined in a further paper by MacKinnon and Milbourne (1988). If the price level is endogenous then the Carr–Darby equation [12.68] should be inverted to make the price level the dependent variable

$$p_t = -\mu \bar{m}_{Dt} + (1 - \theta)m_t + \theta m_t^* - (1 - \mu)m_{t-1} + (1 - \mu)p_{t-1} - u_t \quad [12.78]$$

Clearly equation [12.78] implies two restrictions. Firstly, the coefficients on m_t and m_t^* should sum to one and, secondly, the coefficients on m_{t-1} and p_{t-1} should sum to zero. However, MacKinnon and Milbourne estimate [12.78] using the Carr–Darby US data and find the restrictions to be overwhelmingly rejected. This they interpret as strong evidence against price adjustment of the Carr–Darby kind.

The Cuthbertson–Taylor version of the buffer stock model has also come under attack. For example, Muscatelli (1988) makes three criticisms. Firstly, he queries the logic of a model in which adjustment costs are balanced against disequilibrium costs. Money is the buffer asset because its adjustment costs are zero. The model only makes sense if portfolios are fixed in size and assets can be divided into money which has no adjustment cost and non-money which has positive adjustment costs. Then, any change in money holdings must be matched by an equal and opposite change in non-money holdings. But if portfolio holders save then portfolios will not be fixed in size and the asymmetry is lost.

Secondly, M1 may not be the appropriate definition of money to use in a buffer stock model. It can be argued that, certainly in the UK, M1 is demand determined and that other very liquid assets undertake the buffer role. This suggests that M3 or some other broad money aggregate might be better used to represent buffer stock money. But the buffer stock proponents have always used M1.

Thirdly, the rigid lag structure implied by equation [12.76] rests on the assumption of the multiperiod quadratic cost function [12.75]. Other cost functions would obviously imply different lag structures. In the absence of any clear information about the cost function, Muscatelli argues that it is better to allow the data to determine the lag structure.

In a later paper Muscatelli (1989) uses UK M1 data to compare a forward-looking buffer stock model of the Cuthbertson–Taylor kind with a backward-looking general to specific Hendry-type error correction model. In terms of diagnostic tests of model performance the buffer stock model proves disappointing compared with the error correction model. Serial correlation problems emerge when the backward-forward restrictions are imposed. This appears to result from forcing the lag structure into the *a priori* form suggested by the restrictions. Muscatelli also compares the two models using the encompassing test mentioned in section 7.2 and by nesting them within a more general model. These tests also favour the backward looking model.

12.8 Conclusions

It would be idle to pretend that the vast amount of empirical work performed during the last two decades has been successful in resolving all the outstanding issues concerning the demand for money. Nevertheless, one proposition seems to be established beyond reasonable doubt. Few economists would now deny that the demand for money is to some extent interest-elastic. The elasticity, however, appears to lie between zero and unity – far less than originally suggested by 'Keynesian' economists, and there appears very little evidence in favour of a 'liquidity trap'.

A second issue on which there is a large measure of agreement is that the appropriate scale variable, particularly for broad money functions, is some measure of wealth rather than measured income. Choosing between non-human wealth and permanent income for this measure is less easy, and is handicapped for most economies by a general lack of data on the net worth of the private sector. For narrow money it is still possible to argue that, as suggested by the inventory theoretic approach, measured income is the appropriate scale variable.

The original belief in the stability of demand for money functions has obviously been eroded during the past twenty years, both by the behaviour of M3 in the UK and that of M1 in the US. Indeed, no sooner does one publication proclaim a 'stable' function then another publication appears to demonstrate that function's instability. However this may well be inevitable. Such have been the institutional changes and innovations in cash management during the past two decades that it is almost certainly too much to expect that any short-run demand function could remain unaltered. Short-run dynamics are almost bound to vary and even long-run properties are unlikely to remain unchanged.

Empirical work will obviously continue on both error correction and buffer stock models. The general-to-specific approach clearly has enormous potential for analysing the stability of at least demand for narrow money functions. However, many would argue that the assumption of, for example, the Taylor (1987) model, that the supply of money will always adjust to the short-run demand for it, is implausible when referring to broad money. For this reason buffer stock modelling needs to be applied to the analysis of the demand for broad money aggregates.

One possible promising area of development is that of multi-equation disequilibrium/buffer stock models. We saw at the end of section 12.3 that the various adjustment processes that have been suggested are not mutually exclusive. An exogenous increase in the supply of money is likely to result in adjustments in all the arguments in the demand for money function. A single-equation approach is therefore almost certain to be unsatisfactory. A complete system approach is needed that permits the simultaneous adjustment of a full range of real and nominal variables. A start on developing the required models has in fact already been made. For example, Davidson (1987) has successfully estimated such a system for the UK economy.

Increased attention will also have to be paid to the effects of innovations in cash management on demand for money functions. The results of Johnston (1984) and Hall, Henry and Wilcox (1989) demonstrate clearly the importance of such innovations. For example, the increased use of credit cards makes it possible to economise in the use of narrow money. It is in these areas, and on the increased use of co-integration techniques, that future empirical research is likely to concentrate.

Appendix: Empirical exercise

In this exercise we shall estimate demand functions for the UK narrow money aggregate, M1. We concentrate on M1 since it is not unreasonable to regard this quantity as 'demand determined' throughout the post-war period. As section

12.2 indicates, this means that we can hope to obtain consistent estimators of demand for M1 parameters by the straightforward application of OLS.

Using an approach similar to that of the exercises at the ends of Chapters 10 and 11, we shall use co-integration techniques in an attempt to determine whether a long-run or equilibrium demand for money function exists. However, unlike in previous exercises, we shall use two alternative approaches to estimating short-run functions. Firstly, we shall make use of the Engle–Granger two stage approach described in section 7.5 (page 167). Secondly, we shall adopt the Hendry-type general to specific approach in which both short-run and long-run parameters are estimated simultaneously. Finally, having arrived at preferred short-run equations we shall employ the Chow tests of section 4.3 to test for parameter stability and predictive failure. We shall be particularly interested in whether any instability occurs after the last quarter of 1972 with the introduction of Competition and Credit Control.

We use quarterly seasonally adjusted data for 1963–74, defining the following variables:

M = nominal M1 money balances held by the private sector.
Y = total personal disposable income in 1975 prices.
R = yield on long term (20-year) British Government securities (a long term rate of interest).
P = implied consumers expenditure deflator.

Data on M1, Y and P can be obtained from ETAS 1983. Those for M1 are on pages 146–7 and those for Y on pages 21–2. The series for the price index P is obtained by dividing the figures for total personal disposable income in current prices on pages 21–22 by those for the Y variable. Data for R can be obtained from the Bank of England Statistical Abstracts No. 1 (1975) pages 177–8 and No. 2 (1975) page 166. Note that coverage of the money series M varies so that care has to be taken in obtaining a consistent series. To obtain a quarterly series for R you will have to take an average of monthly values. The final data set used is presented at the end of this appendix.

Working, as usual, in natural logarithms, we first look for co-integration between our four variables M, Y, R and P. Only if our search is successful can we justifiably maintain that a long-run relationship exists between them. Our first step is to determine the order of integration of the variables $\ln M$, $\ln Y$, $\ln R$ and $\ln P$. That is we wish to know whether they are stationary in their levels or whether they have to be differenced once or more before they become stationary. We begin with the M1 series.

To test $\ln M$ for stationarity we compute augmented Dickey–Fuller regressions of the type [7.57]. Remember again, however, that the Dickey–Fuller tests lack power, are not precise and have to be applied with care and discrimination. It is unwise to rely on a single Dickey–Fuller regression. In the present case, typical ADF equations are

$$\Delta m_t = 0.80 + 0.002T - 0.091m_{t-1} + 0.036\Delta m_{t-1} + 0.137\Delta m_{t-2}$$
$$\quad\ (0.69)\ (0.001)\quad (0.079)\qquad\ (0.190)\qquad\quad (0.202)$$

$$\quad - 0.070\Delta m_{t-3} + 0.120\Delta m_{t-4} \qquad (1964(\text{ii})-1973(\text{iv})) \qquad\qquad [\text{A}12.1]$$
$$\quad\ (0.203)\qquad\ (0.212)$$

$$R^2 = 0.15, \quad Z14 = 6.65, \quad Z18 = 9.37, \quad F(2,32) = 2.10$$

and

$$\Delta m_t = 0.37 + 0.001T - 0.042m_{t-1} \qquad (1963(\text{ii})-1973(\text{iv})) \qquad [\text{A12.2}]$$
$$(0.49) \quad (0.001) \quad (0.056)$$

$$R^2 = 0.06, \qquad Z14 = 1.42, \qquad Z18 = 8.85, \qquad F(2,40) = 1.33$$

Lower case letters again denote natural logarithms. In [A12.1] and [A12.2] the largest available sample period has been used in each case. In [A12.1] the earlier values of m are required to compute the higher order lagged values.

$Z14$ and $Z18$ are the LM statistics for up to fourth and up to eighth order autocorrelation respectively (remember that, unlike in most previous exercises, we are using quarterly data). At the 0.05 level of significance, the critical values of χ^2 are 9.49 and 15.51, with 4 and 8 d.f. respectively. Hence there do not appear to be any autocorrelation problems with the residuals of either equation.

To test for stationarity of the m series we have to examine the 't-ratios' on the coefficients of m_{t-1} in equations [A12.1] and [A12.2], that is the ADF statistics. These take the values -1.2 and -0.7. They have to be compared with critical values taken not from normal t-tables but from the right-hand side of Table 7.1. It is clear that we cannot reject the hypothesis that the true coefficient on m_{t-1} is zero. That is, we cannot reject the hypothesis that m is non-stationary.

The F-values given in equations [A12.1] and [A12.2] are those for testing the joint hypothesis that the coefficients of m_{t-1} and the time trend, T, are both zero. Referring to the critical values in Table 7.2 we see that in neither case can this joint hypothesis be rejected. m_{t-1} and T appear to add nothing significant to the explanatory power of the equations. Hence we can regard Δm as being determined either by past values of itself and a disturbance or simply by a disturbance. It certainly does not appear to be subject to a deterministic trend.

To determine whether Δm is stationary we estimate Dickey–Fuller equations for $\Delta^2 m_t = \Delta m_t - \Delta m_{t-1}$, the second difference in nominal money. This gives for example

$$\Delta^2 m_t = 0.006 + 0.0004T - 1.01\Delta m_{t-1} \qquad\qquad [\text{A12.3}]$$
$$(0.006) \quad (0.0003) \quad (0.16)$$

$$R^2 = 0.50, \qquad Z14 = 1.19, \qquad Z18 = 8.67 \qquad (1963(\text{iii})-1973(\text{iv}))$$

and

$$\Delta^2 m_t = -0.60\Delta m_{t-1} \qquad\qquad [\text{A12.4}]$$
$$(0.14)$$

$$\rule{2cm}{0.4pt} \qquad Z14 = 6.83, \qquad Z18 = 8.41 \qquad (1963(\text{iii})-1973(\text{iv}))$$

The sample period in [A12.3] and [A12.4] again depends on how many of the initial observations on m are required to construct the lagged values.

The DF statistics now refer to the coefficients of Δm_{t-1} in the above equations and take the values -6.3 and -4.3 respectively. Comparison with the critical values in Table 7.1, (using the left-hand side of the table for [A12.4] because the intercept and time trend have been omitted), indicates that we can reject the hypothesis that Δm is non-stationary. Our tests thus suggest that the nominal money series is integrated of order one. That is it is non-stationary but becomes stationary after differencing once.

The reader should now determine the order of integration of the remaining three variables defined initially. You should find that all three, Y, R and P are non-stationary in the log-levels but become stationary once log-differences are taken. That is they are all integrated of order one.

Having found that each of our four variables is integrated of order one, we can now proceed to the second part of the test for co-integration – computing the so-called static regression. Regressing m on all three variables y, r and p, using the full sample period yields[13]

$$m_t = 2.71 + 0.76y_t - 0.21r_t + 0.87p_t, \qquad R^2 = 0.990 \qquad \text{[A12.5]}$$
$$(1.33) \ (0.13) \quad (0.04) \quad (0.09)$$

Notice that the elasticities in [A12.5] all have the expected signs. However, contrary to theory, the price elasticity is less than unity, although not significantly so.

If the variables in [A12.5] are co-integrated then the residuals, e, taken from this equation should form a stationary series. To test the residuals for stationarity we need to compute Dickey–Fuller regressions excluding constant and time trend. We use Δe terms lagged up to four quarters and obtain, for example

$$\Delta e_t = -0.635e_{t-1} + 0.173\Delta e_{t-1} \qquad \text{[A12.6]}$$
$$(0.162) \qquad (0.157)$$

$$Z14 = 1.80, \qquad Z18 = 8.15 \qquad (1963(\text{iii})-1973(\text{iv}))$$

and

$$\Delta e_t = -0.542e_{t-1} \qquad \text{[A12.7]}$$
$$(0.137)$$

$$Z14 = 1.65, \qquad Z18 = 6.72 \qquad (1963(\text{ii})-1973(\text{iv}))$$

The LM statistics indicate no autocorrelation problems in either equation, despite the exclusion in these cases of Δe_{t-2}, Δe_{t-3} and Δe_{t-4}. The ADF statistic is the 't-ratio' on e_{t-1} and takes the value -3.92 in [A12.6] and -3.96 in [A12.7]. Comparison with the critical values in Table 7.3 indicates that we can, at least at the 5 per cent level of significance, reject the hypothesis that the residuals form a non-stationary series. They appear to be stationary, that is they are integrated of order zero.

Since the variables m, y, r and p are all integrated of order one, while the residuals from the static equation [A12.5] are integrated of order zero, our four variables appear to be co-integrated. We can therefore reasonably assume that a long-run demand for money function involving these variables does exist.[14]

As noted at the outset, we shall adopt two approaches to estimating a short run demand for money function. First, we adopt the Engle–Granger two-stage (EGTS) approach outlined in section 7.5. Since the variables appear to be co-integrated, we can assume that a long run relationship exists and that any short-run demand for money function can be given an error correction representation involving disequilibrium errors. This follows from the Granger representation theorem mentioned in section 7.5. In the EGTS approach the residuals from the static regression [A12.5] are used as estimates of the disequilibrium errors, and we estimate equations of the kind [7.63]. Since we are using quarterly data, there can be no certainty about the lag to be placed on the disequilibrium errors or residuals. However our data is seasonally adjusted so we shall concentrate our attention on the two ECMs

$$\Delta m_t = \beta_0 \Delta y_t + \gamma_0 \Delta r_t + \delta_0 \Delta p_t + \lambda e_{t-1} \quad\quad\quad [A12.8]$$

and

$$\Delta m_t = \alpha \Delta m_{t-1} + \beta_0 \Delta y_t + \beta_1 \Delta y_{t-1} + \gamma_0 \Delta r_t + \gamma_1 \Delta r_{t-1} + \delta_0 \Delta p_t$$
$$+ \delta_1 \Delta p_{t-1} + \lambda e_{t-2}$$
$$[A12.9]$$

Notice that neither [A12.8] nor [A12.9] contains an intercept term. This is because the long-run relationship [A12.5] already contains such a term and an estimate of it is included in e_{t-1} the disequilibrium error.

Estimating, first, [A12.8] for 1964(i) to 1973(iv) we obtain

$$\Delta m_t = 0.459 \Delta y_t - 0.075 \Delta r_t + 0.842 \Delta p_t - 0.551 e_{t-1} \quad\quad [A12.10]$$
$$(0.126) \quad\quad (0.058) \quad\quad (0.178) \quad\quad (0.129)$$

$$\sum e^2 = 0.00817, \quad dw = 1.82, \quad Z14 = 1.49, \quad Z18 = 9.90, \quad Z2 = 0.077.$$

There appear to be no autocorrelation problems with [A12.10]. $Z2$ as usual is the LM heteroscedaticity statistic covered in section 5.2.1 and its low value suggests we have homoscedastic residuals. Notice that no value for R^2 is quoted in [A12.10]. This is because the equation contains no intercept, so that R^2 is not a valid measure of goodness of fit. If an intercept is added to [A12.10], it proves insignificantly different from zero as expected and R^2 takes the value 0.44. Although this may seem a little low, remember that we are attempting to explain variations in the quarterly change in money balances. This is a much tougher proposition than explaining variations in the level of money balances or variations in their annual change. In fact, since all the variables in [A12.10] are stationary series we have no spurious correlation problems.

All the variables in [A12.10] have statistically significant coefficients apart from Δr which has a t-ratio of -1.29 (with 36 d.f. the critical t-value is $-t_{0.05} = -2.02$). However, since the t-ratio for Δr at least exceeds one in absolute value we shall retain this variable in the equation.

The coefficients on the rate of change variables represent short-run elasticities. The long-run elasticities are contained in the disequilibrium error term, e_{t-1}, and are simply the coefficients in the static equation [A12.5]. Notice that the income and interest rate variables have much larger elasticities in the long run than in the short run. The price elasticity is also slightly larger in the long run but is still less than unity. The coefficient on e_{t-1} indicates that 55 per cent of any disequilibrium in one quarter is made up during the next.

Estimation of the second order ECM [A12.9] yields

$$\Delta m_t = -0.446 \Delta m_{t-1} + 0.410 \Delta y_t + 0.345 \Delta y_{t-1} - 0.046 \Delta r_t - 0.147 \Delta r_{t-1}$$
$$(0.176) \quad\quad (0.147) \quad\quad (0.156) \quad\quad (0.067) \quad\quad (0.073)$$

$$+ 0.526 \Delta p_t + 0.821 \Delta p_{t-1} - 0.597 e_{t-2} \quad (1964(i)-1973(iv)) \quad [A12.11]$$
$$(0.445) \quad\quad (0.435) \quad\quad (0.165)$$

$$\sum e^2 = 0.00766, \quad dw = 2.04, \quad Z14 = 0.848, \quad Z18 = 10.34, \quad Z2 = 0.02$$

While the diagnostic statistics for [A12.11] are satisfactory, two of the regressors have insignificant coefficients – Δp_t and Δr_t. If you drop the variable with the lowest t-ratio, that is Δr_t, from the equation you will find that the t-ratio on

Δp becomes even smaller than in [A12.11]. Also dropping Δp yields

$$\Delta m_t = -0.425\Delta m_{t-1} + 0.419\Delta y_t + 0.367\Delta y_{t-1} + 1.242\Delta p_{t-1}$$
$$\quad\ (0.172)\qquad\quad (0.140)\qquad (0.150)\qquad\quad (0.256)$$

$$\quad - 0.140\Delta r_{t-1} - 0.602 e_{t-2} \qquad (1964(i)-1973(iv)) \qquad\qquad\qquad [A12.12]$$
$$\quad\ \ (0.064)\qquad\ (0.163)$$

$$\sum e^2 = 0.00801, \quad dw = 2.12, \quad Z14 = 1.75, \quad Z18 = 9.75, \quad Z2 = 0.003$$

All the coefficients in [A12.12] are significantly different from zero and the diagnostic statistics are again satisfactory.

It is difficult to choose between equations [A12.10] and [A12.12]. Unfortunately, neither equation is nested within the other so we cannot apply the F-test statistic [4.45]. Tests for choosing between non-nested equations exist and were mentioned in section 7.2 but their application is beyond the scope of this book. In terms of goodness of fit, there is little to choose between the two equations but [A12.10] contains only four variables while [A12.12] has six. [A12.10] is therefore the more parsimonious equation and for this reason we shall select it as our preferred equation from the EGTS approach.

We now adopt our second approach to estimating the short-run demand for money function. We adopt the Hendry-type general to specific (GS) methodology from the outset, starting with a general short-run model and testing down to a suitably parsimonious final model. Both long- and short-run elasticities are estimated together in this approach. However, because our co-integration analysis suggests that a long-run relationship exists, we can be hopeful that, unlike, for example, the case in the exercise at the end of Chapter 10, we will be able to express the short-run relationship in ECM form.

Since our quarterly data is seasonally adjusted we adopt a general model involving up to two quarter lags only, that is a model, of the type [7.23] but with three explanatory variables y, r and p. However, as is demonstrated below [7.23], such a model can be reparameterised into a second-order ECM. We shall therefore estimate our general model in ECM form. This yields

$$\Delta m_t = 2.76 - 0.581\Delta m_{t-1} + 0.431\Delta y_t + 0.358\Delta y_{t-1} - 0.071\Delta r_t - 0.201\Delta r_{t-1}$$
$$\quad\ (2.09)\ (0.195)\qquad\quad (0.204)\qquad (0.221)\qquad\quad (0.076)\quad\ (0.082)$$

$$\quad + 0.960\Delta p_t + 1.38\Delta p_{t-1} - 0.742 m_{t-2} + 0.510 y_{t-2} - 0.223 r_{t-2}$$
$$\quad\ \ (0.560)\qquad (0.708)\qquad (0.203)\qquad\ (0.229)\qquad (0.068)$$

$$\quad + 0.733 p_{t-2} \qquad (1964(i)-1973(iv)) \qquad\qquad\qquad\qquad [A12.13]$$
$$\quad\ \ (0.229)$$

$$R^2 = 0.53, \quad \sum e^2 = 0.00688, \quad dw = 2.07, \quad Z14 = 5.61,$$
$$Z18 = 13.16, \quad Z2 = 0.05$$

The diagnostic statistics do not suggest any mis-specification in [A12.13]. However, the reader should verify that adding third-order lags to the equation leads to a serious deterioration in the autocorrelation statistics. Also, if you are able to compute the RESET statistic for mis-specification, described at the end of section 7.1, verify that, with just the square of the dependent variable among the regressors, the value of the statistic is only 0.50. Since this statistic has a x^2-distribution under the null hypothesis of a correct specification, (critical value with 1d.F is $x^2_{0.05} = 3.84$ this confirms that we can safely ignore lags of more than two quarters on all variables.

Examination of the t-ratios in equation [A12.13] reveals that a number of variables, particularly Δr, are below or near the critical value. However, before we start omitting variables from [A12.13] recall, from the discussion following [7.23], that a special case of the general second order ECM is a first order ECM of type [7.15]. Estimating such a model with our three explanatory variables yields

$$\Delta m_t = 2.96 + 0.318\Delta y_t - 0.080\Delta r_t + 0.972\Delta p_t - 0.572 m_{t-1}$$
$$(1.71)\ (0.172)\quad (0.071)\quad (0.540)\quad (0.144)$$

$$+ 0.316 y_{t-1} - 0.189 r_{t-1} + 0.642 p_{t-1} \qquad (1964(\text{i})-1973(\text{iv}))[\text{A12.14}]$$
$$(0.176)\qquad (0.053)\qquad (0.176)$$

$$R^2 = 0.50,\ \textstyle\sum e^2 = 0.00739,\ dw = 1.95,\ Z14 = 2.11,\ Z18 = 7.71,\ Z2 = 0.21$$

Four restrictions have to be placed on [A12.13] to obtain [A12.14]. What are they? Since the latter equation is nested within the former, we can use the F-statistic [4.45] to test these restrictions. The value of the F-statistic is 0.52 which compares with a critical F-value, with (4, 28) d.f., of $F_{0.05} = 2.72$. Clearly, the restrictions are not rejected by the data. Since there is also no deterioration in the diagnostic statistics, ($Z18$ has in fact fallen sharply), we therefore prefer [A12.14] to [A12.13].

With the exception of Δr, (t-ratio = -1.13), all the variables in equation [A12.14] have coefficients which are statistically significant from zero. However, since its t-ratio at least exceeds unity, we retain Δr in the equation as we did for equation [A12.10]. [A12.14] is therefore our final preferred equation obtained using the Hendry GS approach.

Testing down to a final equation was a relatively easy process in this case. This was because our co-integration analysis, performed prior to the GS estimating procedure, suggested to us in advance that the short run relationship we were seeking would have an ECM representation. This provides a good example of how helpful co-integration analysis can be in estimation even when we do not adopt the EGTS approach.

We now have two preferred short-run demand for money functions – [A12.10], obtained by the Engle–Granger procedure, and [A12.14] estimated using the Hendry–GS approach. They are non-nested equations so we shall not attempt to choose between them. Although [A12.10] has a slightly higher residual sum of squares, it has only four variables while [A12.14] makes use of eight, including the intercept.

Table A12.1   Long- and short-run elasticities

Variable elasticity	Income		Interest rate		Price level	
	Short run	Long run	Short run	Long run	Short run	Long run
[A12.10]	0.459	0.764	−0.075	−0.207	0.842	0.871
[A12.14]	0.318	0.553	−0.080	−0.330	0.972	1.122

The two equations are in fact not at all dissimilar. The implied short- and long-run elasticities are shown in Table A12.1. The long-run elasticities for equation [A12.10] are of course obtained from the co-integrating regression [A12.5]. In both short- and long-runs the elasticities obtained from the two equations are of the same order of magnitude, although the income elasticities are smaller in the GS equation [A12.14] with the reverse being the case for the other variables. More importantly, the EGTS and GS approaches lead to equations with very similar lag structures, long-run effects being fully felt after just one quarter. Also, if we rewrite equation [A12.14] in ECM form as

$$\Delta m = 0.318\Delta y_t - 0.080\Delta r_t + 0.972\Delta p_t \qquad [A12.15]$$
$$- 0.572[m_{t-1} - 5.17 - 0.553y_{t-1} + 0.330r_{t-1} - 1.122p_{t-1}]$$

we see that the coefficient on the disequilibrium error in the GS equation is 0.572. This compares with a value of 0.551 for the EGTS equation [A12.10]. Thus both equations imply that between 50 and 60 per cent of any disequilibrium between actual and equilibrium money balances in any one quarter is made up within the next quarter.

Theory suggests that the demand for nominal balances should have unit elasticity with respect to the price level in both the short and long run. The price elasticities in Table A12.1 are all close to unity, particularly those for the GS equation [A12.14]. This suggests that we might impose short- and long-run homogeneity of degree one with respect to the price level on [A12.14] thus achieving greater parsimony. The restrictions implied could be tested using the usual F-test. However, if we did this we would be implicitly assuming that a long-run relationship existed between real money balances, income and the interest rate. Before adopting such a procedure we need to check whether real balances, income and the interest rate are co-integrated. This task is left to the reader. You will need to check the log-level and log-difference of real balances for stationarity and then estimate a static regression involving real balances, income and the interest rate. If the variables prove to be co-integrated then you can adopt both the EGTS and the Hendry GS procedures to estimate short-run demand for real money functions.

One of the criteria, listed in section 7.2, that a satisfactory model should satisfy was parameter stability. We shall now use the Chow tests of section 4.3 to test equations [A12.10] and [A12.14] for such stability. We shall use both Chow statistics [4.22] and [4.24].

First, we examine the EGTS equation [A12.10] using the first Chow test. We arbitrarily divide our 40 period sample into the sub-periods 1964(i) to 1968(iv) and 1969(i) to 1973(iv). Estimation then yields

$$\Delta m_t = 0.436\Delta y_t - 0.100\Delta r_t + 0.556\Delta p_t - 0.410e_{t-1} \qquad [A12.16]$$
$$\quad\;\; (0.144) \qquad (0.082) \qquad (0.272) \qquad (0.140)$$

$$\sum e^2 = 0.00205, \quad dw = 1.78, \quad Z14 = 1.46, \quad Z18 = 13.83, \quad Z2 = 0.5$$

for the first sub-period, and for the second

$$\Delta m_t = 0.482\Delta y_t - 0.150\Delta r_t + 0.932\Delta p_t - 0.732e_{t-1} \qquad [A12.17]$$
$$\quad\;\; (0.193) \qquad (0.078) \qquad (0.238) \qquad (0.208)$$

$$\sum e^2 = 0.00477, \quad dw = 1.79, \quad Z14 = 1.44, \quad Z18 = 7.03, \quad Z2 = 0.0002$$

The first Chow statistic [4.22] yields

$$\left[\frac{\sum e_p^2 - (\sum e_1^2 + \sum e_2^2)}{\sum e_1^2 + \sum e_2^2}\right]\left[\frac{n_1 + n_2 - 2k}{k}\right] = \left[\frac{817 - (205 + 477)}{205 + 477}\right]\left[\frac{32}{4}\right] = 1.56$$

With $(4, 32)$ d.f. critical F-values are $F_{0.05} = 2.68$ and $F_{0.01} = 3.98$. So we should not reject the hypothesis of parameter stability.

One of the difficulties with the test just performed is that it often involves an arbitrary split of the sample period into two sub-periods as above. However, in the present case we have a more natural breakpoint at which to split our sample. The new system of Competition and Credit Control (CCC) was introduced by the monetary authorities at the end of 1971. It is therefore natural to check the predictive ability of our demand for money function after these changes were introduced. Since we have only eight post-CCC observations in our sample, the obvious test to apply is the second Chow test for 'predictive failure'. This requires estimating our equation for 1964(i) to 1971(iv), the period prior to the introduction of CCC. We obtain

$$\Delta m_t = 0.270\Delta y_t - 0.041\Delta r_t + 0.834\Delta p_t - 0.485 e_{t-1} \qquad [A12.18]$$
$$\quad\;\; (0.162) \qquad (0.063) \qquad (0.203) \qquad (0.133)$$

$$\sum e^2 = 0.00591, \quad dw = 1.82, \quad Z14 = 2.20, \quad Z18 = 11.33, \quad Z2 = 0.72$$

Table A12.2 Demand for money data set

	M	Y	R	P		M	Y	R	P
63Q1	6683	13 100	5.66	0.4025	68Q3	8 530	14 880	7.63	0.4972
63Q2	6812	13 235	5.36	0.4032	68Q4	8 640	15 042	7.93	0.5011
63Q3	6931	13 667	5.21	0.4058	69Q1	8 490	15 243	8.63	0.5111
63Q4	7149	13 758	5.47	0.4081	69Q2	8 310	15 220	9.22	0.5170
64Q1	7218	13 796	5.75	0.4126	69Q3	8 380	15 213	9.30	0.5209
64Q2	7268	13 842	5.93	0.4163	69Q4	8 660	15 403	9.09	0.5275
64Q3	7377	14 065	6.01	0.4213	70Q1	8 640	15 551	8.81	0.5350
64Q4	7387	14 064	6.23	0.4270	70Q2	8 920	16 002	9.40	0.5449
65Q1	7426	14 145	6.46	0.4329	70Q3	9 020	16 097	9.22	0.5530
65Q2	7506	14 160	6.72	0.4378	70Q4	9 420	15 935	9.63	0.5654
65Q3	7555	14 411	6.60	0.4424	71Q1	9 820	15 710	9.37	0.5765
65Q4	7545	14 466	6.45	0.4464	71Q2	9 900	16 154	9.22	0.5930
66Q1	7843	15 083	6.63	0.4500	71Q3	10 210	16 253	8.89	0.6035
66Q2	7763	14 474	6.88	0.4550	71Q4	10 310	16 427	8.13	0.6105
66Q3	7674	14 433	7.33	0.4598	72Q1	10 897	16 923	8.00	0.6157
66Q4	7535	14 477	6.90	0.4654	72Q2	11 223	17 886	8.86	0.6245
67Q1	7714	14 478	6.52	0.4653	72Q3	11 529	17 600	9.42	0.6418
67Q2	7813	14 770	6.66	0.4674	72Q4	11 836	17 805	9.60	0.6576
67Q3	8091	15 114	6.93	0.4704	73Q1	11 931	18 320	9.76	0.6650
67Q4	8180	14 978	7.14	0.4744	73Q2	12 630	19 074	10.07	0.6776
68Q1	8210	15 300	7.28	0.4778	73Q3	12 401	18 845	11.28	0.6951
68Q2	8340	15 237	7.57	0.4895	73Q4	12 458	18 820	12.02	0.7212

The second Chow statistic [4.24] yields

$$\frac{(\sum e_p^2 - \sum e_1^2)/m}{\sum e_1^2/(n_1 - k)} = \frac{(817 - 591)/8}{591/28} = 1.34$$

With $(8, 28)$ d.f., critical F-values are $F_{0.05} = 2.30$ and $F_{0.01} = 3.23$, so the EGTS equation also passes the test for predictive failure.

We next apply the Chow tests to the final preferred GS equation [A12.14]. If the sample period is again split up into two equal sub-periods then you should find that the residual sums of squares obtained are 0.00180 for the earlier sub-period and 0.00408 for the later. The first Chow statistic therefore yields a value of 0.77, compared with critical F-values of $F_{0.05} = 2.36$ and $F_{0.01} = 3.36$. Like the EGTS equation then, the GS equation passes the first Chow test for parameter stability.

To apply the second Chow test to the GS equation we must estimate over the pre-CCC period. This yields

$$\Delta m_t = 3.46 + 0.173\Delta y_t - 0.028\Delta r_t + 1.13\Delta p_t - 0.567m_{t-1}$$
$$(3.17)\ (0.219) \quad (0.079) \quad (0.69) \qquad\qquad (0.193)$$

$$+ 0.257y_{t-1} - 0.176r_{t-1} + 0.647p_{t-1} \quad (1964(i)-1971(iv))[A12.19]$$
$$(0.237) \qquad (0.068) \qquad (0.266)$$

$$R^2 = 0.40, \quad \sum e^2 = 0.00556, \quad dw = 1.89, \quad Z14 = 4.00, \quad Z18 = 9.78,$$
$$Z2 = 0.95$$

Referring back to the residual sum of squares for equation [A12.14] you should find that the second Chow statistic takes a value of 0.99. This compares with critical F-values [$(8, 24)$ d.f.] of $F_{0.05} = 2.36$ and $F_{0.01} = 3.36$. The GS equation therefore also passes the Chow test for predictive failure.

We have had little difficulty obtaining stable demand for M1 functions whether we use the EGTS procedure or adopt a Hendry-type GS approach. This is the case despite the introduction of CCC towards the end of our sample period. This confirms the findings of a number of investigators during the past ten to fifteen years. However, the reader should now attempt a similar analysis of some broad money aggregate such as M3, using the above sample period. Note though that it will no longer be adequate to use personal disposable income as the scale variable. M3 balances are by no means confined to the personal sector so the income measure needs to be broadened to GDP or total final expenditure. Series for these quantities can be found in ETAS 1983, pages 5 and 15. Also, it has to be remembered that broad money satisfies more than the transactionary motive. Wealth measures therefore may prove superior to income measures as the scale variable.

Notes

1. A high coefficient of determination is, in fact, a necessary but not sufficient condition. If a third variable were important, but during the sample period happened to be highly correlated with R and Y, a high coefficient of determination could still be obtained if the effect of the third variable is captured by the R and Y variables.

2. Later work by, for example, Weinrobe (1972), suggested that the precautionary demand for money may also be dependent on the 'brokerage fee' and on the rate of interest.
3. The resultant function is that implied by the old 'Cambridge version' of the quantity theory of money, i.e. $M_D/P = kY$ where k depends on the level of interest rates.
4. In the Tobin analysis risk is measured by the standard deviation of the possible rates of return on the portfolio.
5. The variable most commonly used is the 'consolidated' net worth of the private sector including ownership of government debt. It is consolidated in the sense that 'double-counting' is avoided so that in cases where, for example, households own firms, the value of firms' wealth is counted only once despite the fact that it also forms part of household wealth. Such empirical evidence as exists (see, for example, Meltzer 1963) suggests that the extent of consolidation makes little difference to results. The inclusion of government debt implies that the private sector does not regard future tax liabilities as reducing its net worth.
6. Teigen's demand for money equation included a lagged money stock variable m_{t-1} to allow for partial adjustment of actual to desired balances. The steady state elasticity is found by setting $m_t = m_{t-1}$ in his estimated equation.
7. Equation [12.56] is obtained in the usual manner. First lag equation [12.55] by one period and multiply throughout by $1 - \rho$. Then subtract the equation thus obtained from [12.55]. On rearrangement, the equation eventually obtained becomes [12.56].
8. Hacche's assumption that v_t in [12.54] follows a first-order scheme, implies that, for some unstated reason, the disturbance $\mu\varepsilon_t$ in equation [12.26B] follows the second-order scheme

$$(\mu\varepsilon_t) = (1 + \rho)(\mu\varepsilon_{t-1}) - \rho(\mu\varepsilon)_{t-2} + u_t$$

9. For example, if short-run adjustment is via interest rates, and only in the long run is there a rise in the price level, then the initial fall in interest rates would have to be much greater than that eventually necessary to restore equilibrium. Thus the interest rate would have to 'overshoot' its long-run equilibrium value.
10. Permanent income is estimated by equations similar to [10.24] and [10.25] with λ set equal to 0.025 since the data is quarterly. Transitory income is then computed as the difference between measured income and permanent income.
11. The interest rate overshooting referred to in note 9 need not therefore occur.
12. Equation [12.76] can be regarded as a generalisation of [12.26], with λ in [12.76] the equivalent of $1 - \mu$ in [12.26].
13. The CRDW statistic discussed in section 7.5 take a value of 1.08 for equation [A12.5]. However, as usual in these exercises we prefer to rely on the Dickey–Fuller procedures when testing for non-stationarity.
14. Since we are looking for co-integration between more than two variables, it is very possible that more than one co-integrating vector exists. That is, the vector given by the estimated coefficients of [A12.5] may not be unique. However, the Johansen (1988) procedure for handling this situation is beyond the scope of this book, so we have restricted ourselves to the original Engle–Granger approach. Some justification for this, in the present case, can be seen in the similar results obtained for long-run parameters obtained later using a Hendry-type testing down procedure.

13 Macroeconomic models

The history of macroeconomic model-building stretches back to the early business cycle models of Tinbergen (1939; 1951). During this time the size of macroeconomic models has grown considerably – whereas in the early 1950s the largest was the Klein–Goldberger annual model of the US economy with twenty-two structural equations, the largest models currently in use are quarterly models and contain many hundreds and occasionally thousands of equations.

Macro-models have come increasingly into use as aids to government policymaking. Forecasts from models are published regularly and are of use not only to governments but also to private firms in the planning of their investment programmes. However, the provision of forecasts is not the only use to which, ideally, macro-models can be put. As we shall see, 'simulation' of macro-models can hopefully increase understanding about the workings of an economy and, in addition, they have been used to assess the likely effect of alternative government policy measures.

Different theoretical perspectives led to two different approaches to model-building. Since Keynesians believed that disaggregation both by sector and expenditure category was necessary for a proper understanding of a complex modern economy, they tended to favour large structural models. Others, however, tended to bypass the detailed structure of an economy and stressed the effect of monetary changes on aggregate money income, ignoring individual expenditure categories. This naturally led to smaller-scale models. However, most of the macro-models now in use, particularly in the UK, have been developed out of earlier models constructed at a time when 'Keynesianism' dominated the thinking of most economists. They have therefore tended to retain a basic Keynesian income–expenditure structure, although in recent years far more attention has been given to channels by which monetary variables make their influence felt and also to the supply side of the economy.

We begin this chapter by introducing some basic ideas about macro-models, illustrating them by means of an early six-equation model. Next, we outline the development of macroeconometric modelling in the UK. Finally, we describe how, in practice, models are used for making forecasts and also consider the use of models in their so-called 'simulation mode'.

13.1 Some basic ideas

Consider the following very simple model of an economy

$$C_t = \alpha + \beta Y_t \tag{13.1}$$

$$I_t = \gamma(Y_t - Y_{t-1}) \tag{13.2}$$

401

$$Y_t = C_t + I_t + G_t \qquad\qquad\qquad\qquad\qquad\qquad\quad [13.3]$$

Equation [13.1] is a simple Keynesian consumption function relating consumption, C_t, to income, Y_t. I_t is investment which is determined by a simple accelerator mechanism and G_t is government expenditure. The model is a three-equation system in three endogenous variables C_t, Y_t and I_t, with two predetermined variables, Y_{t-1} and G_t. Y_{t-1} is, of course, a lagged endogenous variable and G_t is exogenously determined. The system is, in fact, a version of the famous Samuelson–Hicks multiplier–accelerator model.

Notice first that, if we wish to assess the immediate current period effect of a change in G_t on the endogenous variables, we must consider both direct and indirect effects. For example, there will be a direct effect on Y_t because of the appearance of G_t in the income identity [13.3]. But there will also be indirect effects because any rise in Y_t leads to increases in C_t and I_t via equations [13.1] and [13.2]. These increases lead to further increases in Y_t via equation [13.3]. To obtain the overall effect within the current period of a change in G_t it is simplest to consider the reduced form which for the above model is

$$C_t = a_1 + b_1 Y_{t-1} + c_1 G_t \qquad\qquad\qquad\qquad\qquad [13.4]$$

$$Y_t = a_2 + b_2 Y_{t-1} + c_2 G_t \qquad\qquad\qquad\qquad\qquad [13.5]$$

$$I_t = a_3 + b_3 Y_{t-1} + c_3 G_t \qquad\qquad\qquad\qquad\qquad\; [13.6]$$

The reduced form gives the endogenous variables as functions of the predetermined variables, Y_{t-1} and G_t, alone. The as, bs and cs are, of course, functions of the parameters in the original structural equations. In fact, for example

$$c_1 = \frac{\beta}{1 - \beta - \gamma}, \quad c_2 = \frac{1}{1 - \beta - \gamma}, \quad c_3 = \frac{\gamma}{1 - \beta - \gamma}$$

We can now see that the overall *immediate* effects of a unit increase in G_t on C_t, Y_t and I_t are given by c_1, c_2 and c_3 respectively. The quantities c_1, c_2 and c_3 are known as *impact multipliers*.

However, the impact multipliers do not give the total effect of a change in government expenditure on the endogenous variables but only the effect within the same time period. The appearance of the lagged endogenous variable, Y_{t-1}, in the model means that our model is *dynamic* and that a change in G_t has further effects after the current period. The impact effect leads to an immediate increase in Y_t, but the appearance of Y_{t-1} in all the reduced-form equations [13.4–13.6] ensures that there are further changes in C, Y and I during period $t + 1$.[1] This change in Y_{t+1} then leads to further changes in C, Y and I during period $t + 2$, and so on.

We can examine these long-run effects on, for example, consumption by successively substituting for Y_{t-1}, Y_{t-2}, Y_{t-3}, etc in equation [13.4]

$$C_t = a_1 + b_1(a_2 + b_2 Y_{t-2} + c_2 G_{t-1}) + c_1 G_t$$
$$= a_1 + a_2 b_1 + b_1 b_2 (a_2 + b_2 Y_{t-3} + c_2 G_{t-2}) + c_1 G_t + b_1 c_2 G_{t-1}$$

402

$$= a_1 + a_2 b_1 (1 + b_2) + b_1 b_1^2 (a_2 + b_2 Y_{t-4} + c_2 G_{t-3}) + c_1 G_t$$
$$+ b_1 c_2 G_{t-1} + b_1 c_2 b_2 G_{t-2}$$
$$\cdots$$
$$\cdots$$
$$= a_1 + a_2 b_1 (1 + b_2 + b_2^2 + b_2^3 \ldots) + c_1 G_t + b_1 c_2 G_{t-1}$$
$$+ b_1 c_2 b_2 G_{t-2} + b_1 c_2 b_2^2 G_{t-3} + \cdots$$

That is, provided $b_2 < 1$

$$C_t = a_1 + \frac{a_2 b_1}{1 - b_2} + c_1 G_t + b_1 c_2 (G_{t-1} + b_2 G_{t-2} + b_2^2 G_{t-3} \ldots) \qquad [13.7]$$

Similarly, successive substitution for Y_{t-1} in equations [13.5] and [13.6] yields eventually

$$Y_t = \left(\frac{a_2}{1 - b_2} \right) + c_2 (G_t + b_2 G_{t-1} + b_2^2 G_{t-1} \ldots) \qquad [13.8]$$

and

$$I_t = a_3 + \frac{a_2 b_3}{1 - b_2} + c_3 G_t + b_3 c_2 (G_{t-1} + b_2 G_{t-2} + b_2^2 G_{t-3} \ldots) \qquad [13.9]$$

Equations [13.7–13.9] represent the *final form* of the system. They express the endogenous variables in terms of the exogenous levels (both current and past) of government expenditure only. To obtain the long-run final effect of a sustained change in government expenditure, suppose such expenditure remains constant at a level $G_t = \bar{G}$. The final-form equation for C_t then becomes

$$C_t = a_1 + \frac{a_2 b_1}{1 - b_2} + \{ c_1 + b_1 c_2 (1 + b_2 + b_2^2 + b_2^3 \ldots) \} \bar{G}$$

or, again assuming $b_2 < 1$,

$$C_t = a_1 + \frac{a_2 b_1}{1 - b_2} + \left\{ c_1 + \frac{b_1 c_2}{1 - b_2} \right\} \bar{G} \qquad [13.10]$$

Similarly, equations [13.8] and [13.9] become

$$Y_t = \frac{a_2}{1 - b_2} + \left\{ \frac{c_2}{1 - b_2} \right\} \bar{G} \qquad [13.11]$$

and

$$I_t = a_3 + \frac{a_2 b_3}{1 - b_2} + \left\{ c_3 + \frac{b_3 c_2}{1 - b_2} \right\} \bar{G} \qquad [13.12]$$

403

We can now see that the *long-run effect* of a *sustained* unit increase in government expenditure on consumption, income and investment is given by the coefficients of $\bar{G}$ in equations [13.10–13.12]. These quantities are known as *equilibrium dynamic multipliers*. Notice that the change in government expenditure we are talking about here is a change from one continually recurring level to another continually recurring level.

The equilibrium multipliers may also be obtained by setting $Y_t = Y_{t-1}$ in the reduced-form equations and solving for C_t, Y_t and I_t in terms of G_t. The advantage of deriving the final-form equations first is that this enables us to derive the time paths of C_t, Y_t and I_t after the change in government expenditure. Given values for the exogenous Gs we can use [13.7–13.9] to obtain the values of C, Y and I for any time period. Also, it may not be the case that the model converges to a new equilibrium after a disturbance or, alternatively, if it does, convergence may take many years. The long-run equilibrium multipliers will then have no useful meaning and we may be more interested in the effects of a change in G after two or three years.

The condition for convergence in the above model is $b_2 < 1$[2] and, in fact, substitution of typical values for the MPC, β, and the capital/output ratio, γ, into the expression for b_2 suggest that the condition is not met.[3] To obtain the effect of a sustained increase in government expenditure after, for example, two years, it is simply necessary to add the additional effects one year and two years hence to the impact effect. For example, the effect on consumption one year hence of a unit increase in G is given by the coefficient of G_{t-1} in equation [13.7] and the effect two years hence by the coefficient of G_{t-2}. These coefficients are, in fact, known as *interim multipliers*. The total effect in two years time is therefore given by

$$c_1 + b_1 c_2 + b_1 c_2 b_2$$

In general, the total effect, n years hence, of a sustained unit change in government expenditure on consumption is

$$c_1 + b_1 c_2 (1 + b_2 + b_2^2 + b_2^3 + \cdots + b_2^{n-1}) \qquad [13.13]$$

On income it is

$$c_2 (1 + b_2 + b_2^2 + b_2^3 + \cdots + b_2^n) \qquad [13.14]$$

and on investment

$$c_3 + b_3 c_2 (1 + b_2 + b_2^2 + b_2^3 + \cdots + b_2^{n-1}) \qquad [13.15]$$

As has been already pointed out, the expressions [13.13–13.15] may have more operational content than the equilibrium multipliers and hence be of more interest for policy purposes. Notice that if the condition for convergence is met, i.e. if $b_2 < 1$, then the additional effects of the increase in G becomes less and less over time and, as n increases, the expressions [13.13–13.15] approach the equilibrium multipliers given by [13.10–13.12].

Klein model I

To illustrate the above ideas we shall use the six-equation model of the US economy constructed by Klein (1950) and generally referred to as Klein model I. Although a small model by present standards, it has been extensively examined and we can take advantage of the fact that values for the various impact, interim and equilibrium multipliers are readily available. The model has, in fact, been used as a testing ground for many of the new estimation techniques that have since been developed.

The model contains three behavioural equations and three identities. The first equation is a consumption function which allows for different MPC out of profits and wage income

$$C_t = \alpha_0 + \alpha_1 \Pi_t + \alpha_2 \Pi_{t-1} + \alpha_3 (W_{1t} + W_{2t}) + \varepsilon_{1t} \qquad [13.16]$$

where C_t is aggregate consumption, Π_t profits, and W_{1t} and W_{2t} are the private industry and government wage bills.

Investment is determined by a profits rather than an accelerator theory so that the second equation is

$$I_t = \beta_0 + \beta_1 \Pi_t + \beta_2 \Pi_{t-1} + \beta_3 K_{t-1} + \varepsilon_{2t} \qquad [13.17]$$

where I_t is aggregate net investment and K_{t-1} is the beginning of period capital stock.

The third equation is an employment equation. The private wage bill (as an indicator of employment) is related to current and previous period total private product and a time trend. Total private product is measured as net national product, Y_t, plus business taxes, T_t, minus the government wage bill.

$$W_{1t} = \gamma_0 + \gamma_1 (Y_t + T_t - W_{2t}) + \gamma_2 (Y_{t-1} + T_{t-1} - W_{2t-1}) + \gamma_3 t + \varepsilon_{3t}$$
$$[13.18]$$

The time trend t is included to account for the effect of growing trade union strength on the private wage bill.

The above three equations contain disturbances ε_{1t}, ε_{2t} and ε_{3t} respectively but the remaining three equations are definitional identities

$$Y_t = C_t + I_t + G_t - T_t \qquad [13.19]$$

$$Y_t = \Pi_t + W_{1t} + W_{2t} \qquad [13.20]$$

$$I_t = K_t - K_{t-1} \qquad [13.21]$$

The first identity expresses net national product as the sum of all expenditures less taxes. The second defines net national income as the sum of profits and wages while the third simply states that net investment equals the change in capital stock. Equations [13.16–13.21] represent a six-equation income–expenditure model in six endogenous variables C_t, I_t, W_{1t}, Y_t, Π_t and K_t. There are four exogenous variables – the government sector variables W_{2t}, G_t and T_t plus the time trend and three lagged endogenous variables Y_{t-1}, Π_{t-1} and K_{t-1}. Lagged values of two of the exogenous variables W_{2t-1} and T_{t-1} also appear.

Since there are fifteen variables in the model altogether, the first three equations are clearly overidentified. Klein estimates their parameters by three different models – OLS, limited information maximum likelihood (LIML) and full information maximum likelihood (FIML). Alternative two-stage and three-stage least squares estimates were later provided by Zellner and Theil (1962). Klein's FIML estimates are presented in Table 13.1.

The reduced-form for this set of estimates has been calculated by Theil and Boot (1962) and is given in Table 13.2.

Table 13.1 Full information maximum likelihood estimates of parameters in Klein model I

i	0	1	2	3
α_i	16.78	0.020	0.235	0.800
β_i	17.79	0.231	0.546	−0.146
γ_i	1.60	0.420	0.164	0.135

Source: Klein (1950)

The impact multipliers defined in the previous section are shown in the columns underneath the policy instrument variables W_{2t}, G_t and T_t in Table 13.2. Thus the immediate current period impact of $1 m increase in taxation is a reduction of $0.188 m in consumption, a reduction of $0.296 million in investment, and so on. The impact effect of a $1 m increase in government expenditure on, for example, income, is an increase of $1.930 m. Since the tax-multiplier in this case is − 1.484 we can obtain a value for the balanced budget impact multiplier of $1.930 − 1.484 = 0.446$ for income. Similarly, the balanced budget multiplier for the private wage bill is 0.607 while for profits it is − 0.162. Thus balanced increases in government expenditure and taxation initially benefit wages rather than profits.

Theil and Boot also calculate long-run equilibrium multipliers (of interest provided the process is convergent) for the three policy instruments. These are shown in Table 13.3.

The long-run dynamic multiplier effects on investment are zero because, in equilibrium, capital stock is constant so that no investment takes place. The long-run effect of a $1 m increase in G is a rise of $2.323 m in income, while that of a similar increase in T is a fall of $1.569 m. Thus the long-run balanced budget multiplier effect on income is $2.323 − 1.569 = 0.754$. This compares with an impact multiplier of 0.446, so that roughly 60 per cent of the effect of a balanced increase in government expenditure and taxation is felt immediately. Similarly, the long-run balanced budget multiplier effect on W_1 is

Table 13.2 Reduced-form parameters for Klein model I

Endo-genous variable	Reduced-form coefficient of								
	Y_{t-1}	Π_{t-1}	K_{t-1}	W_{2t}	G_t	T_t	t	W_{2t-1}	Y_{t-1}
C_t	0.189	0.743	−0.098	0.666	0.671	−0.188	0.155	−0.189	0.189
I_t	−0.015	0.746	−0.184	−0.052	0.259	−0.296	−0.012	0.015	−0.015
W_{1t}	0.237	0.626	−0.119	−0.162	0.811	−0.204	0.195	−0.237	0.237
Y_t	0.174	1.489	−0.283	0.614	1.930	−1.484	0.143	−0.174	0.174
Π_t	−0.063	0.363	−0.164	0.224	1.119	−1.281	−0.052	0.063	−0.063
K_t	−0.015	0.746	0.816	−0.052	0.259	−0.296	−0.012	0.015	−0.015

Source: Theil and Boot (1962)

Table 13.3 Long-run multipliers for Klein model I

	C	I	W₁	Y	Π	K
W_2	0.536	0	−0.271	0.536	−0.192	−1.024
G	1.323	0	1.358	2.323	0.965	5.123
T	−0.569	0	−0.333	−1.569	−1.237	−6.564

Source: Theil and Boot (1962)

$1.358 - 0.333 = 1.025$ while on Π it is $0.965 - 1.237 = -0.272$. Thus the long-run effect as well as the impact effect of such a policy is to benefit wages rather than profits.

Theil and Boot also compute interim multipliers which measure the effect of a change (not sustained) in one of the exogenous variables on the endogenous variables a finite number of periods j later. These are, in fact, equivalent to the coefficients on the current and lagged G variables in equations [13.7–13.9]. These multipliers, in fact, change sign as j increases, indicating that the system oscillates after an external shock. By adding these interim multipliers together we can find the effect of a sustained change in any of the exogenous variables as was done to derive equations [13.13–13.15]. It is then possible to plot the time paths of the endogenous variables after a disturbance. Such time paths are shown in Fig. 13.1 for a sustained increase of $1 m in government expenditure.

It can be seen from Fig. 13.1 that the first-period impact effects of the change in G give little indication of what the long-run equilibrium effects will be. While this is already apparent from study of the impact and equilibrium multipliers

13.1 Time paths for the endogenous variables in Klein model I.

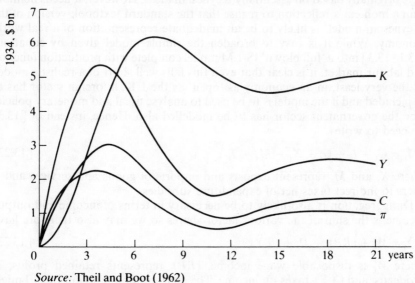

Source: Theil and Boot (1962)

in Tables 13.2 and 13.3, what Fig. 13.1 also illustrates is that neither impact nor equilibrium multipliers give any indication of the effect of the change after, for example, two to three years. As already noted, for policy purposes we are often more interested in such effects as these than in the final long-run effects.

The time paths of Fig. 13.1 also confirm that Klein model I is, in fact, a stable system.[4] The endogenous variables do eventually converge on their long-run equilibrium values after the change in G, although clearly the system oscillates on its way to its new equilibrium. The long-run equilibrium multipliers of Table 13.3 do then have some operational meaning although, since the system only begins to converge on its equilibrium after fifteen to twenty years, they have limited practical significance.

Before leaving the Klein model it is worth asking why, since all the use we have made of that model has involved only the reduced-form parameters, so much effort was put into estimating the structural parameters? Why not simply estimate the reduced-form directly, thus bypassing the problems of simultaneity and overidentification? The reason is that any *a priori* information about the sign and perhaps size of parameters provided by economic theory almost always refers to the structural parameters. Hence, the plausibility of estimates can be best assessed when they refer to the structural equations. Furthermore, suppose we have reason to believe that one of the parameters in the model is likely to change during the forecast period. If the parameter is a reduced-form parameter there is no problem, but it is much more likely to be a structural parameter, e.g. the MPC wage income in Klein model I. If we only have estimates of the reduced-form parameters it becomes far more difficult to adjust forecasts to allow for the suspected change.

13.2 The development of United Kingdom macro-models

As noted at the outset all the major macroeconomic models of the UK economy were originally based on essentially Keynesian ideas. However, it needs no more than a moment's reflection to realise that the standard textbook version of the 'Keynesian model' is likely to be an inadequate representation of a real world economy. While it is easy to broaden the simple model given by equations [13.1–13.3] into a 'full blown' IS-LM model complete with production function and labour market, it is clear that even this falls well short of a realistic model. At the very least, in an economy as 'open' as the UK, a foreign sector has to be included and if the model is to be used to analyse fiscal and monetary policies then the government sector has to be modelled also. Hence, instead of [13.3] we need to write

$$Y_t = C_t + I_t + G_t + X_t - M_t - T_t \qquad [13.22]$$

where X_t and M_t represent exports and imports of goods and services and T_t refers to indirect taxes net of expenditure subsidies.

Disaggregation is also likely to be necessary in terms of income and output. Income is the sum of the various factor shares so we may also therefore have

$$Y_t = W_t + (RP)_t + D_t + (TY)_t \qquad [13.23]$$

where W_t is disposable wage income, $(RP)_t$ represents retained profits, D_t dividends, and $(TY)_t$ taxes on income. The consumption function [13.1] might then be respecified to allow for different propensities to consume wage and non-wage income, as in Klein model I, and/or by replacing total income, Y_t, by personal disposable income, $Y_t - (TY)_t - (RP)_t$.

Output may need to be disaggregated into at least the major sectors of the economy, so we might also have, for example

$$Y_t = A_t + N_t + S_t \qquad [13.24]$$

where A_t, N_t and S_t are the outputs of the agricultural, manufacturing and service sectors.

The three identities [13.22–13.24] all introduce additional variables, most of which cannot be treated as exogenous, and which therefore imply a need for additional equations. For example, imports in [13.22] and taxes on income in [13.23] are obviously going to depend on income Y_t and, to explain any split between retained profits and dividends, it is likely to be necessary to introduce the yield on equities and the return to capital.

When it is also realised that the major expenditure components in the textbook Keynesian model will also need to be split up – consumption into its durable and non-durable components, investment at least into fixed investment and inventories – it is not difficult to understand how we can soon find ourselves with a very large simultaneous equation model indeed.

Another important manner in which the econometric models differ from those of the textbook is in the attention paid to the dynamic structure of equations. The typical textbook model is entirely static in nature, yielding equilibrium solutions but having nothing to say about the time path by which an economy moves to such an equilibrium. While such models, suitably disaggregated, may be satisfactory for the analysis and forecasting of long-run developments in an economy, most macroeconomic models are built for short-term forecasting and policy analysis. Since initial changes in response to any disturbance are likely to be significantly less than the overall long-run effects, the manner in which an economy approaches its long-run position becomes of overriding importance. As in our discussion of Klein model I, we are interested in impact and interim multipliers rather than long-run multipliers. This requirement necessitates careful specification of the lag structures in the behavioural relationships since it is through such lagged responses that the models link one period to the next.

Of the major current macroeconometric models of the UK, some such as those of the Bank of England and the Treasury exist within the government sector, one is operated by the National Institute of Economic and Social Research, while others such as those of the London Business School (LBS), the Cambridge Economic Policy Group (CEPG), Cambridge Econometrics and the Liverpool University model, were built and developed largely in the universities. Since all but the Liverpool model developed out of Keynesian ideas, they originally adopted an income-expenditure approach, similar to that outlined at the beginning of this section. However in recent years, as we shall see, there has been considerable divergence in their structures. The degree of disaggregation and hence the size of the models also varies. For example, the Cambridge Econometrics model contains over 3000 equations whereas the National Institute (NI) model contains little more than 150. The models are continually being revised and any description of their current structure would very soon become out of date. In this section we shall therefore be content with a summary of the progress of macroeconometric modelling in the UK over the past two decades. For a more detailed account see, for example, Ball and Holly (1989).

Most of the large-scale models mentioned above developed out of earlier smaller prototypes constructed in the 1960s. The mainly Keynesian orientation of these early models reflected the mainstream of economic thinking at that time, with effective demand and hence GDP being determined by the expenditures of private, government and overseas sectors. The experience of the 1930s and the belief (based on survey evidence) that investment expenditure was interest inelastic had led to a general consensus that it was fiscal rather than monetary policy that was the more effective in influencing the economy. Moreover, under the Bretton Woods fixed exchange rate system, monetary adjustments tended to occur via the balance of payments so that the government had little control over the total money supply. The supply of money was largely demand determined. Such conditions encouraged the belief that 'money did not matter'.

The development of macroeconometric model building during the 1960s was handicapped by a lack of finance and a general scepticism among leading British economists as to the usefulness of such an exercise. This situation gradually changed and by the mid-1970s forecasts and simulations from large-scale models played an established and significant part in debates on policy making.

As the models developed and became larger, their original Keynesian orientation gradually changed. First, the Cambridge Economic Policy Group was formed at this time. The model the CEPG developed was based on what was then called the 'New Cambridge Economics'. The basic idea behind the model was that fluctuations in the balance of payments current account were largely the consequence of changes in the public sector borrowing requirement. Thus short-term forecasts could not be anywhere near adequate unless proper account was taken of the effect of financial flows on the balance of payments.

Also during the 1970s, fundamental differences in beliefs about how the economy actually worked began to divide the various modelling teams. At the LBS, for example, the model, while still retaining a basic income-expenditure framework, was developed in a way which reflected the ideas of 'international monetarism'. When the UK moved to a flexible exchange rate it became clear that monetary movements could have an important influence on the sterling exchange rate. Fiscal changes were now 'crowded out' not merely through rises in interest rates but by changes in the exchange rate. The likelihood of such effects was built into the LBS model.

Another aspect of the LBS model that distinguished it from its competitors at that time was its treatment of consumption behaviour. The dramatic rise in the savings ratio that occurred during the 1970s had not been predicted by any of the main macro-models. The LBS model was revised so as to explain consumption and saving in terms of a stock adjustment process, with savers seeking to restore the real value of monetary assets that had declined as a result of accelerating inflation.

A further issue over which disagreement arose was that of whether relationships within models should be based solely on available data series or whether they should reflect *a priori* constraints imposed before estimation. For example, should the slope of the long-run Phillips curve be determined empirically? Theory suggests a vertical long-run curve but should this be built into a model before estimation? At the LBS such prior beliefs began to be imposed before estimation whereas, for example, at the National Institute and in the CEPG the view seemed to be that models should reflect the data and the data only. It is only recently that the development of co-integration analysis and the extensive use of error correction models has opened the way for a more rigorous testing of long-run theoretical predictions.

The combination of the LBS view concerning the link between monetary movements and the exchange rate and that on the nature of the long-run trade off between inflation and employment had one important consequence. It led to models which, while Keynesian in their short-run behaviour, implied that under flexible exchange rates fiscal expansions led eventually to inflation rather than any permanent change in employment or output. The developments at the LBS had a considerable impact on both the Treasury and the Bank of England models so that, particularly after the election of a Conservative government in 1979, economic thinking at this level became increasingly non-Keynesian in approach.

The change of government in 1979, with the consequent end of demand management policies, in fact presented all the main macro modelling teams with a major challenge. The empirical effects of factors such as large cuts in marginal tax rates, the adoption of the medium-term financial strategy, financial deregulation and even trade union reform all needed to be incorporated into the various models. This led, firstly, to serious attempts at introducing 'forward looking' expectations into models and, secondly, to extensive work in the modelling of the supply side of the economy.

The Lucas (1976) critique of econometric policy making has been referred to in previous chapters. Lucas questioned whether, given rational expectations and instantaneous market clearing, parameters in macro-models could ever remain unchanged when there were shifts in policy regime. This had obvious implications for all UK macroeconometric models. The assumptions of rational expectations and market clearing in addition imply that there may be no way in which macroeconomic policy can bring about changes in output and employment. However, while forward-looking rational expectations were introduced into some of the main UK macro-models, quantity adjustments remained possible because prices in labour and quantity markets were permitted to remain 'sticky' rather than completely flexible. For example, in the LBS model, while asset markets cleared instantaneously, product and labour markets adjusted only gradually. It was the Liverpool model, however, that led the way in introducing rational expectations into UK macro-models. This model is described in more detail in the next section, but here it should be noted that it incorporated both rational expectations and instantaneous adjustment in all markets, thus ruling out quantity adjustments even in the short run.

Two factors led to the increased attention taken to modelling the supply side of the economy in the 1980s. There was a rapid rise in unemployment during the 1980–81 recession, and the Conservative government elected in 1979 emphasised a supply-side policy of increased incentives and labour market reforms to combat it. Consequently, most of the UK macro-models now include an important labour market and wage determining sector. In general the models work in terms of real rather than nominal wages. It now appears to be generally accepted that money illusion plays little part in the labour market even in the short run. Since the level of employment is included in the wage equations this means that all the models imply a natural rate of unemployment. However, there remains disagreement about what factors influence the real wage rate and hence the natural level of unemployment. For example, there is much argument over the importance of rates of tax and benefits. The relative importance of unemployment in influencing real wages is also now disputed. It is possible, for example, that the level of long-term unemployment has much less effect on wage rates than does that of short-term unemployment. Despite these differences however, it is probably correct to say that none of the major UK models now predict that any substantial long-term gains in real income and output can result from fiscal policy without serious consequences for the inflation rate and/or the balance of payments current account.

13.3 Two smaller macro-models

While the size of the models discussed above stems from their essentially Keynesian origins, non-Keynesian economists have often preferred much smaller models, stressing the link between monetary aggregates and money income. The best known of the smaller UK models is that developed at Liverpool University. The Liverpool model is an annual model which comprised at one time just 20 equations.[5] It differs from other major UK models not merely in its size and the stress it gives to monetary factors but in a number of other crucial aspects. As noted in the previous section it was the first UK model to incorporate rational expectations. In the Liverpool model, even in its early form, expectations were not generated by past observations on variables but were based on the models own predictions of the future values of variables. This has the effect that anticipations of government policy even beyond the forecasting horizon are capable of influencing model behaviour within the horizon itself.

Another unusual feature of the Liverpool model is that it belongs to the class of new classical 'equilibrium models'. Markets are assumed to clear instantaneously – that is there is a full rather than any partial adjustment of prices to expected changes in supply and demand. This full adjustment occurs during the current period. Unlike in other UK models this assumption is applied not merely to, for example, asset markets but even to labour and product markets.

The original version of the Liverpool model effectively exogenised the natural rate of unemployment and hence output but later a significant supply side was added. The natural rate of unemployment is now determined within the labour market by such factors as the tax rates on both employees and employers, the level of unionisation in the labour force and the rate of unemployment benefit. Movements from the natural rate can occur solely because of 'price surprises'. The aggregate supply curve is not completely vertical, however, because the natural rate of unemployment is also made to depend on the real exchange rate. Such an open economy effect gives an upward slope to the aggregate supply curve.

In the Liverpool model the rate of inflation is closely linked to monetary growth. Whereas in most UK macro-models monetary influences on the real sector are felt mainly via the exchange rate, the monetarist aspect of the Liverpool model is seen strongly in the importance it attaches to real balance effects. The level of real wealth (both financial and physical) held by decision-makers plays a key role in the determination of both their investment and consumption expenditures. Since real wealth levels are influenced by changes in the price level and because nominal long-term interest rates are an important factor in determining the market value of financial wealth, money has a more direct impact on aggregate demand than in most other UK models. Uncertainty about future inflation rates is also held to influence expenditure decisions.

The Liverpool model also contains an explicit demand for money function in which the ratio of money demanded to total financial wealth is made dependent on interest rates, total wealth and the measure of future uncertainty about inflation. While under fixed exchange rates the money supply is assumed to be demand-determined, under flexible exchange rates it is regarded as determined by the government via such factors as its long-run budget deficit. Given the demand for money equations, variations in the money supply are therefore transmitted to the real sector via the effect of interest rate changes on the level of real wealth and through changes in the expected rate of inflation.

An even greater contrast to the large-scale Keynesian models is the so-called *St Louis model*, which we shall also describe briefly. The model is named after the link between its builders and the Federal Reserve Bank of St Louis in the US, but has also been estimated from UK data. As presented by Anderson and Carlson (1970) it is an eight-equation model with just five behavioural relationships and three identities. The equation of most interest, however, is one determining changes in total spending $\Delta(YP)_t$

$$\Delta(YP)_t = g(\Delta M_t, \Delta M_{t-1}, \Delta M_{t-2}, \ldots, \Delta M_{t-k}, \Delta E_t,$$
$$\Delta E_{t-1}, \Delta E_{t-2}, \ldots, \Delta E_{t-1}) \qquad [13.25]$$

where ΔM_t is the change in the money supply and ΔE_t the change in 'high unemployment' government expenditure (both assumed exogenous). Equation [13.25] is very much a 'monetarist' equation. Since the cumulative effect of the government expenditure variable is expected to be zero, it implies that in the long run changes in spending depend solely on changes in the money supply. Changes in total spending are defined as identically equal to changes in output, ΔY_t, plus changes in prices ΔP_t

$$\Delta(YP)_t = \Delta Y_t + \Delta P_t \qquad [13.26]$$

Changes in prices depend on expected price changes and demand pressure (itself partly dependent on $\Delta(YP)_t$). Once $\Delta(YP)_t$ and ΔP_t are determined, changes in output are determined by the identity [13.26]. The rest of the model is concerned with determining the expected rate of price change, the rate of interest (assumed endogenous) and the level of unemployment.

Equation [13.25] is usually estimated from quarterly data using the Almon lag technique described in section 6.5. Anderson and Carlson used a fourth-order polynomial with β_{-1} and β_5 pegged to zero. The sum of the coefficients on the ΔE variables was indeed zero while changes in the money supply had a rapid effect on changes in total spending. The equation forecast nominal GNP very well – over 1963–64 its forecasts have a root mean square error of 1.49 per cent.[6] This compared with 2.00 per cent of nominal GNP for the much larger 'Wharton model' of the US over the same period.

Matthews and Ormerod (1978) obtained similar results with the St Louis model for the UK. The sum of the coefficients on the ΔE variables in [13.25] was again insignificantly different from zero, although the effect of changes in the money supply was less rapid. The UK version of the model also forecast well with a root mean square error of 4.16 per cent of nominal GDP over 1975(i) to 1976(ii). This compared with a root mean square forecast error of 3.14 for the National Institute (NI) model over the same period. Matthews and Ormerod however found that, for the UK, the equation is far less robust to changes in the definition of the money stock.

The forecasts obtained with the St Louis model illustrate the fact that it is by no means clear that large models forecast more accurately than small ones. The advantage of the large model, however, lies in the detail of the forecasts they produce and their ability adequately to represent the many different channels through which various policy instruments can influence the economy.

13.4 Forecasting in practice

In theory the procedure for obtaining a one, or more generally, a k period ahead forecast is simple. If data is available up to period t, the model can be estimated using this data. Forecasts for period $t + 1$ are then obtained by substituting into the model the period $t + 1$ values of the predetermined variables and solving for the endogenous variables. If the reduced-form is easily obtained then the values for the predetermined variables can simply be substituted into the reduced-form equations. Similarly, forecasts for period $t + k$ are obtained on substitution of the period $t + k$ values of the predetermined variables. In practice, however, the procedure is far more complicated with judgement playing as important a part as standard statistical procedures. For example, it should immediately be obvious that future values for the exogenous variables will not be available at the time of making the forecast. It is true that future values of lagged endogenous variables will be generated by the forecasts themselves, but any errors in forecasting these variables will have a cumulative effect in subsequent periods because of the dynamic structure of the model.

Osborne and Teal (1979) summarised the procedure by which the quarterly forecasts of the NI model are prepared. The procedure consists of five main steps:

1. First, the data base is updated, making use of all new quarterly observations on variables and any revisions to past data. Values in the most recent quarter may have to be estimated for variables on which data are not available. When making the February forecast, for example, National Accounts are not yet available for the fourth quarter of the previous year and have to be estimated using data on such variables as industrial production and retail sales.
2. Predictions are now made for values of the exogenous variables during the forecast period. This involves considerable background work in assessing recent trends and likely future developments. The exogenous variables mainly concern the world economy and government policy. For example, projections have to be made about the future path of commodity prices – particularly that of oil. Variables influenced by government policy, e.g. public expenditure and tax rates, are forecast under the assumption of unchanged government policies.

3. Making use of the latest data, residuals for the past two or three years are obtained for each of the structural equations in the model. These residuals are the differences between the actual and predicted values of the endogenous variables when actual values of all variables, both endogenous and exogenous, are used on the right-hand side. For equations estimated on the basis of random disturbances one would not expect to find any systematic pattern in such residuals. However, since in practice the model is neither respecified nor re-estimated every quarter, it is possible that a sequence of, for example, positive residuals might be obtained for an equation during the past, say, four to six quarters.
4. Any systematic pattern found in the residuals for any equation is next extrapolated into the forecast period. The extrapolation is performed subjectively and not by some mechanical rule. This judgemental procedure enables other factors not explicitly allowed for in the model to be incorporated into the forecast via these residual terms. For example, it may be necessary to allow for the effect of North Sea oil on imports or for the possibility that a pre-Budget spending spree may have an offsetting effect on expenditure during the quarter after the Budget.
5. The predictions for the exogenous variables and extrapolations of the residuals are combined throughout the model to provide forecasts of all the endogenous variables.

Steps (4) and (5) above are, in fact, iterative. Initial forecasts of the endogenous variables are assessed for plausibility and consistency in the light of expected developments in the economy. If the forecasts are considered to be implausible in any sense, some of the predictions for the exogenous variables may be altered or the values for the residuals revised and the forecasting redone. Several 'runs' of the model may be necessary before the forecasters are satisfied, and the final forecasts are as much the product of judgement as of the econometric model. Such a procedure is, in fact, typical of all macroeconomic forecasting not merely that with the NI model.

The forecasts of all macroeconomic models are continually checked for their accuracy. Osborne and Teal (1979) decompose the error that can be observed between the forecast value of an endogenous variable and the actual outcome into four parts: (a) that due to errors in predicting the values of exogenous variables; (b) that due to errors in the specification of the model; (c) that due to judgemental errors in the extrapolation of residuals; and, (d) that due to revisions to published data using in making the forecast. These sources of error are not independent, however. For example, revisions to data, had they been known at the time of the forecast, might have affected the predictions made for the exogenous variables.

Osborne and Teal consider the NI forecasts for the UK economy made in February of 1975 and 1976. First, they compare the published *ex ante* forecasts with the actual outcome. Next they calculate the forecasts that would have been made had the 'actual' values of exogenous and lagged endogenous variables been available at the time of the actual forecast. These *ex post* forecasts are also compared with the actual outcome. For 1975, in six out of nine categories the *ex post* forecast proves more accurate than the *ex ante* forecast. However, more interestingly, for 1976 the forecasts using revised data are less accurate in six out of the nine cases. This illustrates that not having access to final revised

415

data does not necessarily increase forecast errors but can sometimes fortuitously reduce them. Osborne and Teal also find that the relative importance of data revisions and errors in predicting the exogenous variables is different in the two years. In 1975 data revisions are the more important but for the 1976 forecast the effect of the two is very similar.

The Osborne and Teal study is unusual in that they were able to decompose *ex post* forecast error into its various components. It is rare for independent assessors of forecasts to be able to obtain forecasts under alternative assumptions about the paths of exogenous variables. The models used are not normally available to them. An exception, however, is the ESRC modelling bureaux, based at the University of Warwick, which now makes a regular analysis of the forecasts of the major UK models which includes a decomposition similar to that originally made by Osborne and Teal.

Forecasters now regularly make assessments of their own forecasting performances. Also, in the past ten years, numerous comparisons of the *ex ante* forecast performances of the various models have been published by various authors – see Wallis (1989) for an account of some of these. Such comparisons are made both with respect to different variables (e.g. real GDP or the rate of inflation) and with respect to different forecast horizons. By and large no model can be said consistently to outperform the others. For certain periods one model may do best for a particular variable but such superiority has rarely been maintained for long.

In assessing the performance of forecasters it must be remembered that the economic data series being forecast are themselves only accurate up to a margin of 2 or even 5 per cent. The series are also continually being revised and average absolute forecast errors are generally within the range of adjustment of the series. Given the level of accuracy of most economic data. it is unlikely that forecast errors are likely to decline much below their present levels.

13.5   The simulation of macro-models

In section 13.1 we analysed the impact and long-term effects of changes in the values of the exogenous variables in Klein model I. This involved the derivation of the reduced-form and final-form of the model and the calculation of impact and dynamic multipliers. Clearly, if the far more complicated macro-models of the succeeding sections are to be used to provide information on the likely effect of policy changes, e.g. in taxation or public expenditure or in monetary policy, then some similar form of analysis has to be performed. Unfortunately, such is the complexity of most recent macro-models that calculation of reduced-forms is rarely feasible and the elaborate lag structures in many of the equations make *analytical* study of the dynamic properties of the model impossible. That is, we cannot determine, analytically, whether the system returns to equilibrium after an exogenous 'shock'. Neither, if the system is, in fact, stable, can we derive the time paths of the endogenous variables as they move to their new equilibria or, for that matter, determine at what levels equilibrium is again reached. The answer to these difficulties is to run the model in what is known as 'simulation mode'.

Simulation is a purely numerical technique which is possibly the closest we can get to an experimental situation in the social sciences. A simulation may be performed either over the sample period used for estimation or over any future period. The procedure followed is to run the model, first with one set of values for the exogenous variables (probably actual present values) and then re-run it with an alternative set of values. The changes could involve merely a single change in one exogenous variable for just one period, or a change in more than one perhaps sustained indefinitely.

A further important use of simulation is that it enables the model builders to check whether the time paths for the endogenous variables generated by the model approximate the actual time paths. The properties of a model are analysed in this way since an obviously important criterion for judging a model is whether its behaviour resembles adequately the behaviour of the economy it is supposed to represent. For example, does the model generate the 'cycles' characteristic of most modern industrial economies?

Let us illustrate the simulation technique by considering again Klein model I, introduced in section 13.1. Klein estimated this model from annual data for 1921–41 and we consider how a simulation over the actual sample period would be performed. We have available actual 1921 values for the exogenous variables W_2, G, T and t and also 1921 values for the lagged endogenous variables Y_{-1}, Π_{-1} and K_{-1} (these will be actual values for 1920). We can therefore substitute these initial values into the estimated versions of equations [13.16]–[13.21] and solve to obtain 'simulated' 1921 values for all the endogenous variables C, I, W_1, Y, Π and K. These values form the first points in our simulated time paths for these variables. To obtain simulated 1922 values for the endogenous variables, we again substitute into the model actual (this time 1922) values for the exogenous variables, but instead of using actual (1921) values for the lagged endogenous variables, we use the simulated values for these variables obtained in the 1921 calculations. For all successive years we proceed in this way, using actual values for exogenous variables but simulated values for lagged endogenous variables. Eventually we obtain simulated time paths for 1921–41 for all the endogenous variables which may then be compared with the actual time paths. Such a comparison is, in fact, made by Desai (1982: ch. 8) and it is immediately clear that the simulated time paths differ significantly from the actual time paths. They show no sign of the large cyclical fluctuations characteristic of the inter-war US economy. This, of course, is not particularly surprising, since Klein model I is a very simple model which can hardly be expected to capture adequately the workings of such a complex economy as the US, particularly during the traumatic inter-war years.

Notice that the use of simulated values for lagged endogenous variables after the initial period means that divergences of simulated from actual time paths are likely to be compounded as we move through the sample period. This is because differences between actual and simulated values are incorporated into subsequent calculations. However, the simulation has to be performed in this way, since we wish the system to be moved ultimately only by the exogenous variables. We do not wish the simulated time paths for the endogenous variables to be influenced by their actual time paths because we wish to compare the two. Notice also that in simulation exercises we are analysing the properties of the model alone – the time paths are generated by the model alone, unmodified by the 'judgement' described in the previous section and necessarily a part of published forecasts.

It should be clear that, given initial values for the lagged endogenous variables, simulation exercises, such as that described above for Klein model I, can be performed over any time period for given paths of the exogenous variables. They need not necessarily be restricted to the sample period over which the model was estimated. The technique therefore provides a valuable method of assessing various policy options. Simulations obtained by use of values of the exogenous variables forecast under the assumption of unchanged policies can be compared with simulations arising when various policy changes are assumed. In each case the initial values for the lagged endogenous variables will be their current or latest available values.

An example of this type of exercise is the analysis in the *National Institute Economic Review* for November 1981 of the effects on the UK economy of alternative reflationary fiscal policies each costing £5 bn (gross) in 1981 prices. The results of the simulations made using the National Institute model are shown in Table 13.4.

The simulations suggest that an increase in government spending on goods and services is the most potent way of increasing output and the effects are felt immediately. This form of stimulus also causes the most inflation, although the effect on prices is relatively small. The effect of a reduction in income tax on both output and employment is much weaker and takes longer to be felt. On the other hand, the effect on prices is such that the rate of inflation is reduced from what it otherwise would have been. Cuts in indirect taxes and in the National Insurance Surcharge have similar effects on output and employment as an income tax cut, although the insurance surcharge cut takes longer to work. These latter two forms of fiscal stimulus have, however, a distinctly better effect on the price level than the income tax cut.

The National Institute concluded that the most important result yielded by the simulations was that it was possible simultaneously to reduce both unemployment and inflation. This was true in both the short run and the medium term. (The figures in Table 13.4 refer to a version of the model which

Table 13.4 Effects of alternative reflationary policies each costing £5 bn

Policy	Effect in first year		Cumulative effect after 5 years			
	Output (%)	Price level (%)	Output (%)	Price level (%)	Unemployment ('000's)	Budget deficit (% of GNP)
Increase in government spending on goods and services	1.8	0.0	1.7	1.1	−330	1.0
Income tax cut	0.5	−0.2	1.1	−0.2	−190	1.5
Indirect tax cut	0.6	−2.6	1.0	−6.6	−180	1.2
National insurance surcharge cut	0.3	−0.7	1.2	−5.4	−190	1.0

Source: National Institute Economic Review, November 1981

contains a Sargan (1964)-type 'real-wage' equation. Effects on prices are greater when this is replaced by an 'expectations-augmented Phillips curve' but it still remained possible to reduce unemployment and prices at the same time.)

Limitations of simulation studies

While the use of macro-models in their simulation mode has obviously many attractions, the models also have important limitations when used to analyse the effects of changes in policy. We therefore close this section by considering some of these limitations.

Simulations are almost always performed under the implicit assumption that the estimated coefficients of a model are fixed and unchanging constants. In fact, there is always a margin of error associated with point estimates – sampling variability means that parameters cannot be determined precisely and estimates will always have standard errors associated with them. Since even slight changes in parameters can have considerable effects on the simulation properties of models, it is clearly desirable that all predictions should have confidence intervals attached to them. Unfortunately, the computational burden of calculating such intervals for the larger macro-models of the present day is a heavy one. However, if such confidence intervals were known it could well be the case that apparent large differences between the effects of different policies could simply be accounted for by sampling variability. For example, the appearance of confidence intervals on the numbers in Table 13.4 might well have served to reduce any belief in the differences between predictions for the first policy option compared with the other three.

Even if it were possible to estimate parameters with complete precision there are additional reasons why impact and long-run multipliers should not be regarded as unchanging constants. Most macro-models contain some non-linearity in their variables, e.g. deflation of monetary variables by price indices to produce real variables involves introducing the ratio of two variables. The existence of non-linearities is one of the reasons why the derivation of reduced- and final-forms for large models is so difficult and, hence, why the analysis of the effects of changes in exogenous variables is undertaken through simulation. However, non-linearities can also result in the size of multipliers being itself dependent on the values of variables in the models (see Wallis 1979: 152 for an example of this). This means that the results of simulations may vary depending on the initial conditions of the simulation run. Laury, Lewis and Ormerod (1978) provide an example of this using the National Institute model. When the base set of data began with the first quarter of 1972, simulation of the effects of a 5 per cent sterling devaluation suggested that such a devaluation would not improve the balance of payments until more than three years later. However, for a base data set beginning in the first quarter of 1976, simulation suggested an improvement after only one year. Thus conclusions drawn from simultaneous performed with the economy assumed to be in one state can by no means necessarily be assumed to apply when the economy is in some other state.[7]

Perhaps the most fundamental criticism of the use of macro-models for simulation studies is that of Lucas (1976). As we have noted, Lucas argued that the parameters in a macro-model may well vary with the policy in operation. Thus, while the short-term forecasting accuracy of a model may be adequate, it may be of little use for comparing the effects of alternative policies. It is relatively obvious that, if a policy remains in force long enough or has been tried on a number of previous occasions (e.g. successive exchange rate devaluations), then rational individuals will learn how the policy effects the economy and hence adjust their behaviour to allow for it. However, under rational expectations, even a sudden change of policy, provided it has sufficient credibility, will influence the behaviour of rational agents and hence lead to significant changes in the relationships in macro-models.

The criticisms of Lucas and other 'new classical' economists have undoubtedly led to a complete rethink about how expectations are handled in UK macroeconometric models. Although the models have by and large survived the new classical onslaught, the criticisms (see for example Kydland and Prescott, 1977) have also changed the manner in which modellers view simulations. The 'credibility' of an economic policy is now regarded as important. The obvious example here is the introduction of a new counter-inflationary policy. If it is generally accepted that the government will adhere determinedly to its policy, then it is conceivable that the economy will adjust relatively swiftly to a new inflation rate. However, if it is widely believed that the government is likely to falter, in the face of maybe rising unemployment, then serious output losses are likely before inflation is reduced. The general view nowadays is that, while macro-models incorporating forward looking expectations can be usefully employed for policy simulations, account must always be taken of the credibility with which government policy is viewed by economic agents.

13.6 Some outstanding issues

The last two decades have seen an increase both in the number of full-scale macro-models in the UK and the US and in the average size of these models. More rapid and sophisticated computing facilities together with greater disaggregation in data series have made this possible and maybe inevitable. However, there remain a number of unresolved issues. For example, it is still by no means proven that large models forecast better than small models. We have seen that small monetarist models such as the St Louis model can provide forecasts comparable in accuracy with large Keynesian-type models. It is also the case that far less disaggregated Keynesian models also provide equally adequate forecasts, at far less cost in time and effort, of broad aggregate measures such as GDP and total consumer expenditure. Where the large models score, of course, is in the range of information that they provide. The separate effects of many variables can be allowed for and detailed questions about the alternative effects of the many policy instruments available to governments can be tackled. It is not often that complex policy measures can be translated adequately into, for example, broad changes in G or T as would be required by Klein model I. Maybe the ideal solution is for model-builders to maintain small models for forecasting purposes side by side with large disaggregated models to be used for simulation and detailed policy analysis. Re-estimation of the smaller model using latest available data series then takes place at more frequent intervals than does that of the larger model.

One issue concerning the structure of the main UK models over which there is still much debate is the nature of links between monetary and real variables.

In contrast to the situation in the US, there has been less success in the UK in establishing significant interest rate effects on expenditure – the traditional Keynesian transmission mechanism. Neither, with the exception of the Liverpool model, have UK models permitted any significant real balance effects, the orthodox short-run monetarist channel of influence. Rather than working through domestic demand, changes in the money supply affect prices more directly. For example, in the Treasury and particularly the LBS models, the effect is felt via the exchange rate. In the NI model, on the other hand, the link comes about through changes in interest rates affecting the exchange rate via domestic demand and capital flows.

A practical issue which causes some argument concerns the extent to which judgement should be allowed to influence forecasts. Forecasts are adjusted by projecting residuals from estimated equations into the future and also to allow for any recognised events during the forecast period, for example the imposition of an incomes policy. All forecasters make such residual adjustments. There is no disagreement about making such extrapolations *before* the first forecast is made. The controversial issue is whether forecasters should be prepared to modify forecasts to make them conform to intuitive ideas of how the economy should behave. Adjustments made *after* the forecast to ensure internal consistency of the forecast values for different variables obviously make sense. The important question is the extent to which *a priori* notions should be allowed to influence the forecast.

There remains continued controversy over the extent to which the tenets of the new classical macroeconomics should be incorporated into macro-models. While most models now include forward-looking expectations in their relationships there is a divergence over the manner in which this should be done. For example, while at the National Institute stress has been placed on expectations of future output, in the Treasury model attention is paid to expected movements in the exchange rate. Also, as we have already noted, there is a sharp distinction between the Liverpool model, in which instantaneous clearing occurs in labour and product markets, and other UK models. Finally, the dispute, noted in the last section, over the extent to which macro-models can be usefully employed in simulation exercises is not yet fully resolved.

Notes

1. For example [13.5] may be rewritten as

   $$Y_{t+1} = a_2 + b_2 Y_t + c_2 G_{t+1}$$

2. This can easily be seen if we regard equation [13.5] as a simple first-order difference equation. The single root of its characteristic equation is b_2 which must be less than unity for stability.
3. b_2 is in fact given by $b_2 = -\gamma/(1 - \beta - \gamma)$. Substituting in typical values for β, the MPC, e.g. $\beta = 0.8$, gives $b_2 = \gamma/(\gamma - 0.2)$ which exceeds unity for any value of γ the capital-output ratio.
4. The stability or instability of a dynamic equation system can, in fact, be determined analytically (see, for example, Baumol, 1970: ch. 10).
5. For a detailed description of the model see Minford *et al.* (1984).
6. If there are n forecast errors, e, then the root mean square error is $\sqrt{(\sum e^2/n)}$.
7. In the devaluation example the difference between the two simulations arose because capacity utilisation was high and rising sharply during 1972–73 but very low during 1976–77.

References

Allen, R.G.D. and Bowley, A.L. (1935) *Family Expenditure.* Staples Press.

Almon, S. (1965) The distributed lag between capital appropriations and expenditures, *Econometrica,* **33,** 178–96.

Alogoskonfis, G. and Smith, R. (1990) On error correction models, specification, interpretation, estimation. Discussion paper in *Economics,* 6/90, Birbeck College, University of London.

Anderson, G. and Blundell, R. (1983) Testing restrictions in a flexible dynamic demand system: an application to consumers' expenditure in Canada, *Review of Economic Studies,* **50,** 391–440.

Anderson, G. and Blundell, R. (1984) Consumer non-durables in the UK – a dynamic demand system, *Economic Journal,* **94** (Supplement), 35–44.

Anderson, L.C. and Carlson, K.M. (1970) A monetarist model for economic stabilisation, *Federal Reserve Bank of St Louis Review,* **52,** 7–25.

Ando, A. and Modigliani, F. (1963) The life-cycle hypothesis of savings, *American Economic Review,* **53,** 55–84.

Ando, A.K., Modigliani, F., Rasche, R. and Turnovsky, S.J. (1974) On the role of expectations of price and technological change in an investment function, *International Economic Review,* **15,** 384–414.

Arrow, K.J. (1962) The economic implications of learning by doing, *Review of Economic Studies,* **29,** 155–73.

Arrow, K.J., Chenery, H.B., Minhas, B.S. and Solow, R.M. (1961) Capital–labour substitution and economic efficiency, *Review of Economics and Statistics,* **43,** 225–50.

Artis, M.J. (1982) *Why Forecasts Differ.* Bank of England Panel of Academic Consultants, Panel Paper 17.

Artis, M.J. and Lewis, M.K. (1974) The demand for money–stable or unstable, *The Banker,* **124,** 239–43.

Artis, M.J. and Lewis, M.K. (1976) The demand for money in the United Kingdom: 1963–73, *Manchester School,* **43,** 147–81.

Baba, Y., Hendry, D.F. and Starr, R.M. (1985) US money demand, 1960–84. NBER Universities Research Conference on Money and Financial Markets, Cambridge, Massachusetts.

Ball, R.J. and Drake, P.S. (1964) The relationship between aggregate consumption and wealth, *International Economic Review,* **5,** 63–81.

Ball, R.J., Boatwright, B.D., Burns, T., Lobban, P.W.M. and Miller, G.W. (1975) The London Business School quarterly econometric model of the UK economy, in: Renton, G.A. (ed.), *Modelling the Economy.* Heinemann Educational Books.

Ball, R.J. and Holly, S. (1989) Macroeconomic model building in the United Kingdom, Centre for Economic Forecasting, Discussion paper, No. 16, 16–89.

Barrow, M. (1988) *Statistics for economics, accounting and business studies,* Longman.

Barten, A.P. (1964) Family composition, prices and expenditure patterns, in: Hart, PE., Mills, G. and Whitaker, J.K. (eds.), *Econometric Analysis for National Economic Planning.* Butterworth.

Barten, A.P. (1966) Therie en empirie van een volledig stelsel van vraagvergelijkingen, doctoral dissertation, University of Rotterdam.

Barten, A.P. (1969) Maximum likelihood estimation of a complete system of demand equations, *European Economic Review,* **1,** 7–73.

Baumol, W.J. (1952) The transactions demand for cash: an inventory theoretic approach, *Quarterly Journal of Economics,* **55,** 545–56.

Baumol, W.J. (1970) *Economic dynamics – an introduction*. Macmillan, New York.

Bean, C.R. (1978) *The Determination of Consumers Expenditure in the UK*. Treasury Working Paper 4.

Blanciforti, L. and Green, R. (1983) An almost ideal demand system incorporating habit effects, *Review of Economic Studies*, **65**, 511–15.

Blinder, A.S. and Deaton, A. (1985) The time series consumption function revisited, *Brookings Papers on Economic Activity*, **2**, 465–521.

Blundell, R. (1988) Consumer behaviour: theory and empirical evidence – a survey, *Economic Journal*, **98**, 16–65.

Blundell, R., Pashardes, P. and Weber, G. (1987) *A household expenditure model for indirect tax analysis*, Institute for fiscal studies (Mimeo).

Boughton, J.M. (1991) Long run money demand in large industrial countries. International Monetary Fund Staff Papers, **38**, 1–33.

Box, G.E.P. and Pierce, D.A. (1970) Distribution of residual autocorrelations in autoregressive–integrated moving average time series models, *Journal of the American Statistical Association*, **65**, 1509–26.

Brady, D. and Friedman, R. (1947) Savings and the income distribution, *Studies in Income and Wealth*, **10**, National Bureau of Economic Research, New York.

Branson, W.H. and Klevorick, A.K. (1969) Money illusion and the aggregate consumption function, *American Economic Review*, **59**, 832–49.

Bronfenbrenner, M. and Mayer, T. (1960) Liquidity functions in the American economy. *Econometrica* **20**, 355–71

Bronsard, C. and Salvas-Bronsard, V. (1984) On price exogeneity in complete demand systems. *Journal of Econometrics* **24**, 235–47.

Brown, T.M. (1952) Habit persistence and lags in consumer behaviour, *Econometrica*, **20**, 355–71.

Brunner, K. and Meltzer, A.H. (1963) Predicting velocity: implications for theory and policy, *Journal of Finance*, **18**, 319–54.

Budd, A. and Holly, S. (1986) Economic viewpoint: does broad money matter? *London Business School Economic Outlook*, **10**, 16–22.

Budd, A. and Hobbis, S. (1989) Cointegration, technology and the long run production function, Centre for Economic Forecasting, Discussion paper 10-89.

Byron, R.P. (1970a) A simple method of estimating demand equations under separable utility functions, *Review of Economic Studies*, **37**, 261–74.

Byron, R.P. (1970b) The restricted Aitken estimation of sets of demand relations, *Econometrica*, **38**, 816–30.

Cagan, P. (1956) The monetary dynamics of hyperinflation, in: Friedman, M. (ed.), *Studies in the Quantity Theory of Money*. University of Chicago Press.

Campbell, J.Y. and Mankiw, N.G. (1989) Consumption, income and interest rates: reinterpreting the time series evidence, *NBR Macroeconomics Annual*, **4**, 185–216.

Carr, J. and Darby, M.R. (1981) The role of money supply shocks in the short run demand for money, *Journal of Monetary Economics*, **8**, 183–99.

Carr, J., Darby, M.R. and Thornton, D.L. (1985) Monetary anticipations and the demand for money: reply, *Journal of Monetary Economics*, **16**, 251–57.

Carruth, A. and Henley, A. (1990a) Can existing consumption functions forecast consumer spending in the late 1980s? *Oxford Bulletin of Economic Statistics*.

Carruth, A. and Henley, A. (1990b) The housing market and consumer spending, *Fiscal Studies*, August.

Chiang, A.C. (1984) *Fundamental Methods of Economics*, 3rd Edition, International Student Edition, McGraw-Hill.

Chow, G. (1957) *Demand for automobiles in the U.S.: a study of consumer durables*. North Holland, Amsterdam.

Chow, G. (1960a) Statistical demand functions for automobiles and their use for forecasting, in: Harberger, A.C. (ed.), *The Demand for Durable Goods*. University of Chicago Press.

Chow, G. (1960b) Tests of equality between sets of coefficients in two linear regressions, *Econometrica*, **28**, 591–605.

Chow, G. (1966) On the long-run and short-run demand for money, *Journal of Political Economy*, **74**, 111–31.

Christensen, L.R. and Greene, W.H. (1976) Economics of Scale in US electric power generation, *Journal of Political Economy*, **84**, 655–76.

Christensen, L.R., Jorgenson, D.W. and Lau, L.J. (1973) Transcendental logarithmic production frontiers, *Review of Economics and Statistics*, **55**, 28–45.

Christensen, L.R., Jorgensen, D.W. and Lau, L.J. (1975) Transcendental logarithmic utility functions, *American Economic Review*, **65**, 367–83.

Clower, R.W. and Johnson, M.B. (1968) Income, wealth and the theory of consumption, in: Wolfe, N. (ed.), *Value, Capital and Growth*. Edinburgh University Press.

Cochrane, E. and Orcutt, G.H. (1949) Application of least squares regressions to relationships containing autocorrelated error terms, *Journal of the American Statistical Association*, **44**, 32–61.

Coghlan, R.T. (1978) A transactions demand for money, *Bank of England Quarterly Bulletin*, **18**, 48–60.

Courakis, A.S. (1978) Serial correlation and the Bank of England's demand for money function: an exercise in measurement without theory, *Economic Journal*, **88**, 537–48.

Curry, D., Holly, S. and Scott, A. (1989) Savings, demography and interest rates, Centre for Economic Forecasting, Discussion Paper 1-89.

Curry, D., Holly, S. and Scott, A. (1990) A seasonal-error correction model of UK aggregate consumption. Centre for Economic Forecasting, Discussion Paper 22-90.

Cuthbertson, K. (1980) The determination of expenditure on consumer durables, *National Institute of Economic and Social Research Review*, Nov, 62-72.

Cuthbertson, K. (1986) Monetary anticipations and the demand for money: some UK evidence, *Bulletin of Economic Research*, **38**, 257–70.

Cuthbertson, K. (1988) The demand for M1: a forward looking buffer-stock model, *Oxford Economic Papers*, **40**, 110–31.

Cuthbertson, K. and Taylor, M.P. (1986) Monetary anticipation and the demand for money in the UK: testing rationality in the shock-absorber hypothesis, *Journal of Applied Economics*, **1**, 355–65.

Cuthbertson, K. and Taylor, M.P. (1987a) Monetary anticipations and the demand for money: some evidence for the UK, *Weltwirtschliches Archiv*, **123**, 509–520.

Cuthbertson, K. and Taylor, M.P. (1987b) The demand for money: a dynamic rational expectations model, *Economic Journal*, **97** (Supplement), 65–76.

Cuthbertson, K. and Taylor, M.P. (1988) Monetary anticipations and the demand for money in the US: further results, *Southern Economic Journal*, **55**, 326–35.

Cuthbertson, K. and Taylor, M.P. (1989) Anticipated and unanticipated variables in the demand for M1 in the UK, *Manchester School*, **57**, 319–39.

Daly, V. and Hadjimatheou, G. (1981) Stochastic implications of the life cycle – permanent income – hypothesis: evidence for the UK economy, *Journal of Political Economy*, **89**, 596–99.

Daughety, A.F. and Nelson, F.D. (1988) An economic analysis of changes in the cost and production structure of the trucking industry, 1953–82. *Review of Economics and Statistics*, **60**, 67–75.

Davidson, J. (1987) Disequilibrium money: some further result with a model of the UK, in Currie, D.A., Goodhart, C.A.E. and Llewellyn, D.T. (ed.), *The Operation and Regulation of Financial Markets*, Macmillan.

Davidson, J.E.H., Hendry, D.F., Srba, F. and Yeo, S. (1978) Econometric modelling of the aggregate time series relationship between consumers' expenditure and income in the UK, *Economic Journal*, **88**, 661–92.

Davis, T.E. (1952) The consumption function as a tool for prediction, *Review of Economic Statistics*, **34**, 270–7.

Deaton, A.S. (1974) The analysis of consumer demand in the United Kingdom 1900–1970,

Econometrica, **42**, 341–67.

Deaton, A.S. (1975) *Models and Projections of Demand in Postwar Britain.* Chapman and Hall.

Deaton, A. (1978) Involuntary saving through unanticipated inflation, *American Economic Review*, **68**, 899–910.

Deaton, A.S. (1990) Price elasticities from survey data: extensions and Indonesian results, *Journal of Econometrics*, **44**, 281–309.

Deaton, A.S. and Muellbauer, J. (1980) *Econometrics and Consumer Behaviour.* Cambridge University Press.

Desai, M. (1982) *Applied Econometrics.* Phillip Allen.

Dhrymes, P. (1965) Some extensions and tests for the CES class of production functions, *Review of Economics and Statistics*, **37**, 357–66.

Dickey, D.A. and Fuller, W.A. (1981) The likelihood ratio statistics for autoregressive time series with a unit root, *Econometrica*, **49**, 1057–72.

Douglas, P. (1948) Are there laws of production? *American Economic Review*, **38**, 1–41.

Duesenberry, J.S. (1949) *Income, Savings and the Theory of Consumer Behaviour.* Harvard University Press.

Durbin, J. (1953) A note on regression when there is extraneous information on one of the coefficients, *Journal of the American Statistical Association*, **48**, 799–808.

Durbin, J. (1960) Estimation of parameters in time series regression models, *Journal of the Royal Statistical Society*, Series B, **22**, 139–53.

Durbin, J. (1970) Testing for serial correlation in least squares regression when some of the regressors are lagged dependent variables, *Econometrica*, **48**, 410–21.

Durbin, J. and Watson, G.S. (1950; 1951) Testing for serial correlation in least squares regression, *Biometrika*, **37**, 409–28; **38**, 159–78.

Durbin, J. and Watson, G.S. (1971) Testing for serial correlation in least squares regression III, *Biometrika*, **58**, 1–19.

Dutton, D.S. and Gramm, W.P. (1973) Transaction costs, the wage rate, and the demand for money, *American Economic Review*, **63**, 652–65.

Engle, R.F. and Granger, C. (1987) Co-integration and error correction representation, estimation and testing, *Econometrica*, **66**, 251–76.

Engle, R.F. and Yoo, B.S. (1987) Forecasting in co-integrated systems, *Journal of Econometrics*, **35**, 143–59.

Enzler, J., Johnson, L. and Paulus, J. (1976) Some problems of money demand, *Brookings Papers on Economic Activity*, **1**, 261–80.

Evans, M.K. (1969) *Macroeconomic Activity.* Harper and Row, New York.

Farrar, D.E. and Glauber, R.R. (1967) Multicollinearity in regression analysis: the problem revisited, *Review of Economics and Statistics*, **49**, 92–107.

Fase, M.M.G. and Kune, J.B. (1975) The demand for money in thirteen European and non-European countries: A tabular survey, *Kredit und Kapital*, **3**, 410–19.

Feige, E. (1967) Expectations and adjustments in the monetary sector, *American Economic Review*, **57**, 462–73.

Fisher, F.M. and Kaysen, C. (1962) *The Demand for Electricity in the United States.* North Holland, Amsterdam.

Fisher, I. (1907) *The Theory of Interest.* Macmillan, New York.

Flavin, M. (1981) The adjustment of consumption to changing expectations about future income, *Journal of Political Economy*, **89**, 974–1007.

Fox, K.A. (1958) *Econometric Analysis for Public Policy.* Iowa State College Press.

Friedman, M. (1953) The methodology of positive economics, in *Essays in Positive Economics*, University of Chicago Press.

Friedman, M. (1956) The quantity theory of money, a restatement, in: Friedman, M. (ed.), *Studies in the Quantity Theory of Money*, University of Chicago Press.

Friedman, M. (1957) *A Theory of the Consumption Function.* Princeton University Press.

Fuchs, V.R. (1963) Capital–labour substitution: a note, *Review of Economics and Statistics*, **45**, 436–8.

Fuller, W.A. (1976) *Introduction to Statistical Time Series*, Wiley, New York.

Gilbert, C.L. (1986) Professor Hendry's econometric methodology, *Oxford Bulletin of Economics and Statistics*, **48**, 283–307.

Goldberger, A.S. and Gamaletsos, T. (1970) A cross-country comparison of consumer expenditure patterns, *European Economic Review*, **1**, 357–400.

Goldfeld, S.M. (1973) The demand for money revisited, *Brookings Papers on Economic Activity*, **3**, 577–638.

Goldfeld, S.M. (1976) The case of the missing money, *Brookings Papers on Economic Activity*, **6**, 683–739.

Goldsmith, R.W. (1955) *A Study of Savings in the United States*. Princeton University Press.

Green, H.A.J. (1964) *Aggregation in economic analysis, an introductory survey*. Princeton University Press.

Grice, J. and Bennett, A. (1984) Wealth and demand for M3 in the UK 1963–78, *Manchester School*, **52**, 239–71.

Griliches, Z. (1967) Distributed lags: a survey, *Econometrica*, **35**, 16–49.

Griliches, Z. and Ringstad, V. (1971) *Economies of Scale and the Form of the Production Function*. North Holland, Amsterdam.

Hacche, G. (1974) The demand for money in the United Kingdom: experience since 1971, *Bank of England Quarterly Bulletin*, **14**, 284–305.

Hadley, G. (1965) *Linear Algebra*. Addison-Wesley, Reading, Mass.

Hall, R.E. (1978) Stochastic implications of the life cycle permanent income hypothesis: theory and evidence, *Journal of Political Economy*, **86**, 971–87.

Hall, R.E. (1988) Intertemporal substitution in consumption, *Journal of Political Economy*, **96**, 339–57.

Hall, R.E. and Mishkin, F.S. (1982) The sensitivity of consumption to transitory income: estimates from panel data on households, *Econometrica*, **50**, 461–81.

Hall, S.G., Hendry, S.G.B., Wilcox, J.B. (1989) The long run determination of the UK monetary aggregates, Bank of England Discussion Paper No 41.

Hall, R.E. and Jorgenson, D.W. (1967) Tax policy and investment behaviour, *American Economic Review*, **57**, 391–414.

Hamburger, M.J. (1977a) The demand for money in an open economy: Germany and the United Kingdom, *Journal of Monetary Economics*, **3**, 25–40.

Hamburger, M.J. (1977b) Behaviour of the money stock. Is there a puzzle?, *Journal of Monetary Economics*, **3**, 265–88.

Hamburger, M.J. and Wood, G.E. (1978) Interest rates and monetary policy in open economies, Federal Reserve Bank of New York Working Paper, May.

Hansen, L.S. and Singleton, K.J. (1983) Stochastic consumption, risk aversion and the temporal behaviour of stock market returns, *Journal of Political Economy*, **91**, 249–65.

Harrod, R. (1948) *Towards a Dynamic Economics*. Macmillan.

Harvey, A. (1989) *The Econometric Analysis of Time Series*. Philip Allen.

Hausman, J. (1978) Specification tests in Econometrics, *Econometrica*, **46**, 1251–71.

Heathfield, D. (1971) *Production Functions*. Macmillan.

Henderson, J.M. and Quandt, R.E. (1980) *Microeconomic Theory, a Mathematical Approach*. McGraw-Hill.

Hendry, D.F. (1974) Stochastic specification in an aggregate demand model of the UK, *Econometrica*, **42**, 559–78.

Hendry, D.F. (1979) Predictive failure and econometric modelling in macroeconomics: the transactions demand for money, in: Ormerod, P. (ed.), *Economic Modelling*, Heinemann, London.

Hendry, D.F. (1985) Monetary economic myth and econometric realities, *Oxford Review of Economic Policy*, **1**, 72–84.

Hendry, D.F. and Mizon, G.E. (1978) Serial correlation as a convenient simplification, not a nuisance: a comment on a study of the demand for money by the Bank of England, *Economic Journal*, **88**, 549–63.

Hendry, D.F. and Richard, J.-F. (1983) The econometric analysis of economic time series, *International Statistical Review*, 51, 111–63.

Hendry, D.F. and Ungern-Sternberg, T. von (1980) Liquidity and inflation effects on consumers' expenditure, in: Deaton, A.S. (ed.), *Essays in the Theory and Measurement of Consumers' Behaviour*. Cambridge University Press.

Hicks, J.R. (1956) *A Revision of Demand Theory*. Oxford University Press.

Hildebrand, G.H. and Liu, T.C. (1965) *Manufacturing Production Functions in the United States 1957*. New York State School of Industrial Relations, Ithaca.

Hildreth, C. and Lu, J.Y. (1960) *Demand Relations with Autocorrelated Disturbances*. Michigan Agricultural Experiment Station Technical Bulletin 276, Michigan State University.

Houthakker, H. (1960) Additive preferences. *Econometrica* 28, 244–56.

Houthakker, H. and Taylor, L.D. (1970) *Consumer Demand in the United States 1929–1970* (2nd edn). Harvard University Press, Cambridge, Mass.

Jarque, C.M. and Bera, A.K. (1980) Efficient tests for normality, homoskedasticity and serial independence of regression residuals, *Economic Letters*, 6, 255–9.

Johansen, S. (1988) Statistical analysis of cointegration vectors, *Journal of Economic Dynamics and Control*, 12, 231–54.

Johnston, J. (1972) *Econometric Methods* (2nd Edition). McGraw-Hill.

Johnston, J. (1984) *Econometric Methods* (3rd Edition). McGraw-Hill.

Johnston, R.B. (1984) The demand for non-interest bearing money in the UK, Treasury Working Paper, 28.

Jones, H. (1975) *An Introduction to Modern Theories of Economic Growth*. Nelson.

Juster, F.T. and Wachtel, P. (1972) *Inflation and the Consumer*. Brookings Papers on Economic Activity 1, pp. 71–114.

Kahn, M. (1974) The stability of the demand for money function in the US, 1901–1965, *Journal of Political Economy*, 82, 1205–1220.

Karni, E. (1974) The value of time and the demand for money, *Journal of Money, Credit and Banking*, 6, 45–64.

Kavanagh, N.J. and Walters, A.A. (1966) The demand for money in the United Kingdom, 1877–1961: preliminary findings, *Bulletin of the Oxford University Institute of Economics and Statistics*, 28, 93–116.

Kelejian, H.H. and Oates, W.E. (1989) *Introduction to Econometrics – principles and applications*. Harper and Row, New York.

Kendall, M.G. and Stuart, A. (1973) *The Advanced Theory of Statistics*, Griffin.

Keynes, J.M. (1936) *The General Theory of Employment, Interest and Money*. Macmillan.

King, M.A. (1972) Taxation and investment incentives in a vintage investment model, *Journal of Public Economics*, 1, 121–47.

Klein, L.R. (1950) *Economic Fluctuations in the United States, 1921–1941*. Cowles Commission Monograph 11.

Klein, L.R. (1953) *A Textbook of Econometrics*. Row Peterson, Evanston, Ill.

Klein, L.R. (1958) The estimation of distributed lags, *Econometrica*, 26, 559–65.

Kmenta, J. (1967) On the estimation of the CES production function, *International Economic Review*, 8, 180–9.

Kmenta, J. (1986) *Elements of Econometrics*, Macmillan, New York.

Koyck, L.M. (1954) *Distributed Lags and Investment Analysis*. North Holland, Amsterdam.

Kuznets, S. (1942) *Uses of National Income in Peace and War*. National Bureau of Economic Research Occasional Paper 6.

Kydland, F.E. and Prescott, E.C. (1977) Rules rather than discretion: the inconsistency of optimal plans, *Journal of Political Economy*, 85, 473–92.

Laidler, D. (1966) Some evidence on the demand for money, *Journal of Political Economy*, 74, 55–68.

Laidler, D. (1971) The influence of money on economic activity: a survey of some current problems, in: Clayton, G., Gilbert, J.C. and Sedgwick, R. (eds), *Monetary Theory and Policy in the 1970s*. Oxford University Press.

Laidler, D. (1977) *The Demand for Money: theories and evidence.* Harper and Row, New York.

Laidler, D. (1981) The demand for money in the United States yet again, in: *On the State of Macroeconomics.* Carnegie–Rochester Conference Series on Public Policy, 12, pp. 219–71.

Laidler, D. (1982) *Monetarist Perspectives.* Philip Allen.

Laidler, D. and Parkin, J.M. (1970) The demand for money in the United Kingdom, 1956–1967: preliminary estimates, *Manchester School*, **38**, 187–208.

Laumas, G.S. (1978) A test of the stability of the demand for money, *Scottish Journal of Political Economy*, **25**, 239–51.

Laumas, G.S. and Mehra, Y.P. (1976) The stability of the demand for money function: The evidence from quarterly data, *Review of Economics and Statistics*, **58**, 463–8.

Laury, J.S.E., Lewis, G.R. and Ormerod, P.A. (1978) Properties of macroeconomic models of the UK economy: a comparative study, *National Institute Economic Review*, **83**, 52–72.

Leamer, E.E. (1978) *Specification searches.* Wiley.

Leamer, E.E. (1983) Lets take the con out of econometrics, *American Economic Review*, **73**, 31–44.

L'Esperance, W.L. (1964) A case study in prediction: the market for water-melons, *Econometrica*, **32**, 163–73.

Liu, T.C. (1960) Underidentification, structural estimation and forecasting, *Econometrica*, **28**, 855–65.

Lluch, C. (1971) Consumer demand functions, Spain 1958–64, *European Economic Review*, **2**, 277–302.

Lucas, R.B. (1976) Econometric policy evaluation: a critique, in: Brunner, K. and Meltzer, A.N. (eds), *The Phillips Curve and Labour Markets.* North Holland, Amsterdam.

McAleer, M. and Pesaren, M.H. (1986) Statistical inference in non-nested econometric models, *Applied Mathematics and Computation*, 271–311.

McCallum, B.T. (1976) Rational expectations and the estimation of econometric models: an alternative procedure, *International Economic Review*, **17**, 484–90.

MacKinnon, J.G. and Milbourne, R.D. (1984) Monetary anticipations and the demand for money, *Journal of Monetary Economics*, **13**, 263–74.

MacKinnon, J.G. and Milbourne, R.D. (1988) Are price equations really money demand equations on their heads? *Journal of Applied Econometrics*, **3**, 295–305.

Maddala, G.S. (1989) *Introduction to Econometrics.* Macmillan, New York.

Maddala, G.S. and Kadane, J.B. (1966) Some notes on the estimation of CES production functions, *Review of Economics and Statistics*, **48**, 340–4.

Mankiw, G.N., Rotemberg, J. and Summers, L. (1985) Intertemporal substitution in macroeconomics, *Quarterly Journal of Economics*, **100**, 225–51.

Matthews, K.G.P. and Ormerod, P.A. (1978) St Louis models of the UK economy, *National Institute Economic Review*, **84**, 65–9.

Mayer, T. (1972) *Permanent Income, Wealth and Consumption.* University of California Press.

Meltzer, A.H. (1963) The demand for money: the evidence from the time series, *Journal of Political Economy*, **71**, 219–46.

Minford, A.P.L., Marwaha, K. and Sprague, A. (1984) The Liverpool macroeconomic model of the United Kingdom, *Economic Modelling*, **1**, 24–63.

Mishkin, F.S. (1982) Does anticipated monetary policy matter? An econometric investigation, *Journal of Political Economy*, **90**, 22–51.

Mishkin, F.S. (1983) *A rational expectations approach to macroeconomics.* Chicago University Press.

Mizon, G.E. (1974) The estimation of non-linear econometric equations: an application to the specification and estimation of an aggregate putty–clay relation for the UK, *Review of Economic Studies*, **41**, 353–69.

Mizon, G.E. and Richard, J.F. (1986) The encompassing principle and its application

428

to testing non-nested hypotheses, *Econometrica*, **54**, 657–678.

Modigliani, F. (1949) Fluctuations in the savings income ratio: a problem in economic forecasting, *Studies in Income and Wealth*, **11**, National Bureau of Economic Research, New York.

Modigliani, F. (1966) The life cycle hypothesis of saving, the demand for wealth and the supply of capital, *Social Research*, **33**, 160–217.

Modigliani, F. and Brumberg, R. (1954) Utility analysis and the consumption function: an interpretation of cross-sectional data, in: Kurihara, K. (ed.), *Post-Keynesian Economics*. Rutgers University Press.

Muellbauer, J. (1974) Household composition, Engel curves and welfare comparisons between households: a duality approach, *European Economic Review*, **5**, 103–22.

Muellbauer, J. (1975) Aggregation, income distribution and consumer demand, *Review of Economic Studies*, **62**, 525–43.

Muellbauer, J. (1976) Community preferences and the representative consumer, *Econometrica*, **44**, 979–99.

Muellbauer, J. (1980) The estimation of the Prais-Houthakker model of equivalence scales, *Econometrica*, **48**, 153–76.

Muellbauer, J. (1983) Surprises in the consumption function, Economic Journal, Conference Papers, 34–49.

Muellbauer, J. and Bover, O. (1986) Liquidity constraints and aggregation in the consumption function under uncertainty, Oxford Institute of Economics and Statistics, Discussion Paper No 12.

Muellbauer, J. and Murphy, A. (1989) Why has UK personal saving collapsed? Credit Suisse First Boston Research Note.

Muscatelli, V.A. (1988) Alternative models of buffer stock money: an empirical investigation, *Scottish Journal of Political Economy*, **35**, 1–21.

Muscatelli, V.A. (1989) A comparison of the rational expectations and general to specific approaches to modelling the demand for M1, *Oxford Bulletin of Economics and Statistics*, **51**, 353–75.

Muscatelli, V.A. and Hurn, S. (1992) Co-integration and dynamic time series models. *Jornal of Economic Surveys* **6**, 1–43.

Nelson, C.R. and Plosser, C.I. (1982) Trends and random walks in macroeconomic time series, *Journal of Monetary Economics*, **10**, 139–62.

Nerlove, M. (1958) *Distributed Lags and Demand Analysis*. Agricultural Handbook 141, US Department of Agriculture, Washington.

Nerlove, M. (1963) Returns to scale in electricity supply, in: Christ, C. (ed.), *Measurement in Economics*. Stanford University Press.

Nerlove, M. (1967) Recent empirical studies of the CES and related production functions, *Studies in Income and Wealth*, **31**, 55–122. National Bureau of Economic Research, New York.

Osborne, D. and Teal, F. (1979) An assessment and comparison of two NIESR econometric model forecasts, *National Institute Economic Review*, **88**, 50–62.

Pagan, A.R. (1984) Econometric issues in the analysis of regression with generated regressors, *International Economic Review*, **25**, 221–47.

Pagan, A.R. (1987) Three econometrics methodologies: a critical appraisal, *Journal of Economic Surveys*, **1**, 3–24.

Permon, R. (1991) Co-integration: An introduction to the literature. *Journal of Economic Studies* **18**, 3–30.

Pindyck, R. (1979) Interfuel substitution and the industrial demand for energy: an international comparison, *Review of Economics and Statistics*, **51**, 169–79.

Pindyck, R. and Rubinfeld, D.L. (1991) *Economic Models and Economic Forecasts*, 3rd edition. McGraw-Hill.

Pissarides, C.A. (1978) Liquidity considerations in the theory of consumption, *Quarterly Journal of Economics*, **93**, 279–96.

Pollak, R.A., Sickles, R.C. and Wales, T.J. (1984) The CES-Tranlog: specification and estimation of a new cost function, *Review of Economics and Statistics*, **56**, 602–8.

Pollock, R.A. and Wales, T.J. (1969) Estimation of the linear expenditure system, *Econometrica*, **37**, 611–28.

Porter, R.D., Sproat, P.A. and Lindsey, D.E. (1989) Econometric modeling of the demands for US monetary aggregates: conventional and exponential approaches in structural change and economic modeling. Papers and proceedings of the 7th Pacific Basin Central Bank Conference on Economic Modeling. Sydney, Ambassador Press, 218–30.

Prais, S.J. and Houthakker, H.S. (1955) *The Analysis of Family Budgets*. Cambridge University Press.

Ramsey, J.B. and Schmidt, P. (1976) Some further results on the use of OLS and BLUS residuals in specification error tests, *Journal of the American Statistical Association*, **71**, 389–90.

Revankar, N.S. (1971) A class of variable elasticity of substitution production functions, *Econometrica*, **39**, 61–71.

Rowan, D.C. and Miller, J. (1979) *The Demand for Money in the UK, 1963–1977. University of Southampton Discussion Paper 7902, University of Southampton*.

Sargan, J.D. (1964) Wages and prices in the United Kingdom, in Mort, P.E., Mills, G. and Whitaker, J.K. (eds.), *Econometric Analysis for National Economic Planning*. Butterworth.

Sato, R. and Hoffman, R.F. (1968) Production functions with a variable elasticity of factor substitution, Some analysis and testing, *Review of Economics and Statistics*, **50**, 453–60.

Schmidt, P. (1976) On the statistical estimation of parametric frontier production functions, *Review of Economics and Statistics*, **58**, 238–9.

Schultz, H. (1938) *The Theory and Measurement of Demand*. Chicago University Press.

Shapiro, A.A. (1973) Inflation, lags and the demand for money, *International Economic Review*, **14**, 81–96.

Silvey, S.D. (1975) *Statistical Inference*, Chapman and Hall.

Sims, C.A. (1980) Macroeconomics and reality, *Econometrica*, **48**, 1–48.

Slovin, M.B. and Sushka, M.E. (1983) Money, interest rates and risk, *Journal of Monetary Economics*, **12**, 475–82.

Solow, R.M. (1957) Technical change and the aggregate production function, *Review of Economic Statistics*, **39**, 312–20, reprinted in: Meuller, M.G. (1969), *Readings in Macroeconomics*. Holt, Rinehart and Winston.

Solow, R.M. (1960) Investment and technical progress, in: Arrow, K., Karlin, S. and Suppes, P. (eds), *Mathematical Methods in the Social Sciences*, Stanford University Press.

Spiro, A. (1962) Wealth and the consumption function, *Journal of Political Economy*, **70**, 393–54.

Starleaf, D.R. and Reimer, R. (1967) The Keynesian demand for money function: some statistical tests, *Journal of Finance*, **22**, 71–6.

Stewart, J. (1976) *Understanding Econometrics*. Hutchinson.

Stewart, J. (1984) *Understanding Econometrics* (2nd edition). Hutchinson.

Stewart, J. (1991) *Econometrics*. Philip Allen.

Stewart, M.B. and Wallis, K.F. (1981) *Introductory Economics*. Blackwell.

Stock, J.H. (1987) Asymptotic properties of least squares estimators of cointegrating vectors, *Econometrica*, **55**, 1035–56.

Stoker, T.M. (1986) Simple tests of distribution effects on macroeconomic equations, *Journal of Political Economy*, **94**, 763–95.

Stone, J.R.N. (1954) Linear expenditure systems and demand analysis – an application to the pattern of British demand, *Economic Journal*, **64**, 511–27.

Stone, J.R.N. (1964) Private saving in Britain, past, present and future, *Manchester School*, **32**, 79–112.

Stone, J.R.N. (1973) Personal spending and saving in postwar Britain, in: Bos, H.C., Linneman, H. and De Wolff, P. (eds), *Economic Structure and Development*. North

Holland, Amsterdam.

Stone, J.R.N. and Rowe, D.A. (1957) The market demand for durable goods, *Econometrica*, **25**, 423–43.

Suits, D.B. (1955) An econometric analysis of the water-melon market, *Journal of Farm Economics*, **37**, 237–51.

Taylor, M.P. (1987) Financial innovation, inflation and the stability of the demand for broad money in the UK, *Bulletin of Economic Research*, **39**, 225–33.

Teigen, R. (1964) Demand and supply functions for money in the United States, *Econometrica*, **32**, 477–509.

Theil, H. (1965) The information approach to demand analysis, *Econometrica*, **33**, 67–87.

Theil, H. (1975) *Theory and Measurement of Consumer Demand*. North Holland, Amsterdam.

Theil, H. and Boot, J.C.G. (1962) The final form of econometric equation systems, *Rev. Int. Statist. Inst.*, **30**, 136–52, reprinted in: Zellner, A. (ed.) (1968), *Readings in Economic Statistics and Econometrics*. Little, Brown, Boston.

Thomas, R.L. (1981) Wealth and aggregate consumption, *Manchester School*, **49**, 129–52.

Thomas, R.L. (1987) *Applied Demand Analysis*. Longman.

Tinbergen, J. (1939) *Statistical Testing of Business Cycle Theories, II: business cycles in the USA, 1919–1932*. League of Nations, Geneva.

Tobin, J. (1956) The interest elasticity of the transactions demand for cash, *Review of Economics and Statistics*, **38**, 241–7.

Tobin, J. (1958) Liquidity preference as behaviour towards risk, *Review of Economic Studies*, **25**, 65–86.

Townend, J.C. (1976) The personal savings ratio, *Bank of England Quarterly Bulletin*, **16**, 53–61.

Vogel, R.C. (1974) The dynamics of inflation in Latin America, 1950–1969, *American Economic Review*, **64**, 102–14.

Wall, K.D., Preston, A.J., Bray, J.W. and Peston, M.H. (1975) Estimates of a simple control model of the UK economy, in: Renton, G.A. (ed.), Modelling the Economy. Heinemann Education Books.

Wallis, K.F. (1979) *Topics in Applied Econometrics*. Blackwell.

Wallis, K. (1989) Macroeconomic forecasting: a survey, *Economic Journal*, **99**, 28–61.

Walters, A.A. (1970) *An Introduction to Econometrics*. (2nd edn). Macmillan.

Weinrobe, M.D. (1972) A simple model of the precautionary demand for cash, *Southern Economic Journal*, **39**, 314–24.

Wickens, M.R. and Breusch, T.S. (1988) Dynamic specification, the long run and the estimation of transformed regression models, *Economic Journal*, **98**, supplement, 189–205.

Wickens, M.R. and Molana, H. (1984) Stochastic life cycle theory with varying interest rates and prices, *Economic Journal*, **94**, conference papers, 133–47.

Wold, H.D.A. (1958) A case study of interdependent versus causal chain systems, *Review of the International Statistical Institute*, **26**, 5–25.

Working, H. (1943) Statistical lows of family expenditure. *Journal of the American Statistical Association* **38**, 43–56.

Wright, C. (1969) Estimating permanent income: a note, *Journal of Political Economy*, **77**, 845–50.

Wu, D.M. (1973) Alternative tests of interdependence between stochastic regressors and disturbances, *Econometrica*, **41**, 733–50.

Zellner, A. and Geisel, M.K. (1970) Analysis of distributed lag models with applications to consumption function estimation, *Econometrica*, **38**, 865–88.

Zellner, A., Huang, D.S. and Chau, L.C. (1965) Further analysis of the short-run consumption function with emphasis on the role of liquid assets, *Econometrica*, **33**, 571–81.

Zellner, A. and Theil, H. (1962) Three stage least squares: simultaneous estimation of simultaneous equations, *Econometrica*, **30**, 54–78.

431

Index